Saint Peter's University Library
Withdrawn

The Very Young

Guiding Children from Infancy through the Early Years

Second Edition

George W. Maxim
West Chester University

Wadsworth Publishing Company
Belmont, California
A Division of Wadsworth, Inc.

Education Editor: Bob Podstepny
Production Editor: Jane Townsend
Managing Designer: MaryEllen Podgorski
Cover and Interior Design: Adriane Bosworth
Copy Editor: Jonas Weisel
Illustrator: Patty Kinley
Print Buyer: Barbara Britton

© 1985, 1980 by Wadsworth, Inc. All rights reserved. No part of this book may be reproduced, stored in a retrieval system, or transcribed, in any form or by any means, electronic, mechanical, photocopying, recording, or otherwise, without the prior written permission of the publisher, Wadsworth Publishing Company, Belmont, California 94002, a division of Wadsworth, Inc.

Printed in the United States of America

1 2 3 4 5 6 7 8 9 10—89 88 87 86 85

ISBN 0-534-03861-1

Library of Congress Cataloging in Publication Data

Maxim, George W.
   The very young.

   Bibliography: p.
   Includes index.
   1. Education, Preschool.   2. Child development.
3. Socialization.   I. Title.
LB1140.2.M398   1985   372'.21   84-19521
ISBN 0-534-03861-1

B
40.2
398
'85

To Libby
My partner in living
and learning

Preface xii

Brief Contents

Contents

Saint Peter's University Library
Withdrawn

v

Chapter 6   Physical and Motor Skills: Patterns of Fitness, Coordination, and Control   179

Chapter 7   Early Learning Experiences   213

Like the first edition of *The Very Young,* this second edition is directed toward prospective teachers and day-care personnel who plan careers working with infants, toddlers, and young children in group settings. It is designed to influence professional teaching and caring by drawing its recommendations from several major sources:

1. *Sound research and theory.* Researchers and evaluators help educators understand the complexities of childhood and provide guidelines by which certain aspects of teaching can be measured. Their contributions will be acknowledged throughout the text.

2. *Classroom visitations.* During my professional career I have visited scores of early childhood settings in all kinds of communities. Observations and discussions with outstanding teachers have furnished me with a wealth of knowledge about teaching that supplements the reliable suggestions offered by researchers and theorists.

3. *Teaching experience.* Every new day in a nursery school, kindergarten, or day-care center is a day of enlightenment and learning for the teacher. The suggestions I present are drawn from my teaching experiences, and I hope they will stimulate interest and increase understanding of early childhood education.

As in the first edition, this edition covers the early childhood years from infancy through kindergarten. This range is a feature that sets *The Very Young* apart from most other books in its field. By providing such a concentrated treatment of infancy, it addresses a vital period of life that has perhaps the greatest potential for growth. By starting the examination of young children at this critical stage, the book helps readers to understand the sequential needs of children as they progress throughout childhood.

Many changes were made in this second edition. Three new chapters have been added. Chapter 1 focuses on the personal and professional aspects of teaching and asks readers to carefully consider whether a teaching career is really what they want. Chapter 5 addresses the valuable contributions of play in meeting children's needs within all areas of development and provides suggestions for creating an environment for play. Chapter 6 offers illustrative materials and activities that promote learning without confining readers to rigid subject matter designations such as "math" or "reading." It comprehensively describes what is meant by "early childhood subject matter." In addition to these chapter additions, so many ideas were added to the original chapter on social-emotional considerations that two chapters (3 and 4) now treat important areas such as self-concept, personal feelings, interpersonal relationships, and behavior management.

Now included as separate topics are new or expanded discussions of non-sexist education, first-day-of-school considerations, lesson planning, computer utilization, room arrangement, classroom routines, movement and music, exploration and discovery, informal classroom communication, and IEPs. Although all the information available today could never be presented in any one book, I have attempted to be as comprehensive as possible in my coverage of these topics. I have also tried to make the information as interesting and meaningful as possible by providing specific examples, vignettes, and practical suggestions throughout.

The second edition benefited from valuable comments and suggestions offered by the many readers and users of the first edition. They enlightened me in several areas by offering specific ideas and by asking challenging questions. This was one of the most exciting parts of the entire revision process. Readers and users have contributed to my growth as an early childhood professional; I hope I can be as helpful to those to whom I am privileged to offer my ideas.

ACKNOWLEDGMENTS

Many people contribute to the publication of a book. Unfortunately, only the author's name is prominently displayed alongside the title for all to see. But, because so many others contributed to this second edition, their names and accomplishments deserve special mention here.

I am eternally grateful to my wife Libby. Her early childhood background helped her to offer useful suggestions, and I appreciated her understanding nature as she offered encouragement and praise. Libby was also the major photographer for this project. She did all these things while fulfilling her critical role of mother to our two sons who were born during the revision phase of this book. I don't know how she did it, but I do know how much it meant to me. In addition, my two sons Mike and Jeff deserve special mention. Although they did not fully comprehend, their energy and spirit helped sustain my efforts whenever those "writing-day blues" began to descend. I am also appreciative of the industriousness of my parents, Rose and Stanley Maxim. They taught me the value of persistence in tackling a job as immense as writing a book.

Roger Peterson, former education and family studies editor at Wadsworth, and friend, was the stimulus for the first edition of *The Very Young*. Without Roger's vision, my dream would never have become reality. Marshall Aronson provided energetic leadership for the new edition by soliciting and offering suggestions for change. The second edition was completed under the direction of Bob Podstepny, education and family studies editor at Wadsworth. I am grateful to Bob for his persistence in examining and re-examining the proposals for change until a clear focus was established. Bob's technical knowledge and skill as well as his genuine personal warmth were invaluable. Jane Townsend, production editor, smoothed over the rough spots of the manuscript and skillfully pulled together the text and art program. It was a sincere pleasure to have worked with her.

Typing for this edition was done by Terri Dero. I am deeply thankful for the hours she spent deciphering my handwritten copy and expertly transforming it into beautifully typed drafts.

My colleagues in the early childhood area at West Chester University deserve recognition for their special efforts: Edward Gibson, Elizabeth Hasson, Mary Ann Morgan-Porter, Ruth Petkofsky, Carlos Ziegler, and Connie Zimmerman. I also appreciate the encouragement of my department chairperson, Joan Hasselquist, and the support of Kenneth L. Perrin, president of West Chester University.

Several early childhood professionals helped provide direction for this second edition by offering their insightful suggestions and critical comments. Those reviewers were Leah D. Adams, Eastern Michigan University; Sandra Anselmo, University of the Pacific; David G. Bird, Millersville University; Bonnie Booker, Merced College; Thomas J. Buttery, University of Alabama, Tuscaloosa; Vivian L. Cox, University of Arizona; Sister Imelda D'Agostino, Mt. St. Mary's College; Doris E. Dittmar, Wright State University; Carol R. Foster, Georgia State University; Martha H. Nelson, Western Washington University; Alice M. Pieper, Virginia Commonwealth University; Sherrill Richarz, Washington State University; Jo Rosauer, Iowa State University; Nancy J. Wanamaker, University of Idaho; Jane H. Washington, Riverside City College.

Chapter 1

So You Want to Work with Young Children!

Picture a laughing, spirited group of children chanting this catchy rhyme as they twirl and tumble to the actions suggested in the verse:

We are tops of red and blue.
We spin round and round for you.
We twirl 'round and 'round some more,
'til we tumble to the floor!

"Let's do it again, teacher . . . please?" they call as the last youngster plops to the floor with glee. The teacher immediately knows that they enjoyed this activity and continues once again. The children repeat the rhyme, laughing and moving and subsequently begging for more.

Do you see yourself in this scene? If so, do your facial expression and manner of leadership communicate enthusiasm for working with energetic, twirling, tumbling youngsters every day, indoors or out? Or, how about a less pleasant situation? Suppose a child in your care unexpectedly wets himself or spills a jar of paint on the floor? Are you in this picture? If so, what does your reaction tell you about your sensitivity to the situation?

Even though the tumbling was a planned activity while the accidents were obviously unplanned, both called for a great deal of knowledge and sensitivity. The teacher had to anticipate each situation in order to respond quickly when each one occurred. This course and your other education courses draw upon current research and knowledge in child development and early childhood education in order to help you become a competent leader of young children. The role is a very challenging one and, at the same time, a very rewarding one. Special people work with young children—they understand the long-range implications of their work for the children and also for the children's families, communities, nations, and world. That responsibility cannot be taken lightly, and the purpose of this text is to help you develop strategies and attitudes appropriate for establishing positive relationships between yourself and children. Am I good person for the job? How shall I teach? What should I do? What do I expect from the children? In helping you answer these questions, this book attempts to fuse personal and professional experiences to reach an understanding of what is important in the lives of young children. It is hoped that the resulting blend of theory and practice will help you to understand not only *what* to do and *how* to do it but also *why* what you are doing is important.

Before moving toward these goals, take a few minutes to draw your image of an early childhood teacher. Do not read ahead until you have completed your drawing.

This activity, based upon the work of Harmin and Gregory (1974), is referred to as a *projective description.* This means that your unconscious desires or feelings may be *projected* into descriptions of stimuli, in this case, the early childhood teacher, when you draw a picture. Some people believe you reveal much more about your true feelings this way than you do by simply responding verbally to a question such as, "What is an early childhood teacher?" These projections are not always valid, and interpretations are sometimes impossible to make. But your picture probably reflects aspects of early childhood education that truly concern you or of which you are especially aware. What does your drawing reveal about your subconscious impressions of early childhood education? Try to determine the answer by discussing the following questions with your classmates:

- Is the teacher you? If not, why not?

- Is the teacher drawn in greater proportion to the rest of the picture or in greater detail? What does that suggest to you?

- Are children shown? If not, what does that suggest to you?

- Are the children drawn alike, or are they all "individuals"?

- Are the children active or passive? Does the teacher dominate the scene?

This activity was tried at the beginning of a semester with a group of college students. The drawings were not discussed at that time but were placed in a "time capsule" and displayed prominently in the classroom for the entire semester. On the last day of classes, the students were asked again to draw an early childhood teacher. The time capsules were opened, and the differences in the two pictures were discussed in terms of the preceding questions. Two sample drawings are shown here. Examine them—they represent a common change from the beginning of the semester to the end. At the beginning of the semester, many students unconsciously define teaching as something done *to* the children under total direction of the teacher. Often, the teacher is shown disproportionately larger than the children and is drawn with greater detail. She is the center of attention and, if children are present in the drawing, they are passively gathered about as they listen to their teacher talk. By the end of the semester, however, the students' perceptions have often changed. Their drawings show an *active* classroom: Children are everywhere—working at tables, reading books, building with blocks, painting at easels, and talking with one another. The teacher assumes a less conspicuous role. Teaching is shown as something done *with* children rather than as something done to them. What contributes to such change? The answer cannot be given in a sentence or two, because such change occurs as part of a highly sophisticated process. That process is what your course and this book are all about—developing ideas and attitudes about teaching that reflect what we know about the growth and development of young children.

WHAT ARE MY RESPONSIBILITIES AS A STUDENT?

Your responsibility for becoming an effective leader of young children involves taking an active role in learning all you can about the types of experiences most beneficial to young children. This means going beyond what is presented to you in class or in this book and examining all the ideas you encounter in an open, critical way. It does not mean you should consistently search for negative qualities in ideas; that sort of thinking is more often unconstructive than helpful; it might even be called "cynical" thinking. Critical thinkers examine ideas with open, unbiased minds, always considering reasons for either supporting or rejecting them. This text will often place you in the position of a critical decision-maker who must realize that there is no single, guaranteed right way to lead young children. In order to determine what works best, you will need to examine different styles of adult–child interaction, weigh the positive and negative features of each, and then choose the approach (or combination of approaches) that seems most appropriate for any particular group of children. This ability to associate what you do with young children (practical applications) with the reasons those practices are important for the children (theory) helps you become a true early childhood professional. A large part of professionalism is having the ability to combine knowledge about the development of children with a mastery of teaching techniques. You will learn how to stimulate growth in children within each of the major areas of development: (1) *physical development* (body growth and muscular, or motor, skills), (2) *intellectual development* (thought processes, intelligence, and language), and (3) *social-emotional development* (emotions, feelings, morals, and the ability to get along with others). See Figure 1-1.

In this course you'll learn how these three domains (areas) of development interact as

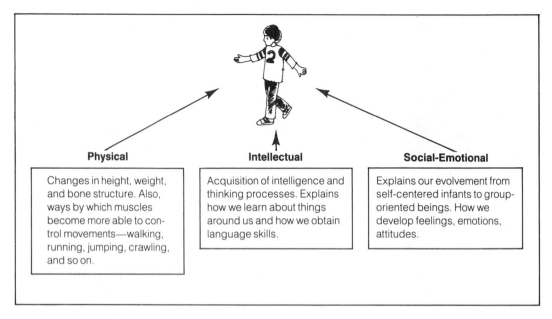

Figure 1-1 The three domains of development

they contribute to the total development of the young child. This means that one area cannot be separated from the others as you plan experiences for youngsters, because each depends upon the others. For example, consider the acquisition of an infant's first word—a developmental phenomenon studied with much care by those interested in language research. The infant might never be able to form that first word if it were brought up in an environment devoid of human encouragement and support or in the absence of opportunities to listen to others speak to and around her (social-emotional domain). Likewise, the infant would have great difficulty with that first word if the brain, ears, tongue, lips, vocal chords, or breathing apparatus were impaired (physical domain). This shows how any single developmental domain (in this case, language) interacts with the others as the child moves from one level of maturity to another.

WHAT IS PROFESSIONALISM?

Success in gaining professional abilities does not happen simply by chance. You may have heard of effective parents referred to as "natural teachers." Some might suggest that their work with their own children was so successful that they could experience the same level of success as teachers in a group educational setting. That kind of suggestion compares to one recommending that a person could successfully defend a client in court or perform delicate heart surgery without specialized training in those fields. Graham and Persky (1977), realizing that both the untrained and the trained individual are well meaning and work toward providing the best experiences for youngsters, provide several examples of how the untrained person may lack specific

Teachers must choose the approach, or approaches, that seems most appropriate for a particular group of children.

knowledge for maximizing the child's opportunities. One such example follows:

> The untrained person, recognizing the importance of establishing rapport and communication with a child, will show a book to a toddler and ask, "Do you like the pretty pictures?" She does not realize that a question asked in this way boxes the child into a "yes" or "no" response. The person who understands that there is a relationship between thought and language and that verbal interaction can promote thinking skills will word her comments so that they evoke a more thoughtful and complex response— e.g., "Why do you think the puppy is running after the little boy?" This can be the beginning of a conversation and an exchange of ideas rather than a simple question and answer episode. [p. 336]

This illustration highlights the fact that there is a body of knowledge and a specialized range of skills to be mastered before you can consider yourself an early childhood education professional.

Professionals are responsible individuals who prepare for careers in many fields by acquiring specialized knowledge and skills. Early childhood education is one of those areas, an area requiring individuals with intelligence and the will to learn. The demands placed upon early childhood professionals are greater than ever before. As the need for full-day services for children from low-income families rises, as the number of families with two working parents increases, and as the number of single-parent families expands, the more need there is for trained professionals who are knowledgeable and able to function in a variety of settings. Many of these settings are different from the typical preschools, day-care centers, or kindergartens you may already know about. Exactly what are those settings?

TYPICAL EARLY CHILDHOOD SETTINGS

The first category of specialized programs for young children can be classified as those most often found in an educational setting, such as a _nursery school_ or _kindergarten_. The second major category can be classified as those directed toward caring for children, usually referred to as _day-care_ or _child-care_ facilities. Day-care and school type programs are often found in such common settings as homes, churches, or schools, but nontraditional settings now show interesting growth potential: shopping centers, hospitals, health clubs, businesses and industries, and recreation facilities, for example. Regardless of where they are located, these specialized programs are popularly grouped under the title of early childhood education. So, when we refer to early childhood education in this book, we are describing all those programs designed for the very young: _nursery school_ (commonly for children from two-and-one-half to five years of age), _kindergarten_ (commonly for children five years old), _day care_ (generally for children through age six, but also offering after-school care for school-age children), and _primary grades_ (usually grades 1–3). From these categorical descriptions, then, we will define early childhood education as any program offering services to children between the ages of birth through eight. Because the emphasis of this book is on the preschool child (through age six), however, nursery school, kindergarten, and day-care strategies will be given more attention than primary grades.

The differences between _care_ programs and _school_ programs are minimal, usually involving the reasons children have been enrolled and the amount of time they spend in them. Similarities between the two are many—they share goals, emphases, and values. The differences and similarities are summarized as follows:

SIMILARITIES

1. Both provide similar opportunities and experiences.

2. Both furnish the same basic equipment, supplies, and materials.

3. Both require nearly the same basic amount of space.

4. Both require similar professional training and experience for their staff.

5. Both are based on an understanding of children's needs and their stages of development.

6. Both promote maximum development in all areas (social, emotional, physical, and intellectual), although some programs may stress one area more than others.

7. Both are subject to similar regulations for state licensing and certification.

8. Both are funded and/or organized through public or private agencies.

DIFFERENCES

1. The primary function of day care is to provide care and protection for children whose parents must be outside the home; the essential function of the nursery school is to train and develop the child.

2. Day-care centers usually offer services throughout the workday; nursery school programs are frequently offered for half a day.

3. Day-care centers must be equipped to serve meals; preschools usually offer only small snacks.

4. Day-care centers must be equipped so that children spending long hours at the center can nap when necessary.

5. Day-care centers often extend their services to school-age brothers or sisters, through before-school or after-school programs.

Table 1-1   A Typical Nursery School Morning

9:00–9:20	Opening Activities. *May include show-and-tell sharing, short songs, or fingerplays.*
9:20–10:00	Self-Selected Activities. *Free choice from among various interest centers such as painting, drawing, water or sand play, puppets, blocks, creative dramatics, toys, or other educational materials.*
10:00–10:30	Outdoor Play. *Vigorous outdoor play, including swinging, running, sliding, climbing, riding tricycles, throwing, and other physical activities.*
10:30–10:50	Bathrooming and Snack. *Toileting and cleaning up in preparation for a short snack of juice and crackers.*
10:50–11:20	Work Period. *Selected activities designed to promote language development and other creative or academic skills. These activities are carried out individually, in small groups, or as a large group, depending on the children's needs.*
11:20–11:30	Dismissal. *Cleaning up and dressing in readiness for parents' arrival.*

Table 1-2   A Typical Day in a Day-Care Facility

7:00–9:00	Arrival. *Children arrive at irregular times. Some require breakfast. While some children are engaged with quiet art activities or toys, or with storybooks, others may be taking short naps.*
9:00–9:30	Outdoor Play. *Active play on the playground is first on the schedule. There is much running and use of equipment.*
9:30–10:00	Large-Group Activity. *Music activities, story time, or a special language development program may be offered.*
10:00–10:20	Toileting and Snack. *Children use bathroom facilities and prepare for the snack.*
10:20–10:30	Rest Period. *Children are encouraged to rest on mats or cots.*
10:30–11:15	Special Activities. *Children are free to choose among special activity centers designed to build cognitive skills in math, reading, and language.*
11:15–12:00	Group Project. *This may be a special art or music activity associated with a special holiday, or it may involve cooking, watching television, show and tell, and so on.*
12:00–1:00	Lunch. *Children help prepare for lunch by setting up the table. A warm lunch is usually served, followed by cleanup.*
1:00–3:00	Sleep. *Children are allowed to sleep on cots during this time. A period of quiet rest is offered for those children who do not nap.*
3:00–3:15	Snack. *A refreshing snack of juice and crackers or cookies and milk is offered to children as they awaken or complete their rest time.*
3:15–3:45	Outdoor Play. *Active outdoor play follows the snack. Some special game or physical activity may be planned.*
3:45–4:30	Free Play. *Children are free to paint, draw, listen to records, play with puppets, and so on.*
4:30–5:00	Going Home. *Parents arrive at irregular times to take their children home.*

You can gain further understanding of the similarities and differences between day-care and other preschool programs by examining typical schedules for each in Tables 1-1 and 1-2. Notice that the activities are basically the same; the major difference is simply the length of time involved during the day.

Characterizing the variety of contemporary nursery school or kindergarten and day-care facilities available and putting these facilities into a meaningful, comprehensive framework is difficult. However, personal visits, interviews with program directors and staff members, professional reading, and research study allows us to provide general descriptions of the types of facilities you will encounter when you begin your career as an early childhood professional. Remember this as you examine the descriptions in Table 1-3.

COMMON CAREERS IN EARLY CHILDHOOD EDUCATION

When I die, I hope it will be my good fortune to go where Miss Blake will meet me and lead me to my seat.
—Bernard M. Baruch

Bernard M. Baruch, advisor to presidents, held this lifelong image of a teacher who made a significant impact on his life. Surely we all hold dear memories of a loving, caring teacher who made life in school a pleasant and eventful experience. The Miss Blakes of this world possess an immeasurable talent that often determines the kind of individuals many young children will eventually become. So, within each of the different types of early childhood settings discussed previously, one main ingredient determines the degree of success or failure: the early childhood specialist. She or he is the key to making all the resources of the center come together into a sound, effective program concerned with each aspect of the child's development. A room full of happy, active children enjoying varied activities is a strong reflection of a confident, competent, caring person.

Although most of you reading this book are preparing to become teachers of young children, I have hesitated to use that career label up to this point. The reason is that it no longer characterizes the wide range of opportunities available in the early childhood field. For example, all of the early childhood settings described thus far can be broadly characterized as *educational/caring facilities*. However, other important fields either directly or indirectly influence the lives of the very young, too (see the following lists).

EDUCATIONAL/CARING SETTINGS

- Teachers
- Directors
- Assistant teachers
- Aides

SUPPORT SETTINGS

- Social workers
- College faculty
- Family therapists
- Extension agents (county)
- Licensing officials

GENERAL SERVICES AFFECTING CHILDREN

- Sales representatives
- Writers
- Researchers
- Child advocates
- Government officials

Since this book most closely addresses the skills and attitudes necessary for working in an educational/caring setting, the term *teacher* will be used as a role label. The field of early childhood education provides much flexibility for a specialist: You can open your own center, manage an operation owned by someone else, or you can become a teacher, a vital, direct link with the children. Depending upon your motivation, purpose in life, and initiative, the field of early childhood education provides a wealth of possibilities for you. A

Table 1-3 *Characteristics of Major Early Childhood Settings*

Facility	Characteristics
Home-care center	The belief that the home is the proper place for the care of young children has motivated some parents to seek men or women who offer child-care programs in their own homes. Federal funds are provided for some home-care facilities, but such aid is limited to needy families with dependent children. Such home centers provide full-day services, serving preschoolers during the day and older children after school. Usually, up to ten children can be accommodated in the home setting. If licensed (only about 5 percent are), the home setting must meet minimum health and safety standards.
Day-care center	Located in hospitals, factories, universities, private buildings, public schools, or a number of other settings, day-care centers are designed as full-day programs for children whose parents work. Day-care programs usually offer health, medical, and social care, along with educational experiences. The centers are open approximately 11 to 12 hours per day, from about 7 A.M. to 6 P.M. Most day-care centers cater to preschoolers, but they also provide after-school services for school-age children. Federal funding is normally available for day-care programs serving low-income families.
Infant-care center	Often found in settings similar to those described above, infant centers provide comprehensive, continuous care for babies usually age six months or older. In order to ensure constant supervision, infant-care centers usually specify a ratio of one adult to three infants so that firm relationships as well as adequate feeding and toileting routines can be maintained. Many include programs of infant "stimulation."
Drop-off centers	Shopping centers, hospitals, colleges, libraries, health clubs, and other facilities visited by parents for short periods of time on an irregular basis often organize special care for children. Such care may be extended on an informal basis, usually of a custodial nature. This means that the children's health and safety needs are met, and they are given ample opportunity for play and exercise, but the sporadic nature of attendance prohibits any meaningful type of a continuous, regular program.
High school centers	More and more high schools (especially those of the vocational/technical variety) have organized day-care or nursery school centers in an effort to train students to become aides in child-care settings. Most states require only a high school diploma for aides, so the campus centers provide an excellent opportunity for the students to gain firsthand experience with an experienced teacher and the children.
Nursery school	Nursery schools are usually privately operated programs or cooperatives located in churches, private buildings, some public schools, or homes. They offer half-day sessions providing varied educational experiences for the child. The goals of nursery schools vary widely, ranging from formal education to the open philosophies. Funding is normally not available, so parents must assume the cost.
Parent cooperatives	Formed by parents primarily to save costs, cooperative schools have the dual purpose of providing an educational program for children and instruction for the parents themselves. Parents share educational responsibilities with the teacher, while they plan and implement the program. Cooperatives are usually nonprofit operations, financed by the parents or by fund-raising projects such as bake sales or auctions.
Child-development centers	These centers, which include Head Start centers, offer programs supported by federal, state, or local funds. The purpose of such support is twofold: It allows low-income parents to work, and it stimulates employment for teachers. The programs are comprehensive and include health services, nutrition, social services, and parent counseling. Perhaps central to the purpose of child-development centers is a concern for sound educational programs for children from low-income families to improve their chances for

(continued)

Table 1-3 (continued) Characteristics of Major Early Childhood Settings

Facility	Characteristics
	later success in school. Parents are involved to a great extent; they serve as classroom aides or participate on advisory boards.
Campus schools	Commonly referred to as laboratory schools or demonstration schools, these college-based programs are primarily aimed at providing both good education for young children and a good training facility for future teachers. Services range from day care to various nursery school or kindergarten programs. The schools may also be set up as experimental research programs where newer ideas are tested. Because of their strong influence on prospective teachers, campus schools are usually strongly committed to excellence in teaching and programming.
Kindergarten	These programs are offered primarily to five-year-old children by either public schools or private agencies. They are intended as a transition experience between the home or other early childhood program and the elementary school.

description of the varying responsibilities held by those in educational/caring facilities follows:

DIRECTOR

- Develops and executes the center's program
- Supervises and evaluates all personnel
- Maintains the physical environment to meet licensing standards for safety and cleanliness
- Enrolls children and establishes fees
- Keeps financial records
- Plans and conducts regular staff meetings
- Establishes schedules for all staff members
- Supervises the purchase and distribution of supplies and equipment
- Keeps all records required by governmental or other agencies
- Teaches groups of children, when necessary

TEACHER

- Plans and conducts daily activities
- Prepares materials appropriate for the maturity of the children

- Maintains an environment conducive to optimal development of the children
- Attends and contributes to staff and parent meetings
- Cooperates with other staff members
- Observes, evaluates, and reports significant individual and group behavior
- Maintains and extends professional knowledge and competence

ASSISTANT TEACHER

- Assists classroom teachers when appropriate and necessary
- Supervises activities as requested by the teacher
- Prepares the daily environment for the children
- Maintains an orderly environment
- Observes and records children's behavior
- Aids children who need individual attention
- Assists at meal and snack time

AIDE

- Assists with activities, when requested by teacher or assistant teacher

An understanding, loving teacher is essential in helping young children handle many of life's complications.

- Supervises children during free play or other group activities
- Assists at meal and snack time
- Helps maintain an orderly environment
- Provides clerical help when requested

CERTIFICATION REQUIREMENTS AND QUALIFICATIONS

The positions described here are those typically found in a privately owned nursery school or day-care facility. In public school programs, the positions and job descriptions are similar, except that the director is usually called the principal. The basic qualifications for early childhood personnel in both nursery school or kindergarten and day-care facilities are basically the same, although some variations do exist. That is a unique feature of our field; we recognize that standards for the training of early childhood personnel are important, but no set of common expectations exist at any level—national, state, or local. This does not imply that individuals and groups concerned with the welfare of young children haven't tried. For years there have been concerted efforts by federal and state agencies, professional organizations, and concerned individuals to ensure the adequate training of those who work with youngsters by suggesting *certification requirements.* All states, for example, require that teachers in all grade levels of our public schools be certified to teach according to standards established by their respective departments of education. Today these standards are influenced by the popular concept of *competency-based education;* state departments of education require that individuals demonstrate specific professional knowledge and abilities before they are certified to teach. This excerpt, taken from the general standards for certification of public school teachers at any level through high school in the state of Pennsylvania, describes the competencies required for certification (Pennsylvania Department of Education, 1977).

Each certification candidate shall demonstrate the ability to:

1. apply theory and research concerning the development, behavior and learning of children including those with exceptional characteristics and/or special needs.

2. prepare, select and use materials and media; modify commercial materials; and produce original materials.

3. use appropriate methods to carry out his/her role.

4. prepare, select and use evaluation procedures.

5. apply knowledge, techniques and skills of describing and analyzing professional, institutional and political situations in order to make educational decisions.

6. assess and improve reading, writing and speaking skills and/or make appropriate referrals.

7. promote better understandings and interrelationships among individuals and groups, of different races, sexes, religious beliefs, national origins and socio-economic backgrounds.

8. make the students aware of the world of work, its opportunities, and to assist students in making the transition from the school to the community.

Candidates who satisfy these competencies must do so at colleges or universities with approved four-year programs in order to teach in the state's public schools. Since many public schools now provide early childhood programs in addition to programs covering grades one through six, there has been a call to extend teacher training programs to include children five years of age or younger, so that prospective teachers may extend their developmental knowledge base. The National Association for the Education of Young Children (NAEYC) initiated a move in 1980 to develop national guidelines for the preparation of teachers of early childhood education in four-year colleges. Its work is still in progress. A second organization, the Association for Childhood Education International (ACEI), also worked toward professional standards of academic preparation for teachers of children age three through eight. Rather than focusing upon teacher competencies, the ACEI group focused instead on program content itself. Their recommendations follow (Hostler, 1958, pp. 65–66):

1. The teacher should have studied in the areas of physical and biological sciences, mathematics and philosophy, language and literature, social and behavioral sciences, and fine arts.

2. The teacher should have a minimum of twenty-four semester hours of professional preparation in the field of early childhood education, including courses in human growth and development; school, parent, home, and community relationships; history and philosophy of education; and school administration.

3. The teacher should have supervised experiences with young children for approximately 360 clock hours.

4. For professional advancement, teachers should be required to take refresher courses

One of the essential competencies to be learned in teacher training is helping children with communication skills.

and to keep active affiliation with professional organizations.

Notice that a minimum of 24 semester hours of professional preparation in the field of early childhood education is recommended. Those semester hours are usually subject to general competencies, such as these of the Pennsylvania Department of Education (1977):

The program shall provide competencies for the prospective teacher which will enable the teacher to lead children in developing:

1. positive self-concepts.
2. favorable attitudes toward school and learning.
3. concepts fundamental to academic success.
4. initial skills in the basic process of learning such as inquiring, observing, generalizing, experimenting, discovering and classifying, verifying and quantifying.
5. growth in verbal and non-verbal communication skills in the cognitive, affective and psychomotor areas . . . reading readiness and developmental reading.
6. knowledge and understanding of the physical and natural world.
7. appreciation of the aesthetic world.
8. physical skill, motor coordination and knowledge of sound health and safety practices.
9. emotional control and the beginning of self-discipline.
10. social competency and understanding.

Colleges with approved teacher training programs throughout Pennsylvania must provide evidence that these competencies are being met and that even more specific competencies are identified by each college. Examine the competency requirements for your state or for your college's certification program. You may be surprised to find that some are listed in fairly general terms, while others may contain dozens or hundreds of specific statements such as, "The student will be able to administer standardized tests to a group of children."

Thus, teachers in public school early childhood programs must hold teaching certificates appropriate for working with youngsters of that age and meet all other competencies as established by state departments of education. Some types of certification are explained in Table 1-4. Twelve states require that teachers of young children go beyond the normal four-year preparation program to complete a fifth year of study or a master's degree in order to receive certification beyond the receipt of the initial (provisional) teaching certificate.

In addition to certification for teachers in public schools, many states now require certification for teachers in private schools. Standards for certification vary from state to state, with some specifying a minimum number of semester hours in early childhood education and others requiring "demonstrated competency," shown by a minimum number of sucessful years as a teacher in a nursery school or kindergarten. Many teachers in private schools attain their formal schooling in four- or two-year college programs that specifically prepare individuals for work in early childhood education. While graduates of four-year programs receive bachelor's degrees, graduates of two-year programs receive an associate's degree from their institutions. While the associate's degree indicates specialized training in a field of study, it does not result in public school certification. Associate's degree holders, though, do assume important leadership roles in the private sector as they serve in the capacity of assistant teacher, teacher, or director in nonpublic day-care or nursery school settings.

Another category of professional credentialing in early childhood education is that of Child Development Associate (CDA) personnel. This program was initiated by the U.S. government's Office of Child Development (OCD) in 1972 in response to the need for trained personnel for nursery school and day-care centers. The goal of the CDA program was to enhance the skills of child care workers outside the traditional, formal educational setting and provide a "career ladder" by which they could advance from jobs as teachers' aides or volunteers to actual teaching positions in which they would have primary responsibility for planning and carrying out the day-to-day activities of a group of children. Originally, the CDA program was a competency-based system by which individuals were credentialed on the basis of what they could actually do in the nursery school or day-care setting rather than on the completion of a college-based two- or four-year program. Six general categories of competencies were developed (Galler, 1981):

1. Setting up and maintaining a safe and healthy learning environment.
2. Advancing physical and intellectual competence.
3. Building positive self-concept and individual strength.
4. Organizing and sustaining the positive functioning of children and adults, in a group, in a learning environment.
5. Bringing about optimal coordination of home and center child-rearing practices and expectations.
6. Carrying out supplementary responsibilities related to children's programs.

Although these competencies can be developed in a college setting, prospective CDAs have the option of being trained through fieldwork programs, work-study programs, or special independent study programs. Regardless of the nature of the program, the CDA must demonstrate competence in performing with young children.

Individuals interested in obtaining the CDA credential need to enroll with The Child Development Associate Consortium at the following address:

Suite 500, Southern Building
805 Fifteenth Street
Washington, D.C. 20005

Table 1-4   *Types of Certification in Early Childhood Education*

Certifying Agency	Type of Certificate
Four-year college (through the state)	Public school certificate allowing one to work as an assistant teacher, teacher, or director in public or private schools (bachelor's degree)
Two-year college (through the state)	Private school certificate allowing one to work as an assistant teacher, teacher, or director in private nursery school or day-care centers (associate's degrees)
CDA Consortium	Noncollege, competency-based credential allowing one to progress up a career ladder from aide or volunteer to assistant teacher or teacher on the basis of demonstrated abilities (CDA credential)

Applicants will be sent an application packet if they qualify for CDA training. Minimum qualifications include being at least sixteen years old, having access to an approved child-care center, and having at least eight months of full-time experience working in a group of three- to five-year-olds. A Local Assessment Team (LAT) designated by the Consortium will evaluate the candidate's overall progress and performance as they relate to the six competency areas just described.

Individuals receiving certification through each of the avenues described thus far are qualified to direct or teach not only in nursery school programs, but also in day-care settings. However, the minimum requirements for day-care employment are not always so stringent. Although day-care professionals are at times subject to separate professional requirements, they know that the adult leader is a most important element in the success of any program for young children. Teachers and other caregivers influence the development of children more than any other element, especially since they are responsible for the children's welfare during the entire day, often from 7 or 8 A.M. until 4 or 5 P.M. Obviously, the need for selecting outstanding staff members exists. Who are the professionals responsible for the direct care of the children, and what qualifications must they hold in order to secure a position in a day-care center?

Basic professional staffing considerations revolve around two specific areas: the individual competencies desired and the number of staff members required for a quality program. Of course, the range of competencies required for the staff of a large day-care center is much greater than that of a small center or a home-based day-care program. More specialists are needed, for example, because the large center represents a more complex relationship to the parents and to the community. Like the private nursery school, private day-care centers are administered by a director, who must demonstrate a basic knowledge of child development and of the health, nutritional, mental, and physical caring practices appropriate for young children. She or he must be able to select, train, and evaluate staff members, oversee the physical plant, work with parents, collaborate with community agencies, secure funding for the program, and fulfill the other complex responsibilities as described for the nursery school director. The job is a demanding one, calling for a person of ability and experience—one whose background includes a college degree in a field such as early childhood education or child development or whose accumulated experience has resulted in equivalent competency.

Regardless of the formal title assigned to them, primary caregivers are defined as group supervisors, assistant group supervisors, teachers, assistant teachers, or any other individuals assigned the responsibility of providing for the direct, day-to-day care of children. Although the qualifications required for these professional positions vary from state to state and from agency to agency, most reflect these basic requirements as defined by the U.S. Office of Child Development (Cohen, 1975, p. 115):

- Each caregiver should be at least 18 years old and able to read and write. (Younger people may help as aides or assistants but should not be considered as primary caregivers.)

- Each caregiver should be healthy enough to perform all duties safely and should have no disease that could be communicated to the children.

- Each caregiver must be willing and able to carry out the activities required by the curriculum.

- Each caregiver must be able to work with children without using physical or psychological punishment; be able to praise and encourage children; be able to provide them with learning and social experiences appropriate to their ages; be able to recognize physical hazards and either eliminate them or take precautions against them; and be willing and able to increase his or her skills and competence through experience, training, and supervision.

- In a program with about 30 or more children, it is advisable for at least one caregiver who is present half the time or more to meet any one of the following qualifications: to have a college degree with course work in child development, child psychology, child health, education, or other directly related fields; or have a high school diploma or its equivalent, plus substantial experience in an educational, early childhood, or day-care program; or be certified as a child development associate or have similar status because of obvious competence.

- In a program where some of the families do not speak English, there should be at least one caregiver who can communicate with parents and children in their native language. [pp. 115–116]

You may have been surprised to learn that the minimum qualifications for such a responsible position are an ability to read and write

and to be at least 18 years old. Individual states may define additional requirements for their day-care personnel, however. For example, the following selection is taken from the Regulations for Child Day Care Centers in the state of Pennsylvania (Pennsylvania Department of Public Welfare, 1981).

- All direct caregiving staff shall be at least 17 years of age.

- The director shall have the following qualifications:

  completion of a graduate program at an accredited college or university with a master's degree in administration, early childhood education, child development, special education, elementary education, or the human services field; *or,*

  completion of an undergraduate program at an accredited college or university with a bachelor's degree in administration, early childhood education, child development. . . ; and two years work experience related to the care and development of children; *or,*

  completion of an undergraduate program at an accredited college or university with an associate's degree or its equivalent in administration, early childhood education. . . ; and four years' work experience related to the care and development of children. [pp. 12–15]

Compare these requirements to the regulations established for private nursery school personnel given earlier. You may notice that qualifications differ in areas such as minimum age and minimum recommended training. Part of the reason for this is that the Department of Public Welfare established the standards for day-care facilities while the State Board of Private Academic schools established those for private nursery schools and kindergartens. Find out about the day-care regulations for your state. How do they compare with your state's nursery school regulations? Do you need to write to separate agencies in order to find this information?

Like the director, group supervisors

(teachers) must possess a bachelor's degree or an associate's degree in the same recommended fields but with two years' work experience instead of four. Assistant group supervisors (assistant teachers) require only a high school diploma, 15 credit hours in early childhood education, and one year of work experience in the field *or* a high school diploma and three years of work experience.

In addition to these positions some programs may employ *aides* for the purpose of assisting with daily activities under the guidance of the group supervisor. The kinds and numbers of aides and other personnel are usually determined by the number of children attending the day-care facility. An adult–child ratio of 1:7 is usually recommended for a group of children from three to four-and-one-half years of age, and of 1:10 from four-and-one-half to six. Younger children require much more individual attention, so a ratio of 1:3 is recommended for children up to eighteen months, and of 1:4 for those eighteen months to three years (see Table 1-5).

In addition to these paid day-care personnel, many centers encourage the involvement of supervised volunteers to work directly with the children. These volunteers, usually par-

ents, help the teachers with daily routines so that the children's needs can more adequately be met. They also serve to lower the adult–child ratios in centers with limited funds and, importantly, also help interpret the varying cultural patterns and expectancies of the children for the teacher. Most states require volunteers to be a minimum of 16 or 18 years of age and able to read and write.

The personnel described to this point, then, are those who work directly with the youngsters in providing caregiving services to children. This category includes the director, teachers, assistant teachers, aides, and volunteers. A second category of personnel, *nonprogram personnel,* also serve important roles in the success of day-care programs, as they furnish services that support or facilitate the caregiving program. This group includes dieticians, food-service personnel, medical staff, psychologists, caseworkers, maintenance staff, office staff, and transportation staff. Their professional qualifications will not be discussed at this point because most of you will be entering the professions mentioned earlier. However, all must meet licensing standards in their states and the qualifications established by their respective professions.

Table 1-5 *Adult-Child Ratios for Day-care Facilities*

Age of Child	Adult-Child Ratio	For a Group of 12 Children
Birth to 18 months	1:3	1 group supervisor 1 assistant supervisor 2 aides
18 months to 3 years	1:4	1 group supervisor 1 assistant supervisor 1 aide
3 years to 4½ years	1:7	1 group supervisor 1 assistant supervisor
4½ years to 6 years	1:10	1 group supervisor 1 aide
6 years to 8 years	1:10	1 group supervisor 1 aide

Of course, some of the nonprogram personnel may be hired directly by the center, while others may be retained on a need basis. For example, special funds may be set aside in order to make medical attention available on a daily basis for those children who need it (the physician is paid only as services are required). However, a permanent cook or maintenance worker is necessary in day-care centers because of the need for quality nutrition and for the cleaning and maintenance of a healthy, safe environment. Nonetheless, the major success of a day-care center depends on a clear commitment, from all program and nonprogram personnel, whether full- or part-time, to the welfare of young children.

PROFESSIONAL ETHICS

Knowledge and skill related to early childhood, then, contributes to your becoming a true professional. But this aspect of your training does not stand alone. A second component, that of possessing appropriate attitudes and feelings of responsibility, must be considered. These attitudes and feelings are often identified as "private systems of law" by professional groups, and one of the characteristics of a profession is that its members share a special code of ethics. Statements of professional ethics (personal responsibilities) in early childhood education describe an individual's role in the professional field and help to clarify his or her relationship with the children, their parents, and the community served by the child-care facility. The statements identify desirable professional behaviors that help to guide the proper functioning of child-care workers. Most professional groups create such statements as a way of offering standards for members. In 1978, the National Association for the Education of Young Children (NAEYC) published a handbook in which Lilian G. Katz

and Evangeline H. Ward (1978) proposed the following set of commitments for members of the early childhood profession:

AN INITIAL CODE OF ETHICS FOR EARLY CHILDHOOD EDUCATORS

Preamble
As an educator of young children in their years of greatest vulnerability, I, to the best of intent and ability, shall devote myself to the following commitments and act to support them.

For the Child
I shall accord the respect due each child as a human being from birth on.

I shall recognize the unique potentials to be fulfilled within each child.

I shall provide access to differing opinions and views inherent in every person, subject, or thing encountered as the child grows.

I shall recognize the child's right to ask questions about the unknowns that exist in the present so the answers (which may be within the child's capacity to discover) may be forthcoming eventually.

I shall protect and extend the child's physical well-being, emotional stability, mental capacities, and social acceptability.

For the Parents and Family Members
I shall accord each child's parents and family members respect for the responsibilities they carry.

By no deliberate action on my part will the child be held accountable for the incidental meetings of his or her parents and the attendant lodging of the child's destiny with relatives and siblings.

Recognizing the continuing nature of familial strength as support for the growing child, I shall maintain objectivity with regard to what I perceive as family weaknesses.

Maintaining family value systems and pride in cultural-ethnic choices or variations will supersede any attempts I might inadvertently or otherwise make to impose my values.

Because advocacy on behalf of children always requires that someone cares about or is strongly motivated by a sense of fairness and intervenes on behalf of children in relation to those services and institutions that impinge on their lives, I shall support family strength.

For Myself and the Early Childhood Profession
Admitting my biases is the first evidence of my willingness to become a conscious professional.

Knowing my capacity to continue to learn throughout life, I shall vigorously pursue knowledge about contemporary developments in early education by informal and formal means.

My role with young children demands an awareness of new knowledge that emerges from varied disciplines and the responsibility to use such knowledge.

Recognizing the limitation I bring to knowing intimately the ethical-cultural value systems of the multicultural American way of life, I shall actively seek the understanding and acceptance of the chosen ways of others to assist them educationally in meeting each child's needs for his or her unknown future impact on society.

Working with other adults and parents to maximize my strengths and theirs, both personally and professionally, I shall provide a model to demonstrate to young children how adults can create an improved way of living and learning through planned cooperation.

The encouragement of language development with young children will never exceed the boundaries of propriety or violate the confidence and trust of a child or that child's family.

I shall share my professional skills, information, and talents to enhance early education for young children wherever they are.

I shall cooperate with other persons and organizations to promote programs for children and families that improve their opportunities to utilize and enhance their uniqueness and strength.

I shall ensure that individually different styles of learning are meshed compatibly with individually different styles of teaching to help all people grow and learn well—this applies to adults learning to be teachers as well as to children.

After examining this list, you may wonder how these statements of ethics differ from competency statements as described earlier. This distinction is a fairly sophisticated one for you to make at this early period of your training, but the differences can best be made by sharing an illustration of each:

COMPETENCY

• The teacher will choose strategies appropriate for the developmental level of the children. (We are stating the behavior we intend to exhibit as we carry through the program.)

ETHIC

• The teacher will respect each child as a human being. (We are identifying specific ways of conducting ourselves as we carry through the program.)

Keep these ethical principles in mind as you progress not only through this course but also as you enter the early childhood profession. Try to grow within the spirit of each statement, for the degree to which you accept the standards will influence the quality of life for each child entrusted to you.

PERSONAL CHARACTERISTICS OF TEACHERS OF YOUNG CHILDREN

Professionalism, therefore, is a critical feature in your training to become an effective leader of young children. What you as an individual bring to your teaching, however, is equally important. Genuine warmth, friendliness, sense of humor, affection toward children—all these personality factors count as much as professionalism in determining the level of your success (see Figure 1-2). Working with children

Professionalism   +   Personality   =   Success

Figure 1-2   *Factors contributing to success in working with young children*

is a serious responsibility, one that combines what you as an individual bring to your work with your knowledge of the tasks of your position, how to do them, and why.

A willingness to learn about yourself and to examine your attitudes toward young children is important in determining whether your personal characteristics are appropriate for a career with children. How do you see yourself as a leader of children? What three words best describe your leadership behavior? How do others see you as a leader? These are important questions to consider as you begin your career, for your personal interactions with children are critical.

This book cannot deal in depth with the personal aspects of successful teaching, but you can make the most of your preprofessional training by doing the following:

1. Keep a written record of what you learn about yourself during your college training and how you behave in leadership situations with children.

2. Be open about your feelings and reactions during any experiences with young children.

3. Be willing to experiment with positive changes in personal behaviors and feel-

ings as they relate to leading young children.

4. Seek out and be receptive to feedback provided by those around you.

We can also be more specific. Since we all have our own feelings of what we think the personality of an effective leader or teacher is, write down your impressions of "good leadership." You may simply write words as they pop into your head (powerful, kind), or you may write a paragraph. Share your results with your classmates the next time you meet.

You may want to try this exercise again at the end of the semester or periodically throughout your college career to see how your ideas change with the passage of time. You can also gain a good sense of what qualities you bring to the child-care profession by reviewing the following checklist, which touches on some of the personal characteristics desirable for an effective child-care worker:

• I love young children.

• I know youngsters are active, so I eat and sleep well and exercise in order to stay physically fit.

• I observe young children so I can evaluate their levels of maturity and plan accordingly.

- I get along well with people.
- I am a hard worker.
- I am willing to put in extra time to complete a job.
- I am punctual and dependable.
- I can keep secrets regarding confidential matters.
- I admit mistakes and work hard to correct them.
- I observe the rules of the groups to which I belong.
- I leave my problems at home and do not let them affect my work.
- I ignore rumors and refuse to gossip.
- I keep myself groomed and neat.
- I keep my work area in order.
- I use supplies and equipment as carefully as if I purchased them myself.
- I take pride in my work.
- I follow directions and respect the leadership of others.
- I have a good sense of humor; I can laugh with others.
- I am a flexible person; I can vary my approach if the situation calls for it.
- I am curious and want to explore new ideas for working with young children.

Much can be said about each item in this list, but one especially deserves elaboration. That is the first item on the list: "I love young children." Once, while I was discussing this feature with a group of graduate students, one raised her hand and commented in a fairly forceful manner: "We've been talking about loving children for some time now and, frankly, I'm getting tired of it. I don't think you can *love* all your children. I love my husband, my parents, and my own youngsters at home, but

I don't love the children I teach. Sure, I have a close attachment to them or I wouldn't be teaching, but I don't *love* them." Naturally, this unexpected reaction created a great deal of discussion. The class attempted to convince the skeptic that *love* certainly was a way to describe the feelings of a teacher toward the children in his or her care. Finally, someone said something that seemed to hit home: "There are many different kinds of love among people, and the love for your spouse or parents is much different than the love of a teacher for her children." This statement was enlarged upon when the class brought me a special item for our next session. Figure 1-3 illustrates the kind of love teachers have for their students. The strong tie between teacher and child is very close to that between parent and child. Can you add any additional descriptive phrases to the list?

As an individual interested in a career with young children, you become trusted by parents, colleagues, and the community as someone who can make a significant positive contribution to the growth and development of young children. You must prepare for this responsibility by examining and reexamining your personal and professional characteristics as you progress through your training so that you can enter the profession as a confident, responsible, happy person, willing and able to move forward in the development of a unique leadership style.

STARTING OUT AS A TEACHER

Now let us suppose that you have met the minimum qualifications necessary for the attainment of a position in early childhood education. You begin your search for a job by checking the Career Development Center at your college, by reading the want ads of news-

√ SAINT PETER'S COLLEGE LIBRARY
JERSEY CITY, NEW JERSEY 07306

Love in a classroom is—

A teacher who helps you with your coat and boots!

Being asked to feed the fish!

A teacher who laughs at something funny you did!

A teacher who holds your hand when you're scared!

A teacher who pushes you on the swing!

A teacher who REALLY listens!

A teacher who hugs you at a special moment!

Caring

Sharing

Touching

Accepting

Feeling

Helping

Understanding

Figure 1-3   *One description of "love of a teacher for children"*

SAINT PETER'S COLLEGE LIBRARY
JERSEY CITY, NEW JERSEY 07306

papers in the communities in which you wish to live, or by making personal contacts with administrators of centers or schools. Several places ask you to fill out an application. Should your qualifications merit further consideration, you may be invited to an interview. Interviews are usually carefully planned by the administrators in charge, not as inquisitions but as comfortable discussions during which the organization gets to know you and you get to know the organization. Questions are usually designed to elicit all of the personal and professional information about applicants that the organization needs to make its decision. Generally, you will be given a careful explanation of the position and its requirements, along with salary expectations. Salaries vary widely in the early childhood field. Some private day-care centers or nursery schools offer minimum wage to beginning teachers, with little or no payroll benefits such as health insurance or retirement. Starting public school day-care, prekindergarten, kindergarten, or primary grade teachers often receive in excess of $10,000 for a nine- or ten-month school year, with a full range of payroll benefits. Although salary is often a major factor when deciding whether to accept a professional position, it is wise to give careful consideration to other factors, too. Get to know the facilities, the administrators to whom you will be responsible, the number of children you will have in your care, the staff with whom you will be working, and anything else that can influence your job satisfaction.

To further develop this scene, imagine that a feeling of satisfaction exists between you and the school or center. You are selected for the teaching position and you accept. You now face the first big question of your professional career: "What do I do now?" This is the main concern of most new teachers, and in this situation, you are not alone. Lilian Katz (1972) described this concern for survival as a characteristic reaction of teachers in Stage 1 of her *four developmental stages of preschool teachers:*

Stage 1: You are preoccupied with survival. You ask yourself questions such as "Can I get through the day in one piece? Without losing a child? Can I make it until the end of the week? Until the next vacation? Can I really do this kind of work day after day? Will I be accepted by my colleagues? (first year)"

During this period, according to Katz, teachers need support, understanding, encouragement, reassurance, comfort, and guidance. They need instruction in specific ways of handling complex behavior in children, especially since classroom management problems can cause intense feelings of inadequacy at this stage. Katz went on to characterize the remaining three developmental stages of teachers:

Stage 2: You decide you *can* survive. You begin to focus on individual children who pose problems and on troublesome situations, and you ask yourself these or similar questions: "How can I help a shy child? How can I help a child who does not seem to be learning?" (second year)

Stage 3: You begin to tire of doing the same things with the children. You like to meet with other teachers, scan magazines, and search through other sources of information in order to discover new projects and activities to provide for the children. You ask questions about new developments in the field: "Who is doing what? Where? What are some of the new materials, techniques, approaches, and ideas?" (third and fourth years)

Stage 4: This is the stage of maturity. You now have enough experience to ask deeper, more abstract questions calling for introspective and researched replies: "What are my historical and philosophical roots? What is the nature of growth and learning? How are educational decisions made? Can schools change societies? Is teaching really a profession?

The point Katz made in describing the four stages of preschool teachers is that the need for furthering your education and becoming exposed to new ideas changes as you gain experience. Just because you have completed a specialized professional program and begun your first job, your concern for further training should not come to a halt. Administrators usually realize this and follow a plan for staff development in order to make their operation more effective and efficient. Generally, such staff development programs address areas in need of special attention, such as:

- orientation of new staff members to the facilities of the school or center
- planned field trips, workshops, or speakers to gain new ideas
- staff meetings where concerns or ideas can be shared
- financial assistance to enable staff to take further course work or receive other kinds of formal training

In addition to these training programs, your personal effort to keep up to date with innovations in the field can be enhanced by seeking membership in major professional groups. A brief list of some of those groups especially influential in advancing programs and policies for young children are given below:

Association for Childhood Education International (ACEI)
3615 Wisconsin Avenue, NW
Washington, D.C. 20016
Journal: *Childhood Education*

National Association for the Education of Young Children (NAEYC)
1834 Connecticut Avenue, NW
Washington, D.C. 20009
Journal: *Young Children*

Day Care and Child Development Council of America
1401 K Street, NW
Washington, D.C. 20005
Publications: *Voice for Children; Action for Children*

Participation in these groups at the early stage of your professional preparation can be very rewarding as you get to know the problems and successes of others in the field. You may even become interested in forming a student organization on campus, where ideas can be shared freely in a more relaxed setting than in the regular classroom.

SOME FINAL THOUGHTS

The most important ingredient of a successful early childhood program is a good teacher. The physical setting is important, but the skills and enthusiasm of the teacher is of primary importance. The teacher's personality, attitude, and behavior determines the tone of the environment and makes a lasting impact on the children, on their families, and, indirectly, on society in general. Few individuals are more important in the lives of young children than their parents, close relatives, and teachers. Teachers are admired and imitated; they are expected to display courage, cleanliness, honesty, openmindedness, generosity, faithfulness, sensitivity, tact, and other admirable qualities. Teachers of young children should be among the finest people we can imagine. But being a fine person does not in itself guarantee success in teaching. A superior teacher must also possess a sound educational background. The successful teacher is a person and a professional who considers it a privilege to be an early childhood educator.

Professional skills develop through an effective combination of education and experience. As they grow, teachers constantly re-evaluate themselves, their children, and their techniques, so that they can provide the most well-balanced, educationally sound environment possible. As you are faced with career choices throughout the next few years, you will undoubtedly ask yourself two questions: Am I happy with what I am? With the skills I now possess, what can I become? The early childhood field can provide answers to these questions, because it offers many careers involving young children. In deciding which career is most appropriate for you, consider these questions now and as you progress throughout your professional training:

- Why am I interested in a career with young children?
- What do I enjoy most about working with young children?
- What special experiences, skills, and abilities will I bring to my work with young children?
- With what age child do I feel most comfortable?
- Can I work with children demonstrating special needs?
- Am I sensitive to the differences of children from racial, cultural, ethnic, or socio-economic groups other than mine?

- What kind of early childhood setting is most attractive to me?
- How much responsibility can I handle while working with young children? other adults?
- Do I find the contributions of early childhood professional groups and organizations to be of value to my career?
- How will I continue to accumulate specific learning experiences and educational background as I grow into my career serving young children and their families?

Now that you have examined the variety of careers available in the early childhood field and the qualifications necessary to ensure success in each, the next chapter will introduce you to the major historical influences that have helped make our profession what it is today. Although much of the information may surprise or even shock you, the message contained in Chapter 2 is one of constant hope that the lives of young children may be made as safe and productive as possible.

A PERSPECTIVE ON HISTORY

Examining the Evolution of Our Profession

"Why do we need to study all those ancient educators anyway? They're not going to help us once we begin teaching; their ideas are so old." Either through such complaints or their body language, my students in introductory early childhood courses often communicate their displeasure at the prospect of going back into history to examine the contributions of prominent philosophers and educators. Rather than offering clichés such as "We learn from their successes and mistakes" or "Their ideas are still very much a part of our current thinking," I often tell this old tale.

There is an old story that bears retelling because it illustrates so well how easily things can go on being accepted without ever being questioned.

When Bismarck was Prussian ambassador to the court of Alexander II in the early 1860s he looked out a window and saw a sentry on duty in the middle of the vast lawn.

He inquired of the Czar as to why the man was there. The Czar asked his aide-de-camp. The aide didn't know. The general in charge of the troops was summoned.

In answer to the question the general replied, "I beg to inform his majesty that it is in accordance with ancient custom."

"What was the origin of that custom?" interrupted Bismarck.

"I don't recall at present," answered the general.

"Investigate and report the result," ordered Alexander.

The investigation took three days. They found that the sentry was posted there by an order put on the book 80 years before.

It all started one morning in the spring of 1780. Catherine the Great looked out on the lawn and saw the first flower thrusting above the frozen soil.

She ordered the sentry posted to prevent any-one's picking the flower, and in 1860 there was still a sentry on the lawn.

The sentry was a memorial to custom, habit, or just everyone saying, "But we've always done it that way."

And so it is today. Far too few ask, "Why?" When told that something can't be changed, far too few ask, "Why not?" "Why can't we find a new or better way?" "How can it be done more easily and effectively?" "What is worth saving?"

After telling the story of the flower, I ask my students to interpret its implied message. I would ask you to do the same. Stop reading now and jot down some of your own imme-diate impressions. The following comments are representative of my students' responses:

The flower was guarded every year and people didn't really know why. Even though it was a ridiculous idea, no one suggested a change for over eighty years. I hate to think what would happen to early childhood edu-cation if everyone in our field refused to examine what we're doing and why we're doing it.

The people really didn't suggest change because they didn't know why the practice of guarding the flower was started in the first place. If they would have tried to find out earlier, the dumb custom wouldn't have been around so long. I guess that's why it's important to examine the history of early childhood, too . . . so we wouldn't lock our-selves blindly into past practices merely because that's the way it was always done.

Yes, all you've said is true. But, if the custom was a good one, it would have been interest-ing to see how *it* was started, too. I can think of a couple of old customs that are parts of our lives such as celebrating holidays like Groundhog Day or Valentine's Day, and I have no idea as to how they got started. They're something we do automatically every year and enjoy, but don't even realize how they ever began. It would be interesting to find out. I guess the same is true for early childhood—it would be interesting to see

how some of our good practices also got their start in the past . . . how and why did they happen?

If we didn't know what happened in the past, how could we be convinced that what we consider innovative today is really new?

Most of us do not think of history in these terms. We often associate history with mem-orizing dates of battles, the names and order of presidents, and so on. The "living spirit" of history, however, should transcend facts and become transformed into experience. Natu-rally, such an approach does not eliminate facts, but rises above them by introducing signifi-cant events into our lives and encouraging us to reflect upon their meanings. The American philosopher George Santayana wrote that a nation not remembering its history is doomed to repeat it. I am sure he was referring to the failures, not the successes, of the past. Perhaps the same is true for the field of early child-hood education and those of us who are involved in it.

This "historical consciousness" is difficult to achieve. Most of us are bound by particular forms of immediacy. An event one month in the future often seems a generation away. Chronological time is remote and unreal, and is often bound by the limits of our memories. People begin to develop a true sense of his-tory as they gain a sense of personal relation-ship to the past. An example of this character-istic is how indifferent many of us felt when parents, grandparents, or other older relatives tried to relate their "history" to us. Later, per-haps after they had passed away, we hungered for the opportunity to quiz them about all they had experienced. Obviously, our interest in history grew as we became personally involved and were able to accumulate the level of per-sonal attachment to enable us to reflect upon past experiences with meaning. That charac-teristic is not easily promoted in this course, especially since at this point in your profes-sional training many of you have not yet developed that "personal attachment" necessary to gain meaning from the history of early childhood education. I will attempt to overcome this handicap by representing history as something that exists as much in the present as in the past. I will attempt to make you aware of the power of history in your professional life and ask you to become conscious of yourselves as makers of history.

In summary, then, do not investigate the following material for the purpose of storing a conglomeration of facts to be recalled on a quiz. Instead, look at it in the same light as the general in the story who searched for a reason why the flower was kept so closely guarded for generations. Investigate the past to explain what we are presently doing in early childhood education and examine the present in order to understand its historical significance for the future.

As you examine the history of early childhood education, you will realize that things have changed dramatically over the years. The reason is not simple; many forces combine to contribute to change. Mostly, however, changes in early childhood education can be described on two fronts: the conditions of society and the beliefs people have about the nature of childhood. The conditions of society often influence our views of childhood, and the ways we view children often determine how we interact with them, the expectancies we have, and the care we provide. As your conception of childhood will influence how you teach or care for young children, so the way adults understood children in the past influenced their behaviors and attitudes toward their children. Lloyd DeMause went as far as to state that those changing adult–child relationships were a greater factor in the overall human condition throughout history than any other single influence. DeMause (1975) said: "*the major dynamic in historical change is ultimately neither technology nor economics* [italics mine]. More important are the changes in personality that grow from differences between generations

in the quality of the relationship between parent and child. Good parenting is something that has been achieved only after centuries as generation after generation of parents tried to overcome the abuse of their own childhoods by reaching out to their children on more mature levels of relating" (p. 85).

Such an observation serves to convince us of the importance of good child care, for the ways by which we provide for youngsters influence not only their personal development, but the conditions of society for generations. Thus, we need to consider some key questions as we examine childhood history: Did adults always act toward children as they do today? What was it like to have been a child during particular historical eras? How did the ways in which children were viewed affect their growing up?

Going back to earliest historical accounts of childhood, we can easily understand that the treatment of youngsters was as primitive in comparison to contemporary views of childhood as the original abacus is to today's field of computer technology. The history of childhood could be considered a nightmare; the farther back we go, the more likely were children to have been killed at birth, abandoned, beaten, sexually abused, or mistreated. It would be easy to discount such treatment of children because of society's general conditions at the time—poor housing, a lack of food, medical ignorance, and inadequate health care—but the resentment and hostility toward children at a very early age often was greater than associated feelings toward animals. As a matter of fact, societies for the prevention of cruelty to animals sprang up earlier in England and the United States than did societies for the prevention of cruelty to children. The following story of Mary Ellen illustrates this dilemma (Wallace, Wallechinsky, and Wallace, 1981).

Before 1875, U.S. authorities had no legal means to interfere in cases of battered children. The laws were changed with the help

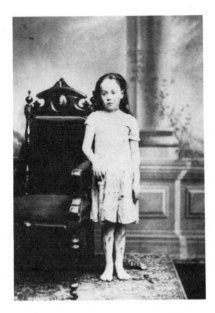

SPCA's before-and-after photos of Mary Ellen, with scissors used to punish her

of the Society for the Prevention of Cruelty to Animals (SPCA).

A 9-year-old named Mary Ellen became the exemplar of the battered children's plight. Indentured to Francis and Mary Connolly (and rumored to be the daughter of Mary's ex-husband), the girl was whipped daily, stabbed with scissors and tied to a bed. Neighbors reported the situation to Etta Wheeler, a church worker, in 1874. When Wheeler found that there was no lawful way to rescue the child from her brutal guardians, she went to Henry Bergh of the SPCA for help.

Under the premise that the child was a member of the animal kingdom, the SPCA obtained a writ of habeas corpus to remove Mary Ellen from her home. On April 9, 1874, she was carried into the New York Supreme Court, where her case was tried. She was pitifully thin, with a scissor wound on her cheek. Mrs. Connolly was sentenced to a year in prison. Mary Ellen was given a new home. The following April, the New York Society for the Prevention of Cruelty to Children (NYSPCC) was incorporated.

Before-and-after photos of Mary Ellen (as a pathetic waif upon her rescue and as a

healthy child a year later) still hang at the New York SPCA, framed with Mrs. Connolly's scissors.

Such cruel treatment of young children was not uncommon during the past. Do not assume, however, that similar treatment was accorded all youngsters throughout history, for there have always been parents who loved and cared for their children. For them and for many others, mistakes were made because of a basic ignorance of childhood rather than hatred. Also, although we may live in an enlightened time, we cannot ignore the fact that cases of abused children today are shockingly common. The point is that as we look further into the history of childhood, we find that the disregard of feelings and rights of children was much more prevalent than today. We can almost assume that such disregard was more the "rule of thumb" than the "exception to the rule."

Unfortunately, it was not until the mid-nineteenth century that some of the worst conditions of childhood began to be alleviated. Spurred on by various *child advocacy* (children's rights) individuals and groups, child welfare reforms gradually emerged to relieve situations such as those of little Mary Ellen and the thousands of youngsters, who, even after 1863 when Lincoln freed the slaves, legally remained "chattel." Considered the property of their parents, children could be used to augment the family income, pay off a debt, or enhance a business deal. What led to such a hardhearted, merciless view of childhood? To answer that question, we must go all the way back to medieval times because the attitudes toward children then, although generally cruel, were maintained well into the 1700s and 1800s.

CHILDHOOD THROUGH THE EIGHTEENTH CENTURY

Perhaps the most meaningful way of examining the plight of children during the earliest phases of this historical treatment is to describe the period of infancy during medieval times. The historical period we usually associate with knights in shining armor, castles, and quaint villages was replete with ignorance about babies and young children. Babies were delivered at home, usually with the mother reclining in bed but sometimes while she was seated in a chair. Midwives commonly received the child since physicians saw the practice of delivering babies as below their level of proficiency. After receiving the infant, midwives severed and tied the umbilical cord, cleaned the baby, and rubbed the gums with honey to cleanse the inside of the mouth. If the baby was illegitimate, however, he or she was probably killed at birth. However, the killing of legitimate children was a fairly common practice during medieval times and continued well into the nineteenth century. The reasons for such a merciless practice are too complex to elaborate upon here, but may in part be due to two

major influences. First, DeMause examined documents from the past and found that the killing of newborns ("infanticide") stemmed from a powerful urge of women to "undo" motherhood. Infanticidal acts, which included stabbing, mutilation, decapitation, and strangulation, were commonly carried out because no law at that time prevented them from happening to infants. Second, any child who cried too much, had some sort of birth defect, was not perfect in every way, or was a girl (boys were more highly favored) was an unfortunate candidate to be thrown into a river, flung into dung heaps, starved to death, or left exposed on a roadside as prey for wild animals. For those fortunate enough to live, some were used as payments for debts and medical services or simply given away for various reasons: "to learn to speak" (Disraeli), "to cure timidity" (Clara Barton), "for health" (Edmund Burke), and because they simply were not wanted (Yeats, Swift) (DeMause, 1974, p. 33).

For those children who were kept, the midwife would "harden" them by first salting them and bathing them in ice water. Later the babies were tied up in *swaddling* bands. The act of swaddling children involved wrapping them in endless cloth bandages with the arms and legs bound tightly to the body; the process took more than two hours to complete. The supposed purpose of such binding, which lasted the entire first year of infancy, was to prevent the baby from damaging its eyes or ears, breaking an arm or leg, touching its genitals, or "crawling like a beast." However, DeMause believes that the real reason for swaddling was that it made infants easier to care for since they withdrew themselves into sleep. Hung on pegs on the wall or laid behind hot ovens, the infants led an extremely quiet, passive life. Parents and caretakers regularly amused themselves with the swaddled infants, often throwing them around from one to another like a ball. Many babies suffered broken bones because of such tossing and some were even killed. The brother of Henry IV of

France, for instance, was dropped and killed while being tossed by his nurses from one window to another (DeMause, 1975).

The amount of time parents actually spent with their babies was minimal. Infants were sent away to "wet nurses," who furnished breast milk and care for the infant. Wet nursing was one of the very few sources of income for poor young women of Europe; therefore, it was especially attractive for them to become pregnant so they could produce their own breast milk. Unfortunately, however, this meant that the wet nurse would often neglect or kill her own baby, being concerned only that she had enough milk to sell. The wealthy upper classes frowned upon breast feeding their babies, so they sent them to wet nurses for two years or more. Even the poorest of mothers refused to feed their own babies, often putting them to the nipple of an animal to suck. The milk of many different animals including the cow, goat, dog, horse, and reindeer was used. Breast feeding was very unpopular in medieval Europe; mothers who did so were considered to be "swinish and filthy." The results of this attitude were horrifying. According to one estimate, prior to 1850, if newborns were not breast fed, chances were only one in eight that they would survive to see their first birthday.

Children were weaned from the breast in two major ways. First, the mother or wet nurse simply chewed the solid food before it was fed to the child. Second, a mixture called *pap* was prepared. Although there are many recipes for pap, the most basic consists of a mixture of animal milk or water with bread or grain. Another pap recipe was boiling stale bread in water, beer, or wine and then straining it through a sieve and seasoning it with honey or sugar.

At about the age of three or four, those children who were not abandoned, sold, given as security for debts, or simply given away to someone else were returned home by the wet nurses. Although we now consider this to be

the age of young childhood, the idea of childhood did not exist in medieval society. The particular awareness of what distinguishes children from adults was lacking. "That is why, as soon as the child could live without the constant solicitude of his mother, his nanny, or his cradle-rocker, he belonged to adult society" (Aries, 1962, p. 128). Not knowing why this "adult" was acting in such ways foreign to adulthood, parents often found young children difficult to care for. Their actions were interpreted as "demonlike" and, if allowed to continue, making them susceptible to "the power of the devil." To keep their youngsters in line, adults regularly terrorized them in a variety of ways. Opium and liquor were often given to children to keep them from crying. Children were tied to chairs to keep them from crawling, and, even into the nineteenth century, strings were attached to the children's clothes to control their movements in a manner much as a marionette is controlled. Acts of discipline would be described as child abuse by today's standards. Beatings were administered with instruments such as whips, shovels, canes, and rods. Such "discipline" was widely advocated through the nineteenth century (when it gradually began to go out of style) as century after century of battered children grew up into adulthood and battered their own. Public objection was rare, and even humanists such as John Comenius and Johann Pestalozzi approved of beating children (DeMause, 1974).

As beatings began to decrease, other forms of punishment had to be found to control children. Shutting children in dark closets or drawers for hours was a popular technique. Another method was to threaten children with hideous masks, with "ghosts" who would steal bad children and suck their blood, or with "devils" who would take the children away to Hell, where they would live forever in a red hot oven. Some parents went as far as taking their children to the gallows where they were forced to view the executions. This experience was intended to serve as a lesson to the youngsters of the consequences of wandering from acceptable behavior.

Thus, prior to the age of six, most children were neglected and despised; they were things to be tolerated until they could learn to live without constant care and careful control. At the age of six, children became "real people" and entered the adult world. From medieval times into the 1800s, children dressed as adults, worked with adults in tasks around the home and in the fields, drank with adults, and even participated freely in sexual activities. Children could be everything an adult could be; they were husbands or wives, field or factory workers, and kings or queens. In effect, they were "miniature adults"—the same as adults but maybe just a bit weaker and less intelligent. Louis XIV, for example, became king of France in 1643 at the age of five. He dressed as any king, wearing a heavy crown and ornate clothes. Furthermore, he led the daily life of an adult king. He drank wine, partied through the night, and even played sexual games with his nursemaids (Plumb, 1974).

Even though ideas of childhood innocence began to surface during the 1600s and 1700s, the view of miniature adulthood was maintained well into the 1800s. As soon as children became toilet trained, learned to feed themselves, mastered the skill of dressing and undressing, and avoided possible dangers, they became working members of the family. Placed in the fields, mines, or shops, they worked along with the older adults and were expected to assume the same responsibilities.

CHILDREN AS VIEWED FROM THE EIGHTEENTH THROUGH THE NINETEENTH CENTURIES

The eighteenth century reflected economic and social conditions somewhat improved from those during the preceding era, but they still were far different from today's. The nineteenth century was characterized by industrial revolutions throughout Europe, so the acceptance of children now became one of increasing economic advantage. Because they could be made to work long hours in badly ventilated, cramped coal mines (often only 22 to 28 inches in height) or factories, five- or six-year-old boys and girls were now accepted as advantageous to the economic survival of families. They often worked six days a week, starting before the sun rose and ending after the sun set. Surprisingly, until 1833 there were no child labor laws restricting the conditions under which children worked, and it was only in 1833 that a European law restricted the work of nine- through thirteen-year-olds to 48 hours per week and those older than thirteen to 68 hours. This law, though, applied only to children working in factories; those working in mines (even as young as four years old) were not legally protected (Kessen, 1965). Thus, although children were still viewed as miniature adults during the nineteenth century, they now became objects of social worth rather than burdens; they were exploited as an economic advantage because of their cheap labor.

Despite the popularity of these practices and for reasons not completely understood, there began to emerge humanitarian and religious movements to distinguish children from adults. Perhaps tied to the Reformation, this movement began on a small scale, but gradually it convinced parents and other adults to accept a new attitude toward the child and education. The child was soon to become a "special person," no longer subject to the conditions described in the following poem.

THE CRY OF THE CHILDREN

The young lambs are bleating in the
 meadow,
The young birds are chirping in the nest,
The young fawns are playing with shadows,
The young flowers are blowing toward the
 west—

Working in factories for up to twelve or sixteen hours a day was not seen as an unreasonable expectation for young children even at the turn of this century. These "miniature adults" were viewed as having the same capabilities as mature adults, only on a smaller scale.
(Culver Pictures)

But the young, young children, O my
     brothers,
They are weeping bitterly!
They are weeping in the playtime of the
     others
In the country of the free.
They look up with their pale and sunken
     faces
And their looks are sad to see
For the man's hoary anguish draws and
     presses
Down the cheeks of infancy.

        —Elizabeth Barrett Browning

As we enter this entirely new phase in the evolution of views regarding the nature of childhood, keep in mind that the descriptive characteristics are merely summarizations of the behavior of parents and other adults at any given time. Presumably many parents throughout the years responded sensitively and humanely to their children or else humanity would not have survived until today. We must recognize that some individuals were brought up to be kind and sympathetic people or else we would not have had "advocates of childhood" arguing against the inhumane treatment of children.

The Child as Innately Bad

The roots of child development theory originated during the nineteenth century mainly through the writings of theologians and humanitarians. Even though most people at the time refused to recognize childhood, the major fundamental issues raised by these theologians and humanists were in regard to the basic nature of children. For instance, if there is such a state of individual development, are children, by nature, basically good or inherently evil? The earliest widely acceptable ideas were those espoused by theologians who told parents that the "misbehavior" of their children was due to "inborn wickedness." Thomas Martin, as well as other philosophers of the 1800s, described this inborn wickedness as "native depravity." In 1818, Martin said:

> *Native depravity* [italics mine] is certainly the source of all moral evil in the conduct of mankind; and as we bring with us into the world a nature replete with evil propensities ... so the first emotions of a mind ... will be emotions of evil, and the first efforts of powers so depraved will be evil; and hence it will be easy to trace the follies of youth ... to the impurities of the heart, which is declared by the highest authority to be Deceitful above all things, and desperately wicked. [Kessen, 1965, pp. 37–38].

Those advocating these notions of "innate wickedness" drew their support from Christian writings that stressed that original sin was the act of defiance committed by Adam in the Garden of Eden. It was believed that, from that time on, original sin was inherited by all children, causing their "bad behaviors." Although the prevailing attitude of childhood was such a disturbing one at the turn of the nineteenth century, a positive note was achieved. It was the first time in the history of humanity that a separate stage of childhood began to be widely recognized. Despite his admonitions of native depravity, Martin went on to say these things about the hope of children: "It [childhood] is the morning of life when every thing is beginning; the dawn of wisdom, when every thing is yet to be learned; the preparation for effort, when every thing is yet to be done ... Ah, happy day! the sweetest and fairest of life!" (Kessen, 1965, p. 36).

Because childhood, although basically wicked by nature, was mercifully viewed as the "dawn of wisdom," techniques of educat-

ing individuals at such a formative period of development were a major consideration. Advocates of early education sought the salvation of youngsters through the establishment of schools designed to develop good character, obedience, honesty, industry, and other socially acceptable qualities.

A belief in the inherent sinfulness of children implied a basic mistrust between child and adult. Severe discipline extracted moral behavior from children long before they could understand the reasons for such behavior. Because behaviors were formed primarily through such harsh disciplinary techniques as beatings and isolation, interactions between children and adults were characterized by distance and mutual incompatibility. Parents were cautioned against being too fond of their children or too familiar with them, lest their children should undermine their authority. Such fondness and familiarity were believed to breed contempt and irreverency in children (Illick, 1974). As bleak as this description appears to be, this is progress from earlier times when most adults refused to admit that such a stage as childhood even exists. And even though childhood was now considered to be a special phase of development, the view of infancy was much less enlightened. Doctors, who once considered mother's milk to be "white blood" that transmitted the mother's characteristics to the child, now warned mothers that breast feeding infants when the mother was depressed or irritable could prove fatal to the child. Even into this century, experts warned against playing with babies because it ruined their nerves; tickling, tumbling, and tossing were thought to make the baby fretful, thereby ruining the child for life. Such ideas were not confined to the distant past. John B. Watson, a prominent psychologist during the early 1900s, said this about handling babies as late as 1930: "Treat [children] as though they were young adults. Never hug or kiss them; never let them sit on your lap. If you must kiss them, kiss them once on the forehead when you say good night.

Shake hands with them in the morning . . . you will be utterly ashamed of the mawkish, sentimental way you have been handling [them]" (pp. 81–82).

As foreign as this message must appear to you in today's world, the basis of medieval thinking was still espoused by widely respected theorists of childhood development until less than 60 years ago.

The Child as Innately Good

Not satisfied with negative interpretations of childhood, humanists concerned with life's dreadful conditions during the 1800s focused special attention on the plight of young children. These reformers were repulsed by the popular description of chidren during their time and proclaimed, instead, the value of childhood as a period of innocence during life in need of special protection. They introduced the earliest notions not only of childhood as a positive stage of development, but also of an individual's development as a progression through a series of periods, or stages, each one dependent upon the preceding.

This philosophy was quite a reversal on the traditional view of children; it offered innocence and natural goodness as a description of childhood. Although we commonly attribute such thinking to the nineteenth century, earlier writers, who went against the grain of popular thought, provided the groundwork for positive views on the nature of children. For example, in 1628 John Earle announced that: "A child is a man in a small letter, yet the best copy of Adam before he tasted of Eve or the apple . . . His soul is yet a white paper unscribbled with observations of the world . . . he knows no evil" (Earle, 1928, pp. 191–192).

Despite such admonitions, it was not until well over 100 years later that Jean Jacques Rousseau, the individual commonly cited as the most influential in advancing the notion

of a positive childhood, wrote the popular treatise *Emile,* in which he described his concept of childhood's nature:

> God makes all things good; man meddles with them and they become evil. He forces one soil to yield the products of another, one tree to bear another's fruit. He confuses and confounds time, place, and natural condition. He mutilates his dog, his horse, and his slave. He destroys and defaces all things; he loves all that is deformed and monstrous; he will have nothing as nature made it, not even man himself, who must learn his paces like a saddlehorse, and be shaped to his master's taste like the trees in his garden. [1762, p. 5]

Rousseau felt his thoughts regarding the natural goodness of children and the negative influence adults may have on their development were especially important for mothers, the primary source of child rearing during his time. Because of this conviction, Rousseau believed in the relevance of education at home and saw the mother as the most important educator of the child. This idea brought about an emphasis on early education, reflecting feelings that the child could be truly educated through active intellectual and moral techniques.

Such counsel was openly offered primarily to mothers rather than teachers because there were few schools for children younger than age twelve during the eighteenth century. Although his thoughts on motherhood were revolutionary and stirred some new child-rearing practices, Rousseau's view on education in general reserved him a prominent place in the history of early childhood. Rousseau felt that schools should not be based on the harsh methods so popularly used during his time, but, instead, should be restructured so that the innocent children were placed in an environment of freedom, where adults could not corrupt their essential purity. Educators slowly began to follow this advice as they patterned methods to allow children full utilization of their senses and open contact with nature. Books, the common teaching tool of the 1700s, were totally excluded from schools based upon the thinking of Rousseau. "I hate books," wrote Rousseau. "They only teach us to talk about things we know nothing about" (1762, p. 124). Rousseau's only exception would be *Robinson Crusoe,* because of the way Crusoe learned all about survival on a desert island by being totally immersed in those surroundings. Likewise, Rousseau recommended that children should learn by being totally immersed in their surroundings and left free to explore, to imagine, to gather firsthand knowledge, and to use these naturally kind feelings in their relationship toward others.

In contrast to the harsh methods of discipline advocated by the "innately bad child" orientation, Rousseau recommended "well-regulated liberty" in moral education: "never punish [the child], for he does not know what it is to do wrong; never make him say, 'Forgive me,' for he does not know how to do you wrong. Wholly unmoral in his actions, he can do nothing morally wrong, and he deserves neither punishment nor reproof" (1762, p. 61).

According to this philosophy, children are born with only goodness in their heart and, if left alone without the vanity, jealousy, and envy of adults permeating their environment, would flower into fit moral beings. Rousseau often referred to "flowering" or "unfolding" to describe internal processes by which children gradually develop and mature from special developmental periods such as infancy and childhood into adulthood: "Nature requires children to be children before they are men. By endeavoring to pervert this order, we produce forward fruits, that have neither maturity nor taste, and will not fail soon to wither and corrupt" (Rousseau, 1762, p. 120).

Rousseau's educational ideals were applied to European schooling and eventually led to the development of two especially significant schools—those of Johann Pestalozzi and Friedrich Froebel. Both of these men could

be described as individuals who built the bridge between the philosophy of *Emile* and the community of educators in the late 1700s.

JOHANN HEINRICH PESTALOZZI (1746–1827)

Johann Pestalozzi was born in Switzerland. He was not as well educated as Rousseau, but he became a great teacher, whose methodology reflected a genuine concern for the poor villagers and farmers of rural Switzerland. Although not a strong writer of educational theory, Pestalozzi's innermost feelings about education closely resembled the writings of Rousseau. The following appeared in a letter written in 1799.

> I believe that the first development of thought in the child is very much disturbed by a wordy system of teaching, which is not adapted either to his faculties or the circumstances of his life.
>
> According to my experience, success depends upon whether what is taught to children commends itself to them as true, through being closely connected with their own personal observation and experience . . . I hold it to be extremely important that men should be encourged to learn by themselves and allowed to develop freely. It is in this way alone that the diversity of individual talent is produced and made evident. [1972, pp. 54–55]

Convinced of this education through nature philosophy, Pestalozzi purchased a farm and started a school there in order to test his ideas. The establishment of his school, called *Neuhof,* actually represented a distinct turning point in the history of early childhood education because it was the first time a prominent philosopher actually went beyond speaking or writing his ideas to actually teaching in a real school setting. Admonishing teachers that their role was to teach children, not subjects, Pestalozzi designed a method to follow the natural path of a child's development. The teacher, according to Pestalozzi, should allow children to explore their environment through their senses.

Pestalozzi, like Rousseau, felt that the most influential teachers were mothers, so he wrote two books in an attempt to educate mothers in detailed procedures for teaching their own children: *How Gertrude Teaches Her Children* and *Book for Mothers*. With these ideas on the importance of parenthood, Pestalozzi anticipated other educators by more than 150 years!

Pestalozzi was criticized because he could not describe his teaching approach precisely, and, consequently, others could not seem to duplicate Pestalozzi's methods. However, his overall feelings of love, trust, and physical exploration of the environment marked Pestalozzi as a great and dedicated teacher.

FRIEDRICH WILHELM FROEBEL (1782–1852)

Friedrich Froebel was born in Germany and brought up in a secluded home by a strictly religious father and an overbearing, rejecting stepmother. Having never experienced a warm home life, he left as an adolescent to become apprenticed as a forester. This was a period of his life when Froebel developed a strong love for nature, a feeling that would permeate his later educational philosophy. After the forestry position, Froebel moved from job to job and even attended several universities, where he studied science and philosophy. These accumulated experiences resulted in a personal philosophy that ultimately extended into Froebel's educational theory. That philosophy, "The Law of Universal Unity," emphasized the unity of all living things—a oneness

of God, nature, and man. Thus, Froebel viewed children as basically good since God is within all.

Froebel never received formal training in education, but he was a natural teacher, who developed strong interests in young children. Concerned with the overwhelmingly restrictive child-rearing and educational practices of his time, Froebel sought alternatives. He became interested in the work of Pestalozzi and visited the school in Yverdun to study Pestalozzi's methods. Froebel was both impressed and alarmed by what he saw. He was elevated by the application of Rousseau's ideas to schooling young children, but he was bewildered and depressed by Pestalozzi's lack of ability to explain what he was doing. According to Froebel, Pestalozzi's response to questions about his method consistently seemed to be, "Go and see for yourself." Because Froebel's rigid nature would not allow him to accept such an ambiguous explanation, he ventured to originate a more planned, specific, and useful method. A brief period in the army interrupted the project but also brought a positive influence. The army was a constructive socializing experience for Froebel, inspiring him to grow from a basically solitary individual to an open, engaging person. Back from the army, Froebel became completely involved in developing a program designed for very young children.

The fruit of Froebel's labor ripened in 1837, when, now in his 50s, Froebel established his first *kindergarten* in an old powder mill near Blankenburg, Germany. Unlike today's kindergarten programs, which accept children aged five years, Froebel's first kindergarten accepted children from one to seven years of age. Froebel chose the word *kindergarten* ("children's garden") for his school because he frequently compared the development of young children to leaves, plants, or gardens. He saw the child's natural growth process as being like that of plants; with the proper love and care, the child grows naturally and blooms into full beauty. Interestingly, Froebel did not use kindergarten as the first name for his school. He initially called it the *Child Nurturing and Activity Institute* but finally settled on the kindergarten title during a reflective walk in the woods that he enjoyed so much.

Froebel developed a carefully planned, systematic program in which the teacher was responsible for guiding and directing the child. He based his curriculum on the idea of play, which was a revolutionary idea at this time. During Froebel's time, play was popularly viewed only as a natural childhood activity with no particular educational benefit, but Froebel believed in the educational value of play. With this goal in mind, Froebel designed three basic elements for his curriculum: *Gifts, Occupations,* and *Mother Plays.*

Gifts were concrete objects to be manipulated by the children in accordance with the teacher's instructions. They were used for learning colors, shapes, and concepts of counting, measuring, contrasting, and comparing. The first Gift, originally intended for infants and toddlers, was a set of six colored worsted (smooth, hard woolen surface) balls with six lengths of yarn the same colors as the balls. The Gift was to teach color recognition and to serve as a valuable plaything. However, Froebel's Law of Universal Unity was abstractly applied to the use of the balls and, as a matter of fact, to the other gifts, also. In this instance, by the action of moving their hands over the smooth, hard surface, children would begin to sense it as a symbol of unity between man and the divine. The following song was used in a learning activity involving colorful cloth-covered balls (Chandler, 1972, p. 72):

> Now take this little ball
> And do not let it fall,
> Balls of yellow, red, and blue
> Some for me and some for you.
> Now take this little ball
> And do not let it fall.
> Hold it in your hand
> Then quite still let it stand

> Balls of yellow, blue, and red
> You are round just like my head.
> Hold it in your hand
> Then quite still let it stand.

Notice how concepts of size, shape, and color were introduced and reinforced through this hands-on, joyful learning experience.

The second Gift consisted of a wooden ball, cube, and cylinder. Each object was to be used repeatedly in situations such as the following (Morrison, 1980, p. 50):

Step 1. Hide the cube in your hand and sing to the child:

> "I see now the hand alone.
> Where, oh, where can cube be gone?"

Purpose: To encourage the child to fix his attention in an effort to find the cube.

Step 2. Open the concealing hand and sing to the child:

> "Aha! Aha!
> My hand has hid the cube with care,
> While you looked for it everywhere.
> See, it is here!
> Look at it, dear."

Purpose: To encourage the child to look at the cube sharply and compare it to the hand.

Step 3. Clasp the cube again, allowing one surface to be seen and sing to the child:

> "Only one side here you see.
> Where can now the others be?"

Purpose: To understand that several parts comprise the whole.

As this passage illustrates, Froebel encouraged children to observe the Gifts carefully and to recognize similarities and differences through their use. The third through sixth Gifts were sets of wooden cubes, each set subdivided into smaller blocks of different sizes and shapes (see Figure 2-1).

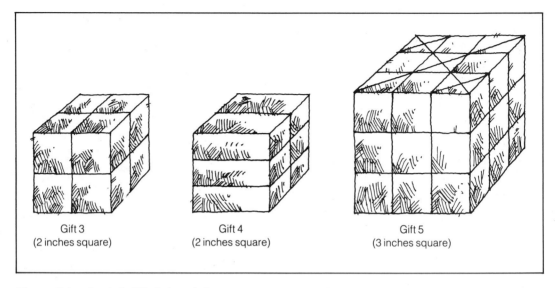

Gift 3
(2 inches square)

Gift 4
(2 inches square)

Gift 5
(3 inches square)

Figure 2-1. _Froebel's Gifts 3 through 5_

Notice that the fifth Gift consisted of twenty-seven 1-inch cubes (three bisected and three quadrasected). The sixth Gift was also a 3-inch cube, but with even a more sophisticated division—three bisected, 1-inch squares and six quadrasected squares. The third through sixth Gifts were presented as whole cubes to the children, separated into parts according to Froebel's directions, and always returned to the whole. Can you sense how this activity reflected Froebel's Law of Universal Unity? Gifts 7 through 10 consisted of various other mathematics-oriented materials:

- Gift 7: colored square and triangular tablets

- Gift 8: small wooden sticks

- Gift 9: circular metal rings

- Gift 10: beans, pebbles, seeds, and other natural objects

Since Froebel's philosophy reflected a strong belief that mathematics should be the starting point of all education, the Gifts were specifically designed as basic materials to gain initial mathematics experiences. Initially, the child would be encouraged to explore the Gifts freely, but then, with the teacher's guidance, the child would manipulate the Gifts in set ways. For example, the child would divide Gift 4 into two equal parts while accompanying his or her actions with the words, "One whole equals two halves; two halves equal one whole." Words always accompanied action in Froebel's scheme because he recognized the relationship between language and learning. See Figure 2-2.

As Figure 2-2 illustrates, mathematical concepts advanced by the use of Froebel's Gifts were not limited to fractions; number combinations and geometry were also taught in this innovative manner.

In addition to the Gifts, the basis of Froebel's program also contained "Occupations" and "Mother Plays." _Occupations_ were basically craft-type activities such as making designs by poking holes in paper with sharply pointed

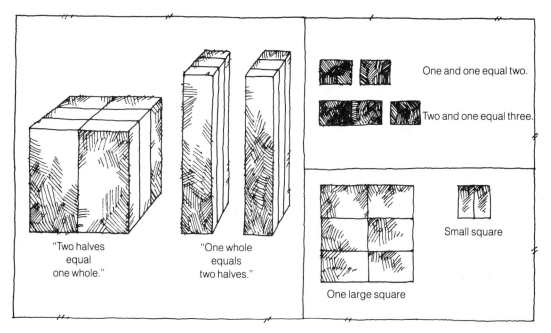

Figure 2-2 *Mathematical concepts taught by Froebel's Gift 4*

sticks, sewing outlines on pattern cards, cutting with scissors, folding paper, weaving, drawing, and modeling with clay. *Mother Plays* were simple songs, poems, or games that Froebel suggested for use with very young children. These included rhymes such as pat-a-cake and other appropriate interactive activities for either teachers or mothers to use with their children.

Froebel's recognition of the educational value of play and his gentle approach to the teaching of young children were received with a great deal of respect and enthusiasm by teachers throughout Germany. Carrying a large box containing his materials, Froebel visited schools throughout the country to describe his kindergarten ideas. His natural magnetism and enthusiasm for the program resulted in a zealous acceptance of the kindergarten. Wherever possible, Froebel demonstrated his methods and materials with children, but sometimes he used adults when children were not available. Kristina Leeb-Lundberg cites Froebel's firsthand account of one such session:

There being not children enough present, I said, "If we want to educate children, we must become children ourselves." There was no getting out of it; all the dignified school masters had to become children again. They felt rather strange at it at first, but were soon so completely filled with the joyous spirit of the occasion that all worked together in perfect harmony.... It was not until eleven at night that we parted in a cheerful mood, and resolved to meet again the next day. [1977, p. 306]

Froebel's kindergarten program sounds so innocent, yet in 1851, not even 15 years after it first became a reality, the Prussian minister of education banned kindergartens because he believed they promoted socialism. The probable reason for such drastic action was that the minister had apparently confused Froebel with his nephew Karl, a radical and outspoken critic of the Prussian government. That possibility was pointed out to the minister, but he did not rescind his decree. The action so affected Froebel that his death in 1852 may have been a result of the severe disappointment and depression accompanying the ban on his kindergarten.

Throughout Europe and into the United States, however, educators promoted the ideas of Froebel. The swiftness and completeness by which the kindergarten swept into the United States will be discussed in the "Children in America" section later in this chapter.

MARGARET McMILLAN (1860–1931)

Another trend in early childhood education began in the early part of this century when Margaret McMillan developed the first nursery school in England. McMillan was a vocal member of a group of social activists in England that included such luminaries as playwright and critic George Bernard Shaw. Her concern with the social, political, and economic conditions of the time led to her election to the Bradford School Board. In that position she became aware of the widespread health problems of the children in the city's slum area. Convinced that such problems had already advanced too far by school age, McMillan chose to establish "day nurseries" for children aged two to seven. These nurseries were to make up for the neglect in health and hygiene the children experienced at home. Since a basic educational program was also part of her plan, the "day nurseries" came to be called *nursery schools.* The overall philosophy of the McMillan school, though, was that of "nurturance." Nurturance was viewed as the process of supporting the total development of the child, including the social, emotional, physical, and intellectual aspects of each individual. In general, McMillan's program can be compared very closely to a contemporary day-care setting.

In an effort to compensate for the neglect the poor children received at home, McMillan designed the school's program to emphasize the qualities of child rearing that characterized the more affluent homes. Central to the program for the very youngest children was a self-caring aspect (buttoning, lacing, tying, washing, dressing, hair brushing, and so on). The self-care responsibilities also included keeping clean—children were often bathed in waist-high tubs (a dozen or more children at a time)—wearing clean clothes, eating nourishing meals, and receiving fresh air and exercise. This concern led to the school taking the form of an "Open Shed," or open-air nursery school. The building had one side that opened into a garden or play area, ensuring that fresh air and sunshine were always present. In nice weather the children spent most of their day outdoors at play in the garden or play area. To further stress the health care aspect of their program, McMillan called the teacher a "nurse-teacher," a practitioner with educational and health care duties.

The self-care component of the McMillan program was influenced by a prominent French educator of the mentally retarded, Edward Seguin. Seguin gained much recognition for his ideas regarding the physical care of young children and also for the prescriptive perceptual-motor and sensory activities that he designed as important components of early learning. Because of Seguin's influence, McMillan provided a great deal of muscular activity for the young children. Play was encouraged in the herb, vegetable, and flower gardens, as well as in the "junk piles" containing mounds of ashes or nuts and bolts. These activities helped the children learn to control their muscles and develop sensory images of taste, smell, touch, and vision. Older children used form boards, color wheels, alphabet boards, and other pieces of sensory apparatus seen as important prerequisites to the development of reading, writing, and number skills. In addition to the perceptual-motor experiences, McMillan provided the children with many activities for self-expression including clay modeling, coloring, drawing, and block play. Rhythmic movement or other musical activities encouraged the children to move creatively and extend their physical skills.

Although play was such an important component of the program for the young children before age five, formalized instruction was provided once the children grew older. Lessons in the three R's (readin', 'ritin', and 'rithmetic), similar to what was found in the traditional schools of the time, were taught to the children after the age of five.

Margaret McMillan was a strong person, who spearheaded the nursery school movement with boundless energy. For instance, her book *The Nursery School* (1919) influenced educators for many years. Her work was so well received that the Fisher Education Act of 1918 was passed mostly through the influence of her nursery school data (see Figure 2-3). The act provided tax money to English communities requesting nursery services. In fact, her influence was so great that the McMillan Training College and the nursery school she started still stand in London as a testimony to her innovative work. Unfortunately, the government financial problems stemming from World War I led to the demise of the Fisher Act and resulted in a temporary slowing down of the nursery school movement in London. The movement in the United States was correspondingly slow and continued that way until the late 1930s. The "Children in America" section later in this chapter will explain the development of the nursery school movement in the United States.

MARIA MONTESSORI (1870–1952)

Maria Montessori's glorious career as an educator has made her name as recognizable as any name in the field of education. But Montessori, who was born and raised in Italy, was known throughout her life as a woman of many roles. As a young woman, for example, Montessori had no intention of becoming an educator. Her great interest was directed toward biology and medicine. Despite the fact that females had been traditionally excluded from medical practice in Italy, Montessori overcame all barriers and emerged as the country's first female to win a medical degree. Her initial appointment as a physician was with the Psychiatric Clinic at the University of Rome, where she was responsible for caring for the insane. At this time, interestingly, insanity was popularly explained as having physical causes. Because the behavioral sciences of psychiatry and psychology were not yet accepted as professional fields, the care of the insane came under the auspices of medical doctors such as Montessori. Also, since insanity and mental retardation were considered to be the same, Montessori came into frequent contact with retarded youngsters who were unmercifully called "idiot children," a harsh but scientifically acceptable label at this time. Montessori's original plans were to observe the children carefully and study their maladies with hope that she could more effectively treat them. Her observations eventually led her to believe that educational principles rather than medical care would be most effective in curing such childhood problems as rickets, paralysis, deafness, and "idiocy."

First, Montessori observed the children carefully in an effort to diagnose their problems. Then she created an innovative, activity-centered, sensory method of education using *didactic* (teaching) materials as the focus of her program. Her efforts were so successful that all her children passed an achievement test, which they took along with the children from regular Roman schools; not all of the "normal" children passed this same test. While others were admiring the "miracle" she had accomplished, Montessori began to search for the reasons that brought the normal children to such a low level as to allow her unfortunate children to equal or surpass them. Thus she

To the Electors

THE OPEN-AIR NURSERY SCHOOL

UP to the present our national system of education has no foundation and no roof. Of the roof and towers this leaflet has nothing to say. But of the foundation—that is, of nurture and education for little children, we have new information and new figures.

The average of delicate and diseased children entering the Elementary School to-day at the age of five years is—*30 to 40 per cent.*

The average of Open-air Nursery School children (who have attended this type of school from two to five years old) is—*7 per cent.*

RICKETS

The average of ricketty children entering the Nursery School at the age of two years is enormous— Dr. Annis, of Greenwich, says 90 per cent., Dr. Thomson, Medical Officer of Health, says 80 per cent., in their respective boroughs. *Within one year* these cases of rickets are all *cured* in an Open-air Nursery School.

MEASLES

INFECTIOUS DISEASE.—Epidemics of measles are very fatal to young children. The Public Health Report of the L.C.C. states that over 1000 children who died of measles in the epidemic of *1925-6* only 55 were over five years old. The death roll of infants was heavy, but not so heavy as was that of children of Nursery School age. *Over 700 children of 1 to 5 years old perished.*

The incidence of measles during the same period *in an Open-air Nursery School* was .7, *that is 2 out of 252 children* had measles. There was no death. The two recovered quickly, having good resistive powers, and were back in school in two weeks.

SKIN DISEASES

SCABIES, IMPETIGO, RINGWORM, etc. These diseases are very common in crowded areas, so common that Doctors and Nurses spend a great part of their time in treating them. They make up the enormous group known as *Minor Ailments. With proper treatment in Nursery Schools they should disappear* and be as rare as leprosy. They do not disappear. They persist from year to year in spite of the work of Nurses and School Nurses. *In the Open-air Nursery Schools, Scabies disappeared in 1925 and 1926.* No case was found. *Ringworm fell to .5. Impetigo rapidly disappeared.*

EDUCATIONAL VALUES

In Mr. Cyril Burt's tables, issued by the L.C.C. to Teachers, etc., the distribution of Intelligence is shown as follows: 46% of all school children are normal; 20% are bright or super-normal, and a very small number, viz.: one or two, stand even higher. This leaves 30% of dull or sub-normal children. *Of these, however, 39% are dull only through neglect in the first years.* Thus there are not more than 18% who can be classed as dull. This number might be found to be still lower, and *lessening* if nurture were the birthright of all.

COST OF THE NURSERY SCHOOL

The cost of such schools should average *£12 to £14 per annum. There is no added danger in large schools* (see L.C.C. Health Report issued in October, 1927, where the incidence of a School of over 200 was as low as that for schools of 20 to 40).

Parents in the North pay as much as 10/- per week to have children " minded." There is no need for such costly and unscientific treatment of the young.

Furthermore, *financial help is given by parents in the poorest areas.* One Nursery School alone has a steady income of £1,000. The full cost in large schools is £11 15s. per annum.

These facts are incontrovertible. They are more forcible than pleading or eloquent speech. The rate-payers have never before been put in possession of them. We believe that now publicity having been given to them *the case for Open-Air Nursery Schools is established.*

Issued by the NURSERY SCHOOL ASSOCIATION OF GREAT BRITAIN, 32 Bloomsbury Street, London, W.C.1

Printed by THE WILLIAM MORRIS PRESS LTD., 41 Gartside Street, Manchester

Figure 2-3 *Message from Margaret McMillan to the voters in London in which she stressed the health and educational values of her nursery school*

spent several years modifying her method for use with normal children. She got an opportunity to try out her methods when Edoardo Talamo, the director general of the Roman Association for Good Building, asked her to organize a school for young children from families living in Roman tenements. Montessori accepted, and her "Casa dei Bambini," or "Children's House," for children aged three to seven opened in 1907. The school began opening branches in other locations as her successes became known. Her special rules and regulations are shown in the following statement (Montessori, 1964, pp. 70–71).

The Roman Association of Good Building hereby establishes within its tenement house number, a "Children's House," in which may be gathered together all children under common school age, belonging to the families of the tenants.

The chief aim of the "Children's House" is to offer, free of charge, to the children of those parents who are obliged to absent themselves for their work, the personal care which the parents are not able to give.

In the "Children's House" attention is given to the education, the health, the physical and moral development of the children. This work is carried on in a way suited to the age of the children.

There shall be connected with the "Children's House" a Directress, a Physician, and a Caretaker.

The programme and hours of the "Children's House" shall be fixed by the Directress.

There may be admitted to the "Children's House" all the children in the tenement between the ages of three and seven.

The parents who wish to avail themselves of the advantages of the "Children's House" pay nothing. They must, however, assume these binding obligations:

(a) To send their children to the "Children's House" at the appointed time, clean in body and clothing, and provided with a suitable apron.

(b) To show the greatest respect and deference toward the Directress and toward all persons connected with the "Children's House," and to cooperate with the Directress herself in the education of the children. Once a week, at least, the mothers may talk with the Directress, giving her information concerning the home life of the child, and receiving helpful advice from her.

There shall be expelled from the "Children's House":

(a) Those children who present themselves unwashed, or in soiled clothing.

(b) Those who show themselves to be incorrigible.

(c) Those whose parents fail in respect to the persons connected with the "Children's House," or who destroy through bad conduct the educational work of the institution.

Montessori's method was based on her ideas of child development. She thought that children move through "sensitive periods," stages of life during which they are able to learn certain skills or behaviors more easily than they can during others. Using this idea, she devised an environment with activities and materials designed specifically for the special needs of children during three basic periods of growth: (1) the period of practical life experiences; (2) the period of sensory education; and (3) the period of academic education.

Practical Life Experiences

Montessori saw care of the self as an extremely important initial stage in the educative process. Therefore, the first phase of her program was designed to address the following important self-care areas.

Care of the Person Montessori advises that children are to be inspected for cleanliness as soon as they enter school. This includes an examination of the hands, nails, neck, ears, face, teeth, and hair. Also, clothing is checked for rips, soil marks, or missing buttons; shoes are checked for dirt or scuffs. By encouraging teachers to do this, Montessori hoped that the children would soon begin to take interest in their own appearance. From this point, children are taught to button, lace, fasten, zip, snap, or buckle their clothing. In addition, children are encouraged to polish their shoes, wash their hands, clean their nails, comb their hair, brush their teeth, and so on.

Care of the Environment As Montessori observed children, she noted that they appeared to take a great deal of interest in watching adults prepare the classroom for their activity

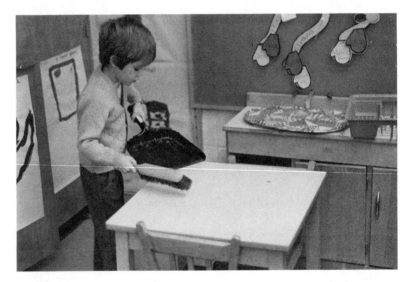

The Montessori program helps children develop physical skills by providing opportunities for self-care activity such as polishing, scrubbing, and the like.

or clean up once they were finished. Capitalizing on this interest, Montessori included activities such as dusting, sweeping, washing table tops, raking leaves, mopping, shoveling, setting the table for a snack, caring for plants and animals, and so on. Importantly, the children carried out these activities with scaled-down brooms, mops, rakes, and other utensils, not with toy-type reproductions of adult tools. Here we sense Montessori's strong commitment to a respect for children and their activity.

Muscular Education Montessori sought to organize and control the children's natural movements through planned exercises such as walking, marching, running, kneeling, rising, bending, breathing, jumping, swinging, rhythmically moving and other simple gymnastics. She felt that muscular education was extremely important, not only because of its physiological advantages, but also because of its influence on learning. For example, she considered breathing activities important because they helped the child develop control necessary for the exact articulation of words. She felt finger exercises were necessary because they readied the fingers for buttoning, lacing, manipulating objects, and, later, for writing. According to Montessori, without such motor coordination, the acquisition of higher mental processes later would not be as effective.

Sensory Education

Sensory education was designed to help the child develop discrimination in sight, taste, touch, and sound through the use of graded didactic materials (materials designed to teach by themselves). The children were deemed ready to move from the earlier practical life experiences to the sensory materials only when they showed an eagerness to work with these materials. Following the children's lead, the teacher then slowly introduced them to the didactic materials. Each piece of sensory equipment exhibited two important characteristics: *gradedness* and *error control.* The *graded materials* increased in difficulty following the normal cognitive development that Montessori observed. *Error control* allowed the material itself to reveal an error. She considered these two characteristics important because they helped the children become autonomous, or self-motivated, learners. The following are examples of didactic sensory materials. Illustrations of the manipulative activities are shown in Figure 2-4.

- *Knobbed Cylinder Blocks.* Three separate wooden blocks with holes and three corresponding sets of wooden cylinders (with knobs on top) that fit into the holes. One block has holes that vary in diameter only while the depth remains constant; another block varies in depth only while the diameter remains constant; and the third block varies in both diameter and depth. The children remove the knobbed cylinders from the wooden blocks, arrange the cylinders in mixed order, and then attempt to match each to its proper hole.

- *Pink Tower.* A set of ten pink wooden cubes that diminish in size from 10 cubic centimeters to 1 cubic centimeter. The child begins with the largest block and attempts to build a graduated tower so that the smallest block is at the top.

- *Broad Stairs.* A set of ten blocks of wood, each 20 centimeters in length but varying in height and width (from 1 to 10 square centimeters). The child arranges the blocks in order, from largest to smallest, so that they resemble a staircase.

- *Sound Cylinders.* Two sets of closed wooden cylinders that are filled with materials such as sand or rice. The child attempts to match a cylinder from one set to the appropriate cylinder from the other set.

- *Musical Bells.* Two sets of bells, one white and one brown, which are alike in shape and size. The child matches the bells according to tonal quality.

- *Sandpaper Tablets.* Two sets of sandpaper tablets that vary in texture. The child rubs his or her fingertips over the tablets to identify two of the textures.

- *Herb Jars.* Two identical sets of jars made of white opaque glass. The tops allow odors to pass but do not allow the children to see inside. The child matches pairs of jars according to likeness of smell.

- *Red Rods.* Ten red wooden rods increasing in length from 10 to 100 centimeters. The child arranges the rods

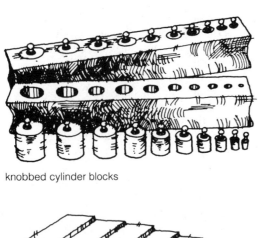

knobbed cylinder blocks

yellow knobless cylinders

broad stairs

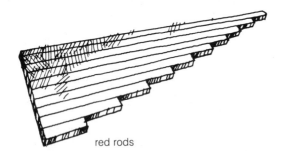

red rods

pink tower

Figure 2-4 *Sensory materials found in Montessori classrooms*
(Nienhuis Montessori catalogue)

next to each other from largest to smallest.

You may have noticed that some of these materials are somewhat similar to those used by Froebel for his kindergarten program. Montessori herself said, "The first didactic material used by us is made up of the bricks and cubes of Froebel" (1964, p. 188). Despite this affinity to Froebel's materials, Montessori differed in her approach to how the materials should be used. Her lesson technique was highly prescriptive; the teacher was advised to use each piece of material in a planned, systematic way:

1. *Isolate the object.* Children are exposed only to the object they will be working with. Everything else is to be cleared from the table so there will be no distraction.

2. *Work exactly.* The teacher is to show

the children the proper use of the material, performing the activity once or twice so they can develop a complete understanding of its use.

3. *Rouse the attention.* The teacher is to display a lively interest as the object is offered to the children. The goal is to attract their attention to the new material.

4. *Finish well.* The teacher is to show the children how to put the finished material back on the shelf. Children are to carry each item securely in both hands and replace it exactly where it belongs.

This sequence gives some idea of the degree of organization that characterizes the Montessori approach. The sensory materials were considered not just toys, but rather tools necessary to develop the concentration needed for later learning.

Academic Education

The final area of Montessori materials involved academic learning. Montessori found that once the children had appropriate early experiences with the sensory materials, they were ready to be led from sensations to the internalization of ideas. An essential component of this process was the use of exact nomenclature as new ideas were presented to the child. The following example illustrates the procedure.

1. The children associate sensations with a letter sound. The teacher says, "This is *b;* this is *a.*" Immediately, the children trace these letters, which are mounted on cards. Once they master this skill, they attempt to repeat it with their eyes closed. The goal of the activity is to enhance muscular memory.

2. The children recognize letter shapes when they hear the corresponding sounds. The teacher says, "Give me *b;* give me *a.*" If the children recognize the

correct letter, they hand it to the teacher. If not, the lesson is ended and begun again on another day.

3. The children recognize the letter and generate its name. The teacher spreads out the letters on the table and asks, "What is this?" They are expected to respond with the appropriate letter name.

Academic concepts were introduced as early as age four through this three-step lesson and the use of a variety of didactic, concrete teaching materials. Some of those materials are as follows:

• *Geometric insets.* Ten geometric shapes that introduce writing skills. The children choose one alphabet letter inset and trace around it. Then they fill in the letter outline with a colored pencil.

• *Activity cards.* A set of red cards with an action word printed on each. The children read the word on the card and perform the identified command—jump or sing, for example.

• *Sandpaper letters and numerals.* Letters or numerals cut from sandpaper and mounted on individual cards. The teacher uses these letters or numerals in the three-stage lesson just described.

The Montessori method became extremely popular in the United States during the first part of this century, and Montessori visited this country to deliver lectures on her system of education. This popularity was short-lived, however, as discontent with her emphasis on academics grew among "child-centered" early childhood educators, who believed a higher value should be placed on expressive activities such as play, music, and art. Since the 1960s a revival of interest in academic instruction has led to what many have described as "the rediscovery of Montessori." Nancy Rambusch also provided much of this impetus with her

This Montessori teacher guides a young child in a musical activity.

"Americanization" of Montessori. Rambusch opened a Montessori school in Connecticut in 1958 and changed the curriculum to include greater opportunities for music, art, imaginative play, and social activity. Others followed Rambusch's lead and the movement eventually led to the formation of the *American Montessori Society* (AMS). Presently, however, most Montessori programs are private in nature, follow the international philosophy, and usually enroll children only to the age of five or six (as do most typical American nursery schools). Since the Montessori program is very specialized and requires at least one year of formal training from Montessori specialists, it is not described in greater detail in this text. Nevertheless, you should become aware of the basic components of the program and of its impact on early childhood education today. If you are interested in knowing more about either the international Montessori program—Association Montessori Internationale (AMI)—or the American program, write to the following addresses:

- The American Montessori Society
  175 Fifth Avenue
  New York, New York 10010

- The Montessori Institute
  2119 S Street, N.W.
  Washington, D.C. 20008

CHILDREN IN AMERICA

In America, as in Europe, the strict maintenance of family discipline was the key consideration in raising children during the 1800s. There are no written records to suggest that swaddling or wet-nursing were practiced in America. The only substantial evidence of a concern for childhood is literature recommending that parents repress their child's natural tendencies and discipline their children to respect an adult's higher authority, whippings were advocated as the primary means of treating children who did not obey.

This youngster is performing a higher-level Montessori mathematics task. Notice that learning materials remain concrete even into this highest phase of the Montessori program.

It must be noted that most of America's children were not educated in schools during the 1700s and 1800s. Apprenticeships took many children out of the house as early as six years of age, and, for the others, most education took place in the home. For those who did go to school, the six-day school week began at seven in the morning and ended at four or five o'clock in the afternoon; this long period of time was established to make sure attendance at school would not "soften" the children. These schools were based on the philosophy of the Calvinists, who brought the ideas here from England. The English, who came to America in large numbers, spread their doctrine that children are born wicked and filled with evil inclinations. Every child has to contend with the influence of the Devil. The prevailing purpose of schools was to help children avoid the way of the Devil by developing into "saints," since "saints were wiser than other people because they knew God. In one way or another everything done in the schools tied into the overall purpose which was the development of saints"

(Ford, 1879). Children were required to memorize passages from the Bible, such as: "He that spareth his rod hateth his son: but he that loveth him chasteneth him betimes" (Proverbs 13:24). In other instances, religious views of childhood were reflected in the children's reading books. This passage was taken from the presentation of the alphabet in the *New England Primer:*

A	In *Adam's* Fall We sinned all.
F	The idle *Fool* Is whipt at school.
J	*Job* feels the Rod Yet blesses GOD.
R	*Rachel* doth mourn For her first born.

Children dressed and acted as adults once they reached the age of six, although they were not legally extended the rights and privileges of adulthood. Given this scant information, Walzer (1974) advised us that the seventeenth to nineteenth centuries are a very difficult period of time to describe as regards children. He said, "We can learn far more about the cultivation of flax in the colonies than how mothers raised children" (p. 365). Any major parenting recommendations we know of during this time were directed toward lessons in obedience, manners, and religion. Direct action was the course taken toward any misbehavior; a large round ruler was the teacher's usual aid for keeping children in line, while parents often concocted even more violent techniques. One parent, for example, "made Eugene drink a pint of [urine]" (369) in order to cure bed-wetting problems. Other gruesome practices were devised for children whose actions could not be tolerated by adults.

American scholars, influenced by the emerging works of Rousseau, Pestalozzi, Froebel, and others in Europe, examined this form of child care and became disturbed by it. They sought to change the traditional negative view of childhood toward one reflecting compassion and respect.

Kindergartens

The interest generated by concerned Americans was allowed to grow into reality during the mid-1800s when America's Industrial Revolution began to flourish. The promise of freedom, wealth, and a fresh start in life influenced thousands to emigrate from Eastern European countries to the cities of the United States. Many of these immigrants were well educated and, naturally, had strong feelings about the care of their children. As they moved into urban neighborhoods and searched for schools for their youngsters (younger than age six), they found to their dismay that there were none. The only schools available were for older children, and disappointingly, the prevailing concept of childhood in America at that time dictated that the children be taught in a strict, moralistic manner. Fortunately, however, a number of German women trained by Froe-

bel to teach kindergarten children in a manner consistent with the emerging European philosophies were part of the immigration movement. They set up private kindergartens in their own homes to serve their own families and those of their closest friends and relatives. Soon the word of the revolutionary kindergarten began to spread as American educators sought to learn more about such a new view of childhood and method of child care.

The first kindergarten was opened in Watertown, Wisconsin, in 1855 by Mrs. Margarethe Schurz, who had been a student of Froebel's in Germany. This German-speaking kindergarten was originally intended only for her own children and those of close relatives, but it soon became known to others. Schurz's application of Froebel's teaching materials, creative activities, and warm classroom technique attracted other parents, and her school gained widespread interest. The greatest opportunity for the spread of Froebel's program to America, however, came when Mrs. Schurz and her statesman husband, Carl, attended a social gathering with their five-year-old daughter, Agathe. Also present at the gathering was Elizabeth Peabody, a prominent socialite who was especially noted for her strong interests in the conditions of young children. Peabody was very impressed by Agathe's demeanor while at play with the other children, calling her enchanting behavior a miracle and asking how the girl was raised. Mrs. Schurz told Elizabeth Peabody about the kindergarten, introduced her to the ideas of Froebel, and later sent her a copy of Froebel's book, *The Education of Man*. Peabody became so interested in what she learned that she eventually established the first English-speaking kindergarten in Boston in 1860 and became one of the leading proponents of kindergartens in the United States.

The kindergarten movement spread rapidly from this beginning. In 1870 less than a dozen such private kindergartens existed in the United States, but by 1892 the number of classrooms had risen to approximately 2,500 and involved over 33,000 pupils. This rapid growth was confined mainly to the large cities of the East and Midwest, where support came from private associations such as mothers' clubs and other philanthropic agencies concerned with the lives of young children. Interest in the movement spread to public school systems, too. Encouraged by supporting letters from Elizabeth Peabody, Susan Blow opened the first public school kindergarten in St. Louis in 1873. Although attendance in the public kindergartens was not mandatory, enrollments surged to over 130,000 children by 1900. Professional organizations whose main interest was educating kindergarten children also arose at this time; the largest of these organizations, the International Kindergarten Union, became the third largest educational organization in the world by 1918 (Lazerson, 1972, readings, p. 54).

Why was Froebel's impact in the United States so monumental during the early 1900s? Patty Smith Hill offered these thoughts about the kindergarten movement being "in the right place at the right time":

> The kindergarten appeared on the horizon at the right moment. . . . Society turned to the young child as the one great hope, and kindergartens opened under religious and philanthropic influences all over America. They were located in the worst slums of the cities, and highly cultured and intelligent young women prepared themselves in normal schools [teacher-training schools] supported by philanthropists. These young women entered upon the work with rare enthusiasm and consecration to the cause. No neighborhood was too criminal, no family too degenerate, no child too bad. Into Little Italy, Little Russia, Little Egypt, and the Ghettos they went, offering daily care to humanity in its early years. [1941, pp. 1948–1972]

Unfortunately, this initial enthusiasm toward the development of the Froebelian

kindergarten in America was hindered by the fact that the followers of Schurz, Peabody, and Blow were unable to study Froebel's program directly. Froebel had died in 1852, and his program had been banned in Germany. Instead, they studied under proponents of Froebel's theories in the United States; these followers often advocated a more rigid use of materials than was originally intended. Programs in the United States gradually lost the freedom and activity that characterized earlier kindergartens, and interest in Froebel waned. An example of how formalized instruction became is illustrated by Joseph Mayer Rice (1893):

> Before the lesson there was passed to each child a little flag, on which had been pasted various forms and colors, such as a square piece of green paper, a triangular piece of red paper, etc. When each child had been supplied, a signal was given by the teacher. Upon receiving the signal, the first child sprang up, gave the name of the geometrical form upon his flag, loudly and rapidly defined the form, mentioned the name of the color, and fell back into his seat to make way for the second child, thus: "A square; a square has four equal sides and four corners; green" (down). Second child (up): "A triangle; a triangle has three sides and three corners; red" (down). Third child (up): "A trapezium; a trapezium has four sides, none of which are parallel, and four corners; yellow" (down). . . . This process [was] continued until each child in the class had recited. [pp. 39–46]

Thus, the first reason for the retreat of the new European philosophy of childhood from the American scene during the late 1800s was an inability to sustain or enlarge the less formal philosophy of the original Froebelian kindergarten. A second major reason for such a decline was the growing skepticism of many American psychologists, who viewed the informal European philosophy with reservations. They questioned the belief of educators, who echoed Rousseau's philosophy that culture destroys a child's natural instincts and that we violate children if we do not allow them to "do what comes naturally," Spodek (1973) summarized the thoughts of these protesters:

> Unfortunately the arguments using natural childhood as a source of [schooling] do not hold up well. There is nothing natural about any school, even a [kindergarten] . . . kindergartens cannot be directly derived from the natural activity of children. The very nature of the educational process requires that if it is effective, the child ought to be different as a result of his experiences within it. The child should exit from the program in a less natural state than the one in which he entered. All schools, as a matter of fact, are cultural contrivances to do things to children to change them. [p. 83]

While rejecting the new "natural childhood" philosophy, the dissenters asked questions such as: How can we believe that such radical, new ideas about children are true? and How did these scholars gather information in order to form such ideas? The answers to these questions were disturbing to the critics, since, rather than gathering their information through "scientific" means, Rousseau, Pestalozzi, Froebel, and other early advocates of childhood had formed their ideas through "introspective" techniques. This means that they had simply pondered the concept of childhood and speculated what the characteristics of that stage of human life might be. They did not formally observe children, but simply "meditated" about childhood and wrote down their theories for others to read. Although these writings were not exact scientific explanations of childhood, however, the early philosophers did mark an important start of characterizing childhood as being more than a time of "helplessness" or "miniaturized adulthood." They also saw the value of education (at home or at school) as a central part of childhood because it provided nurture for development and support for a natural unfolding process of development.

The Progressive Kindergarten

Groups of educators in the United States who reacted against the rigid formalism, and sought to return to the more flexible, play-oriented settings originally conceived for five-year-old children turned for the first time to new educational reformers from America rather than directly to the European philosophers and educators discussed earlier. Educators were now searching for a scientific approach to study the characteristics of young children, an approach emphasizing formal observation and data collection rather than simple speculation on the uniqueness of childhood. Their interest in scientific information was given great impetus by G. Stanley Hall, commonly referred to as the "father of the child study movement."

Beginning with a formal study of children's thinking in 1891, Hall verified that children are not miniature adults—they had skills and abilities much different than those found in adults. Hall's students adopted his point of view and became interested in studying all aspects of children's growth and development. Arnold Gesell is among the most prominent. He and his co-workers Louise Bates Ames and Frances Ilg extended Hall's original research by observing large numbers of children and describing their intricate development in terms of normal developmental stages. They recorded, averaged, and tabulated physical and behavioral data from large groups of children at various age levels in order to create a "composite" picture of the typical one-, two-, three-, four-, or five-year-old. By describing the early years as the most important, Gesell's (1923) ideas renewed the enthusiasm of those interested in young children.

> The preschool period is biologically the most important period in the development of an individual for the simple but sufficient reason that *it comes first*. Coming first in a dynamic sequence, it inevitably influences all

subsequent development. . . . This remarkable velocity of mental development parallels the equal velocity of physical growth during these early years.

The character of this mental development is by no means purely or preeminently intellectual. Almost from the beginning it is social, emotional, moral and denotes the organization of a personality. [pp. 2–8]

Gesell's information gave early childhood educators a wealth of knowledge about the uniqueness of children and about the need for developing environmental conditions conducive to optimal growth. Many other theories were developed at this time, some agreeing with Gesell's ideas and others opposed. However, every theory seemed to agree with Gesell on one major point—the early years are the most important.

A popular educator, John Dewey, embraced these new views on the value of the early childhood years. He pushed for the immediate application of these findings to school programs for young children. His suggested program, often referred to as "progressive education," emphasized learning through real experiences and an atmosphere that encouraged healthy social and emotional growth in young children. This progressive philosophy was very close to that of earlier European educators—with one major difference. As Martin Dworkin explained, "In education, progressivism brought . . . a romantic emphasis upon the needs and interests of the child, in the tradition of Rousseau, Pestalozzi, and Froebel—but now colored and given scientific authority by the new psychology of learning and behavior" (1959, p. 9).

Patty Smith Hill, who became a leader in the "progressive" kindergarten movement, also accepted this new philosophy and dedicated herself to reintroducing the concepts of play and purposeful activity into the kindergarten setting. Hill developed her concept of the "progressive" kindergarten while teaching at

the Louisville Free Kindergarten with Anna Bryan. Together, Hill and Bryan proposed a program that used the child's personal experiences as a basis for learning. The program involved concrete, child-oriented activities and classroom play based on the natural activities of childhood, set in a free, informal atmosphere. It was similar to Froebel's original program, except that blocks, dolls, and other toys replaced his "Gifts" and more time was devoted to expressive activities such as housekeeping, art, and music. The basic form of Hill's progressive kindergarten became extremely popular and remained so through the late 1960s. It eventually became known as a *traditional approach* to early childhood education. The types of activities provided during a typical day are shown in the box on traditional program activities.

Dolores Durkin (1976) offers this explanation of why Hill's program resisted change for so many years:

> The reason might have been the general tendency of people to resist what is new and different, but it might also have been the tendency to hang on to what was difficult to achieve. Here I refer to the great effort required in earlier years to break out of the Froebelian rut. It is easy to believe that once the new ideas won approval and the new program was accepted, those who worked hard for the approval and acceptance would not be eager to abandon what they had achieved in favor of something else. Further, it is also likely that once the newer ideas became a program, inertia took over. How much simpler to do what was done last year than to try something different! [pp. 12–13]

Although the types of programs offered to kindergarten children remained stable over the years, the number of children enrolled in the programs has now risen to over 2½ million, or about 65 percent of all five-year-olds. Predictions of future growth are optimistic, especially in light of increased state and federal tax support. Texas and West Virginia, for

TRADITIONAL PROGRAM ACTIVITIES

Work Period The children choose their own activity—painting, working with clay, building with blocks, or participating in dramatic play at the housekeeping center.

Story Time The children listen while the teacher reads or tells a story. The story is usually about children their own age or about animals.

Music Time The teacher leads the children in singing short, simple songs in which the children are encouraged to move their bodies rhythmically or to experiment with rhythm instruments.

Outdoor Play The children spend a generous amount (30–40 minutes) of time on the playground,

using equipment such as boxes, slides, swings, tricycles, and digging equipment.

Rest Time and Cleanup The children return to the room, where they are encouraged to use the bathroom facilities and to wash up. The room is then darkened and the children are encouraged to stretch out, relax, and sometimes take a short nap.

Snack Time The children gather around small tables and have a half-pint of milk or glass of juice along with a cookie or cracker.

Real Experiences Field trips, resource people, and other active experiences help the children acquire information and develop increasingly sophisticated ideas about their growing world.

---

example, have included kindergartens under state funding, thus making them available to all children. Other states are likely to follow this trend, and provide funds for programs designed for all five-year-olds.

Day Care and Nursery Schools

The first kindergartens in the United States were established to meet the needs of European immigrants during the mid-1800s. Most early programs were privately funded, so only people who were the most able to pay were able to send their children. However, the need for care of children from less fortunate families also became apparent during that time. As the dreams of many immigrants faded before the harsh realities of life in a new world, they soon realized that a single source of income could not meet their needs. Consequently, many mothers were forced to go to work, thereby creating a serious dilemma in their lives. Mothers were considered negligent at this time if they were not at home caring for

their children. Could the mother be considered any less negligent, however, if she did not utilize her power to earn money to feed and clothe her children? Some mothers, especially those who were widowed or abandoned, addressed this dilemma by sending their children to orphanages or foster homes so they (the mothers) would be free to enter the work force. For the larger percentage of working mothers, however, this type of arrangement was not suitable, and they searched for other alternatives. One alternative, the *day nursery,* surfaced during the 1850s. The day nurseries were primarily funded by philanthropists, or charitable individuals, concerned about the lives of young children. The day nurseries were staffed by women who cared mainly for the health and safety needs of young children for up to 12 hours per day while their mothers worked.

Such "custodial" care characterized the early programs until word of the emerging European programs reached the United States. Soon the day nurseries began to reflect the European influence. The first such program was established in New York City in 1915 by a Montessori teacher named Eva McLin. It used Montessori strategies to teach the fundamentals of health care and nutrition. However, because Montessori's method was felt to be too regimented, her popularity was not great, and soon McLin's school was closed.

In 1919 a nurse named Harriet Johnson opened a nursery, the *City and County School,* in New York City patterned after the McMillan philosophy. By 1920 a number of teachers trained by Margaret McMillan had come to the United States from England, either to demonstrate her ideas or to set up "nursery schools" in the United States. One of the first of these trained teachers was Abigail Eliot, who was hired in 1922 by the Women's Education Association of Boston to lead the Ruggles Street Nursery School, which was located in a low-income neighborhood. Before Eliot's arrival the purpose of the school, like the others at her time, had been group day care. There was no educational program. Physical protection, sterile cleanliness, orderliness, and obedience had been stressed. Under Eliot's direction, however, the school's program changed to reflect the educational views of Froebel and McMillan. For example, child-size furniture was put into the main room, and a garden and sandbox were set up in the playground. Health concerns were addressed by watching for contagious diseases and by teaching habits of cleanliness. Large group activities included music, art, water play, sand play, games, and stories; independently chosen "occupations" were performed using Froebelian or McMillan learning materials such as chalk, scissors, and blocks. The children were provided with sound nutrition during a daily lunch and then given about two hours of sleep or quiet rest. The difference between a "day nursery" and a "nursery school" became simply that the day nursery offered custodial care only while the nursery school usually had a planned program, including an educational component.

Nursery schools similar to Ruggles Street were soon organized, often by privately funded organizations or departments of home economics in state-supported land-grant colleges. The privately funded Merrill-Palmer Institute in Detroit, for example, was begun in 1922 by a provision in the will of philanthropist Lizzie Merrill-Palmer. She had been concerned about the quality of motherhood in America and had bequested money to found a school—to be known as the Merrill-Palmer Motherhood and Home Training School. Young women were to be educated and trained, especially for wifehood and motherhood. The school was first directed by Edna Noble White, who also organized a nursery school so the women could gain firsthand practical knowledge by working with and observing young children. At land-grant colleges, the first program of this motherhood type was offered at Iowa State in 1924.

Despite the dreams and good intentions, the nursery school movement grew slowly during the 1920s, primarily for the following reasons:

- Often the schools were overcrowded and staffed by untrained personnel.
- They were seen as a factor in weakening family unity.
- Many believed that by encouraging mothers to work, the father's role of breadwinner was being undermined.
- It was felt that mothers neglected their child-rearing duties if they went to work.

By 1931, only about 200 nursery schools were in operation throughout the United States. But, by 1935, that number had increased to over 1900 schools. What caused such significant growth?

One factor was the *Work Projects Administration* (WPA), an agency established by the federal government in 1933 to combat the problems caused by the Great Depression. The WPA appropriated money to various groups throughout the nation to create jobs for the unemployed and to combat the conditions imposed upon young children by the economic and social difficulties caused by the depression. Nursery schools benefited from this funding, and they became a source of jobs for unemployed teachers. The WPA also made it possible for mothers, normally tied to their homes and children, to seek employment and support their families. Most of these schools were, once again, day-long nurseries that provided full-day care for parents who either worked or were too poor to care for their own children. Beyond this immediate benefit, however, was the popularization of the nursery school movement. The movement was gaining status as a growing "profession" because institutions were providing formal training for nursery school teachers, and opportunities for early childhood education became valued by all socioeconomic groups. Middle- and upper-income families sent their children to private nursery schools rather than the publicly funded schools of the needy. "Self-realization," "personal growth," and "social adjustment" became the key phrases. Perhaps the greatest impetus to the growth of schools of this type was the emerging stature of Sigmund Freud. Popular among the more intellectual members of the community, Freud was one of the first to point out the effects of children's experiences during their earliest years on their future personality. Freud viewed the first five years of life as a period when children's basic drives are directed toward sexual gratification; Freud's ideas of sexuality were that as children grow, they seek pleasure from sensations received from different parts of their bodies.

Freud described stages of sexual interest beginning with birth—each stage characterized by a different source of sexual gratification accompanied by conflicts with parents and other caretakers over the satisfaction of each sexual need. The relationship between the child and parent or caretaker during any of these stages could cause the child to take one of three different routes for development. The first route is to progress normally through the stages of development. "Normal" development occurs when neither excessive gratification of sexual urges nor unreasonable suppression of them occurs during each stage. If excessive gratification is allowed, the child may develop a *fixation*. This means that he or she may cease to develop beyond any single stage and no further personality development ensues beyond that stage. However, when sexual impulses are not allowed to be satisfied at any particular stage, the child may experience the third route of development—*regression*. In this case, the child returns, or regresses, to an earlier, happier stage of development. Table 2-1 summarizes the major characteristics of each stage of development and offers the associated normal character traits. It also shows the character traits exhibited by individuals who become fixated at a particular stage or regress to an earlier stage.

These Freudian ideas became nearly a revelation to "informed" parents. Nursery schools assumed the responsibility to help young children fulfill needs and to grow toward a full and free maturity. The role of the nursery school changed, in many instances, to providing experiences basic to emotional and social stability.

Intellectual activities for young children were not encouraged; such matters were considered "old-fashioned" by many and not appropriate during the child's early years. Because the new ideas of Freud were in vogue, nursery schools stressed social, emotional, and physical growth to the total exclusion of intellectual growth. Grace Owen (1920), one of the great leaders of the nursery school movement, made the position clear when she wrote, "No mention has been made of instruction in the nursery school because in any formal sense it has no place. No reading, no writing, no number lessons should on any account be allowed,

Table 2-1 *Freud's First Three Stages of Psychosexual Development*

Stage	Age	Behaviors	Normal Character Traits	Fixations
Oral	0–8 months	Derives pleasure from the mouth—sucking, biting, or swallowing anything that can be put into the mouth.	Develops feelings of acceptance and trust.	Chews gum, smokes, bites nails, overeats, overdrinks, kisses excessively, talks a lot.
Anal	8 months–1½ years	Derives pleasure from moving the bowels or retaining the feces.	Develops traits of punctuality, orderliness, and cleanliness.	Stingy, hoarding, obsessively exacting, sets rigid schedules and routines, excessively clean and orderly or extremely messy, perhaps overly aggressive.
Phallic	1½ years–6 years	Stimulated by manipulating the genitals.	Develops feelings toward others, especially adults. Social strivings guide the individual.	Feelings of inferiority or jealousy. Oversatisfaction of sexual strivings may lead to rape or sadism.

for the time for these things has not yet come" (p. 25).

Despite this emerging new philosophy of early childhood education, many of the public day-care programs closed down as WPA funds were phased out. They were revived at the start of World War II. During World War II, women were forced into the jobs vacated by men entering the armed services, and again day-long child care became a problem. The federal government intervened and passed the Lanham Act, which provided funds for the establishment and staffing of more day-care facilities. Like those in the depression years, these war-time centers provided children with food, rest, shelter, and a kind, loving mother substitute. There was little or no desire to go beyond this basic care in most centers by offering educational programs. Day-care provisions even spread to industry as some employers sought to provide for the care of employees' children. The Kaiser Shipyards on the West Coast were instrumental in providing quality care. Led by James Hymes, these programs provided attractive facilities at each shipyard, staffed by trained teachers who patterned their programs after the most innovative ideas of the time. This day-care concept was popular during the war years and paved the way for future changes.

Shortly after the war, federal support for child-care services stopped because it became the prevailing view once again that the mother's place is in the home. Local, state, and philanthropic agencies, however, continued to operate many of the facilities. The most significant growth in preschool offerings, though, came through expansion of nursery school programs. Supported by various private funds such as churches or parent groups, nursery school programs steadily grew through the 1940s and into the 1950s.

During this period, nearly all nursery schools, kindergartens, and child-care facilities were identified with health care, play-oriented activities, concern for social and emotional growth, and the teacher as a mother substitute. During the 1960s, however, major changes occurred in nursery school and kindergarten education. In the following section, major contemporary influences affecting the growth of preschool programs in the United States are discussed.

THE EMERGING SCENE: EARLY CHILDHOOD EDUCATION TODAY

At the beginning of this "modern period" of innovation and growth in early childhood education, most kindergartens were under the auspices of the public schools, although a number of private programs also existed. In many parts of the country, kindergartens were the only preschool experiences available. In areas where nursery schools and day-care programs were available, they were operated mostly through private funds. In many ways, however, the programs of the kindergartens, nursery schools, and day-care centers were the same.

By 1965, though, changing views of childhood, along with unresolved social problems, stimulated attention to the young child and ushered in the greatest period of experimentation and growth ever experienced in the field of early childhood education. This period was originally touched off by the launching of the Russian space satellite Sputnik I in 1957. At that time, Americans became overwhelmingly concerned about falling behind the Russians in the technology race; some even predicted disaster and doom for the nation. One of the first areas to be attacked by these critics was the field of education. The public called for a careful examination of schools and demanded new programs to close the gap between the Russians and the United States. Among the areas that received the greatest study were those

related to the education of young children and the social problems that directly affected their lives.

A New View of Children

In 1959 the National Academy of Sciences sponsored a conference in Woods Hole, Massachusetts, to determine how science and mathematics programs could be improved so that the gap in technology between the United States and Russia could be closed. Jerome Bruner chaired the conference and was responsible for compiling and reporting on the group's recommendations. The result was his popular book, *The Process of Education* (1960). One of the strongest recommendations in the book was that science be taught in the early elementary grades. To emphasize why early contact with science was possible, Bruner wrote: "We begin with the hypothesis that any subject can be taught effectively in some intellectually honest form to any child at any stage of development" (p. 33). Originally the statement was meant to support the request to educators that science offerings in their schools be reexamined and restructured so that even kindergarten children were exposed to very simple science concepts. However, some interpretations distorted Bruner's true intent and led to attempts to teach complex concepts to youngsters without first translating them to their level of understanding. For instance, in some schools two- and three-year-olds were being taught to read and write, and first graders were being asked to deal with fundamentals of economics and algebra. Despite such misinterpretations, Bruner's assumption was a valuable contribution to early childhood education. It renewed interest in the potential of children to learn during the earliest years of development.

J. McVicker Hunt stimulated additional interest in the abilities of youngsters when he published *Intelligence and Experience* in 1961. The book describes and interprets previously completed research studies dealing with optimal early learning environments for young children. Its greatest impact was on the widely accepted contentions of Hall and Gesell that intelligence is hereditarily predetermined. Hunt mounted his attack with statements such as: "The assumption that intelligence is fixed and that its development is predetermined by the genes is no longer tenable" (p. 342). Hunt explained that learning experiences and academic stimulation are as essential to sound intellectual growth during the early years as play and a Freudian-inspired loving, understanding adult are to healthy social-emotional growth. He concluded that we should be able to prepare the young children's environment so as to increase their intellectual development (IQ) by up to 30 points. The clue to this growth process is similar to Bruner's—a "match" has to be found between the current level of children's understanding and the new experience to which they will be exposed. Hunt felt that through such a carefully designed, organized plan, young children could gain information and acquire academic skills at an age rarely thought possible before.

Benjamin Bloom also helped focus attention on the significance of the early years. In 1964 he published *Stability and Change in Human Characteristics,* in which he studied the relationship between selected environmental forces, early experiences, and intelligence. Bloom found that "in terms of intelligence measured at age 17, about 50 percent of the development takes place between conception and age 4, about 30 percent between ages 4 and 8, and about 20 percent between ages 8 and 17" (p. 88). Bloom also estimated that the long-term overall effect of living in a "culturally deprived" as against a "culturally abundant" environment to be 20 IQ points, and hypothesized that this effect was spaced developmentally as follows: from birth to 4 years, 10 IQ units; from 4 to 8 years, 6 IQ units; from 8 to 17 years, 4 IQ units (p. 72). Bloom's conclusions emphasized both the importance

of providing suitable learning experiences during children's early years, and the fact that those environments could affect the intelligence of young children.

Other educators of the early 1960s supported the push for early experiences as the key to raising children's intelligence levels during their early years. Martin Deutsch (1964) reported that children who attended preschools did better in fifth grade than those who did not. William Fowler (1962) rejected the recommendations of early developmental psychologists like Hall and Gesell, who stressed play and social-emotional growth in the early years, and called for specialized teaching methods designed to increase intelligence during that period.

These views on the importance of intellectual stimulation during the early years began a controversy unequaled since Patty Smith Hill began the progressive kindergarten movement in the early 1900s. Supporters felt the preschool years were important for intellectual growth, and advocated more formal academic types of instruction. Opponents believed in continuing an unstructured preschool experience emphasizing social and emotional growth.

David Elkind (1970) described the positions of both groups. According to Elkind, the group advocating more structured preschool instruction felt:

> (a) The earlier we start a child in the formal academic path, the earlier he will finish and the cheaper the total educational cost; (b) learning comes easy to the young child and we should take advantage of the preschooler's learning facility and eagerness to learn; (c) intellectual growth is rapid in the preschool years and instruction will help to maximize that growth while failure to provide appropriate intellectual stimulation may curtail the child's ultimate level of achievement and (d) traditional preschool experience is too soft, too directed toward emotional well-being and too little concerned with cognitive stimulation. [p. 133]

The traditional group reacted with these defenses:

> There is no preponderance of evidence that formal instruction is more efficient, more economical, more necessary or more cognitively stimulating than the traditional preschool program. Indeed, while there is room for improvement in the traditional preschool, it already embodies some of the most innovative educational practices extant today. It would, in fact, be foolish to pattern the vastly expanded preschool programs planned for the future upon an instructional format that is rapidly being given up at higher educational levels. Indeed, it is becoming more and more apparent that formal instructional programs are as inappropriate at the primary and secondary levels of education as they are at the preschool level. [p. 133]

This controversy over the role of intellectual development in the preschool setting has continued to grow. During the late 1960s and early 1970s cognitive growth became more important than social-emotional growth (see Table 2-2). During the late 1970s, however, most early childhood educators began to feel that a good balance among all areas of the child's development—including both the intellectual and the social-emotional—would be desirable. That feeling, popular today, identifies the preschool as an experience designed to address the needs of the "whole" child; that is, programs reflect a balance of activities that lead to physical growth and development, intellectual stimulation, healthy social-emotional growth, and the encouragement of creative potential.

Head Start and Follow Through

In addition to a *changing view of young children,* a second factor that stimulated change in the field of early childhood education was a social concern for *equalizing educational opportunity among children from low-income families.* The ideas of Bloom, Bruner, Hunt, and others made us aware that if youngsters from lower socioeconomic groups do not receive early intellectual stimulation they are destined to fail in public schools. In 1964, therefore, President Lyndon B. Johnson created the Office of Economic Opportunity (OEO) to find solutions to educational inequality. One solution was Operation Head Start, which was conceived as the nation's major weapon in this fight. Head Start funds were sent to community-action agencies throughout the country to establish programs for preschool children from poverty-stricken urban and rural areas to meet the following goals:

1. Improve the child's physical health and physical abilities.
2. Help the emotional and social development of the child by encouraging self-confidence, spontaneity, curiosity, and self-discipline.
3. Improve the child's mental processes and skills with particular attention to conceptual and verbal skills.
4. Establish patterns and expectations of success for the child which will create a climate of confidence for his future learning efforts. [Cook, n.d., p. 2]

The goals were general in nature so local communities could interpret and adapt them to their own special needs. As a result of this leeway, many programs were aligned with the new trend toward intellectual development in the preschool setting, but most maintained a more traditional alignment. Whatever the form, however, all educators were concerned about providing school readiness experiences that would eliminate the disadvantages children from low-income families assumed when they entered middle-class-oriented schools.

During its first summer, in 1965, Head Start programs served over 580,000 children in approximately 2,500 preschool child-devel-

Table 2-2 *Contrasting the Traditional and Newer Views of Intellectual Growth in the Preschool*

Pre-1960s: Traditional View of Intellectual Development	Post-1960s: Redefinition of Intellectual Development
Intellectual growth occurs in stages that are hereditarily predetermined and sequential in nature.	Intellectual growth depends on both hereditary *and* environmental factors.
Growth through stages is exclusively the result of biological maturation.	Growth occurs through experience and practice as well as through biological maturation.
When a child's biological "alarm clock" sounds, he is ready to begin intellectual pursuits.	The environment can be arranged so movement through the developmental stages is accelerated.
Social-emotional development is of major concern because preschool children are not yet "ready" for intellectual functioning.	Intellectual development has the highest priority; social and emotional development are less important.

opment centers throughout the country. Classes were limited to 20 children, although 15 were preferred. Each class had one teacher and at least one aide, both of whom were trained in special Head Start training programs. These first programs were similar to established nursery school and kindergarten routines, although there was a somewhat greater emphasis on labeling and on sensory and academic experiences.

Table 2-3 describes a typical day in the summer program (8:45 A.M. to 3:30 P.M.).

Social workers, medical personnel, parents, and teachers worked together in this nationwide effort to develop comprehensive programs. Each group assumed special responsibilities. *Social workers* identified the need for clothing, food, toys, and learning materials that were absent from the home. Where child-rearing practices were involved, they were responsible for conducting parent or parent-child counseling sessions. *Medical personnel* examined the children and provided care when needed. In addition, they stressed good nutritional practices. *Parents* did volunteer work in the classroom and helped establish programs and formulate policies for

the community preschools. They were also often asked to try learning activities with their children at home. *Teachers* were responsible for planning and providing the high-priority learning activities and for coordinating the efforts of the supporting personnel at Head Start centers.

Early short-range studies of the effectiveness of various Head Start programs were predominantly positive. The short-range data showed evidence of growing interest in school, gains in IQ scores, better results on reading readiness or language tests, and even growth in initiative, imagination, and expressiveness. Although encouraged, project directors and researchers were, nevertheless, looking for long-range studies; these would give a better idea of the lasting effectiveness of Head Start experiences.

The most prominent early long-range study of Head Start was conducted for the Office of Economic Opportunity from June 1968 through May 1969 by the Westinghouse Learning Corporation and Ohio University (1973). Although the goals of the Head Start program were much wider in scope, the basic question posed by the study was, To what extent are the children

Table 2-3 *Head Start Schedule*

8:45–9:15	Arrival and independent work time (easel painting, puppets, blocks, dramatic play)
9:15–9:30	Morning group time (story, music, rhythm activities, sharing)
9:30–9:50	Snack and cleanup
9:50–11:00	First work period (math, reading, language, cooking projects, and other organized learning activities)
11:00–11:45	Outdoor play
11:45–12:30	Lunch
12:30–12:45	Cleanup
12:45–1:40	Rest period
1:40–2:05	Story and snack
2:05–3:10	Second work period (creative dramatics, caring for pets, language activities, and so on)
3:10–3:30	Discussion period and preparation for home
3:30	Dismissal

now in the first, second, and third grades who attended Head Start programs different in their intellectual and social-personal development from comparable children who did not attend?

To answer this question, the researchers studied children from 104 Head Start centers across the country. A sample of children from the centers who had gone on to first, second, and third grades in local area schools (experimental group) were matched with a sample of children from the same grades and schools who had not attended Head Start (control group). Both groups were given a series of tests covering various aspects of cognitive and affective development; parents were interviewed for information on their children's attitudes; and directors and other officials of the Head Start centers were interviewed about the various characteristics of their programs.

The major conclusions of the study were startling to many people.

1. Summer programs appeared to be ineffective in producing any gains in cognitive and affective development that persisted into the early elementary grades.

2. Full-year programs appeared to be inef-

fective as measured by the tests of affective development used in the study, but were marginally effective in producing gains in cognitive development that could be detected in grades one, two, and three.

3. Head Start children, whether from summer or from full-year programs, still appeared to be considerably below national norms on the standardized tests of language development and scholastic achievement.

4. Parents of Head Start enrollees voiced strong approval of the program and its influence on their children.

Head Start programs, then, did not achieve all the planners had hoped. Nevertheless, rather than give up, the planners looked more carefully at the results and prepared a critique of the Westinghouse study. Their basic arguments were as follows:

1. All new programs are bound to have "bugs"—many new programs were growing into large-scale operations, and there was little time to iron out the problems.

2. Very few standards existed for Head Start programs. The Westinghouse study lumped the poor with the good without noting the specific characteristics of successful programs.

These major arguments, together with the mixed results of the full-year findings (conclusion 2), the positive reactions of the parents, the value of the health and nutritional aspects of the program, and the urgent need to remediate the effects of poverty all influenced the planners to recommend the following:

1. Summer programs should be converted as early as possible into full-year or extended-year programs.

2. Full-year programs should be continued, but every effort should be made to make them more effective.

3. Since preschool educators are not sure about what constitutes effective early childhood programs, some full-year programs should be set up as experimental programs (strategically placed on a regional basis) for new procedures and techniques.

Project Follow Through, initiated in 1967, was a large-scale program designed to extend Head Start services through grade three. Its purpose was to maintain and extend short-term gains children made as they continued through elementary school. Both projects had similar goals and encouraged program experimentation to find the best programs for various kinds of settings. Also, Head Start and Follow Through became known for the "planned variation" of their educational approaches. These approaches fell into three categories:

1. *Basic Skills Models.* These programs stressed the acquisition of reading, language, and number skills through programmed teaching with highly structured and sequenced learning activities. (A *product* approach)

2. *Cognitive/Conceptual Models.* These programs stressed the development of concepts and learning processes through activities such as problem solving, observation, and manipulation. (A *process* approach)

3. *Affective/Developmental Models.* These programs tried to strike an even balance among all areas involved in child growth and development: physical, intellectual, and social-emotional—but with primary emphasis on the last.

Abt Associates, Inc., of Cambridge, Massachusetts, was commissioned from 1969 to 1975 to look at these Follow Through program variations and determine which program model was most successful. The Abt evaluation (1977) found, however, that the effectiveness of each model varied from site to site and that no model suceeded everywhere it had been tried. In basic skills development, the report indicated, direct instructional models (Basic Skills Models) had a higher average effect on basic skills scores than the other models. Conversely, the models that put their emphasis on cognitive/conceptual or affective/developmental approaches to learning had more negative effects on basic skills scores. The study also concluded, "It appears that [non-Follow Through] children are receiving educational experiences that teach them the basic skills by third grade more effectively than would the . . . programs offered by Follow Through" (Harris, 1977, p. 3).

Why did these programs have so many negative effects? The main reason advanced was that the tests used for gathering data were designed exclusively to assess the general goals of schooling, and so did not equally reflect the unique goals of all the models. In addition, the same arguments that had been presented to explain the negative Head Start results were also used to explain the negative outcomes of the Follow Through experimental programs.

Rather than discouraging preschool educators, studies like the Westinghouse Report and the Abt Planned Variations Study have stimulated them to discover more about the relationships between the environment and children's learning. For example, Dr. Irving Lazar of Cornell University recently conducted studies of Head Start children ten years after they had left preschool. He found that there were 50 to 90 percent fewer special education placements among these children than among children from identical backgrounds with no preschool experience, and that significantly fewer children with preschool experience had been retained one or more grades.

Currently, Head Start and Follow Through programs are still receiving support from the federal government through the Office of Economic Opportunity. Although studies indicate the effectiveness of these programs to be mixed, the OEO has to consider their overall educational benefit. Strong community support nationwide has made the government aware that determining the general educational benefit of programs must indeed include consideration of their overall effect on those who are served.

Changes in Day Care

The dynamically changing American society stimulated growth not only in the nursery school and kindergarten, but also in the area of day care. Most of the growth has been stimulated by social factors, including the problems facing children of low-income families, the changes brought by the movement for equal rights for women, the economic need for two-income families, and changing family patterns such as single-parent family units.

Today, according to 1980 Census Bureau reports, 9.6 percent of all American families are living in poverty, but the figure is 40 percent for families headed by single women; 20 percent of all children in America are living with a single parent, usually the mother. These 1980 figures contrast sharply to those from 1960, when only 12.4 percent of children lived

in single-parent households. By 1990, 25 percent is projected. This large number of single-parent families means that the parent with whom the child lives is normally the parent employed outside the home. Since many single-parent families today are not as apt to be living near grandparents and other relatives as they did in the past, those parents require child-care services to assist them in their role as parents.

During the late-1960s and early-1970s parents requiring the child-care services on a day-long basis were not always satisfied with what was available for them. Child care then was popularly described as "custodial"—that is, it simply provided a safe and healthful place for children to stay, and did not consider their total developmental needs. Many child-care centers were unlicensed, private operations whose services amounted to group babysitting at best. M. D. Keyserling (1972) described one child-care situation:

> When Mrs. ———— opened the door for us, we felt there were probably very few, if any children in the house, because of the quiet. It was quite a shock, therefore, to discover about seven or eight children, one year old or under, in the kitchen; a few of them were in highchairs, but most were strapped to kitchen chairs, all seemingly in a stupor.

> Mrs. ———— takes care of two families—six children which the Bureau of Children's Services subsidizes. The other children (41, for a total of 47 children) she takes care of independently, receiving two dollars per day per child. She told us that she has been doing this for 20 years and seemed quite proud to be able to manage as well alone, with no help. [pp. 135–136]

And even today such situations may cause tragedy. Here is a recent report adapted from the *Philadelphia Bulletin:*

> Temperatures over 100 degrees apparently killed two infant girls in a Miami apartment that served as an unlicensed nursery yesterday. Police said Louise H————, 32, had

been caring for 22 children, ranging in age from 6 months to 10 years, in partially closed rooms with no air-conditioning or fans. Two infants, 6 and 10 months old, died Thursday and charges are pending against Mrs. H———.

The quality of child-care programs alarmed those interested in gaining daylong care for young children. They were appalled at the number of centers run by unskilled staff and at the lack of adequate facilities. The 1970 White House Conference on Children addressed the need for higher quality daylong child-care facilities when it called for child-care centers to develop *comprehensive* family-oriented child-development programs. The Conference made 25 specific recommendations, including reordering national priorities to indicate the importance of quality nursery school and kindergarten programs that present "opportunities for each child to *learn, grow,* and *live creatively*." Gathering support from political groups as well as professional organizations, educators, and parents called for the establishment of comprehensive daylong child-care facilities that would meet the *social, emotional,* and *intellectual,* as well as the *physical* needs of children. In other words, they wanted daylong child care patterned after good, half-day preschool programs.

In addition, federal, state, and local agencies began to establish licensing requirements for child-care facilities. However, not all states established such standards of operation, and no national licensing laws have been developed. Newman and Newman (1978) explained:

Requirements for licensing differ in each state. Usually they include specifications about the kind of building, the amount of indoor and outdoor space, fencing for the outdoor play area, a staff-pupil ratio, provision for nutritious meals, and health and safety regulations. These latter requirements usually involve inspection of the site by the health and fire departments of the community. The program of the day-care center and the effectiveness of the center are not subject to direct requirements for licensing or for renewal of the license. As compared to the amount of standardization of the public school curriculum at each grade level, there is enormous variety in the goals and activities of day-care programs even within the same state. [p. 381]

This lack of curriculum standardization is favored by some early childhood educators whose states do have licensing standards for the physical facility. They feel that the variety of children's needs, program philosophies, ways of working, and community desires make national or statewide standardization of programs inappropriate. Thus, most regulatory agencies consider that planning, organizing, and carrying out actual programs are outside their jurisdiction. Many do, however, offer guidelines and models for establishing improved day-care programs. Perhaps the most effective of these aids is a government publication entitled *Day Care: Serving Preschool Children* (Cohen, 1974). Because of the variety of the nation's child-care needs, different types of day-care programs are now widely available in a variety of settings, such as industry, in apartments or condominiums, labor unions, colleges, and hospitals. There is also a growing number of private day-care centers such as those made possible by Head Start and other programs aided by government funds.

In the early and middle 1970s this initial growth in quality preschool services for working women slowed. At the beginning of his administration, President Nixon (1969) had made this reassuring statement:

As I mentioned previously, greatly expanded day-care center facilities would be provided for the children of welfare mothers who choose to work. There is no single ideal to which this administration is more firmly committed than to the enriching of a child's first five years of life, and thus helping the poor out of misery at a time when a lift can help the most. Therefore, these day-care centers would offer more than custodial care; they would also be devoted to the development of vigorous young minds and bodies. As a further dividend, the day-care centers would offer employment to many welfare mothers themselves. [p. 1108]

Despite this promise, Nixon vetoed a $2.1 billion Comprehensive Child Development Program bill in 1971. The bill would have provided funds for increased comprehensive child-care facilities throughout the country and would have emphasized a nationwide commitment to early childhood education. It was turned down as fiscally damaging, administratively unworkable, and potentially damaging to the family. Attempts to strengthen the nation's child-care services persisted during the 1970s, but the legal clout necessary for formal action was missing. One attempt was made in 1974 when Albert Shanker and his union, the American Federation of Teachers (AFT), launched a program called Educare, which was designed to provide preschool jobs for public school teachers laid off by declining enrollments and tight budgets. The AFT estimated that 150,000 to 200,000 teachers could be put to work if the nation's 10.4 million children three to five years old were provided quality child-care facilities. Despite strong efforts, Educare has not yet gathered enough support to become a reality. The AFT also endorsed the $1.8 billion Child and Family Services Bill of 1974. The bill, sponsored by Senators Walter Mondale and John Brademas, was designed to provide money for the establishment of comprehensive child-care centers for low- and middle-income families throughout the country. The bill was defeated in Congress because it was seen as too expensive. In 1979, Senator Alan Cranston of California introduced a bill designed to subsidize child-care services for all children up to age 15, provided the children were enrolled in licensed centers. Cranston's bill was attacked on many fronts—as socialistic, expensive, and administratively

unworkable. Those charges led to its demise that same year.

Such political disagreement as to the best means of providing child care has caused the United States to be the only major industrialized country in the world that does not provide basic child-care services for its citizens. Political debate continues as to whether financial support should be provided by the federal government, how much should be provided, and what the delivery system should be. The AFT is still the major voice calling for action by the government, but it has now been joined by many other national organizations including the AFL-CIO, the National Education Association (NEA), the Parent-Teacher Association (PTA), and various influential women's organizations. Despite the fact that the federal government has not decided on the appropriate delivery vehicle for such comprehensive child care services, these organizations overwhelmingly endorse one system as the most responsible vehicle for delivering services to young children—the public schools. The reason for this recommendation is that if one major sponsoring agency (public schools) were responsible for child-care programs, the agency could coordinate quality services for all children regardless of social or economic status.

What is the future of early childhood education in America? If the federal government is willing to make a commitment to young children in the form of public school services, the public schools may well turn out to be a total community service. However, responsible critics of public school-based child-care services argue that if this happens, the close relationship that has always existed between the smaller day-care operations and families using their services will be eroded. And this has always been a desirable aspect of early childhood education. They also argue that a centralized delivery system will tend to eliminate the flexibility that exists in early childhood programming today. The various nursery schools and day-care centers now offer a wide assortment of services and experiences through home, school, center, industrial, and other program sites. Could those accommodations and variances in program approach be preserved? Should they be preserved? Should day care be educational, too? A last issue is whether those teachers responsible for the caring operations within public school systems would possess the essential training required for teaching children younger than age five. Critics point out that many teachers assigned to these facilities will be those trained mainly as elementary school teachers who already were employed by a school district but who face the danger of losing their jobs due to dropping school enrollments. According to the critics, even though these teachers have the best intentions, they would find it difficult to adjust to the different educational approach of prekindergarten programs.

These issues seem central to change for early childhood education and comprise an area of historical significance of which you are an important part. How many of you will be eventual leaders in the movement to bring day-care services under public school control or to allow them to remain as diverse as they presently are? What new possibilities might you offer for a situation that has often been described as public day care for the poor, private nursery schools or day-care centers for affluent, and potluck for families in neither category?

SOME FINAL THOUGHTS

Early childhood education is not a new movement in our country. Based upon their European roots, day nurseries became available in the mid-1800s, kindergartens in the late 1800s, and nursery schools in the early 1900s. Today, early childhood programs are available in a variety of settings and for a variety of pur-

poses. Generally, their contemporary popularity can be attributed to two major sources: the realization of the importance of the early years in the lives of children and changing social conditions, including those created by mothers who work for economic reasons or for the pleasure associated with the fulfillment of a career. A major issue for all early childhood educators is whether the situation should be allowed to remain as it is with different kinds of preschool programs or whether the government should become involved to the point of centralizing all child care within the public schools. You, the readers, are the dynamic new forces who will shape early childhood education in the future. What is your view toward assisting families and providing early opportunities for children in an effort to make them responsible adults in the future?

The historical review presented in this chapter was intended to give you an idea of how the first six years of a child's life came to be considered a distinct period of an individual's development and how early childhood programs were developed over the years to reflect those views. This is the foundation upon which the future will be built. What the future will bring is open to conjecture. One thing, however, is certain: That which comes will be created mainly out of love and concern for young children. As you consider major issues in early childhood education and begin to develop your own philosophy, you may wish to sort your thoughts into these categories:

- *Who* should have early childhood programs available—children from low-income families, handicapped children, all children?

- *What* form should early childhood programs take; what should their content be; what activities or teaching strategies should be used?

- *Where* should these programs be located—in homes, private buildings, public schools, or separate settings?

- *When* should early childhood education begin—in infancy, before age three, in kindergarten?
- *Why* is early childhood education important—for intellectual growth, social and emotional development, physical development?
- *How* should early childhood programs be made available to the people who want or need them—government support or through the variety of channels that presently exist?

Finally, Table 2-4 is an organized "time-line" of the historical milestones in the development of early childhood education as they were described throughout the chapter.

Table 2-4   *History of Early Childhood Education*

1400–1700s	Period of childhood is not recognized as a separate stage of development.	1913–1915	Montessori spreads word of her program by visiting America and delivering speeches at the White House and Carnegie Hall. McLin opens first Montessori school in New York City.
1700s–early 1800s	Period of childhood is recognized in a crude form—children are described as naturally bad.		
1760s–1800s	Rousseau and other humanists try to advance the idea that children are basically good. (Emile)	1919	Harriet Johnson establishes the first nursery school in New York City.
1760s–1800s	Pestalozzi's school in rural Switzerland applies the education principles of Rousseau. (How Gertrude Teaches Her Children and Book for Mothers)	1922	Abigail Eliot begins the Ruggles Street Nursery School in Boston. Merrill-Palmer Institute is founded in Detroit.
1837	Froebel establishes the first kindergarten in Germany. (The Education of Man)	1923	Arnold Gesell influences early childhood education with publication of The Preschool Child in which he establishes the importance of the early years.
1856	Margarethe Schurz opens the first American kindergarten in Watertown, Wisconsin. "Day nurseries" become available for working mothers in the United States.	1900–1920s	Patty Smith Hill organizes and establishes the progressive kindergarten. Dewey's "progressive education" philosophy becomes popular through America.
1860	Elizabeth Peabody starts the first English-speaking kindergarten in Boston.	1930s	Freud's psychosexual theories point out the importance of personality development throughout the preschool years.
1892	International Kindergarten Union (IKU), later to become the Association for Childhood Education International, is organized.	1933–1942	WPA nurseries are funded for the purposes of providing jobs for teachers during the depression and encouraging women to enter the work force.
1890s	G. Stanley Hall begins the scientific era of child study in the United States.	1941–1946	The Lanham Act provides funds for nurseries so that women are able to work in our country's defense plants.
1907	Maria Montessori opens her "Casa dei Bambini" in Rome.		
1911	Margaret McMillan establishes the "open-air" nursery school in England.	1960	Jerome Bruner writes The Process of Education.

Table 2-4   *(continued)*

1961	*J. McVicker Hunt publishes* Intelligence and Experience.	*1974*	*Educare, a comprehensive, federally funded, universal child-care program is proposed by the American Federation of Teachers.*
1964	*Benjamin Bloom authors* Stability and Change in Human Characteristics.	*1977*	*Abt Associates studies the effect the "planned variations" of the Follow Through programs.*
1965	*Head Start is funded by the federal government in an effort to provide early schooling for four- and five-year-old children affected by the conditions of poverty.*	*1980s*	*Federal and state rulings establish strong advocacy for children's rights. Equal opportunities for handicapped children and a search for answers to the child-care dilemma dominate this era.*
1967	*Project Follow Through extends Head Start services through grade three.*		
1970	*Westinghouse Report studies the effect of Head Start programs.*		

Chapter 3

For I want what I want when I want it!
That's all that makes life worth the while.
For the wine that tonight fills my soul with
    delight,
On the morrow may seem to me vile.
There's no worldly pleasure myself I deny,
There's no one to ask me the wherefore or
    why,
I eat when I'm hungry, and I drink when I'm
    dry,
For I want what I want when I want it!
I want what I want when I want it!

—Victor Herbert

Nurturing Personal Feelings and Interpersonal Relationships of the Very Young

SOCIAL-EMOTIONAL DEVELOPMENT

Although not referring specifically to infants, Victor Herbert's lines from *Mademoiselle Modiste* give us a succinct description of the basic drives of infants. Their major reactions are to satisfy basic physical needs and discomfort; if they desire to be fed or cleaned, their cries inform you so. When and how you meet those cries transforms the strong drive to satisfy physical needs into social and emotional reactions as well. Babies quickly recognize those responsible for their care, and, as time goes on and the care becomes consistent, babies begin to develop feelings about their encounters. Rage and hostility accompany the absence of immediate help, while pleasant coos and babbles inform you of the baby's satisfaction. From these early experiences, infants go through a special developmental process called *social-emotional development*.

The term *social* refers to the establishment of relationships between two or more people through which they mutually influence each other's behavior. Notice the word *mutually* in the preceding sentence. This word reflects the contemporary view of the nature of caregiver–child interaction. Until the

1970s, many child psychologists had adopted the stance that caregiver–child interaction is basically a one-way street; according to this position the caregiver is the active agent in shaping the infant's or child's behavior while the infant or child merely reacts to the efforts of the caregiver. We now understand, however, that even infants in their earliest days influence the caregivers' behavior and, just as the caregivers play a major role in shaping the social behavior of children, infants become a major factor in determining the caring behaviors of their caregivers (Bell and Harper, 1977). One of the most important considerations of planning programs for young children, therefore, is the process of understanding how youngsters and caregivers reciprocally influence one another as they respond to the commonly accepted behaviors and values of the early childhood environment.

The term *emotion* refers to the expression of feelings in a variety of ways. Some emotions, such as love and happiness, are positive and enjoyable; others, such as anger and fear, may be negative and unpleasant. Youngsters generally develop greater abilities to acquire emotional maturity as they experience positive social contacts with their family members, peers, teachers, or other significant individuals in their lives. Conversely, negative social experiences tend to bring about emotional problems such as temper tantrums, jealousy, and aggression (Gander and Gardiner, 1981, p. 354). Social experiences and emotional expressions are clearly inseparable; one influences the other. For that reason, we'll term social-emotional development the evolving process of realizing and acquiring the behaviors and values of any particular group and learning how to express specific feelings.

Over the years, social and emotional development has been a primary concern to parents and educators responsible for choosing or providing programs for children prior to the first grade. Both groups have traditionally valued goals such as "ability to get along with others," "establishing self-control," "learning to deal with feelings in an age-appropriate manner," "developing a positive sense of self-worth," "behaving in socially acceptable ways," and other crucial social or emotional considerations that might be globally referred to as *mental health*. We don't need to justify concern for this extremely important aspect of our children's lives; we need only take a close look at social conditions such as rising crime rates, dishonesty in government, the self-preoccupation of many young adults labeled the "Me Generation" in the 1970s, and other disturbing social conditions. We now know that the experiences occurring before a child usually enters school have far-reaching consequences, both positive and negative, on lifelong patterns of behavior. But we still don't know how early before the child normally enters school to emphasize the social and emotional needs of children. How early is early enough? Although this question still remains completely unanswered and serves as a focus of heated discussion even today, many educators recommend that we must assume responsibility for the social and emotional development of children from the moment of conception onward throughout life.

Burton White (1975) believes that the period from eight months to three years of age is perhaps the most crucial of all. "To begin to look at a child's educational development when he is *two* [italics mine] years of age is already much too late, particularly in the area of social skills and attitudes" (p. 108). With this knowledge comes great responsibility, for we as teachers of young children must be ready to meet the exciting challenge of preparing environmental surroundings suitable to the current developmental state of each youngster in our care. Before we directly address this area of responsibility, however, we will discuss four basic theoretical positions that will serve to guide your efforts.

FOUR DESCRIPTIONS OF SOCIAL-EMOTIONAL DEVELOPMENT

The following four philosophies represent the four major ways of characterizing social-emotional development and working with the very young. First, and most historically rooted, is the *environmentalist* position. This position has its foundation in the philosophies of Rousseau, Pestalozzi, and Froebel, who all compared young children to plants or animals allowed to live freely in nature. They felt that, given freedom within optimal environmental conditions, the young child would unfold from within into a beautifully mature adult. As the single major determiner of development, only environmental conditions could either benefit children or impinge upon their individual progress.

The second position was derived from those who thought it wise to gather scientific evidence to either support or reject the ideas of the environmentalists. Known as *maturationists,* these individuals studied and systematically recorded the characteristics of children from birth through the early years. They concluded that the environment alone cannot account for development. Instead the child's development is governed by a genetically inherited "internal alarm clock," which determines the times at which certain behavioral expectancies emerge. Articulated primarily by G. Stanley Hall, Arnold Gesell, Frances Ilg, and Louise Bates Ames, this position observed that "normal" behavioral characteristics are predictable for any particular age. There is no need, therefore, to be concerned about manipulating the environmental conditions in order to facilitate the development of those characteristics; all we have to do is wait for the biological maturity associated with various ages to appear naturally.

Supporters of the third position, like the environmentalists, maintained that optimal environmental conditions are the sole determiners of development. They believed, however, that the complete freedom within the environment as espoused by Rousseau and others is inappropriate. Associated with *behaviorist* theories, individuals such as John B. Watson and B. F. Skinner believed behavioral changes to be totally contingent upon the ways by which we structure and regulate the environment. Behaviors resulting in positive reactions will tend to be repeated while those resulting in negative reactions will diminish. This school of psychology was concerned only with externally observable behavior within an environmental context rather than with internal factors such as "unfolding" or "maturing."

These three positions appear to create a dilemma that lasts in some quarters even until today. It is often referred to as the *nature vs. nurture controversy.* Do children become uniquely individual because of the special genetic structures each inherits at conception, or do children become socialized through the unique environment each experiences throughout life? If development is a combination of both, is one aspect more influential than the other? We still do not have definitive answers to all these questions, but the general feeling in early childhood education today, and our fourth basic alternative, seems to be that behaviors are determined primarily through sophisticated interactions between environmental and genetic influences. This position, therefore, is known as *interactionism.* For example, if we observe children, we will find that the sequential patterns of change as described by Gesell, Piaget, Erikson, and contemporary researchers such as Kohlberg do exist in children. Children do appear to move through the stages of development. We know that "stranger anxiety" is characteristic of most infants at about six to nine months of age and that two-year-olds differ in their play patterns from six-year-olds. Children do seem to exhibit common behaviors during separate developmental stages of their lives.

This is a fascinating aspect of child development, but equally as interesting is the aspect of individuality. For instance, the individuality of infants can be observed in the degree of crying during the first six months of life. Some may be easily calmed and docile while others scream at the slightest provocation. Some babies are roused by little stimulation; others require much more. Some infants need a great deal of sleep; others get by with relatively little. Some infants display alertness by constantly scanning their environment; others do not. These characteristics appear to be something biological that the baby brings into this world. This biological information results in two phenomena: (1) it may influence the response of the primary caregiver to the child, or (2) the response of the primary caregiver may influence future behavior of the child. Parents often play games with babies involving the interaction of both. For example, saying "peek-a-boo" every time eye contact is made encourages infants to gurgle or coo. Parents enjoy such games because of the positive feedback received from the baby, while babies continue because they enjoy such warm interaction. Infants, therefore, become socialized not entirely through events beyond their control; they become an active part of the process as they respond to and initiate physical contact, vocal interchange, and other forms of interpersonal contact.

Contemporary views of the social and emotional nature of children assign an active role to the child and describe the process of development as a reciprocal interaction between the child and the environment. As Baumrind (1980) explained: "Socialization is [a] ... process ... in which ... individuals become what they are in reciprocal interaction with the environment, and the crucial environmental context for young children ... will limit or expand in important ways potentialities that can become manifested as socially

useful and personally satisfying attitudes and actions" (p. 640). Although eclecticism is a major goal of this text, we have chosen the interactionist viewpoint as the major underlying theoretical structure to support the teacher's role in working with the very young. It helps to solidify the contention that the child actively imposes changes on the environment and that the environment similarly brings about changes in the child. However, this is not meant to presuppose that traditional prospectives such as behaviorism will not be mentioned. You should know about alternative approaches to social and emotional development, because every child is like every other child and every child is unlike every other child. One approach can work with some children but not with all. Interactionism does appear most dominant in early childhood education today, but alternatives, including forms of behaviorism, also extend valued possibilities for teachers whose children indicate a need for its use. Children must be steadily led through the process of development as they grow toward maturity, so far as their ability to express personal feelings and to develop a social sense is concerned. What social and emotional characteristics do children go through as they progress from birth through early childhood? What kinds of things can their caregivers provide in order to facilitate this movement?

To begin to answer these questions, let us start at the very beginning—birth.

SOCIAL-EMOTIONAL GROWTH IN INFANTS

Crying

The infant experiences a radical environmental change at birth. It is taken from protective surroundings in which all survival needs were supplied by the mother, and abruptly put into a new world requiring quick adaptations for survival. The infant begins to breathe air; it adjusts to new temperatures; it begins to take in, digest, and excrete food; and it communicates reactions to the environment. It struggles to alter objectionable experiences and takes comfort in an environment filled with love and physical support. Thus, tiny infants receive their first lessons in social behavior as they acquire new behaviors and adjust old ones to satisfy basic needs. Naked and helpless, babies are dependent for nearly everything from the adults around them. Hunger, thirst, wetness, weariness of the same position, discomfort from being too cool or too warm, boredom, and a host of other conditions bring out babies' cries. Should you become responsible for infant care in any of the growing numbers of infant-care centers around the country, you should know that such cries are the infant's first basic form of communication. You'll quickly become successful at "translating" cries, such as the hungry cry and the wet cry, and learn to take appropriate measures to supply the necessary relief.

Sometimes, however, when a baby just cries and cries, you know there is nothing wrong; there is no apparent physical reason for it. This phenomenon is quite common. Some frequent periods of crying and fretting can't be explained by physical causes. In fact, by the time they are one month old, nearly all babies develop fretful periods. Some babies limit their crying to a particular time in the morning while others choose the afternoon or evening. Usually, such behavior vanishes by three months of age, perhaps because the infant's immature digestive and nervous systems are beginning to adjust to life in the outside world. Infrequently, you may experience fretfulness and irritable crying in babies past three months of age. The cause for such behavior is unknown, but it should be acknowledged, as individuals caring for babies often become frustrated when their best efforts fail to soothe the infants in their care. The

screaming and thrashing reactions are difficult for them to accept, especially since the infant seems to be saying, "Try your best to comfort me, but it just won't work!" The caregivers' initial feelings of compassion soon change to feelings of inadequacy and, often, to feelings of outright frustration and anger. Such negative feelings eventually turn into guilt and the caregivers become more strained as the strong feelings continue to intensify.

Rather than just holding the baby and attempting to quiet it, try these suggestions:

- Rock the baby.
- Walk with the baby.
- "Dance" with the baby.
- Sing or talk in a quiet manner.
- Shake or rattle a toy.
- Lay the baby across your lap on its stomach and genty stroke its back.
- Lay the baby on its stomach across a warm hot-water bottle.
- Swing the baby in a wind-up swing.
- Give a pacifier to the baby (the "Nuk" brand pacifier allows less air to enter into the baby's mouth and lessens potential gas pains).
- Breathe deeply and slowly as you hold the baby; the baby may become quieted by your relaxation.
- Turn on some loud music or let the water run for a few minutes.
- If all else fails, try an old parents' strategy; run the vacuum for a short period of time.

Social Interactions

In addition to knowing how to respond to babies' cries or when and how to quiet a crying baby, a second major issue faced by caregivers and parents is how to extend our social contacts with babies in ways that go beyond simply satisfying basic physiological needs. T. G.

R. Bower (1977) gave us valuable help in this area when he made the observation that infants even in the first days of life are able to interact socially.

> One of the more spectacular demonstrations . . . is the fact that babies less than a week old will imitate other people. If the baby's mother, or some other adult, sticks out her tongue at the baby, within a relatively short time the baby will begin to stick his tongue back out at her. Suppose she then stops sticking her tongue out and begins to flutter her eyelashes; the baby will flutter his eyelashes back. If she then starts to open and close her mouth in synchrony . . . the newborn actually seems to enjoy engaging in this mutual imitation game.
>
> . . . And all these [imitative] capacities are bent toward what is clearly, I think, a social purpose. The newborn enjoys social interaction with adults. Imitation at this stage is a social game. The responses are quite specifically directed toward human beings and seem to me to be testimony that the newborn considers himself human too. . . . The newborn baby imitates the facial gestures of the adults around him for no reward other than the pleasure of interacting with them. [pp. 28–30]

Therefore, through an imitative game—interaction with adults—the infant begins to participate in his or her first *socialization experiences* (see Figure 3-1).

Social Smiles   *Emotional* expressions (or feelings) become part of the newborn's repertoire, but only in very limited ways. Discomfort or distress of any kind—hunger, pain, heat, cold—is usually expressed through techniques such as crying, thrashing, or turning red all over. At about six weeks of age the infant begins to develop a highly positive *social smile*. The social smile can be triggered by a number of pleasing experiences: human voices, faces, familiar objects, gentle touches, stroking, tickling, or rocking. Accompanying the smile may be gentle humming or cooing vocalizations and the smooth movement of

arms or legs. Parents are usually elated at the emergence of the social smile and its accompanying behavior that the baby directs to them, and they take great pleasure from this interaction. The infant's smile is not only enjoyable for all parties involved, but also socially significant because it is the first obviously positive social response emitted by the newborn. Gradually, during the next two or three months, the child extends the smiling response to other family members and possibly even to some strangers. However, during the sixth to eighth month babies tend to reject the advances of all others and relate only to a loving, mothering person.

Stranger Anxiety   This notion of mothering person–infant attachment has received more emphasis today than almost any other area of social-emotional development in infancy. Researchers have found that the period of social attachment between the mothering person and infant is signalled at first by a fear of strangers and anxiety at separation. Bower stated that:

> Smiling is a pleasant social behavior. . . . The second half-year is marked by the emergence of behaviors which are much less pleasant in affective tone. Somewhere around the age of eight months, the baby begins to manifest quite clearly a fear of strangers. At this stage, at the approach of a strange adult, the baby will cry, scream, or otherwise try to avoid the encounter. If the baby is mobile, he will try to crawl away. At a slightly later age, a baby will begin also to show fear of separation from his mother. Separation from the mother will lead to attempts to rejoin her, screaming, stillness, tears, and other signs of distress. Both these behaviors are an unmistakable sign that the baby has formed a critical social attachment. [1977, p. 49]

The infants' decided fear of strangers is commonly referred to as *stranger anxiety*. Stranger anxiety ushers in a phase in children's lives when they reject strangers and form

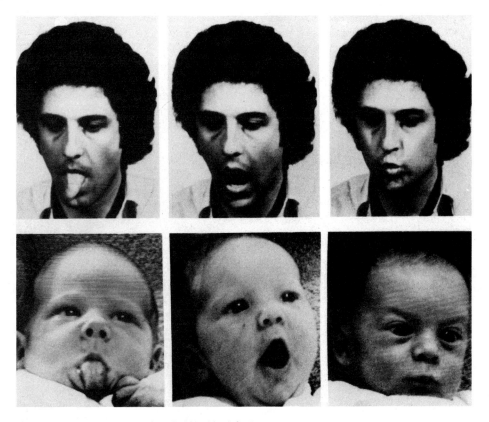

Figure 3-1   *Facial expressions imitated by infants*
("Imitation of Facial and Manual Gestures by Human Neonates," Meltzoff, A. N., and Moore, M. K., Science, vol. 198, pp. 75–78. Photos 7 October 1977. Copyright 1977 by the American Association for the Advancement of Science.)

strong emotional attachments only to mother figures.

Often the person who cares for the infant most will become the object of such mothering feelings. That person is able to soothe and comfort the baby when others are unsuccessful; it is to this person the baby turns, gives the most special smile, or stretches out its arms in an appeal to be held. Gladys Jenkins and Helen Shacter (1975) feel that, "There are indications that babies thrive best when there is one central mothering person to whom they form an attachment by the middle of this first year. This attachment provides the feelings of security and trust which make it possible for

the baby to grow into warm relationships with other people all through life." (p. 48) These authors also feel, however, that other mothering people, including fathers, need to contribute significantly to the child's social growth at this stage in order for subsequent growth to develop optimally.

The intensity of stranger anxiety has become a popular topic for researchers. They have found that its strength seems to depend on how varied the baby's caretakers have been. Schaffer and Emerson (1964) found, for example, that babies who have interacted with greater numbers of adults show a lesser degree of stranger anxiety than those who have had less contact. Bettye Caldwell (1963) discovered that children raised in environments where child care is a shared responsibility of many adults (such as the kibbutzim of Israel or some communes in the United States) tend not to show a marked degree of stranger anxiety.

This discussion about stranger anxiety may raise a question in your mind as to whether it is good or bad. L. Joseph Stone and Joseph Church offer an answer to this question:

> It is our hunch that it is good insofar as it reflects a strong emotional attachment which should facilitate cultural learning and may foretell a later generalized capacity for strong affection. It seems to be good, too, in that it shows clear perceptual discrimination among people. On the negative side, stranger anxiety may mean excessively limited social contact or it may represent an attachment so strong as to interfere with the normal weanings from infantile ways. [1973, pp. 67–68]

They go on to stress the significance of stranger anxiety in terms of practical considerations:

> Stranger anxiety is important in practical terms, since it affects leaving the baby with new caretakers while the mother goes outside the home, and because many a visiting grandparent or aunt or uncle has suffered wounded feelings at the hands of a rejecting baby who has been rushed through the process of getting acquainted or reacquainted. The wise stranger keeps his distance, knowing that the baby's reaction to a novel stimulus has components of both fear and curiosity. With a bit of patience on the visitor's part, the baby's curiosity dominates his fear, and aversion soon changes to friendliness. [p. 66]

Stranger anxiety, then, should be a strong consideration of child-care workers involved with caring for infants. If you find yourself in a professional position working with infants six months and older, keep these ideas in mind as you plan your approach:

1. Proceed slowly as you become acquainted with the baby. Quick movements or sudden talking may cause crying, screaming, or other rejection responses from the child.

2. Encourage the mother-figure to stay at your facility for short periods of time as you slowly gain the baby's approval.

3. Use toys and playthings to capture the child's interest while you slowly allow the baby to become comfortable in the new surroundings.

4. Develop a warm, loving atmosphere reflecting mothering characteristics so that the baby will form trusting, positive emotional attachments to you.

5. Encourage mother-figures to receive their children with warm affection when they are taken back home at the end of the day.

Interaction Games Infants at about the age of eight months normally begin to enjoy the company of other familiar adults. They revel in simple games such as having adults hide their faces behind their hands in a game of peek-a-boo. They enjoy being picked up to exchange nonsense sounds with adults. They always smile and gurgle during their exchanges of "Da-Da," "Ma-Ma," or "Ba-Ba." Infants captivate adults with such social games and quickly learn new behaviors needed to cue their participation—slaps on the high chair tray, fake coughing, or a special smile.

At about the tenth month babies are able to participate in more advanced social games, such as pat-a-cake. (As hard as they may try, though, it is difficult for infants to clap palms together. Their first motion in a pat-a-cake game is clapping their fists together instead of their palms. Eventually, they are likely to clap their palms together, but they won't make clapping sounds.) Slowly, infants begin to understand simple commands and requests, along with special cue words for familiar games and daily routines. These patterns of socialized play indicate a stable pattern of social-emotional growth. Children are fascinated with repetitive play and enjoy duplicating their new experiences many times—to the point where it often becomes monotonous for an adult. Don't lose your patience when this happens, but keep in mind that children behave like this because they are thrilled with their new discoveries. As they are continually encouraged by adults to extend their interests, their growth is stimulated and reinforced. Several kinds of social play are described in the accompanying box.

Stages of Growth

From about eight months of age until toddlerhood, infants prefer to strengthen ties with their caregivers, and they make every effort to stay close. They crawl after the caregiver, cry out if the caregiver is elsewhere, clutch an apron or trouser leg, gladly return hugs and kisses, and cuddle comfortably in the caregiver's arms. Infants feel emotionally secure in their newly developed social environment, and they seek to keep close contact with those they trust. This developing confidence encourages further explorations into new relationships.

Thus, during the period of infancy, children progress through three definable stages of social-emotional development. These stages are summarized in Table 3-1.

The following are suggestions to help you in your social-emotional contacts with infants.

1. Remember that infants understand the language of touch much earlier than the language of speech. As the person caring for infants, you must be mindful to hold them in a calm, relaxed manner. Handle them confidently, cuddle them, and talk in soothing tones.

2. Don't become overanxious when first handling an infant. Many caregivers are too excitable during their initial experiences with the child and tend to cause

anxiety and insecurity within the child. Relax and try to follow the advice in suggestion 1.

The key to healthy social-emotional development appears to assume its significance during the special, tender period of infancy when the babies learn to trust those around them to provide for their care. This idea of trust was made especially clear to early childhood professionals by the noted psychologist Erik Erikson. A close associate of Freud, Erikson agreed with most of Freud's theory regarding the need to satisfy differing drives during our lifetime and the importance of the early years upon later emotional characteristics, but he felt that Freud's theory was somewhat narrow in its focus upon the satisfaction of sexual desires as the major factor in development. Remaining as loyal as he could to his good friend and respected colleague, Erikson adhered to Freud's basic psychoanalytic theory, but centered his conviction that development of "self" or "self-identity" is a product more of cultural, or social, factors than of sexual factors. Erikson's (1963) resulting *psychosocial theory* is based on the premise that all individuals progress through eight stages of development; during these stages they are confronted with unique "conflicts" that demand an adjustment of personal needs to the social expectations of the culture in which they live. Erikson described each stage as a *crisis period,* a time when individuals experience stresses and strains as they attempt to regulate their behaviors to the demands of their particular culture. In each period the crisis is expressed in terms of dichotomies, or two opposing divisions, of orientation, each seeking to control the individual. For example, the first pair of competing dichotomies is trust vs. mistrust; the second pair is autonomy vs. shame and doubt. Erikson proposed that the goal of personality development is to resolve such conflicts by encouraging positive qualities to

SOCIAL PLAY FOR INFANTS

Mimicking The caregiver encourages the baby to imitate gestures or sounds. Waving "bye-bye" or stretching out the arms to indicate "so big" are favorites. Coughing, sniffing through the nose, or making simple sounds such as "ahr-r-r-r" amuse the infant for great periods of time.

Drop and Fetch Babies seem to drop things at first simply to see what happens. They hear the noise and turn to see what transpired. Their great joy comes, however, when the caregiver becomes involved and picks up the object. This soon becomes great entertainment; the baby drops and the caregiver fetches. To some caregivers, this repetition seems pointless and boring. However, when we consider the social play resulting from this interaction, we realize that the game is an important source of learning about the world.

Peek-a-Boo Babies enjoy this traditional adult–infant participation game. The caregiver begins the game by hiding his face in back of his hands or a blanket, suddenly showing his face, and saying, "Peek-a-boo. I see you," to the baby.

Pat-a-Cake This simple rhyme is greeted with enjoyment by infants long after the caregiver may become tired and bored with it.

> Pat-a-cake, pat-a-cake, baker's man. *(Clap baby's hands together.)*
> Bake me a cake as fast as you can.
> Roll it *(Roll baby's hands.)*
> And pat it *(Pat baby's hands.)*
> And mark it with a B *(Make a letter B on baby's tummy.)*
> And put it in the oven for baby *(or baby's first name)* and me!

Action Games Traditional favorites are jiggling the baby above one's head, swinging it from the chest to between the knees, tickling the baby's trunk, or bouncing it on a knee to a familiar rhythmic verse. Here are two rhymes to accompany the bouncing activity:

TO MARKET, TO MARKET

> To market, to market, to buy a fat pig;
> Home again, home again, jiggety jig.
> To market, to market, to buy a fat hog;
> Home again, home again, jiggety jog.

FIDDLE-DE-DEE

> Fiddle-de-dee, fiddle-de-dee,
> The fly shall marry the bumblebee.

> They went to church, and married was she;
> The fly had married the bumblebee.

Sound Games Interaction with infants is greatly enhanced when the caregiver plays sound games involving parts of the body. Games combining movement and rhymes include these popular selections:

BABY BUMBLEBEE

> I'm bringing home a baby bumblebee. *(Cup hands together.)*
> Won't my mommy be so proud of me?
> I'm bringing home a baby bumblebee.
> OUCH! *(Clap hands.)*
> He stung me!

KNOCK ON THE DOOR

> Knock on the door. *(Tap on baby's forehead.)*
> Peek in. *(Lift up an eyelid.)*
> Open the hatch. *(Pretend to turn baby's nose.)*
> And walk right in. *(Tickle baby's lips.)*

Give and Take This is a popular favorite, which begins with the caretaker giving the child a favorite toy and saying, "Now I'll give it to you." Back-and-forth activity is encouraged as the caregiver says, "Now you give it to me."

Gotcha Once the baby is able to creep or crawl, he or she enjoys the challenge of moving away and being chased to a warning, "I'm gonna getcha." The caregiver should let the baby crawl for a while and grab him or her, exclaiming, "Gotcha!" The baby should be given a big hug or tickle after each episode.

Hide-n-Seek Babies laugh with glee as their caretakers repeatedly call their names while searching behind doors or into wastebaskets or drawers of the "lost infant."

Facial Examination Older infants punctuate their growing social awareness by showing an interest in a caregiver's facial features. The baby may grab the nose, grasp eyeglasses, touch an ear, or poke at one's eyes. By guiding the infant with words such as "Easy, easy," the caregiver informs the baby that such exploration must be done carefully. One may want to name each feature as the child touches it, eventually encouraging the child to touch the same feature on his or her face. By continually following this pattern, the child may be able to respond appropriately by the end of the first year when asked to "Show me your nose (or other feature)."

Table 3-1   *Three Stages of Social-Emotional Development through Infancy*

Stage	Age	Social-Emotional Characteristics
Stage 1	Birth to six months	Infant imitates facial gestures of adults and begins to respond to the mother-figure. The infant enjoys simple imitative games. The social smile begins to appear as the child reacts positively to varieties of positive stimuli. Negative stimuli are usually met by crying or thrashing.
Stage 2	Six months to one year	Infant becomes closely attached to mother-figure. Stranger anxiety ushers in this period. Baby gradually begins to cooperate in social games such as peek-a-boo or pat-a-cake and begins to show greater interaction with those who are trusted.
Stage 3	One year to two years	Infant needs to be close to the caregiver. Babies anticipate expressions of love and gladly return such expressions. Intense positive and negative reactions signal likes and dislikes.

Table 3-2   *Erikson's First Four Crisis Periods*

Stage	Age	Positive Outcome	Negative Outcome
Trust vs. Mistrust	Birth–1½ years	Learns to place faith in others and have confidence in them. Develops feelings of security and comfort.	Is fearful and unsure of the environment. Fear, anxiety, and apprehension characterize the personality.
Autonomy vs. Shame and Doubt	1½ years– 3 years	Accepts independence, learns to make decisions, does things for herself.	Overcontrol leads to inhibitions, shame, and loss of self-esteem.
Initiative vs. Guilt	3–6 years	Plans and carries out own activities, tests new powers confidently, enjoys achievement, and attempts to master new challenges.	Fears failure in trying new things. Failure may lead to punishment, leading to guilt feelings.
Industry vs. Inferiority	6–12 years	Learns to seek recognition by learning the skills of a culture or by producing things. These successes help the child develop a positive self-concept.	Lack of recognition or consistent failures lead to feelings of frustration, inadequacy, and inferiority. Neglects forming relationships with others.

emerge during each stage. Accordingly, warm, understanding adults help move the child toward a positive sense of self by furnishing continuous, consistent care for the infant during the stage of trust vs. mistrust. Consequently, the ways by which stresses are met during each of the following stages combine to form the individual's personality. Table 3-2 describes the first four stages and associated

characteristics of conflict as proposed by Erikson.

Erikson assumed that developmental changes occur during separate stages of a person's life and that social-emotional maturity is developed as a result of a person's ability to resolve conflicts within each stage. The influence of such thinking was significant, especially as it added to the contemporary concern

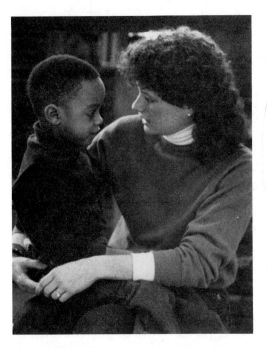

Acceptance and approval from caring parents and teachers help satisfy the child's basic drive for self-esteem and provide the confidence necessary for later expressions of independence.

for children during their early years. Barman (1969) explained:

> What do Erikson's formulations tell the teacher about handling the [young] child? Put in very rudimentary form, they tell her, "Let him trust you as a consistent adult who cares for and about him. Encourage him in his growing independence, avoid shaming him and making him doubt his own worth. Provide him with a climate where new experiences with people and materials challenge his learning and give him goals to reach. [p. 20]

The message of all teachers and adults is that it is important to communicate to the child that they are able to satisfy the child's needs and that they want to satisfy those needs. In turn, the child will become more attached to them and will be more willing to regulate his behaviors to reflect his expectations of them.

One additional important matter concerns questions we all have in our first experiences with infants: "How do I show the infant my love?" or "What do I do?" There is no one way to show your love to a baby. Some caregivers physically demonstrate their feelings with great effusion; you may envy their joyful and excitable freedom of expression. Others are soft and quiet in their manner, and tenderly hold and caress the child in a tranquil, nurturing way. Surprisingly, both types of loving expressions probably elicit positive responses from babies. The reason for this is that babies are individuals and need different amounts, as well as different kinds, of love. They are responsive and develop trust in you only as you are reliable and consistent in the types of affection you offer. Be yourself: You, too, are an individual and you have your own special ways of expressing real affection.

SOCIAL-EMOTIONAL GROWTH IN TODDLERS

Autonomy

From about 15 months until about 2½ years, children live in a period commonly referred to as *toddlerhood*. During this time they become walking, talking individuals full of energy, curiosity, exploration, and discovery. Many of their babylike competencies remain, but new and more childlike behaviors begin to emerge. As children master their own bodies, they begin to strive for autonomy; they want to do things by and for themselves. However, this autonomy does not happen all at once. Toddlers initially alternate between a clinging attachment to the caregiver and an interest in moving away and trying things for themselves. For example, outdoors they may toddle off to pet the family cat but suddenly stop short and scamper back to a caregiver's protective hug. At the grocery store they may eagerly explore the wonders of the packages on each shelf and suddenly burst into tears at the realization that mother has moved out of sight. New tasks, such as riding tricycles, are tried with more confidence if a familiar adult is near and offers a secure finger or hand to cling to.

This drive for autonomy is surprisingly strong in toddlers. We need only examine how quickly they move from the clinging attachment and begin to assert their independency by pushing away our well-intentioned hands after gaining confidence with their first steps. Their constant pleas of "Me do it!" or "I want to do it!" are usually dispatched with such zealousness that their very lives seem to hinge on whether or not they are allowed to do so. Their complete happiness seems to weigh on whether they are permitted to do even such seemingly unimportant things as opening or closing a storage closet door, stretching up and up to turn off the light switch, or operating the water fountain all by themselves. Their bright eyes and eager expressions appear to be telling us, "If I can only learn to do this myself, I will indeed be a worthy individual!" If we, however, through our impatience or lack of knowledge fail to realize this deep need of early childhood and complete the task for the children, they appear crushed.

This strong quest for independence has unfortunately resulted in an unfair reputation for toddlers. Perhaps you have heard them referred to as the "Terrible Twos," signifying belligerent, feisty individuals dominated by a compulsion for negative behavior. It is somewhat easy to label toddlers like this, especially since their drive for autonomy often leads them to test boundaries; the frustration accompanying the need to accept limits is often accompanied by tantrums. Try to understand that these behaviors are not a "master plan" among toddlers to make adults as miserable as possible, but a normal manifestation of a need to be persons of their own. It is to be expected that

the bouncy, cuddly calmness of babyhood transforms into new behaviors as the children master new skills, allowing them to explore and make new discoveries in their rapidly unfolding surroundings. Imagine the excitement of using emerging skills such as walking and talking as keys to unlock new doors of curious surroundings. Naturally, toddlers want everything and want to get into everything.

But, on the brighter side, think about the positive features of toddlerhood: the delightful, spirited youngsters calling on boundless sources of energy to become involved in vigorous activity; the curious, creative individuals using their emerging abilities to experience new things; the increasingly attentive children becoming absorbed in stories or with their toys; the imaginative tots spontaneously playing "mommy" or "daddy"; and the friendly, loving youngsters offering hugs and kisses as their open way of sharing affection. These are the rewards to help temper the negative images of toddlerhood. If you try to understand what the children are going through, your growing patience will help you relax and help lead the children to emerge and grow through a very delightful period of development.

Need for Guidance

Toddlerhood is a time of contrasting characteristics; the time of "I want to do it myself" is also a period during which a child's favorite word is "no." Children who used to smile and coo as you helped them dress now shriek, "No! No!" as you attempt to put on their jackets to go to the playground. She may have been anxious to go, but as soon as you grabbed her jacket, the fun began. During free play time, he balked at playing with blocks, but ten minutes later he was screaming because he did not want to stop in order to go home. Children who, until about the age of two accepted things congenially, now almost constantly seek to exert their growing independence.

Tears and tantrums become almost commonplace for two-year-olds who are not able to fulfill their wishes. The great challenge for those in charge of toddlers, therefore, is to encourage appropriate behavior without punishing the children into submissiveness or tears every time a clash of wills surfaces. Such a challenge is best addressed by developing a sound system of *discipline*. This seems to be the magic word awaited by all teachers as the key to making living with children a comfortable experience. What do we mean by discipline? Too often, the word *discipline* is equated with "punishment." We prefer to think of discipline as "guidance." Guidance implies an emphasis on teaching and learning—leading children toward the goal of self-discipline. It is something you do *for* children rather than *to* children as you talk and explain about things they can and cannot do. Guidance does not mean yelling at or spanking the child. Children may misbehave because limits were not set, and their behavior may be a way of asking for control. Or they may misbehave because you are inconsistent—sometimes lenient or sometimes harsh for the same issue. It is easy to start a habit of punitive control to control the resulting misbehavior. Since you are the "boss," you gain the behavior you desire through physical or verbal punishment. But toddlers, who are just learning all about their environment and are so eager to explore it, often become inhibited, rebellious, or aggressive because they are consistently experiencing this abuse of adult power. Furthermore, this form of adult control teaches children a very real lesson; if you don't like what someone is doing, you yell at or hit him or her. To overcome these possible outcomes, children must know what is acceptable behavior and what is not, and they depend a great deal on you to teach them.

A Safe Physical Facility Realizing that your toddler's quest for independence is also a learning time, you will need to take some

basic precautions to make sure that your facility is a relatively safe place to explore. Be sure to examine the room itself for safety features such as the following: All tall, unstable furniture such as bookcases are anchored; stairways are protected by safety gates; stairs are protected by carpeting; harmful medicines and/ or cleaning equipment are stored where children cannot reach them; and windows are protected by grilles if they can be reached by the children. Safety basics should also be followed on the playground: The area is fenced in; grass or sand areas under the equipment serve as protection for jumps (or falls); the equipment is child-size; the equipment is safe (no splinters, no protruding sharp points, and no moveable joints to squeeze the children's fingers).

Guidance Techniques Despite these considerations for the safety of your facility, you cannot guarantee that your youngsters will never take a tumble or have a minor accident. However, such circumstances can be minimized if you encourage behavior appropriate for the situation, prepare the environment for safety, and have a few, consistent rules for the child to follow.

Each nursery school, kindergarten, or child-care facility is different, so there is no single set of universal rules to apply to all situations; your children and their parents will most certainly need and expect what they view as appropriate for them. Talk about guidance in advance with the parents and plan your strategies before the children actually enter your facility. In our case, even after we changed the environment to suit our children's growing independence, we found there were some tasks that were simply too unsafe for toddlers. Plugging in the projector or other electrical cords and walking out of the room alone were but two tasks we felt were in need of limits. But, rather than sharply saying no if a child tried these tasks, we made sure to explain our reasons. Children like to listen to such explanations if they are accompanied by the assurance that the tasks can be tried once the children are older. If they persist once you've given them your best reasons, it may be wise to grasp their hands firmly or pick them up and remove them from the situation. After explaining the behavior expected in that situation, encourage them to participate in another activity.

Be careful not to use angry, critical statements beginning with phrases such as, "What's the matter with you? Don't you ever . . ." or "You never . . ." or "You'll always be a . . ." Instead, use statements that would most likely achieve the goals you wish, but that help you do so by helping the child maintain dignity and self-respect: "It would be helpful if. . ." or "I would be happy if . . ." Toddlers may react with frustration when you prevent them from doing tasks that they just can't do yet, and they may react in intense ways. The emotions of toddlers are sharp and often appear to be lacking in degrees of strength. They may respond to a seemingly trivial episode with as much vigor as they do to a major one. Expressions of fear, anger, and joy may be intensely brought to the surface, but typically last only a few minutes and then end abruptly. The youngster may blurt, "I hate you, I hate you!" for preventing him from trying a dangerous task but then shortly throw his arms around you and give you a giant hug. Children are much different than adults in that they do not bottle up their emotions, but "clear their systems" quickly. Their behaviors rapidly change from laughter to tears, from frowns to smiles, or from affection to hostility. Keep this point in mind because many beginning teachers often develop feelings of inadequacy or frustration as they experience such rapid shifts in emotions among their children. This is a normal characteristic of toddlers, however, and it helps to explain why this period of life is much different than all others.

In addition to the preceding suggestions, the following ideas may help you guide the toddler in your care.

- *Allow plenty of opportunities for informal dramatic play.* Toddlers love to get into everything, and a large part of their day will be spent playing with the contents of cupboards or toy boxes. Encourage children to explore dolls, stuffed animals, adult clothes, household items, or tools and to express the feelings that each causes.

Toddlers prefer to play by themselves. Although they are somewhat attracted to other children, they tend to treat them all alike and hesitate to develop individual friendships. They keep their distance from one another and look on their peers with a sense of wonder rather than of friendship. Social contacts are rarely, if ever, achieved. It is almost as though they were thinking, "You mean there's another one like me?" *Parallel play* is normally a characteristic of peer social relationships by about the age of two years. Toddlers do not know how to actually play with one another, but they are willing to be near each other while playing in a sandbox, or with stuffed animals and dolls. They can sit near each other for extended periods of time and yet remain unaware of what the others are doing. You should remember that it can be hazardous to leave two toddlers alone in these situations because toddlerhood is marked by strong individualism; it is a period during which everything is "mine." Toddlers find it extremely difficult to share and will often bite, push, or hit others who attempt to take something they consider their own. When you do wish to have children share their toys with each other, remember to have a substitute toy ready to place in their hands immediately when they relinquish the other.

Toddlers enjoy taking part in *dramatic play* activities in which they mimic the roles and activities of the adult models to whom they are exposed. Beginning dramatic play is extremely simplified, consisting mainly of imitating single social events such as "using" the

Toddlers enjoy being near other children but are content to play by themselves.

telephone, "writing" with a crayon, "cooking" a meal, "reading" the newspaper, or "drinking" a cup of coffee. The child may also follow a family member around the house and imitate the activities or chores being performed by that member. This imitation can lead, in many instances, to the child's actually cooperating in the performance of family duties rather than merely playing at them. Probably the most important contribution you can make at this time is simply to provide many opportunities for such interactions and support the child's experimentation. This type of play strategy seems vital in helping the child toward self-identification and a better understanding of family and societal roles.

- *Use a happy, positive approach to control.* Toddlers respond best to fun and humor rather than to direct interference. Don't attempt to reason with the child—it is not very effective at this age. If a problem occurs in a sandbox, simply distract one child with a happy

word, place him on your shoulders, and give him a happy "horsey" ride to another activity. Removing the child from the situation and diverting his attention is much more effective than some arbitrary negative punishment can be.

- *Choose direct, simple statements that can be communicated in positive terms.* For example, the statement "Jimmy is playing with the wagon now, so you play with the tricycle, Laura" is much more effective than "You can't play with the wagon, Laura, because Jimmy has it."

- *A simple, negatively oriented statement designed to clarify consequences of actions may be used if direct interference by the caretaker is necessary.* A statement such as "You shouldn't hit Barry, Fran. It hurts him" helps the toddler realize that her actions affect others. However, stay away from comments such as "Don't be a bad boy, Bobby.

Come over here and behave yourself." Helping children understand the effects of their actions is important in helping them develop systems of self-control.

• *Establish reasonable, consistent limits and help the toddlers learn to cope with them.* Try to keep the child's frustration at a minimum and think of "discipline" as a sensitive guidance skill instead of a form of punishment. Toddlers have a very difficult time understanding why their personal desires need to be compromised in a spirit of cooperation. Punishment may tend to frustrate and bewilder them even more since it is difficult for them to understand your motivations or why it is necessary for them to cooperate and share. Excessive punishment may result in fear, anxiety, or temper tantrums that include head banging, breath holding, or kicking.

• *Learn to forestall things that are likely to happen.* Anticipate the child's readiness to hit another, to wander away from supervised play, or to grasp a dangerous object. You may be able to stop the child beforehand, saying no firmly as you do. For example, suppose a child suddenly darts from an area of supervised play into a parking lot. You bring him back and divert his attention with a tricycle or wagon. After a minute or two, however, the child begins to dart back into the parking lot. You have anticipated his action, though, and you cut him off. Now you have to do something different because the original diversionary tactic simply didn't work. Don't get angry—you'll only make the situation worse. Calmly take the child inside and explain firmly, "When we are on the playground, you must always stay on the grass." The child may cry or kick or pout,

but don't feel bad! By the time he calms down and becomes friendly with you again (he will!), he'll have learned a very important lesson: There are certain *limits* he must know, adults are *consistent* in their treatment of those limits, and he must learn to *accept* such limits.

• *View the child from the proper developmental perspective rather than from an adult perspective.* Remember that at this stage children fervently seek independence and do things that often frustrate us, such as refusing to put on a sock while getting dressed. This is not the advent of "bad" behavior, only the beginning of independence. Be patient—wait for the child—give her a chance. A minute later she may be only too happy to put on the sock—only this time she'll do it all by herself!

During this period, as during infancy, children develop as unique individuals, differing in temperament and mood. Some are energetic and bold; others are timid and shy. Some conform readily to behavioral norms; others strongly resist. Some respond to social situations; others do not. Some are serious; others smile a lot.

We must remember that these characteristics only emphasize the fact that every child is different and that our role is to know how to treat each one. Katherine Baker and Xenia Fane (1971) expressed this idea well when they stated:

> We help children most when we accept them as they are. We all need to feel that we are loved for what we are. This feeling gives each of us the courage to grow and improve. We are likely to want to change at our own rate and in our own way. It makes us uncomfortable or even unsure of ourselves to be pushed. Being pushed often makes it harder to change. Children

feel the same way. . . . Each one wants to be accepted and liked for what he is. Each needs to be helped to grow in his own way and at his own rate. [p. 21]

You, the child's parents, and the culture in which the child is raised each have specific ideas about the kinds of affection, quantity of interaction, and experiences necessary to stimulate individual social-emotional growth. However, the child's own personality will combine with your efforts to become a major force in shaping the eventual socialized individual. How children act in organizing and interpreting the experiences you provide for them accounts for their continued, systematic social-emotional growth.

SOCIAL-EMOTIONAL GROWTH IN YOUNG CHILDREN

The toddler displays wide varieties of intense emotions—love, joy, anger, sadness—each surfacing freely for all of us to share. Those emotions also change rapidly—smiles to tears, kicking to kissing. These emotions are mainly expressed through physical means; an angry child screams or kicks and an affectionate child throws his arms around you for a hug or kiss. Toddlers are seemingly unable to express their emotions verbally. As they enter the late twos or early threes, though, children gradually become increasingly conscious of their emotions and begin to use words as well as actions to express them. A precious moment for beginning teachers, for example, is when a child first throws her arms around the caregiver, gives a big hug, and gushes out the words, "I love you!" However, there are times when this same child will also express angry feelings by pouting and sharply exclaiming, "You're a

dummy, I hate you!" As children grow linguistically, they gradually realize that their emotions can be shared with others and that others will respond to those expressions. Such children have formed their individual temperaments and begin to emerge more completely as individuals expressing their emotions in unique ways.

Development of Self-Concept

Children's characteristics of dealing with people are becoming established as they form personalities and social patterns that will define their individuality in the years to come. By four years of age, they begin to play with groups of other children and are quite active. They begin to see themselves from the perspective of others, which is a characteristic greatly affecting their personalities as they grow. Children internalize their interactions with others in the environment and begin to form feelings and ideas regarding their own personal worth, often called *self-concept.* Figure 3-2 illustrates this sophisticated process.

Teachers exert a tremendous influence on a child's self-concept when they interact verbally during various daily routines. One teacher realized this fact when she needed to decide whether to allow a child, Vanessa, to climb the steps to the top of the playground slide and glide down all by herself. The teacher spent a great deal of time hovering over Vanessa, worrying about whether she would fall and hurt herself. Even though the teacher taught Vanessa how to grip the guardrail carefully as she climbed the steps and to sit firmly before starting down, she just couldn't bring herself to let the little girl try it alone. The teacher appeared to communicate the message "You're not good enough to do that by yourself," a message damaging to a positive self-concept. Charles Horton Cooley (Bierstedt, 1974) is famous for a theory, called the *Looking-Glass Self,* which is related to this idea. The theory can be sum-

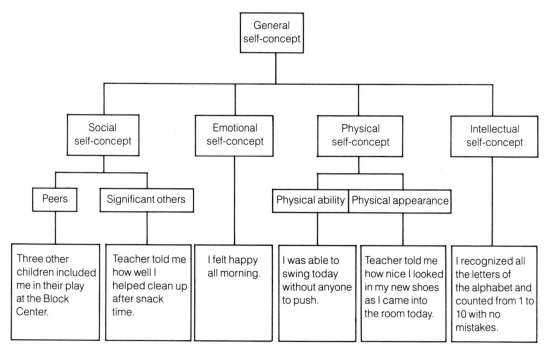

Figure 3-2   *Factors influencing general self-concept*
Adapted from F. J. Shavelson, J. J. Hubner, and G. C. Stanton, Self-concept: Validation of construct interpretation. Review of Educational Research, 1976, 46, 413. Copyright American Educational Research Association, Washington, D.C. Reprinted by permission.

marized as "I am what I think you think I am." Closely related to this theory is Merton's (1968) famous concept of the *self-fulfilling prophecy.* He pointed out that what people learn to think about themselves from the messages they receive from others will eventually come true. For example, if Vanessa is constantly told that her efforts are certain to end in failure, she will stand a good chance of eventually avoiding all challenges for fear of possible injury or failure.

Vanessa helped alter her teacher's approach one day through her sudden and straightforward statement, "I don't want you to help. I want to do it myself!" The teacher backed off and suffered inwardly, but the result was positive. Vanessa is now nearly four years old and hasn't had an accident yet. She was

ready for this new experience, but the teacher wasn't! It is important to keep an eye on your children but also to realize that children don't know what they can do until they are at least allowed to try.

Thus, the self-concept of an individual is developed as a direct result of the experiences permeating the entire day. But, even more importantly, the very young child appears to react to those experiences not primarily on the basis of whether he or she was successful at something, but more often on the basis of what the important people in the environment seemed to think of the child's efforts to accomplish something. The views that people appear to have of children are revealed through their reactions to the children's behaviors—through reward or punishment, love or withdrawal of love, approval or disapproval, acceptance or nonacceptance. From the very earliest years, children learn to read messages from such reactions. They learn how capable they are at activities deemed important by people of significance and how "valued" they are as individuals. Therefore, if a teacher communicates to a child that specific behaviors or skills are important but reacts in ways that indicate that the child is incompetent, the child forms a negative self-concept. Because of strong needs to feel important, though, children may react to the situation in ways that are not even conscious:

- They may hide or disguise their failures.
- They may minimize the importance of the activity.
- They may make it apparent that they will no longer extend an effort toward accomplishing a behavior or skill because of the possibility of failing again.

With the current emphasis on reading and math ability in youngsters, kindergarten children learn that inability to read or recognize numbers is socially unacceptable. The second posture is, therefore, difficult to assume. Children may choose either of the remaining options—to hide their failures or to quit trying altogether. Since it is nearly impossible to hide such shortcomings, youngsters are often forced into the third option—to give an appearance that they are not actually trying. They may show disinterest, refuse to participate in planned activities, exhibit carelessness, or state a hatred of reading or math. If teachers have realistic expectations for children and help them to recognize successes, they will develop a positive sense of self and gain confidence to learn more and to take pleasure in attempting further learnings. The role of self-concept is important in all areas of development, not only in this single area that we have discussed so far and identified as social-emotional. The self-

concept assumes a vital role in the total picture of what eventually forms each child's unique personality. Another part of that picture is the development of a large repertoire of easily recognized and highly differentiated emotional responses: fear, jealousy, affection, fantasy; and many other feelings such as frustration and control, patience and impatience, imitation and originality, or happiness and sadness. To discuss each is more within the realm of a course in child psychology or development, so we will address ourselves more to the point of recognizing what to do to help young children develop and maintain positive personality traits conducive to an atmosphere of good mental health.

Enhancing Personality Development

What *can* adults do to enhance early personal development? Burton L. White, director of Harvard University's Preschool Project and author of an influential book for parents and teachers, *The First Three Years* (1975), contends that the first priority in helping children reach their maximum potential is for caregivers "to do the best possible job in structuring experiences and opportunities" (p. 264). That job requires four highly important tasks:

1. *Arranging the children's world.* This task ranges from designing a safe environment to providing for maximum opportunities within the environment and supplying stimulating materials.

2. *Being a consultant to the children.* This task involves interacting with the children in a sincere, genuine way while conversing or asking questions.

3. *Accepting a role of authority in the children's lives.* This task directs the caregiver to assist children in understanding and accepting the limits for their behavior.

4. *Providing for many play opportuni-*

ties. Play is a natural and important activity for children. Play has many benefits, but, for our immediate concerns, it serves not only as a means of social adaptation but also as a medium of understanding and expressing emotions.

Because your ability to satisfy these tasks is of critical developmental importance and reflects upon your success as an early childhood professional, they will be discussed in detail throughout the remainder of this text. Tasks 1, 2, and 3 are essential to the development of a sound social-emotional climate and resulting self-concept and they are primarily addressed within the context of Chapter 4. Task 4, to provide for many play opportunities, is a complex charge that will be specifically analyzed in Chapter 5. However, it must be noted that ramifications of the four tasks involve much more than what will be offered in those two chapters and will weave their way within each of the succeeding chapters of this text.

SOME FINAL THOUGHTS

Between the time of birth and six years of age, children make great leaps forward in terms of sociability and management of their emotions. They move from complete dependency upon caregivers toward personal independence. As infants grow into toddlerhood, they begin to realize that they are individuals with separate identities from all others in their surround-

ings. They begin to develop what is described as a personality. Each child's personality develops from a combination of environmental and genetic factors, but all children progress through a series of stages during which common social and emotional characteristics are apparent. Toddlers, for example, tend to reject involvement in group activities, because they are busy struggling to form their own identities. They want everything to be their own, especially toys and the attention of adults. Because the concepts of rightness and wrongness or goodness and badness are somewhat vague in toddlers, they use any means they can think of to get what they want. Grabbing, screaming, and aggressive behavior often characterize their efforts. This phase of development requires delicate leadership and support on your part, for abandonment or lack of guidance from adult caregivers causes confusion and even fear in toddlers.

When they receive love and understanding, three-year-olds become increasingly confident as individuals. They become interested in playmates and learn to control their behaviors and feelings in ways that permit them to engage in a variety of activities with others. Social and emotional growth, then, like all other areas of development, evolve through a combination of learning and maturing. The process begins at birth, and your skill in leading youngsters will play a large role in their growth and in the way they learn to express their feelings, to show concern for the feelings of others, and to develop skills for getting along with others.

Chapter 4

Helping Children Achieve Maximum Personal Growth

Let us leave the confines of the environment in which you now find yourself as you read this book. Imagine yourself at the threshold of your first teaching experience. Suppose that you are standing in the center of a large room awaiting the arrival of kindergarten children on their first day of school. Many of them have not experienced nursery school and are anticipating this special day for the first time in their lives. Think of all the essential provisions you need to make as you prepare for this significant childhood experience.

Certainly, you realize that the ways by which we get children started at the beginning of the school year, whether or not they have ever been a part of a sustained group experience previously in their lives, have a significant impact on the ways children adjust to school and to the individuals who will be with them in succeeding months. This initial concern is very critical in a youngster's life, for the young child's social and emotional life had been firmly anchored in his or her immediate family or child-care surroundings prior to this time, and any major change could fill the child with apprehension and fear. Therefore, you must consider the first of White's four tasks (introduced in Chapter 3): accounting for the ways in which environmental arrangement affects a child's transition from the comfort of home to the uncertainty of school.

ARRANGING THE CHILDREN'S WORLD

Starting the Year

As an early childhood professional, you will be faced with the responsibility of introducing most young children to group-oriented life outside the home. If the introduction is well planned and effectively implemented, your children will develop a positive attitude toward school and toward meeting the daily challenges involved in this new setting. Therefore, the means by which you encourage children to take this first step away from home is of utmost importance not only to a successful beginning of the new school year but also to the formation of overall attitudes that will become part of the children as they progress upward through the schooling ladder. Certainly it is possible later to overcome the effects of a poor start at school, but it is much easier for children to enjoy school when they have had a favorable introduction.

Do not take this charge lightly, for coming from the loving safety of home to an unknown world represented by your classroom involves a move much more significant than we may imagine through our adult perceptions. Most youngsters eagerly anticipate entrance into school and will rush into your room, fervently looking forward to everything that school will bring. Adjustment for these youngsters is no problem and they will normally like everything they see. But, for a disconcerted few, school may be viewed as a place where childhood's fragile lives will certainly come crumbling down. They are threatened by a host of concerns: experiencing a new adult; leaving their parents for an extended time; discovering a new physical setting; losing their individuality by being placed with so many other children; following new routines for toileting, eating, resting, or playing; and adjusting to behavioral expectancies or modes of conduct that may be much different than those practiced in the home. Under your skillful and sensitive guidance, this diverse collection of children needs to be offered a good beginning so that they are able to progress through the year as a responsible, cohesive group where individuality is maintained, group standards are understood and practiced, and links to home and parents are sustained.

Obviously, all early childhood settings have unique goals, populations, and priorities. They each have their own special strategies for getting started and establishing a routine throughout the year. Because it is impossible to describe all of those possibilities in the limited space available, only a sampling of methods for this critical teaching area will be discussed. Some of these methods are based on the valuable ideas of K. Eileen Allen and Betty Hart (1984).

Early Visits by Parents Perhaps the safest way to introduce your facility to parents and children is to plan for school visitations a week or two prior to the actual beginning of the school year. Usually done on an appointment basis, this visit helps parents and children to become familiar with the new setting and to feel at ease in the teacher's presence. Here are some suggestions for this important introductory meeting:

1. Call the parent on the telephone to set up a time for the meeting. Such a method establishes a personal touch to the arrangement and allows for questions or comments in ways that go beyond a written invitation.

2. Arrange the room with displays, materials, and furniture, much as they will be seen on the first day of school. Since the purpose of this meeting is to establish a smooth transition between home and school, you will want to assure the child that the new environment will look the same upon his or her return to your room. A drastic change from this meeting day to the first day will only create confusion in the young child.

3. Plan a comfortable seating area where you can sit and talk with the parent. Refrain from sitting behind a desk and asking the parent to sit on a chair in front of you. Such a practice establishes roadblocks to good communication by setting up an artificial barrier between you and the parent. Instead, arrange two or three child-size chairs facing each other or sit around a children's table.

Try to have a beverage (coffee, tea, or milk) for the parent along with a small snack. A small nutritious snack along with juice or milk might also be available for the child.

4. Arrange a separate display area with photographs of activities from the school program, advertising brochures, program descriptions, and other informational materials concerning items such as policies regarding health, field trips, meals, fees, and so on, for the parents. These "hands on" items usually create good topics for discussion and often serve as excellent resources to "break the ice" conversationally.

5. When the parent and child arrive, emphasize the idea that the program and setting are there for the *child* by directing your first comments to the child: "Good morning. You must be Charles and this is your dad. Hello, Charles, and good morning, Mr. Goodwin. Please come in; I've been expecting you. This will be where you will come to school, Charles."

Children vary enormously in terms of how they greet their first day at school.

6. Extend your initial comments to the child by calling his attention to the play materials arranged about the room. Try not to overwhelm the child with too much, but have popular materials such as puzzles, books, crayons, blocks, or other items that require a minimum of supervision with single children. Lead the parent and child on a short walking trip around the room pointing out these items for the child. End the tour at your prearranged conversation area, inviting the child to return to an area he seemed to be attracted to on the walking tour: "Charles, your dad and I will sit at this table and talk for a little while. We have a Mickey Mouse puzzle you can play with or you might like to draw with crayons. They're right here at another table. They are two kinds of things children like to play with at school. Your dad and I will be right at that table if you need us."

7. If the child appears distressed when asked to leave his parent (most will leave), do not force him to go. Just say, reassuringly, "Charles would like to stay and listen to us talk. That's okay, too. But, if you want to visit the blocks in just a short while, Charles, we'll all go and you can show us how to build with them." When you actually do this, try to get the parent to help interest the child in the blocks. If that fails, simply bring a puzzle, book, or toy to your conversation area and let the child play there as you talk. Or walk from one display to the other as you hold your conversation with the parent; the child may become interested in one or another as you move along.

8. Briefly discuss your program along with special policies (health, field trips, birthday celebrations, meals, fees, and so on). However, most of this information should have been shared with the par-

ent through the mail. See Figure 4-1 for a sample letter. The visit should focus on questions parents may have had about the mailed information and on the child—special needs, interests, hobbies, talents, and so on. Encourage parents to center on positive aspects at this initial meeting. Some will criticize the child or want to talk about a special problem. Indicate interest in such concerns, but schedule a later meeting when they could be explored in a much deeper manner.

9. Plan to spend about 45 minutes to one hour for each visit. This allows sufficient time to talk with your visitors as well as to make any preparations for the next visitors. You may want to jot down a few special notes while the parent talks with you or wait until the end of the visit to record special information. On the one hand, taking notes during the visit formalizes the process; on the other hand, waiting until the end of the day often causes confusion and incompleteness.

10. End your visit with something personal for the child. Go with the parent to where the child is playing and say, "Charles, I know you're having fun, but it is almost time to leave. You may play with the crayons again when you come back to school." You may want to have Charles's cubby (locker) nametag ready and direct him to that very special place that will be all his own. To do this, prepare a set of nametags beforehand along with a variety of pictures of the same dimension (animals, vehicles, cartoon characters, story characters, and so on). Make sure you have different ones for each child. Invite the child to choose from among the pictures one that he would like to have on his cubby. Then see if the child can select his nametag from a group of three or four. If not, reassure the child that you can help. Attach the selected picture along with the nametag to the child's cubby. Prepare a duplicate set so the child can take

it home (a *special* gift) and bring it back to school on the first day. Then the child can match either his animal or nametag in order to find his cubby. The purpose of this practice is to establish a crossing link between this initial introductory visit and the first day of school.

First Day of School   Let's assume that your initial meetings with parents and children were successful. We are ready to ask the question "What do I do on the first day of school?" This question causes great concern among not only prospective teachers but also experienced teachers; everyone wants to get off on the right foot. To begin formulating an answer, we start with the obvious; your initial responsibility is to *make sure you know your children*. You will have learned some basic information in advance from your parent conference, but it is also important to read each child's record file carefully. Those children who have been to school in years prior to entering your classroom will have accumulated more information than those entering school for the first time, but a cumulative folder should be available for each child. The folder should contain information such as the following:

- *Enrollment form,* showing the child's name, age, birth date, address, phone numbers, parents' occupations, emergency phone numbers, and the date of enrollment in school.

- *Information form* on which you will find a record of the child's physical and dental examinations, results of mental or intelligence tests, previous preschool experiences, and various special considerations such as family conditions, handicapping conditions, or observations of the child's personality.

Cumulative folders do help you know your children well and respect them as individuals. However, among some teachers, the prospect of reading and rereading cumulative records

Dear Parents,

    It is a pleasure to welcome you and your child to Happy Day Nursery School. Being four, your child is among a group of other children at the magical age when they are full of questions, just loving to get into things. They are full of boundless energy! We want to capitalize on their spirit and do things with your children, explore with them, encourage them to solve problems. To meet this goal, your children have to experience things - so there are times your children may become wet, or dirty, or messy, or rumpled. Becoming involved often means these things.

    To help your children, send them to school in clothes-for-fun. Please try not to send them in clothing accompanied by "Don't get them dirty," but dress them in durable wash-and-wear items that are able to withstand the challenges of childhood.

    (Other policies inserted here)

    As a final note, occasionally your children will be asked to bring home special messages like this, perhaps pinned to their clothing. Please read them in the company of your children so that they understand your interest in their school. By the way, please compliment your children on being good messengers!

    Thanking you in advance, I remain

                Sincerely yours,

Figure 4-1   *Sample introductory letter to parents*

to gain that information is a controversial topic. Some teachers see very little or no value in keeping records. They view such "paperwork" as taking away from time necessary for preparing materials and activities for the children. Others reject the start-of-a-year reading of cumulative records because they want to offer each child a "fresh start," free of all the preconceived attitudes others had formed. They do not wish to risk the possibility of labeling children as either "good" or "bad" before any personal contact has been established. Both groups, however, fail to understand that cumulative records are kept for valid reasons and that shortcomings are primarily the fault of teacher usage rather than the records themselves. How can records be used intelligently? Here are eight ways:

1. to help you understand each child;
2. to help parents understand their children;
3. to outline evidence of growth and development;
4. to discover and address special needs;
5. to detect personality or behavioral problems;
6. to provide data should the child switch to another school;
7. to serve as a guide in planning programs based on individual needs; and
8. to offer background information for confidential reports to specialists or for research purposes.

Do not be fearful that cumulative information will cause you to prejudge your children. The file materials are only words, numbers, and figures. Your true and lasting perception will not be formed until you actually meet the real, flesh-and-blood individuals so eager to step into your room on the first morning.

A second responsibility involved in arranging for the first day of school is to *plan an effective entrance program*. A staggered entrance program is one way to achieve this goal. Entrance can be staggered by scheduling only one-third of your group to appear on each of the first three days of school. Or you may wish to schedule one-third of your children to enter during the first hour, another third to come during the second hour, and the final third during the last hour of the daily session. That way, every child in the group can have equal daily school opportunities during the crucial first week. You may prefer to schedule a few experienced children in each group; their confidence and knowledge of equipment usage will serve as a good model for the inexperienced children.

A third responsibility during the first day of school is to *consider a wholesome parent-child separation procedure*. Most youngsters, especially by kindergarten age, will eagerly and wholesomely manage the great adventure of the first day at school and enthusiastically greet it as a sign of "growing up." A few, however, may not be as responsive and protest the fact that they are going to be left alone in the new situation. For those who adjust well, you need only exchange a few casual pleasantries with the parent and child. Then the parent can assure the child that she will be picked up at session's end, and the child is encouraged to join in with the others at one of the interest centers you had arranged. The parent should be advised to depart quickly so that the child is able to participate with her new "school family." For instance, the parent may say, "I'm going to go now, but I'll be back in a while and we'll go home together."

It is easier for the enthusiastic child to adjust to his new setting when he is not torn between school and parent, as is the case when parents linger to observe their children. Oftentimes, when parents stay, the child will actually become confused, soon refuse to leave the parent, or become involved in such a way that he looks for a parent's approval with every action. Sometimes, this child may even become embarrassed at his parent's lingering presence. One kindergarten mother, for example, appeared especially apprehensive upon delivering her child to school. Bending down and peering directly into her son's eyes, she asked, "You're not going to cry when I leave, are you, Frankie?"

"No," responded Frankie confidently.

"It's okay if you want to cry," offered mother. "Remember how we talked last night about crying and about how people feel better when they cry. So, cry if you think it will make you feel better."

"I really don't want to, mommy," blurted the youngster.

"I'm sure going to miss you, Frankie. It will be lonely at home without you," added mother.

"Oh, mommy. You're treating me like a baby," Frankie said. "I think you better go home now."

With Frankie's admonition, his mother gave him a big hug and went on her way. Frankie eagerly went about sizing up his new situation. This scenario, variations of which occur each year, indicates that separation problems may, in some instances, be greater for the parents than for the children. The parents may fear losing the central role they have held in their children's lives up to this time.

It is easy to become overly critical of such protective parents, but there are some very good reasons why a parent fears separation. First, the love between parent and child is very strong and, as such, there is a great conflict between wanting to hold onto the child and giving the child the opportunity for independence. Second, parents may be apprehensive about the experience itself (some, by necessity, must leave their children for full days as early as three or four months of age). You must encourage these parents and reassure them to support their children at this very critical time.

At the other extreme, we find an even greater professional challenge. Here we have a child so timid, so insecure, and so inexperienced that it would be just short of emotional abuse if we forced him to stay during the first day without a parent. The popular temptation (and practice) for some parents and teachers is to have the parent silently sneak away at the first sign that the child is becoming interested in a puzzle, toy, or other activity. Their justification for such a tactic is that the parent's anxiety will actually compound the child's if the parent stays. Also, it is argued that interrupting the child to say goodbye will actually cause him to stop playing and resume his clinging, cranky behavior. Perhaps these parents and teachers are correct in their views, but consider what the child may do if, a few minutes after the parent has left, he searches out and cannot locate him or her. We must realize that with his protesting manner the child is attempting to communicate a feeling in ways that words cannot express. He is not ready to be left alone, but he does not possess the mental maturity to translate his anxieties to us in any other way. Both parents and teachers must be aware of the hesitant child's needs and join together in a psychologically safe plan to help the child make the adjustment from home to school. You may consider these steps in setting up your program:

1. Ask the parent to stay at least during the first whole session.

2. Encourage the parent to leave for a short while if the child becomes engrossed in an activity. Don't suggest that the parent "steal away." He or she could approach the child and say, "I'm glad you are building with the blocks. I'm going to leave for ten minutes, but I'll be right back to see how you're doing." Some children may stop playing at this point and hold onto the parent in an effort to keep him or her from leaving. The parent should then be instructed to sit down near the child's play area and say, "Okay, I'll watch just for a short while before I go." After a

few minutes, the parent should leave with a message such as, "It's time for me to go. You finish playing with the blocks, but I'll be back in ten minutes (or a short while) to see what you built."

3. At times, parents will not be able to progress through these suggestions because of uneasiness or their own separation anxiety, so you may need to be near to initiate the conversation. Should that be necessary, you might say, "Your mother (father) will be leaving for ten minutes. I will be near if you need me."

4. Meanwhile, insist that the parent leave immediately but return exactly as promised. You must give the child every reason to trust you and the parent during this often traumatic transition period.

5. Once the parent returns to the classroom, he or she can go straight to the child and comment about the progress he has made. Then the parent and teacher can come together to discuss the child's reaction to this initial separation. If he continued playing with little or no negative reaction, you might encourage the parent to try leaving until the end of the session. On the other hand, if he seemed uneasy or anxious during the departure, you should plan a subsequent exit-return sequence. This exit-return sequence should be continued for as long as it takes a youngster to become acclimated to his new environment.

Some children will adjust in just one day, while a rare child may take as long as two weeks. The key to the entire process, however, is joint parent-teacher planning and execution within a confident, unpressured sequence of exit-return strategies. Successive positive experiences in which the child observes parent and teacher working as partners will form the foundation of adjustments and serve to help him assimilate himself into his new group.

A fourth responsibility for the first day of school is to *organize a safe, friendly orientation for all the children*. Take the time to greet each child in a warm, friendly manner as he or she appears at the classroom door. The children should return with the nametags they had chosen during parent meeting day. If such a day had not been held, you may want to point out the need for name and cubby tags and ask the children to select from an assortment of basic geometric shapes cut from various colors of construction paper on which their names will be printed. From the beginning, you are showing the children that they are worth consulting in manners involving choices. Headley (1966) informs us that children's responses can tell a great deal about their social, emotional, and intellectual maturity. What do each of these responses tell us about the child?

1. He refuses to make any response.
2. Her parent chooses a tag.
3. He simply points to a tag but does not name it.
4. She points to a yellow circle but says, "The green circle."
5. He pays little or no attention as you print his name.
6. She volunteers to spell her name or even write it herself.

When the nametag is finally complete, you should pin it with a large safety pin to the front of the child's shirt. Then invite the child to find, from the remaining tags, a matching tag that will be used to identify his cubby. What do each of these subsequent responses tell you about the child?

1. He refuses to accept the second tag.
2. Her mother takes it for her.
3. He takes the tag but is confused about which cubby to select.
4. She posts her name upside-down.

Displaying children's names on the first day of school and on the days that follow present exciting opportunities to foster emotional and social behaviors as well as motivating learning experiences. What are some intellectual skills that can be developed by examining nametags?

5. He posts the tag in a meticulous fashion and indicates readiness for the next business at hand.

You should be encouraged to observe the children's actions to the various challenges presented during such a nametag orientation, but be careful not to overanalyze or to set your expectations too high. For example, some two- and three-year-olds may be able to read their names, but it is unreasonable to expect even an entering kindergartner to do so. You are providing such an experience only to inform yourself of the characteristics and abilities of the individuals you have just met. The children delight in posting their tags; through such

experiences the young children eventually perceive that the classroom is really theirs.

From this initial orientation experience, you address your fifth responsibility: *to arrange the room into various centers of interest.* Once the children claim their cubbies and feel comfortable in their new surroundings, they should be encouraged to explore the variety of manipulative toys, puzzles, paper and crayons, dolls, building blocks, and books made available for them. All materials should attract the children's attention while graciously inviting them to explore the environment. You may want to make passing comments as they play or even sit with the children to look at books. Further information about interest centers will be offered later in this chapter under the heading "The Room Itself."

Finally, you are ready to approach your last major opening day responsibility, *helping the children get to know each other*. At some time, after about one-half hour to three-quarters of an hour of free play, you will need to signal the children to join together for a group experience. If you sound a few notes on a piano or even a small xylophone, the children will naturally turn toward you. When they do so, explain that your signal means that all must put away their playthings and come together to sit in a circle on the rug. It may take a week or two before all the children all respond to the signal, but such a signal is established so that a safe, comfortable routine can be instituted. Once the children are gathered in the circle, you may wish to initiate an introduction game (see the box on p. 105) to help the children learn each other's names and become familiar with each other. We used this particular sequence successfully with four-and-five-year-olds. Adjust the content to meet age, maturity, and experimental differences.

These special efforts for children to learn to know each other are key components of any early childhood program. Some children entering your setting may be extremely anxious about the presence of other children. Opening activities such as these are, therefore, necessary for helping each child maintain his individuality while, at the same time, developing a feeling of becoming an integral part of a group.

Teaching Individuality and Participation From these and other introductory activities, you get to know the children's names and help the children get to know one another's names. It usually takes preschool children about five or six separate sessions to learn to share other personal information about themselves with the others in a smooth fashion. However, such activities should be practical throughout the school year. Before the

child can begin to understand her role in society, she needs to develop a positive sense of her own individuality—her uniqueness as a person. Move from such introductory activities toward experiences that help to reinforce the idea that individuals are distinguished by physical attributes. Some suggestions for this phase follow in the box on p. 106.

Besides being chosen for their creative way of introducing children to parts of their bodies, these action verses (or fingerplays) were selected for their ability to encourage children to participate together in an activity. To use such action verses, first say the entire verse for the children and demonstrate the accompanying actions. Invite the children to join you as they feel comfortable. Don't worry about the children becoming bored with repetition; they enjoy the rhythm and action to the extent of begging for a chance to do it again and again.

Daily Routines As the children experience an initial period of free play followed by large group activity, they become acclimated to your daily routine. Their awareness of social roles and responsibilities grows as they become involved in these special daily routines. Given their structure within a carefully planned daily schedule, these routines inform the children what is expected of them during specific times of each day. Most children learn routines quickly and should sense your pattern after only a few days. Table 4-1 shows a typical one-half day routine schedule.

The schedule illustrated in Table 4-1 is typical of half-day nursery schools or kindergarten classrooms. Of course, each teacher has his or her own priorities and adjusts the schedule to meet certain needs, but the scheduling plan should be carefully followed each day so that the children master the technique as quickly as possible. Day-care centers often follow a similar format during the mornings, but, since they are full-day programs, provide lunch for the children at noon. Following lunch,

AN INTRODUCTION GAME

Invite the children to sit in a circle to meet you and a very special friend—Charlie the puppet. Say to the children: "Good morning, boys and girls. I am your teacher *(your name)*. I'm so happy you came to school today. Each day when you come back we will have fun playing, talking, and learning."

"Now I have a special friend to *introduce* to you. Does anyone know what the word *introduce* means? (If not) *Introduce* means to tell names. Telling names is called *introducing*. Now I will introduce our puppet friend. Are you ready? Boys and girls, meet Charlie. Charlie, meet *(child's name)*, and *(child's name)*, and so on." Call attention to the nametags as you call each child's name. Some teachers prefer to ask the children to stand up as the names are called; this not only gives the children physical movement, but also helps others identify them more easily.

After this introduction game, ask the children to repeat a familiar nursery rhyme or join you in a fingerplay. Such activity helps develop a spirit of camaraderie on this very important day. For example, say, "Let's have some fun together. Listen and watch what I do." Before you start, make sure the children are all seated and facing you. Place your hands behind your back and sing the following popular tune (to the tune of *Frere Jacques*):

Where is Thumbkin? *(Hands behind back)*
Where is Thumbkin?
Here I am. *(Right hand out, thumb up)*
Here I am. *(Left hand out, thumb up)*
How are you today, Sir? *(Right thumb "bows")*
Very well, I thank you. *(Left thumb "bows")*
Run away. *(Right hand behind back)*
Run away. *(Left hand behind back)*

"Now, where are your thumbs? Can you make them Thumbkins by pointing them up like this? Very good!

Let's sing the song together and this time you be Thumbkins, too."

Repeat the song as many times as the children show interest. Be sure to allow extra time for the children to move their thumbs to the song's actions. As the children gain confidence in future sessions, add verses for "pointer," "tall man," "ring man," and "pinky" following the actions indicated.

On the second day, some teachers prefer to adapt the initial "Thumbkin" activity by using children's names. For example:

Where is *(child's name)*?
Where is *(child's name)*?
There she is. *(Child stands up.)*
There she is.
How are you today *(sir* or *ma'am)*?
Very well, I thank you. *(Child bows.)*
Run away. *(Child sits down.)*
Run away.

Repeat the song several times, using each child's name and inviting the children to stand and sit according to the verse. The introducing phase of the routine can be extended on the third day with an activity called "This Is My Friend." The game begins with the children seated in a circle, holding hands. The puppet starts things off by covering his eyes with his hand and saying, "Peek-a-boo. Who are you?" Uncovering his eyes, Charlie looks at a child while the child gives her name. The game continues until all the children are introduced.

The concluding activities of this routine can be organized in the form of a "Who's Who" bulletin board. The bulletin board is composed of photographs of each child with nametags printed beneath. To help children recognize their names (and the names of others), "Thumbkin" is sung as before but, in this instance, the children place their nametags with their pictures.

---

the children clean up, use the toilet, and prepare for a nap or quiet rest period. If some parents do not wish their children to sleep or if some children simply do not need a nap, they are usually taken to an adjacent room where they may read a book, listen to songs or stories on earphones, or participate in other quiet activities. Following this period, toileting and cleanup again take place. The children then are provided an extended period of active

outdoor or indoor play prior to departure; this last period may be intermingled with singing songs or listening to stories.

The daily schedule is designed not only as a guide for you, but it also helps the children bring comfort and order to their rapidly changing lives through their knowledge of *what* is happening *when*. The dynamic nature of early childhood education will periodically result in minor changes to the daily routine, but this,

**GAMES AND ACTION VERSES TO
TEACH INDIVIDUALITY AND
GROUP PARTICIPATION**

- Play a good listeners game. Say, "We are going to do what *(Puppet's name)* says."

   (Puppet's name) says,
   "Close your eyes."
   "Open your eyes."
   "Stand up."
   "Sit down."
   "Clap your hands."
   "Hold your nose."
   (To make more complex, give two directions at one time.)

- Say, "We just used and named some parts of our bodies. Let's say them and point to them together."

   "Eyes."
   "Nose."
   "Hands."

- Say, "Let's say and point to some others."

   "Ears."
   "Neck."
   "Feet."
   "Arms."
   "Legs."

- Use fingerplays to stimulate attention to parts of the body. The topic of fingerplays will be comprehensively discussed in Chapter 7, but here we'll present specific fingerplays that can be used to stress individuality:

   Me

   On top of the mountain is a bunch of grass. *(Point to hair.)*
   Under the grass are two bright lights. *(Point to eyes.)*
   Under the lights is a little hill. *(Point to nose.)*
   Under the hill is a little pond. *(Point to mouth.)*
   Inside the pond are ten white stones. *(Point to teeth.)*

And a little fish jumps in and out. *(Tongue moves in and out.)*

My Fingers (good for calming a group)

I stretch my fingers way up high, *(Raise hands.)*
Until they almost reach the sky. *(Stretch hands upwards.)*
I lay them in my lap, you see, *(Place hands on lap.)*
Where they're as quiet as can be!

Stretch

Stretch, stretch, way up high; *(Reach upward.)*
On your tiptoes, reach the sky. *(Stand on toes.)*
See the bluebirds flying high. *(Wave hands.)*
Now bend down and touch your toes; *(Bend and touch.)*
Now sway as the North Wind blows; *(Sway body.)*
Waddle as the gander goes! *(Waddle freely.)*

Follow Me

(Follow actions as rhyme indicates.)
Hands on shoulders, hands on knees,
Hands behind you, if you please;
Touch your shoulders, now your nose,
Now your hair and now your toes;
Hands up high in the air,
Down at your sides and touch your hair;
Hands up high as before,
Now clap your hands, one, two, three, four.

One Little Body

(Follow actions as rhyme indicates.)
Two little feet go stamp, stamp, stamp,
Two little hands go clap, clap, clap,
One little body stands up straight,
One little body goes round and round,
One little body sits quietly down.

too, is a learning experience for the youngsters. We must all learn to adjust to unforeseen circumstances in our lives.

The schedule contains large-group activities, small-group activities, structured activities, unstructured activities, active times, and quiet times. Therefore, the schedule is both specific and flexible. Each area of the schedule will be discussed further in the succeeding chapters of this book, but there are a few topics that should be expanded here because their specific nature is especially appropriate to social-emotional considerations.

Table 4-1   *Sample Half-Day Schedule*

9:00 – 9:45	Arrival, Greeting, and Independent Activities. *The first time block during the day should be set aside as an informal period during which you talk to the children and their parents upon arrival. This special recognition helps get the day off to a positive start by showing each child that you have some special words especially meant for her. The short conversation could relate to something as seemingly trivial as the weather or to a special accomplishment experienced during the previous day's activities. As the children organize their belongings, they could slowly become involved in a number of activities that interest them—housekeeping corner, block play, easel painting, and so on. This flexibility activity period allows you to comfortably include even those children who may be late for school by not making them enter a formal group activity once it has begun.*
9:45 – 10:00	Cleanup. *Upon signal, the children complete their activities and put away the materials. If necessary, they use the toilet or wash their hands. Those children who finish before the others are encouraged to take part in quiet activities such as looking at books, observing classroom pets, or listening to a story. Basically, you are providing a transition between an active period of time and a more quiet time.*
10:00 – 10:30	Large-Group Time. *All of the children come together for singing songs, listening to a story, or participating in a movement activity. Special daily routines such as the calendar, weather charts, or attendance charts may culminate this time period.*
10:30 – 10:50	Snack. *The children are provided a light meal, usually consisting of cookies, crackers, a vegetable, or other healthful food and a beverage. During this time, socialization is encouraged through the stimulation of informal conversation. In addition, you may wish to spend some time discussing the food—what it is, its sensory characteristics, where it comes from, and so on.*
10:50 – 11:20	Small-Group Activities. *Small groups of children, usually consisting of five or fewer members, work with an adult aide or volunteer in a special learning activity. For example, one group may engage in picture discussion, another in a counting game, and the third in an art project. They change stations every ten minutes. You may lead one of the groups or be on hand to supervise the entire program.*
11:20 – 11:30	Cleanup and Toileting. *This period is basically similar to the 9:45 – 10:00 time block, except that it culminates with dressing for an outdoor play time.*
11:30 – 11:50	Outdoor Play. *The children participate in self-selected outdoor activities. They may slide or swing or simply mingle together for creative play. In some instances, you may wish to play a special outdoor group game. Regardless, you should be constantly aware of what each child is doing. Proper supervision is essential during this time block.*
11:50 – 12:00	Departure. *The children are encouraged to organize the classroom and to make sure whatever they want to take home is ready. As with the start of the day, a special smile or word to each child and their parents brings the day to a happy closing.*

Transitions Between Time Periods A major responsibility in learning to adapt to classroom routines is to know what to do as one period comes to a close and the next period begins. If you do not inform the children of your expectations during these times, you may find children bickering among each other because of a longer wait than can be tolerated or bumping into each other as they try to put away materials in an unreasonably short transition time. Careful planning, however, will serve to ensure the greatest possibility for the children moving through the day's routine with confidence and ease. Here are some useful techniques for moving children through transition times.

- Signal the children with a special tune played on the piano or other instrument. Such a tune need not be longer than five or six notes; however, the children should know that when you play it, they have a responsibility to bring their activity to a close and begin to move to the next one.

- Ring a bell or set an egg timer to go off at a special time.

- If you are moving from a large group activity to snack, for example, play a simple game with the children such as, "The children wearing red may go to snack now" or, on another day, "Tell me the opposite of _up_ and you may go to snack."

- Adapt a familiar rhyme or song to move the children from one activity to another. One teacher adapted "Twinkle Twinkle Little Star" to inform children when it was their turn to move:

  Snack is ready,
  At the table.
  Come as quickly
  As you are able.

- Mount close-up photographs of each child on tagboard cards and glue a clothespin to each card. Large tagboard

signs depict the various areas within your classroom. Clip the photos to a sign to indicate the area to which each child will move during small-group activity periods. (See Figure 4-2.)

- Choose about three animals that make distinctive sounds such as a bird, dog, and cow. Whisper an animal's name into each child's ear and ask him or her to make the sound of that animal. Be sure that one-third of your group is assigned one animal. The children then make the sounds until they have all grouped themselves according to the animal you assign.

The Room Itself The _classroom environment,_ as much as the _established routine,_ serves to contribute to a positive social-emotional climate. It should be a colorful, comfortable place, where the children are able to live together in a congenial atmosphere. The classroom can be designed to provide the children with the structure they require in order to exhibit the behavior expected of them. If, for example, you expect the children to work independently with classroom materials and put them away when they are finished, you will need to place the materials on low shelves in an area of the room where they are to be used and clearly mark the shelf or container where the materials belong with a silhouette outline of the material. If you expect only four children to participate in an art activity at once, only four brushes or four chairs should be provided.

Classroom structure can be used to establish guidance and to help solidify the scheduling routine. Many buildings housing preschool programs were designed to provide rich environments for preschool children, but a large number of rooms (especially those found in churches, homes, or abandoned commercial buildings) were not designed with preschoolers in mind. There may be no low windows (if there are windows at all), no natural alcoves for a carpentry area, or no bare

Figure 4-2 *Display indicating movement among small-group activities*

ground that can be turned into a garden plot. Such an environment may seem uninviting and hopeless, but with your ingenuity and creativity, you can meet the challenge and make the most efficient use of the usable space. Colorful, light paint or patterned walls can brighten the room; lamps add to its attractiveness and comfort. Low shelves or screens can be arranged to form the boundaries for a private dramatic play corner, carpentry area, or doll corner. Live plants placed on shelves or tables as well as in hanging baskets provide the children with both beauty and opportunities for experiences; large wooden or metal boxes filled with dirt and placed in a sunny area of the playground make splendid outdoor planters for vegetables or flowers. Don't be frustrated by the initial appearance of the place in which you will be teaching—it is professionally very rewarding to make acceptable and comfortable a room that originally seemed frightful.

Most preschool teachers, regardless of their basic philosophy, prefer to divide their rooms into several basic areas, among which are:

1. art activity

2. block building and other large construction activity

3. dramatic play

4. books, records, and other language-related activity

5. manipulative toys, puzzles, and games

6. woodworking area

7. water and/or sand play

8. a large area for creative movement, dancing, storytelling, cooking, or other large-group activity

9. child-size tables and chairs for eating or individual projects

10. storage areas for clothing and other supplies

The way in which these areas are organized and maintained influences young children's acceptance of school and the learning process. The skillful teacher decorates and equips the room to provide continual motivation and a suitable climate for development. Of course, the preschool setting for three-year-olds would need to be somewhat different from that for four-year-olds; the setting for four-year-olds, somewhat different from that for five-year-olds. Sample room arrangements for these three age groups are presented in Figures 4-3 through 4-5.

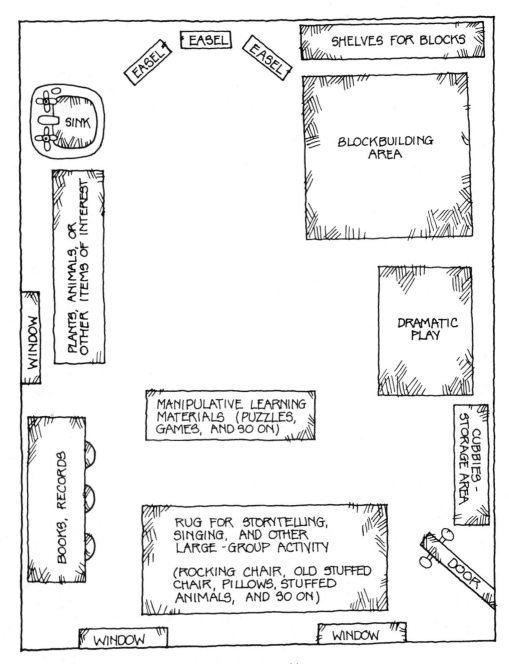

Figure 4-3 *A sample classroom design for three-year-olds*

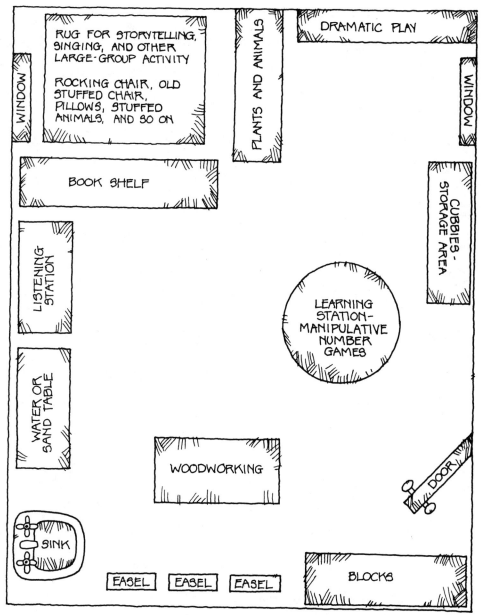

Figure 4-4   *A sample classroom design for four-year-olds*

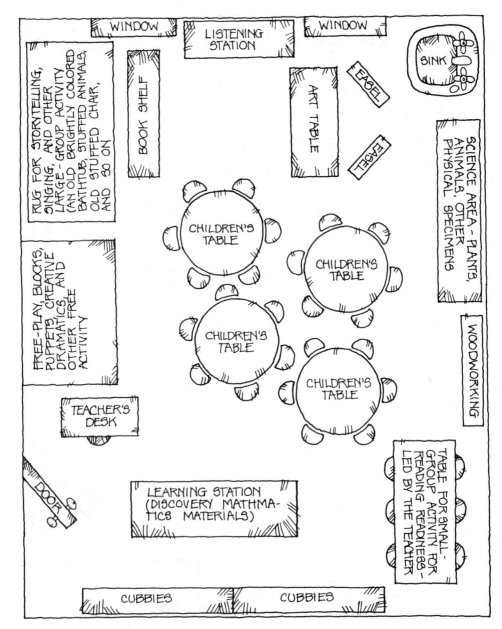

Figure 4-5 A sample classroom design for five-year-olds

After you have studied these and other sample classroom arrangements, you must decide which is most closely aligned to your personal ideas of what best serves growing and changing children. As your personal plan begins to evolve, however, remember that any arrangement and selection of equipment and materials must contribute to the goals of the program. There are several key points to remember as you progress through this phase of decision making.

- *Have good reasons for choosing your room design.* Consider the needs and strengths of your children and reflect these characteristics in the various activity areas. It may be wise to draw different arrangements on paper before moving furniture.

- *Equipment utilization is multifaceted.* Many different learnings often result from the use of one type of material. For example, an ice cream store complete with signs can help the children with reading readiness, numeral recognition, color identification, language growth, creative expression, social skills, and a variety of other valuable learnings.

- *Store toys and supplies conveniently so they are easily accessible to the children.* Place them on low shelves so the children can easily reach them, and place them as close as possible to the area in which they will be used. It is unnecessarily difficult to store blocks in one corner of the room and to locate the block play area in another.

- *Locate painting and other art activities near a sink.* This point is important not only for clean-up purposes, but also for the times when paints and pastes need to be mixed, spills need to be cared for, and the like.

- *Separate, as much as possible, noisy play areas from those areas requiring a quieter setting.* It would be unwise, for example, to locate the library corner next to the woodworking center or the painting area next to the block corner. Children should be able to pursue individual tasks free from unnecessary disruptions or distracting stimuli. A quiet nook, isolated from the normal classroom routine, should be provided for the child who needs to be alone for a short period of time.

- *Furnish individual lockers (cubbies) where the children can store their belongings.* Youngsters take comfort in knowing that a special part of the room has been designed for their personal use and will enjoy assuming responsibility for keeping it neat and orderly. The children should be provided with individual lockers (cubbies) in which they are able to store their wraps or personal belongings. These cubbies should be child-sized but still contain adequate space for the children to use them easily. Photographs with name labels help children identify their locations as well as provide them with practice in recognizing their own names.

- *Do not put all the equipment and materials out at one time.* It can be dangerous to overstimulate young children with many new materials. The children become literally overwhelmed by everything around them and may demonstrate two basic behaviors: withdrawal from all activity because of too much stimulation too soon or uncontrolled darting about from one part of the room to another in an attempt to experience as much as possible in the shortest amount of time. Lori Fisk and Henry Lindgren (1974) illustrate this concern with the following example:

Introducing a number of [classroom materials] all at once produces a situation in which children's cognitive systems collapse under an "overload of input," as my computerized friends and colleagues would say. Once, as a teenager, I babysat for a day, while the child's mother attended a confer-

Isolated quiet areas encourage children to read, listen, or participate in other less physically active pursuits.

ence. As she went out the door, she paused for ninety seconds and told me how to run the dishwasher, washing machine, clothes dryer, garbage disposal unit, and toaster oven. Before I could open my mouth to say, "Just a minute, you're going too fast!" she was gone, with a cheerful, "Have a good day!" Needless to say, I touched none of these household devices during her absence, since I was afraid that I would do something to break them. Children are of course less mature than teenagers and can absorb even less information if it is delivered all at once. [p. 58]

  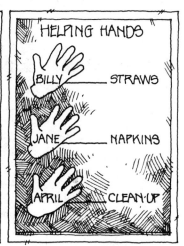

Figure 4-6   *Classroom helpers bulletin boards*

Introduce only a few materials at the beginning of the preschool year and gradually add others as time goes by to maintain a comfortable, challenging environment.

• *Make every effort to create a warm, friendly physical environment.* Remember that, in many instances, you are providing the children with their first real educational experience and that the feelings they develop during this experience will most likely accompany them throughout the remainder of their schooling. For that reason, the rooms they enter should be friendly and alluring. This does not mean that an interior decorator has to design the room, but only that even the most unattractive room can be transformed into a more attractive one by painting, using colorful draperies, decorating with discarded store displays (such as animals, cartoon characters, story characters), exhibiting children's artwork, providing a small carpeted area, and a variety of other techniques.

Classroom Helpers   Individual contributions to group welfare can be effectively dem-

onstrated by assigning helpers for specific classroom duties. Deciding who the helpers should be can be done on a daily or weekly basis, but it should be a consistent part of the schedule. There are several ways to organize this facet of your program; the following suggestions may prove helpful (see Figure 4-6).

• Start off the year by utilizing concrete materials to indicate individual responsibilities. For example, a child's photograph and a sponge may be placed next to each other on a "Our Helpers" bulletin board to indicate who is responsible for cleaning the table after snack. A straw and a photograph indicate the straw arranger, a photograph and napkin for the napkin passer, and so on.

• As the children begin to recognize their names, print them on smile faces and follow the preceding procedure by associating the smile faces with the labeled concrete object. A "Happy Helpers" bulletin board is an attractive way of organizing the materials.

• As a final stage in this developmental process, organize a special "Helping Hands" bulletin board, on which one

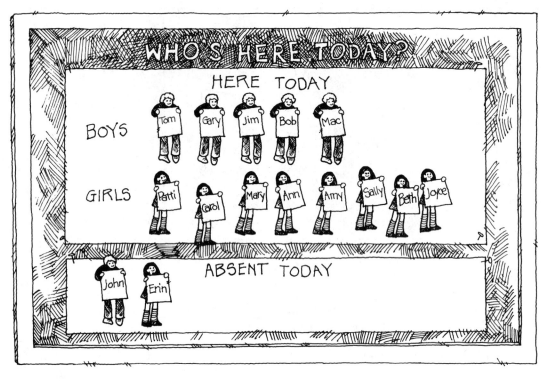

Figure 4-7 Attendance chart

hand is labeled with the classroom responsibility and the other identifies the child assigned to it. To avoid disagreements as to whose turn it is to do what job, print the job completed by each child on the back of the hand with her name.

Children enjoy assuming responsibility in the classroom and enthusiastically meet their tasks each day, especially if they are motivated by colorful charts or bulletin boards.

Attendance Charts Charts designed to record who is present or absent each day help young children recognize that separate individuals comprise their group and aid them in recognizing each other's names.

- Mount the children's photographs or small self-portraits on red construction

paper apples labeled with their names. Make a large apple tree from green and brown construction paper. As they arrive at school each day, the children find their apples and place them on the apple tree. The children can look at the chart during large group time and determine who is absent that day.

- Mount library book pockets on a bulletin board, each pocket illustrated with the child's photograph or self-portrait. Print each child's name on a card large enough so that when the card is placed into the pocket, the child's name can be read. As the children come to school each day, they place their name card into the corresponding library pocket.

- To promote counting skills, make a series of cardboard dolls representing the boys and girls in your classroom. Label each doll with the children's names. As they enter the classroom, the children place their dolls in the "Here Today" row; when everyone has arrived, you take the absent children's dolls and place them in the "Absent Today" row. During large group time, you may help the children count the number present, the number absent, the number of boys present, girls present, boys absent, or girls absent. (See Figure 4-7.)

Birthdays One of the major highlights of the school year is the celebration of special days, but no party or experience seems to bring as much excitement as the planning and execution of a birthday party. Most preschool teachers set aside a special time during the day when the birthday child is allowed to share her special day with the others. Some suggestions for this special day follow.

- Paint a special chair with bright paint and decorate it. This is a "Birthday Chair" to be used by the birthday child only on his birthday.

- Make a crown from construction paper, decorate it, and label it with the child's name, date, and age. She may wear it during the birthday party and keep it to take home as a souvenir.

- Sing "Happy Birthday" and/or "For He's a Jolly Good Fellow" as a group to the birthday child.

- Recite a special poem, such as the following, to add special significance to the child's birthday.

FIVE

Say, everybody, look at me,
For I am five-years-old, you see.
And nevermore will I be four,
Never, never, anymore.
I won't be three, or two, or one,
For that was when I'd just begun.
Now I'll be five for a while and then—I'll be
something else again.

—Author unknown

Birthday celebrations are happy times that contribute a great deal to positive self-concepts.

BEING A CONSULTANT TO THE CHILDREN

Some psychologists, including humanists such as Carl Rogers and Thomas Gordon, say that if children are put into a supportive social environment and encouraged to tune into their feelings and the feelings of others, and if they are taught communication skills that maximize interpersonal interaction, they will relate directly and openly to their peers and the adults in the classroom. And once they do so, they are able to develop fuller social relationships in a climate of openness and trust. Children enjoy communicating with others during planned or informal situations throughout the day; these interpersonal interactions can be greatly enhanced by teachers who are familiar with basic consulting skills.

If we expect children to share their ideas and feelings, we as consultants must seize each worthwhile opportunity for meaningful verbal interaction. It's not easy to do this, though, for learning when and how to talk with children is a skill that most effectively develops with experience. The following suggestions, based upon the work of M. K. Weir and P. J. Eggelston (1978), may be used as a basic guide in motivating children to communicate and in moving children toward verbal self-expression. You will need to adjust the specific wordings in order to reflect your own personality as well as the personality of the class, which is indicated by its age span, ethnic culture, neighborhood setting, and so on.

- *Provide a warm, accepting greeting when the child enters for the day.* For example, you may say: "Good morning, Maria. What nice, cool clothes for this warm day." Such a greeting not only signals your direct attention to the child but also helps her notice physical characteristics, colors, relationship of clothing to weather, or other important details considered as basic to conceptual development.

- *Take time to listen to children who are ready to tell you something.* For example, suppose a child bursts out, "Teacher, guess what! Yesterday mom got a new yellow living room set." A young or inexperienced adult might be unsure how to respond with anything other than "Oh, that's very nice," or "Did you like it?" Most authorities, however, recommend that the teacher assume the role of an *active listener* in such situations. You "feed back" to the child a question or statement—usually a paraphrase—that informs him that you really heard what was said. For example, you might say, "So mom got a new living room set. What kind of furniture was in her set?" Such a response indicates that you heard what the child said, you are interested in his family and his home, and you would like to hear more.

- *Use language to help develop concepts.* Keep your eyes and ears open for the many daily opportunities during which the children's attention may be directed to specific learnings. For exam-

ple, Oren, busily at work in the art center, suddenly called to the teacher, "Teacher, look what I did. I put red paint and white paint together." Oren's teacher quickly seized the opportunity and said, "Yes, you did. That's a pretty new color. What is its name?" Oren thought for a second and replied, "Uh-uh." "Then let me help you," offered the teacher. "That color is called pink. Did you ever see the color of pink before?" "Oh, now I remember," said Oren, "my dad got a new pink shirt for his birthday yesterday. Now I made pink with my paints!" Through such patterns of communication, children learn informally as they play.

- *Seize opportunities to expand upon the child's language.* By elaborating on a child's language, we help him primarily by serving as a good model for further refinement of language skills. For example, a toddler may approach you with a crayon in hand and say, "Picture." You may ask, "Do you want to make a picture?" The child may nod yes and accompany you to a table where you can supply paper and more crayons.

- *Share the child's day with the parent who picks her up.* Such conversation helps to give the parent something to talk about with the child and extends the school day to the home. For example, the teacher may say, "Carrie really had a great time making salad today. I know she'd like to tell you what she did." Such an ending to the day encourages conversation between parent and child and makes the end of the day a transitional rather than a final experience.

Communication within a supportive social environment, however, should occur not only from teacher to children, as in the case of the examples we have read about so far. In a supportive environment, children are encouraged to express their thoughts and feelings openly as they explore behavioral patterns. The premise is that, if children are taught communication skills that encourage them to express their feelings, then they will naturally tend to make wise behavioral decisions and will use their accumulated experiences to correct unwise behaviors. A key extension of this idea is that teachers organize group experiences allowing for freedom of personal expression, interpersonal communication, and direct exploration of feelings of self and others. Uvaldo Palomares and Harold Bissell (1967) created a popular program to help teachers provide such group experiences in their classroom. They call it the *Magic Circle*.

Magic Circle The Magic Circle program involves small-group exchange sessions, lasting 15 to 20 minutes, that encourage group interaction and acceptance of feelings and attitudes. The Magic Circle box gives a typical script for the program.

A teacher sensitive to the Magic Circle technique of dealing with children's feelings would plan sharing and discussing sessions such as the following situation described by Mary Olsen:

Teacher: "Some words people use make us feel bad or make us feel happy. Different words make different people feel bad. I don't feel happy when someone calls me stupid. Did someone ever use words that made you feel bad or unhappy?"

Billy: "My sister calls me 'stinky.' "

Teacher: "How does that make you feel?" *(no response from child)*

Teacher: "Do you like to be called 'stinky'?"

Child: "No. It makes me feel bad."

Teacher: "Would someone else like to share a word."

Susan: "It makes me feel bad when someone says, 'Shut up.' "

Teacher: "I know what you mean; it makes me feel angry when someone says 'shut up' to me."

John: "Big boys say, 'Get out of here.' "

Teacher: "How does that make you feel?"

John: "I don't like it."

Susan: "My sister calls me 'stupid.' "

Chris: " 'You can't play.' I don't like it when they say that."

Teacher: "I can tell by your voice that you feel hurt when someone won't let you play. Alice, you look like you have something to say."

Alice: "My brother calls me 'puny.' I don't like it."

Teacher: "It isn't a nice feeling inside when a brother calls you 'puny.' Did anyone ever say some words that made you feel happy?" *(Two children start to smile but don't respond verbally to the questions.)*

Teacher: "I can tell that you're thinking of something that makes you happy because you're smiling."

Chris: "You get to ride a trike."

Teacher: "How would that make you feel?"

Chris: "I'd say, 'Goodie,' and I'd tell everyone."

Susan (blurts out): "I like you!"

Teacher: "How does that make you feel when someone says, 'I like you'?"

Susan: "It makes me feel good."

Teacher: "It makes me feel happy when my son says to me, 'Mom, that pie was delicious.' John, what did someone say to make you feel good?"

John: "Someone said, 'You're nice.' "

Teacher: "How did that make you feel?"

John: "I liked it."

Susan: "I like it when it's my birthday."

Teacher: "What do you like about your birthday?"

Susan: "The presents make me happy."

Teacher (smiles and nods): "I like presents, too. Words can make people feel happy or sad. Different words can make people feel happy or sad. I'm going to say something that might make you happy. I think you did a very nice job of sharing how you feel." [1970, pp. 120–121]

In this example, the teacher encouraged the children to talk openly about their feelings and emotions. You will no doubt have noticed that the Magic Circle guidelines were not rigidly or mechanically followed, but the teacher's active and friendly leadership helped the children recognize and accept each other's feelings. The Magic Circle program, under the leadership of Palomares and Bissell, has available lesson plans and teacher's guides to direct teachers in improving children's self-confidence and awareness. (Complete teachers' guides and session formats can be obtained from: Human Development Training Institute, Inc., 7574 University Avenue, La Mesa, CA 92041.)

ACCEPTING A ROLE OF AUTHORITY IN THE CHILDREN'S LIVES

Regardless of the care and diligence you bring to the establishment and execution of the previous suggestions, there are bound to be times when the children's behaviors will exceed the bounds of what is normally described as acceptable behavior. You've prepared the environment carefully, but Janie knocked over Barbie's block tower as she went on her way to the sand table. You need to step in now and directly handle the situation, but what do you do? When children don't do as they were told or when they act in ways that we disapprove of, a special system of guidance or control is called for. Some teachers strike out with a harsh word or statement because instant obedience is their major concern—no matter what they must do to get it. Others feel that open affec-

tion is so important at a time like this that anything other than patience and niceness would be unthinkable. These two views are described here along with a third point of view—a middle-of-the-road view that believes in caring deeply about children but still recognizing the need for good control and firm discipline by an authoritative figure sensitive to the caregiver's role in helping children toward the development of their own inner control.

1. *The Authoritarian:* This teacher "rules the roost" with forceful control. She punishes children who exhibit undesirable behaviors but does not explain the reasons, often simply commanding, "Stop talking" or "Take turns." The teacher determines the rules and standards for behavior and makes each child conform, not taking individual differences into account. This teacher may normally appear friendly while leading the children, but the "friendliness" often appears only on the surface.

2. *The Permissive:* This teacher does not appear to understand what a leader is. Children "run the roost" by being given the freedom to do whatever they wish. The teacher does not enforce rules or set standards and offers too much freedom, feeling that restrictions will eventually inhibit the child. The teacher is willing to help the children, but frowns upon enforcing rules to control the disruptive or disobedient child.

3. *The Democratic:* This teacher understands the social and emotional characteristics of young children and uses this knowledge as a basis for determining why certain behaviors surface. She is flexible and applies rules in a way that gradually increases the children's individual competence and independence. The teacher responds to the children and values their self-assertion.

Democratic teachers recognize the value of behavior management, understanding that

THE MAGIC CIRCLE PROGRAM

1. Teacher and about seven or eight children sit in a circle.

2. Teacher gives a cue and waits for a child to respond. Cues for discussion are grouped into three categories:

   a. *Awareness:* For example, "Something that made me feel bad," or "What I like about my pet," or "A bad feeling I once had."

   b. *Mastery:* For example, "Some things at school that I can do for myself," or "Something I was afraid of but I did anyway," or "Some things I can't do for myself."

   c. *Social Interaction:* For example, "A time we did something for each other," or "How I made someone feel good," or "Somebody did something that I didn't like."

3. Teacher encourages active listening. Child 1 talks on the cued subject and the teacher feeds back to that child. She may feed back a feeling, such as "How did that make you feel?" or she may paraphrase a child's statement, such as, "When you were telling us about the lake, you mentioned how much you like to swim. You said it as if it made you very proud." As each child talks, the teacher calmly looks at him and nods, smiles, or uses other gestures to indicate interest. When each child is finished contributing, the teacher should thank him for his idea.

4. Teacher begins to vary the procedure.

   a. As conversation slows she may review what each child has said by saying, "Let's see where we've come" and then asking if anyone in the group would review what was said.

   b. She may focus on similarities and differences by saying, "Jim said something that sounds like what Amy was saying. Who can tell us what it was?"

   c. Encourage the shy children through an invitation such as, "Jane, would you like a turn today?" Children should not be forced to speak, however.

5. Teacher leads a roundup. At this point, all the contributions are summarized and the feelings associated with each event are identified. The teacher may say, "Let's go back and tell what each person did," or "Who can feed back just the feeling?"

children must eventually develop the skills of managing their own behaviors. They reason that by either neglecting to establish and enforce behavior standards (permissive) or by using forceful, commanding control (authoritarian), teachers fail to provide children with experiences whereby they learn to manage failures as well as successes. Standards for behavior are either neglected by the permissive teacher or imposed by the authoritarian teacher in ways that take away from the children all opportunities to learn. Democratic behavior management, on the other hand, strives to help children learn socially acceptable self-management skills that will guide them in new situations not covered by any past experiences. Children learn behaviors, either appropriate or inappropriate, as they interact with those in their environment. Through such interactions they learn ways of behaving as well as how others respond to their behaviors. Young children continually internalize those reactions and eventually assume behaviors that appear to them to be accepted or valued by significant others in their environment; during early childhood, those significant others are usually adults. Both socially acceptable and problem behaviors evolve in this way. The first step in acquiring either type of behavior pattern is the child's attempt to meet the expectations of significant others.

Many early childhood texts or articles on managing young children's behavior start with suggestions for guiding children who exhibit socially unacceptable behaviors. Hitting, spitting, biting, and other common misbehaviors dominate the pages of these resources as they offer guidance suggestions to the teacher. Such a negative focus often communicates to the prospective teacher that the major behaviors to be recognized and attended to in the class-room are those identified as socially unac-ceptable. Likewise, "good teaching" is often associated with an individual's ability to con-trol the misbehavior of children; adults are admonished to assume their role of power while guiding children who are obviously less skilled and less experienced than they. Thus, the major type of behavior directly recognized in preschool settings is problem behavior because "my effectiveness as a teacher is directly related to my ability to handle such behav-iors." A major problem with such an approach is that, if problem behaviors are constantly recognized and attended to in greater pro-portion than acceptable behaviors, children continue to exhibit problem behaviors because those behaviors are what normally attract the greatest attention from the teacher. Con-versely, many positive behaviors brought to the classroom by the children may slowly become discontinued because they are nei-ther recognized nor rewarded. Therefore, the basic premise of this text is that children are able to learn most of their self-management skills if they receive meaningful attention and praise while successfully exhibiting socially acceptable behaviors in the early childhood setting.

Verbal and Physical Feedback

Most of the time, you inform the children if they are successful at managing their own behavior by offering them verbal or physical feedback. You may offer *verbal feedback* in one of three ways: (1) bringing attention to the child's behavior, (2) offering praise, or (3) sharing a special feeling. Of course, a combi-nation of any of these three is often used, too. Such techniques are especially important dur-ing the first school sessions, when children are learning about you and your expectations.

Here are some samples of what you can do to offer verbal comments in each area.

1. *Bringing attention to the child's behavior*
   - "You placed the cup back on the shelf. That's where it belongs."
   - "You picked up the eraser and erased all your chalk lines. Now the chalkboard is clean again."
   - "You rode your trike around the bench. You were careful not to knock it over."
   - "You took little bites and all of the food stayed in your mouth."
   - "You put the puzzles back where they belong. Now they're ready for someone else to use."

   With such statements, you not only focus the children's attention on socially approved behaviors, but also inform the children that you have accepted the ways they have applied what they already know to their new environment. Most children will be highly pleased to know this and will be motivated to further seek your approval. Eventually, the children will openly seek your feedback by asking, "How's that?" or other such questions.

2. *Offering praise*
   - "Great job! You did it."
   - "That's good."
   - "Good for you, Carlos."
   - "Wow, that was quite a job."
   - "That's a clever way to do it."

   These phrases, rather than informing the children of their positive behaviors, serve mainly to communicate that they have done something good and that you appreciate their efforts. Often such short praise statements are used alone, but they can also be used together with statements describing the child's positive behavior: "It was really great of you to let Lucius help you build that house with the blocks. He likes to play with you."

3. *Sharing a special feeling*
- "That makes me very proud of you."
- "I'm happy that you were able to do that."
- "I like the way you helped Warren pick up the blocks. Thank you."
- "I'm very proud of the way you listened so well to the story."
- "It makes me feel good to see you share the blocks with Megan."

These kinds of "special feeling" comments are normally shared for the purpose of informing children about exactly what effect their positive behaviors have on those people who are very important in their lives. However, the use of such statements should be judicious, for their overuse may wrongfully communicate to the children that self-management primarily involves assuming certain behaviors simply to please others. Self-management involves much more than that, but it is certainly beneficial to let children know just how much you appreciate their positive efforts.

All of these special verbal feedback and communication techniques are very effective, but they often gain further effectiveness when used in partnership with forms of positive *physical feedback.* Physical feedback involves all the "body language" you utilize while reacting to a child's positive behaviors. A smile, a nod of approval, a hug, or a pat on the back all inform the children that you appreciate their efforts and value what they have accomplished. By physically getting down at the child's level when talking or listening as well as maintaining direct eye contact, you let the child know that what is being communicated holds a very important place in your life. Such friendly physical feedback helps children get to know

you as a person who values them and establishes a sound initial bond between you and the children.

Structuring the Environment

A second major technique for avoiding emphasis on negative behavior is to arrange the environment in ways that prevent behavior problems from occurring in the first place. Although there is no single, superior organizational plan for preschool or kindergarten classrooms, you can influence children's behaviors by the ways that you arrange and distribute furniture, materials, and supplies. For example, if you have a large, open space, many children will naturally use it for running or other rowdy play. However, if the furniture is arranged so as to form pathways of travel, many discipline problems can be prevented. Arrangements of chairs and tables, cabinets, and screens will cut off long running areas and will reflect an understanding of behavioral maturity. Conversely, crowded situations tend to provoke misbehaviors such as hitting or hurting others. You may also want to examine your classroom to see that materials are age-appropriate and that there are enough of them. If the materials are too simple, too difficult, or scarce, boredom or frustration can lead to undesirable behaviors. For example, if you believe there are youngsters in your setting who are likely to waste or spill paint, you will carefully supervise their use and keep the supplies in a locked cabinet.

Thus, a room arrangement is based upon your perception of children's needs and just what behavioral management competencies the youngsters have mastered when they come to you. Be prepared, especially in the early weeks of the school year, to watch the children in action and see what changes need to be made in order to ensure that the children's needs are adequately met. Most often, your first arrangement will not reflect the best use of the room and you will rearrange the setting several times.

Classroom Rules

Management of behavior does not stop with the feedback of positive behaviors nor with the organization and utilization of physical space. Self-management also involves learning and following classroom rules. Rules are expressions or expectations that you have for the children's behavior. We discussed the possibilities of communicating rules through informal, positive verbal feedback—"Good work. You kept the sand from falling outside the sandbox when you dumped it." The children learn many rules this way. However, when children enter your program, they must be aware that formally established rules do exist so that the safety and welfare of all are ensured.

Your responsibility in this area is to know what rules are commonly required in early childhood settings and how those rules are presented to the children. First, let us consider the question of what rules are most commonly required. A simple answer would be to identify all the daily events in need of rules:

- arrival procedures
- sharing materials with others
- toileting procedures
- indoor and outdoor safety
- storage and care of personal property
- transition between routines
- consideration toward others
- mealtime, snacktime, or rest
- care and use of materials and supplies
- departure procedures

At the beginning of the year, examine your children's needs and interests and present as few explicit rules as are needed to maintain the safety and well-being of your group. Once you have identified the essentials (don't have so many that you "suffocate" the children), you must come up with the best wording so that the rules are as clearly and simply stated as possible. Some rules are better stated to individual children in a positive way when the situation arises ("We walk indoors"); other rules are more effective when presented to small groups. For example, involved toileting rules are best communicated to small groups. A whole group introduction to rules is probably the least often used technique, but it would be appropriate in whole-class situations such as field trips, where you may want the children to always follow their adult leader, walk in a two-by-two arrangement, or always line up in a particular order.

Regardless of the technique you choose for teaching rules to young children, children need much practice and patience while learning them. Learning a rule is basically no different than learning anything else in an early childhood setting. You would probably agree that an initial recitation of the alphabet in no way constitutes the only learning experience necessary for children to internalize the names and order of the letters. Much reinforcement and repetition of related skills are required. Likewise, the process of learning rules for behavior requires extensive learning opportunities before children can be expected to become completely competent at self-management.

Lawrence Kohlberg's popular ideas of moral development provided early childhood educators with evidence supporting the need for providing opportunities to learn rules for behavior. By carrying out intensive studies of children around the world, Kohlberg found that, despite differences in cultural, social, economic, and religious backgrounds, individuals progress through a series of stages of moral development. Although he never assigned age designations to his stages, it is basically accepted that most children through

Children learn by observing the behaviors of adults around them. Providing a model of sincere caring will build skills within the children and help them to extend caring behaviors toward each other.

the kindergarten year operate at stage one. This is a period of development during which children believe that to be "well behaved" means blind obedience to an adult authority figure. Children do not understand why certain behaviors are expected of them, but they determine "goodness" or "badness" of an act solely on the basis of whether an adult will punish or reward them. If we interpret Kohlberg properly, we realize that a unilateral respect for the behavioral expectations of adults is an unavoidable stage in the development of children. For this reason, they call out for guidance by adults and require behavior standards to be established for them. However, those standards must be chosen thoughtfully, for children do not completely understand the reasons for your choices.

Although this message may be interpreted as indicating a need for strict classroom authority, the only way a child can move from this initial stage to more mature stages is not through authoritarian leadership, but through experience. Otherwise, the child will remain locked into the patterns of behavior management just described. Experience can be gained through involving children in understanding both the motives behind behavioral expectations as well as the reasons for the rules themselves. We thereby help them gain increasingly mature patterns of self-guided behavior so that they move from the least mature behavioral motivation of being concerned about reward or punishment for their actions toward a higher Kohlberg stage such as behaving in ways that take into consideration other people's feelings and what a "good" person should do. For example, Erin displays a higher level of moral development when she decides that she should share the cookie cutters with Luis because that is what a "good person" does in the classroom rather than because she would be rewarded by the teacher if she does, or possibly reprimanded if she does not.

This entire area of handling personal behavior management is extremely sensitive. Katherine H. Read (1971) supported this view when she said that guiding the young child requires a great deal of personal insight: "Overdirection may distort his development; so may the lack of direction. He needs time to learn through suitable experiences. He is sure to make some mistakes in the process of learning. . . . If we deal calmly and confidently with unacceptable behavior, we will create the kind of climate in which the child is helped to master his impulses and to direct his own behavior. We will be using authority in constructive ways" (pp. 108–109).

Behavioral Problems

Regardless of your attempts to prevent misbehavior, behavioral problems will occur. Sadly, at this point, the idea of punishment immediately rushes into some people's minds—especially if the misbehavior tends to be

repeated. "What else can you do?" they ask in frustration. Before that question can be answered effectively, let us start with the premise that your actions should be in direct proportion to the severity of the misbehavior. Minor misbehaviors that neither disturb others nor threaten their safety or well-being oftentimes are best ignored. For example, Jerry, a calm, easy-going child, rarely displayed open signs of intense emotion. One day he accidentally knocked over a container of paint and blurted out, "Damn!" so loudly that everyone heard. The teacher saw Jerry start to clean up his accident and decided it would only embarrass Jerry if she brought attention to this short-lived infraction. So she ignored it. The ability to overlook such minor misbehaviors, which cause neither inconvenience nor harm to others, is an extremely mature professional competency.

If a rule is broken, and there is reason to step in, you must enforce the rule. But this does not mean that you punish the children. Your responsibility is to talk with the offender and go over the rule step by step so that the youngster understands that the rule is important. You want the offender to understand the rule, the reason for its existence, and its value to the group so that he can internalize it as his own. You enforce your rules, but you do not punish children. Enforcement implies teaching: You talk, discuss, and offer reasons for rules repeatedly until your standards become the children's and they freely accept the rules as guides for their own behavior.

Some parents and teachers become frustrated at such frequent talking. "You've got to punish them!" these adults say as a last resort. "Come on! The children are asking for it." Keep teaching is my only retort. Have patience and try to understand that self-management is not an easy skill for many youngsters to develop, especially since they are at the very beginning of a lifetime of experiences. Teaching need not imply a "soft" approach, but a serious, matter-of-fact process by which you use words and actions to get ideas across. Specific teaching suggestions will be offered shortly, but, for now, let us examine the topic of punishment a bit more closely and try to understand why it is an inappropriate technique for guiding young children. James L. Hymes (1981) gave the following reasons for eliminating or minimizing punishment when working with the very young:

1. *Punishment is subject to "inflation."* For example, you may choose a punishment such as making a child sit while the others play and it seems to have a tremendously positive initial impact on controlling misbehavior. Then, at some point, the child may say, "Aw, that doesn't bother me anymore," and you've got to control his behavior with a new punishment that hurts him even more than the original.

2. *Punishment opens up a "bargaining" process.* The child soon learns she has a choice: is the right to misbehave worth the punishment that results? Soon, your classroom may assume the character of an auction, where children are not guided by a sincere desire to adopt socially acceptable behaviors, but by whether or not their misbehavior is worth a degree of mental or physical pain that results.

3. *Punishment jeopardizes positive adult–child relationships.* Youngsters are intimately dependent upon the love and support of nurturing adults. An angry face, a cross word, a sharp voice, or a caustic glare all strike more fear into young children's hearts than we can ever imagine. Our punitive expressions of displeasure to their behaviors hurt children deeply because they need our understanding, patience, and approval so much.

In summary, effective teaching does not mean that we allow children to walk all over us nor does it mean that we shame, ridicule, or use other punitive measures to guide young children. Effective teaching does mean that a loving, caring adult reaches out with words and actions to help children learn to master their behaviors. This adult realizes that such a goal involves a long, slow journey replete with frustration: "I've told that boy a dozen times and he still doesn't listen!" Do not allow such frustrations to tempt you to resort to punishment techniques. Children need to succeed and to feel pride in their accomplishments. Here are some suggestions for helping them on their way.

1. *Gather all available information about the behavior before you attempt to deal with it.* Search for possible clues as to why the behavior occurred. Conscious observation yields valuable information about the cause of misbehaviors and also helps provide the basis for handling the situation. Think, for example, of an infant who suddenly cries. She is clearly exhibiting a behavior you wish to change, but what do you do about it? Certainly, you know not to yell at her, give her a scowl, or, even worse, hit her. Your training and sensitivities tell you that much. You must find out what is causing the behavior before you can do anything about it. Is the baby hungry, sleepy, or sick? Does she have a rash? Does the diaper need to be changed? Has the baby been burped after the most recent feeding? Was she possibly frightened or startled by something? Did you lay her on a small toy? Is she in discomfort? You consider the possibilities and, if you find the apparent cause, deal with the situation accordingly. In this case, you find that the baby's diaper needs changing, perform your job, and are rewarded with the coos and gurgles of a comfortable baby.

   However, suppose that you change the diaper and still find no change in behavior; the baby keeps on crying. What then? Certainly your frustrations do not dictate that you "punish" the baby. Sincere, caring adults would pick up the baby, talk softly to her, offer her hugs and kisses, rock her gently, and offer a number of other loving gestures. Likewise, you examine many causes when you search for the factors that encourage certain behaviors among toddlers and young children. And, if your first hunches are not on target, you search for alternatives rather than inflict punishment or withdraw affection in order to find a base for eliminating the problem.

Here is an example: You see Tara, a four-year-old, assume leadership in the block area, building an elaborate structure with three other children. The children appear to enjoy playing with each other until Tara hits Doreen. Hitting is a behavior that cannot be allowed in your classroom. You approach Tara, explaining the rule she had broken and why she should not hit. However, despite all of your well-intentional talking, you become aware that Tara's penchant for hitting is becoming a habit. Now what do you do?

As physicians know that a fever is caused by certain health problems, teachers must understand that misbehavior may be caused by a variety of reasons. Before physicians treat the fever, they must perform a battery of observations in order to determine its cause. The teacher, too, must be observant and aware so that she can discover the causes for misbehavior in her classroom and use this knowledge as a base for altering that behavior. This observant teacher would look for things such as:

• Did Doreen take something from Tara?

• Was Tara frustrated in the situation?

• Was Tara provoked in some way?

• Did excessively crowded conditions contribute to Tara's behavior?

• Were the blocks age-appropriate for Tara and her playmates?

• Does a particular home situation have Tara upset?

In order to avert hitting in the future, you must know the reasons for Tara's

behavior. If crowded conditions provoke Tara (and it does in some children), you will need to rearrange the block area so that more space is available. If Tara hits because she has difficulty sharing her toys with others, you will need to stress the positive value of sharing. From your informal observations you might find a simple remedy for your problem. But, if you always treat the symptom (hitting) rather than the cause (Tara was provoked), you may regularly experience frustration in eliminating undesirable behavior.

Here is another example of how one teacher solved a behavior problem by understanding its cause. Manuel was playing with some clay at a table when Jennifer intruded and took almost half of what he was using. Manuel reacted by slapping Jennifer and ordering, "Give it back, you *(obscenity)!*" The primary cause of this confrontation, of course, was Jennifer's intrusion into Manuel's activity. It would be wise to address that component first with a comment such as, "Manuel was using the clay, Jennifer, and I can't let you take it from him. I'll get you some and you can use it at this table." Then you should address the *result* of the confrontation by explaining to Manuel, "I know that Jennifer took some of your clay without asking, but I can't let you hit her and use words like that in our classroom. She made a mistake."

The way you handle situations involving children's feelings is important to the develpment of healthy personalities and budding social relationships. You must always use constructive methods to cope with the various stumbling blocks that can affect positive growth.

When dealing with causes of misbehavior, you must try to anticipate problems before they happen. Perhaps more than any other teaching behavior, this comes with experience. Learning to prevent problems before they happen is important because children may not always benefit from mistakes. For example, while watching two children playing in the block corner, you observe that Michael is unknowingly moving closer and closer to Benny's block tower. In another minute, an errant foot may kick over a carefully constructed tower and cause calamity. You carefully appraise the situation, approach Michael, and say, "If you want to play with your truck in the block city, Michael, you should come over here where you won't kick over Benny's tower." If you wait for the situation to unfold before taking action, the children may be unable to learn anything constructive.

2. *Know what to say and how to say it.* In spite of our most sincere intentions, we often compound or complicate matters by failing to allow the child to express his emotions or by misinterpreting his intentions. Negative emotions that go unexpressed or unrecognized may eventually be expressed in highly destructive, hostile ways. For example, in recognizing that Arnie's behavior—slamming his paper cup on the table—was a result of his desire to quench a deep thirst, the teacher may say, "It's hard to wait for your juice when you're thirsty, isn't it, Arnie? You want your juice right now." Arnie may answer, "Yes. I wish Judy would hurry." The teacher may suggest, "Then you should tell her. I cannot allow you to throw things like you did because I want this school to be a safe place for all children. Please tell Judy what you want." Arnie may now go on to express his desires to Judy and receive his juice in return. You should describe the child's feelings only if you can identify them accurately and also give a description of the situation that goes beyond a simple statement, such as "You're feeling angry, aren't you, Arnie?"

The following examples and suggestions illustrate some techniques used by teachers as they try to get ideas across to children. They are specific examples used by some teachers, but you will certainly develop your own unique way of saying these things and resolving problem situations. Examine these ideas and search out ideas of other educators in order to develop your own personalized guidance. No recipe will ever teach you how to guide *all* children; you need to understand the child, the situation, and the reasons behind the behavior.

- *Use your voice as a tool for preventing problems.* When the daily routine evolves without problems, your voice maintains a mellow, casual, soft tone. The children should react positively to your relaxed demeanor and maintain their comfortable environment. When you sense a need for specific control, you should adjust the volume or tone of your voice in a way that indirectly communicates what you would like to say directly in words. For example, if you are leading children in a group math activity, they may become so motivated that they appear to be reaching a point of excitability. Not wanting to squelch this motivation with a direct statement such as, "All right, take it easy, we need to calm down a little bit here," you may simply bring the excitability level down but keep the enthusiasm high by continuing on with your normal dialogue, but adjusting your voice to communicate the authority of an adult in charge. At other times, it may be appropriate to use words directly along with the change in your voice, especially when it appears that a degree of mischief is starting to appear: For example, "Slide down *feet first*," is all that is needed when you want to prevent misuse of playground equipment.

- *Speak to individuals* whenever possible unless large groups are involved in the situation. Squat, sit, or kneel down and get the child's attention by facing him squarely. Look intently into his eyes, reach out and hold the shoulders gently, and talk about the difficulty in words easily understood by the child. If the situation warrants, you may also augment your statements with action. For example, Amanda developed the habit of putting small objects such as beads into her pocket and taking them home. As this happened one day, Amanda saw the teacher and, reacting quickly, popped the bead into her mouth. A suitable reaction to this situation might be to say, "I know you want this bead, Amanda, but it belongs to all the children in our room so I can't let you take it. Open your mouth and give it to me because you might swallow it and that would be very dangerous. That's good. We put only food in our mouths here at school."

• *Use a tone of voice suitable* for the age of child with whom you are working. Some teachers adopt an extra slow, smooth, high-pitched voice that virtually drips of sugar and honey. Such an extremely sweet approach is often artificial and staged. The problem with such artificiality is that the teacher's mood often appears to shift radically when she needs to control a child or group and brings a firm tone to her voice. This may lead to confusion and ultimate distrust from the children as they seemingly ask, "Who is my *real* teacher?" Other teachers seem to feel that the only way to guarantee respect and control is to use a strong, aggressive voice that communicates, "I'm boss in here and what I say goes." Such an extreme approach may create anxiety and fearfulness among the children, causing them to tense up, to use aggressive behavior, or to begin to adopt the same behavior patterns with their peers. Listen to yourself when you work with young children. Look at the children's faces as you talk to them. What do you hear and see? Would you be happy with yourself as a teacher?

• *Develop skill in talking with children.* Although you should not overreact to every little act and place it under a microscope for deeper study, you must react with spontaneity to situations demanding your authoritative leadership. Such leadership can be effectively established and maintained as you become skilled at using these suggestions:

Give directions in a positive form. In other words, don't use *don't*. I could perform a great disservice and stop after that statement with no other explanation and illustrate to you what we often do to children. We create confusion when we say what *not* to do because the receiver of our message is unsure where to go from there.

Although youngsters must learn the meaning of *no, stop, don't,* and other words that may be needed to get the children's attention on those occasions when immediate compliance is necessary, their constant use is confusing to the children and fails to help them learn to handle situations through positive, constructive means.

SAY THIS	NOT THIS
"Walk in the room. You can run outside."	"No running in the room."
"Stay with the others until the others are through. You're part of the group, too."	"Don't leave until we're finished with our snack."
"Drive your truck around the blocks or it will knock down Peter's tower."	"Don't knock over the blocks with your truck."

SOMETIMES THIS

"No pushing on the slide; someone can get hurt. First Lucy, then Jaime, then Ricardo, and Matthew."

"I can't allow you to bite other children. It hurts them."

"I will not let you spit on Marcie. You can spit in the toilet."

Direct your comments to what has happened, not to the child. You are disapproving of the behavior, not the child. Avoid labeling the child with descriptors such as "bad," "stubborn," or "attention-seeker." Which would obviously tear down the child's confidence if used to handle a classroom situation? (1) "You're so clumsy to spill the water on the floor." (2) "Water makes the floor very slippery and someone could fall. Take this mop and try to mop it up." You are not only helping children change behaviors with positive guidance, but you are also helping them understand the consequences of their actions.

Give choices only when you mean it. "Do you want to come indoors now?" the teacher calls to the children as she waits by the door for the children to come in from the playground. "Do you want to eat your snack now?" and "Would you like to clean up now?" are the kind of questions that back us into a corner because they give children a choice that we are not willing to accept. "No!" they will probably answer in response to each. The teacher may have used the questions because she felt that children need real experiences to learn to make decisions, but she actually set up situations in which she could not accept the children's choice. A question such as "Would you like to listen to *Pelle's New Suit* or to *Madeline*?" or "You may either swing or ride the trike" offers the children a choice we can accept.

Redirect an activity to help the child change behavior. Detouring the child or changing the environment in which the behavior takes place is often an effective means of dealing with unacceptable behavior. For example, if the children are playing with ropes to simulate gasoline hoses as they fill up the tanks of their wheel toys and the ropes appear to have the potential of tripping children or knocking over block structures, you may step in and say, "The gasoline pumps seem to be in a dangerous place here. Let's put them in a special place so they won't harm the other children." Then you can move the ropes to a safer location while averting a potential crisis.

Give only one or two requests at a time. Anything more than, "Walk to the closet and bring back the sponge" may confuse young children.

Reinforce your directions when necessary by actually showing the child what you mean.

Avoid comparisons that communicate a preference for one child over another. For example, "Carrie washed her hands so much better than you did, Alice."

Do not shame the child or make him feel guilty with comments such as, "You're acting just like a baby."

3. *Use physical guidance when appropriate.* When early childhood educators speak of physical guidance, they do not mean techniques such as shaking, slapping, spanking. What do you teach children when you hit them to make them stop hitting? If you were to discipline children simply by doing to them what you don't want them to do to others so that they can see how it feels, why not knock over their block towers, spill their juice, or overturn a jar of paint? If you

did these things, you would be acting very childish indeed. What the children need in a problem situation is a supportive adult with enough self-control to encourage them and make them feel safe. Here are a few physical means of guiding behavior:

- *Lend a helping hand.* Children feel safe and secure while attempting new or complicated tasks if they know the steadying hand of their teacher is warmly extended. For example, "Pour the juice carefully so it will not spill. Here, I'll hold the cup while you fill it. There . . . you did a great job." Or, "I'll hold your hand while you try to climb up onto the tree stump, Carmen. You let me know when you've practiced enough to do it by yourself."

- *Restrain children to prevent them from hurting themselves or others, or damaging property.* Sometimes, due to factors such as overfatigue or anger, children erupt in explosive outbursts. Often teachers remove such children from the situation and direct them to activities such as pounding clay or punching a punching bag in an effort to reduce angry feelings. Other children may need even more direct physical guidance when they lose control. When you need to step in during such outbursts, catch the child and hold her firmly with your hands or arms with the child facing away from you. The child should be led to understand that you are trying to help through a firm, supportive attitude. The child needs to come out of such a crisis knowing you can be trusted and that you are near to help when control is lost.

4. *Love your children.* It is only human nature to want to have all the answers when you face situations involving the behavior of young children, but in some instances you will simply not know enough to solve a problem situation. However, you shouldn't stop short of trying to discover the cause when there

continue to be indications that something just is not right and give up with defeatist statements such as "He'll always be a brat!" or "She's a perfect slob." Instead, continue on with combinations of practical recommendations you glean from many sources and act much as our caregiver of the crying baby discussed earlier. If the mother could find no cause for the baby's crying after she examined all the possibilities, she would most probably resort to one last behavior: She would pick him up, cuddle him, and croon a soft, soothing lullaby. Likewise, older children benefit by our reassurance and love when they face complicated problems having to do with emotions or feelings. However, if severe behaviors persist over a period of time with no apparent cause, do not play "amateur psychologist" and try to solve those problems by yourself; turn for help to professionals trained to deal with such problems.

COPING WITH DISLIKE FOR A PARTICULAR CHILD

Until now we have focused our attention on the emotional reactions of children to their new classroom, to the other children, and to the teacher. One area that has not yet been addressed is the topic of your own emotional reactions to the classroom situation. Most of your feelings will probably be those of compassion, understanding, empathy, pleasure, acceptance, and enthusiasm. Whenever you think of outstanding teachers, you probably imagine qualities such as those. Would you add descriptors such as jealousy, dislike, ambivalence, fear, or anger to that list? Probably not, yet teachers do have those emotions, and children frequently are the cause (Parker, 1962). Despite this fact, teachers are usually

Young children need to know that they are loved.

reluctant to admit such feelings, especially one important emotion we shall consider here—the feeling of dislike for one particular child. Guilt often accompanies the realization of dislike, and teachers oftentimes agonize as they attempt to repress it. However, Greenberg (1969) states that such dislike should be accepted as a normal emotion: "It is impossible to feel the same way toward all children. Human beings react uniquely or specifically to other human beings. [Teachers] have had a lifetime to form personal likes and dislikes. [They] cannot shed them in class." Although we will find it difficult to admit dislike for any single child, it is important to recognize the fact that such emotion may exist in our professional life. Only through such recognition can we expect to cope with the situation. Fordyce (1982) offered these coping strategies:

1. *Pinpoint the specific reason for disliking a child.* Is it the physical appearance such as obesity or a constantly running nose? What about specific mannerisms such as biting or hair pulling? A list of these specific behaviors could stretch out for pages. After identifying the irritating behaviors or characteristics, you should accept them as problems to be solved.

2. *Analyze why a personal chord has been struck.* Once you have pinpointed the bothersome behavior, try to understand why it is so dominant in your attitude toward the child. Is it because the behavior itself is so foreign to your own behavioral repertoire? Can it be that the behavior is so much like you, for example, a quick temper? By discovering this source of personal aggravation, you can begin to direct strong feelings away from the child.

3. *Recognize which characteristics or behaviors are genuinely liked.* Try to look beyond your dislikes and develop a well-rounded view of the child, searching for positive characteristics. For example, you may strongly dislike a five-year-old clinging to his mother upon arrival to school, but may truly enjoy his creative play at 9:20. These feelings of delight will help you overcome your dislikes and form a more well-rounded view of the child.

4. *Determine whether the disliked behaviors are actually age-appropriate.* Be sure to solidify your knowledge of child development so that you can establish realistic expectations. Rather than labeling a two-year-old "restless" because she is unable to participate in a whole-group activity for twenty minutes, you should understand that such behavior is characteristic of all children at that level. Understanding this developmental stage can be an excellent way to displace dislike.

5. *Share your concerns with a colleague.* Although you may be "turned off" by a child, a co-worker may feel differently. You can then be assured that the child will get fair and objective treatment from that co-worker who enjoys the child's company.

Dislike for a child is but one emotion you can expect to surface as you teach. To explore each would be impossible, but let us consider an interesting opposite feeling—intense warmth toward a child. Could you imagine how it is possible for strong positive emotions to interfere with your professional judgment?

As with dislike, even this emotion should be aired out and examined. It is only through this process that you can effectively cope with your emotional reactions to children.

ALTERNATIVE BEHAVIOR MANAGEMENT APPROACHES

In addition to the democratic approach to behavior management discussed thus far, several other methods may be used. Here we discuss behavior modification and modeling.

Behavior Modification

When teachers work on changing particularly inappropriate behaviors, they often choose a technique called *behavior modification*. This classroom management model is based on the idea that adults can systematically control children's behavior through external motivation techniques such as reinforcement, withdrawal of attention, or even punishment. Behavior modification approaches are primarily derived from the theories of B. F. Skinner and his process of *operant conditioning*. Guy Lefrancois (1973) defined operant conditioning in this way: "The simplest explanation of operant conditioning is that a response followed by *reinforcement* will be more likely to occur when the organism [again] finds itself in a similar situation" (p. 90). To understand how that process works, let us examine a special piece of equipment known as the Skinner Box. In its most basic form, the box can be an enclosure containing a food tray and a lever that is designed in such a way that when it is pressed a pellet of food drops into the tray (see Figure 4-8). Operant conditioning is demonstrated when a hungry rat is placed into the box and learns to press the lever to receive a reward (food pellets). Of course, simply putting a rat into such a box and waiting for it to press a lever may result in a starved rat, for something has to be done to aid the rat in learning to press the lever or it may never press it. The process of helping the rat is called *shaping*. The eventual pressing of the lever to receive food is called operant conditioning. McCarthy and Houston (1980) describe the process of shaping:

> In the shaping process the experimenter, who has control over delivery of the food pellets, rewards closer and closer approximations of the desired behavior. First, he rewards the animal if it faces the lever; then he rewards it only if it approaches the lever; and finally the rat only gets rewarded if it touches and presses the lever. This procedure can usually be accomplished in a matter of minutes, as opposed to an indeterminate amount of frustrated time if the experimenter would wait for the animal to press the bar itself. [p. 33]

What does this example of the Skinner Box have to do with classroom life? Behaviorists believe that this simple learning process contains much of what goes on in human learning, too, and that shaping techniques along with a carefully selected reward system can be an effective means of teaching young children appropriate behaviors.

Identifying Behaviors Before you make any attempt to change children's behaviors, you must first carefully observe the extent to which undesirable behavior is practiced. Teachers can keep track of that behavior on a simple graph throughout the period of changing the behavior.

The first step of this process is to collect *baseline data*. This is an initial collection of information regarding how often a behavior occurs. Usually collected over a three-day period, the baseline will be used as a starting point with which to compare later change. Data are often recorded on a graph; the vertical axis provides information on how often a behavior

Figure 4-8 *A Skinner Box*

occurs and the horizontal axis identifies the time frame in which a behavior occurs. Let us suppose that swearing is a behavior that you are concerned about. Figure 4-9 shows that the child swore four times on Day 1, six times on Day 2, and five times on Day 3. Your goal is to decrease swearing to the point where it occurs zero times. How can that be done?

Ignoring and Reinforcing Once you have identified the specific behavior you want to change, you must ignore unacceptable behavior and reward acceptable behavior much as we found in our Skinner Box example. Ignoring by itself is not usually sufficient to change behavior, so you must reinforce desirable behaviors until the behavior is changed. Reinforcement, or reinforcers, may take one of four basic forms:

1. *Token reinforcers:* Chips, counters, stars, labels, and check marks.
2. *Food:* Candy, raisins, juice, cookies, peanuts, cheese, fruit, popcorn, cereal, carrots or celery, and milk.
3. *Activities:* Toys, games, puzzles, and art.

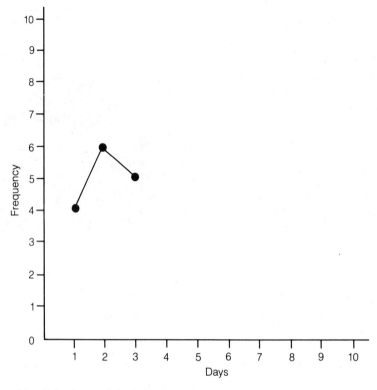

Figure 4-9   *Behavior graph for 3 days*

4. *Social reinforcers:* Smiles, hugs, hand-shakes, pats on the back, and verbal praise, such as "I like the way you did that"; "You're doing a great job"; "Wow! Thanks for helping out"; or "Good boy (girl)!"

If you want to change a child's swearing behavior, you ignore the swearing whether it is out of anger or for whatever other reason. You do not express shock or admonish the child in any way. Such attention may actually be a reinforcer for the child and increase his swearing behavior. If the other children act up or imitate, you try to divert their attention. You also reward the child for times when non-swearing takes place and continue to record the occurrences of swearing each day. Your chart may look like Figure 4-10.

Notice the rapid rise in frequency of swearing behavior on Day 4. The reason for such a drastic change is that when you begin to ignore behavior that had been previously attended to, the child tries harder and harder to regain your attention. Here is where you need patience and determination. Remember that this is a natural phenomenon and that your program will soon bring about change. Your ultimate goal, of course, is to get a zero frequency count for three or four days in succession; then you begin measures to maintain the new behavior. You continue to reinforce desirable behaviors and ignore occasional swear words. Remember, however, that reinforcers may not be effective unless they are:

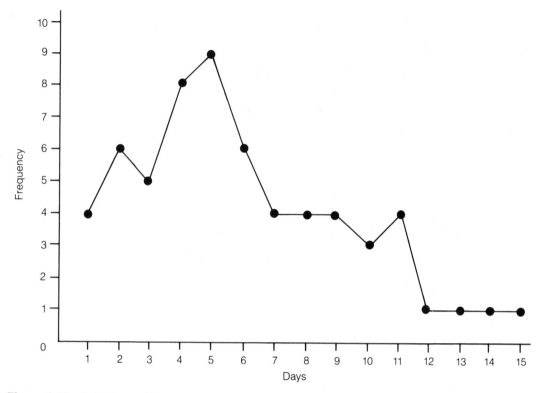

Figure 4-10   *Behavior graph for 15 days*

- *sincere* (You genuinely communicate an approval of the child's behavior.),
- *valued by the child* (For some children a hug may work as a reinforcer, while, for others, food works better.), and
- *closely matched with the desired behavior* (You smile at the child and say, "I like the way you're playing daddy. You talked so nicely to the baby.") (O'Leary and O'Leary, 1977).

Reinforcement is most effective when it follows an observable behavior as closely as possible. For that reason, teachers employing behavior modification principles often combine positive reinforcement techniques with a reinforcement system that uses *tokens*. In this system whenever children exhibit a positive social characteristic, such as saying "Thank you," they are immediately given a token (a chip or a counter of some kind) and a verbal reinforcement, such as "Way to go. Your manners are super." The children accumulate these chips during the day and use them to "buy" an activity later in the day. For example, the special art activity may cost them five chips, free play may cost three chips, and so on. Teachers using this technique discover what the children like to do and then use that activity as a reinforcing consequence. The reinforcer tends to have its greatest strength the first time it is used. Over a period of time, the children tire of the same reinforcer, and eventually it will begin to lose its desired effect. When you notice that the reinforcer is not having the effect you desired, substitute an alternative reinforcer. In the first stages of your program to change behaviors, you must immediately reinforce desirable behavior every time it occurs. Once the behavior shows indications of changing, you can extend intermittent reinforcement, spacing your reinforcement in even intervals rather than each time it occurs. Oftentimes, teachers introduce contingencies along with the reinforcer. For example, they say, "You may have more time at the learning centers if everyone continues to work so well." Notice that the reward is contingent upon desirable behavior.

Those using a behavior modification approach recommend that teachers ignore disruptive behavior because attending to it acts as a reinforcer. Since a principle of behavior modification is that behaviors tend to weaken if they are not reinforced, ignoring undesirable behaviors will cause them to decline eventually. When you first begin to ignore a behavior, that behavior will initially get worse, but it will continue to decline as you continue to ignore it. An ignoring technique often employed to extinguish negative behavior in some preschool classrooms is *time out*. For example, if a child is misbehaving during story time and begins to disrupt the others in the group to the point where the teacher is not able to ignore his actions, the child is sent to a special time-out corner in the room where he is isolated from the rest of the group. During this time, the child cannot earn chips and will be unable to collect enough to participate in an anticipated activity. Behaviorists feel that by placing such restrictions on the disruptive child, teachers will be able to extinguish undesired behavior eventually. However, the program itself must be of high quality if this technique is to be used. Some children may actually rejoice at being sent to the time-out area in a poor program, because "I didn't want to do those dumb things anyway!"

Time out is not a punitive area where the child sits in a corner accompanied by harsh words from the teacher, but is simply an area removed of activity to which the child is asked to move when he is not able to exhibit appropriate behaviors. The teacher may tell him that he is welcomed back to join the group, "When you are ready to control yourself." If the program is interesting enough, the child will be ready very soon.

Critics of this approach believe that it is wrong to assume that undesirable behaviors can be extinguished simply by ignoring them (Caldwell, 1977). Oftentimes, they argue, youngsters interpret the ignoring aspect as a permissive stance to management and tend to continue the misbehavior or increase it. For that reason, the critics recommend that teachers reject the ignoring principle and assume an active, authoritative stance to handling situations involving undesirable behavior.

Punishers Punishers are consequences of behaviors that tend to weaken or extinguish those behaviors. Some examples of punishers are (1) spanking, (2) reprimanding, (3) withholding privileges, and (4) isolating or ignoring.

There seems to be no conclusive evidence that punishment is an effective deterrent to negative behavior. There is evidence that it can cause temporary suppression of negative behaviors, but negative social or emotional reactions frequently reappear. Evidence shows that these reactions reappear because punishment techniques are often associated with the punishing person rather than with the disapproved behavior, resulting in a strong dislike for a teacher or parent.

If you use punishers, you must be very careful for there is danger in using punishers the wrong way. The use of punishment can cause the child to form a resentment toward you rather than to change her undesirable behavior. And, aside from legal implications, spanking or other forms of physical punishment serves as a model for youngsters that it is acceptable to hit others in order to get what they want or to relieve pent-up emotions. Sometimes, though, teachers choose to use punishment by withholding privileges. In doing so, they must provide a warning signal and carry out their plan in a deliberate way. For example, if a child is throwing water onto the floor from the water table, you may wish to provide the warning, "If you cannot keep the water in the table, you may no longer play there." Now the ball is in the child's court; her actions will determine the future course of events. If the child persists, you must step in and carry out your plan by removing her from the situation. Notice that the teacher warned the child only once and then carried out her warning. Some teachers wrongfully insert a second, third, or fourth warning that goes something like this: "Remember what I said about throwing sand?" or "If you do that one more time . . ." Once the child is removed, you need to redirect the child to another activity or require her to sit next to you (or in the time-out chair). Always accompany your withdrawal of privileges with a clear-cut method of getting them back. In this instance, you may wish to say, "When you think you can keep the water in the water table, tell me, and I will let you go back." When the child goes back, you must be ready to reinforce her desirable behavior: "Now you are playing well, I'm very proud of you!"

In summary, preschool classrooms reflecting the behavior modification approach to assisting social-emotional development would employ these basic principles:

1. identify the behaviors to be reinforced;
2. determine the appropriate reinforcer (undesirable behaviors should not be reinforced);
3. develop a system of implementation;
4. reinforce or ignore behaviors as they occur; and
5. periodically evaluate progress toward desired goals.

Although not as widely accepted as the democratic approach, behavior modification nevertheless does contribute positive practices that we might use as part of our democratic system. For example, behaviorists insist that children be made aware of what is acceptable and what is not, that desired behavior tends to be repeated if it is rewarded with sincerity, and that we must observe children carefully for possible clues as to the causes of certain behaviors. However, critics point out that there are enough shortcomings to the behaviorist system as a whole to prevent them from using it. Among their arguments are the following:

1. The approach works better with individuals than with entire classes, so it cannot be used as a whole system.
2. The use of reinforcers is seen as manipulative and impersonal.
3. The effects of ignoring children and using practices such as "time out" may be negative in the long run.
4. Teachers may be tempted to utilize techniques of punishment. Even though behaviorists do not openly advocate punishment as a favorable practice, it is implied as a tool that might be used.

Modeling

Some preschool educators prefer to combine strong features from each of these major contrasting philosophies. For example, inherent in the beliefs of both Freud and Erikson is the idea of *identification*. Identification is a method of solving crises or conflicts by following an adult model who shows an ability to make successful life adjustments. The young child, for example, first identifies with parents because of their continual presence, but as he grows older, he seeks other significant adults to emulate. As the child's horizons widen further, he has additional opportunities to observe and *imitate* the different people he meets.

A. Bandura and R. Walters (1963) concentrated on this imitation feature and formulated a theory of socialization that stresses that the acquisition of prosocial or antisocial behaviors comes about not primarily through internal motives but through behavioristic principles of extrinsic environmental stimuli, especially *modeling*. When children imitate the behavior of an adult model, they frequently are rewarded, particularly if the behavior is approved. If children are exposed to aggressive models, for example, they will likely be aggressive in their behaviors; if they are exposed to helping models, they will likely become helping, caring people. If a child sees that a behavior is successful for someone else, he is likely to try that behavior for himself. And, if the child is rewarded for exhibiting that behavior, he will be inclined to repeat it.

Two examples illustrate this concept. First, consider the child who uses vulgar expressions in your child-care facility. He may have heard his parents and other adults using these words and was looked upon as being cute or amusing when he repeated them. The amused recognition of his language was a reward to the child and encouraged him to repeat the behavior. He may not have been aware of their meaning, but he repeated the words because they were positively reinforced. Second, consider Ricky, who comes from a home environment where help is constantly extended to those in need. When another child spilled his paint on the floor, Ricky was there with a mop to help clean up. The teacher recognized Ricky's effort by giving him a warm smile and thanks for a job well done. In both examples, children repeated model behavior that was rewarded, although the behaviors range from undesirable to desirable in most instances. The process of imitating behavior is not extremely complex, but it does help to explain further the many influences that account for the social-emotional development of children. Keep in mind, of course, that a portrait of the complex social-emotional world of the child painted by only one artist can be very restrictive and distorted. The key to choosing one method or combination of methods is to understand the children in your care, to establish limits that are fair and reasonable, and to extend firm and consistent intervention whenever any child goes beyond the limits.

Very few persistent social-emotional problems will be solved, however, if you do not develop a plan that is consistent with parents' actions so that the home interaction patterns parallel those of the school. Most parents are willing to cooperate in such a venture and to establish parent–child relationships similar to the teacher–child relationship. This home–school connection is essential to reinforcement of your practices since the parent–child relationship is normally far deeper than the teacher–child relationship.

Strong parent–child ties may at times cause problems, however, for they sometimes prevent parents from perceiving a situation with the same objectivity as you. For example, some parents in your child-care facility may become upset because they want a program stressing group conformity in behaviors while you value individual pursuits more highly. In these instances, you need to resolve the differences by thoroughly discussing them in a professional manner. In other words, explain your philosophy of social-emotional development so that the parents can see the value of your beliefs. They need to understand your position completely so that their strong concerns can be alleviated. Also, remember that your discussion with the parents must be a two-way process. Listen to what they have to say—perhaps their mode of operation is based on deep convictions, such as cultural expectations, very different from your own. In these cases, you must take the time to understand and respect the parents' concerns; a quick resolution is rarely possible. Instead of forcing your beliefs on the parents and risking alienating them and their community, try to empathize with their position and work out an amicable agreement.

This takes skill to accomplish, but you won't win them over with a "take it or leave it" attitude, and you can't provide the best situation for their children if you can't offer the type of program you think is most professionally sound—it's a real dilemma. Take the case of young Charles, for example. Charles was brought up in a rough neighborhood, and was taught by his parents to fight whenever possible to protect his possessions. Naturally, when playing in the child-care setting, Charles frequently protected his toys and games with physical force. Concerned for the safety of the other children, Charles's teacher approached his parents. The parents refused to support any of the teacher's suggestions for changing Charles's behavior because they felt it was a necessary quality for survival in their neighborhood. Thoroughly perplexed, the teacher realized that any techniques used in school would not be carried through in the home so she decided that her responsibility would be to do the best possible job at school. Whenever Charles resorted to punching or hitting, she would immediately step in and sternly state, "I cannot allow you to hit other children in school." Respecting the parents' feelings, the teacher did not warn the child that his behaviors were wrong in *all* situations, but she did communicate the limits of his behavior in the classroom in a firm, direct way. Become familiar with the various techniques of parent–teacher cooperation, for a partner-type relationship between parent and teacher is essential to solving social-emotional problems and helping a child grow.

SOME FINAL THOUGHTS

According to an old saying, two of the most enduring gifts a teacher can give to a child are roots and wings. What do the gifts involve?

Consider the profiles of these two children as we determine a suitable answer to the question. First, let us consider Monica, age five. She is attending kindergarten, where she seems to thrive. She appears to be the most intelligent youngster there, although she has no more native intelligence than the others in her class. She is openly responsive to the teacher's questions and comments, eagerly offering her own responses even if they are only guesses. She meets every daily opportunity with enthusiasm and persistence. If something fails, Monica freely asks the teacher for help. Likewise, she takes pride in her accomplishments. For example, Monica is proud that she has just learned to skip across the room with no help. Monica openly converses with her peers and with the teacher, showing growing competence each day.

Holly, also age five, is not progressing very well in kindergarten. Although she appears to be one of the least intelligent children in class, Holly has as much native ability as the others. She never volunteers to answer questions and often shrugs her shoulders when asked questions by her teacher. Holly hesitates to try new things and often performs those tasks she does try with apprehension of failing. She has few friends and becomes shy and withdrawn whenever involved in group activities. Holly appears more content to be a spectator than a participant. Holly and Monica are thoroughly different from each other, although the differences are not in native ability.

The differences in these two children are more accountable to social and emotional factors than they are to native factors. Monica is confident and self-assured. She has a positive view of herself and those around her. She looks at life as an adventure and believes she can achieve through effort. Holly, on the other hand, is filled with self-doubt and apprehension. She has no confidence in those around her and expects failure when she attempts new tasks. She does not feel she can achieve because she is not as competent as the others.

Why do some children become Hollys and others become Monicas? Most early childhood educators today, especially those associated with the work of Burton White, feel that early experiences during infancy and young childhood play an important role. What kinds of early experiences are we talking about? First, we must provide quality interactions as well as a close, warm relationship with adult and child. Second, we must provide a stimulating environment, where children have the freedom to explore within limits. And, third, we must stimulate the children with many opportunities for play. Basically, the charge to preschool teachers is to create an environment that responds to the child in ways that encourage the development of Monicas rather than Hollys.

As you face the challenges of daily interaction with youngsters, try to have a sense of balance. Although most of your days will be filled with joy and the pleasant reward of watching children respond to your efforts with enthusiasm and glee, you must be ready to accept the fact that all days will not be as carefree as you hoped they would. Don't become discouraged if your classroom isn't perfect every day. We all have days when things do not go the way we want. Our moods, home situation, the weather, and many other influences affect our routine, as well as the child's. When we allow such events to affect our classroom disposition, minor problems tend to compound themselves. Keep a realistic outlook and a faithful confidence in yourself and your children.

Chapter 5

DEFINING PLAY

Providing for Many Play Opportunities

When I started working at my child's cooperative day-care center, I was dismayed by the lack of "structure." Each week I came with activities, projects, and worksheets to keep fingers busy and territorial and toy fights to a minimum. I was disappointed when the children preferred to play independently or changed my ideas to suit their purposes.

Over the years I have mellowed. The children have helped me, and I have learned much from watching and listening to them. I now try to enter their world whenever possible, instead of imposing my world on them. I see more creative learning result from the children's games and their own ideas for projects than from most of the pre-packaged, child-guidance, store-bought, or parent-made "let's learn" ideas. I've watched them experience joy, sadness, anger, aggression, and compassion as they share their fantasies.

These children have had the freedom of time and space to pursue their own ideas. Consequently, they "play with" any idea or suggestion from grownups and have often expanded a single suggestion into a whole afternoon of play. Cut and pasted pictures of ships, sea creatures, and pirates have led to making eyepatches, hats with skulls and crossbones, and to hours of treasure hunts and sea adventures.

I feel sad that when my child enters school his playtime will be more structured, ordered, or even missing. Panel members share my concern about play in our schools. Valerie Suransky writes in her book, *The Erosion of Childhood* (1982), that childhood is a natural phase of life, "but the particular forms of childhood created through the social ideology of "schooling" embedded in early childhood institutions have, in many ways, eroded that life phase. . . ." Suransky thinks that preschools often do not permit children to play or even work in a meaningful way; *process* becomes subordinate to *producing* artifacts, and space, time, and toys are often rigid and one-dimensional. [Strother, 1982, p. 1]

The concern of D. B. Strother for providing free play in early childhood settings mirrors the extremes of reaction many have associated with the process of _play_ over the years. For some, play is considered the most valued aspect of childhood, while for others, play is regarded apathetically or even aversively. In order to clarify this polarization, go back to your own childhood or recall the activities of youngsters you are able to observe. Most of you will visualize opportunities such as climbing trees, jumping in leaf piles, zooming around the house imitating a race car, rocking a "baby" to sleep in the cradle, molding a chunk of mud or dough into a "pie" or "cake," building the tallest "skyscraper" in the world, or staging a _Star Wars_ battle with friends. Can you recall how you did those things "just for the fun of it"? These are probably among the childhood memories you cherish most. If so, you may wonder why, if something is that prized and so much fun, some people view it as a frivolous and time-wasting activity?

Perhaps the most common reason for such feelings can be tied to the historical influence of the work ethic. This ethic implied that anything associated with fun was not work. And, since work was valued highly, something that was fun could not be valuable or necessary. Because the primary purpose of our schools was to instruct, play was interpreted as something that really didn't matter too much. This attitude regarding the value of play may even be seen today in some parents of preschool youngsters in your classroom. They may oppose play activity because they see your role as teaching their children how to count and say the alphabet, not to "waste" their children's educations on something they could do at home on Saturday or Sunday. One group of parents, for example, became so apathetic toward a start-of-the-morning free play hour in their children's nursery school that they consistently brought their children to school up to a half-hour late because the youngsters "weren't missing anything." Their pattern changed, however, once the teacher renamed the period a "work hour." The children arrived on time each day because of the new emphasis. Even though the children continued doing the same activities, the parents felt better because their suspicious view of "fun" at school was eliminated by the change (Riley, 1973).

A second factor contributing to a negative view of play in an early childhod setting is that the direct benefit of instruction in reading or spelling is fairly clear for most educators and parents to see, but what children learn through play is not as obvious. Until a few years ago, educators even became apologetic in their efforts to justify the existence of play in their programs. Instead of using the term _play_ to describe the children's activity, they substituted phrases such as "exploring the physical features of objects." Instead of "playing with a leaf," children were "exploring the physical features of a leaf."

Before we continue, we must examine what we mean by the term _play_. Of all the aspects of this book, this challenge of defining play is perhaps the greatest, because play is such an integral part of every child's life. It is natural, enjoyable, voluntary, spontaneous, and nongoal directed. It is important to emphasize this nongoal directed aspect since, once we begin to assign goals to the children's play and make play a goal-directed activity, the act becomes work. For example, scrubbing the snack table may have a definite goal associated with the activity—to clean the table—and is defined as work. However, the free use of dress-up clothes in the dramatic play center has no preconceived goal for the youngsters and is defined as play. Despite this fact, play does result in very valuable outcomes. It helps children clarify and master many fundamental aspects of development in all basic areas: physical, intellectual, social, and emotional. In the physical realm, play develops the large muscles as children lift blocks, ride trikes, dig with shovels, climb ladders, or throw balls. It develops small muscles as the children cut with scissors, draw

Figure 5-1   *The many contributions of play to the total development of the child*

with crayons, paint with brushes, complete puzzles, or button, lace, zipper, and tie articles of clothing. Play develops intellectual skills as children share and communicate thoughts through language; examine color, shapes, sizes, and relationships through block play, sand play, painting, and other experiences; make decisions and solve problems; and begin to sense the difference between fantasy and reality. Play develops social skills when numbers of children become involved in an activity. Whenever one child becomes involved with another, that child must learn how to be accepted, how to get along with the other so that everyone enjoys the activity, how to give and take, and how to develop empathy for and a consideration of others. Finally, the emotional realm is enhanced as the children learn to express, control, and manage their feelings; play out tensions, frustrations, and fears; or, simply, take comfort in knowing that it's okay to "act like a child."

Play reflects more than any of these separate aspects alone (see Figure 5-1). One separate play activity—block play, for example—benefits the child in more areas than a singular area such as physical development. All aspects are interwoven in the child's play experience and become separated only when play is analyzed for academic purposes and broken down into its components. For example, let us continue our examination of block play for the purpose of illustrating some of the benefits derived by the children in each realm of the activity.

- *Physical:* Large muscle—lifting, stacking, pushing, pulling, climbing
  Small muscle—manipulating toy cars or trucks; cutting a construction paper road

- *Intellectual:* perceiving size relationships; recognizing similarities and differences among shapes; counting similar items; perceiving length differences; discovering balance; noticing weight variances

- *Social:* sharing responsibility; coordinating efforts; cooperating
- *Emotional:* relieving strong emotion such as jealousy by knocking down her own tower; gaining pleasure by completing an enjoyable activity

Play begins with the exploratory behavior of infants and continues as a central part of our lives even into adulthood as we become involved in our competitive games or recreational pursuits. Although its basic characteristics change as we get older, the enjoyment of play doesn't change. Youngsters do not enjoy competition nor do they pursue play for its recreational value alone. Play is necessary in the lives of youngsters and is a vital component of their development. And, true play occurs only when children are active and are given some degree of freedom. In fact, Jerome Bruner (1975) has stated that "play is . . . the principal business of childhood" (p. 83).

DEVELOPMENTAL STAGES OF PLAY

According to the available research on play, there are two major categories, or dimensions, of play. The *social dimension* deals with the ways children become more and more collaborative and cooperative as they begin playing with parents and gradually learn to plan and interact with others. The *content dimension* refers to the composition of play, or what children play with or at, such as sand, blocks, or serving tea. The key point to remember about those two dimensions is that they each are developmental, meaning that the patterns of play enjoyed at infancy develop into new patterns as children grow older and participate in play experiences. But the earlier patterns do not disappear as new behaviors emerge. The new patterns do not enhance the earlier ones; they bring maturity to children's play as new experiences are encountered.

The Social Dimension

Perhaps the most time-honored view of play is Mildren Parten's description of social play during the early childhood years. In her classic study, Parten (1932) discovered that social participation among two- to five-year-olds increases with the child's age through six separate stages of development, beginning with a desire to play alone and growing into a desire to play and cooperate with others.

1. *Unoccupied behavior.* The children are not actually playing, but they occupy themselves by watching anything of momentary interest. When nothing interests the children, they lull around, play with their own bodies, follow an adult, or simply sit in one spot glancing around the room. (pre-two-year-olds)

2. *Onlooker behavior.* One child spends his time watching the other children play. He may talk to the others, ask them questions, or give suggestions, but he does not enter into the play situation itself. This stage differs from the preceding one in that the child is specifically observing a group of children at play rather than anything that happens to be exciting at the moment. (two-year-olds)

3. *Solitary play.* The child actually engages in play activity, but by herself. She may choose toys that are different from those used by the children within speaking distance and makes no effort to move near to the others. She pursues her own activity without concern for what others are doing. (two- to two-and-one-half-year-old children)

4. *Parallel play.* The child still plays by himself, but deliberately chooses a toy

or activity that will bring him among the other children where he can enjoy other children's company. He may choose a toy that is like those the other children are using but plays with it the way he wants, not as the others may be playing. Likewise, he does not try to influence or modify the play of the children near him. He plays near to, rather than with, the other children. (two-and-one-half- to three-and-one-half-year-old children)

5. *Associative play.* The child begins to play with other children in groups. There is borrowing and loaning of play materials; following one another with wagons or trains; and mild attempts to control who may or may not play in the group. All the group members engage in a similar activity, but there is no organization of the activity around any specific purpose, material, or individual. Therefore, a group of children may flock together in the sandbox, each doing her own activity. The children do not subordinate their individual interests to those of the group; each child plays as she wishes. The interest is obviously in developing interpersonal associations rather than on the play activity itself. (three-and-one-half- to four-and-one-half-year-old children)

6. *Cooperative play.* The child plays in a group that is organized for some specific purpose. That purpose may be to make something, to dramatize situations of adult or group life, or to play a formal game. Regardless of the purpose, the major social significance is that there is a marked sense of group membership. (four-and-one-half-year-old and onward)

Parten's research has received great interest since the 1930s and has resulted in a number of subsequent studies, some supporting her findings and others challenging them. One of the most interesting aspects of current research into Parten's work is the finding that three- and four-year-olds in today's society dis-

Play fascinates young children and involves them in naturally enjoyable activity for long periods of time.

play significantly more unoccupied, solitary, and onlooker activity and significantly less associative and cooperative play than Parten's children (Barnes, 1971). Reasons for such change are not clear, but some have cited cultural and social-class differences over the years. For those researchers who have supported Parten's classifications of play, some have questioned her conclusion that solitary play is less mature than succeeding kinds. They argue that the child who plays alone may be exhibiting very mature behavior; independence can be seen not as poor social adjustment but as a sign of growing independence and maturity. In light of these new developments, therefore, the traditional application of Parten's categories needs to be reconsidered. We must be aware that children's play progresses from playing alone to playing with others; however, as children develop increasing social maturity, they do not outgrow their need for solitary, individual play.

Generally, very young children may or may not want to become involved with others as they play with a watering can, wagon, doll, stick, or truck. But, as they seek to extend the possibilities inherent in their play, youngsters eventually look for other children to play with.

These significant peers are very important to children because only they can share the imaginative thinking so much a part of the early years. Do adults understand that the empty orange crate is really a race car, that the pile of leaves is obviously a nest of baby birds, or that the mud patty is the juiciest, tastiest cherry pie ever made? This "private" world of make-believe appears to be the exclusive property of children. The line between reality and fantasy is a very flexible division for the very young, and they move back and forth very freely. For this reason, youngsters bring wide ranges of behavior to their play situations. They may become mommies, daddies, babies, mail carriers, firefighters, barking dogs, or elephants, all on the same morning. This reality-fantasy play constitutes a serious effort on the part of young children to explain this new environment of which they are now such an integral part.

As children become increasingly aware of their environment, they begin to realize that others must be involved in their play activity if that environment is to be portrayed most effectively and efficiently. Think how limited our "firefighter" would be if there were no "kitty" on top of a burning building to save, or how restricted our "baby birds" would be if there were no "momma" or "pappa" bird to feed them their "worms." Such a need for playmates must be met in the early childhood setting. However, these play opportunities may present critical interpersonal conflicts as the children stubbornly refuse to participate in ways their companions deem as suitable. For example, Kacie, who had been content for weeks to be Nikki's "mommy" now finds it more attractive to move away from the housekeeping center and move on to the block center where she sets up shop as a gasoline station attendant. Nikki, sensing the loss of a crucial play partner, pleads with Kacie, "But I *need* a mommy. The baby *needs* her mommy!" and breaks down into tears.

The teacher must meet the needs of both children. In such situations you must apply one of the many suggestions offered in Chapters 3 and 4 for leading young children. During play youngsters learn to give and take, solve conflicts, and perceive things from others' points of view. Your leadership in this area is critical, for inherent in the idea of social growth through play is the children's ability to learn about their place in the world from each other. They must learn how much to expect from others and how much of their own personal desire they will need to compromise in order to become a functioning group member. To learn these concepts is not a major problem for many, but it may be painful for some children. Conflicts will arise over play areas, sharing or using equipment, or how group projects can best be carried out. You must be able to help children solve such conflicts and work toward acceptable group behavior. The following are examples of typical play conflicts in early childhood settings with recommended solutions for each. Think of how you would solve each conflict before you read my suggested approach.

SITUATION 1

A group of four-year-olds eagerly stands in line to take turns on the playground sliding board. Suddenly, Chuck shoulders in ahead of everyone so that he can be the next to go. Lawrence, Chuck's best friend and the second child in line, blurts out an extreme threat of violence: "You old meanie. Get back or I'm gonna chop your head off!"

SOLUTION

Arguments and fights frequently occur over taking turns. This can happen with playground equipment or with classroom toys. Some children, like Chuck, operate as though they should be first with everything and as though they "own" all the toys and equipment. You must help Chuck realize that he needs to share and take turns. For example, you can say to him, "I understand how much you want to slide, but you've just had a turn. It's now time for Lawrence to go. You wait with me and I'll make sure you get another turn."

Another theme in this situation has to do with children using certain words for their shock value. When confronted with social difficulties, some children resort to intimidating insults that often involve mutilation of a peer's body parts. At the preschool age, children are becoming increasingly aware of their bodies and frequently become concerned with keeping them together. Therefore, when faced with frustrating situations, as Lawrence was, children will react in ways that threaten the body of the aggressor. The reaction of some teachers in this situation might be, "Lawrence, I'm surprised at you. If you can't say something nice, don't say it at all." Such a reaction, however, may not be constructive and, in fact, may cause further interpersonal conflicts. Instead, you should simply let the child know that you understand his feelings and that you're willing to listen to him talk about what made him angry or what he thinks can be done about it. "I know how much you like to slide. You don't like it when someone jumps in line in front of you," is a much more effective approach. The child knows you sincerely understand his concerns and that you have confidence in his ability to make appropriate social adjustments.

SITUATION 2

Three children are busily working together making a snowman after a newly fallen snow. Laura walks over to the area and begins to join in. Alice immediately runs over to Laura and complains, "This is our snowman and you can't play with us. We hate you. We hate you." Laura rushes over to the teacher and tearfully cries, "Alice hates me. She won't let me play."

SOLUTION

Most teachers expect youngsters to allow others to share equipment and to join their play. However, frequently you will find two or three children who enjoy going off by themselves for a period of time to work on a special project in their own way. They cannot tolerate interruptions by their peers, and their emotions often flare when such circumstances occur. You must respect the right of the small group to pursue its goal, and diplomatically divert the offended child's attention to another area.

You may say, "Alice, Cathy, and Betsy are working on a very special snowman. They don't hate you—they are just upset because they wanted to build it by themselves. Let's go over here and ask Jeanie if she'd like to build a snowman with you."

SITUATION 3

A group of four-year-old girls enjoys playing with the variety of dolls in the doll corner. When Brad walks over and attempts to join them, Mary Ann complains, "Get out of here, Brad. We're playing with dolls and you can't because boys aren't supposed to. Go away!" Brad runs to the teacher and says, "I want to play dolls. The girls won't let me."

SOLUTION

As you watch this situation unfolding, you may probably begin to examine your own feelings about sexism. You might recall other situations in which girls were excluded—from those "masculine" activities such as working with woodworking tools or digging in the dirt. In this situation, the girls have turned the tables, and, in effect, are protecting "their turf" as fervently as the boys protected "their" trucks and tools in other situations. In essence, the boys and girls have subconsciously established separate territorial rights to activities associated with stereotyped sex roles. What do you do for Brad, who wishes to play in the doll corner?

You must realize that it is perfectly normal for children to explore activities and materials in the preschool regardless of the sex stereotype with which the materials have been traditionally associated. Through their play, they enjoy trying different roles and pretending to be mothers or fathers, or boys or girls, regardless of their sex. A boy may enjoy dressing like the *mother, a girl like the father; a boy may enjoy serving tea, while the girl may enjoy sitting on the chair reading the evening paper. This is all very common and very healthy. Allow children to explore and try out these roles.*

In this situation, it may be wise for you to suggest to the girls that it is all right for boys to play with dolls. You could say, "Brad would like to play with the dolls. There are enough dolls for everyone. Boys like to play with dolls, too. Let's help Brad find a doll he would like." In the same way, you must make sure the boys don't exclude girls from traditionally male stereotyped activities.

SITUATION 4

Most children in this room for four-year-olds seem to enjoy playing with one another. One day, however, while a group is busily digging a hole with shovels, Billy suddenly walks over and hits Amy because she refused to allow him to use her shovel. The teacher intervenes and explains to Billy that he must wait his turn. He lashes out shockingly at the teacher, "I hate you. You're a mean old rotten egg [or worse]."

SOLUTION

You must remember that a frustrating social experience may trigger a personal verbal attack, often with a special vocabulary, sometimes of the four-letter variety. Such circumstances are especially common when the teacher has not yet had ample opportunity to build up satisfying social relationships with all members of the group. It is a rare three- or four-year-old, however, who does not develop a friendly relationship with the teacher after a short period of time.

Some teachers react to statements like Billy's with surprise and displeasure, and may express their disapproval by saying something like, "You should never speak to me like that again. You're a naughty boy." Such reactions, however, do not help build positive relationships between the teacher and child, and, in fact, may intensify the child's practice of using such language. The best way to deal with such behavior is to accept it casually—it does not signal the child's moral breakdown, but is merely a frustrated

attempt at handling interpersonal conflicts. Often, such language can be ignored and, when the child senses that it has lost its shock appeal, it soon disappears. However, in this instance, Billy's physical action of hitting Amy, combined with his verbal aggression, called for some positive action from the teacher. You should remove Billy from the area and take him to a quiet area. Then you should firmly explain to him, "It hurt Amy when you hit her. You mustn't hit other children. You must remember that other children would like the toys just as much as you do and you must wait your turn." Then, addressing the verbal attack on you, say, "You're angry at me, Billy, but I like you. When you feel better, come back with the others and I'll help you find a shovel. Maybe after a while you'll learn to like me, too."

SITUATION 5

This classroom for four-year-olds is fairly congenial and a cooperative attitude seems to prevail. Occasionally problems surface, but they nearly always work themselves out. However, one child, James, seems to be always singled out as the object of excessive teasing and taunting. He apparently doesn't have the courage to stand up for what is his and often reacts immaturely to social situations. One day, James falls while running on the playground and tears a small hole in the knee of his trousers. Trying to suppress tiny sobs, James looks embarrassed as some children begin to chant, "James is a crybaby! James is a crybaby!" James runs to the teacher, tears streaming, wounded more by the ridicule than by the small bruise on his knee.

SOLUTION

In almost any group of three-, four-, or five-year-olds, one child will occasionally be singled out for excessive teasing. This child is one who reacts passively or babyishly to many situations. Often, the child comes from a home where he received an overabundance of strong affection, and where his every need and demand were met. As he grew up, he found that continued displays of babyish behavior made him the center of attraction, and adults thought him cute and amusing. Therefore, long after he should have left his immature behavior behind, he continues to entertain and delight those who reinforce such behaviors.

Now, in the school situation, James becomes confused and frustrated when other children react negatively toward behaviors that win him pampering treatment at home. Your role in such situations must be to attempt to help the unassertive child move beyond his babyish reactions, while helping all the children realize that it is their responsibility to treat each other with consideration. Often the immature child presents problems that are almost impossible for teachers to cure. The trouble may have begun very early and may now extend too deeply. You must recognize such handicaps, but be willing to do what this teacher did to help James:

1. *She was a giving person, but she wouldn't allow the child to "push." When she couldn't give James all he wanted, she said no in a firm and assertive way. She didn't lay down the law harshly, however, because it would only have led to further disruptive behaviors.*

2. *She met James's frequent outbursts by removing him from situations and inviting him to return when he was ready not to disturb others. "You must not take another child's crayons while he's using them, James. Wait here until you're ready to share the materials."*

3. *She met his temper tantrums with patient understanding. She stopped him firmly and let him know she meant business. "James, you must stop that," or "When you get done yelling, you can finish your picture," are comments she frequently made. The teacher was careful, however, to stay away from "bribe" statements such as, "If you don't stop kicking your feet, you won't be able to play on the playground later."*

4. *James's desire to get everything he wanted was allayed somewhat as the teacher helped him share and turned his attention to other things. For example, she would say, "You cannot have the hammer now, James. Mar-*

tha is using it. I'll help you use the saw while you're waiting."

5. *The teacher watched James very closely to make sure he would meet situations only when he was ready for them.*

SITUATION 6

Four children are busily painting in the art center; the teacher is standing by the block corner watching with obvious pleasure. All the children in the room seem thoroughly engrossed in separate little projects and are paying little attention to each other. Richard, who has just completed his picture, turns with excitement to the teacher to share what he has done. Just as he is about to approach her, however, he stumbles into Francine's block city. As her city crumbles, Francine's contentment turns to anger. With tears streaming, she hits Richard with a solid blow and exclaims, "I hate you!" Confused, Richard begins to cry and soon tears and sobs from both parties fill the air.

SOLUTION

Accidents frequently cause strong anger and disagreement among young children. In this case, Richard's excitement led to an incident where he destroyed Francine's block city without meaning to. In these instances, the teacher should assume the role of an interpreter rather than that of a disciplinarian. She must help the children understand that the circumstances caused irritating results, but that these results were unavoidable. She must help them perceive the intent of the incident and lead them to respond to it rather than to the actions.

For example, you could have squelched Richard's enthusiasm by rushing to Francine's aid and stating, "Richard, take your time and watch where you're going. You ruined Francine's block city." Instead, you should try to help both children cope with the situation by saying to them, "Francine, Richard didn't mean to knock your blocks down. He was just coming to show me something and forgot all about your blocks. Let's both calm down a little so we can be friends again." Normally, the children will work things out for themselves. As you place Rich-

Young children learn to join together and cooperate with one another in play pursuits. However, sometimes conflict arises.

ard's picture in a special area of the room, you can watch him and Francine busily at work rebuilding the block city.

The Content Dimension

The social dimension of play does not explain by itself all of the major facets of the play experience. We must now examine what children play with or at—the content dimension. As described earlier, play enables children to transform or explain their world; they are communicating a level of understanding as they "fit" their play to the degree of experience they bring to it. If they have had very limited experiences, children will not have rich play opportunities because they will have very little to express through their play. Conversely, children having full, varied life experiences will find much to play with or at. The content dimension of play, therefore, is a reflection of the experiences children have had throughout their lives, beginning in infancy. What are the kinds of play children normally enjoy at various developmental stages? Perhaps the best way to answer this important question is to combine the common features of two of the most currently popular explanations of the content dimension of play—Piaget (1962) and

Smilansky (1968). The resulting explanation groups the content dimension into three basic categories: *sensorimotor play, symbolic play,* and *games with rules* (see Figure 5-2).

Sensorimotor Play This form of play begins early during infancy and continues as a dominant form of play up until about age two. The term *sensorimotor* was chosen for this initial phase because it describes the two major kinds of play experiences infants enjoy— *sensory* experiences and *motor* experiences. Butler, Gotts, and Quisenberry (1978) describe these two play activities as follows:

- *Sensory play:* emphasizes the processes of (1) sucking and mouthing (fingers, toys, or anything else they can bring to their mouths); (2) making sounds and listening; and (3) gazing at and following objects visually, including their hands and feet.

- *Motor play:* emphasizes the simple movements of infancy that result in (1) control of grasping and handling objects (fine motor skills); (2) physical mobility, from sitting up to walking (gross motor skills); and (3) exploration and knowledge of one's own body.

This interest in using the senses and motor skills does not stop when the child becomes a toddler, but merely becomes refined to accommodate new mental processes. Muscular activity and sensory awareness cannot be separated from other play characteristics during toddlerhood but actually become a framework upon which those new play orientations are built. The banging together of pots and pans by a nine-month-old, therefore, serves to stimulate sensory play (making sounds and listening) and motor play (grasping and handling objects). But, in addition, the skills gained by repeating such action will help the child to gain confidence of his own abilities and eventually lead to the physical and sensory exploration of blocks and other manipulative mate-

GAMES WITH RULES
(5 YEARS AND UP)

COOPERATION AND
PLANNING TOWARD
GROUP-ORIENTED
GOALS

SYMBOLIC PLAY
(2-5 YEARS)

INCREASED SKILL IN
USING PLAY MATERIALS;
DRAMATIC
PLAY BEGUN

SENSORIMOTOR PLAY
(0-2 YEARS)

SIMPLE MUSCULAR
ACTIVITY

Figure 5-2 *Developmental sequence of play*

rials during toddlerhood. Since sensorimotor play is most appropriately associated with physical and intellectual benefits, specific suggestions will be provided in Chapters 6 and 7.

Symbolic Play By the age of two, children still enjoy the pleasures associated with sensorimotor play, but they begin to move toward an interest in using simple play materials to construct or reproduce things they have experienced. The term *symbolic* refers to the use of objects or images for the purpose of integrating these new environmental experiences into their lives. For example, the child may handle an inanimate object such as a toy truck and transform it through imagination into a real truck struggling up a hill with a heavy payload. Thus, the interaction between the child and truck takes on a deeper meaning than simply the action involved in manipulating the truck for sensory or motor purposes. It becomes an avenue by which the child can show what he understands about his physical and social world. Likewise, dolls, blocks, and other materials help children develop a greater and more accurate understanding of their environment by allowing them to reproduce the realities of people, places, and events within their realm of experiences.

Typical symbolic play among young children involves experiential themes such as house, school, farm, zoo, doctor, dentist, place of worship, animals, community helpers (fire-fighter, police officer, sanitation worker, or street sweeper), construction workers, bus driver, bride and groom, television characters, and innumerable other possibilities. The variety and content of the children's play serve as valid indicators of the amount and quality of firsthand experiences provided the children in a setting. Children from a remote Kentucky mountain home could be expected to bring different content and materials to their play episodes than children from a city home exposed to artists, actors, and a variety of other people and things.

Games with Rules   According to Piaget and others, children remain content to express themselves through the vehicle of symbolic play during the preschool years and into the primary grades. As a matter of fact, it is not until about six or seven years of age that children leave the major thrust of symbolic play and begin to govern their activities with rules. The following example illustrates this transition: If we give a one-year-old a ball, she would roll it on the floor or grasp it (sensorimotor play); a three-year-old might place it on a pillow, lay on it and "pretend she is an eagle in her nest" waiting for the baby bird to hatch (symbolic play); a six-year-old, however, would probably gather a group of friends for a game regulated by an agreed-upon set of rules (game with rules). The rules are serious business for these youngsters and any violation is usually met with verbal abuse or even physical aggression by the others. Because children themselves begin to establish guidelines for the purpose of limiting their own behaviors, rather than having restrictions placed by others, games with rules are usually considered the highest form of play activity.

However, since we are primarily addressing children through the kindergarten level in this book, we will examine the teacher's role in providing for sensorimotor and symbolic play only. Your role in these areas is crucial

and goes far beyond the directing and controlling aspect discussed earlier. You must learn two very important skills: provide for play areas both inside and out; and supply the materials necessary for the children to bring out their ideas effectively.

PLAY DURING INFANCY

Every caretaker is eager to provide the best possible attention during the first years of life. Sensory experiences comprise one of the most important processes of early life and are characteristic of the activities caregivers need to stimulate through play. In an infant's first few weeks, even before he can grasp a toy, stimulation occurs through the senses of vision and hearing. Mobiles or objects hanging above the crib are excellent first playthings. Fasten the mobile so it won't fall and make sure there are no small removable parts for the baby to swallow. Babies prefer to gaze at faces; therefore, a mobile with pictures of faces on the bottom is a good choice. Also, babies enjoy mobiles with bright, contrasting colors or a variety of shapes. During these early days, infants are amused mainly through sensory stimulation. Tease the infant's senses; even the day-old child can follow moving objects, feel changes in temperature, and move the head in response to sounds. The joy of each new discovery is an exquisite sensation for infants.

Infant Play Activities

The following list offers some examples of what you might try. It is by no means complete, so look for activities in other sources and keep adding to your accumulation of ideas to use with infants.

- Rub smooth satin on the child's cheek.
- Tickle the baby's lips with a soft piece of terry cloth.

- Hold a favorite toy in front of the baby and encourage him to reach for it.

- Suspend a favorite toy above the baby with elastic so she can look at it, reach out and bat it, and watch it move.

- Get a toy that can be attached to a flat surface by means of a suction cup. Encourage the baby to reach for and grasp it.

- Hold the baby on your lap. Place a favorite squeaky toy in front of him so he must reach for it. Squeak the toy and reinforce the baby's efforts with praise and smiles.

- Occasionally place a brightly patterned sheet on baby's crib so he can be visually stimulated.

- Babies are attracted by bright objects. Move a bright object or penlight across the baby's line of vision until she follows the light with her eyes.

- Place a mirror above the child in the crib.

- Lay the baby on a variety of surfaces during feeding, changing, rest, or play.

- Provide toys with different kinds of surfaces, such as plastic, cloth, furry, soft, smooth.

- Stimulate the baby's hearing by tying a bell to his bootie or around his wrist, putting a rattle in his hand, setting a metronome near him, talking or singing, rustling paper near his ear, or playing soft music periodically.

- Say a series of babbles (*ma, pa, ba, ga*) so the child hears them easily. Say these sounds or the baby's name in various situations. Reward the baby's attempts to imitate you.

- Call the baby's name from the side of the crib opposite where she is looking. If she doesn't respond, gently turn her toward you and offer a bright smile.

- Say the baby's name to her over and over again. Sometimes sing it and some-times vary your pitch and inflection. Try to get her to look at you when you do this.

- Smile and talk as you hold the baby. Hold him about 12–18 inches from your face. Tickle him or toss him gently, trying to make him laugh and gurgle.

- Use a pull toy that makes some type of sound. Pull it slowly back and forth in front of the baby.

- Seat the child upright in a soft chair and support his head with pillows. Hold a toy or bright object in front of the baby and encourage him to initiate head support. Gradually reduce the support until you see how well the baby keeps his balance. Repeat the procedure.

- Place a soft, small object (sponge or soft cloth) in the baby's hand and wrap her fingers around it. Take your hand away. Repeat the procedure if she drops it. Then vary the texture of the objects placed into the baby's hand.

- Seat the child on your lap facing you and pull her up by having her grasp your fingers.

- Stand the baby on your lap and bounce her up and down, smiling and saying a series of babbles.

- Help the child to stand by placing her hands on the corners of the crib.

The Infant Setting

The physical setting in an infant-care center goes beyond the selection of toys and a provision for adequate sensorimotor activity. It includes the items you will need to complete the baby's clothing needs, feeding equipment, and other basic nursery needs. Some of these items may be donated by families or agencies, others may be gathered at used furniture shops, while yet others may be required to be brought by parents. Whatever the source, here is a checklist of things you will find to be basic to the physical welfare of infants in your care.

This baby is experiencing both sensory and motor play. Those play activities stimulate him and serve as solid foundations for future growth.

CLOTHING

- diapers (10–12 per day per baby)
- cotton shirts
- stretch suits
- waterproof pants
- socks or booties
- gown, sacque set, or kimono
- shoes (only to protect feet if walking)
- diaper pail

FURNITURE

- crib

  snugly fitting mattress

  siderails with childproof releases

  hardwood construction

  2-⅜-inch maximum space between rail slats

  safety bumper pads running around entire crib

plastic teething guard on top slats

crib sheets

waterproof mattress pads

crib blankets

comforter or quilt

- refrigerator
- clothing hamper
- changing table
- chest of drawers
- playpen (play yard)

  hinges that lock tightly

  firm floor support (foam pad)

  padded rims

  mesh netting

- infant seat
- portable baby swing
- toy storage box
- high chair

  strong tray latch

  crotch strap to prevent sliding

  adjustable footrest adaptable to growing child

  high, padded seatback for head support

  raised edge tray to catch spills

- stroller

  wide diameter wheels for stability

  padded seat

  shock-absorbing suspension

  easy-to-operate brakes (two brakes are preferable)

  no easily removed wingnuts or other easy-to-swallow parts

- walker

  long wheelbase to prevent tipping

  sturdy materials

  protection covering springs and hinges

- body carrier

well padded

adjustable

no sharp or protruding edges

- rocking chair

FEEDING

- presterilized nurser kits, or eight bottles per child and sterilizer kit
- bottle warmer
- baby dishes and utensils
- food strainer
- bibs
- food warmer

BATHING

- towels (3–4 per child)
- washcloths (3–4 per child)
- baby soap and shampoo
- brush and comb
- toiletries: moist towelettes, petroleum jelly, cream, powder, lotion
- cotton swabs
- baby nail scissors
- baby thermometer

If you reacted to this list of essentials for an infant-care center in a way similar to most who are considering the rapidly growing infant-care business, your first thoughts were probably, "The cost!" To get a good idea of exactly how much it would cost to provide for one infant for one year, including wardrobe, equipment, feeding, and other needs, we went to retailers, furniture manufacturers, and infant-care centers. Our best estimate is that an average start-up cost per infant per year in an adequate facility could add up to about $2000. Naturally, the cost would be lower if you require parents to supply certain clothing and nursery equipment or if you receive gifts and donations. However, the cost figure does serve as an indication of what to expect if you start from scratch and receive little or no outside financial or in-kind (material goods) help. If you are like most individuals interested in infant care, however, your decision to work in or operate such a facility is primarily a personal one, and only secondarily an economic decision.

You must be able to meet all of the needs required by infants, including the social needs of play. You must think not only about the amount of time you spend with an infant, but also about the quality of interactions you choose. Regardless of the number of activities you have in your repertoire, you can be successful only to the degree that you bring sensitivity and appropriate timing to the situation.

THE PLAY OF TODDLERS AND YOUNG CHILDREN

Having grown in life experiences and physical control, toddlers still are uncertain and relatively inexperienced in the social realm. Their growing physical skills permit toddlers to play by themselves for longer periods of time, but they still welcome and demand adult attention. Thus, many of the social games enjoyed during infancy continue into toddlerhood largely unchanged.

Even so, a new awareness that often ushers in an entirely new social play orientation develops during toddlerhood. That awareness has to do with noticing other children. For the first time, toddlers begin to realize that there are others in this world just like them and—to make sure their impressions are accurate—poke, prod, and touch their counterparts to see if they are correct. Imagine the thoughts rushing through one toddler's head as she meets another for the first time. She doesn't talk, but the touch and smile tell us that she just encountered a wondrous and amazing being. This apparent interest in other toddlers, however, seldom blossoms into enjoy-

able play. Seemingly content to play side by side, toddlers enjoy each other's company but still prefer to explore and examine the environment by themselves. They seem to be most interested in trying out their rapidly developing motor skills in frisky, spirited play. Because of their need to move about, toddlers cannot be expected to stay in one place very long. One minute they may be quietly playing with puppets and the next crawling gleefully through a crawling tunnel. Free, uninhibited play assumes an enormously important role in the lives of toddlers as they learn things about themselves that would not otherwise be learned so well. The entire center and outdoor play area become a stage for manipulation and experimentation that lead to new skills and understandings.

Since young children enjoy many of the same kinds of play activities found during toddlerhood, the actual materials and activities for both groups may be essentially the same. The major differences between the two groups lie in these general areas: (1) because toddlers are less socially mature, they will use the materials individually rather than in groups; and (2) toddlers use the materials more for their sensory pleasure and exploration rather than for more purposeful, guided reasons. Keeping these ideas in mind, you should provide many opportunities for spontaneous as well as planned periods of play. Children should be given plenty of time to play freely with materials or come together for specially organized play under the teacher's direction. Regardless of the form, opportunities for play must be provided at different levels to conform to the varying needs of all the children in your care.

SPONTANEOUS PLAY

Opportunities for free, spontaneous play should be provided daily in every childhood setting. One widely accepted method of planning for such play is to arrange the room into special play areas commonly referred to as *interest centers*. Generally, this method of organization suggests that equipment and supplies for any unique play activity be organized into special areas where that particular play could occur. A "block area," for example, would be cleared of all other materials and be set aside specifically for block play. Some of the more popular interest centers follow.

Dramatic Play

The most popular form of play during the preschool years is *dramatic play*. Children assume the roles of other people as they act out events experienced in their growing new world. This strong interest begins in toddlerhood with acting out home life events and gradually moves into dramatic depictions of the world at large. You may observe children assuming the various roles of the people they have seen: housewives, husbands (they still pretty much stereotype these roles regardless of social changes), doctors, nurses, gasoline station attendants, firefighters, police officers, construction workers, taxicab drivers, truck drivers, airplane pilots, or dentists. Children normally enjoy depicting roles in which specific, active functions are apparent rather than a role in which the person's role is somewhat general or sedentary; a lawyer or bookkeeper, for instance, would hold little appeal for dramatic play.

When they engage in dramatic play, youngsters enjoy putting themselves as completely as possible into their assumed roles. Simple costumes or props, therefore, often enhance their play: dressing up in other people's hats, jackets, or shoes; using a carpenter's tools; serving guests from a tea serving set; or listening to heartbeats with a real stethoscope. Many times, though, the youngster's creativity will overcome the lack of materials. A large box or crate may become a truck, a block serves as a horse, or a piece of rope

becomes a gasoline hose. The older the children, the greater their need for accurate representational materials. For example, a three-year-old "farmer" may seem perfectly content to allow blocks to represent animals or sticks to represent people. Four-year-olds would feel more comfortable as "farmers" with toy animals and perhaps some plastic food and a straw hat. Five-year-olds would most likely feel most satisfied only when provided a full supply of materials for the part they are playing. A word of caution, though: The emphasis on dramatic play does not switch to amateur theatricals as the children's needs for increasingly sophisticated play materials grow; the emphasis remains on imaginative, spontaneous play.

Dramatic Play Centers and Housekeeping Centers   While arranging dramatic play centers, teachers usually try to fight the tendency to supply the children with every piece of material needed to involve the youngsters in a role situation. Even five-year-olds must be encouraged to use inventive thought in adapting unrelated materials to suit new purposes. Teachers usually organize dramatic play centers according to one of these three basic plans:

1. Some teachers have only a permanent *housekeeping center* where the children are provided hats, dresses, vests, jackets, shoes, and a variety of other garments worn by household members. The children are encouraged to try on the clothes, regardless of sex, and to assume the roles of interest. Boys may become "mommies," and girls become "daddies"; even today, however, the youngsters appear to gravitate toward like-sexed roles. Luncheons, tea parties, baby's bath time, telephone calls, and even reenactments of unpleasant arguments involve the children. This fantasy outlet permits the children to reduce their intensity of emotion associated with real experiences or to redefine and

clarify the meanings of real-life experiences. In addition to the clothing, common household items make great vehicles for dramatic expression: old electric shaves, lunch boxes, pots and pans, sweepers, magazines, briefcases, alarm clocks, toasters, purses, clip-on earrings, and a variety of other easily obtained, inexpensive materials.

2. Other teachers have a permanent housekeeping center *and* a second dramatic play center that varies as the interests of the children change. In this changeable center, the children are provided with garments and props associated with particularly meaningful experiences. For example, your group may have recently visited the fire station, the children may have had regular medical exams, the children may be particularly interested in a popular movie or television show, or a special story may have created special interests in space exploration. The play materials in these special centers usually are not as plentiful as those in the housekeeping area, but they provide a nice variation for children who need and enjoy them.

3. Finally, some teachers prefer to gather a variety of dramatic play kits for the children and introduce them one at a time throughout the year, keeping only one center equipped at a time. A housekeeping center may be one of the possibilities, but it does not remain out for the entire year as it did in the previous examples. In this option the teacher observes the children's level of interest and varies the materials as the children's needs dictate.

Regardless of the organizational pattern you choose, it is important to arrange attractive, neat areas. Display the materials invitingly and hang the special costumes neatly so they can be easily seen. Children respond more positively to clean, fresh costumes. Whatever the design of the area at any one time, furniture and equipment should be child-size

whenever possible. The *housekeeping corner* generally includes a table and chairs; wooden kitchen equipment such as a stove, refrigerator, or sink; a wide selection of dolls; and cupboards containing cups, saucers, pots, spoons, pitchers, and so on. These materials do not need to be purchased—a little imagination turns orange crates into stoves or storage cabinets, and a little resourcefulness leads you to used and outgrown toys. The *dramatic play corner* offers children a wide variety of creative possibilities. Changeable items should be provided so that children can shift roles whenever they have such inclinations. In this area children can explore the lives of people in varying occupations and locations. For example, the following locations can be depicted with their equipment:

- *Ice cream store:* Ice cream scoops, empty ice cream containers, white aprons and caps, a table with chairs
- *Automobile repair shop:* Overalls, work caps, tools, hose for gasoline, miniature vehicles or crates to represent cars and trucks
- *Hamburger stand:* Aprons, caps, paper bags, napkins, fast food containers, pad and pencil, cash register, play money, trays
- *Hospital:* Doctor bag, stethoscope, bandages, doctor or nurse uniforms, bed, crutches
- *Tailor shop:* Table, measuring tape, variety of cloth, scissors, needle, thread, dolls to be fitted with clothes
- *Beautician parlor:* Hair curlers, aprons, shampoo and makeup bottles, hair dryer, old electric shaver, mirror
- *Bakery:* Cookie cutters, bowls, baker's apron and cap, flour sacks, rolling pin, pie tins, cash register, toy money

Of course, these are only a few of the dramatic play situations youngsters can get involved in. Other creative possibilities for role-

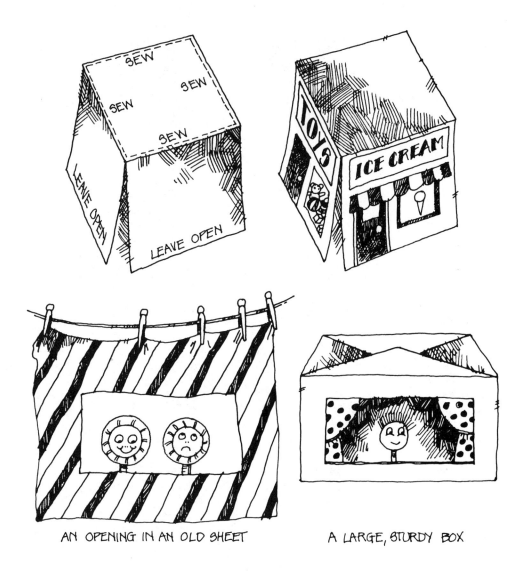

AN OPENING IN AN OLD SHEET   A LARGE, STURDY BOX

playing include: shoe repair persons, launderers, jewelers, service station attendants, firefighters, police officers, factory workers, secretaries, farmers, barbers, postal workers, race car drivers, and the like.

One interesting variation on this approach to the dramatic play corner is to invite your children to take turns making the dramatic play corner into an area that represents their lifestyle, hobby, interest, or fantasy by bringing in materials from home (see Figure 5-3). This activity offers a child a chance to share something personal about herself with the other children. Creative play is one of the most effective forms of children's communication.

In addition to the dramatic play materials discussed so far, teachers have traditionally supplemented their programs with other interesting dramatic activities, such as the following.

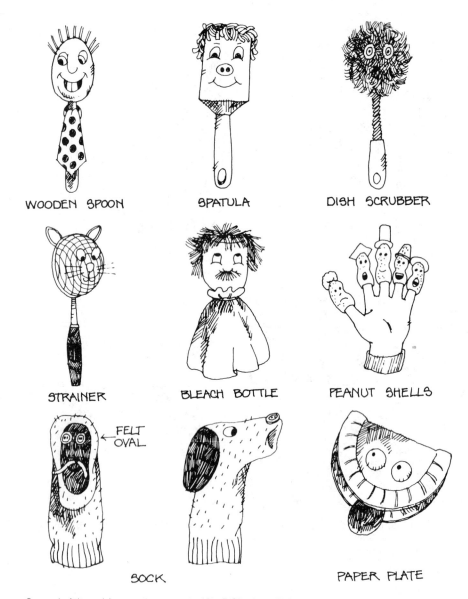

WOODEN SPOON   SPATULA   DISH SCRUBBER

STRAINER   BLEACH BOTTLE   PEANUT SHELLS

FELT ←OVAL

SOCK   PAPER PLATE

Several of these ideas were suggested by F. Charlene Fink.

TV Stars   Make a television set from a used packing box or look for a discarded television set from which the screen has been removed. Secure a large mirror to the inside of the set so that when the children look at the "screen" they see themselves as the actors or actresses.

Hide-a-House   Sew four pieces of an old sheet to a fifth one so that you have a large top-to-floor cover for a table. Draw different houses, stores, or buildings on the four side squares. The children can enter the structure through slits in the corner and assume any roles they desire.

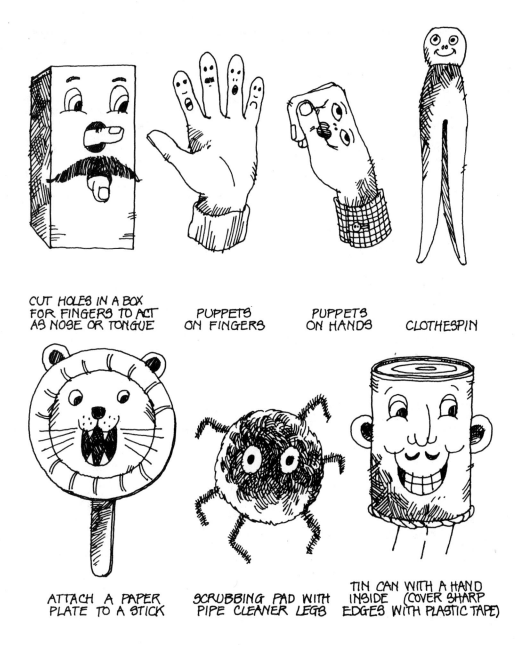

CUT HOLES IN A BOX
FOR FINGERS TO ACT
AS NOSE OR TONGUE

PUPPETS
ON FINGERS

PUPPETS
ON HANDS

CLOTHESPIN

ATTACH A PAPER
PLATE TO A STICK

SCRUBBING PAD WITH
PIPE CLEANER LEGS

TIN CAN WITH A HAND
INSIDE   (COVER SHARP
EDGES WITH PLASTIC TAPE)

Puppets

Still another major form of creative dramatic play, puppets, engage preschool children in individual or small group dramatizations. Whether commercially made or constructed by the children and the teacher, puppets pro-mote valuable play-oriented goals. Puppets can help children project their wildest thoughts into characters and make amazing ideas come true: Buildings fly, automobiles sing, and alligators disappear in front of our eyes. The magic ingredients for making puppets are all around the school, center, or home. Just look around

PUPPET-MAKING ACTIVITIES

Simple Hand Puppets

• Common household items such as wooden spoons, spatulas, dish mops, strainers, or hair brushes can be used to form the base for simple hand puppets. Decorate the items with wiggle eyes, yarn, felt, ribbon, sequins, pan scrubbers, and so on, and create a bunch of lovable characters for your classroom.

• A plastic detergent or bleach bottle makes a creative puppet head. Use an old mop head, yarn, or a discarded doll's wig for hair, a piece of cloth attached to the bottle's opening with a rubber band for a body, and paints or marking pens to create a face. Hold the bottle from underneath the body or by the bottle handle at the rear.

• Puppets with moving mouths are easily made by using a sock. Cut a slit through the toe of the sock and turn it inside out. Fold open the mouth and pin an oval piece of felt to the slit. Stitch the felt to the sock. Turn the sock right side out and add buttons, scraps of yarn, or fabric for facial features.

• Paper plates form the beginning of interesting puppet friends. Fold a plate in half and glue two Ping-Pong balls to the top. Decorate the paper plate creature with fabric, yarn, or paper. Operate the puppet by placing your fingers on the top of the plate and your thumb beneath.

Peanut Puppets

Carefully cut one end of the peanut shell away. Hopefully the peanuts will fall out—don't forget to eat them! Use paint or marking pens to draw the puppets' faces. Have the children place the puppets on their fingers and perform a peanut puppet production.

Other Puppet Ideas

• *Box puppets*—Use an empty box for this puppet. Draw a face on a piece of paper and cut it in half at the mouth. Glue the upper part of the face on the top half of the box and the lower part of the face on the bottom half. Operate the puppet by placing the hand in both halves of the box.

• *Paper bag puppets*—Draw the upper part of a face on the bottom of a bag and the lower part of the face on the side. Yarn may be glued on for hair.

• *Stick puppets*—Draw and color a figure or face on a piece of cardboard and glue it to a tongue depressor or ice cream stick.

• *Finger puppets*—Draw a head on a piece of drawing paper and leave a tab at the bottom. Tape the tab around the index finger as it forms a tube.

Puppet Stage

Make a handy stage for your puppets and use them in a variety of ways, or just enjoy them out in the open!

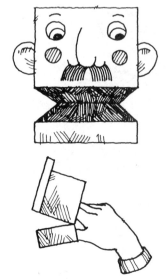

BOX PUPPET

PAPER BAG PUPPET

←FINGER

FINGER PUPPET

Figure 5-3 *Children may take turns using the dramatic play corner to share a personal interest.*

in drawers, wastebaskets, or cupboards for items such as cardboard tubes or boxes; yarn, string, or ribbon; scraps of cloth or paper; paper plates, bags, or cups; and plastic bottles. See the accompanying box for more ideas.

Be near the area of dramatic play as the children participate with whatever interests them, but try to suppress the temptation to join the children as a peer participant. Often, beginning teachers do this without realizing that they stifle the children's enthusiasm and creativity by doing so. Your function is that of a facilitator—someone who can arbitrate or forestall a hassle, suggest or supply additional materials as needs arise, or help maintain order in the area. Inform the children when the play period begins to draw to a close so that they

can restore the arrangement back to its original condition and get ready for the next activity on the schedule.

Block Play

While some children are involved at the dramatic play centers, others will be participating in an alternative play center—*the block center.* Perhaps the oldest toy created for children, blocks are the classic play materials for young children. Blocks can promote social skills when groups of children participate in a common block play activity, but the greatest apparent advantage of blocks is the development of motor skills such as reaching, grasping, balancing, stacking, sliding, and carrying. In addi-

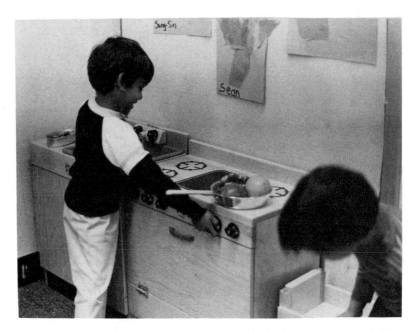

The housekeeping corner is a traditionally favorite area for dramatic play activity.

tion, blocks enrich the development of imaginative play. Since blocks often become animals, people, or objects in the child's mind, the block center should be placed somewhere near the dramatic play center; the children can thereby use materials from either center to supplement their play in the other. For example, on a typical day you might see "construction workers" or "truck drivers" from the block area drop by the housekeeping area's diner for a quick bite to eat.

A well-equipped block center should have a variety of materials differing in size, shape, color, texture, and material of construction. Basic to most classrooms are the *unit blocks*. Unit blocks are durable, their natural wood color is pleasing to the eye, and the smooth finish makes the blocks pleasant to touch. They may be purchased as a complete set (over 750 blocks), half sets, or individual pieces. Each set of blocks contains many different shapes so that children at various levels of ability may

use a set with success. These blocks are made in multiples of a unit (5½ inches × 2¾ inches × 1⅜ inches), with increasing size along one dimension only—length—to the size of 22 inches × 2¾ inches × 1⅜ inches. Also part of the unit block assortment are pillars (1⅜ inches × 1⅜ inches × 5½ inches), cylinders (1⅜ inches or 2¾ inches diameter × 5½ inches), curves (1⅜ inches × 2¾ inches × 90 inches), arches (1⅜ inches × 5½ inches × 11 inches), and hardwood boards of various sizes (see Figure 5-4).

Unit blocks should be made of unvarnished durable hardwood; all corners and edges should be rounded and smooth, and, above all, accurate to avoid frustration in building. *Hollow blocks* are often used as a supplement to unit blocks in an early childhood facility. These are large, wooden blocks that allow children to make a variety of structures—some even large enough to play within (see Figure 5-5). Despite their size, hollow

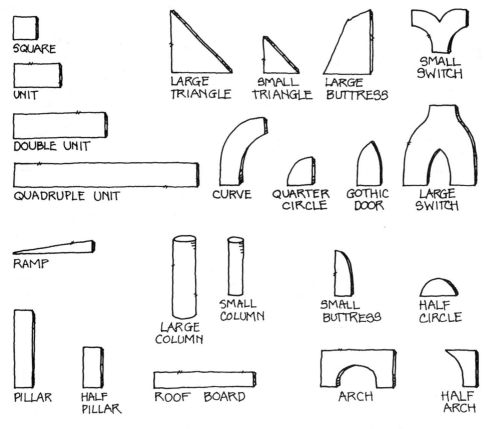

Figure 5-4 *Unit building blocks*

blocks are light enough to handle and easy enough for small hands to grip. When selecting hollow blocks, be sure to choose those made from unvarnished wood such as oak or maple durable enough to resist splintering or cracking and with rounded edges and corners to facilitate picking up and handling comfort. Hollow blocks come in the following sizes and shapes:

- *square:* 5½ inches × 11 inches × 11 inches (28 in a full set)
- *double square:* 5½ inches × 11 inches × 22 inches (16)
- *half square:* 5½ inches × 5½ inches × 11 inches (16)

- *short board:* ⅝ inches × 3¾ inches × 22 inches (8)
- *ramp:* 22 inches long × 5½ inches high × 11 inches wide (4)

A complete set of hollow blocks contains 80 pieces. Other popular plastic or wooden block-type construction toys include *bristle blocks, Tinkertoys,* and *Lincoln logs.* Examine these and other types as you select the right kinds of block play equipment for your youngsters.

Because most early childhood facilities operate on limited budgets, teachers often find that they are not able to purchase all the blocks they would like. You don't have to buy everything; discarded, donated, or homemade equip-

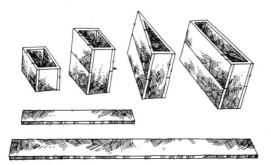

Hollow blocks serve as excellent play materials to help children explore new territories, master new skills, and make new friends.

ment can serve your needs well. Some excellent materials of this type include milk cartons, cans, boards, spools, styrofoam, lumber scraps, boxes, barrels, shoeboxes, and cardboard tubes.

Arrange the block corner in an area of the room where the children can move freely and be safe from distractions or accidents caused by other children in unrelated play. For example, don't put the block center near riding toys or the climbing equipment. Likewise, the sand or water table would invite problems if they were located near the block area. Place storage shelves or cabinets on the perimeter of the area to separate it from other areas of vigorous activity. Be sure the children have a flat, steady surface on which to work; a wobbly table or a carpeted floor are too unstable for building large structures such as towers. Store the blocks on low shelves so that the children can easily take them out or put them back without difficulty. Be sure to inform the children that all blocks are assigned a special position on the storage shelf and that the appropriate blocks should always be returned to that place. Organize the blocks by size, shape, or some other quality, and label the shelves with outlines or pictures of the blocks that belong in each section. This makes cleanup time go smoothly and gives children practice in grouping and ordering objects, which we will consider in Chapters 7 and 9.

Some children start at the block corner using only one large block, which represents to them a store, gas station, house, and so on. They often do this because they do not have the muscle control necessary to manage a two- or three-block structure. It would be appropriate for these children especially to start with cardboard boxes somewhat larger than the customary wooden blocks. By pushing, lifting, crawling into and out of, and carrying these boxes, the children begin to develop increased muscular control and confidence. Eventually, when the youngsters arrange the boxes to represent bridges, caves, tunnels, and other earthly or imaginative features, this random activity becomes more meaningful.

Once children gain the control necessary for manipulating the smaller blocks, they may be ready to manage two- or three-block structures. When they reach this point, you may wish to provide accessories such as toy vehicles, hoses, wagons, road signs, figures of people or animals, and other objects that encourage imagination and dramatic play. It is interesting to watch how the children's creative minds transform their block structures into super highways, city streets, or rural farmyards.

Children in any culture enjoy block play for all the pleasurable experiences such play contributes. Your role in maintaining an environment that encourages purposeful block play is critical. Basically, the role involves these responsibilities:

1. Observe the block area carefully. Your presence not only communicates an interest in what is happening, but it also helps to prevent unpleasant situations before they occur.

2. Provide support for the children engaged in block play. Encourage them to talk about their problems and accomplishments with well-timed questions such as "How can we get your gasoline station to stand?" or "How did you get it

Figure 5-5   Hollow blocks

to stand up?" Do not set patterns for a child to copy.

3. Allow sufficient time for the block play. This amount, of course, should remain flexible and is usually determined by the children's interests and spans of attention.

4. Encourage the children to get their own blocks and to put them away when finished.

Block play is recognized as perhaps one of the two most popular activities used by pre-school teachers. One of the major reasons for this popularity is the realization of educators that block play, like dramatic play, integrates experiences in a total developmental context.

Sand and Water Play

An area of sensory stimulation, social inter-action, and physical exercise involving won-derfully messy, squishy, sticky materials is sand and water play. Experiences with water and sand are probably among the most memora-ble of our lives, but often we forget their plea-sures and deny them to youngsters because "they're dirty," "they get wet," or "they take so much time." Anyone who has ever observed children at the beach, however, can testify to the enjoyment children experience with sand and water.

Sand play usually takes place outdoors in a sandbox. The sandbox should be fairly large (about 10 feet square) with a wide ledge around it to serve as a seat for the children or as a

SAND PLAY ACTIVITIES

Sand Sculptures

The children pack wet sand into any kind of container such as milk cartons, matchboxes, plastic bottles, and so on. These forms are transformed by the children's imagination into houses, automobiles, spaceships, skyscrapers, and other objects. Use these tools as molds:

cans of all sizes	plastic containers of all sizes and shapes
buckets	shoe boxes
milk cartons	cardboard tubes
funnels	pie tins
matchboxes	cake pans
cookie cutters	jello molds
paper cups	nut shells
sea shells	

Sand Script

Wet the sand surface and make it smooth by pulling a ruler over it. Encourage the children to draw designs, print their names, or write messages on it with sticks.

Sand Designs

The children may wish to create original designs or patterns on a smooth, wet sand surface. Provide a variety of tools for this kind of activity:

combs (see the sand comb activity)

potato mashers

spatulas

forks

hand rakes

sticks

Sand Hands (or Feet)

Put wet sand into a small box and ask the child to press her hand into it so she makes a distinct impression. Fill the impression with a thick plaster of paris mixture (like a milkshake) and allow it to set for about 40–50 minutes. It should feel cool and hard. When it is dry, the child should be able to lift a solid replica of her hand

Play with dry sand or dirt often fascinates young children and involves them in imaginative thought, physical activity, and intellectual stimulation.

from the sand. The children may try to match the sand hands to the original owners.

This technique can also be used as the children make molds of shells, bones, keys, or any other interesting objects.

Sand Combs

Help children make textures and patterns in the sand play area by constructing sand combs. Cut a 4- × 8-inch piece of quarter-inch plywood. Draw a comb pattern on the wood and cut it with a saw.

Sand Timers

Children not yet ready to read time on clocks may be introduced to the concept of keeping time by making a simple sand timer to measure how long they want to play a game or perform some activity.

Glue the tops of two identical jar lids together with a strong epoxy adhesive. Make sure it's dry and then punch holes in the lids with a hammer and a thin nail. Alternate the sides into which you punch the holes. Add sand to one of the jars until it is nearly (but not totally) full. Screw the lids onto that jar and attach the other jar to the top. Then, turn the timer over and begin timing.

SAND CASTLES (FINGERPLAY)

I dug in the sand
    (Make digging motion.)
And carefully made
Five sand castles
    (Hold up five fingers.)
With my pail and spade.

I felt like a king
    (Stand up tall.)
With a golden crown
    (Form circle overhead.)
Till a big blue jay
    (Flutter hands.)
Knocked my castles down.
    (Hold five fingers up; knock them down
    with the other hand.)

So I dug again
    (Make digging motion.)
In that sandy shore
Till I had ten sand castles
    (Hold up ten fingers.)
And was king once more.
    (Stand up tall; make circle overhead.)

table for different activities. A special value of the ledge is that it serves as a frame to keep loose sand from spilling over the edges. You may be wise to locate the sandbox as far away from the classroom door as possible so much of the accumulation on children's clothes can fall off or be brushed off on the way in. Keep the sandbox covered when it is not being used to prevent it from becoming contaminated with animal elimination or excess rainwater.

Children enjoy sand for many reasons. It pours; it forms into shapes; and it smells, looks, and feels good. Children enjoy pouring sand, molding it into castles, building roads, digging rivers or lakes, and making sand cookies or cakes. Imagination is allowed to flow during such activity; the children almost always accompany their construction with the "brrm, brrm," of a steam shovel, a "whoosh" of a jet plane, or other inventive expressions. Small dump trucks, pails, shovels, funnels, refrigerator trays, road graders, animals, and other props encourage children to dramatize and verbalize events within their sandbox environment. Some sand play suggestions are described in the accompanying box.

Water play is often feared by teachers because of their concern that the children may become too overstimulated, resulting in a wet and messy area. The opposite is usually true, however. If the water play experience is carefully planned and organized, the children become absorbed to the point that their cooperativeness and behavior is more controlled than during most other daily activities. Water play usually takes place with a water table—a raised, rectangular galvanized container resembling a table in appearance. A washtub or other large container holding up to 25 gallons of water to a depth of 8–10 inches is suitable for water play either indoors or out. Protect the children with full-length plastic aprons, boots, or plastic bags over the shoes, and sleeves pushed up over the elbows. Cover the floor with plastic if you are indoors and then add several layers of newspaper. Rugs or mats may

WATER PLAY ACTIVITIES

Straight Water Play

Children love to experiment with the water itself:

- Measuring cups, funnels, egg beaters, medicine droppers, strainers, watering cans, squeeze bottles, sieves, ladles, sponges, and brushes help children observe and feel water as they experiment with it.

- Encourage the children to swish their hands through the water, swirl their hands in circles, try to grab a handful of water, stir it with a spoon, and so on.

Water and Soap

Add a mild nondetergent soap to the water and try these activities:

- Blow bubbles with a straw.
- Beat the water with an eggbeater or whip.
- Wash dolls, furniture, dishes, and other materials.
- Add glycerine to the soapy water. It will make larger and stronger bubbles from a bubble ring.

Floating and Sinking

Collect a variety of objects and see what will sink or float:

- Beverage bottle caps, bits of wood, paper clips, rubber bands, styrofoam shapes, and other materials can be used.

- Invite the children to construct a variety of sailing boats: spool boats, jar lid boats, cork boats, nutshell boats, styrofoam boats, plastic box boats, or milk carton boats.

- Use sailboats in races. Stretch string along a large tray or pan of water to make racing lanes. The children choose their boats and a lane and attempt to win the race by blowing their boats with straws.

Water and Color

Add food coloring to the water and try these activities:

- Try a drop or two at a time into a small container to see how vivid it becomes as more coloring is added.

- Dip fabrics or a sponge into the water to see how the water is absorbed.

- Drop one color onto wax paper. Add other drops from different colors to see, for example, what happens when a red and yellow drop come together.

- Get a number of jars with watertight lids. Fill the jars halfway with colored water and fill it the rest of the way with vegetable oil. Have the children screw the lids on tightly and rock the jars back and forth to see the changing designs.

also be used. Also, good preparation includes provisions for cleanup should accidents occur; sponges, mops, and paper towels should be handy. When these steps are taken, you are ready to try a variety of activities involving water. Here are some suggestions to get you started.

There should always be an adult present whenever sand or water play is in progress—not to participate in the play with the children or to tell them how to play, but to keep a watchful eye should problems arise. One of the most frequent of these problems is a ten-

dency to throw sand or splash water. Another problem is that youngsters need a great deal of room while using shovels, sand rakes, or other tools. They may become so enthusiastic in their play that they sometimes bang another child with their tools. Still a third problem lies in the condition that some two- or three-year-olds have a propensity for putting sand into their mouths or rubbing their eyes while sand is sticking to their hands. Be near to forestall these problems before they happen. Otherwise, the sand and water should be among the

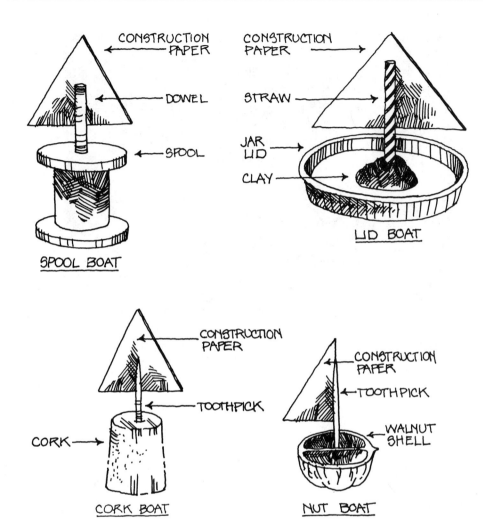

freest play activities we can provide for children. They are absorbing, soothing, and free from pressures and tension. Besides, sand and water play provide excellent stimulants for social interaction.

Woodworking Bench

As three-, four-, and five-year-olds gain more accurate control of their muscles, working with real tools can be an important experience offered to youngsters two or three times per week. To boys and girls alike, the satisfaction of making something real comes from the use of real tools. Real tools are necessary; toy tools such as a die-cast light metal hammer only insults or frustrates the enthusiastic builder. These tools are recommended for an active woodworking area:

sturdy workbench with two vises	screwdrivers
claw hammers	assorted nails (large heads) and
saws (crosscut), 12 and 16 inches	screws
	C-clamps to hold

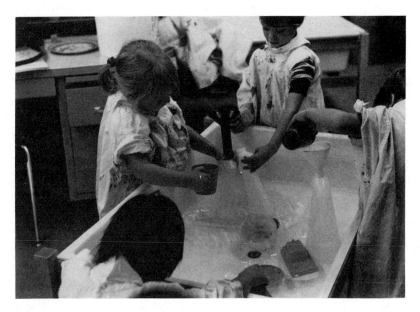

Water play, either indoors or out, provides the children with delightful activity. Careful supervision must be provided to keep clothes dry, but the opportunity to take a cool bath on a hot city playground may be a temptation some youngsters may find too difficult to resist.

hand drills and bits
pliers
sandpaper
   (wrapped around
   a wood block)
cotton work gloves,
   cap, carpenter's
   apron

wood steady
rasp or smoothing
   plane
chisels
nuts and bolts
wrenches

Provide an abundance of soft wood (pine is especially good), which is easily obtainable as scraps from lumberyards, home builders, parents, or even high school shop classes. The major initial interest on the part of your children will not be to construct something; they simply enjoy the physical and sensory sensations of pounding nails into the wood, sanding or sawing the wood and smelling the fragrance of the wood dust, turning the hand drills to make holes, and performing other jobs they have seen adults do. Since the emphasis in woodworking during the early childhood years

is upon experience and enjoyment rather than constructing a final product, you should provide careful guidance rather than detailed carpentry skills. Such guidance should be both directed and informal. For example, since many of the tools are potentially dangerous if not used properly, you will want to demonstrate their proper uses. Show the children how to hold a hammer and nail, where to place their hand so it would not be in the path of the saw, and how dangerous pliers could be if used to clamp onto things (such as other children's fingers) not originally intended. You will also want to explain the importance of keeping the woodworking area neat and orderly. Hang a large pegboard near the area and paint or glue construction paper outlines of the tools available in the center. Mount hooks above the outlines and direct the children to replace the tools on the appropriate hooks when they are finished using them. You may need to be somewhat more wary of the children in this center than in some of the others. Your physical presence often is one of the best incentives for appropriate behavior. Avoid being too directive, but display enough interest to offer suggestions or words of encouragement periodically. Do not take over the woodworking play; make sure it is always the child's activity.

As they gain confidence and skill, some children will move from the sensory aspects of woodworking to a desire for actually making things. Of course, their creations will be crude, but imagine the joy when a child decides that the piece of wood she just sawed would make an excellent train engine once a nail is driven in just the right place. The values of experimentation, creativity, muscular coordination, emotional pleasure, planning, and social exchange far outweigh the accuracy of the final product.

Other Interest Centers

The centers just described are some of the best ones you can provide for the very young. Here are a few more—they will not be discussed in such depth because they are treated comprehensively in other areas of this book:

- *Manipulative Materials Center:* puzzles, beads, pegboards, lotto, bingo, parquetry, small table blocks
- *Art Center:* paints, brushes, easels, crayons, scissors, paste, glue, paper, modeling dough, scrap materials
- *Listening Center:* television, record player, tape recorder, records, cassette tapes, books with taped stories, ear phones
- *Book Center:* rug, shelves, books, cushions, rocking chair, pictures, magnetic letters
- *Science Center:* plants, aquarium, balance scale, magnifying glass, magnets, items from nature

THE TEACHER'S ROLE DURING FREE PLAY ACTIVITY

Although children should feel free to experiment and create, play time does not mean an unbridled "free-for-all" environment where anything goes. Realistically, it needs to be a rich experience for children—one in which there is a great deal of planning, guidance, and understanding.

Alert supervision implies a system of guiding children that allows them to participate in their active experiences confidently and safely. This means that careful observation of the children and their equipment is necessary at all times. Guidelines for supervising young children follow.

- *Use casual, noninterfering guidance.* Remember that although the play process is providing the children with most of their learning, you must be ready to give support and guidance when needed. You act as a stimulant to the child in this regard as you introduce new materials, stimulate thought, and pull together random experiences into a meaningful whole.

- *Create an atmosphere of freedom.* In order for children to enter freely into play activity, they must know that they have your acceptance and trust. You must remember that some children will have had more limited experiences with toys and play than others, so they must be allowed to approach materials at their own pace. On the other hand, some children will have had numerous opportunities for such experiences at home and will more quickly adapt to their use at school. Remember to begin where the children are, and encourage their entry into play when things become familiar to them.

- *Keep a constant eye on the children.* Two- and three-year-olds naturally wander off from the play area to explore new wonders. Since they have little idea of what is dangerous, they need firm, positive control. Direct special attention to swing or slide areas and give children directions on the use of this equipment. Don't hesitate to tell children to "Wait until Levi comes down the slide before you climb the ladder," or "Run in the grass, not through the sand box."

• *Check the equipment to make sure it is safe.* Be sure that the equipment is not faulty and that children can use the equipment safely. For example, if some children still put things in their mouth, postpone activities that involve shells, rocks, sticks, and the like until these children can safely attempt them. Also, arrange the play areas so that effective supervision can be maintained and the possibility of accidents is kept to a bare minimum.

• *Anticipate possible safety problems.* Position yourself close to a group of children who may be playing with potentially dangerous equipment. If you need to give a group of children special attention, stand facing the other children so you can minimize the possibility of accidents there. With experience you will learn to anticipate trouble spots and take steps to eliminate problems before they erupt. The safety and welfare of young children are major responsibilities. Regardless of the quality of supervision, however, accidents are always possible. For that reason, it is wise for every school to carry accident insurance to cover its children and staff.

• *Arrange equipment in an attractive and safe manner.* A wide variety of materials is necessary in order to have an effective play atmosphere. If not arranged and kept in neat order, however, they can eventually become disorganized to the point of becoming unattractive. Children must understand that a great deal of responsibility for this organization is

theirs. They should be warned that cleanup time is near and that "I'll help you put the truck in the shed if you bring it to me." Children can be encouraged to clean up and put things back in their original places through the use of a puppet or a catchy tune. Children are more than willing to help clean and organize the room—give them a chance and you will be richly rewarded by their willing cooperation.

• *Observe children by listening and watching.* Your careful observation of children during play will tell much about their interests, abilities, emotional state, social adjustments, and all other areas of child growth and development. Such information can be used as an evaluative tool when you plan further individual and group experiences.

OTHER BASIC EQUIPMENT FOR PLAY

In addition to the major types of classroom centers designed to encourage free play, teachers of preschool children should arrange for other kinds of educative play. This means that particular attention should be paid to all areas of the child's needs so that a broad range of purposes can be met. For example, three areas of play that will be addressed more comprehensively in succeeding chapters include *manipulative play, physical play,* and *creative play,* each involving specially selected materials. Manipulative play is characterized by a child's handling equipment with small pieces: puzzles, cuisenaire rods, pegs and peg boards, nesting blocks, color cones, and beads. The values of these materials are derived specifically from the child's handling of them. Physical play is characterized by the child's ability to use and refine skills in which the large or

Careful supervision of areas designed to encourage vigorous outdoor exercise is a must. Encourage parents, grandparents, and other interested adults to join you on the playground to help prevent accidents.

small muscles must be used. Activities such as running, marching, climbing, walking, and skipping help children increase their large muscle skills; experiences with cutting, lacing, and weaving facilitate control of the small muscles. Creative play involves a variety of art, music, and language activities designed specifically to encourage the rich inventiveness, originality, and freedom of thought and expression commonly exhibited by young children. Varieties of materials in all areas will keep the preschool experience interesting and encourage growth in all areas of development.

SOME FINAL THOUGHTS

When adults dismiss play, the very serious business of childhood, as "just having fun," they are minimizing one of the most valuable activities during childhood. Play, a process observed in virtually all children within all cultures, provides an avenue of rich activity that takes up most of youngsters' waking hours. Surely, play is fun or children wouldn't expend so much effort with it, but play is something that also develops skills, helps children learn, and provides an outlet for emotions. In dramatic play children learn how to get along with one another as well as to practice the roles of people observed in the environment. Other play areas, such as outdoor play, contribute to physical growth and development. Academic skills are enhanced, too, as children compare shapes of blocks or decide upon colors for their painting. Young children also gain pleasure or express other feelings from play materials such as paints, clay, or crayons. Although these benefits may be unknown to the children, play is an all-encompassing activity through which many values are attained.

Because play is an expression of the children's own private world, we must respect their right to enter their own personal, creative worlds through play. As teachers, however, we may be conditioned to judge activities that are not goal-specific to be inappropriate. For instance, we tend to deemphasize those activities that do not seem to be supported by cognitive goals. But play does involve thinking in addition to imagination and spontaneity. By providing for play, we are allowing children to figure out where they fit in this new world by associating it with a world of their own.

Chapter 6

Physical and Motor Skills: Patterns of Fitness, Coordination, and Control

Billy, a rather active five-year-old, normally gained great pleasure from outdoor play. He reveled in the variety of available physical activities but seemed to find the greatest satisfaction from participating in throwing and catching games with a partner. Billy's choice of partners was not extremely selective as he basically enjoyed playing with whoever would be willing to join him at the time. There never seemed to be cause for any conflicts as only a few children were interested in such activity, and those children were all generally at about the same ability level. One day, however, Andrew became interested in throwing the ball with Billy and a friend and eagerly rushed to the corner of the playground to join them. Billy willingly tossed the ball to Andrew and watched in surprise as the ball sailed by his rigid arms and rolled away. "Pick it up, Andrew, and throw it back," shouted Billy. Andrew, quite paunchy and slow, ambled toward the ball, fumbled with it for a moment, and finally picked it up. In preparing to toss it back to Billy, Andrew had great difficulty in coordinating his arm and leg movements. Finally, deciding that his left arm would be the best, Andrew awkwardly cocked it back, bent his body at a cumbersome angle, and stepped forward on the wrong foot to give the ball its momentum. It flew off, but landed only a short distance from Andrew's feet, much short of its target. At this time, Billy's original partner began to sense their superiority and soon began to badger and criticize Andrew. "C'mon, Fatty!" he shouted. "My grandmother can throw better than you." "Yeah," others joined in, "I never saw a whale try to throw a ball before." Crushed beyond words, Andrew shrunk from the area and slowly withdrew from the active game of ball.

After this episode, one that indicates relationships between physical growth and mental health, Andrew may feel too rejected and discouraged to continue his "friendships." He may begin spending more and more time alone in order to avoid the cruel jokes of his peers. Such situations often result in crying spells and lead to additional rejection, learning problems, or possible behavioral abnormalities. An ability to throw a ball, as well as the condition of being overweight, is, of course, a very special attribute. Knowing about these physical attributes and how they affect the entire realm of behavior and intelligence is necessary for all early childhood educators, because many aspects of development depend on children's bodies and their physical growth. Consider the ability of Andrew to throw a ball, for instance. The act involves many complex physical tasks and demands the development of many complex physical systems, beginning with a visual system, which is necessary for looking at and recognizing a ball. It includes the development of the hand and arm, including the bones and muscles, all of which allow the child to grasp the ball in a proper manner. It involves the development of the brain and nervous system, which are essential for choosing whether to hold the ball in the left hand or the right and for coordinating precise muscular movements such as opposition of movement between the arms and the feet; for example, as the throwing arm moves back, the opposite foot moves forward, shifting the child's weight to the front when the ball is released. Naturally, as the child grows older, factors such as physical maturity, appropriateness of experiences, and opportunities for practice determine just how much better his throwing skills develop. Nevertheless, this one seemingly simple activity paves the way for more complicated tasks involving movement, coordination, and control.

Of course, the ability to throw a ball is a very personal skill, but it illustrates exactly how much each child's life can be affected by physical attributes. Throwing a ball well; running fast; jumping high; being tall, short, fat, skinny, clumsy; having red hair, black hair, or brown— all of these physical features have a great effect on the way children are treated by others. "Fatty," "Clumsy," "Canary Legs," "Tubby," "Bag of Bones," and other tags are often directed at physical attributes and often cause children critical emotional problems. Sound physical

development, then, is important to the total growth of a child, and the teacher has the big responsibility of providing maximum opportunities for optimal physical growth.

The years between two and five years include times of enormous refinement of physical skills. Children acquire increasingly mature limb and body control as well as improved small muscle abilities during these years. These accomplishments certainly benefit the area of total development we commonly refer to as physical development, but they also influence the acquisition of a positive sense of self—that is, who I am and what I can do. Rapid progress is made as youngsters are provided opportunities by knowledgeable adults for physical play at home and in the preschool classroom. Preschoolers enjoy all kinds of physical play: They seem to run tirelessly, climb up or over all kinds of structures, perform balancing feats on curbs or low walls, and delight in pedaling simple riding toys. In its purest form, such play emerges freely from within children. Each child brings his or her own unique set of interests, needs, and abilities to the play situation, trying out novel approaches to play as new situations and new materials are encountered. Free play, as we learned in Chapter 5, has many values in the total developmental scheme of young children, but one of the most apparent benefits is the acquisition and refinement of physical skills, popularly referred to as *perceptual-motor skills.* Perceptual skills refer to all the sensory modalities that transmit environmental information to the brain:

auditory . . . . hearing
visual . . . . seeing
tactile . . . . touching
gustatory . . . . tasting
olfactory . . . . smelling

These perceptual skills are naturally developed as children play informally and can be further refined and enhanced through formal instruction in the preschool setting. Motor skills, on the other hand, involve the use of the body's large and small muscles to perform basic movements and movement patterns such as the following:

- *gross motor* (large muscle) *skills:* throwing, catching, running, kicking, jumping, and so on.
- *fine motor* (small muscle) *skills:* cutting, lacing, buttoning, pasting, pouring, and so on.
- *body awareness:* identifying body parts, performing tasks, moving, exploring, imitating, and so on.

Perceptual and motor skills interact with one another as children play. However, such skills will not develop if the child is left alone; development requires play opportunities within challenging play environments and sensitive, informed professionals who understand that physical development is a major area of development in the very young. The purpose of this chapter is to aid you in both of those areas.

PRINCIPLES OF PHYSICAL GROWTH

Physical development is usually discussed in terms of what is "normal" for children at a certain age level. For example, the normal height and weight of three-year-old boys has been determined to be 38 inches and 32¼ pounds. These figures were established through a process of carefully measuring and observing thousands of growing children and arriving at an *average* weight and height figure. A "norm," then, is the average for a child at a certain age level, not some *ideal* level of development for that period. Keep these thoughts in mind as "normal" patterns of physical development are discussed throughout this chapter.

A number of developmental principles account for the variations in rates of growth in different parts of the body for different individuals. Such principles are classified by researchers in their own unique ways, but they seem to fall into seven basic categories.

1. *Directional Growth:* In general, this principle of physical growth states that growth proceeds from the head down to the toes and from the center of the body outwards. In particular, the principle breaks down into two basic areas:

- *Cephalocaudal:* This Latin term meaning "from head to tail" states that the infant's development proceeds from the head to toe. For instance, the child's head at birth comprises about one-quarter of its body, the rest being evenly divided between trunk and legs. In contrast, the adult's body is made up of about one-eighth head, one-half legs, and one-third trunk. Likewise, the muscles closest to the head are the first the child is able to control. Therefore, infants placed in a lying position are first able to raise their heads; then, as shoulder, arm, and stomach muscles develop, they become able to raise their shoulders, and eventually they are able to raise the entire upper part of their bodies. Gradually, as leg and thigh muscles develop, the children become able to raise their hips from the surface.

- *Proximodistal:* Another Latin term, this one meaning "from near to far," states that physical development proceeds from the center of the body to the extremities. The child first learns to control the shoulders and pelvis; then later, the elbows, wrists, knees, and ankles. For example, infants first use their shoulder muscles when reaching for an object, but, by the end of the first year, they begin to use and control their arms at the elbow, wrists, hand muscles and fingers.

2. _General to Specific Growth:_ This principle of development explains that the developing being has a general shape when it is forming in the mother's womb and then it becomes progressively more specific. Likewise, the baby's original reflexive reactions progress from general to specific behaviors. For example, a pin prick to the bottom of a baby's foot may initially result in a general whole-body reaction—kicking, thrashing, and screaming. Later, the same stimulus may evoke a more specific, coordinated response, such as a quick withdrawal of the foot. The overall tendency in physical development is toward minimum, specified muscular involvement: large muscle to small muscle control. The child gradually moves from the large, random movements of the arms and legs during infancy to the refinement of specific movements necessary for special skills such as cutting, pasting, or drawing.

3. _Differentiation and Integration in Growth. Differentiation_ refers to the process through which the child eventually gains control over specific parts of the body in order to perform certain tasks. For example, even into toddlerhood, young children have great difficulty controlling and coordinating their movements in order to catch a ball. However, if a five-year-old is thrown a ball, it is very likely that the child will catch it. Once children have discovered, or differentiated, which parts of the body can do certain things, they are ready to perform more complex activities that involve the coordination of movements centered in different parts of the body _(integration)._ Climbing a stair, drawing a picture, or building a block tower are all complex activities for certain children, depending upon their abilities to understand which parts of their bodies result in the control of certain movements and how those movements can be coordinated in order to achieve a specific goal. Some of these

movements, such as crawling, walking, sitting, or grasping, develop naturally if the environment allows the child a reasonable degree of freedom. Others, such as riding a bicycle, skipping (for some children), or roller skating require a certain degree of help.

4. _Variations in Growth:_ Individuals vary in their growth rates in these two ways: (1) they vary from person to person, and (2) the various organs and systems within each individual grow at different rates. Anyone who has ever observed children recognizes that rates of growth vary from one child to another—some grow quickly; others more slowly. One of the most apparent demonstrations of this principle is that girls are more physiologically mature than boys until adolescence. This principle should help us understand what we can expect from children at various chronological ages, but to temper that understanding with a realization that each child is a unique human being and will grow according to his or her own personal rate.

5. _Optimal Tendency in Growth:_ This principle states that individuals seek to reach their full potential for development. For example, suppose growth during a certain period is interrupted by a lack of food or exercise. The child attempts to make up for that lean period as soon as adequate provisions are made available; he soon catches up to normal growth expectancies and then resumes a characteristic pattern of growth. Only if the deprivation is severe will the child exhibit permanent effects from it.

For children afflicted with some type of physical disability, this principle is especially apparent. Blind children, for example, learn to compensate for their lack of sight by sharpening other senses such as touch or hearing.

6. _Sequential Growth:_ This principle, mainly influenced by the work of Gesell, explains that physical growth evolves through an orderly sequence; that is,

children must learn to crawl before they venture to walk. Sequential patterns of growth have been described for nearly all physical skills including locomotion, use of the hands, and other abilities. Gesell's original work described such sequential growth as a natural "unfolding" process, but the currently popular view is that the child's environment, together with heredity factors, is basic to the process of physical development.

7. *Growth During Critical Periods:* This final principle contends that there are certain key times in a child's development during which the presence or absence of specific interactions can be especially important. For example, the first three months of an infant's life are extremely critical for the development of the eyes, ears, and brain. In order to foster optimal development of these organs, the child should be provided with a rich variety of visual and verbal stimulation. A critical period, then, is the time when certain physical growth can be most readily enhanced.

What does all this mean to you, the teacher of young children in their early years? Consider, for a moment, this scene, which is all too typical of an average day at a preschool center.

Mary and Barbie carefully scoop up dirt with their small trowels and place it in their pails, preparing a neat bed for their seeds. Jeff and James, on the other hand, dig into the soft dirt with their hands and toss it aside, letting it fall where it will. James, suddenly bored with the activity, decides to join other children at the swings and stands up quickly. Unfortunately, the short fence surrounding the garden catches him on the legs and sends the boy sprawling. Unhurt, James runs to his friend Dan at the swings. Meanwhile, Jeff is unaware that James has left, and he continues tossing the dirt about. One of Jeff's tosses inadvertently lands directly on Mary's neat seed bed and partially on Mary, and she gives a loud cry of despair. The teacher's attention is directed to the area at this

Remember that children develop to different degrees, so some children will feel comfortable in activities that may seem dangerous to adults. Do not discourage such activity simply because you are fearful. In general, children will normally choose only those activities in which they feel safe.

point and she quickly moves in. The teacher hugs Mary and consoles her the best she can. Eventually, Jeff is directed to another activity and soon all four children are busily involved in new tasks—the garden incidents forgotten by all.

If we examine this situation in depth, we discover several principles of physical growth that have a direct impact on the children's behavior. One principle of growth and development, for example, states that girls mature more quickly than boys (variations in growth).

You will note that Barbie and Mary were purposefully scooping up the dirt and placing it into their pails while the boys were tossing their dirt about in an unplanned way. The girls may have been able to control their muscles more effectively than the boys and therefore were able to carry out their work more precisely (general to specific growth). Also, James's fall may have been the result of his lower body not being as well developed as his upper body region (directional growth). If this were so, his center of gravity would be high and would cause him to fall for the slightest reasons. Since his legs are short in proportion to the rest of his body and he is usually in a hurry to go somewhere, the preschooler often prefers to run rather than walk—oh, for longer legs!

It is important for you to know the patterns of physical growth in young children because there is some general agreement that physical appearance has a major influence on how children view themselves and how others, in turn, view them. Karen Dion (1972) found that physical attractiveness plays an important role in how nursery school children are viewed. In the study, women were given reports describing severe classroom problems. Along with one problem, the researcher attached a photograph of an attractive child. A photograph of an unattractive child was attached to a second problem situation. In response to the first problem, the one involving the attractive child, disturbing behavior was excused because "a bad day can occur" and the child's behavior "need not be taken too seriously." However, with the unattractive child, the response was, "I think the child would be quite bratty and would probably be a problem to teachers." Attractiveness, then, seems to be a quality that allows adults to be more tolerant of negative behaviors.

In a study of preschool girls, Kenneth Dion (1973) found that young children are well aware of the value of attractiveness; they respond to picture cues with responses such as, "People like you if you're pretty." Clifford and Walster (1973) did a study evaluating to what extent physical attractiveness influenced the behavior and judgment of others. Their study showed that teachers thought of attractive children as having greater potential for academic success than unattractive children, even though both groups of children were identical in all other qualities. These studies and others show that we are influenced by the physical characteristics of others; we tend to focus more on the appearance of others than on trying to discover the qualities of the inner person.

Individual differences make it imperative that teachers avoid establishing rigid expectations for physical growth and appearance. Each child grows differently; each is distinguished by body builds, different sizes and shapes, hair color, eye color, skin color, physical abilities, and different levels of physical maturity as a distinctive entity. What are some of the factors accounting for such differences in individual physical growth and development? Basically, these factors fall into two broad categories: *heredity* and *environment*. Our genes help determine such things as body size, build, facial characteristics, hair color, and so on. However, heredity provides only a potential for development; the actual growth and maturation process must be considered within an environmental context. We must therefore look back to an old principle of child development: Growth is a product of the interaction of an organism with its environment. Suggestions for creating an environment that encourages optimal physical growth are discussed in the following section.

ENCOURAGING OPTIMAL PHYSICAL GROWTH

Teachers who work with young children have long known the importance of physical growth and maturation in the total development of the child. Recall the concerned efforts of educational pioneers such as McMillan and Montessori who reacted most strongly to environmental conditions that related directly to children's physical growth. Their schools contained facilities designed to promote health and physical care. The same is true for schools today. Among the major factors that we now recognize as having a positive influence on physical growth are (1) a balanced program of activity, rest, and relaxation and (2) a safe, healthful environment. Suggestions for preparing and maintaining a balanced program of activity, rest, and relaxation are presented in this chapter. Suggestions for preparing and maintaining a safe, healthful environment are offered in this chapter and in Chapter 13.

MOTOR DEVELOPMENT DURING INFANCY

General basic changes in the body—height, weight, muscles, bones, nervous system, and hormones—are commonly dealt with in courses of child development, so they will not be treated here. However, all these changes operate together to influence how infants, toddlers, or young children are able to use their bodies. This process is referred to as *motor* (muscular) *development*. For parents, as well as teachers, the development of a child's motor skills provides some of their most momentous occasions—seeing an infant take a first faltering step or a three-year-old child learning to catch a ball. All children require active physical experiences in order to exercise their growing muscles; a child learns to ride a bike or to skip only when these new skills are built upon a great number of prerequisite and less obvious skills. For that reason, we will break down motor development into two distinct categories: (1) large motor control *(gross motor development)* and (2) small muscle control *(fine*

motor development). Gross motor development involves the use of large muscles such as those in the arms, legs, or trunk; fine motor development involves the use of the smaller muscles such as those in the fingers. Both gross motor skills and fine motor skills follow certain predictable patterns of attainment; these are valuable to know because they influence our expectations for young children. Only if our expectations are accurate and result in the preparation of associated experiences can we establish a classroom with a proper emotional tone.

Motor development during the period of infancy progresses very rapidly. The child advances in two years from a seemingly uncoordinated individual capable of only reflexive actions to a walking, toddling, exploring wonder. This development, of course, does not happen simply by chance but is a product of two interrelated factors: maturation and environment. These two influences work together to help children achieve their greatest developmental potential. Remember that the overall sequence of growth is head-to-toe and center-outward. The individual first controls the facial, neck, and shoulder muscles and lastly the legs and toes. Likewise, voluntary control of the arms is achieved before control of the hands and fingers. Mary Shirley (1933) conducted a study of infants that illustrates the predictable sequence of motor development during infancy. Her results are illustrated in Figure 6-1.

Taking into account what you know about the child's physical development and motor coordination, what sort of games or toys would be appropriate for an infant? Let us try to answer this question by constructing a list of gross and fine motor activities appropriate for children through 12 or 15 months of age (see accompanying box).

Special care must be taken with the toys selected for an infant's play. For example, one 13-month-old boy was tragically strangled when a pull-cord from a cradle gym looped around his neck and pulled tight as he struggled. Brittle plastics, loose beads, and glued-on doll parts all present similar potential dangers. Since infants manipulate toys via hand and mouth, you may wish to try this important infant toy safety quiz as you choose their toys.

INFANT TOY SAFETY QUIZ

1. Can tiny toys or toys with removable parts be swallowed or lodged in a baby's windpipe, ears, or nose?
2. Are there sharp edges?
3. Can eyes or limbs be pulled apart from stuffed animals?
4. Are crib toys securely fastened?
5. Is the length of string attaching the toy to a crib or playpen so long that it can be accidentally wound around the infant's neck?
6. Does the toy have holes, slots, or hinges that can pinch or injure the child?
7. Can the toy be punctured allowing beads or other small objects to spill out?
8. Is the toy flammable?
9. Has lead-based paint been used in making the toy? (If so, it can be dangerous.)
10. Will the baby really use this toy or am I buying it for my satisfaction?

Some basic toys you may wish to select for your infant-care facility include the following, arranged in order for use during the infant's first weeks of toddlerhood.

- multicolored rattles in different sizes and shapes (Infants respond most actively to red, and then yellow, blue, and green; they also like contrast.)
- bath toys that are easy to push
- small plush toys such as "animal grabbers" or stuffed animals (Babies like to grasp.)
- crib activity centers that include buttons to push, dials to turn, doors to open, bells to ring, wheels to spin

- soft, pliable cloth clutch balls or animals that allow the baby to grasp and squeeze
- balls that can be pushed as the infant learns to crawl
- large, nonglass, unbreakable mirrors
- multicolored pop beads that snap together and pull apart
- multicolored plastic stacking rings
- play telephones that include dials and bells
- scooter board toys that allow the baby to lie upon the toy and crawl about
- ride-on toys such as buses or ponies that allow the baby to sit or be on and move with her feet
- baby carriages (Babies love to use them for support when they are learning to walk.)
- pull toys with strings for crawlers and walkers
- tumble balls—large-size air-filled or soft foam balls that allow children to push or squeeze
- stacking toys
- nesting toys
- plastic bottles with objects such as clothes-pins to take out and put in
- simple puzzles, especially with knobs
- rocking boats designed for two children at a time
- spinning toys such as tops (especially those activated simply by pushing down)
- small-scale playground equipment such as slides or climbing toys
- blocks strong enough to stand or sit on
- other types of building blocks
- puppets

Although gross motor skills usually develop before fine motor skills, your first objective is for the child to gain control over related movements; once control is established, the

Figure 6-1   *Motor development in infants. (Reprinted by permission of the University of Minnesota Press.)*

MOTOR ACTIVITIES FOR INFANTS

Varied fine and gross motor activities contribute to the infant's and toddler's muscular growth and encourage increasingly sophisticated explorations of the environment.

Gross Motor Activities for Infants

1. Dress the child in loose clothing so he will be unrestricted in creeping, crawling, turning, or pushing activities.

2. Initiate exercise activities with the infant: move his arms and legs; hold him in a sitting position; encourage him to turn, push, creep, and crawl. Hold the child and toss him gently into the air. Hold him upright while giving him gentle support; bounce and dance to music while giving the child his first feelings of motion.

3. Hold an attractive, colorful toy above the infant as he lies on his back. Keep it steady until you are sure he sees it, then move it slowly from one side to another so that he is encouraged to turn his head and exercise his neck muscles.

4. Use crib toys to attract the infant to new objects and to give him practice reaching and grasping. Toys varying in color, texture, and sounds have great appeal for the infant.

5. Infants spend much time on their tummies. Hold a colorful noisemaking toy in front of the baby's head while he is in this position. Gently shake

the toy. Initially, the baby will try raising his head to find the toy; then use his arms for support while lifting the head and chest. These are strengthening exercises.

6. Provide a safe, clean area in which the child can freely crawl about. There should be several toys and books in the area for him to look at, explore, and grasp.

7. Grasp the child's hands and pull him from a lying position to a sitting position. After a period of time, the infant will learn to pull himself up as you help by continuing to hold his hands.

8. Pull the infant to a standing position and allow him to feel the weight on his legs. Support him by the hips or waist as he struggles to maintain balance. Later, the infant can be urged to pull himself up by using the rail of his crib or playpen.

9. Place the baby in a walker where he can practice extending his legs and making walking movements without having to support his full weight. Gradually, he will learn to stand by himself. When this happens, squat in front of him, grasp both his hands, and encourage him to step toward you. He may seem reluctant or scared—if he does, don't force him; stop and try again at a later time. Slowly increase the distance as the child gains skill, comfort, and confidence.

10. Roll a ball toward the infant. He will watch it roll and want to roll it himself.

Fine Motor Activities for Infants

1. Hold an attractive toy about 8 to 10 inches from the infant's eyes. After you are sure that he sees it, move it slowly until he follows it with his eyes.

2. Make a crib gym that gives the infant plenty of practice in reaching and grasping. Stretch a length of heavy gauge elastic across the crib and secure each end. Tie several shorter lengths to the first at intervals, allowing them to hang a short distance. To each of these short lengths of elastic securely attach a rattle, plastic spoon, beads, bells, or other toys too large for him to swallow. The infant will begin to use his

gym by hitting the toys and enjoying the bouncing action. Later, he will begin to grasp the objects with his fingers.

3. Give the infant a variety of toys to explore. He will initially select the ones that are easiest to grasp (such as a plastic ring), but will eventually move to ones that require greater finger control (plastic rattles). Vary the toys so that the child will be exposed to many textures, shapes, and sounds.

4. Make squeeze toys from vividly colored fabric stuffed with old pantyhose. A doughnut-shaped toy is probably the most appropriate because babies can easily hold the shape and squeeze it with their fingers. Variety stores sell toys like this with noisemakers inside, but before selecting one make sure that it is safely constructed so the noisemaker won't fall out.

5. Bath time is an excellent opportunity for the child to exercise his fingers. Allow him to pick up and squeeze the sponge or washcloth.

6. Show the infant some pop-beads. Pull them apart and hold the pieces close to each other. The child may at first only look at the two parts, but eventually he will attempt to grasp them and put them back together. Be sure to give the infant constant attention while he is playing with objects that can be easily swallowed. Infants enjoy placing new toys or objects into their mouths and can often swallow dangerous things.

7. Allow the child to use his fingers during feeding time, but remember that he will be messy. This is an important initial step in getting the infant to feed himself.

8. Give the infant a spoon to play with as you feed him. Soon you will be able to help him fill the spoon and put it into his mouth. Naturally, he will miss the target a few times at first, but have patience; he will slowly improve with practice.

9. Let the infant play with an unbreakable empty cup while you are feeding him. When he seems to gain control, fill the cup with a few drops of a favorite liquid and let him try to drink from it. Again, there is bound to be some spilling, so give a small portion at a time and allow plenty of practice.

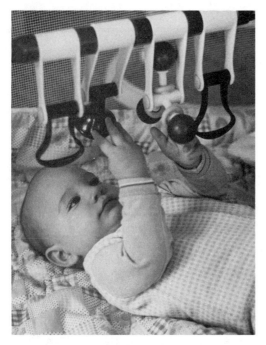

This crib toy encourages sensory exploration as well as the exercise of motor skills.

infant must be given frequent opportunities for practice. Such practice affords the child a chance to refine the quality of movements so that they are correctly sequenced and rhythmical. With such growing ability, the child can explore her world more fully; this ability is useful for all other areas of an individual's total development.

MOTOR DEVELOPMENT DURING THE PRESCHOOL YEARS

Although infants are fairly active during their waking hours, most of their energy is directed toward just growing rather than toward physical activity. This, in fact, is the period of fastest physical growth. Growth in height and weight begins to slow during toddlerhood (at about age two children are approximately half their adult height), so the energy required for rapid growth is now redirected toward increasing physical activity. Children are now beginning to walk and feed themselves so new experiences and new needs are beginning to surface rapidly. Table 6-1 summarizes the motor skills developing in the youngster between the ages of two and five years old.

Gross Motor Development

Perhaps the most obvious area of growth during the preschool years lies in the area of gross motor (large muscle) development: running, jumping, galloping, hopping, climbing, skipping, or throwing, catching, and kicking a ball.

Children enjoy practicing these skills through frequent repetition. A child stands on a balance board or kicks a ball using many different techniques until he finds one that actually works. It gives him confidence to develop skills through such active self-initiated play. Some of the play activities involving the large muscles with which children may be involved during a normal preschool day include swinging on a swing, climbing on a jungle gym, digging with a shovel in sand or dirt, throwing and catching a ball, jumping with a rope, walking on low balance boards, riding a tricycle, sliding down the slide, pulling a wagon, pushing a small wheelbarrow, painting with water, running through fresh grass, pounding nails, and sawing, planing, or sanding wood.

Katherine Read (1971) emphasized the importance of such physical activities: "A child builds self-confidence from control of his muscles. He gains when he is 'in tune' with his own body, able to use it freely following his own rhythms. . . . The child with good motor skills can do more about what he perceives"

Table 6-1 *Physical Characteristics of the Child from Two to Five Years Old*

At Two Years Begins to	At Three Years Begins to	At Four Years Begins to	At Five Years Begins to
Walk	Jump and hop on one foot	Run, jump, and climb with close adult supervision	Gain good body control
Run	Climb stairs by alternating feet on each stair	Dress self using buttons, zippers, laces, and so on	Throw and catch a ball, climb, jump, skip with good coordination
Actively explore his environment	Dress and undress self somewhat	Use more sophisticated eating utensils such as knives to cut meat or spread butter	Coordinate movements to music
Sit in a chair without support	Walk a reasonably straight path on floor		Put on snowpants, boots, and tie shoes
Climb stairs with help (two feet on each stair)	Walk on balance beam	Walk balance beam with ease	Skip
Build block towers	Ride a tricycle	Walk down stairs alone	Jump rope, walk in a straight line
Feed self with fork and spoon	Stand on one foot for a short time	Bounce and catch ball	Ride a two-wheel bike
Stand on balance beam	Catch large balls	Push/pull wagon	Roller skate
Throw ball	Hop	Cut, following lines	Fold paper
Catch	Gallop	Copy figure ×	Reproduce alphabet and numbers
Jump	Kick ball	Print first name	Trace
Push and pull	Hit ball		
Hang on bar	Paste		
Slide	String beads		
	Cut paper with scissors		
	Copy figures ○ and +		

(pp. 194–195). Verna Hildebrand (1976) stated that, "The imaginative games ... observed during children's [physical] activity challenge the child's creativity, concepts, percepts, and memory. All are part of the child's mental development. Vigorous physical activity stimulates all vital processes, such as circulation, respiration, and elimination. Eating habits improve, and rest is more welcome" (p. 119). Physical activity, then, has values that go beyond mere physical gains; it enhances emotional, creative, and cognitive areas as well.

In order for children to benefit in these ways from physical activity, however, the environment must offer them many opportunities to develop and refine their growing capabilities. For instance, children must have

- space in which to use equipment and in which they can walk, run, and jump.

- the necessary equipment, such as balls and beanbags to throw and catch, • wagons to pull and push, things to lift and carry, ladders to climb, and fences or rails on which to balance.

- reinforcement from adults to let them know they're doing well.

- adults who are observant and can step in and give help and guidance when needed. [Charlesworth, 1983, p. 125]

In order to apply these considerations to the design of opportunities for physical growth through active play, you need to consider several factors.

Adequate Space Children require outdoor play areas that are safe, spacious, and inviting. Space requirements vary according to the source, but generally they fall into the generous limits of 75 to 200 square feet per child. Using the maximum figure of 200 square feet per child, a playground for twenty children would thus be as wide as a football field and as long as the distance from the goal line to the 25 yard line. Naturally, for some child-

care facilities, especially those in urban settings, it is nearly impossible to obtain the land necessary for such a spacious playground. In these cases, creative and careful planning is necessary so the limited space can be used to its fullest potential. Some of the most exciting limited space urban play areas have been developed on rooftops or on abandoned lots that were cleaned up and prepared by involved neighborhood groups.

Outdoor play areas should be planned extensions of the classroom. Wide, low windows should face the playground and give the child an uncluttered view of the facilities. If possible, a door should connect the classroom to the outdoors so the children are able to move freely from one area to the other. Some teachers find it desirable to fence in the playground for privacy, safety, and security. High shrubs, evergreen trees, fences, or walls are often used for this purpose. Many child-care facilities have asphalt surfaces as well as grassy or dirt surfaces so that activities can occur in appropriate places: riding a tricycle or bouncing a ball on the asphalt or running with bare feet in the grass or digging in the dirt. Play areas should also provide a good balance between sun and shade. Where large shade trees are not present, teachers have requested that simple overhangs be constructed from the side of the building, have brought in beach umbrellas, and have even tacked up strong cardboard or butcher paper in strategic rest areas. In general, the appearance and formation of the playground stimulate children to explore, to become physically active, to create, and to learn in ways that bring happiness, health, and new challenges to their developing lives.

Classroom space recommendations vary from 35 to 100 square feet per child, depending again on the source. However, how the space is filled and planned is at least as important as how many square feet are available. Indoor play areas must be as inviting to physical activity as are the outdoor areas. Children need room to romp and jump, to push buggies and pedal tricycles, and to move about freely without bumping into one another. They need corners or nooks and crannies to serve as private hide-outs—places that give them a chance to be alone. They need areas for clean up and toileting, for activity and rest. Sufficient space and effective equipment arrangements are a must in providing opportunities for large motor activities both in the classroom and out.

Adequate Equipment   Selecting appropriate indoor or outdoor equipment and supplies is often an expensive experience. However, a resourceful teacher can overcome this obstacle by seeking out used toys or equipment from parents of older children; by contacting parents who know carpentry; and by improvising with boxes, crates, tires, barrels, or planks. Some appealing play areas have been created by innovative teachers and parents using free or inexpensive materials that had been destined for the junk heap. Parents with special materials or skills to contribute are often willing to become involved, especially if their responsibilities are kept to the level at which they feel comfortable.

Most inexpensive equipment also stimulates creativity in young children. For example, they add old buttons or dials to wooden packing crates and turn them into cars, trains, garbage trucks, fire engines, buses, airplanes, boats, and other vehicles. Other equipment is limited only by the child's imagination. The following can also serve as materials for the children:

- *Milk crates*—dairies will provide old ones
- *Packing crates*—sanded and painted in a variety of bright colors
- *Rubber tires*—see your service station manager
- *Boards*—large planks 7 to 8 feet long
- *Small crates*—orange crates and the like (paint them)

- *Telephone cable spools*—make excellent outdoor tables
- *Logs and stumps*—good for climbing or sitting
- *Ladders*—4 feet long with 2-inch boards spaced evenly (Lay the ladders on the ground and watch the children climb, crawl, balance, and walk.)
- *Hose*—young firefighters enjoy this important tool
- *Barrels*—great for rolling, climbing through, and so on
- *Cardboard boxes*—cut holes in the sides to encourage crawling (These also make wonderful, secretive "hiding places.")

If you have to buy any equipment, follow suggested criteria for selection and purchase. Questions such as those on the following equipment checklist should be considered before you buy any new equipment.

PURCHASING EQUIPMENT
FOR YOUNG CHILDREN

1. *Will the children enjoy the equipment?*
   The equipment should be challenging, yet not frustrate or defeat the children.

2. *Are the materials safe?*
   Check the material for sharp corners or edges and exposed nails or screws. Make sure it is constructed of materials that would be injury free when used in normal ways. Check whether the paint, varnish, or other finish is nontoxic. Make sure small pieces are securely fastened so they cannot be swallowed or poked into the eyes or ears.

3. *Are the materials durable?*
   Be sure that the materials are strong and resilient. They should withstand extreme weather conditions and hard use.

4. *Are the materials versatile?*
   Look carefully to see if the materials could be used in a variety of ways. Balls, blocks, wagons, and ropes are but a few of the many items that are appropriate.

5. *Will the equipment provide balance to my collection?*
Assess the materials you presently have—evaluate whether you are over-loaded with one or more of these types of equipment: solitary play vs. group play; creative activity vs. closed-ended activity; motor vs. intellectual vs. social-type equipment.

6. *Is the material attractive?*
Determine whether the children will be attracted or turned away by the color, form, or sound of the equipment. Equipment should have a high overall appeal for children.

7. *Will the child be actively involved in its use?*
Many times, equipment is manufactured to appeal to an adult rather than to a child. The simple reason for this is that adults buy the equipment. Therefore, be wary of gimmicky-type equipment that is designed primarily for entertainment and that makes the children passive observers.

8. *Is the material developmentally appropriate?*
Check to see whether the size is correct and whether it would be suitable for the age level of the children.

9. *Am I buying this equipment because the children need it or because I like it?*
Be careful to avoid impulse purchases. Decide what your needs are and stick to your purchase plans. Do not be enticed by sharply reduced prices, flashy displays, or smooth sales pitches.

Many lists of suggested play equipment are available for ready reference. You can consult these lists whenever new equipment is needed. However, the following list of common items will give you a general idea of what is normally found in many preschool centers. Keep in mind that many of these materials can be used either inside or out, depending, of course, on the weather, the space available, and other similar considerations.

STATIONARY EQUIPMENT

1. *Slides.* Standard slides are made of rust-proof metal. They come in various sizes so children of each age level will have a safe, appropriate height to negotiate. Some slides are extensions of raised play platforms or tree houses so children can more readily carry their imaginative play over to the equipment. For some children, the slide becomes a fire-fighter's quick approach to a fire truck, a slipping waterfall, or a parachute jump from an airplane.

2. *Raised play platforms.* These structures are normally 5 to 7 feet in height with a 5-foot-square platform surrounded by a safe railing or fence. Many times the play platform is on top of a playhouse in a quiet area of the playground.

3. *Jungle gym.* This is a sturdy arrangement of strong, rustproof steel pipes that presents the child with a maze of climbing and crawling avenues to attempt to negotiate. Wooden gym structures are available for indoor use.

4. *Trapeze.* A rope secured to a sturdy tree branch or other support comprises this uncomplicated piece of equipment. Children can swing on the rope or attempt to climb up its length, hand over hand. Knots should be tied every foot or so to give the children secure footrests for climbing.

5. *Swings.* If the swing area is not properly supervised, it can be one of the most dangerous areas on the school playground; some teachers of children younger than age four or five don't use swings. For younger children bucket swings should have safety straps so the youngsters can be safely placed on the seat with almost no danger of falling out. Older children should have swings made from canvas or flexible rubber strips. If they hit a child, these swings will not harm him as much as a hard rubber, metal, or wood swing could. Children also enjoy tire swings, which

are made from old tires hung from tree limbs with sturdy supports. Swings should be placed so that they are away from the direct line of normal play; some advocate placing a barrier such as a hedge in front of the swings to prevent any child from being accidentally injured. Also, soft sand or pine mulch should be placed on the ground around the swings to help protect any child who falls.

6. *Sand areas.* As discussed in Chapter 5, the sandbox should be fairly large (about 10 feet wide on each side). The ledge can serve as a seat or table for various activities, as well as a frame to keep loose sand from spilling over the edges. Other sandboxes are easily made from old tires, plastic wading pools, and similar discarded equipment. A variety of toys and utensils—shovels, pails, plastic containers, old pots and pans, toy cars or trucks—should be kept in the sandbox to encourage imaginative play and large muscle activity. The outdoor sandbox should always be covered when the sandbox is not being used. This helps prevent contamination from animal elimination, unhealthiness from refuse collection, or problems of excess rain water.

7. *Water play areas.* Again, as discussed in Chapter 5, a washtub or large galvanized container containing 20 to 25 gallons of water to a depth of 8 to 10 inches is suitable for water play outdoors or inside. Protect the children with plastic aprons as they enjoy experimenting with materials such as measuring cups, funnels, egg beaters, medicine droppers, strainers, watering cans, soap, bowls, squeeze bottles, ladles, sieves, sponges, or brushes. Children enjoy using straws to blow bubbles formed with water and mild detergent and revel in activities such as "painting" the slide or playhouse with a paintbrush and water.

8. *Playhouse.* This structure can provide a quiet retreat for some children and a center of creative play for others. It can be constructed with a variety of stairs and levels to encourage large muscle development by climbing, crawling, pushing, pulling, and so on. Dress-up clothes and various props help stimulate imaginative play episodes.

9. *Storage shed.* A small structure convenient to the various play areas is ideal for storing outdoor equipment. Children can be encouraged to put away their equipment when finished or to assist the teacher if a sudden weather problem arises.

MOVABLE EQUIPMENT

1. *Wheel toys.* Tricycles, wheelbarrows, wagons, tractors, trucks—equipment that can be pulled, pushed, and manipulated by the child—are useful both for physical and for imaginative play.

2. *Gardening tools.* Shovels, rakes, trowels, pails, and similar tools should be available for active digging or raking. Such tools should be durable and child-sized.

3. *Balls.* Balls of different sizes (8–24 inches), shapes (round, elliptical), and composition (rubber, leather) should be available for throwing, kicking, and catching. Beanbags can also be used for these purposes.

4. *Ropes.* Individual jump ropes and longer ropes that can be turned by two people should be available for those children who are able to use them.

5. *Balance boards.* Choose planks of varying widths (4–10 inches) and lengths (4–8 feet) for the children to walk along and exercise their sense of balance. You will need about 10 to 12 planks.

6. *Miscellaneous.* Large sewer pipes make fine crawling tunnels; old telephone cable spools serve as play platforms or tables; used tires can become jumping circles, buried halfway into the ground to form a tunnel, made into sandbox enclosures, or bolted together and hung

Interesting playground equipment can be made from a variety of different materials.

by cables from trees to form climbing or swinging equipment; fallen tree trunks can be sawed into several lengths, anchored vertically in cement (about 2 inches apart), surrounded by sand, and used as a walking or climbing area; barrels can be securely mounted on a platform and used as a tunnel, as a quiet retreat, or as a theater, rocket ship, or other prop in a dramatic play. Other miscellaneous equipment includes wooden storage crates, pulleys, air pumps, small ladders, hoses, or nuts and bolts. All these materials tap the child's imagination and encourage valuable physical activity (see Figure 6-2).

Figure 6-2   *Miscellaneous play equipment*

Table 6-2   Patterns of Fine Motor Development in Preschool Children

Age	Fine Motor Abilities
1–2 years	Can hold large pencil or crayon Can pull off shoes and socks Can begin to drink from a cup and feed themselves with a spoon
2–3 years	Can scribble with pencils or crayons Can open boxes and other simple containers Can begin to use knives and forks when feeding themselves
3–4 years	Can use pencils or crayons to copy circles or simple lines Can print large capital letters Can use modeling clay, make cookies, and sew Can feed themselves well and even wash and dry dishes Can cut paper
4–6 years	Can copy some simple geometric figures: circles, squares, triangles, and rectangles Can print their names, entire alphabet, and numerals from 1 to 20 Can build crude models from wood and other materials Can bathe themselves, brush own teeth and hair Can dress themselves completely, except for tying shoes Can cut following a line

Most of the large muscle play equipment described to this point probably appeared to you as being most appropriate for outdoors on the playground. The main reason we did not specify it as such was that most standard large muscle equipment can be modified to the limitations of the classroom. Poor weather and limited-access outdoor play areas need not hinder your children's large muscle play activity, for this is a very important area of your children's growth. This awareness has led manufacturers to develop durable, flexible equipment appropriate for either indoor or outdoor play. Usually built of hardwood such as maple, this equipment is made so that it is easily transportable between the playground and classroom. Jungle gyms, slides, and other equipment can be used indoors on stormy days and returned again to the playground a week later when the weather again becomes appropriate. Such flexibility allows you to use the same large muscle play equipment over and over again for different activities.

Fine Motor Development

Preschool children are given opportunities to refine many school-related skills. In the realm of fine motor (small muscle) activity, they are given experiences to manipulate puzzle pieces, hold paintbrushes to paint lines and circles, use scissors to cut paper, and handle crayons or pencils to color and draw (see Figure 6-3). Nearly all of these experiences are designed to develop perhaps the most necessary of all fine motor skills: precise hand control. Some common developing patterns of hand control are presented in Table 6-2.

To encourage these fine motor skills, you should provide a variety of materials with which the children can experiment. In contrast to infants, who engage in random motor play as a way to develop related skills, preschoolers prefer to use motor activity in ways that help meet general purposes. For example, they may enjoy running barefoot through cool grass simply for the pleasure it brings, but more

Figure 6-3 *Children learn to develop strength and coordination in small muscles by engaging in many school-related activities such as painting, drawing, cutting, pasting, fingerplays, writing, and so on.*

often they run to catch another child in a game of tag, or twist pipes together to "install" a sink, or dress up to assume the role of a parent or community helper. Because of this functional, purposeful nature of the preschooler's motor play, Maria Montessori was prompted to advise us that *play is the young child's work.*

There are numerous opportunities each day to help the child apply his play orientation to the refinement of fine motor skills. Such activities will be comprehensively discussed in later chapters. The following is only a brief list of some general activities whose primary value is to help develop small muscle skills: pouring, cutting, building (tinker toys), drilling, mixing, printing, constructing puzzles, stapling, pasting, buttoning, screwing bottle tops, manipulating, drawing, zipping, nailing,

grasping, painting, lacing, scribbling, and planting seeds.

Such activities are not only inherently pleasing for young children, but they also serve as readiness for the eventual mastery of handwriting skills and other intellectual growth. Before young children can be expected to write, for example, they must be able to hold a pencil properly and to control movements of their wrist and finger muscles. They gain this control through the activities listed in the preceding paragraph. As children develop the small muscle skills, they learn to coordinate the hand and eye *(eye–hand coordination)*. Children who hammer a nail straight or follow a path with their pencil demonstrate eye–hand coordination. All of these actions help to increase the children's intellectual growth. As Julius

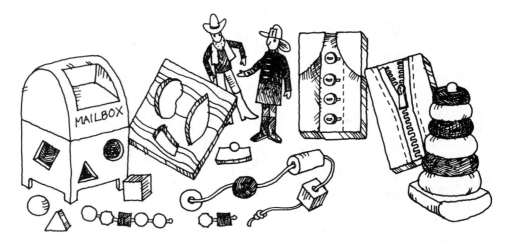

(1978, p. 20) emphasized, "action or move-ment, natural to children, is the raw material for intellectual development."

Equipment designed to foster small mus-cle control is rich and varied. Some common small muscle equipment is shown in the fol-lowing list.

SMALL MUSCLE EQUIPMENT

- *Stacking rings.* Children stack the color-ful plastic rings in order.
- *Snap-lock beads.* These colorful plastic beads snap together and pop apart.
- *Puzzles.* Simple wooden or durable cardboard puzzles should be easy enough for the child and not frustrate him. Some suggestions: For two-year-olds use one- or two-piece puzzles with handles. For three-year-olds and older use puzzles of up to eight pieces.
- *Shape toys.* Children put three-dimen-sional plastic shapes into appropriate openings in a special box.
- *Wooden beads.* Children pick up the beads and either string them or plop them back into the can.
- *Dressing frames.* Children refine their skills of lacing, tying, buttoning, zipping, and snapping on small practice frames.
- *Art supplies.* Children can be helped to control their small muscles through cre-ative art media such as fat crayons, fat pencils, felt-tip markers, note pads and paper, glue, clay, blunt-pointed scissors, brushes and paint, and yarn.
- *Small plastic figures.* Children enjoy manipulating animals, farmers, fire-fighters, police officers, and other small plastic figures.

When choosing materials for small mus-cle development, be sure to separate the good buys from the bad. The following checklist should help you when you look for appropri-ate toys:

CHOOSING TOYS FOR SMALL MUSCLE DEVELOPMENT

1. Is it too large to be swallowed, stuck in the ear, or jammed into the nose?
2. Can the detachable parts be swallowed, stuck in the ear, or jammed into the nose?
3. Can little parts easily break off?
4. Are there sharp corners or dangerous points?
5. Is the construction solid and durable?
6. Is the material nontoxic?
7. Can parts pinch or catch hair?
8. Is it possible for long cords to acciden-tally strangle the child?

Periods of planned, group physical activity are normally included as a part of a pre-school's daily schedule.

9. Can the child use the toy independently?

10. Can plastic bags or large containers suffocate the child?

You should be aware of the importance of providing opportunities for refining gross and fine motor skills. As the children experience learning opportunities in curriculum areas, they do so in physically active ways, and children *need* physical activity during the preschool years. You will find that, except for short periods of quiet (as during story time) or rest (as after vigorous play), nearly all learning activities during a typical preschool day involve the children in physical activity. However, it is important that you individualize your program and make it developmental. That is, all children develop at different rates, and so opportunities for muscular exercise should range from the simple (running, jumping) to the more demanding (cutting, printing). Your

ability to plan activities based on such considerations will help children develop to their full potential when they are ready.

PERIODS OF PLANNED EXERCISE

Many children enter the preschool setting with good coordination and muscle control. These children benefit from opportunities to improve their skills through continued informal exercise, such as we have been discussing. Others are less proficient and need positive encouragement to achieve greater success. Your role in this process is to structure short indoor or outdoor practice activities in which the children can work on developing their muscular coordination to its full potential. Such activities, combining creativity and physical exercise, can be somewhat informal. Consider the following example.

BODY PART SONGS

Fingerplays

THUMBKIN

(Sung to the tune of "Frère Jacques")

Where is thumbkin?
Where is thumbkin?
Here I am.
Here I am.
How are you today, Sir?
Very fine, I thank you.
Run away.
Run away.

Repeat, extending a different finger for each
verse, as follows: thumbkin = thumb, pointer
= first finger, tall man = second finger, ring-
man = third finger, pinky = little finger.

TEN FINGERS

I have ten little fingers and ten little toes, *(point
to body parts)*
Two little arms and one little nose,
One little mouth and two little ears,
Two little eyes for smiles and tears.
One little head and two little feet,
One little chin; that's ME, complete!

ONE LITTLE BODY

Two little feet go stamp, stamp, stamp, *(stamp)*
Two little hands go clap, clap, clap, *(clap)*

One little body stands up straight, *(stand
straight)*
One little body goes round and round, *(turn)*
One little body sits quietly down. *(sit)*

FOLLOW ME

Hands on shoulders, hands on knees, *(follow
actions as rhyme indicates)*
Hands behind you, if you please;
Touch your shoulders, now your nose,
Now your hair and now your toes;
Hands up high in the air,
Down at your sides and touch your hair;
Hands up high as before,
Now clap your hands, one, two, three, four.

CLAP YOUR HANDS

Clap your hands, clap your hands,
Clap them just like me.
Touch your shoulders, touch your shoulders,
Touch them just like me.
Shake your head, shake your head,
Shake it just like me.
Clap your hands, clap your hands,
Now let them quiet be.

Traditional Tunes

The following song is sung to the tune of "There Is a
Tavern in the Town." The children place their hands on
the part of the body mentioned in the song.

*Marge and her friend Terri made an interest-
ing discovery while on the playground one
day. They went down on their hands and knees
and watched in fascination as a large frog
hopped erratically in the tall grass at the edge
of the play area. Soon several other children
joined the two girls and called to their teacher
to observe their discovery. After encouraging
the children to comment on the frog's bumpy
skin and bulging eyes, the teacher was pleased
when the children began to discuss how it
hopped and jumped. "Gee, look how far it
hopped!" "It jumped so high." Suddenly, Terri
kicked up her legs and supported herself with
her hands. "Watch me," she called, "I'm a frog.
Watch me hop." Soon the other children joined
Terri and hopped along with each other. The
teacher, alert to the situation, began to lead*

*the children in a rhythmical chant, "Hippity
hop, hippity hop, watch us jump and flip and
flop. Hippity hop, hippity hop. . . ."*

In addition to these informal experiences,
teachers often plan programs carefully designed
to help children practice their growing physical skills through play activity. Operating with
the motto of "Teach a little and play a lot,"
these teachers realize the importance of
developing guided activities appropriate for
the age level of their children, but, at the same
time, realize the need for the youngsters to do
it their way. "I can do it" and "Watch me" are
frequent exclamations of children who experience the excitement of gaining control over
their movements. Your ability to perceive the

Head, shoulders, knees, and toes,
Knees and toes.

Head, shoulders, knees, and toes
Knees and toes and—

Eyes and ears
And mouth and chin and nose.

Head, shoulders, knees, and toes,
Knees and toes.

To the tune "Hokey Pokey," encourage the following movements:

Put your right hand in. *(toward center of circle)*
Take your right hand out.
Put your right hand in, and shake it all about.
We'll shake it in the morning or we'll shake it afternoon.
That's what it's all about.

(second verse) . . . left hand . . .
(third verse) . . . right foot . . .
(fourth verse) . . . left foot . . .
(fifth verse) . . . head . . .
(sixth verse) . . . whole body . . .

Create new words to familiar tunes as children are encouraged to exercise. This is one of many possible variations of the tune "Jingle Bells."

Clap your hands, clap your hands,

Clap them loud and long,
Oh, what fun it is to clap,
And sing this happy song.

(second verse) Touch your toes . . .
(third verse) Stretch up tall . . .
(fourth verse) Walk in line . . .
(fifth verse) Row your boat . . .
(sixth verse) Throw the ball . . .

"Looby Loo" is a favorite circle-song that encourages children to move different parts of their bodies creatively.

(chorus) Here we go looby loo,
Here we go looby light,
Here we go looby loo,
All on a Saturday night.

Verses follow with:

I put my left hand in
I put my left hand out
I give my left hand a shake, shake, shake
And turn my self about.
(chorus) Here we go looby loo . . .

Continue with right hand, left foot, right foot, round head, and whole self.

world of the child and to see things from that point of view is a necessary prerequisite to sharing happy play experiences such as the following:

KNOWLEDGE OF BODY PARTS

- Ask the children to identify parts of the body by touching them. Start by touching the different parts of your body as you say, for example, "I'm touching my nose. Touch your nose." Continue with the ears, eyes, chin, mouth, shoulder, neck, arm, elbow, knee, stomach, toes, back, side, ankle, and hand.

- A number of traditional early childhood songs stimulate children to recognize body parts and their relative movement

properties. Some examples are shown in the accompanying box.

- Use variations of the first activity:
  –Touch the parts with eyes closed.
  –Touch the parts with two hands.
  –Touch the body parts with a body part other than the hand or finger; for example, "Touch your elbow with your knee."
  –Touch a body part with an object in the environment; for example, "Touch your knees to the floor," or "Touch the tree with your foot."
  –Invite the children to take turns leading the activity.

- Establish relationships of body parts. Say, for example, "See if you can move your hands far away from your feet (or shoulders)," or "Move one foot behind the other," or "Stand next to a partner," or "Wave your hand above your head."

• Use fingerplays, such as those in the accompanying box, to help identify body parts.

REFINING LOCOMOTOR SKILLS

After children are aware of the basic parts and gain control of them, they are ready to pursue activities that refine rudimentary movement skills and encourage creativity of movement.

Note: Most of these activities are best used along with musical accompaniment such as recordings or simply drums or tambourines.

• *Walking:* Walk fast; walk slow; walk backwards; walk on tiptoes; walk on heels; walk sideways; walk with hands on head; walk with hands on hips; and so on. Play games such as Follow the Leader or encourage the children to walk like favorite animals.

• *Standing:* Stand on tiptoes for a count of five; stand on right foot for a count of five; stand on left foot for a count of five; stand in each of the previous ways with eyes shut.

• *Balancing:* Get a 2 inch × 4 inch × 8 foot board for these activities. First, ask the children to stand on the board to see if they can control their bodies. This ability to balance is basic to other activities. When children display good balance, ask them to walk with one foot on the board and one foot on the floor. Then encourage children to take short series of steps with both feet on the balance board. Gradually, children will learn to walk forward on the balance board. Then ask them to walk slowly (forward); walk sideways (first the dominant side leads and then the other leads); walk with a beanbag on their heads; walk slowly (backward); walk

slowly backward with a beanbag on their heads.

• *Running:* Run fast; run slowly; run on tiptoes; run with hands behind their backs; run with long or short strides; run toward the teacher; and so forth.

• *Jumping:* Jump up and down in place; use only one foot while jumping; jump forward; jump backward; jump into the air and make a quarter-turn; jump with eyes closed; and so on. Jump from a low height onto a mat or landing pad. Children can be encouraged to become frogs, grasshoppers, or jumping jacks.

• *Galloping:* Help children learn this skill by showing them the correct procedure. Play some background music appropriate for galloping and invite the children to become galloping ponies or reindeer. Then show them how to gallop—step forward on one foot and bring the other foot up beside it. Then step forward on the first foot and again bring the second beside it. Gradually encourage the children to repeat the process to the music until they achieve a smooth, galloping gait.

• *Skipping:* Skipping is perhaps the most difficult body movement for young children to master. For that reason, you must spend a good deal of time instructing them in this skill. Tell the children to step forward on one foot while holding the second foot in the air (you may want to hold it up for the child). The first foot then makes a hop and the second foot steps forward. The children are led to step and hop on one foot, step and hop on the other, and so on until the step-hop sequence becomes smooth and natural.

CREATIVE BODY MOVEMENT

Once the children have mastered basic large muscle skills, you may wish to capitalize on their imaginations in order to further refine their capabilities. Some suggested activities are presented in the box on p. 206.

As the children use their bodies to explore and express creative movements, they begin to make unconscious rhythmic body movements in response to strongly accented verbal directions or to music. Therefore, the fingerplays described earlier provide an excellent starting avenue of rhythmic expression. Action verses such as the preceding help the children to control new movements such as skipping or hopping and to develop a conscious "inner rhythm," especially if actions are accompanied by a drum beat or other musical rhythm. Movement, therefore, plays an important role in the development of musical concepts in children, because children use their whole bodies to explore and express the dynamics of music. Since the relationship between movement and music is so close, the temptation to include music material at this point is very strong. However, because it is a significant topic in itself, the process of illustrating the transition between movement and music will be comprehensively treated in Chapter 10.

Games With Rules As the children grow through kindergarten into the primary grades, they reach a level of social maturity and physical skill that allows them to benefit from group games involving rules. These organized games should have few rules or directions, since children are more interested in the physical activity than they are in following the directions. Games most appropriate to kindergarten or primary grade play are loosely organized and are frequently of the "circle" type. The few rules guiding such games direct the activities; in spontaneous (free0 play, the materials guided the activity while established rules guide the playing of games.

Since the primary objective of games is to have fun, the actual playing time should be lively and relaxed. Do not become so involved in communicating rules to the children that your anxiety and desires for conformity reduce your children to gloomy and depressed individuals. Remember, instead, that excitement is part of the game and that the fun and thrill of playing is controlled only to the degree that game rules must be followed.

When introducing young children to games, remember to tell them that it is important for them to concentrate on your directions if they expect to play the game correctly. It may be appropriate to give verbal directions while stressing the importance of listening carefully. It may be appropriate to demonstrate certain steps with some children so that the others will understand your directions more clearly. Go through each step carefully before you proceed to the next so that the set rules are clearly established. Here is one teacher's outline of how she organized a game with her kindergarten youngsters.

1. Group the children in a large circle and have them signal how they feel about being there.

2. Have the children use their arms to draw a letter (or numeral) as large as they can in space. Ask them to think about other parts of their body that they can draw with and have them do so.

3. Ask the children to choose partners and form a letter (or numeral) with their bodies on the floor or in a standing position.

4. Form a large letter on the floor with heavy yarn. Then, for example, encourage the children to move around a big "B," "buzzing like a bug" or "bouncing like a ball."

5. Give each child one letter. Then begin this rhyme and ask the first child to make his letter in space as big as he can:

> This is what I can do.
> Everybody try it, too.
> This is what I can do.
> Now I pass it on to you.

After the verse is complete, ask the other children to mimic the action and tell what letter (or numeral) was shared. Repeat for each child.

CREATIVE BODY MOVEMENT ACTIVITIES

Freeze Play lively music on the radio or tape recorder. Invite the children to move freely as the music is playing. Every so often, quickly turn off the sound and ask the children to "freeze." See if they can hold the position for two or three seconds, and start up the music again.

Shadows Two children work together. One child performs a basic body movement and the other child must imitate what was done. They take turns being the leader.

Rope Games

A long length of rope should be placed on the floor or ground. Have the children who are able walk a straight line along the rope forward and backward. Make a circle from the rope and ask the children to walk the circle forward or backward. With the rope in a straight line, have the children hop over it and then hop back again. Make curves in the rope and have the children run or hop so each step will be taken in a new curve. Ask the children to invent a new way of moving with the rope.

Tightrope Walker

Establish a straight line about 10 feet long on the floor of your classroom. Invite the children to walk along the line as far as they can without ringing a small bell held in their hand. For variety, try making a curved line, a circle, and other shapes used previously.

Animal Imitations

Invite the class to walk like animals.

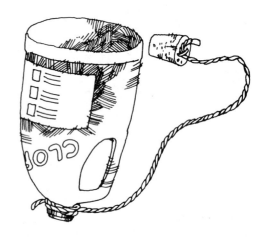

Catch-Ups

Remove the bottom from a large plastic container such as a bleach bottle. Attach a large cork to one end of a piece of yarn and slip the other end into the neck of the bottle and attach it there by screwing the lid on tight. The children hold onto the handle and try to catch the cork in the bottle. This is an adaptation of a traditional Mexican game and should be described as such, especially if Mexican-American children are in your care.

WALK LIKE A SPIDER
(ON ALL FOURS)

PULL YOURSELF
LIKE A SEAL
(THE LEGS
DRAGGING
BEHIND)

SPRING LIKE A KANGAROO
(SQUAT AND JUMP)

SWIM LIKE A FISH
(PADDLING ARMS AND LEGS)

PLOD LIKE AN ELEPHANT
(WITH ARMS AS THE TRUNK)

WADDLE LIKE A DUCK
(BENDING KNEES AND
RAISING ARMS SLIGHTLY)

KICK LIKE A MULE
(HANDS AND FEET ON THE
FLOOR — FEET KICKING
BACKWARDS INTO THE AIR)

CRAWL LIKE A SNAKE

GARBAGE BAG

CREPE PAPER STREAMERS

OLD SHEET

Race Track

Mark out a curvy path on the floor or playground with masking tape, rope, or chalk. The children run from the start of the track to the finish as quickly as they can without touching or going beyond the sides of the track.

Wings

Especially on days when winds are brisk and steady, invite the children to don a variety of wings and run about as imaginary butterflies, birds, superheroes, or anything else that jogs their creativity. Some effective wings include an old sheet; crepe paper streamers stapled onto a cloth strip; and a plastic garbage bag slit to form a large sheet. (Plastic bags can be dangerous, so children playing with them should be closely supervised.)

Going to the Zoo

To encourage creative movements of many kinds, gather the children in a group and invite them to go with you on an imaginary trip to the zoo. On this special trip, the children must choose an animal to imitate as their means of getting there. Lead them by saying this phrase, "We're going to the zoo. How is Diana going to get there?" "I'm going to fly like a bird," says Diana. Encourage the

rest of the children to follow the first child's lead and perform the actions described in the previous activity—flying like birds, hopping like frogs, waddling like ducks, swimming like fish, crawling like snakes, and so on.

Circus Time

Arrange the children in a circle formation, seated on the floor. Select one child to stand in the center to act as "ringmaster." The ringmaster passes out one slip of paper to each child, each slip picturing an animal with a distinctive movement, such as a horse, elephant, bird, and so on (or hang the picture around the child's neck). When signalled by the ringmaster, the child steps to the center of the circle and pantomimes the animal on his slip. After the ringmaster has given each child a chance, she organizes a parade in which the children move in a circle, pantomiming their respective animals.

Tree Stumps

A large tree stump allows children to hammer (with a real hammer) until content. Allow them to pound nails (roofing nails are safest) into the stump throughout the year to see if it can be covered by year's end. Note: It might be wise to provide some kind of protective eye covering to prevent serious accidental injury.

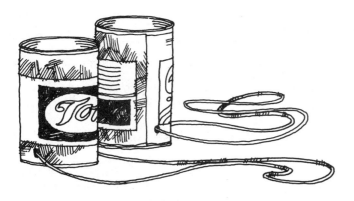

Walking Cans

Get some large cans with one end removed. Punch a hole with a nail in two opposite sides of each can near the closed ends. Cut pieces of heavy twine and string one piece through each can, tying the ends together with a good, secure knot to form a large loop. Encourage children to stand with one foot on one can and one foot on another, remaining steady by holding onto the twine. They may want to walk a short distance on a hard-surfaced play area.

Balloon Bat

Give each child in your group an inflated balloon. Give the children a signal to start, whereupon they throw their balloons into the air. The children see how long they can keep the balloons in the air by tapping them back when they begin to come down.

Jack, Be Nimble

Make several potato chip canister "candlesticks" (make a slit in the plastic top and pull a red kerchief through it). Place one in front of each child in your group. Say the nursery rhyme, "Jack, Be Nimble," and have the children jump with both feet over the candlesticks as the last line is recited. (You may wish to encourage the children to jump one-by-one over their candlesticks by substituting their names for *Jack*.)

> Jack, be nimble,
> Jack, be quick,
> Jack, *jump* over the candlestick.

Say the rhyme again, this time jumping backward over the candlestick. Continue with variations such as jumping sideways or with arms stretched in front.

Action Verses

Compose a set of verses by which you can encourage various body movements. For example, while playing outdoors, these rhymes can be used:

> Little frogs, little frogs,
> Hop to the wall;
> Little frogs, little frogs,
> Please come back, I call.

> Little lions, little lions,
> Run to the door;
> Little lions, little lions,
> Give a great big roar.

> Little ducks, little ducks,
> Waddle to the gate;
> Little ducks, little ducks,
> Hurry—don't be late.

> Little birds, little birds,
> Fly to the swings;
> Little birds, little birds,
> Flap and flap your wings.

GAMES WITH RULES

Red Light/Green Light

Children line up alongside each other at one end of the playground. A leader stands at the opposite end of the playground with his back to the rest of the children. The leader yells so that all can hear, "1—2—3—green light!" and the players run toward the leader as fast as they can. The leader then calls out, "1—2—3—red light!" which is a signal for all children to stop running. The leader turns around quickly to see if all the players have stopped. Any player caught still moving by the leader must return to the starting point. The first player to reach the leader is the winner.

Cross the River

Use 8½- × 11-inch construction paper of various colors and paste different geometric figures on them. Arrange them on the floor and explain to the children that they are going to try to cross a river by stepping on stones (the geometric shapes). The teacher guides the children across the river by saying, "Hop to the green square, . . . the red circle, . . . the blue rectangle," and so on.

Red Rover

Mark off two end boundary lines with lengths of rope. Children stand in back of one line while the leader stands facing them between the two lines. The leader calls out, "Red Rover, Red Rover, let (a child's name) come over." The child called must cross the space and the opposite boundary line before he is caught by the leader. Any child caught must stay in the center to help the leader. The last one caught is the new leader.

Duck, Duck, Goose

Arrange the children in a large circle and designate one child to be "It." "It" walks around the circle and touches certain children and says "Duck" with each touch. When he touches a child and says "Goose," however, that child must get up and run around the circle trying to catch "It." If the "Goose" does that before she returns to her original place in the circle she becomes "It," and the players switch places.

Cross the Stream

Draw two lines on the playground or on the classroom floor. The space between the two lines represents a stream. The children attempt to jump over the stream without getting "wet."

Dog and Bone

One child is chosen to be the dog. He sits with his back to the group with a beanbag (the bone) on the floor behind him. Taking turns, the other children try to sneak up and steal the bone without being heard. If the dog hears a child, he says "Bark, bark!" and that child must go back. If that child is able to steal the bone without getting caught, however, he returns to the group who chants, "Dog, oh dog, where is your bone?" The "dog" then has three chances to guess who has his bone. The one who stole the bone then becomes the "dog," whether or not his name is guessed.

Most games involve a great deal of body activity and mobility such as in the preceding example. The games in the accompanying box can be played indoors or out, but keep in mind that the playground often gives you more area, allowing for greater freedom of movement. These games are enjoyed by kindergarten and primary grade children.

Games should be chosen to help children refine specific skills rather than to establish a winner and loser. If excessive competition results from the game, and a child fails constantly, that child's motivation may be killed.

For that reason, winning or losing should depend on a child's ability to use effective strategy or on a combination of luck and skill rather than on skill alone. Other suggestions for using games effectively are:

1. Use your time efficiently. As a rule of thumb, young children's attention spans during intensive activities are about one or two minutes more than their age.

2. Keep groups as small as possible. This provides greater opportunity for maxi-

mum individual efforts with careful guidance by the teacher.

3. Concentrate on only one or two skills in any game session. More than that number may confuse or frustrate some children.

4. Give clear, simple directions and make sure the children understand how the game is played. You may even demonstrate the actions of the game to give a clear idea of how to play.

5. Do not force each child to play. Try to encourage all to participate, but you will find that the activity will go much better if the children join of their own free will rather than because of the teacher's demand.

6. Keep a watchful eye on the children. Stop the game when their interest wanes and move on to something else. Don't overdo it—too much of a good thing will eventually tire the children of nearly anything.

SOME FINAL THOUGHTS

Play is an important vehicle for physical development. Even during infancy, physical (or sensorimotor) play characterizes the child's simple, repetitive actions. These play behaviors gradually give way to more sophisticated motor responses during toddlerhood and the early years. Building blocks, wheel toys, carpentry tools, paints, scissors, paste, playground equipment, free movement or dance, imitative games, and many other forms of play enter the child's life and make the process of play more complex. By being knowledgeable and sensitive to specific physical abilities at any given point of the children's development, you can extend and enrich the children's play and encourage transition from one developmental level to the next.

It is important to remember that physical growth is best enhanced through free play within stimulating, challenging play environments. Arrange your classroom or playground in ways that offer children opportunities to develop large and small muscles as well as perceptual skills. The first requirement is to provide plenty of safe space in which to play. The second is to choose appropriate play equipment and activities so that all children can be accommodated. The third requirement is to encourage children in certain activities, to observe the interests and skills of the children, and to guide overly aggressive or overstimulated youngsters. Such provisions will certainly foster increased feelings of trust and initiative in young children, leading to increased growth in all areas of development.

Chapter 7

Early Learning Experiences

PLAY TODAY?

You say you love your children,
And are concerned they learn today?
So am I—that's why I'm providing
A variety of kinds of play.

You're asking me the value
Of blocks and other such play?
Your children are solving problems.
They will use that skill everyday.

You're asking what's the value
Of having your children play?
Your daughter's creating a tower;
She may be a builder someday.

You're saying you don't want your son
To play in that "sissy" way?
He's learning to cuddle a doll;
He may be a father someday.

You're questioning the interest centers;
They just look like useless play?
Your children are making choices;
They'll be on their own someday.

You're worried your children aren't learning;
And later they'll have to pay?
They're learning a pattern for learning;
For they'll be learners alway.

—Leila F. Fagg

We have read about play in previous chapters and examined the ways by which it contributes to social, emotional, and physical development. Whether pushing a car up a ramp, fitting pegs into holes, creating a train out of blocks, or putting a doll to bed, children are learning to cooperate, to express pleasures, anxieties, or fears, and to satisfy the need of growing muscles to push, climb, run, bend, and lift. These special moments are exclusive to childhood, and youngsters deprived of them are unfortunate indeed. As Leila F. Fagg so vividly described in her poem, play contributes to early learning when children dig in the earth, complete puzzles, prepare a tea party, climb trees, balance on rocks, or engage in countless other unstructured activities available to them. Children do not engage in these play activities especially to "learn" any special lessons. They choose to participate because play brings them pleasure, and, unknown to them, helps provide keys to discover the world.

As children play, they become active thinkers with a level of diligence and concentration that provides for endless opportunities of exploration and discovery. Consider, for a moment, how these attributes are present during a sand play experience. It is a rare youngster who does not love to play in sand—to let it run through her fingers or through a sifter when it is dry, to mold it into a variety of shapes when it is wet, to poke fingers into it to see what will happen, to pour it from one container into another of a different size or shape, or to create major roadways for construction toys. What do children learn through such play? They discover that sand can flow freely when dry or take a shape when wet, that it changes weight and texture when wet, that it can be spread out or molded into bumps or hills, that its color becomes darker when wet, that it is warm in the sun but cold in the shade, and a variety of other important things. Children naturally learn by making such discoveries through play and should be provided with opportunities for such creative exploration.

Despite this apparent value of play as it contributes to learning, the traditional role of play in the preschool setting has not been defined in ways so as to capitalize on this valuable process. Certainly, early childhood settings through the years have recognized the need for good play equipment and ample space for its use, but teachers have frequently tended to "turn the children loose" and intervene only to prevent accidents or to settle disagreements. The historical role of the preschool was to help children get along with each other and to cooperate—those areas we refer to as "socialization." Once the materials for play had been arranged, the teacher remained removed, expecting the materials and equipment to serve their own purpose.

These teachers defended their position with the argument that *planned* learning activities for young children were not appropriate because the children simply were not "ready" for such education. Grace Owen (1920, p. 25), a popular early nursery school educator, forcefully commented: "No mention has been made of instruction in the nursery school because in any formal sense it has no place. No reading, no writing, no number lessons should on any account be allowed, for the time for these things has not yet come" (p. 25). The "time" for these things, according to these early educators, happened as a natural biological phenomenon when the child reached the approximate age of six and a half years. If instruction was begun before that time, they reasoned, the child would certainly experience pressures and frustrations leading to failure and discouragement. Thus, the concept of *readiness* for learning was based solely on biological maturation—the teacher should wait until the child is old enough to learn and, in the meantime, provide a warm, comfortable social and emotional environment.

Such thinking ran into difficulties beginning in the late 1960s. At that time, educators started looking at the intellectual powers of young children and implored teachers to raise play from its position as contributing only to social or emotional development to a prized method of learning, too. This was not an easy task, however. Scientific evidence was needed to convince teachers that young children could be exposed to planned learning activities prior to the age of six and a half years. Such evidence came pouring out from many sources and resulted in programs with varying degrees and types of intellectual stimulation. Three major philosophies, under which each of those programs can be classified, emerged during the decades of the 1960s and 1970s: Behavioral, Cognitive–Developmental, and Informal (see Table 7-1). The Behavioral stance is patterned closely after the regimented techniques of B. F. Skinner, whose ideas we examined in Chapters 3 and 4. The Cognitive-Developmental and Informal programs, which

Table 7-1 *Summary of Three Major Teaching Philosophies*

Behavioral	Cognitive-Developmental	Informal Classroom
Subject matter foremost	Child foremost	Child foremost
Teacher-centered	Teacher and child work together	Child-centered
Subject matter structure	Content and process equally emphasized	Integrated day stressing process
Formalized instruction	Teacher role somewhat prescriptive	Incidental learning
Specific objectives and learning tasks	Activities inferred from Piaget's ideas and theories	"Messing about"
Learning occurs through a process of "conditioning"	Learning occurs through a process of "equilibration"	Each child is unique and learns in his own way
Motivation extrinsic (material rewards)	Motivation may be combination of external and internal rewards, but primarily intrinsic	Motivation intrinsic (self-reward)
Passive learning: pay attention, listen, follow specific instructions	Active learning with adult providing a supportive role	Active learning: exploring, discovering, experimenting
Emphasis on measuring and testing	Evaluating logical thinking processes so new learning can be associated with past experiences	Informal observation and discussion as evaluation
Rigid time schedule for learning activities	Structured as well as informal activity helps to achieve cognitive objectives	Informal atmosphere: children move freely from one activity to another

offer children more freedom than the Behavioral program, drew their primary support from an individual who influenced current early childhood education more than any other—Jean Piaget. We will begin our examination of intellectual stimulation with Piaget.

THE INFLUENCE OF JEAN PIAGET

Infants

To begin our study of how Jean Piaget provided theoretical support for early learning, it is important to go to the threshold of intelligence—infancy. For some time, the field of psychology had neglected the study of intelligence as it begins in the infant's mind. Pines (1966) found that there had existed some agreement that infants do not really have minds and whatever they do possess is relatively unimportant. Pearce (1977) suggested that even in 1977, our thinking had not yet changed that much since we still viewed the infant as a passive being. Today, of course, psychologists and educators have become increasingly aware of the tremendous potential of the infant's mind. Perhaps the first theories that truly alerted us to the infant's intelligence are those of Jean Piaget. As early as 1920, Piaget began his study of intelligence in human beings—a study that lasted throughout the lives of his own children. His description of the development of intelligence begins during infancy and deals with the growing awareness of infants through their most basic reactions to the environment.

Early childhood educators stress the importance of allowing young children to pursue areas of direct, firsthand learning. This child, for example, is spending time observing some newly hatched chicks scampering about in an incubator constructed, in part, by the members of his class.

Primitive reflexes are present at birth; these involuntary reactions help the infant cope with the environment. Knowledge of why some of the reflexes stay with us (coughing or eyeblink, for example) and others leave (the rooting reflex in which a baby's head turns and the mouth opens to suck when the cheek is stroked) as we grow into adulthood is not fully complete, but Piaget describes infant learning as a process beginning with such reflexes and evolving into higher processes of thought.

Piaget's theory of intelligence is currently the most popular explanation of how play facilitates the process of learning. Piaget talks about intelligence in a broad, biological framework: Some organisms have more complex biological structures, which accounts for higher levels of intelligence. For example, "Amoebas do not explore their environment, but dogs, rats, and human babies certainly do. Primates and humans have hands which immeasurably increase the organism's capacity to manipulate and explore objects" (Kamii, 1970, p. 9). Kamii explained further:

It seems more fruitful to put the emphasis on developing the efferent side, i.e., "the capacity to move freely and to act on and manipulate things of the environment." The importance of developing children's curiosity and eagerness to explore and experiment becomes clear. The more curious the child is, the more he will explore and the more knowledge he will gain. The more knowledge he has, the more advanced the nature of his curiosity will be, and the more systematic his exploration will be. [p. 10]

Piaget (1956, p. 10) used this concept of a child's acting on and manipulating things of the environment to form his own general definition of *intelligence.* He said that intelligence "is the form of equilibrium toward which all the [cognitive] structures . . . tend." The term *equilibrium* was taken from physics and implies seeking a balance between the person's existing mental structures and those things yet to be understood. To Piaget, this self-regulatory process is the most fundamental of all factors of intelligence. Through this process, children encounter something that is new to them and actively work toward relating it to something they already know. As they are able to resolve such discord, they reach a new level of equilibrium (intelligence).

The growth of intelligence can be viewed as an ascent up a flight of stairs, each stair representing a balanced state of equilibrium. As people progress to and through each stair, they are using a process called *adaptation,* a process of adjusting themselves to their surroundings. Adaptation involves combining two processes: *assimilation* and *accommodation.* Assimilation is the process of dealing with the environment in terms of current intellectual or physical structures. Accommodation is the process of changing existing structures in ways that fit the new situation more effectively. The following example illustrates the process of adaptation.

Suppose an infant is presented with a rattle for the very first time. The infant reaches out

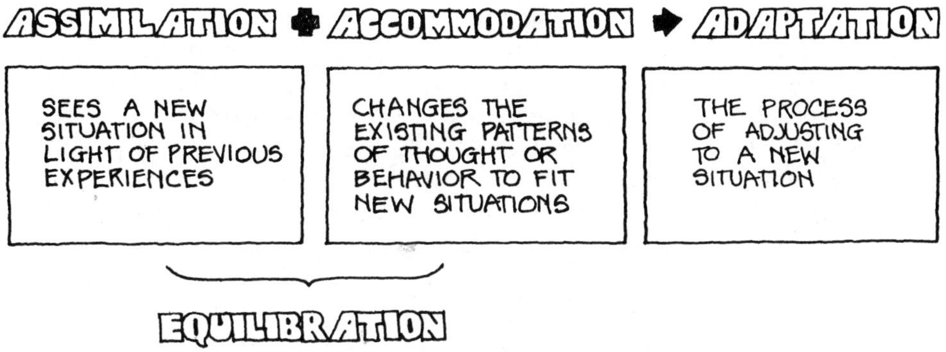

ASSIMILATION ✦ ACCOMMODATION ➔ ADAPTATION

| SEES A NEW SITUATION IN LIGHT OF PREVIOUS EXPERIENCES | CHANGES THE EXISTING PATTERNS OF THOUGHT OR BEHAVIOR TO FIT NEW SITUATIONS | THE PROCESS OF ADJUSTING TO A NEW SITUATION |

EQUILIBRATION

Figure 7-1 *Piaget's conceptualization of intelligence*

and tries to grasp the rattle. He has grasped things like plastic rings and his bottle before, and when he sees the rattle he attempts to pick it up by curving his fingers in one way and then another, trying to use the same grasping patterns he used to fit the shapes of the bottle and rings. The child is comparing the new object with things that he is already familiar with— things that can be grasped. This is the process of assimilation.

The child finds, however, that his grasp must be modified if he is ever to pick up the rattle and hear its pleasing sounds. He eventually curves his fingers in a new way—in a way that fits the long, slender handle of the rattle instead of the more substantive shapes previously experienced. The child has now accommodated *previous grasping reflexes to a shape never before experienced.*

The simultaneous process of assimilation and accommodation, then, is called adaptation. Equilibrium is achieved and the child has grown to a new level of knowledge. Figure 7-1 illustrates this process.

Piaget's feelings about activity, exploration, and direct experience again come to the front as Celia Stendler explains their importance in the process of adaptation:

Self-activity is crucial in the adaptive process; for Piaget, "Penser, c'est operer." If equilib-

rium is to be achieved at a higher level, then the child must be mentally active, *he* must transform the data. The elements to be incorporated may be present in an experience or the child may be *told* of the error in his thinking, but unless his mind is actively engaged in wrestling with data, no accommodation occurs. Children, like adults, are not convinced by being told they are wrong, nor by merely seeing evidence that contradicts their thinking. They have to act upon the data and transform them, and in so doing, make their own discoveries. [1965, p. 330]

Assimilation and accommodation are constantly working in harmony to produce changes in the baby's world and in the ways the baby reacts to it. It is an active process; it requires interaction between the child and something or someone. According to Piaget, the baby does not enter this world with intelligence but attains it as reflexes become refined into planned sensory or motor activity and planned sensory or motor activity evolves into thoughts (or *mental operations*). In Chapter 4 you learned that sensory play during infancy involves sucking and mouthing; making sounds and listening; and gazing at and following objects. Motor play emphasizes control of grasping and handling objects; physical mobility; and knowledge of one's own body. Since we are now addressing a completely different application of these concepts, we want to see how play activities evolve into thought processes. Piaget divided the sensorimotor period of play into six stages, each with its major description of intellectual achievement. See Table 7-2.

As infants grow from the use of only a few basic reflexes at birth through a maturational process by which they gradually perform actual thinking functions, we say they are *learning*. Most definitions consider learning to be a process through which we can observe behavioral changes as a result of experience. This definition should bring a second question to your mind: What kinds of *experience?* Basically, babies are relentless explorers, so the experiences you use to enhance their learning should be of the sensory type, especially those that include materials designed to invite *holding* and *manipulating*. The box on p. 221 lists some activities you might choose as infants begin a developmental process enhanced by your sensory stimulation.

By definition, infancy is a period of life when individuals are not able to talk, but the activities described here help form the foundation for subsequent language and other learnings. They give babies an opportunity to explore their surroundings and form the concepts to which word labels eventually will become attached. The child, then, translates thoughts gathered through direct experience into mental structures, and those mental structures eventually become verbalized in conformance to adult signs (language). Since language acquisition is an involved developmental process in itself, it will be dealt with in Chapter 8.

Toddlers and Young Children

From these beginnings children now enter a transition time between being tied into the concrete, immediate environment of infancy

to a time when they can effectively and efficiently use symbols to represent objects and events. According to Piaget the child's cognitive processes develop in an active way within two major areas: physical knowledge and logico-mathematical knowledge.

1. *Physical knowledge.* Physical knowledge refers to the observable properties of those objects within the child's realm of experience. For example, if we pick up a rubber ball, hold it at eye level, and allow it to drop, we find out something about the physical properties of the ball. In the same way, the child learns about the physical properties in his environment through observation and experimentation—looking, dropping, folding, pouring, knocking, watching, and listening are but a few of the actions he can use on objects to find out how they react. Physical activity is seen as a necessary stimulus for mental activity. The objects themselves, not the teacher, tell the child about their properties.

2. *Logico-mathematical knowledge.* This area of knowledge involves five skill areas: (a) classification, (b) seriation, (c) spatial relations, (d) temporal relations, and (e) conservation.

Classification involves the child's ability to group objects based on some common criterion. The emphasis is not on discovering a "correct" grouping, but on the process of independently grouping and regrouping objects in various logical ways. For example, from the following list we may ask the child to "put together the objects that are the same in some way": three red plastic dogs, four red plastic birds, three yellow plastic cats, and four yellow plastic chickens.

The objective of asking the child to group these things is not to see whether he can figure out how you want them grouped, but to see whether he can group the objects himself

Table 7-2 *Intellectual Achievement during Piaget's Sensorimotor Period*

Stage	Characteristics of Intellectual Achievement
1. Reflexes (birth–1 month)	Infants respond to the environment only with reflexes. They suck to receive nourishment or grasp objects placed in their hands.
2. Primary circular reactions (1–4 months)	Reflexes become elaborated upon and coordinated. Sucking, for example, is an inborn behavior intended to help the baby ingest food. However, if a safe object is placed near the infant's mouth, the inborn reflex would cause her to suck the object and, perhaps, enjoy the experience. The infant would then repeatedly seek out the object not for food-getting, but for pleasure. The change in purpose from food-getting to pleasure is elaboration, while the process of grasping and bringing the object to one's mouth is an example of a higher order of coordination. Active repetition, "habituation," of such activity is characteristic of this period.
3. Secondary circular reactions (4–8 months)	In Stage 2, babies repeat actions because of the pleasure they bring. Now they repeat actions for the purpose of seeing what will happen. The first shake of a rattle may startle a child, but with experimentation the child soon knows that certain regular movements of his arm will cause a sound. Once the child shakes the rattle for the purpose of producing the sound, he is demonstrating a specific skill or repeating actions not only for the pleasure it brings but also to experience the consequence of the action itself.
4. Coordination of schemes (8–12 months)	The child's reactions are now becoming more purposeful. She may initiate an action now because she has a specific goal in mind. For example, if a desired toy is shown to the child and then placed beneath a scarf out of a child's sight, the child will look for it, lift off the scarf, and grasp the toy. This is an example of object permanence, or knowing that an object exists even though it cannot be seen. Object permanence exists only in a rudimentary form at this stage, however. If the toy were taken by the adult from beneath the first scarf and placed beneath a second scarf (even while the baby was watching), the baby would still look under the first scarf and look in wonderment as to why it was no longer there.
5. Discovery of new schemes (12–18 months)	Infants begin to demonstrate a rudimentary form of purposeful, trial-and-error activity at this stage. They still make accidental discoveries of actions as they explore their world, but now they no longer exactly repeat those actions for pleasurable results only. They seem to be "experimenting" with the objects or actions for the purpose of seeing what makes them different than others. Infants also begin to discover new ways of attaining certain goals. For example, instead of crawling to a toy and grasping it to play, the baby may now pull it to herself by means of an attached string. Finally, the concept of object permanence is complete, except for multiple displacements. For example, if you put a small toy in your hand, put your hand inside a box; and brought your hand out for the baby to see, the baby would look for the toy in your hand.
6. Invention (18–24 months)	Children now have a fairly good understanding of the nature of objects and the results of their actions upon objects. They no longer need to perform trial-and-error actions with objects in order to "understand," but can now picture events in their minds in order to solve new problems. In essence, they are learning to think, and words become attached to the mental pictures. For example, an 18-month-old baby is pushing and pulling a sliding screen door back and forth. All is going well until a toy block becomes wedged in the door track and hinders the door's movement. Without needing to experiment in order to determine how to get the door to slide again, the baby visualizes the problem and removes the block from the track. In addition to the development of thought processes, the child is now beginning to use language. The concept of object permanence is also complete at this stage.

These children are involved in a seriation activity: ordering counters from least to greatest.

and give you reasons for his actions. A reasonably mature child may create these groupings:

GROUP 1

all the dogs

all the birds

all the cats

all the chickens

(because they are the same animal)

GROUP 2

all the red animals

all the yellow animals

(because of their common color)

GROUP 3

the dogs and cats

the birds and chickens

(fur versus feathers)

Many types of classifications can be made by the youngsters. Preschool children learn to group things according to size, shape, color, texture, taste, sound, and many other physical attributes.

Seriation involves an ability to order or arrange objects according to size (small to large), quality (rough to smooth), or quantity (less to more). The emphasis is on comparing likenesses and differences among objects in the same category and on ordering them according to their relative differences. Figure 7-2 illustrates several types of seriation activities commonly presented to preschool children.

Spatial relations involve the child's ability to understand his relationship to objects and the relationship of objects to one another in terms of direction, distance, and perspective. For example, the teacher may point to the large ball that is *far* from the child and ask him to bring it *near*. The teacher may ask the child to pick up a toy that is *beneath* the table. The child may be asked to point to the boy who is *in* the doll corner or to name the *closest* child to him.

Temporal relations involve the child's ability to perceive time sequences. He learns that events begin and end and that events can

SENSORY ACTIVITIES FOR INFANTS

Early Infancy (0—6 months)

- Babies require *visual stimulation*.
  - Paint the walls bright colors; hang pictures on them.
  - Use printed crib sheets.
  - Hang a colorful crib mobile (or even pie tins).
  - Place a mirror above the child in the crib.
  - Shine a penlight into the baby's eyes and encourage baby to follow it as you move it slowly; cover the penlight with changeable color cellophane paper.

- Babies respond to *sound*.
  - Offer small rattles, squeeze toys, or bells.
  - Hang wind chimes near the crib.
  - Put on wristbands with bells (also helps them discover their hands).
  - Play a variety of music on the radio or record player.
  - Make sound toys for baby (a tin box filled with marbles or pebbles is a good choice).
  - Play a music box.
  - Say the baby's name over and over in a variety of situations.

- Babies *touch, grasp,* and *feel* things.
  - Offer plastic rings, measuring spoons, keys, rattles, or soft terry cloth clutch toys.
  - Choose toys offering a variety of textures, shapes, and colors.
  - Provide a cradle gym that has moving parts and makes noises.

Middle Infancy (6—12 months)

- Babies enjoy exploring objects.
  - Let baby play with pots and pans to bang them together.
  - Invite baby to put things in and take things out of containers (clothespins dropped into an empty plastic container, for example).
  - Provide plastic pop beads to put together and take apart.

- Supply a variety of paper for the baby to tear and crumble (tissue paper, drawing paper, foil paper).
- Furnish an unbreakable mirror so the baby can see her reflection and begin to recognize herself.
- Have in store a number of different materials for the baby to investigate: milk cartons, wooden spools, empty plastic containers, boxes, bowls, buckets, pie pans, and other safe household objects.

Late Infancy (1—2 years)

- Babies begin to participate in *purposeful* play, or they have a particular goal in mind for their activity rather than performing it simply for the pleasure it brings.
  - Challenge baby to imitate you as you insert geometric blocks into a shape sorter or place stacking rings on a peg.
  - Encourage the following of directions by providing simple one- or two-piece puzzles with knobs.
  - Help baby verbally label objects by drawing attention to picture books with large, uncluttered photographs or simple drawings.
  - Aid baby in sensing the relationships among parts of objects by providing nesting boxes, geometric blocks, or puzzles.
  - To assist baby in developing the concept of object permanence, play games such as putting a favorite toy in one of three boxes in front of the child. Ask the child to find the toy.
  - To encourage baby's continued interest in experimenting with objects, keep providing pots and pans, sound toys, texture toys, and other materials suggested previously.

- As children approach age two, they imitate others and begin to "pretend" in their play.
  - Arrange your facility with dramatic play areas as they were described in Chapter 5.

be sequentially ordered. Concepts of *first, last, before, after,* and *next* are learned. For example, the teacher may tell the child, "*First,* you will need to put one cookie on each plate and *next* you may pour the milk." At story time, the teacher may say, "I'll *start* the story now

and we'll go outdoors to play when I'm *finished.*" Or, during clean-up time, the teacher may promise, "*After* you've put away your toys, we'll *begin* our snack."

Conservation involves the child's ability to conceptualize physical properties of objects.

SIZE:
THE CHILD IS ASKED TO ARRANGE THE PEOPLE FROM SMALL TO LARGE

QUALITY:
THE CHILD IS ASKED TO ARRANGE THE TOUCH TABLETS FROM ROUGHEST TO SMOOTHEST

QUANTITY:
THE CHILD IS ASKED TO ARRANGE THE CARDS IN ORDER FROM THE LEAST TO THE GREATEST NUMBER

Figure 7-2   *Seriation activities*

Young children (2–7 years) usually make sense of the world in terms of the way it looks to them—they focus on only one dimension at a time. They have great difficulty realizing that objects can possess more than one property. These characteristics can be best explained within the context of the examples in Figure 7-3.

Transition from Stage to Stage

The preceding section explained a number of key concepts associated with Piagetian theory. These concepts should help you to form an overall idea of what Piaget means when he uses the term *intelligence*. Essential to the development of higher levels of Piagetian intelligence is movement through a series of

four developmental stages, each describing an orderly pattern through which the child constructs knowledge. Development through the stages follows a sequential order such that each stage is necessary for the construction of the next.

Piaget identifies four specific stages through which individuals progress: sensorimotor, preoperational, concrete operations, and formal operations. The criteria for defining the characteristics of the child's behavior during each stage are explained in the following descriptions.

Stage 1: Sensorimotor (0–2 Years) We learned that the child begins life capable only of two kinds of *reflexive movements:* (1) those such as knee jerks that are not altered by experience and (2) those such as grasping and sucking that can be altered by the child's expe-

	Have the children agree that there are:	Then make this change:	And ask the children:
Conservation of liquids	two equal glasses of liquid. 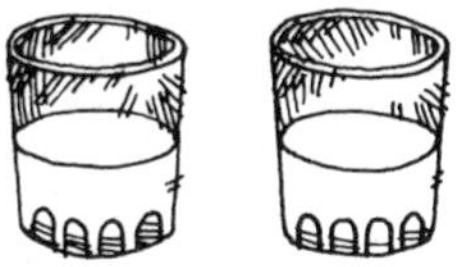	Pour one into a taller, thinner glass. 	Do the glasses contain more, less, or the same amount? Why do you think so?
Conservation of number	two equal lines of coins. 	Lengthen the spaces between the coins on one line. 	Do both lines have the same number of checkers or does one line have more? Why do you think so?
Conservation of matter	two equal balls of clay. 	Squeeze one ball into a long thin shape. 	Which piece has more clay—the ball or the snake? Why do you think so?
Conservation of length	two pencils of equal length. 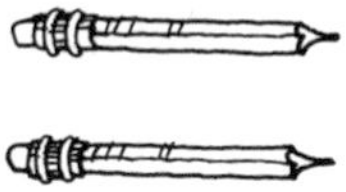	Move one pencil. 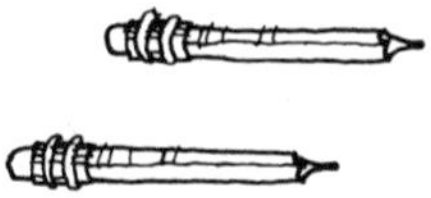	Would two ants starting a hike at the end of the pencils and walking at the same speed both travel the same distance? Why do you think so?
Conservation of area	two identical pieces of green construction paper representing a field of grass on which are placed the same number of red blocks representing barns. Add a toy horse to each field. Establish that both animals have same amount of grass to eat.	Rearrange the barns. 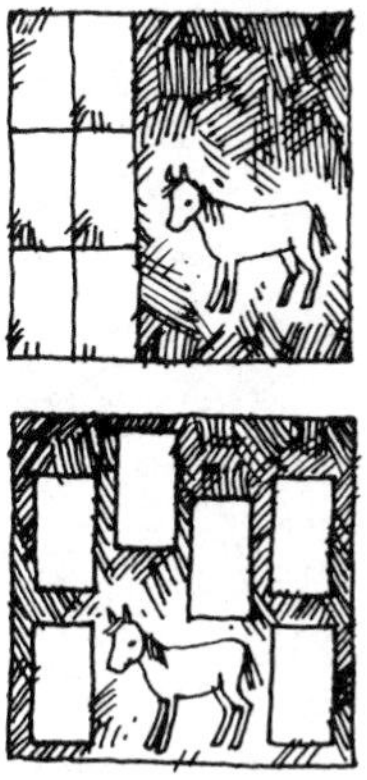	Do the animals still have the same amount of grass to eat? Which has more? Why do you think so?

Figure 7-3   *Piagetian conservation tasks*

riences. The child, with these reflexes as a base, uses the process of assimilation and accommodation to build higher intellectual structures from that reflexive base.

The child's initial *actions* such as arm waving and sucking appear to be aimless since they appear over and over again as primitive reflexes. However, they soon begin to show purpose as the child learns to grasp objects, hold them, push them, manipulate them, and experiment with them. The infant actively attempts to understand single objects and the relationship among objects as he repeats and alters behaviors in an attempt to adjust to his environment.

One of the more important achievements of the sensorimotor period is the development of the idea of *object permanence*. Early in this stage, if a toy is hidden, the infant acts as if it no longer exists. Only gradually, after experiences in which objects are dropped or rolled out of sight, do infants realize that objects continue to exist and begin to look for them. This is a signal that the youngster is moving away from the concept of "out of sight, out of mind" and toward the ability to form mental images of the people and objects in his environment. Another important concept emerging during this period is the idea of causality—an awareness that other objects besides the child himself can be the source of actions. For example, this cause-effect concept is evident at the end of the sensorimotor period when a child is able to understand that the reason he cannot open a playpen gate is not because he lacks pushing power, but because a piece of furniture may be blocking it.

By the age of two, the child possesses the concepts of object permanence and causality—thus making him quite cognitively different from the infant at birth. The ability to experiment is beginning.

Stage 2: Preoperational (2—7 Years)
By stage 2, children have made great progress in cognitive development, but they still have a long way to go. They see the world only from their own point of view (egocentrism) and believe that everyone else sees it the same way.

The child begins to use *words* to represent objects and actions within his environment, perhaps the single most evident development during this stage. However, he describes those objects and actions only in terms of how they look to him. For example, children judge the amount of water in a glass on the basis of the container (a tall, thin glass has more water than a short fat glass of equal volume); a piece of clay rolled out into the shape of a sausage has more clay than that same piece of clay when it was in the shape of a ball. Because of egocentric thought, basic conservation skills remain undeveloped during this stage.

Rudiments of *classification* and *seriation*, however, do appear during this stage. The child can make collections of things based on some criterion, such as separating red horses and blue horses into two piles. He is even able to shift criteria, that is, first sort the horses into piles of red and blue, then sort them according to size: large and small. The child can also compare two or three members of a set within a series and put them in order.

The child begins to understand basic *temporal* concepts at this stage. He shows a rudimentary understanding of concepts such as *first, next, after,* and so on. However, these terms should always be used only in pairs such as, "*First* wash your hands and *then* you can eat the snack." However, sensing logic among more than two things in a series will cause confusion.

The child *learns* by manipulating objects, recognizing pictures, participating in dramatic play, drawing, and using words or objects to represent thoughts.

Stage 3: Concrete Operations (7—12 Years)   The child now is able to learn some things through mental operations involving

symbols (reasoning) rather than through direct physical manipulation (perception). The *previously* developing skills are becoming refined; as egocentrism fades, the ability to *conserve* quantities is beginning to appear. The child understands relationships between the whole and its parts and begins to see things from the viewpoints of others. Logical reasoning brings order to the child's world as he becomes able to understand symbols (reading and math) and is beginning to sense cause-and-effect relationships.

Stage 4: Formal Operations (12–Adulthood) The child is capable of learning entirely through verbal and written symbols—the symbols themselves serve to evoke meaningful mental images. He is able to think logically and perform the previously discussed Piagetian tasks with ease. The child is able to construct knowledge independently of concrete experience and now learns to integrate new knowledge while solving problems with meaning, not only for the present, but also for the future.

Implications of Piagetian Thought: Cognitive-Developmental Instruction

Piaget has described the process by which individuals develop intelligence from infancy into adulthood. Until age two, infants learn as they use their senses. Motor responses accompany sensory experiences—movements such as grasping, banging, and waving. Infants learn to recognize objects through such activity while learning verbal names and functions—that is, a "rattle" is for shaking, a "cat" meows, and so on. An environment full of direct experience in which the child is free to interact is the most effective early learning setting.

After entering toddlerhood, children move to a completely new stage of intellectual functioning—one that builds upon the sensory and motor experiences of infancy. No longer completely restricted by learning through sensory and motor means, toddlers begin to build rudimentary "concepts," or mental pictures, of experiences that are frequently encountered. They learn not only the concepts, but also the verbal labels associated with particular concepts. Thus, we observe the onset of verbal communication; the child uses concept labels (words) to share thoughts with others regardless of whether or not the actual objects being talked about are present. This stage still relies on the manipulation of real objects; for example, the child learns the concept of *farm* by seeing, hearing, touching, smelling, and tasting all of the special things that make a farm what it is. But the difference between toddlerhood and infancy is that these experiences become stored as conceptual perceptions in the mind. As these fresh perceptions accumulate and build, children begin to seek out and build relationships among the concepts; this is another new intellectual means of explaining the environment. Therefore, toward the end of toddlerhood, children learn to group things according to some common characteristic such as color and shape. They constantly examine likenesses and differences among objects. As these experiences accumulate and the children have freedom to manipulate, play, and explore, they build increasingly complex thinking skills. Therefore, through toddlerhood and into the preschool years, children must be primarily exposed to sensory and motor experiences with real objects within a secure, trusting environment. Formal learning experiences can be provided, but they, too, should be approached as play; for example, "Let's see what we can do with these toy animals."

Thus, Piaget helped educators redefine the concept of "readiness" as it was traditionally interpreted prior to the 1960s. Readiness for learning now became viewed within the context of these two principles: (1) every experience takes up something from those that have gone before and modifies the quality of those which come after, and (2) readiness is actually the adequacy of an existing mental capacity to meet the demands of a new learning task. Teachers, therefore, abandoned the time-honored guidelines of waiting six and a half years before introducing academic programs and began searching for a "match" in order to introduce and reinforce sound learnings. Teachers observed and evaluated children for the purpose of assessing current mental capabilities in order to bring about educational challenges.

Teaching young children now implies a careful preparation and presentation of activities that fall into three broad categories: (1) providing the child with direct experiences; (2) presenting many play opportunities where children are free to explore and manipulate, and (3) designing play-oriented learning experiences that center on specific, age-appropriate concepts. Programs reflecting these characteristics are referred to as cognitive-developmental. They are _cognitive_ because they are directed toward the stimulation of active thinking as it contributes to the development of intelligence. They are _developmental_ because they are based upon the assumption that learning occurs in stages and that each stage includes elements of earlier levels but expands upon them in increasingly sophisticated ways.

DIRECT EXPERIENCES

Although you will be given many general suggestions for applying Piaget's theory, Piaget himself never actually designed a method of teaching. Your author, though, has had the opportunity to listen to Piaget speak to groups and sensed his uneasiness whenever individuals concerned about methodology asked questions about the value of presenting the kinds of logico-mathematical tasks outlined earlier as a method of accelerating children through his stages. Piaget consistently commented that only in America were such questions of acceleration asked and that the use of his tasks as teaching tools to speed children through the stages was "idiotic." Instead, he emphasized the value of direct experience and either dramatic play or play with manipulative materials. The traditional play-oriented nature of early childhood programs was easily adaptable to this new mission; only an emphasis on specific "subject matter" needed to be considered as a supplement to the standard curriculum.

The following story of Peter and the Rabbit illustrates Piaget's stress on the importance of providing direct experiences whenever possible.

"Class, look at the picture, and tell me what you see," said the teacher.

Hands went up, but the teacher called on Peter, whose hand had not been one of them.

"Peter, what is it?"

"It looks like a rat."

The class laughed. Someone said, "Peter is so stupid. He doesn't know a rat from a rabbit."

The teacher said, "Peter, what's the matter with your eyes? Can't you see that it has long ears?"

"Yes," said Peter weakly.

"It _is_ a rabbit, isn't it, Peter?"

"Yes," he said.

"Today's story is about a rabbit," said the teacher, pointing to the picture and then the word. It's a story about a _hungry_ white rabbit. What do you suppose a rabbit eats when he's hungry?"

"Lettuce," said Mary.

"Carrots," said Suzy.

"Meat," said Peter.

The class laughed. Someone said, "Peter is so stupid. He doesn't know what rabbits eat."

"Peter, you know very well that rabbits don't eat meat," said the teacher.

"That depends on how hungry they are," said Peter. "When I'm hungry, I'll eat anything my mother gives me, even when I don't like it."

"Don't argue, Peter," said the teacher. "Now, Class, how does a rabbit's fur feel when you pet him?" asked the teacher.

"Soft," said Suzy.

"Silky," said Mary.

"I don't know," said Peter.

"Why?" asked the teacher.

"Cause I wouldn't pet one. He might bite me and make me sick, like what happened to my little brother, the time a hungry one got on his bed when he was sleeping."

The class laughed. Someone said, "Peter is fibbing. He knows his mother doesn't allow rabbits in bed."

After the class had read the story and had their recess, the teacher said to the supervisor, "I hate to sound prejudiced, but I'm not sure that this busing from one neighborhood to the other is good for the children."

The supervisor shook his head sadly and said to the teacher, "Your lesson lacked one very important ingredient."

"What was that?" asked the teacher.

"A rabbit," said the supervisor. [Grant, 1967, back cover]

To avoid the type of situation illustrated in this sample classroom, provide the types of activities that help the children form accurate concepts (ideas) before you ask them to express those ideas verbally. The remainder of this chapter is designed to offer you ideas about the kinds of activities most appropriate for encouraging children to explore and learn about their world. Chapter 8 will extend the discussion by presenting the language skills developed by participating in such activity.

Doing Something Real

Young children learn by doing; they are in that "messing about" stage when it is natural to get into and try everything. They do whatever it takes to discover—to learn the hows, whys, and whats about things. They want to know how things work, why they work, and what can be done with them. They may come to your facility knowing a little about a lot of things, but are thirsty for experiences that will help them find out much more. For that reason, you should have many things for them to do:

- look into a microscope or magnifying glass
- take photographs with a camera
- plant vegetable or flower seeds
- make ice cream or butter
- weigh things on a scale
- use a magnet to see what it will attract
- freeze or boil water
- take care of classroom animals or plants

The most effective way for children to gain knowledge is through firsthand experimentation with special challenges in the preschool environment. Spoken or written words cannot approach the value of such direct learning experiences. Those verbal symbols may effectively grow from, summarize, supplement, or enrich such experiences but, for the very young, should rarely be used as learning experiences in themselves. Because the child's physical and social environments are full of possibilities for direct activity, a complete discussion of related experiences will be treated separately in Chapter 10.

Realia

Sharing real things with children is an important activity. Some typical categories of realia that often interest young children are:

Real experiences help children understand the existence of natural phenomena and clarify their jumbled notions of the earth's many mysteries.

- *plants* (dried flowers, live plants of various kinds)
- *animals* (goldfish, gerbils, earthworms, and so on)
- *clothing* (police uniform, Mexican serape, Alaskan parka)
- *money* (rubles, yen, marks, confederate money)
- *nature* (flowers, animals, plants, rocks)
- *household items* (cooking supplies, eating utensils, furniture, cleaning supplies)
- *tools* (farming tools, carpenter's tools, community helper's tools)
- *foods* (authentic cultural, national, or ethnic foods)

- *toys* (toys of ethnic, cultural, or historical interest)
- *school items* (books from other nations or time periods, hornbook, globes or maps from the past)
- *musical instruments*
- *sports items* (hockey equipment, soccer ball, baseball equipment)
- *historical items* (powder horn, quill pen, old musical instruments)

Such materials serve as excellent learning resources and supply the children with basic materials to more easily understand what life is all about. Whenever we discuss realia with college students and have them examine realia, we get this response: "I really learned a lot and even cleared up some ideas I thought were pretty established in my mind, but I have one problem. How could you expect teachers to bring in realia every time they teach something new? Where would they find it all?"

It is impossible to expect teachers to provide realia for every topic. However, that loophole does not excuse you from extending an effort toward providing as many real objects for your children as possible. If you examine the following three basic resources, you will probably find enough real material for your classroom.

1. *Libraries or museums.* Often you will find items related to your children's interests at your local public library or museum. Some of these places even allow teachers to borrow certain items for short periods of time. If not, a field trip to the library or museum may be appropriate, especially if provisions have been made for a tour guide to explain special items of interest.

2. *Yourself.* Check your own materials for possible classroom value. If you have taken trips, reexamine souvenirs and other memorabilia that may have been stashed away or forgotten. Items such as

seashells, rock or mineral samples, surf-boards, old clothing, records, and the like are often taken for granted in our lives and receive little attention when considered for classroom use. Think about those things and also about bringing back interesting items from any future trips you will take. It is surprising how things of this type add up with time.

3. *Parents and other adults.* In most instances, parents or other adults throughout the community will serve to be your greatest asset for procuring realia for your classroom. Parents, especially, are willing and often anxious to lend things to you once they know what you need and that their items will be properly cared for. A simple letter sent home with your children a few days before the beginning of study on a new topic will often result in a wealth of real classroom materials. A sample letter form of this type is shown in Figure 7-4.

Don't shirk from the responsibility to bring real items into the classroom and don't make excuses to explain why you cannot provide realia. It is your job to search out such items and to get them into the classroom where they can be put to good use. The following are some special techniques to stimulate your children to explore the realia you bring into the classroom.

- After you bring in a special article to class, encourage the children to describe its characteristics: "How does it feel?" "Can you smell it?" "Can you taste it?" and similar questions can be used to elicit information about size, shape, color, texture, and so on.

- If you have introduced more than one article to the children, place them in a box and review the children's observations by asking, "What did I give you?" Vary the game by asking the child to reach into the bag, feel the object, and tell what it is.

- Arrange an "interest table" or "treasure box" where an item of interest is periodically displayed to stimulate children's thinking and arouse their curiosity. Some special items include:

seashells	leaves
tree bark	seeds
dried fruit	an apple sliced horizontally in half
fruit pits	
stones	musical instruments
feathers	
magnets	locks and keys
acorns	telephones
dried flowers	twigs

Field Trips

The setting outside the classroom is also rich in direct learning experiences; it presents varied opportunities for children to get close to things that may otherwise be experienced only through books, pictures, or films. By organizing *field trips* outside the classroom, you help children explore and deal with the real world rather than representations of it. Trips are an important part of children's learnings; children love the excitement, adventure, and new awareness of the world around them.

It is advisable not to take young children on trips until they have been in school for a while (about a week in most instances) and have had a chance to become familiar with their environment and their teacher. As they become accustomed to these new features in their lives, a brief trip around the building might be taken. A short exploratory walk around the facility helps the children place their room in relationship to the other rooms in the building and familiarizes them with your expectations in such settings. They can learn about their school by visiting the director's office, kitchen, nurse's office, storerooms, heating plant, library, and gymnasium. After

```
                                              June 14, 1984
         Dear Parents/Guardians,
              Our children have shown a great deal of interest
         in rodeos. In order to help the children learn about
         rodeos and about the people who are involved in them,
         I am trying to locate and collect as many real items
         as possible in order to organize a classroom display.
         If you have any real items, pictures,and so on from
         rodeos that we could borrow, would you please let me
         know by returning this note to me?
              Thank you for your help in this matter.
                                    With appreciation,


                         Mr. Woodburn
         ------------------------------------------------------

              Parent/Guardian Signature _____
              Phone Number_____
         ____ Sorry, but I cannot help at this time.
         ____ I have items that you can borrow, and
                   ____ they are fragile so please do not allow
                        the children to handle them.
                   ____ they may be handled with care by the
                        children.
                   ____ I will be glad to visit your classroom to
                        show how these items are used.
```

Figure 7-4   _Sample letter requesting realia from the parents of your students_

this first trip experience, the children may be taken on a walk around the block, even though the sights may already be familiar to them. Even the most obvious things are worth pointing out, since your goals should be to develop an awareness of the environment and to help the children articulate the things they see and hear. During one such episode, for example, a rabbit hopped out from among some short bushes as the children walked by. The children watched its movements and had fun doing so: "Look at it hop," "Look how long the back legs are," and other comments were made by the children. The teacher encouraged their animated discussion and occasionally inserted questions, such as "Did you see its fluffy tail?" to guide their observation. The children's interest was evident as several youngsters began "hopping" along the street to their next adventure. Such dialogue is important to encourage

Real experiences and free, active exploration are the keys to early learning.

at this age because it establishes the ground-work for active thinking about what the children will see on future trips. As you expand such walking trips, you will become aware of many things to do and see: traffic lights, fire hydrants, mail boxes, bus stops, telephone booths, and parking meters. It is also exciting to see special activities such as loading and unloading of trucks, repair work on streets involving exposed pipes, or open manholes or large cranes. During the spring months it is fun to notice the leaves coming out on trees on the street or in parks. Pick a "class tree" or "class plant" and follow its progress for a few months. You might want to follow the route that some of the children take from school in going home, stop and talk to a police officer, see the building where the children live, and on your return try to find the windows of the classroom from the street.

The following are some of the places you might like to visit, for shopping or just for looking:

- *stores:* supermarkets, fruit stores, pet shops, bakeries, repair shops, florists, appliance and hardware shops, open air markets, live poultry markets, stationery stores, or automatic laundries.

- *building construction sites*

- *community services:* post offices, fire stations, police stations, public libraries, subway stations, health centers, schools, playgrounds, parks, gardens, factories, garages, lumber yards, or housing projects.

These first experiences away from the classroom should be handled with great care. You should be familiar with the location to be visited and be sure that your visit has a distinct purpose. Don't just go on a trip for something to do; have a genuine reason for doing so. Be sure to establish a secure feeling by telling the children where they will be going, what they will see, and what they will hear or taste or smell. Don't be too informative at this initial point, though, because you will not want to keep the trip from being a learning experience in itself. After you prepare the children for the trip, be sure to consider a few precautions:

- *adequate supervision* (at least a 5:1 child–adult ratio)

- *toileting* (everyone goes before you leave)

- *emergency materials* (Band-Aids, tissues, safety pins, change for the phone)

- *clothing* (extra clothing for winter, rain gear, and so on)

- *rules* (walk in pairs, hold hands, walk with the teacher, stay on the sidewalk, cross streets on signal from the teacher, and don't run)

When the children have had walking experiences of this type and feel comfortable in settings outside the school, you may want to begin locating worthwhile places to visit where transportation is required. Some school systems provide buses for transportation or may offer a special subsidy for these trips. In other cases, parents may offer to pay the costs of transportation with the school district taking care of the charges for families who cannot afford to pay. The same basic considerations for walking trips apply to transportation trips: finding a good place to visit, having a good purpose to visit, informing the children, and being aware of certain prerequisites. However, transportation trips also require many additional considerations:

- Arrange for transportation.

- Schedule the visit with those at the other end.

- Secure written parental permission (usually on a form provided by the school).

- Plan for lunch (either packed at home or at school).

- Arrange for admission costs to places such as the zoo.

- Maintain a 5:1 child–adult ratio (parents are usually willing to volunteer).

- Establish rules for behavior.

Trips vary in kind, as we have seen, but regardless of the type, take a camera with you. Because young children may have never seen pictures of themselves, take individual as well as group shots at the places you visit. If you mount photos on a wall in your room at the children's eye level or use them as a basis of a group scrapbook that is available to the children, you will find that they will be a tremendous source of satisfaction as well as an important learning experience. The pictures come in handy to stimulate discussion long after the trip has been taken.

You can maximize the value of trips if you follow them up with a related activity once the children return to the classroom. An experience story is one good approach; other approaches are illustrations, discussions, creative skits, and comparisons of what was experienced with information from reference books. Whatever you choose, the trip will not be valuable unless you lead the children through activities that help to summarize their experience. You and the children should also evaluate the trip by asking questions such as the following:

- Were we able to answer our questions?

- Did we develop any new interests (hobbies, ideas, and so on)?

- In what ways did our behavior affect the trip?

- Would we recommend this trip for others? Why?

- What suggestions could we give to make the next field trip better?

In addition to careful planning of all phases of a field trip, you should extend courtesy and appreciation by sending group-dictated letters of thanks to all persons involved: chaperones, resource people, bus driver, school nurse, and principal. Letter writing can be done in the early years by asking the children to express their thoughts to you. As the children dictate their thank-you message, you may write it on a chart. If any of the children are able to write, they can copy the letter and send it to the designated person. A strong personal touch is associated with the letter when it is handwritten by the children.

It is also helpful to compile a schoolwide file of successful field trips. This file can be kept in the supervisor's office or in the teacher's room and referred to when desired. Information should be compiled in summary form and stored on a file card, listing:

- place name
- address
- phone
- name of person to contact
- best time to call
- admission charge
- number of people accommodated
- time required
- experiences available

Some good possibilities for field trips in the early years are as follows:

farm	public buildings
museum	bus terminal
department store	shopping center
historical sites	planetarium
airport	children's theater
railroad station	public library
factories	truck terminal
newspaper building	concerts
fire station	cultural events
city hall	zoo
supermarket	repair shop
post office	bakery
camping areas	construction projects

The checklist presented in Figure 7-5 summarizes the major considerations to be addressed prior to, during, and following field trips.

Perhaps the most frequently overlooked source of learning outside the classroom is the world directly outside—nature. Take frequent trips outdoors to walk through a field of flowers or to listen to the noises of a busy street. Stop for a moment to watch a fuzzy caterpillar crawl along the pavement or to watch a rainbow fade into the blue sky. Nature includes the sights, sounds, smells, and tastes all around us. Help the children learn about nature by taking a nature walk and try these things:

- *Listen*—Sit down in a park, near the street, or anyplace else and listen quietly for one minute. Ask the children not to talk or move. Listen to the sounds: birds chirping, wind whistling through the trees, airplanes flying overhead, automobiles driving by, other people talking, insects buzzing, construction equipment hammering, and a multitude of other sounds to talk about.

- *Look*—Children love to look for colors. How many different colors do they see? How many shades of the same color are there? How many basic shapes (circle, square, triangle, rectangle) do they see in nature?

- *Feel*—Find objects that are rough, smooth, soft, furry, cold, warm, wet, or dry. Discuss the textures.

- *Smell*—How many different things can the children smell? How does the freshly cut grass smell? How about a bakery? What does the air smell like after rain?

Before returning to the classroom, ask each child to find three "treasures" that could be picked up and brought back. What are some possibilities for using those "treasures" in teaching situations?

```
                        FIELD TRIP CHECKLIST


PRETRIP EVALUATION

    ☐  I am familiar with the location to be visited.
    ☐  This trip is suitable for the maturity level of my children.

TEACHER PREPARATION

    ☐  My supervisor has been notified of the trip.
    ☐  Administrative approval has been secured in writing.
    ☐  Parental permission slips have been signed.
    ☐  Transportation has been arranged.
    ☐  Proper supervision has been planned (a 1-5 adult-child ratio is ideal).
    ☐  Toilet facilities are present at the location to be visited.
    ☐  Clothing requirements have been communicated to the parents.
    ☐  Safety rules were communicated to the children:
         • Stay together in a group.
         • Walk with a friend.
         • Stay on the sidewalk.
         • Cross only with the green light.

TEACHER-CHILD PLANNING

    ☐  The children are familiar (but not too familiar) with where they are going.
    ☐  Points of interest have been shared.
    ☐  Individual and group responsibilities have been assigned.

THE TRIP

    ☐  All children can see and hear.
    ☐  I offer cues and comments to stimulate the children's interest.
    ☐  I am constantly aware of special problems or emergency situations.

FOLLOW-UP ACTIVITY

    ☐  informal discussion of the trip
    ☐  art projects related to the trip
    ☐  group experience charts
    ☐  creative dramatics
    ☐  bulletin board display
```

Figure 7-5   *Checklist for preparing preschool field trips*

Resource Persons

Resource persons are individuals either within or outside the school who may have certain expertise, experience, skill, or knowledge in a field of special interest to the class. Generally, children enjoy contact with outside visitors and the contributions and interesting materials they share. When studying topics related to the neighborhood or community, for example, you can invite persons who provide goods or services in the specific area, such as police officers, firefighters, farmers, delivery persons, construction workers, doctors, nurses, newspersons, bakers, industrial workers, store workers, craftspersons, lawyers, bankers, clergy, government officials, and so on. When introducing children to different cultures or ethnic groups, you can ask people with appropriate backgrounds to provide information and answer questions. As with field trips, careful planning is essential for a successful visit by a resource person:

1. Determine whether inviting a visitor is the best way to get the intended knowledge and information.

2. Determine whether the speaker's topic and style of delivery are suitable to the maturity level of the children.

3. Inform the speaker about such matters as the age level of the children, the needs of the children, the time alloted for the presentation, and the facilities available.

4. Follow-up and discussion related to the speaker's presentation should be provided. Discussion, art projects, dramatization, and storytelling are all suggestions for summarizing and extending the information.

5. A letter of thanks is highly recommended as a gesture of appreciation and gratitude.

Visitors to the classroom can provide the children with exciting experiences because they offer important adventures in a very personal way. One day, for example, Miss Graham heard a discussion about firefighters among a small group of children while they were examining a book in the reading corner. She listened as the children expressed wonder at the big rubber boots and hard red hat the firefighters wore. Seizing the moment, Miss Graham suggested that a firefighter might be invited to visit their classroom. "Would he really come to see us?" asked Michael. "I'd like him to come here," offered Sarah. "How can we ask him?" Miss Graham had no doubt that her intentions were appropriate and called the fire company to ask if a firefighter could visit the children. She was informed that not only was such a visit possible but that arrangements could be made for two firefighters to bring a small firetruck to the school.

The next day the children eagerly waited at the school parking lot for the truck to arrive. Their anticipation grew into excitement as the bright red and silver truck motored up the winding entrance. Keeping the children well in control, Miss Graham reminded them to stay behind her until the firetruck came to a halt. When it did, the children gingerly approached the vehicle. The firefighters came out to show the children all their paraphernalia and explain their jobs. "The truck is so shiny," remarked Rebecca. "Yeah, and look at all those big hoses!" shouted Ben. "One of the firemen is a lady. Wow, a lady fireman," said Denise, all agog. "Do you have to go to college to learn how to be a fireman?" asked Oren. The children watched, listened, commented, and asked questions as they tried on the hard hats and floppy boots, watched the brilliant lights, and listened to the firefighters talk. The most adventuresome youngsters even accepted an invitation to climb up into the cab and sit in the firetruck. All of this wonderful activity culminated in a well-supervised, short trip around the parking lot on the back of the truck. Miss Graham was rewarded by the fact that this informal learning experience was thoroughly enjoyed by the children and that they had learned a great deal about a valuable community service.

After the firefighters left the school, Miss Graham assembled the children as a group and invited them to share their thoughts. As the children spoke, Miss Graham recorded their comments on an experience chart (see Chapter 8). Later the children dictated a thank-you note that was mailed to the firehouse.

Mrs. Greene, on the other hand, handled her visit by a resource person in quite another manner. Upon learning that a parent of one of her children was a skilled wood-carver, Mrs. Greene invited the parent to give a short demonstration of his skill. When the wood-carver arrived at school, Mrs. Greene quickly admonished the children to move from their free play and join together in a group to meet him: "Quickly, children, put away your materials and join us on the rug. Show Mr. Champion what good boys and girls you are." Promptly and efficiently, the children put away their materials and grouped themselves on the rug hands folded and eyes directed toward Mr. Champion. "Weren't they just terrific?" commented Mrs. Greene, as if attempting to convince the parent of her superlative control. The children, unsure of why Mr. Champion was there, listened as Mrs. Greene continued on with a lengthy introduction of the visitor. Finally, Mr. Champion had a chance to talk, explaining his craft in such minute detail that even the most mature child's interest began to wane. Nervous glances from Mrs. Greene informed each fidgety child that certain behaviors were not to be tolerated. At the end of the long presentation, Mrs. Greene eagerly thanked Mr. Champion for coming and warned the children of the danger of going close to any of his materials. Ending with the comment, "Let's all show Mr. Champion how much we enjoyed his visit by clapping for him," Mrs. Greene lined up the group and led them to the rest room.

Compare and contrast the techniques of Miss Graham and Mrs. Greene. What were the obvious strengths in Miss Graham's style? What were the apparent flaws in Mrs. Greene's approach?

Special speakers are often very willing to share their accomplishments with children. The problem is that teachers often do not know where to find them. Many teachers solve this problem by sending questionnaires home with their children. The questionnaire should show name, address, phone number, area of knowledge, preferred age level, days available, and hours available. It should also ask if the speaker is willing to come to the classroom or if the class should visit the speaker.

Many times, interested schools or parent-teacher organizations keep a centralized card file of persons from throughout the community who are willing to share their expertise, including those who can help break down stereotypes, such as senior citizens with special skills or hobbies, women carpenters, male nurses, and so on. The card file can be organized by subject listing, and all teachers can use it as a ready reference. Care must be exercised, though, in the way contributors are solicited as possible classroom speakers. The practice of sending request forms throughout the community, for example, is a questionable procedure since a small number of persons who have little or no immediate usefulness may volunteer. Undesirable public relations problems may result as these persons may never be called upon to speak. The safest approach seems to be requesting recommendations from other teachers, involved parents, and other school personnel. In this way, you will be able to select speakers who will inform and motivate your children about a variety of new jobs and experiences.

To summarize, children may receive direct experience from four basic sources: (1) real activities within the classroom, (2) realia, (3) field trips, or (4) resource persons. Regardless of the source, they should be actually involved in *doing something real.*

Skillful guidance during such real encounters is an effective teaching tool. You should constantly be offering questions and comments to help the children observe carefully or to engage in higher order thought processes, such as predicting or finding relationships. Examples of pertinent questions and comments include:

• I wonder if the ants will eat the cracker crumbs. Let's try it and see what happens.

• Let's try it again and see if the same thing happens.

• Maybe we can find out if we watch it carefully.

• How can we find out?

• Which twig is longer?

• How long do you think it will take?

• What food does the rabbit eat?

• How many baby hamsters were born?

• Which animal lives in a tree? Underground?

• What word does the worm make you think of?

• What would you do if you could climb a tree like that squirrel?

PLAY ORIENTATION

From our discussion so far, we have learned that the children's intellectual development first begins as they are involved in sensorimotor activities, but as they grow older, youngsters switch from using their senses to building mental pictures. The facilitation of this transition may be one of your most important functions. Perhaps the most evident method

of encouraging the shift in modes is to encourage dramatic play in which the children symbolize the many aspects of their changing world. Children as young as three years old have a tendency to reenact any sensory impression immediately. For example, going on a trip to a construction site may be followed by pointing out the tools available in the woodworking area of the classroom or the blocks in the block area. By making this connection, you are encouraging the children to symbolize their experiences in play and letting them know that such opportunities are desirable activities. Once the child becomes capable of such play, your role is to continually structure the environment with a number of interest centers similar to those we discussed in Chapter 4—blocks, housekeeping, woodworking, and so on. As the children play, you assume the role as a skillful facilitator, recognizing the importance of helping the children translate sensorimotor experiences into symbolic dimensions of thought.

Perhaps the major way you are able to assist in this process is to offer statements or questions as the children are engaged in dramatic play with a goal of expanding such concepts as size, shape, patterns, and spatial relationships. The following is just a short list of sample encounters in the block area:

• Are there more round blocks or square blocks in your building? (shapes; more than–less than)

• Can you find another block just like the one Arnold has in his hand? (matching)

• Your building looks strong with all the big blocks on the bottom. (size)

• The boat will be able to go under the bridge you built over the water. (spatial relationships; over–under)

• Is it shorter to Mike's building from here or to Kate's building? (spatial relationships; longer–shorter)

• Your block building looks just like Lucy's except for one block. Can you see which one is different? (patterns)

Play, therefore, serves as an excellent force to integrate the child's sensorimotor experiences with internal mental processes. This eventually produces patterns of communication enabling the child to express ideas in symbolic forms. Children who are able to engage in dramatic play are offered an avenue in which they can independently, naturally, and effectively pursue the skill and cognitive tasks necessary for later school-related learning.

Constance Kamii, an educator who has made many applications of Piaget to the early childhood classroom, explains how play activities help the young child gain knowledge of his physical world:

In a simple situation like pretending to have coffee with friends, children represent their knowledge of reality in all areas of the cognitive framework. For example, they represent their *physical knowledge* by heating the coffee, pouring it, spilling it, stirring it, and burning oneself with it. They represent the idea of pouring more coffee than cream, or giving a lot of cream and sugar to some people, and less or none to other people *(pre-seriation)*. They construct elementary *number concepts* as they get just enough cups, saucers, napkins, and spoons for everybody. They represent the *temporal sequence* of making coffee, getting the cups and saucers out, pouring coffee, drinking it, and then cleaning up. They learn to serve the guests first *(social knowledge)*. Sometimes, they invite people by phoning them beforehand. In this situation, some children's temporal sequence has been observed to consist of accepting an invitation first before being invited, or dialing first before picking up the receiver! [1972, p. 305]

Such play-oriented situations should be kept open-ended. Eventually, the young child's curiosity will be motivated and she will begin a transition to more academically oriented tasks. Ann Hammerman and Susan Morse use an informal classification example to illustrate such a transition activity:

In the course of her play, Judy began grouping objects by color, making a red group and a white group. She noticed a red pencil with a white end. She put it first into the red group and then into the white group. She was noticeably perturbed. Neither solution satisfied her. Finally, she placed the pencil so that the red end was near the other red objects and the white end was near the white objects. The pencil formed a bridge between the two groups. She was experiencing a moment of tension between a more rigid view that an object can belong to only one group at a time and a realization that groups can overlap. [1972, p. 51]

Play-oriented activities can lead to more academically oriented tasks if the teacher allows children to explore objects in the classroom freely and perform their own actions on them. When children begin to develop an increasing awareness of the objects around them, the teacher may do some systematic questioning leading to problem solving. Hammerman and Morse described the following situation in which a preschool teacher encouraged problem solving.

Teddy approaches the table. The objects available to him are: a rectangular plastic container, funnel, sticks, wooden and plastic discs of different sizes, aluminum tart tins, different shapes and sizes of blocks (rectangular, cylindrical), marbles, different kinds of paper, beads, spools, straws and plastic airplanes.

Teddy begins making a tower alternating metal tins and paper cups. He is ordering the items in a specific way, as well as testing out the balance of forces. I say, "I'll make a tower too. Let's see if I can make mine taller." I decide to bring in the comparison of heights to see if Teddy will pursue this aspect of tower building. Then he picks up the whole pile of cups to add them to the tower. I ask him, "What do you think will happen if you put all the cups on top there?" Since he is silent, I ask, "Do you think it will fall?" He nods. "Do you want it to fall over?" He shakes his head no. "Well, what could you do so that it will not fall over?" He considers the pile of cups. He takes part of the pile and puts it on the tower. I say, "That's an idea, taking some away." The tower does not fall. He has considered a problem and figured out a solution. He now adds the rest of the cups. The pile topples.

He rebuilds the pile in the same spatial pattern as before. When he is at the point of wanting to add the whole pile of cups, he pauses to consider the situation. He places the entire pile of cups on top of the tower pushing down from the top as he does so to compress the pile. I say, "Another good idea, to press down on the cups." He has considered another solution to the problem. This is a sophisticated solution, intuitively using the laws of physical science.

This time the tower does not fall. [1972, pp. 43–44]

Your role in using this problem-solving situation is multifaceted. You must learn to:

• encourage children to explore their physical world.

• point out logical relationships when they occur.

• encourage children to predict and hypothesize.

• encourage children to pursue their own direction in testing their hypotheses.

• verbalize children's actions so they would direct their major efforts toward thinking.

Ask challenging questions and offer comments that help children work toward a solution to their problems.

As their language competencies grow, young children will openly join you in the conversations and freely verbalize their exciting new discoveries. The basic format for cognitive-developmental instruction is as follows:

Play-games, such as this sorting activity, constitute one type of activity derived from Piagetian learning theory.

1. Furnish the children with toys and objects that encourage exploration and experimentation.

2. Capitalize upon the children's interest in all the real phenomena in their world.

3. Offer informal language stimulation to highlight specific concepts.

INFORMAL EDUCATION

Early in the century, John Dewey and William H. Kilpatrick developed ideas of education that urged teachers to form child-centered classrooms. As Kilpatrick (1937) said, "Who can question that there are many ... learnings going on in each child all the time, and that the sum of the ... incidental ... [child-centered] learnings may and does overshadow the *specific* [italics mine] school learnings, and may determine what [the child] shall do in life?" (p. 422). These "progressives" reasoned that knowledge grows from personally meaningful play experiences in a socially oriented, child-centered classroom.

Such ideas regarding child-centered learning have been reshaped and molded over the years. During the 1970s, such ideas were called *informal education;* they were espoused by Carl Rogers, John Holt, and others.

In basic philosophy, informal classrooms are very much like Piagetian classrooms. In fact, Piaget has often been cited as having provided theoretical support for the informal classroom. This is because Piaget called upon others to translate his theories into action, and some of the resulting programs defined the teacher's role as being more directive and learning sequences more prescribed. Programs of this type became known as cognitive–developmental programs. Other programs focused upon direct experiences, dramatic play, and sensory–motor activity espoused by Piagetians, but they differed in the amount of teacher direction that they prescribed. Believing that children should have nearly complete freedom to explore and discover according to their own interests, educators supporting these less structural programs became known as proponents of informal education.

Carl Rogers (1974) implored early educators to think of themselves as *facilitators* rather than as *teachers.* He used his "mug and jug" theory to explain the difference:

> The teacher asks himself: "How can I make the mug hold still while I fill it from the jug with these facts?" The attitude of the facilitator has almost entirely to do with climate: "How can I create a psychological climate in which the child will feel free to be curious, will feel free to make mistakes, will feel free to learn from his environment, from fellow students, from me, from experience? How can I help him recapture the excitement of learning which was his in infancy?" [p. 102]

John Holt's views were similar to Rogers's:

> We do not need to "motivate" children into learning, by wheedling, bribing, or bullying. We do not need to keep picking away at their minds to make sure they are learning.

> What we need to do, and all we need to do, is bring as much of the world as we can into the school and the classroom; give children as much help and guidance as they need and ask for; listen respectfully when they feel like talking; and then get out of the way. We can trust them to do the rest. [1967, p. 187]

Informal education, then, can best be described as a feeling on the part of the teacher that children learn most effectively when they become directly involved in their own learning. It is an attitude that perceives the child as capable of making his own decisions regarding learning. It is a strategy that emphasizes learning as a *process,* not a *product.* Programs based on the informal education philosophy generally hold the following assumptions to be of major importance:

- Children are naturally curious and are eager to explore their environment freely.

- Learning is not done "to the child" but "by the child."

- Active exploration and manipulation enhance learning.

- Play is the child's form of work.

- Children have both the ability and the initiative to make certain decisions regarding their own learning.

- Children learn and develop according to their own unique rates and styles.

- Learning occurs best as it proceeds from the concrete to the abstract.

- Most facets of an individual's learning are best evaluated through direct observation of a child at work (play) rather than through paper-and-pencil tests.

- Learning to interact and cooperate as a group member is essential to the growth of an individual.

- Education must take place in an environment communicating trust, kindness, warmth, courtesy, respect, openness, and security.

Figure 7-6 *Learning from a recipe*

Teacher's Role

The teacher's role in the informal classroom is to guide and support the child's endeavors by accepting the role of facilitator. The teacher prepares the environment with a rich variety of materials and informal learning activities rather than with rigid lesson plans that compel children to dispense common sets of skills, content, or responses. He or she allows children to choose such activities freely, to assist each other, to discuss work freely with one another, and to pursue any one goal for as long as they wish. The teacher encourages children to answer their own questions rather than to respond to his or hers and wants children to look at learning as self-rewarding rather than as dependent on extrinsic rewards or praise.

Informal classrooms are characterized by no single method of instruction, but rather suggest a range of active modes of learning that reflect discovery learning and self-chosen involvement. Basic to all informal education programs, however, is the concept of the *integrated day*. What this means is that learnings are communicated in contexts that closely approximate daily living. For example, the teacher might have available a cookie-making project for those children who are interested (see Figure 7-6). The children would measure cups of flour and shortening or tablespoons of sugar, salt, and baking powder. Learning the various measures as well as counting the number of cookies would be part of the mathematics program. Reading the simplified recipe would be part of the informal reading program. Becoming aware of the physical changes occurring during the mixing of ingredients or during the baking process lends itself to direct scientific observation. The verbal exchange during the entire project lends itself well to language or concept development. And the cooperation and interpersonal exchanges necessary for a group project to be completed provide a meaningful social context in the lives of the children. Obviously, the integrated activity becomes the medium for communicating subject matter to young children. The overall goal of such a strategy is to make the children's education as meaningful and purposeful as possible.

Supplementary to integrating subject matter, some informal classrooms use a variety of learning centers. A *learning center* (sometimes called "interest center") is an area in which activity-oriented materials motivate and enable children to assume individual responsibility for their own learning. Materials for these centers may include commercial, teacher-made, or "junk" items. After analyzing the children's needs and interests, an informal classroom-oriented teacher might decide on several types of independent center activities.

Learning centers can be arranged for a variety of different purposes. Science centers may be established to encourage children to investigate and study nature; dramatic play centers help children express themselves or interact with others; an art center can help awaken the child's desire to create and discover through a variety of media; sand and water play centers encourage children's imagination and cognitive processes; and woodworking or block centers allow children to construct things. You must not be misled by this discussion of the physical organization of learning activities; informal classroom philosophy is more than a set of organizational pattern or a specific teaching strategy. The pattern of organization and method of instruction are merely vehicles through which a feeling of freedom, trust, and motivation for learning grow. Once this atmosphere is established, children are likely to become productive, positive, and successful learners.

A Sample Classroom

At this point, we're going to look at one variation of the informal classroom in some detail. In this classroom children range from age three to age six. This "multiple-age" grouping, or "family" grouping as it sometimes is called, allows children to form groups as they do outside of school—that is, with siblings or with peers having like interests, abilities, or skills.

The preschool classroom has one teacher and an aide for 15 children. The room is large and is organized into many nooks and crannies—messy corners, book corners, display corners, and quiet corners. The children's work, exhibited in many unique ways, is evidence that creative learning activities abound.

As the children enter the room, they move freely to their chosen areas and select the activities they want for this particular time slot. Some children prefer lively activities like painting, woodworking, or puppetry. Others are more passive—they prefer the rug and pillows in the reading corner; this comfortable area is a quiet start to the day.

The aide helps one child insert a card into the Language Master; the child listens intently as his words are recorded and played back for him. Another child puts on a set of earphones and listens carefully to a prerecorded story on the tape recorder. Two more children become involved with the manipulative letter recognition games located at the reading table. The aide works with Martha on an experience story. As Martha tells her story, the aide writes it down for her. When the story is complete, the aide reads it back to Martha; then there is a short session during which Martha is asked to locate a few key words. Finally, Martha decides to illustrate her story at the art center.

As the reading corner activity continues, children move freely throughout the room or take up new activities. They write on paper, build with blocks, observe the polliwogs, make things, move to music, or simply recline peacefully. Periodically throughout the morning, the teacher helps children in need of special guidance to find activities or tasks that will be valuable to them. Some are directed to the arts and crafts center where children are making butterflies out of construction paper and pipe cleaners. Others join the creative dramatics area where their invitation to a "tea party" is issued with friendly smiles.

Basic to this informal classroom is an outdoor learning area. Flower and vegetable gardens, play equipment, and animals are freely accessible through a door leading from the classroom. On this brilliantly warm day, one child has chosen to bring a book with her and is sprawled in the shade of a large tree. Another child is active on the tire swings that hang from the tree. A small group is digging in the vegetable garden, preparing the ground for a fresh planting of beans. Children move freely from inside to out and excitement and spontaneity flow easily from one area to the other.

Rather than bringing materials from their natural settings into the classroom, this school makes every effort to get the children out of the classroom. The city, the countryside, and the neighborhood all provide exciting opportunities for the children to experience new phenomena. Fresh bakery bread, a newly born baby calf, or a ride on the district fire engine create new situations in which children can ask or answer questions related to newly developed interests. The classroom, therefore, is viewed as not merely an area surrounded by four walls, but as a total living environment in which both teachers and children are discovering novel ways of exploring and learning.

Informal classrooms do not need to be as liberal as the examples used to illustrate the philosophy. Basic to the idea, though, is the belief that learning is most effectively carried out when the child is free to initiate his own

learning in an environment rich in materials and activities.

From the time of birth through the preschool years, youngsters learn through an accumulation of all their experiences. In essence, all of life is their curriculum, and children assume the central role in the learning process whether that process takes place in the home, school, or any other environmental setting. The most interesting characteristic of much of this learning is that, whether in a cognitive–developmental or informal setting, it takes place in a play-oriented setting. Even so, the progress made by individuals between the time of birth and eight years of age is fantastic. Lefrancois (1983) considered this phenomenon and reasoned that, "It appears reasonable, then, that if children can learn as much as they do . . . from a curriculum as unsympathetic . . . as parts of their lives, they could certainly learn better from the more organized efforts of people trained in the schooling of young children. Indeed, this reasoning underlies many preschool education programs" (p. 247). And, even though current research evidence to determine whether preschool education actually does enhance learning has been somewhat inconclusive, many studies have indicated that such planned programs do have markedly beneficial effects on the learning of young children (Belsky & Steinberg, 1979; Bronfenbrenner, 1979).

Guided Learning

Children learn a great deal by themselves, but often require help in putting those learnings together to form increasingly sophisticated concepts. Help is usually offered by providing activity and play, but with the teacher assuming a more involved role. For example, you may wish to encourage the child to be able to discriminate among objects on the basis of color. To achieve that goal, you show a child a box full of small toys and say, "Look at all the toys in this box. Let's dump them on this rug and see what we have." Allow the child to play for a time with the toys, then invite him to join you in a game: "Let's play a sorting game with these toys. We'll put the red toy on this red rug (sample) because it is the same color, the blue toy on the blue rug, and the yellow toy on the yellow rug. Ready? Show me a toy. Where will you put it? Good. The blue toys all go together. . . . You sorted all the toys by color. Very good! Please tell me the names of the colors we sorted. You did very well. Let's mix the toys and play the game again." Analyzing this teacher's strategy, we find that she:

1. arranged a special set of manipulative, play materials,

2. encouraged the child to play freely with the materials,

3. demonstrated an activity with the materials that leads to understanding,

4. invited the child to perform the same action until mastery was achieved, and

5. continued the activity until the child lost interest.

Remember that this sequence doesn't need to be followed rigidly each time an informal activity is offered. The exact amount of teacher involvement as well as the number and order of play experiences should always remain open so they can more readily match the child's changing interests and needs.

Once we begin to work with young children in a group while they are engaged in intellectual tasks, though, it is important to provide some structure to the available time so that maximum benefit can be derived by all. Small-group time devoted to intellectual pursuits generally becomes a part of the daily routine for some four-year-old groups and, by kindergarten, most teachers provide for such structured group time. Groups usually consist of five to nine children who meet regularly for 20–30 minutes each day.

A learning goal is usually specified for each group session. This helps give the lesson a focus and provides a major source of professional support for choosing the activity for the group. Examples of goals include "exploring with the senses," "comparing the contrasting objects," or "recognizing colors."

There are two features of goals that you should remember whenever you are called upon to plan for group sessions: First, the goals or objectives are stated in terms of the _children,_ such as, "The children will describe the relative position of a set of objects." An inappropriate objective would be one that describes the behavior of the teacher, such as, "The teacher will furnish the children with information about basic geometric shapes." When you identify objectives, your statements must describe what you want the children to accomplish; your expectations, of course, are to make sure the objectives are realized. Second, there should be only one or two objectives specified for each group session. One characteristic problem of many beginning teachers is to state too many objectives; they seek to accomplish too much. Remember that young children need a special focus and that too many objectives cause your session to become so general that it may lack real meaning.

Critics believe that overly broad objectives are often stated in such indefinite ways that they lack real meaning. For example, they say that an objective such as "The children will understand the four basic geometric shapes" lacks any real focus and could probably apply just as well to the study of high-level plane geometry as it does to the simple recognition of basic geometric figures.

For that reason, some educators prefer to state objectives in terms of direct, observable behaviors; such objectives are called _behavioral objectives._ Behavioral objectives identify the specific behaviors you hope the children demonstrate as they progress through the learning activities you plan. Behavioral objectives consist of three major parts:

1. identifying the *input process,* or the activity you will provide,

2. describing *what the child is to do* during the activity, and

3. stating the child's minimum acceptable *level of performance.*

Behavioral objectives are frequently used to give more specificity to the broader objectives. For example,

- *General Objective:* The children will distinguish among specific sounds made by the teacher.

- *Behavioral Objective:* After listening to five common sounds with their eyes shut *(input),* the children will name the source *(what they are to do)* of at least four sounds *(minimum performance).*

Regardless of the type of objective you wish to state as you plan for small-group learning activities, however, you must give it careful thought. Objectives give you a reason for providing the session for the children and for choosing the learning activity to which the children are exposed. Instead of aimlessly searching through teachers' idea books for a "cute," "gimmicky," or "fun" activity to share with the children, start with a purpose for the session. Ask "Why is this lesson so important?" or "What is it going to do for the children?" Once you have done this satisfactorily, you are on the right road to selecting appropriate activity; cute, gimmicky, and fun now have a purpose. If you go through this process, you are using a sophisticated professional reasoning skill—making *if-then* connections. For example, you may be thinking along these lines:

- *If* we want the children to describe spatial relationships, *then* we may want to place a toy bear at one end of an elaborate construction paper path and a toy house at the other. We'll ask the children to describe how the bear can get

home by using spatial terms such as going "over" hills or "under" bridges.

- *If* we want to help develop fine muscle control appropriate for beginning writing, *then* we may want to encourage the children to use knobbed wooden inlay puzzles so that they use the two fingers and thumb in much the same way that they must be coordinated for writing.

Once you have decided what your objectives are and choose the materials the children will enjoy, you must develop a session, or lesson framework. Such frameworks are most effectively produced when they are thought of in three clear-cut parts: *beginnings, bodies,* and *ends.*

Beginning. In order to prepare a good beginning, keep these tips in mind:

- Have the necessary materials ready at the place they are going to be used.

- Have the material divided into portions for each child, if necessary.

- Get everyone's attention in an interesting way. For example, "I'm going to tell you a secret," or "What do you think happened to this carrot today?"

- Give a brief description of the activity, for example: "Here are some toys. Does anyone have an idea how we can find out which ones will sink and which ones will float?"

- Have the children enter into the activity as soon as they understand what they are to do.

Body. Your role during the actual work time includes these responsibilities:

- Watch and listen to see if things are going smoothly and as anticipated.

- Talk with each child, making sure you stimulate thinking and help them describe the activity with words.

- Challenge the children to solve special problems: "Could we use this piece of styrofoam to help the paper clip float?"
- Give special suggestions to children who may be having trouble.

Ending. To ensure that the children will feel good about the activity, end it with little confusion:

- Caution the children that the activity will soon be coming to an end.
- Ask each child to tell about or show what she has done.
- Make cleanup a part of the activity: "After you put everything away, we can look at books until everyone is ready for the story circle."
- Encourage the children to try the materials again if you have your classroom arranged with interest centers.

This suggested sequence of presenting planned cognitive lessons to young children should be studied carefully. You will most likely be asked sometime soon to plan an organizational sequence for learning activities. Such a blueprint, or plan of action, enables you to predict the course of action you find appropriate for the identified area of instruction. Although forms and styles differ markedly among college instructors and classroom teachers, a lesson plan usually contains sections in which objectives, methods and materials, and techniques for evaluation are specified. Depending on the nature of the lesson, some provisions for individual differences must be indicated. The accompanying box contains a sample lesson plan, which applies the ideas shared thus far. It is my particular style of planning and merely suggestive in intent. Your instructor will certainly express a personal

preference; a comparison of philosophical orientations is recommended.

Because we have so carefully considered descriptions of guided learning, we must also point out a common trap that captures many early childhood professionals. This misunderstanding equates preschool instruction with some commonly abused elementary school approaches—all children sitting at their seats, using workbooks, reciting facts, and so on. Do not bring dull routines and dreariness into the children's lives, but challenge their minds with methods of teaching that appeal to young children. Our concern is not to "cram" information into children, but to develop an interest in learning that will last all through their lives.

Planned programs recommended by most early childhood educators, then, differ markedly from what many nonprofessionals believe to be "learning." The popular misconception of early learning is that it is much like we may have experienced during the early elementary grades—acquiring information primarily from books, films, or by listening to teachers tell us about things. These sources of learning do eventually become an important component of the child's educational experience, but the preschool teacher's role is more suitable to encouraging the kind of developmental learning most suitable for young children before they enter the elementary school. This means planning and carrying out those experiences by involving youngsters in exploring, experimenting, and action-oriented activity. Young children are capable of learning much before they learn to read from books, but exactly *what* learnings should we be providing? Learning experiences especially appropriate for the three- through five-year-old child include opportunities to:

- *understand self and others.* The child knows own first and last name, birthday, age, address, phone number, parents' (parent's) name(s), teacher's name, the

LESSON PLAN

- Group size: 3–5
- Age level: Four-year-olds
- Teacher: Miss Ginny

Objectives

- *General Objective:* The children will understand the concept of "same."
- *Behavioral Objective:* After observing ten common objects, the children will sort all five pairs that are the same.

Methods and Materials

1. Arrange on a large table as many boxes containing five pairs of common objects as there are children in the group: styrofoam cups, pencils, crayons, scissors, and paint bushes, for example. Also, have a separate box for the teacher containing five pairs of different objects.

2. Encourage the children to explore the objects by saying: "Look at all the things in these boxes. Let's take them out to see what we have."

3. Allow the children to play for a short period of time.

4. Invite the children to join along in a game: "Let's play a sorting game with these toys." Start off by placing one block from the teacher's box on the table and saying, "I'm going to find another that is the *same*." Then place a second block with the first.

5. Ask the children to show a styrofoam cup from their boxes and place it in front of them. Then invite the children to find the matching cup. Once that is done, reinforce the concept by saying, "These are the same."

6. Encourage the children to pull one other toy from their boxes and find the other that is the same. Continue until all five pairs are matched.

7. Ask the children to tell you what they have done.

8. Invite the children to put away the materials they had used: "After you put the toys back into the boxes, place them on the shelf and get ready for the playground."

Evaluation

Observe the children during the activity to determine whether all five pairs were accurate.

---

other children in the classroom, and parts of the body.

- *develop language skills.* The child attaches verbal labels to objects, ideas, and feelings; participates in informal conversations; follows directions; listens to stories; plays word games; and develops interests in written words, labels, and books.

- *acquire basic cognitive skills.* The child knows basic concepts such as "shapes" (circle, square, triangle, rectangle, sphere, and cube), "colors" (recognizes color names and shades of color), "locational terms" (front/back, top/bottom, in/out, over/under, inside/outside, on/off, above/below), "time concepts" (yesterday, today, tomorrow; before, after;

morning, afternoon, evening, night; names and order of the days of the week; the calendar), "opposites" (big/small, heavy/light, dark/light, night/day, happy/sad, hot/cold), "classifications" (putting together things that are alike based on common characteristics of size, color, use, and so on).

- *discover the physical world.* The child experiments, explores, and manipulates in order to find out about the nature of things: plants, animals, pulleys, ice, alarm clocks, condensation, boiling, magnets, parts of the body, floating, sinking, and hundreds of other physical phenomena.

- *understand the social world.* The child learns about group life, family structures and responsibilities, and community and its people.

- _develop physical skills and coordination._ The child develops small muscle skills through the use of puzzles, tools, games, cutting, sewing, weaving, pasting, and other manipulative materials or activities; large muscle skills through building, climbing, lifting, running, jumping, swinging, pushing, dancing, and other activities.

- _acquire a basic mathematical understanding._ The child experiences opportunities to estimate, measure, and count.

- _develop interest and skill in expressive media._ The child freely participates in activities dealing with art, music, and creative dramatics.

By analyzing the skills and concepts inherent in each area, teachers provide opportunities for a variety of learning experiences. Sometimes materials are arranged around the classroom, like bait, so that the child is attracted to them. At other times, the teacher may encourage and invite the child to explore materials. However, with either approach, the teacher promotes active involvement, manipulation of materials, problem solving, and exploration. She helps the child develop a sense of mastery and confidence in his abilities through rich and varied learning experiences and is always near to clarify and support during learning activities in order to prevent misinterpretations and misconceptions from occurring. Young children, then, must be provided an environment of stimulation within a climate of emotional support in order to grow in their capacity to learn. Researchers tell us that the environment can be arranged to promote learning in the very young, and early childhood educators mostly agree on the kinds of learning appropriate for youngsters in such an environment, but your responsibility as a teacher becomes greater than ever before as

you decide upon exactly how to arrange that environment and function within it.

Teachers often choose to reinforce and extend the introduced concept by arranging a number of learning centers. Each center would be designed to contain at least one distinct developmental activity to which the children may move in order to become individually involved. In any classroom there may be as many as 15 stations or as few as 1. At a learning station or center (stations usually contain only one activity while centers contain more than one), children may perform tasks by themselves or with assistance from the teacher or aide. The activities in the accompanying box are designed for center use. See if you are able to match the activity with the items identified in the "subject matter" list presented earlier.

AN ALTERNATIVE APPROACH TO PRESCHOOL INSTRUCTION: THE BEHAVIORAL APPROACH

Perhaps the greatest theoretical influence supporting the use of structured learning in the preschool setting has been that offered by the behaviorists. Led by B. F. Skinner and his ideas regarding _operant conditioning,_ the behaviorists view the learning process as a complex system of rewarding desirable behaviors. As discussed in Chapter 3, Skinner's theory conceptualized _operants_ as any behaviors—singing, hitting, walking, talking, playing, and so on—emitted by an organism. The operant behavior takes on its character not so much because it is elicited by any specific prior stimulus, but because its presence in the environment produced a particular response from a child. For example, when a child presses an appropriate key on a typewriter, a teacher may

INDEPENDENT LEARNING ACTIVITIES

Position Game

Use a box with a lid and a variety of objects for this learning activity to reinforce relative terms. Ask the child to "Put the dog *inside* the box," "Put the cow *near* the box," "Put the horse *under* the box," "Hold the truck *above* the box," and so on.

Food Sort

Put a mixture of dried foods into a shoe box. Have the children sort these foods according to whatever characteristic they choose—size, shape, color, type of food, and so on. Egg cartons, cups, or plastic glasses work well as sorting containers. The following dried foods are appropriate: macaroni of various shapes, split peas, lima beans, dried corn, pinto beans, kidney beans, rice, and navy beans.

Feely Box

Get an old packing box and decorate it with bright colors and designs. Cut two holes in opposite sides and stitch old socks (with toes removed) to the holes through which the children will reach their arms. Each day, put a surprise object into the box and ask the children to feel it and guess what it is. Paintbrushes, sponges, drinking cups, combs, strings of yarn, and feathers are but a few of the objects appropriate for this activity.

Lids and Containers

Collect an assortment of containers and lids and place them on a table. Ask the children to match the lids to the appropriate containers.

Photo Match

Take a front view and back view photograph of each child in your room. Mount the photos on oaktag to make them sturdy. Put them all in a box and mix them up. Have the children examine the photos and match each front view with its appropriate back view.

Fabric Match

Glue various fabric scraps onto pieces of square cardboard. Use a wide variety of interesting textures (corduroy, felt, satin, fur, and so on) and a wide variety of colors and patterns. Make two squares of each fabric. Put all the squares into a box. The children will enjoy finding the squares that match.

Hint: Wallpaper samples will work just as well as the fabric squares.

Matching Colors

Select two or three colors that are being taught to the children. Cut a square of each color from construction paper and paste those squares on white oaktag. Have

(*continued*)

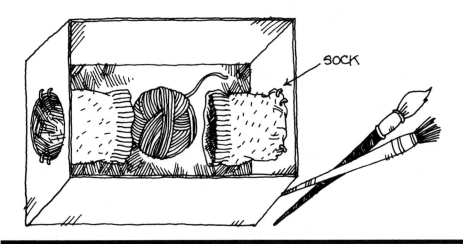

SOCK

the children search through a shoebox of plastic chips, buttons, or farm animals and sort each object onto the appropriate piece of tagboard.

Treasure Hunt

Paint six boxes with tempera paint—one red, one blue, one green, one yellow, one orange, and one purple. Have the children search the room for objects with these colors (or bring things from home) and put the objects into the appropriate boxes.

When all the materials are collected, you may wish to dump them on the floor and invite the children to put them back into the corresponding boxes.

Color Clothespins

Collect several pieces of fabric of various solid colors. Also, buy a bag of plastic clothespins whose colors match the fabric colors (or paint some wooden clothespins the appropriate colors). Ask the children to hang the red fabric with the red clothespins, the yellow fabric with the yellow clothespins, the blue fabric with the blue clothespins, and so on.

Shape Sort

Make a set of four cards (5 × 5 inches). On each card draw or paste one of the four basic shapes (circle, square, rectangle, triangle). Collect objects that conform to each shape, such as circular toy dishes, bottle caps; square blocks, toys; rectangular dominoes, books; and triangular hangers, musical instruments. Ask the children to sort through the various objects and place them on the card with the appropriate shape.

Beanbag Toss

Make three beanbags from old fabric pieces and some dried beans. Make one beanbag a red square, another a green circle, and the third a yellow triangle. Cut a hole of the same shapes in the tops of three cardboard cartons and paint the cartons the corresponding colors. Have the children stand back from the boxes and try to throw the beanbags into the corresponding holes.

Shape Tape

Cut as many strips of 1½-inch masking tape as needed to provide each child in a group with one 12-inch strip. Place one strip on the table with the sticky side up and

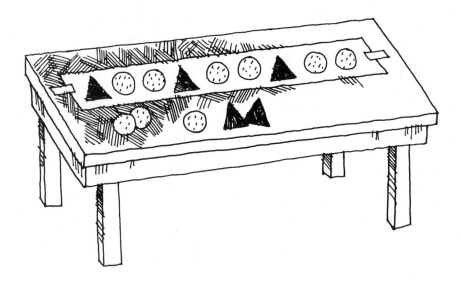

fasten it to the table with two smaller pieces of tape. Cut out a series of 1-inch geometric shapes of various colors. Make a pattern of geometric figures on your tape and ask the children to make a pattern just like yours.

Hint: Flannel strips may be cheaper than masking tape in the long run (they're reusable).

Hint: If you leave a section at the end, some children may welcome the challenge to guess what the next shape might be.

Cross the Stream

Tape a series of geometric shapes to the floor in patterns. Invite the children to join you on an imaginary walk in the woods. Pantomime a series of actions to encourage the children's active imaginations—actions such as, "Look at the pretty butterfly," or "Slap the mosquito that just bit you on your arm." After a short while,

announce to the children that they have approached a wide stream and the only way to cross it is to step on the colorful construction paper shapes. Give directions this way: "Martha, cross on any of the circles," "Will, cross on any of the red squares," "Pam, cross on the biggest green triangles," and so on. The directions can be individualized to account for specific differences in the children's abilities.

Objects and Shapes

Gather a number of everyday objects found at home or at school—items such as a pencil, hammer, screwdriver, doll, cup, fork, and so on. Trace around the objects on dark construction paper and cut out the silhouette. Mount the silhouettes on heavy white tagboard. Have the children match the real object with its corresponding silhouette.

praise him. Pressing the typewriter key is the operant and the praise is the reinforcer—the stimulus that causes the child to press the key is not important.

The process of education, then, in Skinner's theory, is classified as *operant conditioning,* that is, reinforcing desirable operants so they have a strong chance of occurring again. Thus, the mechanical system by which a child's response is reinforced by the teacher reflects the essential character of Skinner's operant conditioning.

When it is applied to the classroom, this philosophy is expressed in terms of programmed instruction. The format dictates that preschool academic instruction be built on three basic principles:

1. identification of the desirable operants (behaviors)

2. careful sequencing of learning experiences from simple to complex

3. use of reinforcers to strengthen and maintain the desired operants when they appear

These ideas became popular among some early childhood educators in the late 1960s—especially because of the strong concern for the education of low-income children. It was felt that these children were handicapped when they entered school because they had lost out on many of the early experiences necessary for success in middle-class-oriented school systems. These experiences had to be provided, therefore, in a short time with a highly efficient, structured, formalized approach. The approach was supported by many, but perhaps the most vocal supporter was Siegfried Engelmann. Educators subscribing to Engelmann's beliefs agreed that time was running out on children from low-income backgrounds and that a structured, highly teacher-directed approach was needed if they were to succeed once they entered the primary grades.

Such programs focused on the systematic development of academic skills and generally followed this sequence of steps that were examined in Chapter 3 within the discussion of behavior management:

1. *Establish terminal behavior.* State the behavior you wish the child to exhibit at the completion of a learning sequence. This must be specified beforehand so that an end point to the sequence is established. For example, one terminal goal would be that children be able to count from one to ten.

2. *Assess entry behavior.* Evaluate the child's present ability (through tests or observation) in the established terminal behavior. Some children, for example, may be able to count to five, others to three, and so on.

3. *Establish a structured, sequential learning system.* Arrange the instructional material in sequential segments and reinforce appropriate behavior at the end of each sequence. Such reinforcement may take the form of *preferred activities* such as free time or playground time; *tokens* (plastic chips) that can be used much like money to buy candy, school supplies, and so on; *food* such as raisins, cookies, or candy; and *praise.* Reinforcement is most effective when it is presented immediately following a desired behavior, so the teacher must be constantly alert to reward the child so behaviors are effectively strengthened along the way.

The curriculum is normally built around programmed materials that:

1. specify the exact behavior the child will exhibit at the end of the sequence

2. require frequent, direct responding by the child

3. contain clear standards for a "correct" response

4. allow for individual rates of progress throughout the sequence

5. provide for periodic testing of progress toward the desired behaviors

Behaviorally oriented programs usually contain hundreds of learning tasks, each arranged in a hierarchical sequence—skills learned earlier are prerequisites for later tasks. The basic process of behaviorism has to do with acquiring learned responses through conditioning so that the responses will automatically occur again in similar situations. Inherent in this process is the principle of learning by *association,* or simply pairing a stimulus (for example, pictures, objects, statements, or questions) with a correct response. The principle here is that if the pairings occur together over and over again they will become associated. Later, when only the stimulus is present, the response will automatically occur. Most of us have been exposed to association learning in our own schooling: You may have repeated, "The first president of the United States was George Washington" over and over. When you saw the stimulus on a test, "The first president of the United States was _____," you responded, "George Washington." Likewise, some early childhood programs stress the process of such drill while teaching youngsters basic concepts. These programs encourage frequent repetition for the purpose of establishing appropriate responses or behaviors.

Teachers using such programs are required to follow a strict sequence of instruction. For example, note the following lesson described by Aukerman taken from a beginning reading exercise in the DISTAR® program:

START THE PROGRAM HERE

Objective: Teaching *mmm* as in "him."
Task 1: (Identify new sound)
a. "Everybody, look at the book." *(Praise children who look)*

b. *(Point to letter m in book)* "Mmm. This is *mmm.* Say *mmm.* Good."
c. *(Point to picture of ice cream cone in book)* "Is this *mmm?*"
d. *(Wait. Praise the response: "No.")* "What is this?"
e. *(Trace m)* "Mmm, say *mmm.*" *(Wait)* "Good."
f. *(Point to letter m in book)* "Look at the book. *Mmm.* This sound is *mmm.* Say it loud. *Mmm.*"
g. *(Wait)* "Good."
h. "Look at the book." *(Point to a picture of an ice cream cone in book)* "Here's *mmm.*"
i. *(Wait)* "You fooled me! What is it?" [1971, p. 450]

Giving the students "Take-Homes" is a reward procedure often used to reinforce those who did a good job during the lesson. Study the following example of teacher instructions for presenting "Take-Homes."

DIRECTIONS FOR TAKE-HOME BLENDING SHEETS 1A AND 1B

Task 1
a. *(Do not show the picture until the children have blended the word)* "Say it fast and you may keep the picture. Say it fast!" Ham *(pause)* burger." *(Award the picture to the first child who gives the correct response)*
b. *(Present the word to each child)* "Say it fast! Ham *(pause)* burger." *(Award pictures for correct responses)* "Good. You get to keep the picture and take it home."
c. *(Present either "Motorboat" or "Hamburger" to each child. Alternate the words.)* "Say it fast! Motor *(pause)* boat." *(Award the picture of the motorboat for the correct response)*. "Say it fast!" Ham *(pause)* burger." *(Award the picture of the hamburger for the correct response)*
Task 2
(Hold up the picture of the hamburger so that the line is at the top. Call attention to the line) "Is this how we hold the paper?" *(Wait. Praise the response: "No")* "Show me how to hold the paper. . . . Yes, with the line at the bottom." [Engelmann and Becker, 1970]

Notice the amount of teacher direction involved in the overall strategy. This is what the behaviorists mean when they refer to their teaching strategies as being highly "teacher-directed" rather than "child-centered." Also, the teacher in this program used two types of positive reinforcers during the activity: verbal praise and the "Take-Homes." Other behavioral programs use a system of token rewards as positive reinforcers. As children master various learning tasks, they are given tokens for their progress and improvement. Later, after they have accumulated a number of tokens, they have opportunities to exchange them for events or activities that are valued. The children may, for example, exchange tokens for a favorite puzzle, game, free play toy, or art activity. These activities give the children motivation to learn and to succeed.

Critics have attacked behaviorally oriented programs for several reasons. First, they feel that because children receive their motivation from outside sources (tokens, hugs, candy, and so on), rather than internal sources (feelings of happiness, accomplishment, and so on), what they learn they soon forget. However, Harris (1977) reported that the comprehensive study of Follow Through programs completed by Abt Associates in 1977 showed that "highly structured programs that emphasized basic skills were more successful than other education approaches" (p. 2). Second, the behavioral approach is seen by some as stifling a child's creativity and self-direction. However, supporters cite independent research that indicates no significant differences in maladjustment among children in various instructional groups (including behaviorist). Third, some have criticized behavioral programs for not addressing themselves to affective objectives such as helping to foster a positive self-image. However, advocates argue that self-image and self-respect are best developed when children acquire the necessary academic skills to help them compete once they enter first grade.

Jessie Stanton (1975) summarized the thoughts of most critics in her stinging poem, "On Behavior Modification":

> Education works just dandy,
> When you use a piece of candy.
> You don't need to use your brains;
> To help a child make splendid gains.
> You don't need to get involved,
> All your problems will be solved.
> Each time a child does something right,
> Pick out a bonbon colored bright.
> Then tell the child to open wide,
> And pop the pretty piece inside.
> Of course he makes the right connection,
> Between the act and the confection.
> It's such a pleasant way of working.
> There is no need for any shirking.
> No play dough, paints or messy clay.
> No cleaning up at end of day.
> The child goes home all full of candy.
> Not weary, Teacher feels just dandy.
> It sounds so simple and so easy.
> Yet somehow it makes me queezy. [p. 22]

James L. Hymes (1968), one of the most popular traditional early childhood educators, attacked both the methodology and the motivation of the behavioral approach when he described the writings of Carl Bereiter and Siegfried Engelmann (two behaviorally oriented educators) as the "best [material] to read to appreciate how devastating a program for young children of the poor can be, once first grade time-panic sets in" (p. 14).

When examining the behavioral approach, keep in mind that it is a relatively new strategy for preschool education and consequently a candidate for careful review and criticism. Remember, too, that it has been used in one form or another for over 50 years with older children and must possess some redeeming qualities in order to last that long. There is no mystery to this new system; its basic principles have been understood and applied for years. Thousands of preschoolers all around our country, though, are now experiencing these behavioral programs and are being exposed to techniques that preschoolers never experienced in the past. Perhaps by choosing one, some, or all of their components, we can apply behavioral concepts to make our personalized programs more effective and enjoyable for the children.

COMPUTERS IN THE EARLY CHILDHOOD SETTING

In addition to all the learning possibilities presented to this point, you must become aware of a recent trend—an interest in the use of computers with young children. Teachers and children are reacting with enthusiasm to this new instructional tool. As a prospective teacher, you need to learn about them, too. The following material describes how computers are used with young children and introduces you to microcomputer applications in the classroom. But you need to know much more—what courseware is available and how to use the computer to fit your needs. For those reasons, try to take at least one course that will get you started in classroom computing and computer programming.

Sammie, age five, watched impatiently as his classmates took their turns at a computer terminal that was spouting merry jingles as colorful images flashed across its screen. Finally, Sammie's turn arrived. A scene appeared on the screen: a deep blue ocean and a fish swimming through the water. Sammie's tiny fingers wasted no time as they moved deftly across the keyboard to strike the numeral 3 in answer to a silent question posed when three bubbles suddenly appeared emerging from the fish's mouth. A snappy jingle rewarded Sammie's successful attempt at counting objects on the screen.

For Sammie, this experience was nothing new. He had been operating the computer for

a year by now. Although he does not understand what the computer did or why it did it, Sammie changed to a program that was designed to familiarize him with words. A word is flashed briefly on the screen and Sammie copies the word by typing it on the keyboard. If he copies the word correctly, the computer responds with a bright jingle and smile face on the screen. If Sammie does not, he must try again.

This sequence is fairly typical of the way most computer experiences work with young children. They begin when a child turns on the computer and is welcomed with a jingle and cheery "hello" printed on the screen. Problems then appear on the screen and the child works them out. If the decision is correct, the child will be rewarded and the next problem appears on the screen. If the response is incorrect, the machine notifies the child with a "buzz" or other signal and presents an alternate problem. In Sammie's number experience, when he is wrong, the computer says, "Uh, no," and the bubbles burst. Then the program starts over. Sammie tries again and again until he selects the correct responses for all the numbers of bubbles. "That's my favorite game," says Sammie. "I like the bubbles when they come out of the fish."

Most of the *software* (instructional programs) for young children are very simple in nature. As a matter of fact, Sammie was performing advanced operations with his counting exercise. A more basic program would find animal images flashing across the screen as the child touches *any* key. The child then sees the animal's name as the terminal plays "Old MacDonald Had a Farm." As the child presses any other key, the same sequence evolves. The conventional formats for storing these programs are in the forms of disks (5¼-inch × 8-inch magnetic devices resembling 45 RPM records), cassettes, or cartridges. A computer by itself can do nothing; it has to be given a systematized set of instructions. The disk, cassette, or cartridge provides these instructions in very special computer languages. Although there are more than 150 languages now in existence, the most popular appears to be BASIC (Beginner's All-Purpose Symbolic Instruction Code). The purpose of this course is not to teach you computer programming, but an example of BASIC language might be expressed as PRINT 2 + 1. The word *PRINT* is called a *command* because it signals the computer, in a very complex way, to take the result of whatever follows and put it on the screen. Therefore, the computer follows the instruction, adds the two numbers, and puts the result on the screen.

Children learn to use computer software very quickly because program operation is a fairly simple procedure. You need only make a picture chart showing the operational steps and guide the children through the following sequence (Hunter, 1984, p. 77):

1. Take the disk out of its paper jacket, holding it with the label under your thumb.
2. Put the disk into the slot in drive 1, holding your thumb side up.
3. Close the door on the disk drive.
4. Turn on the computer.
5. Wait for the program to load into the computer.
6. When the [key word] comes on the screen, press the number 1 key.
7. Play the game.
8. Take the disk out of the drive. Keep thumb on label.
9. When finished, turn off the computer.
10. Put the disk back in paper jacket.

Some educators criticize such computer-aided instruction because it bypasses the human element of teaching with interesting, but nevertheless old-fashioned drill. Proponents of computer-aided instruction counter with the argument that computers were never meant to replace teachers, but simply to offer a tool to assist them with teaching. As far as the emphasis on rote drill, a new computer language, called *Logo,* has been developed specifically for educational purposes. Logo was designed to move from the rote learning aspects of other computer-aided instruction toward problem solving and active learning whereby children could construct their own knowledge. The language began to be developed in the late 1960s by Seymour Papert and finally by the late 1970s was refined for use in microcomputers. Papert's active thinking concept of computer-aided instruction was primarily influenced by Jean Piaget with whom he had worked for a number of years.

Although Logo can be used to do almost everything other computer languages can do (from controlling a robot to designing a simple word-processing program), it is best known for its graphics environment, referred to as *turtle geometry.* Logo's turtle is a small white triangle that appears on the center of the screen. Users can make the turtle move by typing in commands as simple as FORWARD (the turtle draws a straight line in the direction it is headed) or RIGHT (to make the turtle head in a new direction). When each command is followed by a number, the turtle knows just how far to go in any particular direction. Beginning students are often given those two commands (forward and right) and given a chance to see what they could do. They may figure out how to make the turtle draw geometric shapes, such as a square, by typing the following:

```
TO   SQUARE

     FORWARD 50

     RIGHT 90

     FORWARD 50

     RIGHT 90

     FORWARD 50

     RIGHT 90
```

FORWARD 50

RIGHT 90

END

From this point on, the computer will draw a square whenever someone types the command SQUARE. What does this complicated procedure mean for preschoolers and kindergartners who do not have the maturity to create such commands by themselves? Louisa Birch (1983) feels that the eager, curious nature of kindergartners makes them the perfect age to be introduced to Logo on computers. She used a Logo program titled *Instant,* which made it possible for her children to execute any of the preceding commands by pressing only one key rather than typing out the whole statement itself. Choosing a classroom area dubbed "The Turtle's Corner," Birch introduced her children to commands such as these: The turtle moved forward 10 steps when a child pressed *F;* turned right 30 degrees for *R;* drew a square for *S,* a half circle for *C,* and a rectangle for *H;* and would erase when a child pressed *E.* To help them learn this language, Birch made a large picture chart and displayed it in the corner. Children each then had a chance to experiment with these commands for up to 15 minutes daily.

As the children experimented with the commands and created exciting new designs, Birch added new commands: The turtle could be moved to a new location without drawing a line when the child pressed *P;* it drew a triangle when *T* was pressed; and so on. The children welcomed these new commands and added great variety to their designs. One special command they especially enjoyed was UNDO *(U).* It allowed the children to erase only the last command given, leaving the rest of the design on the screen. Actually, the command erases the screen and recreates everything but the last step. Through this process the children could see their designs redrawn before their eyes, thereby observing the process

they had gone through to create their designs. Birch went from this experimentation to teaching her kindergartners how to write their own Logo programs. A new turtle graphics program called *Delta Drawing* (Spinnaker, Cambridge, MA 02142) aided her in this segment of her computer curriculum. Through her experiences with children and computers, Birch enthusiastically believes that kindergarten is an ideal time to introduce children to computers.

Computer utilization with young children is an exciting area just in its infancy stage of development. Although two- and three-year-olds are probably not mature enough to use the computer correctly (most have a tendency to abuse the keyboard), there is no reason why four-year-olds could not be introduced to computer basics. Because the entire field of state-of-the-art technology in education has become so popular today, you are encouraged to assume a strong leadership role by taking computer-literacy courses, training in basic programming, and understanding the impact of computers in our society.

SOME FINAL THOUGHTS

With increasing information about how children learn, parents and teachers sometimes overemphasize the child's intellectual growth. Resulting school programs have tended to transfer the traditional elementary school program into the preschool classroom by teaching facts and skills associated with reading, writing, and math. However, most preschoolers are not ready for such abstract thinking; they want to explore and experiment. They want to form wet sand, observe ant colonies, group sea shells, or investigate the world through their senses. Children want to figure out what things are, how they work, and how they fit into their lives.

You encourage children's natural capacity to learn by organizing a rich environment in which children interact and explore with enjoyment. You do not need a great variety of expensive materials to accomplish this goal; common objects such as spools of thread, pebbles, or pots and pans will suffice. The world outside the classroom is a great resource, too. Just consider the possibilities for learning associated with leaves (shapes, sizes, colors, and textures). Children, however, do not learn simply by being placed in an environment with all these things and left alone. They need adults who talk with them; point out shapes, sizes, and colors; help them perceive relationships among things; and assist them to organize their world in ways that aid the children when opportunities for formal learning come along. Moreover, talking with children is an important consideration because it helps in acquiring and refining the language skills so essential for the growth of higher mental abilities.

Preschoolers learn so much by doing. Be near to provide stimulation and encouragement. By doing so, the youngsters will assume the enjoyment and successes that lead them toward increasingly sophisticated learnings.

The scenes in the following anecdotes reflect the three major philosophies of early learning that we have discussed; scene 1 is based exclusively on the cognitive–developmental theory of Jean Piaget; scene 2 is based on theories of informal learning derived from a combination of Piaget, John Dewey, and Carl Rogers, and can be found in many of today's informal classrooms; and scene 3 is based on the behaviorist theory of B. F. Skinner. These three major theories of instruction were examined in this chapter because such knowledge is essential to help you plan teaching strategies for your own classroom. Grouping the children, choosing classroom materials, deciding on your role, selecting what things to say and how to say them, determining how to evaluate your children, and other key decisions must always be based on a solid theoretical foundation. In short, you should be able to finish this statement for each strategy: "I've decided to try this with my children because . . . ." Answers such as "They have fun doing it" are not satisfactory. Of course, enjoyment is a major consideration, but a true *professional* early childhood educator should have deeper insight into his or her teaching repertoire.

Teachers need to have the ability to understand learning theory and to apply it in planning the curriculum for their own children. Yet, getting teachers to understand or to become interested in such practice is difficult. A great part of the reason for this problem may lie in the way learning theory has been traditionally handled in education courses and/or in professional reading materials. Few attempts have been made to suggest the importance of learning theory to the teacher. Unfortunately, it is often taught as a body of facts to be learned rather than as a strong, applicable tool for teachers. The aim of this chapter, then, was to avoid such common traps and enable you to see how learning theories can help you develop valid, practical teaching practices for the education of young children. The three major classifications of learning theory discussed were: (1) the behavioral view, (2) the cognitive developmental view, and (3) the informal view.

SCENE 1

In a classroom, Ms. Perez is sitting at a table with five of her four-year-olds; the remaining ten children in her classroom have been divided into two other groups, one headed by an assistant teacher and one by an aide. Each group is working on the skill of classifying things according to same *and* different. *Ms. Perez begins this session by stating a rule to the children: "Vehicles are things that take us places." She then asks the children to look at a group of objects (doll furniture, blocks, coins, toy cars, toy trucks) and to select those that take us places by making two groups—*vehicles *and* not vehicles. *When the children accomplish the task, Ms. Perez asks them to tell why they grouped* the particular objects as they did. Supporting their responses, Ms. Perez says, "Yes. These are all the same; they are vehicles. These are different; they are not vehicles. Please tell me, what is a vehicle?"

Ms. Perez follows up the vehicle activities with one in which the children are to classify items that are tools and those that are not tools.

SCENE 2

In another classroom, the children are engaged in several independent activities, either alone or in small groups. Mrs. Field and her assistant do not formally interact with any group, but are nearby to offer encouragement or support when needed. In the science center one child becomes fascinated with a large magnet. Gina finds that by manipulating the magnet and approaching several objects, some materials are attracted to the magnet while others are not. Another child is watching nearby and soon joins Gina. Mrs. field sees their initial interest growing so she takes a box full of small objects and brings them to the children. "Will these stick to the magnet?" Mrs. Field asks.

"Yes, the block will," says Judy.

"No, it won't," counters Gina.

"How do you think we can find out?" asks Mrs. Field.

"We can touch each thing with the magnet," offers Gina.

"Yes, that would be fun," adds Judy.

"Good idea," Mrs. field says. "Do it your way and put all the items that will stick to the magnet in the blue box at the table and all the items that will not stick to the magnet in the red box."

Mrs. Field follows the same procedure with other groups throughout the activity period—she creates a problem situation, asks the children to predict an answer to the problem, and encourages them to discover the solutions by themselves.

SCENE 3

Seated at a table with a small group of children, Mr. Koh enthusiastically announces, "We are really going to have fun today." The children meet his announcement with an approving "Hooray!"

"I want you all to be good listeners and lookers while I show you a picture. What am I going to do?"

"Show us a picture," reply the children in unison.

"You are all very good listeners today," says Mr. Koh. "Look at the picture and tell me what kind of animal you see."

"Bunnies," offer the children.

"Very, very good," replies Mr. Koh. "Now I will count the number of bunnies in the picture. Follow my finger as I point to each bunny . . . one bunny . . . two bunnies. How many bunnies did I count?"

"Two bunnies!" exclaim the children.

"I like your answers," compliments Mr. Koh. "Now you count the bunnies while I point."

"One bunny . . . two bunnies," count the children in unison.

"Oh, you are so smart today," says Mr. Koh. "Now let me see if I can fool you. Here is another picture—a picture of some kittens. There is one kitten in the picture."

"No!" counter the children.

"No?" questions Mr. Koh. "Show me! I'll point to the kittens and you help me count."

"One kitten . . . two kittens," chant the children. "See, you couldn't fool us."

"You're right," admits Mr. Koh. "You're too sharp for me today."

Chapter 8

Transforming Thoughts into Language

Chris, a three-month-old girl, lies quietly in her crib during one of her frequent daily nap periods. Suddenly she begins to sense a feeling of growing hunger and seeks to find a way to communicate her needs to an understanding adult. Initially, Chris's method of communication consisted of thrashing her arms and legs, but since her efforts met with no response, she adopted a more direct form of exchange—she started to cry. Suddenly an adult's footsteps start toward the nursery and Chris stops crying, knowing that help is on the way. Chris's parent lifts her up and comforts her with a series of cheerful words: "Oh, you sound like you're very hungry. Don't worry, I will take care of you." Chris begins to take comfort in the security of her parent's arms, and soon she finds herself advancing through a procedure experienced many times before. "I have your food, Chrissy. Open your mouth wide—oh, that's a good girl. Doesn't this taste good? Yes, yes—Chrissy was hungry."

Her stomach now full, Chris delights in being held over her parent's shoulder while being gently patted on the back. The accompanying humming and singing give Chris a very warm feeling indeed. She responds in ways that communicate her strong feeling of security: as tiny bubbles of gas that developed during feeding burble up, Chris smiles, gurgles, and babbles with delight. Chris's responses elicit smiles and hugs from her parent, completing a sophisticated cycle of parent–child actions and reactions.

Through the entire experience, an observer could have easily detected effective patterns of two-way communication that transmitted feelings of love and trust between parent and baby.

PATTERNS OF COMMUNICATION DURING INFANCY

From patterns of communication during infancy, the difficult task of learning a language begins. The first months of an individual's life are spent in "self-

A caring adult who warmly vocalizes the child's routines contributes immeasurably to language growth.

imposed" practice—the baby listens to sounds and learns to discern their likenesses and differences. Long before he can say words himself, the infant learns how to interpret what others are saying: His caregiver's voice, the sound of his name, or tones of voice all cause him pleasure or frustration. The infant also expresses feelings of pleasure and discomfort during these early months. Loud crying or quick arm and leg movements help communicate a certain need for relief of discomfort. Soft babbling, cooing, and smiling communicate strong positive feelings of comfort and satisfaction. How infants grow beyond these initial phases of communication to acquire and retain formal language is a complex and varied process. You notice how valuable it is for the baby to be with an adult who warmly and pleasantly vocalizes during routines. This gives the baby comfort and a feeling of trust, and also moti-

vates the baby to try to "talk" himself. Beginning speech flourishes under these pleasurable conditions.

The wise parent or caregiver should be encouraged to spend time with the child in verbal interaction. The child should be given many opportunities to "practice" his growing ability to communicate, and he should receive continuing reinforcement from his parents. Before long, the infant delights in vocalizations and begins to experiment with volume, pitch, and different sounds. He begins to listen more intently to words spoken by others and tries to repeat them. After six to nine months, the child may be crudely naming things with word labels. It is at this time, when verbal sounds are associated with objects, people, or activities, that the first true language is spoken. Robert Armstrong and W. J. Gage (1972) say that "from that time on, from a linguistic point

Table 8-1 *Patterns of Normal Language Growth during Infancy*

Age in Months	Listening	Speaking
1–2	Is calmed by familiar voices Listens to voices Listens to noises made by toys	Exhibits undifferentiated crying as a reflexive response to discomfort Makes throaty vocalizations while crying Coos and babbles—undifferentiated vocalizations
2–4	Looks toward sound Moves head and eyes to follow sound	Differentiates cries for different types of discomfort, such as hunger cry or pain cry Babbles in repeated sounds of two syllables: "ba-ba," "goo-goo" Begins loud laughter
4–6	Distinguishes between friendly and angry sounds	Vocalizes, somewhat randomly, over a sustained period of time Imitates the sounds of others Repeats vowel sounds ("a-a-a")
6–12	Responds to hearing own name Looks at other familiar objects when they are named Enjoys listening to own voice Responds to requests ("Give me the rattle.") Understands commonly used words	Begins to say "mama" or "dada" Imitates words or syllables Begins to expand vocabulary to one or two other words
12–24	Follows simple verbal instructions; points to parts of object when named Listens to simple stories of a few sentences, especially about self	Begins to acquire more words by imitating the sounds of others (at 12 months has 10–15 word vocabulary; at 24 months 20–50 words) Begins to use personal pronouns "I" and "me" or own name Asks for objects by name: "ball" or "cookie" Begins to string two words together into simple sentences ("Me go.")

of view, he never looks back. He listens and tries to imitate what he hears. He receives responses in the form of warm milk, dry diapers, or approval. He modifies his speech, listens again, adds words and structures, and when success seems obvious, a pattern of language becomes habitual" (p.9).

Table 8-1 presents patterns of normal language growth during infancy. You should be aware of these patterns for they will help you anticipate normal development at different stages, and help you create an appropriate language program for each child in your care.

Suggestions for Interaction

Of all factors affecting the child's growth during these stages, then, one major factor appears to be the quality of interaction and experience found in the family or child-care environment. Parents and other significant adults, as the child's first teachers, therefore assume primary roles in establishing the child's ability to cope with language. This is not meant to imply that such responsibility ends when the child enters school, but that a good start followed by continuing talking and listening experiences encourages language facility. The following suggestions are offered for parents or child-care workers.

- *Play sound games with the baby.* Let the child know you are interested in her babbling or gurgling. Imitate her sounds for a little while and encourage the baby to alternate her sounds with yours. Eventually, you will become so engrossed in the game that it will be difficult to tell who is leading whom. After imitating sounds for a little while, change your pronunciation of the sound. For example, if the child says "da, da, da" (as in "daddy") change it to sound like the *da* found in "*da*rk."

  Babies enjoy playing with their fingers and toes, and this opens the way for many more games. "This Little Piggy Went to Market," "Thumbkin," "Peek-a-Boo," and other games are fun for infants or toddlers.

- *Talk to the baby.* Although the rhythm, rhyme, and tone of voice used by parents during "baby talk" are pleasing to the baby and encourage infants to respond, standard English should be spoken at regular intervals. When doing so, you should use short, simple sentences. Speak slowly so the child can follow your pattern of speech and repeat key words or phrases when appropriate. Be sure to use the child's name repeatedly in the conversation.

  Your normal routines offer excellent opportunities for you to speak to the baby. You can hum or sing to accompany the caregiving experience, but more often you will probably talk. You can tell him simple stories of a few

sentences about what he is doing. If you repeat the same story during the same activity each day, it helps him learn about language.

Billy is getting dressed now. Now I'll put on his shirt—put his arm through here and that arm through there . . . slip it over your head, peek-a-boo! Now Billy's pants—one leg goes through here and the other leg goes through there. Now his socks—one on this foot and one on that foot. Now, we're almost done. Whoops—we forgot Billy's shoes! One for this foot and one for that foot. Now Billy's all dressed!

- Similar language experiences can be shared during bath time ("Now I'll wash Billy's tummy. Billy laughs so much when I rub his tummy with soap."), feeding ("Here is Billy's bottle. Oh, Billy looks so hungry today."), toileting ("Time to use the toilet, Billy. You did such a nice job. Billy's a *big* boy now."), or other routines. The key thing is to try to put all the child's actions into words.

  A word of caution, however: Don't feel strange about talking to babies. Many beginning child-care workers, especially those who are not parents, sometimes feel peculiar talking to babies. Because babies do not "talk back," these caregivers see infants as being essentially like plants—unresponsive to their talk. But remember, through increasing meaningful interaction, you *are* helping the infant move from simple, random vocalizations to more effective means of communication.

- *Share books with the baby.* Hold the baby comfortably in your lap and turn the pages of a book that has large, simple pictures. Point to different objects in the picture and name them for the child. Tell the child something about the picture, such as, "Look, Amy, here is a doll. It looks just like your doll." Do so in a pleasant voice so that everything will add up to a comfortable experience. Remember that the baby's listening vocabulary is much larger than her speaking vocabulary, so, long before she is able to say the name for herself, she will be able to point to a picture if you say the name for her. For example, if you say, "Amy, show me the kitty," she will proudly point to the picture. By the time the baby is about a year old, she will be able to awkwardly turn the pages of appropriate-sized books or magazines as she "reads" all by herself. Babies find books containing large pictures of familiar single objects, animals, or people most stimulating.

• *Sing to the baby.* Babies love being sung to, especially if the songs are accompanied by activity. Many caregivers hesitate to sing because of a lack of confidence in their voices. Don't worry about your voice—infants don't care if you sound like Barbra Streisand or a worn-out fog horn; they simply love to hear you sing. Also, don't worry about finding a known song for every situation. Make up a tune and lyrics as you do whatever you happen to be doing at the moment. Sing to the baby as you feed him, change him, dress him, play with him, bathe him, and so on. Look directly at the baby while you sing; smile and try to get the baby to "sing" along with you.

Songs help the child learn to associate word labels to his body and to familiar objects in his surroundings. For example, the simple tune "Pat-a-Cake," although old and tired for an adult, is met with enthusiasm time and again by the infant.

Pat-a-cake, pat-a-cake, baker's man *(clap baby's hands together)*
Bake me a cake as fast as you can.
Roll it *(roll baby's hands)*
And pat it *(pat baby's hands)*
And mark it with a *B (or baby's first initial)* *(make initial on baby's tummy)*
And put it in the oven for Billy *(or baby's first name)* and me.

Mother Goose rhymes and other action songs or games are both stimulating and enjoyable for children of this age.

• *Provide a variety of experiences for the baby.* Allow the child to accompany you to the supermarket, to the park, or on any special trip. She will enjoy the stimulation of new experiences, especially if they are accompanied by explanations by the caregiver ("Let's try the swing, Amy.")

Infants enjoy listening to adult conversations. Some become excited when such communication takes place, many to the point of trying to join the conversation. Let the infant listen to adult conversation and encourage her to sputter and gush as she tries to talk along.

Don't be frustrated if your efforts fail to result in immediate success. It takes much repetition and practice before a baby acquires language. Don't always expect the baby to do something correctly the first time or to remember today what she was able to do yesterday. Don't rush her—she loves to experiment, but only in a relaxed, trusting, accepting environment.

Thus, the onset of language finds its base during infancy as babies are provided a variety of direct experiences within an environment rich with language. Figure 8-1 illustrates how these experiences become transformed into mental images and how those images become transformed into words.

LANGUAGE GROWTH IN THE PRESCHOOL CHILD

By the time the child is two years old, he is experiencing a rapid growth in vocabulary and is starting to combine two or three words into rudimentary sentences. Kornei Chukovsky, a famous Russian writer and linguist, wrote: "It

Figure 8-1   *The importance of providing direct experiences rather than verbal instruction*

seems to me that, beginning with the age of two, every child becomes for a short period of time a *linguistic genius*" [italics mine] (1968, p.7). Children begin to feel comfortable with words and use them freely. By the time they are 2½, children's vocabulary is likely to explode to the point where it includes 400 words or more. At this age they are beginning to ask endless questions, and their favorite word seems to be "Why?" Although these questions may bother some adults, they do help the child clarify his understandings and feelings.

Also by 2½ years the child has moved from one-word noun utterances to simple combinations of nouns with verbs. His first combinations take place at about age 2. The following list shows word combinations commonly uttered by children during this early phase of language acquisition:

Sit chair
Timmy go boom
Me go
Janie hungry
Pretty dolly
Papa work
Shoes off
More play

There doggie
It choo-choo
Cars go bye-bye
Where mitten?
See baby
He go out
No nap now
Cookie allgone

How do simple utterances of infancy and early toddlerhood eventually become enlarged and combined into combinations such as the preceding and eventually into more complex sentences during early childhood? Perhaps the most meaningful way to explain this process is to divide the language acquisition process into two basic dimensions: the *content dimension* and the *social dimension*. The most popular "content of language" explanation is that of a group of linguistics labeled the "nativists."

Figure 8-2 *The mechanics of the language acquisition device*

Leading spokespersons for that group—Noam Chomsky, Eric H. Lenneberg, and David McNeill—argue that children are born with internal mechanisms that give them natural powers to combine words into phrases and sentences.

The Content Dimension

Eric H. Lenneberg (1964) talks of an "innately mapped-in *program* for behavior." David McNeill (1966) agrees and speculates on a set of "templates" in the neural system, called a "language acquisition device" (LAD), that allows the child to develop language naturally. He says, "It is as if he were equipped with a set of 'templates' against which he can compare the speech he happens to hear from his par-

ents" (p.36). Courtney Cazden (1974) explains the nature of such abilities:

> When we say that a child knows a set of rules, of course we don't mean that he knows them in any conscious way. The rules are known non-consciously, out of awareness, as a kind of tacit knowledge. This way of knowing is true for adults too. Few of us can state the rules for adding /s/ or /z/ or /iz/ sounds to form plural nouns. Yet if asked to supply the plurals for nonsense syllables such as *bik* or *wug* or *gutch* . . . , all who are native speakers of English could do so with ease. Most six-year-old children can, too. [p.43]

Figure 8-2 summarizes the process by which nativistic language acquisition takes place. The language acquisition device (LAD) helps the child analyze the language that surrounds him and produces a developing rule system that becomes the basis for mature speech.

The LAD receives input from the child's environment, probes this input, and helps the child naturally organize words already a part of his vocabulary into a verbal statement (Figure 8-2A). Notice how similar this initial process is to the explanation of language acquisition illustrated in Figure 8-1. Further attempts at duplicating adult speech result in shortened versions of the adult's language, but the basic sentence and thought forms remain the same (some function words—articles, prepositions, conjunctions, and so on—are eliminated) (Figure 8-2B). With increased exposure and practice, the child gradually acquires an ability to use different forms of verbs and nouns, prepositions, pronouns, and other function words (Figure 8-2C).

A process used by many teachers and parents to encourage children to acquire more complex sentence patterns is *expansion*. When the child says a sentence fragment, an adult expands it, adding appropriate elements. For example:

CHILD'S FRAGMENT	ADULT'S SENTENCE
"Joey eat."	"Joey is eating his breakfast."
"Doggie bark."	"The dog is barking."
"Daddy cookie."	"Daddy has a cookie, too."
"No more play."	"Joey doesn't want to play any longer."

Children love to experiment with language throughout their preschool years in these and similar ways; they are acquiring increased skills in sentence formation through such interaction. The practice they receive often results in a highly creative and imaginative use of the language.

By three years of age, the child's speech patterns have gone beyond the simple two-or three-word phrases uttered earlier. Now they

begin to form four- and five-word sentences such as "The dog is barking." By the age of four or five, most children have acquired all of the basic, common sentence structures of the English language. Although we do not know when and exactly in what order these sentence patterns are learned, we do know that most young children are fairly sophisticated linguistic beings by age three.

The Social Dimension

As the child learns to associate objects with words and begins to create simple combinations of words, he moves through several social phases of language. The first variety, *noncommunicative speech,* is considered egocentric in nature and is divided into three types:

1. Repetition: The child repeats or mimics something he has heard. Often, he uses words that he does not understand, but repeats the phrase for the mere pleasure of doing so.

2. Monologue: The child talks aloud to himself, often at great length. It seems as though the child is thinking aloud when this monologue appears. For example, the three-year-old may busily play alone at the sand box: "My truck goes br-r-r-m . . . I'm building a road. The truck helps me . . . br-r-r-m."

3. Collective monologue: The child talks aloud when other children are present, but the others do not listen to what he says. The speaker may think that others are listening, although he does not expect them to answer or respond in any way. In effect, the child is still talking to himself, but his remarks are directed toward a listener. You can expect to hear the same type of monologue as that described in item 2.

You can expect to hear some of each of these types of noncommunicative egocentric speech from young children. In fact, Piaget is convinced that egocentric language character-

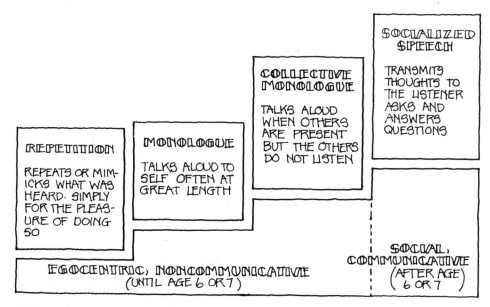

Figure 8-3 *Levels of speech development according to Piaget*

izes most children's speech until age six or seven. M. M. Lewis (1969) said: "this self-addressed speech is more than an accompaniment to action . . . it is part of the action, which is thus both non-linguistic and linguistic. The words are a means by which a child is helped to direct his attention, to regulate what he is doing, to 'think aloud' " (pp. 32–33).

Up to about the age of six or seven, then, children seem to use language as a means of thinking aloud. They do so as they gain increasing knowledge of things through experience and observation. They experience things directly in their environment and they construct mental images of them. These mental "imitations" provide the child with symbols (representations—other than verbal—of some real thing). The symbols then eventually are transformed into words, both symbols and words becoming personal interpretations of real objects or experiences within the environment. Words are eventually combined into meaningful combinations and used in non-communicative, or egocentric, ways to express growing mental images. During this stage, the children love to play with words, to repeat them, to exercise them. New experiences continuously create and reconstruct mental images, resulting in increasing sophisticated language patterns.

Working with children at ages six and seven, Piaget observed a move from egocentric speech toward *socialized* speech—communicative speech intended to facilitate interaction with others. In socialized speech, the child considers the listener and tries to transmit thoughts to him. For example, he may tell another child about the tempera paint: "Mix red and yellow together if you want orange." The child may also criticize the work or behavior of others, ask questions of others, and answer the questions or commands of others. However, children may not be able to explain *why* things are as they seem ("Why does yellow and red make orange?") and tend to focus on events rather than their causes. An illustration of the various levels of language development is presented in Figure 8-3.

To summarize, children move through infancy and into the preschool years according to the language acquisition patterns illustrated in Figure 8-4.

Language growth increases steadily during the preschool years. By the time children are three years old, they are able to use about 900 words. Vocabulary continues at this rapid rate during the next two years, but begins to tail off slightly at about age five or six, dropping from 350–450 word gains per year to gains of only 200–250 words per year by age six and seven. What factors account for such a drop? Some authorities agree that formal schooling experiences contribute a degree of artificiality to the previously natural process of language acquisition and begin to create barriers to verbal experimentation. Pose Lamb (1971) explains:

> These early nursery years of the twos, threes, and fours bring rapid growth in language skills. Funds of knowledge and ranges of interests broaden to include real conversation and social interaction, resulting in an ever-widening range of interests and skills. The nursery school child is bright-eyed at the wonders of his world. He explores, he looks, he feels, he hears, he tries it all on for size, and, curiously enough, the healthy child takes off and discards the parts that don't fit.

> Still wide-eyed with the wonder of it all, the child comes to kindergarten. Here he lives in a world that too often resembles the more formal scene that will come next year upon entry to first grade. The days are too short, the room too small to contain his enthusiasm and exploratory activity. [p.11]

Chukovsky's "linguistic geniuses" somehow slowly lose their momentum and, as he stated, "beginning with the age of five or six, this talent begins to fade" (1968, p.7).

The formality of the child's language learning, according to Lamb, often increases upon entry into first grade. This learning is often characterized by the use of restricted vocabularies in basal readers and by a need to "Sit in your seat quietly so that others aren't disturbed." (This order is especially threatening since children of this age find it frustrating to remain seated quietly for periods of more than 5 to 10 minutes.) It is difficult to determine a true cause-and-effect relationship between the decline of language growth during the primary grade years and the growing formality of the classroom environment, but evidence has clearly indicated a positive relationship between meaningful personal experience and guidance during the preschool years and the acquisition of rapidly growing language skills.

TECHNIQUES FOR ENHANCING LANGUAGE GROWTH

Because the most crucial language learning seems to take place before the child is six, most educators feel that it is the role of the preschool to create programs to facilitate growth in language skills. What helpful advice can be given by early childhood educators and students of language? Alvina Burrows (1971) says that "one admonition leaps out beyond most others: *Use the oral efficiency that children bring to school as the means of developing [further] efficiency in [language]*. To extend, refine, and enhance the oral arts and skills children already possess is the first obligation" (p.90). To achieve this goal, children must be given opportunities to practice language. They must be able to speak in a variety of situations, and they must be exposed to good language as it is spoken by a good model. The following sections discuss activities that can be used to achieve language competence in ways that go beyond opportunities to talk.

Informal Conversation

Children will talk with one another informally and naturally if you establish the conditions for them to do so. They will talk about their

STAGE 1: RANDOM SPEECH SOUNDS

"BA - BA."
"A BAH- BAH."
"GOO. GOO."

STAGE 2: DEVEL-OPMENT OF ONE-WORD UTTERANCES (HOLOPHRASES)

"CAR"

STAGE 3: MERGING OF WORDS INTO PHRASES (TELE-GRAPHIC SPEECH)

"MOMMY GO."

STAGE 4: FULLY DEVELOPED SEN-TENCE PATTERNS

"I WANT TO GO WITH MOMMY."

AGE: BIRTH - 1½ YEARS

AGE: 1½ -2 YEARS

AGE: 2-3 YEARS

AGE: 3 YEARS AND UP

Figure 8-4   *Language acquisition patterns from infancy through the preschool years*

experiences—what happened last night on television, what they are thinking about, or what their cat did to the bird's nest in the back bush—as they enter the room, take off their coats and boots, play at the interest centers, clean up the room, cavort outdoors, or work on special activities. Although planned speaking experiences may be necessary in some components of your curriculum, some activities should be planned especially to interest children in free-flowing oral expression. These activities are usually of the direct observation or participation variety; visits to another part of the school building, excursions to interesting places in the neighborhood, or observations of phenomena such as chicks hatching from eggs in the classroom incubator. Whatever the setting, youngsters will spontaneously talk about the events they observe. Soon, and with very little or no prodding, the children will bring twigs, pine cones, rocks, and countless other objects to the classroom.

They will also develop many new ideas and, consequently, many new words and sentence patterns for their growing language ability. Other possibilities for encouraging personal experiences to lead to informal conversations include:

• Set up an interest table in your classroom. Each day bring something new to display at the table so that curiosity will be tapped while comments are offered. Some interesting objects that serve to stimulate conversation are an apple cut in half horizontally, seashells, pine cones, rocks, leaves, magnets, feathers, interesting pictures, and the like.

• Keep an aquarium, gerbil cage, or other animal habitat.

• Provide tasting experiences.

• Listen to stories and records.

• Participate in singing activities.

By using a real telephone, youngsters capitalize on their imaginations and, at the same time, extend their language skills.

imposed by adult speech. Children speak in rhythm, in pleasing sounds, or even in melodious tones simply for the delight it brings during free play. For instance, while acting as a "daddy" at the housekeeping center, a child may suddenly say, "Daggies, doggles, goo-goo-geeze, too-too-too-too tykle geeze!" Young children acquire language through imitation, reinforcement, and repetition as suggested earlier in this chapter, but they also develop linguistic skills and have fun while "playing" with the language, too.

The Teacher's Role

What about the teacher's role, often referred to as "interaction skills," in the informal language process? If a large part of language acquisition is that of expressing ideas through interaction, the teacher's role is often one of interaction with the children. To be an effective interactor with children, however, you must be aware of these following questions:

Some beginning teachers, however, fail to realize the values inherent in the important process of simply allowing children to talk. Perhaps thinking back as far as they could reach in their own educational experiences, these individuals often characterize the teaching process as giving children information or asking questions in order to get information from the children. Regardless of whether the process is _giving_ or _getting,_ these teachers perceive their role as being the central figure in all classroom talk. However, the primary role of the preschool teacher is not to be the center of classroom talk, but to stimulate good conversation and language use among children. "Good conversation," though, should not be regarded solely as an ability to converse in adult-type talk. Through play experiences, especially, children often express patterns of words and ideas that go far beyond the limits

- _Do I monopolize the interaction?_ Good conversations with young children are more likely to be sustained if initiated by a child. Once interested in something, the child will often launch into a complex discussion of anything from fire trucks to daisies. The difference between the child who will keep on talking and the child who stops is the teacher. Does she thrust herself and her thoughts into the conversation and virtually reduce the child's role to that of a head nodder? If so, she has discovered the secret of stifling meaningful communication.

- _Do I ask good questions?_ Do my questions encourage further communication on the part of the children, or do they guarantee immediate closure. While working with college students in their early field experiences, I often find that they ask children questions resulting in "yes or no" answers. For example, watching a child painting at the easel, the teacher may ask, "Do you like painting with blue paint?" The bewildered child answers, "yeah," but seems to be thinking, "Of course I do, or it wouldn't be splattered all over this paper!" If the answer to your question is so self-evident as this example, then your question is silly and stands a good chance of ending a conversation before it begins. Try to design questions or comments that stand a better chance of eliciting thinking responses from the children. For example, an interaction comment for this child might be "You certainly seem to be enjoying the blue paint today. Please tell me about all the blue paint on your picture." Or you might say, "How would your painting change if there were only green paint at the easel corner today?" Such thought-inducing questions or comments lead to greater thinking and linguistic expression. One other advantage of such questions or comments is that they communicate to the child that you value his thoughts and what he has to say. Other questions that encourage extended language usage include the following:

How many different things can you do with that bucket?

How did you feel when that happened?

What reason do you have for saying that?

How do you know that's the right thing to do?

What would happen if your ideas worked out?

• *Do I encourage and listen to children's questions?* Everyone agrees that good teachers know how to ask good questions. As a matter of fact, practice in asking good questions is an important part of all teacher training programs. But how many of us have ever been given help in becoming good *listeners* to the children's questions? We often cut off interest and a spirit of communicating by not listening. But, when we do listen, we often can get children to offer more

details, to clarify experiences, and to grow in linguistic expressiveness. The following is one example of how one teacher demonstrated the skill of nonlistening to a high degree: The teacher was near as children were observing a jar-type worm environment. They exchanged comments about the worms until one child turned to the teacher and asked, "Do worms have bones?" The teacher looked at the child in a chilling manner and responded, "What kind of silly question is that? Can't you see that they don't?" This type of response is inappropriate, of course, and does nothing to encourage children to explore the new world into which they have been placed. Because of their tremendous curiosity, children's questions will often furnish rich material for exploration and imagination:

What makes this rock sparkle?

Where does the water go when I flush the toilet?

What makes the sky blue?

Why can't my dog talk?

The teacher who listens to these questions and understands that their language production is closely associated with their understandings communicates the feeling that "You are worth listening to and I value your thoughts." That is something we all need to know.

• *Do I encourage the child to "tell me more" during verbal interactions?* Oftentimes, teachers become very predictable in their responses or questions as their interactions with children evolve. For example, you can vary the question "Do you need help?" by saying, "Can I give you a hand?" or "Is there anything I can do for you?" Think of the number of ways you can vary your questions or comments so that children hear similar concepts of ideas expressed in different ways during regular daily routines. Think of how you might change these often repeated comments: "Put away the blocks now. It's time to go outdoors." or "Oh, Nancy, would you please do me a favor?"

- *Do I really listen to the children?* Am I familiar with the various forms of verbal and nonverbal language that communicate an attitude toward the children that they are making valuable contributions? The following suggestions may be useful for you to consider as you interact with your children:

Offer words of praise for sincere efforts on the part of your children. A spontaneous, honest reaction such as "Yes, I understand," "Go on, you certainly are on the right track," "All right!" "Um-hm, that's something to think about," "Right on!" or "I'm listening," lets the children know you are, indeed, paying attention to what they are saying and encourages them to continue.

Another technique of letting the children know that "lines of communication are open" is to *maintain direct eye contact with the child who is speaking.* All too often, however, we tend to glance down at the teacher's guide or lesson plan or think ahead to the next question with faraway looks in our eyes. You must let the child know you are interested in what is being said and that you are trying to understand.

Utilize "body language" as a technique to offer the children support as they contribute to the class discussion. A smile, nod of approval, or pat on the back indicates your satisfaction of a child's efforts and lets him know you appreciate his active participation.

Any of the preceding approval techniques, used alone or in combination with one another, initiates an action system that builds a positive interaction pattern between the teacher and students. Avoidance of eye contact, apparent disinterest, frowning, sarcastic comments, impatience, or the ignoring of children's talk does the opposite; it establishes roadblocks that terminate the children's talk and, in effect, says, "I want you to stop talking." Instead of such roadblocks, consider using the following verbal and nonverbal signals.

ORAL REINFORCEMENT

- *Words:* great, fascinating, positively fabulous, splendid, right, correct, unmistakable, exciting, powerful, wow
- *Sentences:*

That's clever.

That shows a great deal of good thought.

I like the way you explained it.

You make being a teacher very rewarding.

You really thought that one out well, didn't you?

You catch on very quickly!

I like that—I really didn't know it could be done that way.

You did some great thinking today!

EXPRESSIONS

- *Facial:*

smiling, winking, nodding, raising eyebrows, widening eyes

- *Bodily:*

shaking head, thumbs up, signaling O.K., clapping hands, sitting on desk near students, touching, or hugging

In summary, your role as an early childhood teacher is much different than that of some teachers you may have remembered from your past, who operated with the assumption that learning can best be achieved in a quiet setting. Such assumptions are difficult to overcome because we all have a strong tendency to teach as we remember being taught. The most vivid memories (even it they're negative) appear to dominate what we eventually do in a similar situation. A word of caution, however. Because I am trying to convince you of the strong, positive rewards of effective classroom interactions, please do not interpret my message to imply that "anything goes" in your classroom. Children cannot function in a chaotic environment, where there are no ground rules or limits for behavior (see Chapter 4). In other words, the encouragement of effective verbal interaction requires the organization of classroom life in ways that rich communication can take place.

Group-Oriented Conversation

During most of the day, children should be encouraged to speak freely to the teacher and to one another as they plan and execute their daily activities. When we observe four- and five-year-olds, we are often astounded at how free and open they are with their verbalization. They talk to themselves, verbalize to others and listen to their ideas, make up stories or rhymes, and generally participate in a variety of give and take. Through such practice, children steadily improve their vocabularies, sentence patterns, and clarity of expression.

First attempts at having children speak in more controlled situations—for example, before a group—should also be somewhat informal. Many preschool teachers arrange for a special talking time during the day when children are free to share anything of interest with the others. This group-oriented discussion provides an excellent avenue for practicing their speaking skills and the amenities of conversation such as taking turns, listening carefully, articulating carefully, sticking to a point, and constructing good sentences. In sharing-type situations, children are encouraged to bring to the group a book, toy, souvenir, or any object that is of general interest to the entire group. These "props" help the boys and girls feel at ease; the props become the center of the group's attention and help focus attention on the words of the speaker.

In order to make such sharing periods a worthwhile part of the day, however, you should always make sure that they involve more than simply allowing each child in the class to "have his say." In this latter situation, the teacher usually asks the children to each bring in something special for a 15-minute "Show-and-Tell" period. During the period, one child gets up to tell about his object while the others are expected to listen; then a second child does the same; then a third; and so on. Nothing can be so boring and time wasting as a period of this type—children either don't listen, or they wait in fear (or anticipation) of being called on next.

An alternative to the "Show-and-Tell" period is the informal group-sharing time. Perhaps the best way to describe an informal sharing period is to provide this illustration:

When she arrived at school this morning, Belinda was smiling brightly and clutching a colorful stuffed toy hippopotamus. Mr. Roberts noted the pride with which Belinda shared her new toy with him:

"His name is Hippo," offered Belinda.

"He's cute," said Mr. Roberts. "Do you know what kind of an animal Hippo is, Belinda?"

"A hippopa . . . hippopapa . . . a potamus," stuttered Belinda.

"Oh, yes," replied Mr. Roberts. "A hippopotamus. You're a lucky girl to get a nice friend like Hippo. Please show everyone what a nice toy you have."

"Daddy gave him to me. Daddy was away yesterday and when he came home he gave me Hippo," said Belinda.

Mr. Roberts: "Hippo is a nice gift, Belinda. Let's see if anyone can think of another animal that looks like Hippo."

"An elephant," volunteered James. "He's as big as an elephant—I saw one at the zoo."

"That's right, James," commented Mr. Roberts. "I see you remember our trip to the zoo last week."

"I think it looks like a rhino," declared Sally.

"Yeah," "Me too," chimed in the others.

"Does anyone have a toy rhino or toy elephant?" asked Mr. Roberts.

"I think I have a toy elephant—I'm not sure," said Warren. "It's almost as big as Hippo."

"I have a toy elephant," exclaimed Marty. "I can wind him up and he wiggles his ears!"

Mr. Roberts saw that the interest was still high and allowed the children to talk for several minutes. Then, when he sensed it was time to bring the informal conversation to a close, he simply stated, "Hippo was a wonderful gift for you, Belinda. Thank you for bringing him to school today for all of us to see."

The principle of developing good language experience through informal conversation is apparent in Mr. Roberts's technique. He allowed Belinda to talk about her toy, but not in the context of a formal presentation. She simply responded to his question about Hippo. The other children were asked to contribute their own individual experiences as Belinda's toy was shared so their interest level would be maintained. In a few short minutes, then, Mr. Roberts succeeded in involving several members of the group in the conversation rather than forcing them to listen to the often incohesive patter of only one child. The experience was a valuable one, not only for its conversational value, but also for its contribution to intellectual growth.

Teachers often structure an early morning talking time during which a weather chart is organized (see Chapter 11), attendance is taken, the calendar is discussed, or interesting experiences are shared. These conversations can be written down by the teacher on a large chart (usually 24 inches × 36 inches) to elicit added interest from the children in what they had said. Teachers sometimes add special events such as birthdays or holidays as shown in Figure 8-5.

Using Daily Activities for Language Growth

In addition to providing such opportunities for oral expression, you must consider the potential value of regular daily activities for stimulating language growth. Try to associate language as the children become intently involved with their experiences. Do not teach language directly, but simply verbalize the properties of objects and their relationships to each other as the children play. Consider this example of a child working in the art center.

Eugene was at the art corner busily working on a watercolor painting. "You are doing a very nice job, Eugene," commented the teacher. "I like your picture. Please tell me more about it." When Eugene had done so, the teacher added, "Your dog is so big he fills up the whole paper." The teacher made further comments focusing on the other physical characteristics of the painting:

"You made some nice red circles."

"Look at that big yellow line."

"How nicely you've drawn the small circle inside the bigger one."

"Oh, it's nice how your thick red paint flows across your smooth, yellow paint."

"That long curvy line is just above the small blue dot."

Likewise, children learn as language is associated with snack time ("Would you like the *same* amount of juice as Jenny?"), the woodworking center ("You'll need to hit the nail *harder* in order to get it to go *into* the wood."), the block area ("Arlene used *five* blocks to build her tower."), or any other real experience. Such comments help stimulate

Today's News

Today is June 8, 1986.
Today is Thursday.

It is bright and sunny.

June 8 is Michael's birthday.
He is five years old today.

Lisa got a new kitten last night.

Kenny hurt his foot on
the playground.   = ouch!

Figure 8-5   *Daily experiences chart*

children's thinking and help them to experience concretely physical features, comparison, contrasts, and various relationships. Through such informal methods, children gain new names or labels for things, as well as increased concept formation; both are essential to the acquisition of language.

Story Time

Stories, either told or read aloud, have an extremely important place in the language arts program of preschool classrooms. Storytelling is one of the most effective ways of exposing children to rich and varied language; this procedure is basic to the effective development of speaking vocabularies. Children enjoy listening to stories; they discover new words and meanings, develop understandings, and engage in imaginative thought.

Stories Children Like   Of course, the foremost source of stories for children is good literature. It is important to know what kinds of stories appeal to young children, so the stories you choose will meet their developmental interests. Preschool children delight in hearing many kinds of stories, but they especially enjoy stories about things they are already familiar with. Make-believe, humor, new places, animals, family, Mother Goose rhymes, fables, and fairy tales, however, are also favorites. It is difficult to generalize about the type of story enjoyed by all young children since they demonstrate such a wide breadth of interest in stories. They can easily identify with H. A. Rey's lovable monkey *Curious George* or Maurice Sendak's *Little Bear*. They empathize with Dr. Seuss's imaginative Horton as he faithfully attempts to hatch an egg; and their hatred changes to love as Seuss's dreaded Grinch nearly steals Christmas from the citizens of Whoville. All children figuratively hitch up their belts and join the fight with the courageous operator and his brave machine in *Mike Mulligan and His Steam Shovel*. They discover new adventures as they are led through the trials and tribulations of characters in stories such as *Make Way for Ducklings* or *The Tale of Peter Rabbit*. And Mother Goose rhymes are not only enjoyable to listen to, but they introduce children to new concepts and experiences such as planting, shearing, and spinning; the children visit villages and castles, and they meet kings and shepherds.

As you select story materials, remember to start at the children's present level and carefully plan a program to broaden their interests and expand their experiences. The books in the following list have been found to be successful with young children. Remember, though, this is just a representative list; many other books will prove equally popular. With experience, you will develop insights into what is good for your children and be able to add to the list as your favorites appear.

- H. A. Rey, *Curious George*
- Marcia Brown, *Three Billy Goats Gruff*
- Marcia Brown, *Stone Soup*
- Virginia Burton, *Mike Mulligan and His Steam Shovel*
- Virginia Burton, *The Little House*
- Marguerite De Angeli, *Book of Nursery and Mother Goose Rhymes*
- Ludwig Bemelmans, *Madeline*
- Ezra Keats, *The Snowy Day*
- Dr. Seuss, *Horton Hatches the Egg*
- Dr. Seuss, *The Cat in the Hat*
- Wanda Gag, *Millions of Cats*
- Hardie Gramatky, *Little Toot*
- Robert McCloskey, *Make Way for Ducklings*
- Robert McCloskey, *Blueberries for Sal*
- Tasha Tudor, *A Is for Annabelle*
- Emily Kingsley et al., *The Sesame Street Book of Fairy Tales*
- Charles Perrault, *Puss in Boots*
- Marjorie Flack, *Angus and the Cat*
- Clement Moore, *Night Before Christmas*
- Beatrix Potter, *The Tale of Peter Rabbit*
- Clare Newberry, *Mittens*
- Lois Lenski, *Cowboy Small*
- Maurice Sendak, *Where the Wild Things Are*
- Berta and Elmer Hadar, *The Big Snow*
- Richard Scarry, *Richard Scarry's Best Story Book Ever*
- Esphyr Slobodkina, *Caps for Sale*
- Taro Yashima, *Umbrella*
- Taro Yashima, *Crow Boy*

- Gene Zion, *No Roses for Harry*
- Charlotte Zolotow, *The Sky Was Blue*
- Munro Leaf, *The Story of Ferdinand*
- Louise Fatio, *The Happy Lion*
- Marie Hall Ets, *Another Day*
- Ruth Carroll, *Where's the Bunny?*
- Elsa Beskow, *Pelle's New Suit*

Libraries are full of good books for young children. When making your choice to read, however, you must remember that regardless of how attractive the book is to you, the needs of the children are foremost. Be sure to consider the backgrounds and attitudes of your children as well as their abilities and interests. Most young children like stories about animals, machines, transportation or construction vehicles, and about situations similar to those found regularly in their own environment. They enjoy rhythm and rhyme and take special delight in stories that contain a fanciful wish come true. The best way to get to know such books is to read them. A major concern in choosing books is to select those free of stereotypes—Black, Hispanic, Native American, or Asian children should be portrayed in realistic settings. Likewise, steer clear of books perpetuating sexist stereotypes, such as a little girl in a frilly dress running to a boy to have her doll fixed. Remember that male roles as well as female roles have been traditionally stereotyped in children's stories. Try to avoid the establishment of such unfair role expectations by providing stories portraying men and women in a variety of roles.

Reading and Telling Stories Two of the primary early childhood education teaching skills are telling a story and reading one. After you select a story, you must decide which to use. This decision is sometimes difficult, since both methods help us share good literature with young children. Many stories are just as effective read aloud as told, but some are written so that telling them would ruin them. This is especially true of some rhyming stories or other stories in which words are used to create a specific mood. Dr. Seuss's stories, for example, must be read, because their creative use of rhyme and nonsense words, and the nonsense sounds they make, create certain feelings. Also, many books for preschoolers are written in such a way that pictures help tell the story. Because of this close relationship between picture and script, it is advisable to read liberally illustrated books.

Often, a beginning teacher is tempted to memorize a story word for word before telling it. This, however, often makes a performance stiff and stilted, and should be done only rarely, if ever. Of course, you should know the story well; you should read it carefully beforehand so important events are logically organized in your mind. This is important because it helps you prepare for changes in mood or expression as you go along.

Storytelling and reading are highly personal skills; there is no special "formula" for ensuring success in either. The technique one person uses may work magic with a group of youngsters, whereas the same technique might fail terribly if someone else uses it. Nevertheless, there are some generally accepted guidelines that are helpful in planning and reading or telling a story.

The physical setting should be comfortable and relaxing. Usually all the children will be together in a special area away from other activities and distracting materials; the posibility of inattentiveness can, thus, be minimized. However, there will be times when some children do not care to listen, so they should not be forced to join the group. Such coercion often results in unnecessary behavioral problems. These children should be given an opportunity to play quietly in other areas of the room or playground, perhaps in the company of a teacher's aide or volunteer.

When a quiet, comfortable nondistracting area has been selected for the story, you should establish some sort of special technique, or gimmick, to arouse the children to join you. Many creative techniques have been used by innovative teachers over the years:

- Play a special little tune on the piano indicating to the children that story time is at hand.

- Use a favorite hand puppet to announce that story time is ready to begin. Then, a simple little dialogue between teacher and puppet can introduce the story to be shared. For example, a simple message from Ellie the Elephant encourages the children to listen, and also helps develop interest in the forthcoming story: "Hello, boys and girls. It's so nice to see you again today here at the story time corner. Miss Alley is going to tell us an exciting story today about a brave little boat named Little Toot. Let's all listen carefully to Miss Alley because I think she's about to start." Miss Alley may then thank Ellie and begin the introduction to the story. When using puppets in this manner, look at the puppet when *it* is "speaking" and look at the children when *you* are speaking.

- Capitalize on the children's creative imagination by engaging them in a simple role-playing experience. For example, the children can be asked to pretend that they are all taking a walk in the woods. Point out some interesting features and have the children imagine that they are actually seeing them: "Oh, look at that tree—it's so tall. Look at how tall it is. Let's all stretch ourselves and try to be as tall as that tree" or "There goes a little rabbit—watch it hop through the grass. Let's all hop like the rabbit." After sharing three or four such experiences, you may all pretend to be getting tired from the long walk and decide that it would be a good time to find a safe, cool place to rest. Ask everyone to pantomime looking for a place to rest. As the children look around the "forest" for a suitable place, you find a little

meadow in the trees that would be a good spot. So no dangerous bears or lions will hear them, encourage the children to gather as quietly as they can into a compact group and sit in the meadow. After the children are quietly gathered in their safe little area, you may begin to tell them the story. Depending on the type of story to be told, the children can be similarly led to swim across a river to a safe island where a story is told, build a safe treehouse, and so on.

Children will want to be as close to you as possible while the story is being told so you will need to organize them in a way that is satisfactory for all. Perhaps the best arrangement is an informal semicircle facing you. The children may be comfortably seated on chairs, on individual rugs, or on the floor, but the most important consideration is that they can easily see your face and any pictures or illustrations to be shared.

Selecting the story is particularly important. Once the children are properly seated and in a mood to listen, the telling or reading of the story may begin. Although a seemingly uncomplicated task, the storytelling or reading process is nevertheless one that involves a great deal of careful preparation and thoughtful presentation. The following questions may be helpful as you select a story that is appropriate both for the children and for you and prepare to tell it:

SELECTING STORIES FOR PRESCHOOLERS

- Is the plot simple and uncomplicated?
- Are the situations presented in generally familiar contexts?
- Does the plot evolve around a great deal of direct conversation, or dialogue, among story characters?
- Is the story written with carefully chosen words that will mostly be familiar to the children?
- Are the story characters interesting and easily identifiable to the children?

Reading and telling stories expose children to new adventures as well as to rich, new language patterns.

- Is the story free from ethnic, racial, or sex-role stereotypes?

- Does the plot include catchy phrases, rhymes, and repetition that can catch and hold the children's interest?

- Can the story be easily related to the experiential background of the children?

- Can the story be completed in one short reading or broken up into short distinctive parts?

- Is the story accompanied by uncluttered, colorful illustrations of animals, people, or objects that are easily identified by the children?

- Does the story appeal to the teacher?

Children are very insightful into your feelings for a story and can easily detect whether or not you are sincere in your desire to share it with them. The children will deepen their respect for good literature only when they know you want to share it with them.

Make sure the story is one that you *can* tell or read. Some teachers have pesonalities that do not match the mood or content of a story. If this is true in your case, either choose other stories, or be extremely careful to practice the story so you communicate a feeling of comfort to the children rather than one of confusion or insincerity.

Choose an appropriate method of presentation. Both reading and telling have a valuable place in the preschool classroom. Reading stories helps children gain respect for books and helps them realize that reading can be an enjoyable experience. Telling stories can be especially helpful in these situations:

- If you want the children to focus on a large number of pictures while the story is being told.

- If the illustrations or pictures are not particularly appealing. In this case, you may need to use your own drawings, puppets, or flannelboard characters to supplement the story. Reading the story and sharing visual aids is difficult, so storytelling may best be used in such situations.

- If the story is of value to your group but is too long for their attention span.

If you decide to tell the story rather than read it aloud, do not try to memorize it word for word. Memorized stories are usually presented mechanically and thereby lose their appeal. If certain key words or phrases are repeated throughout the story, however, you may want to know them—those words should be carefully learned or the story will be spoiled. It should be emphasized, though, that to tell a story well, you should know it and make it a part of you—carefully organize the sequence of events in your mind.

Be sure to _prepare for each story you read or tell._ Even a story that you have read or told several times should be carefully reviewed in order to ensure accurate recall of details and events. In preparing for your story, consider the following suggestions:

1. Read your story silently to get an overall idea of the plot.

2. Read the story aloud so you can develop a "feel" for its mood. Read it two or three times on a tape recorder and analyze each of your readings. Be especially watchful for "uhs" and "and-uhs."

3. Sit or stand in front of a mirror. Try to communicate openly a feeling of comfort and interest while reading aloud.

4. If you possibly can, practice your story in front of a friend and request honest criticism of your technique.

5. Determine how long the story will take to read or tell. Children's attention spans vary from story to story, but a good rule of thumb is to stay within a time limit of 5–15 minutes.

Develop your own personal style of telling or reading a story. Successful teachers seem to weave a magic spell during story time, and you might be tempted to emulate good storytellers you observed in the past. However, what worked for that individual may not work for you. It is important to be yourself—personality and charm are made part of the story only if the children know that the storyteller is the same person who is with them during other parts of their day; periodic personality changes only confuse and unnerve the children. These suggestions for telling and reading stories may be helpful:

1. Plan a good introduction so children are able to get an idea of what the story is going to be about. Be careful not to get too involved with highly detailed descriptions of characters or events, but give the children an idea of the main story characters and what their major situation will be.

2. Use your voice effectively. Speak naturally, but be aware of the ways in which loudness or softness and fastness or slowness can affect the mood of a story. For example, suspenseful parts may call for a soft, slow, mysterious tone while happy parts may call for livelier, louder, joyous tones. Your voice can be used to add surprise, sadness, question, or fear to the story, but remember not to get overdramatic. If you do, you will shift the focus from the plot to the storyteller,

and you will interrupt the children's interest and concentration.

3. Keep good eye contact with the children. A good storyteller looks directly at his audience in order to gain and hold their interest. A few gestures will add to the vividness of the story being told.

4. Anticipate questions and minor interruptions during the reading or storytelling period. Handle children's questions or comments tactfully so the trend of the story is not interrupted. For example, one child became so absorbed in a story that he blurted out just before the climax, "Oh, I wonder how the kitten will be saved." Another child insightfully offered the actual solution: "I know—the mama cat will save her." Although the storyteller could have become flustered at the revelation of the story's ending, she remained composed and simply commented, "Your idea was very good, Robin, but let's all listen and see if you were right." The children, in this case, were drawn right back into the story. Often, teachers themselves cause unnecessary interruptions by throwing out questions or explaining new words along the way. Such digressions add nothing to the story and mainly serve to lessen interest or to interrupt continuity of the plot. Never interrupt the flow of a story yourself except in case of extreme necessity. But, don't think that stories should be exclusively receptive in nature. Welcome the children's comments and questions, keeping in mind that stories should encourage expressive as well as receptive language skills.

5. Share pictures throughout the story if they help clarify or illustrate the evolving sequence of events. By sitting on a low chair or on the floor, you will be in perfect position to hold up the book for the children to see. Hold the book open all the way in a steady position. Some teachers, when reading a story, prefer to hold books at either side; others find it more comfortable to hold them in front.

Whatever the position, be sure that all children can see the picture without having to crane their necks or move unnecessarily. If the children are seated in a semicircle, you may have to move the picture so they all can see. In these cases, it is important to hold the book and pause so the groups seated to your left can focus their eyes on the picture; hold and pause at the center; and hold and pause to your right. Some teachers share poorly by holding the pictures so the children on the left are able to focus and then slowly sweeping to the right without stopping the picture along the way. It is difficult for the children in the center to focus on the moving picture, and they may not be able to see it properly. Short sweeps and pauses are necessary so the focal point can remain fixed for a short period of time.

6. Use flannelboards and other aids to help illustrate a story being told or read. Some supply companies are now producing attractive flannelboard characters and scenery that help to illustrate time-tested favorites such as "Goldilocks and the Three Bears," "Three Billy Goats Gruff," or "Henny Penny."

7. After the story is completed, the children may enjoy discussing the main characters or plot for a short period. This will not always be the case, but if you find that the interest is high, guide the discussion with questions like these:

• Tell us what you liked (or didn't like) about the story.

• If you had been (story character) how would you have felt when _____ happened?

• In what other way could (character) have solved this problem?

• Which character from the story would you most like to meet? Why?

• How do you think (character) felt when _____ happened?

- What story character would you most like to be? Why?

- Why do you think (character) did what he did?

- Did someone in the story change his mind about something? What was it? Why did he do it?

- What do you think happens to (character) now after the story ended?

- Have you ever had a problem like (character)? What did you do about it?

- Did you like the story? Why? Why not?

- Which picture did you like the most? Why?

- What things happened in the story that could really happen? That could not really happen?

- What would you change about the story?

- Did you know another story like this one? What is it? How are the stories alike?

Not all these considerations will need to be examined before each story time. However, they must all be emphasized because your ability to plan and execute storytelling is so important to the success or failure of the children's total language program. Your preparation is central in making story time a delightful and rewarding experience both for your children and for yourself.

Picture Discussions

Large, colorful, uncomplex pictures stimulate verbal exchange in the classroom by motivating children to discuss what they see or by inspiring them to make up related stories. However, simply holding a picture in front of a group is not enough to move the children to discuss it. A carefully planned sequence of questions must be designed to move the children from the simple enumeration of objects observed in a picture to higher levels of inter-

pretation. For example, asking a general question such as "What is the picture about?" will lead only to a response such as "A kitten," or "A kitten and a butterfly." Children will very rarely move beyond responses of this listing type unless you encourage them to do so with appropriately stated questions.

Basically, children respond at three levels when they read and interpret pictures: a *low level*, where they are able to identify the objects in a picture; a *middle level*, where they are able to describe what is happening; and a *high level*, where they are able to communicate personal feelings and establish relationships among objects or events (see Figure 8-6). Most preschool children operate on the low level, but occasionally there will be children who are able to answer questions on the middle or high level. The bulk of your discussion questions should be directed at low-level interpretation, but, because your goal is to encourage increasingly mature patterns of thought and language, you will want to insert higher-level questioning periodically. Thus, the children can experience challenges and successes at individual levels of ability while, at the same time, being exposed to higher levels of thought through the comments and observations of their peers.

Help the children look for a variety of things in discussion pictures by guiding their observations along the lines of these questions:

LOW LEVEL

Tell how many. . . .

Tell me what you see. . . .

Tell me about the picture. . . .

What (animal) is in the picture?

MIDDLE LEVEL

What is _____ doing?

What kind of _____ do you see?

What color is the _____?

How far from the _____ is _____?

LOW LEVEL: LISTS OB-
JECTS IN THE PICTURE

MIDDLE LEVEL:
DESCRIBES DETAILS OR
EVENTS

HIGH LEVEL: DRAWS
INFERENCES AND SEES
RELATIONSHIPS

Figure 8-6 *Levels of picture interpretation abilities*

How large is the _____?

HIGH LEVEL

What will _____ do next?

What kind of _____ do you think
_____ is?

Why did _____ happen?

What title can you give this picture?

Preschool teachers usually draw from several sources when choosing pictures for discussion times. Many good books written for young children can be used for their pictures alone. Excellent picture books often contain a variety of appropriate illustrations—animals, community workers, children at play, cowhands, imaginary characters, and so on.

A second major source of pictures for young children is commercial teaching materials manufacturers. These companies organize picture collections around central themes such as "seasons" or "feelings" and arrange them in sets especially designed for study and discussion. These study prints are normally mounted on durable, attractive backings and are indexed for easy reference. A teacher's discussion and activity guide usually accompanies these sets, either as a separate manual or as a chart on the backs of the pictures. The second method is perhaps the most useful for teachers since the picture can be held up for the children to observe while the question and discussion guide is conveniently in front of the teacher. A separate manual can, at times, cause irritating problems as the teacher shifts back and forth from manual to picture while leading a group discussion.

Still a third major source of classroom discussion pictures is the teacher's own picture file. Developing your own picture file for preschool children is a valuable project you should try to start as soon as possible. Search through magazines, newspapers, old calendars, advertisements, or discarded books to find pictures illustrating subjects of interest to young children. Be sure the pictures are clear and free from confusing details; think of the developmental characteristics of the children. A good source of free or inexpensive pictures for your own picture file is business, industry, or special interest groups like the American Dairy Council.

Once suitable pictures have been discovered, you will need to back them with protective construction paper or tagboard. If possible, run the mounted picture through a laminating machine or cover it with clear adhesive plastic so it will be more attractive as well as more resistant to damage. You may wish to organize your pictures into a permanent file with headings that are attractive to preschool youngsters: animals, food, jobs, play, and so on.

As a method for encouraging language growth, children should be encouraged to make up stories for a small series of pictures. They may not be able to do this for only one picture, but a series of three or four pictures relating to a subject in which they are intensely interested may encourage many excellent stories. Some special place should be available for such experiences—a place where the story could be told to the teacher, to a few select

friends, or to the group as a whole. One child, after a trip to the farm, selected several pictures from a group provided by the teacher (some children may like to draw their own) and told the story shown in Figure 8-7. Photographs taken by the teacher during such direct experiences provide great opportunities for creative storytelling activities, too.

Children's conversation, then, can be stimulated in a variety of ways by the skillful use of picture discussions in the preschool classroom. Children think of many ways to respond to pictures, and your understanding of them will make related conversation highly original and interesting.

Fingerplays

You have read about the usefulness of fingerplays for promoting physical growth, but this form of verbal and physical play also assumes a valuable language role, too. When verses, rhymes, or short stories are shared for the pleasurable repetition of words and for the free use of children's voices in joyous play activity, the children are provided with a strong motivaton to speak. Fingerplays may be enjoyed by the entire group at once or by only a few children, but remember that any fingerplay should be matched to the coordination level of your children. For example, the popular fingerplay "Here is the church and here is the steeple" is much too complex for four-year-olds—they usually feel defeated as they try to lock their fingers into the positions suggested within the verse. The fingerplay time should be one of confidence building and fun-filled word play, so situations that frustrate or defeat the children should be avoided. Suggestions for the use of fingerplays in the preschool setting follow.

- *Use fingerplays in a variety of situations.* Teachers have found that, besides serving as a simple fun-time language activity, fingerplays are a very good means

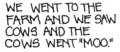

WE WENT TO THE FARM AND WE SAW COWS AND THE COWS WENT "MOO."

WE SAW A BARN. IT WAS BIG AND THE COWS LIVED THERE.

THE FARMER MILKED THE COWS IN THE BARN.

HE GAVE US A GLASS OF MILK.

Figure 8-7 *Pictures used to tell a child's story*

for getting children's attention for a special group announcement, gathering them for story time or any other large-group activity, or keeping them occupied during potentially restless times— toileting, awaiting the arrival of a special guest, or any other time the children must be unexpectedly kept waiting. However, a word of caution: *Never* use a fingerplay to calm overly excited or restless children. One instance that sticks out in my mind vividly involves a student teacher who, for the first time in her career, was asked to organize a group of about ten children and guide them down a hall to a place where their rest room facilities were located. Partway down the hall, the children became extremely restless and began to misbehave. Perhaps remembering that fingerplays hold great potential for organizing children during toileting, or perhaps from her own frustration, the teacher began to sing, "Where is thumbkin . . . " and tried to encourage the children to join her. Naturally, by this time, the children were fidgeting, jumping, talking, and pinching—any chance of getting them to join the fingerplay was lost. This unfortunate teacher, desperately attempting to lure the children to join her, continued singing, "Here I am. . . . Here I am. . . ." while most of the chil-

dren went along totally oblivious of her efforts. The only ones of the entire group who participated in the activity were the teacher and one or two of the children. The true value of fingerplay activities was gone for this time.

- Fortunately, this student teacher grew from her failure. During a self-evaluation of her day's experience, she focused on the toileting incident and recognized her mistake. Her recommendation for improvement was that she should have stopped the fingerplay immediately upon recognizing that the children were not going to respond. Then, speaking in a firm, clear voice, she should have involved them in more active pursuits where they could have released energy in fuller, freer, and more purposeful movements. What alternatives would *you* suggest?

- *Know the fingerplay before you use it.* Many teachers memorize a small number of highly interesting fingerplays before their first experiences with young children. Thus, they have a number of appropriate fingerplays at hand and can use them comfortably whenever unforeseen situations arise. However, if memorizing on your part results in an overly mechanistic presentation, you may wish to consider printing the fingerplays on sheets of oaktag and placing them on the wall or on some fixture near a strategic area in the classroom, for example, the story time corner, file cabinet, or toileting area. In this way, you have a ready reference when your mind needs a little stimulation to help it remember a key word or phrase. Placing the fingerplays on index cards and keeping them ready when needed is not recommended because your shifting from the card to the children during the fingerplay may be extremely distracting.

• *Choose appropriate fingerplays.* Be sure the fingerplays are the type children like. Often, fingerplays are chosen for their literary quality or because of their appeal to adults. Remember, however, that fingerplays must interest the *children* if they are to be useful, and what appears "cute" or "funny" to an adult may be totally disliked by a child. Also, fingerplays need not reflect high literary standards—in fact, most are of poor literary quality. The purpose of fingerplays, however, is not to teach literary appreciation, so the poetic accuracy should not be as important as the fun and interest a fingerplay generates. Some traditionally favorite fingerplays for young children are found in the accompanying "Fingerplays" box.

Poetry

Very young children can be exposed to poetry, either through the action verses described to you in the previous section on fingerplays or simply by hearing poems sung or spoken in a variety of classroom settings. We have already discussed the values of sharing rhymes such as "This Little Piggy Went to Market," or "Pat-a-Cake, Pat-a-Cake" with infants; mothers and teachers have used those catchy ditties for generations. These rhymes are still important for young children, not only because they enjoy hearing the rhythm, repetition, and humor but also because they often delight in learning to

say many of the easy verses. Consider, for example, children's enjoyment as they repeat "Mary Had a Little Lamb," "Jack Be Nimble," "Hickory Dickory Dock," "Humpty Dumpty," "Jack and Jill," "Little Bo Peep," "Hey! Diddle, Diddle," "Little Miss Muffet," "Goosey, Goosey, Gander," "Ding, Dong, Bell," "Jack Sprat," and other traditional nursery or Mother Goose rhymes. Just reading through that list may have provoked beloved memories from your own childhood since rhyming ballads and jingles stimulate some sense of genuine poetic charm in all of us.

The short, rollicking nature of nursery or Mother Goose rhymes makes them an ideal vehicle for introducing choral speaking. Choral speaking is the interpretation of poetry by several voices speaking as one. There are three types of choral-speaking techniques appropriate for younger children:

1. *Two-part:* This requires a leader who says a line and a group that offers the response. The following example serves to evoke humor as the children experience this form of choral speaking.

   Teacher: I went up one pair of stairs.
   Children: Just like me.
   Teacher: I went up two pairs of stairs.
   Children: Just like me.
   Teacher: I went into a room.
   Children: Just like me.
   Teacher: I looked out of a window.
   Children: Just like me.
   Teacher: And I saw a monkey.
   Children: Just like me.

   Nursery rhymes and Mother Goose rhymes provide an endless source of response-type material for teachers of the very young.

2. *Group Arrangement:* This approach to choral speaking simply requires the chil-

FINGERPLAYS

LET'S MAKE A BALL

A little ball, (*Make a circle with pointer finger and thumb.*)
A bigger ball, (*Make a circle with both pointed fingers and thumbs.*)
A great big ball I see; (*Make large circle with arms.*)
Now, let's count the balls we've made;
One, two, three. (*Repeat action of first three lines.*)

THE APPLE TREE

Away up high in an apple tree, (*Point up.*)
Two red apples smiled at me. (*Form circles with fingers.*)
I shook that tree as hard as I could; (*Pretend to shake tree.*)
Down came those apples,
And Mmmmmm, were they good! (*Rub tummy.*)

OPEN, SHUT THEM

Open, shut them; open, shut them;
Give them a clap.
Open, shut them; open, shut them;
Lay them in your lap.

THERE WAS A LITTLE TURTLE

There was a little turtle, (*Make circle with hands.*)
He lived in a box. (*Form box with hands.*)
He swam in a puddle, (*Make swimming motions.*)
He climbed on the rocks. (*Make climbing motions with hands.*)
He snapped at a mosquito, (*Make grabbing motion.*)
He snapped at a flea, (*Make grabbing motion.*)
He snapped at a minnow, (*Make a grabbing motion.*)
And he snapped at me. (*Make grabbing motion.*)
He caught the mosquito, (*Clap hands.*)
He caught the flea, (*Clap hands.*)
He caught the minnow, (*Clap hands.*)
But he didn't catch me. (*Start to clap, but stop short.*)
—Vachel Lindsay

CHOO-CHOO TRAIN

This is a choo-choo train (*Bend arms at elbows.*)
Puffing down the track. (*Rotate forearms in rhythm.*)
Now it's going forward, (*Push arms forward; continue rotating motion.*)
Now it's going back. (*Pull arms back; continue rotating motion.*)
Now the bell is ringing, (*Pull bell cord with closed fist.*)
Now the whistle blows. (*Hold fist near mouth and blow.*)
What a lot of noise it makes (*Cover ears with hands.*)
Everywhere it goes. (*Stretch out arms.*)

RABBIT SONG

In a cabin in a wood (*Draw cabin with hands.*)
A little man by the window stood (*Shade eyes and look around.*)
Saw a rabbit running by, (*Make rabbit hopping with hands.*)
Knocking at my door. (*Knock.*)
"Help me! Help me!" the rabbit said. (*Throw hands in air.*)
"Or that farmer will shoot me dead." (*Point fingers like gun.*)
"Little rabbit, come inside,
Safely you'll abide." (*Wave imaginary rabbit in, and stroke him in your arm.*)

(At end of each verse, leave out the words for one motion and do the motion in silence, until whole song is pantomimed.)

MR. TURKEY

Mr. Turkey's tail is big and wide.
(*Spread fingers.*)
He swings it when he walks.
(*Swing hands.*)
His neck is long,
(*Stretch neck.*)
His chin is red,
(*Stroke chin.*)
He gobbles when he talks.
(*Open and close hands—make gobbling sounds.*)

REST

I know it's best
To take a rest
So I take my little key.
I'll lock the door,
(*Children lock lips.*)
Pull down the shades,
(*Children close eyes.*)
So I cannot talk or see.

FIVE BUNNIES

"My baby bunnies go to bed,"
The little mother rabbit said.
"I'll have to count them first to see

(continued)

If they have all come back to me.
One bunny, two bunny,
  (*Raise one finger for each bunny.*)
Three bunny dear,
Four bunny, five bunny,
Yes, they're all here.
They're the sweetest things alive
My bunnies 1,2,3,4,5.

TEN FINGERS

I have ten little fingers.
  (*Hold up hands.*)
They all belong to me.
  (*Point to self.*)
I can make them do things.
Would you like to see?
  (*Point to eyes.*)

I can open them up wide,
  (*Spread fingers.*)
Shut them up tight,
  (*Make tight fist.*)
Put them together,
  (*Fold fingers together.*)
Jump them up high,
  (*Reach above head.*)
Jump them down low,
  (*Touch floor.*)
Fold them quietly,
  (*Fold fingers together.*)
And sit (or stand) just so.

THE ROBOT

There is a robot
Big and strong;
Watch him stiffly
Walk along.
  (*Move arms and legs like a robot.*)

His head turns left,
  (*Turn head to left.*)
His head turns right,
  (*Turn head right.*)
And both his eyes
Shine wide and bright.
  (*Open eyes widely.*)

Press this button
  (*Press nose.*)
And he will say,
"How are all my friends today?"
  (*Say in low voice.*)
Pull this handle
  (*Pull left index finger with right hand.*)
And he will say,
"I am feeling quite okay."

THE BEEHIVE

Here is a beehive
  (*Close fingers together, thumbs inside.*)
But where are the bees?
Hidden someplace where nobody sees.
Soon they'll come out of their hive.
One, two, three, four, and five.
  (*Open one finger as you say each number.*)

ONE LITTLE BODY

Two little feet go stamp, stamp, stamp,
  (*Stamp*)
Two little hands go clap, clap, clap,
  (*Clap*)
One little body stands up straight,
  (*Stand straight*)
One little body sits quietly down.
  (*Sit*)

dren to speak the entire verse together. Perhaps most appropriate for kindergarten or older children, whole-group speaking is most effective when it is aided by the use of action to accompany the rhythmic nature of the nursery or Mother Goose rhyme. The "Hickory, Dickory, Dock" box (p. 292) is an example. Look for other poems that lend themselves to this setting. Attentions spans seem to increase and the timid children gain encouragement and confi-

dence as they become involved in such enjoyable group activity.

3. *Sequence Speaking*: This form of choral speaking is an advanced form of group cooperation in which one small group speaks a line or two by itself followed by another small group, and so on until the rhyme is complete. The following rhyme, for example, is a very good way of introducing this type of choral speaking:

FOLLOW ME

Hands on shoulders, hands on knees,
   (*Follow action as rhyme indicates.*)
Hands behind you, if you please;
Touch your shoulders, now your nose,
Now your hair and now your toes;
Hands up high in the air,
Down at your sides and touch your hair;
Hands up high as before,
Now clap your hands, one, two, three, four.

BEAR HUNT

Leader: Let's go on a bear hunt.
Children: (*Repeat above*)
Leader: All right?
Children: All right.
Leader: O.K.?
Children: O.K.
Leader: Let's go!
   (*Make walking sounds by clapping hands on
   knees; children repeat or follow all motions
   and words of leader.*)
Oh look!
What's that?
A big tree!
Can't go under it.
Can't go round it.
Can't go through it.
Have to climb it.
All right? O.K.? Let's go!
   (*Make climbing motions; resume walking
   motions.*)

Oh look!
What's that?
A big field!
Can't go under it.

Can't go round it.
Can't go over it.
Have to go through it.
All right? O.K.? Let's go!
   (*Swish palms together; resume walking
   motions.*)

Oh look!
What's that?
A big river.
Can't go under it.
Can't go round it.
Can't go through it.
Have to swim it.
All right? O.K.? Let's go!
   (*Swimming motions; resume walking
   motions.*)
Oh look!
What's that?
A dark cave!
Let's go in it.
All right? O.K. Let's go!
Ooh—it's dark in here.
The walls are wet.
   (*Make feeling motions.*)
Oops—my toe bumped something!
What could it be?
It feels furry!
It has a tail!
A large back!
Two ears!
A big nose!
Two eyes!
Ooh—big teeth!
It's a bear!!
Let's run!

One, two,
Buckle my shoe;   (*First group*)
Three, four,
Shut the door;   (*Second group*)
Five, six,
Pick up sticks;   (*Third group*)
Seven, eight,
Lay them straight;   (*Fourth group*)
Nine, ten,
A big fat hen.   (*Fifth group*)

The musical quality of these verses often prompts requests to "Do it again!" Such pos-

itive introductions to poetry give the children an excellent start to enjoying poetry in other settings. Use a variety of settings to read or speak poetry to children. Many successful teachers of the very young have effortlessly memorized a number of poems that they gaily offer to the children often at times when they don't even realize it. Such spontaneity communicates to the children that you thoroughly enjoy the poems and encourages them to accept the use of poems naturally. In time, you may even find that the children will learn to repeat favorite poems much as they repeat favorite fingerplays or songs.

A number of entertaining poems are appropriate for young children; these poems reflect the consciousness, interests, and play of children. They should reflect the child's everyday world, both real and imagined. Poems can be chosen to enrich all areas of the early childhood curriculum, as illustrated by the following example from _A Child's Garden of Verses_, which applies to self-awareness. Search through collections of poetry to find others that can be used for areas such as weather, transportation, community helpers, playground activities, or animals.

MY SHADOW

I have a little shadow that goes in and out
    with me,
And what can be the use of him is more than
    I can see.
He is very, very like me from the heels up to
    the head;
And I see him jump before me when I jump
    into my bed.

—Robert Louis Stevenson

HICKORY, DICKORY, DOCK

Ask the children if they have ever seen a big grandfather's clock. How does it go? Discuss the "tick-tock" and the pendulum. Share pictures, if necessary. Then offer a yardstick, dowel rod, or any other object similar to a pendulum and swing it back and forth rhythmically. Ask three or four children to be the grandfather's clock by repeating "tick-tock" as the pendulum swings. The cadence suggested by the "tick-tocking" can be used as the rest of the children chant the rhyme:

Hickory, dickory, dock!
The mouse ran up the clock.
The clock struck one.
The mouse ran down.
Hickory, dickory, dock!

Guided Language Instruction

Some teachers prefer to supplement interaction opportunities for language growth with structured group activities designed to teach specific language concepts or to encourage children to describe or label objects with words. In doing so, teachers act primarily as models for children to imitate. For example, a teacher presents the child with two cardboard squares, one covered with sandpaper and the other covered with smooth cloth. The teacher asks the child to run his fingers over the sandpaper, and comments, "This is rough." She does the same thing with the smooth cloth square and says, "This is smooth." She then moves to the next step by asking the child to point to the rough square and then to the smooth square. The child is encouraged to use the terms himself as the teacher asks, "Tell me about this square." If the lesson had a good effect, the child would say, "It is rough (or smooth)." In this final stage, the child has generated the word by himself after the initial modeling procedure. Although the lesson was fairly well sequenced, the child moved from direct, active manipulation of the objects in his immediate environment to the use of words to describe those objects. As further reinforcement, the teacher could follow up the lesson by having the child sort various cards into two piles: rough and smooth. Some sample activities that are commonly used by teachers of the very young to reinforce language concepts are located in the accompanying "Language Growth Activities" box.

Regardless of the concepts or word labels taught through such a guided manner, language maturity evolves most effectively if the child first has had opportunities to explore and interact actively in her surroundings. Through those direct experiences, the child is able to develop a foundation upon which to build mental structures, although she may not be able to express all such concepts in words. This foundation is important, though, because "Piaget defines teaching as the creation of situations where structures can be discovered, not the transmission of structures which may be assimilated at the verbal level only" (Smith, 1972, p.10). Once these structures have been acquired, they may be readily translated into language. According to Piaget, "Mainly, language serves to translate what is already understood: or else language may even present a danger if it is used to introduce an idea which is not yet accessible" (Duckworth, 1964, p.15).

We must allow children to have opportunities to form mental structures through activity before we begin expecting effective language to develop—activity precedes language. Also, we must realize that presenting concepts to children verbally rather than through activity in which the structures are first developed, we keep the child from building a firm language foundation.

TEACHING A SECOND LANGUAGE

The issue of teaching language skills to young children who primarily or exclusively speak a divergent form of English or a language other than English is of concern to early childhood educators. These educators have studied the problems faced by adolescents and adults whose dominant language was something other than standard English and concluded that such problems had their roots in early school experiences. As children, these individuals were unable to meet the expectations of English-speaking public school systems and were often retained in the lower grades and classified as slow or retarded learners. Eventually, these students dropped out of school as the system

failed to meet their special needs and expectations.

Choosing a term that will identify children whose economic, social, or intellectual environment hampers their maximum developmental potential is a delicate task. Educators have often described these children as "disadvantaged," implying that lack of economic, social, or intellectual opportunities caused educational problems that prevented successful adjustment to and performance in school. When these children were compared to "advantaged" children, it was often found that they were behind in most areas of development—most seriously in academic development. Some blamed this lag on inadequate schooling, but others recognized the role of the home and community in meeting educational needs of young children. "Disadvantaged" youth, then, properly became associated with two categories:

- *Children from economically deprived families.* Numerous studies have shown that children from low-income homes have greater school-related problems than do children from homes with higher incomes. They may drop out of school earlier, adjust poorly to school routines, achieve at a lower scale, and generally underestimate the value of schooling.

- *Children from minority groups or identifiable subcultural backgrounds.* The challenge is great today to provide equal educational opportunity to groups that have been, consciously or unconsciously, shortchanged by the American economic, social, and political system: Chicanos, Native Americans, and Blacks, as well as the residents of urban ghettos or rural slums, such as the Southern Appalachian whites. Research studies have shown that a great proportion of low school achievement can be directly associated with children from these groups.

LANGUAGE GROWTH ACTIVITIES

Telephone Talking   Real telephones, connected by wire and powered by battery, can often be obtained free from your local telephone company for an extended period of time. Place these phones in your classroom and encourage the children to talk to one another or act out imaginative roles.

Fooler Game   Choose a set of words that all belong together—for example, colors, shapes, food, animals, rhyming sounds, clothing. Have the children listen carefully as you begin to say one list, and have them say "Stop!" when they hear you make a mistake. For example, you start out slowly, saying "Red, blue, yellow, green, square ('Stop!')" or "Boy, big, Billy, boat, ball, car ('Stop!')."

Classification Charts   Draw, cut from magazines or old workbooks, or buy commercially, pictures of fruits, vegetables, animals, colors, toys, and so on. Have the children classify, name, and describe the pictures on a large pocket chart. Place one card in each row and ask the children to sort out the other cards, placing the

Research evidence, then, indicates a high correlation between (1) low income and low achievement in school and (2) low school achievement and minority group or subcultural affiliation. Despite the popular use of the term _disadvantaged_ to describe any child who, due to some damaging condition brought about by a social or economic cause, falls below the developmental levels of children at any particular age level, we feel that the dangers inherent in establishing such a definition can unreasonably lead to stereotyped views of the children labeled in such a negative way. One danger is that we tend to forget that disadvantages are relative. Any person who tries to function in an unfamiliar milieu will be at a disadvantage. But perhaps the greatest danger is to imply that _all_ members of any group be considered disadvantaged; that is, _not all_ Black, Native Americans, Chicano, urban ghetto, Southern Appalachian, or migrant children should be generalized as being disadvan-

corresponding pictures in the appropriate rows. As they place the card in a slot, ask the children to explain their reasons for doing so.

Story Sequence Cards   This exercise builds on the idea of ordered sequence in communicating ideas. Cut out three or four pictures that tell a story when they are placed in proper sequential order. Mount the pictures onto heavy tagboard so they will be more durable. Mix up the cards and ask the children to examine them and put them into an order that tells a story. Then, ask them to tell you the story.

Guess What I Have   Hide an object inside a colorfully decorated box with a lid. Then begin to describe the object—its size, weight, use, composition, color, and any other distinguishing characteristics. Children try to guess what is in the box.

With experience, the children will be able to choose their own familiar objects and provide the descriptions for the other children. Toys, tools, foods, school supplies, and familiar household objects are highly recommended for this activity.

Flannelboard Stories   Use flannelboard, a large snowman, and a variety of cut-out birds. The birds may all be cut from the same pattern and varied according to color, size, and design. Pass out one bird to each child in a group of five or six children and ask them to put their bird on and take it off the flannelboard in the appropriate spot of the story. Then read this story:

Once there was a nice, big snowman who grew tired of being all alone in the backyard. So the lonesome snowman wished and wished with all his might, "I'm so lonesome, I wish someone would come and play with me." All of a sudden, a plain red bird flew into the yard and landed at the snowman's feet. "I'll play with you," said the red bird. "I'm coming, too," chirped a white bird with large yellow dots, and it landed right on top of the snowman's head. "Wait for me," sang a checkered bird as he flew right beside the snowman, "I want to play, too." Just as the snowman flashed a big, wide smile on his face, the biggest bird of all flew up and perched next to the snowman's head on his big, round shoulder.

"Oh, my! Oh, my!" said the snowman. "Maybe it's not so bad to be lonesome after all." So, he shuffled his feet and the red bird flew away; he wiggled his head and the white bird with large yellow dots left; he waved his arm and the checkered bird scurried away; he jiggled his shoulder and the biggest bird of all sailed into the sky and flew away, too. "There," said the snowman, "now I'm so tired, I think I'll just go to sleep."

Use your imagination to create imaginative flannelboard stories to suit your needs. Just remember to keep the stories short and full of action and repetition—all with rich, colorful language.

Tape Recorder   Explain and demonstrate the use of a tape recorder to a small group of children. Ask each child, in turn, to say something, such as his name, and then immediately play it back. Then, encourage him to talk until he wants to stop—play it back immediately. Children are fascinated by hearing their voices on a tape recorder and will be highly motivated to keep such activity going on their own.

A word of caution: Some children are too shy to do this activity. In these cases, don't force the children to talk; simply wait until they are ready to do so on their own. This is one good way—if it is used properly—of getting children who usually do not talk much to open up and produce more speech.

taged. To do so would be to create biases that are both incorrect and unfair. Because the term *disadvantaged* implied such a stereotyped definition for many years, we frown on its use and wish to substitute the phrase *culturally different* instead. We hope this phrase will not be interpreted as being negative and you will understand that, regardless of the term chosen, *severe economic and social hardships* are most likely to cause limited access to early educational opportunity rather than *member-ship in any particular ethnic or racial group,* and that those hardships seem to be more highly concentrated in some cultural and economic groups than in others.

Preschool programs, beginning primarily with the federally funded Head Start programs of the 1960's, carefully examined the needs of culturally different children and began to develop special teaching materials and instructional techniques, mainly to counteract the negative educational start these children may have received. The models were based on the following theories:

1. *The deprivation theory:* This theory states that the child who is deprived of quality experiences during the early years will not develop the processes necessary for normal acquisition of intellectual skills and abilities.

2. *The critical period theory:* This theory supposes that lack of intellectual stimulation during the early years causes some degree of permanent mental retardation.

3. *The cumulative intellectual deficit theory:* This theory observes that children from "disadvantaged" homes are greatly affected by their early lack of intellectual stimulation. This lack leads to an initial deficit that causes the child great difficulty in reaching newer, higher stages of development. Eventually, the child falls further and further behind children from "advantaged" homes.

Ornstein (1971) carefully examined the three prevailing theories and offered this critical response:

> It might be argued that the three theories constitute a scholary mode for describing the disadvantaged in terms of being "stupid." Although the objective is to make the teacher aware of the intellectual factors related to learning, as well as to counteract the child's limited environmental stimulation with compensatory programs and proper teaching practices, the continuous listing of negative traits and supporting cognitive theories may be used to "alibi" the teachers' and schools' ineffectiveness. It may also be alleged that the social scientists themselves, by delineating these traits and theories, unwittingly contribute to the teachers' acquiring negative attitudes about the disadvantaged students' inability to learn. [pp.267–268]

Teachers, then, must understand low-income and culturally different children in order to avoid stereotyping them and translate those understandings into programs offering them equal educational opportunity. Without this understanding and without viable programs and quality teaching practices, any early educational disadvantages these children may have had will be perpetuated and exacerbated.

The educational problems of culturally different youth are varied and complex. They result from conditions in the home and community that affect learning in that they contribute to traditionally low expectations for educational success. Such conditions include dilapidated housing; poor hygienic practices; inadequate nutrition; low income; substandard medical care; illiterate parents; very little verbal exchange; paucity of educational experiences such as visits to zoos; museums, stores, and so on; poor attitudes toward education.

Improvement of these conditions cannot, of course, be assigned to the schools alone; a joint effort with the home and with community agencies is required. However, preschool educators are becoming increasingly sensitive to their responsibilities and are adapting their teaching methods so that culturally different youth are given every opportunity to learn and grow as much as possible. Some of the special adaptations and considerations are described in the following sections.

Language Factors

Perhaps the most damaging myth that has grown from studies of culturally different youngsters is the myth of "nonlanguage." Observations of these children in traditional middle-class-oriented classrooms led them to be described as "inarticulate" or "unresponsive," "not willing or unable to communicate." However, many of these children came from homes where the language spoken was not the language of the school. They learned their subculture's rich language in the home or neighborhood, and freely expressed their thoughts with their peers. However, they frequently suffered damaging results when speaking in situations where standard English was expected. E. Brooks Smith, Kenneth Goodman, and Robert Meredith (1976) provide two examples to illustrate this point.

A teacher noticed that one of her first-graders was unable to participate in the general discussion after the class returned from the trip to the zoo. She was, in fact, unable to answer the simplest question about the animals. She did not even seem to know the names of such common animals as lions, tigers, elephants, and bears.

A few days later, the teacher tactfully raised the question with the child's mother during a parent-teacher conference. "You know," she said, "it would be very good for Mary if you and her father took her on trips to places like the zoo. She needs experiences like that." The mother was puzzled. "As a family we go on many trips," she said. "We get to the zoo several times a year, as a matter of fact. It's one of the children's favorite trips."

Now it was the teacher's turn to be puzzled. "But Mary doesn't even seem to know the names of the animals or anything about them," the teacher said.

"Oh, she does know about animals," the mother explained, "but, you see, my husband is Old World Chinese. He is very anxious that our children learn to speak Chinese and appreciate their cultural heritage. So when we go on trips he insists that we speak only Chinese. Mary knows the Chinese names of many of the animals in the zoo. I'm sure she could tell you a lot about them in Chinese."

A second-grade teacher had prepared to introduce a story to her reading group. The children all lived in a housing project near the heart of Detroit. The story was about a squirrel. Assuming a lack of experience with squirrels, which she associated with suburban residential districts, the teacher had prepared a large cutout of a squirrel to show the children. "I'm thinking," she said, "of a small animal that likes to climb trees and has a bushy tail." Hands shot up and several children, bursting to answer, almost shouted, "I know, I know!" Triumphantly the chosen child said, "Squirrels! We got lots of squirrels

where we live." "Really?" said the teacher in polite disbelief. "Who can tell me about squirrels?" she called on a black child, literally falling off the front edge of his seat in eagerness to tell about his experiences with squirrels. "My daddy, he go huntin' for squirrel," he said. "Sometime he take me 'long." "Hunting?" the teacher said in a dull tone. "What do you do with the squirrels?" "First we skin 'em. Then we cook 'em," he said. "They goo-oood!" he added, drawing out the last word for emphasis. The teacher responded with a silent look of revulsion. An Appalachian youngster then said, "I know how to skin squirrels!"

Another boy spoke out without the teacher's permission. "My brother, he ten. He catch squirrel and tie tin can to they tail. Man, they sure fun to watch." "That's enough, Thomas," the teacher said coldly. "Class open your books to page 37 and begin reading." [p.51]

Each vignette illustrates one of the two language problems common in today's preschool setting: (1) *bilingual children,* who have difficulty expressing their thoughts in expected school language and (2) *divergent children,* who have difficulty expressing their ideas and experiences in standard English. Teachers who are not sensitive to the needs of these groups can hurt and damage young children who are attempting to discuss their feelings and experiences. As rejections accumulate, children often retreat into the comfort of silence—hence, the label "nonverbal." Many children, then, who *seem* nonverbal in the school setting would be able to express themselves fluently if they were accepted by the teacher and were confident that neither their ideas not their subculture's language would be ridiculed or rejected.

Making young children feel comfortable and wanted implies that teachers understand the language of their children. Sarah W. Zaremba (1975) compiled a list of basic words that English-speaking staffs could use easily with Spanish-speaking children. That valuable list is presented in Table 8-2. Pronunciation of the Spanish phrases is indicated by English

Table 8-2 *Basic Expressions in Spanish and English*

English	Spanish	Pronunciation
Good morning.	Buenos días.	BWEH-nohss DEE-ahs
Good-bye.	Adiós.	ah-TH YOHSS
Thank you.	Gracias.	GRAH-s yahss
Please come.	Venga por favor.	VEHN-gah pohr fa-VOHR
Come tomorrow.	Venga mañana.	VEHN-gah mah-N YAH-nah
Come today.	Venga hoy.	VEHN-ga OY
Yes.	Sí.	SEE
No.	No.	NOH
I don't understand.	No entiendo.	noh ehn-T YEHN-doh
I understand you.	Le entiendo.	leh(ehn)n-T YEHN-doh
Please speak more slowly.	Hable más despacio, por favor.	AH-vleh mahss dehss-PAH-S yoh, pohr fah-VOHR
Please repeat.	Repita, por favor.	rreh-PEE-tah, pohr fah-VOHR
Where do you live?	¿Dónde vive usted?	DOHN-deh VEE-veh oo-STED
What is your name?	¿Cómo se llama?	KOH-moh seh YAH-mah
My name is——.	Me llamo——.	meh-YAH-moh——
Mrs.——will drive you.	La señora——le va a llevar.	lah seh-N YOHR-ah leh-vah-ah-yeh-VAHR
Let me help you.	Déjeme ayudarle.	DEH-hem eh ah-yoo-DAR-leh
Here is the bathroom.	Aquí está el baño.	ah-KEE ehss TAH ehl BAH-n yoh
Wash your hands.	Lávase las manos.	LAH-va-seh lahss MAH-nohs
Soap.	Jabón.	hah-BOHN
Water.	Agua.	AH-gwah
Milk.	Leche.	LEH-cheh
Juice.	Jugo.	HOO-goh
Cracker; crackers.	Galleta; galletas.	ga YEH-ta; ga YEH-tahs
Where is your coat?	¿Dónde está tu abrigo?	DOHN-deh ehss-TAH too ah-VREE-goh,
sweater?	suéter?	suh-EH-ter
What do you need?	¿Qué necesita usted?	KEH neh-seh-SEE-tah oo-STED
What are you planning to do with it?	¿Qué va a hacer con eso?	KEH va ah as-SEHR kohn EH-soh?
You haven't finished.	——todavía no ha terminado.	toh-dah VEE-ah nohah terr-mi-NAH doh
What's the rule?	¿Cuál es la regla?	KWAL ESS lah RREH-glah
Your mother is at home.	Tu mamá está en casa.	too mah-MAH ess-TAH enh KAH-sah
——is not feeling well.	——no se siente bien.	——noh seh see-EHN-teh bee-ehn

Table 8-2   Basic Expressions in Spanish and English (continued)

English	Spanish	Pronunciation
——is taking (child) home.	——va a llevar a (child) a casa.	——vah ah yeh-VAHR ah (child) ah KAH-sah
Sit down on the bus.	Siéntese en el autobús.	see-EHN-teh-seh en ell ow-toh-BUSS
The bus will come soon.	El autobús va a venir pronto.	ell ow-toh-BUSS vah a beh-NEER PRON-toh
After lunch.	Después de mediodía.	dehss-PWEHSS deh meh-dee-o-DEE-ah
Please ask.	Pídalo por favor.	PEE-dah-lo pohr fah-VOHR
Please tell him.	Por favor dígale.	pohr fah-VOHR DI-gah-leh
He's sorry.	El lo siente.	ELL LOH see-EHN-teh
Story time.	Es la hora de los cuentos.	ess lah OHR-ah deh lohs KWEHN-tohs
Please sit down.	Siéntese por favor.	see-EN-teh-seh pohr fah-VOHR
Listen.	Escuche por favor.	ehss-KOO-che pohr fah-VOHR
Walk.	Camine.	kahm MEE-neh
No running.	No corra.	NOH KOHR-rah
Speak softly.	Hable bajo por favor.	ah-ble BA-ho pohr fah-VOHR

Cardinal Numbers		
One	Uno	OO-noh
Two	Dos	DOHSS
Three	Tres	TREHSS
Four	Cuatro	KWAH-troh
Five	Cinco	SEEN-koh
Six	Seis	SEH-eess
Seven	Siete	see-EH-teh
Eight	Ocho	OH-cho
Nine	Nueve	new-EH-veh
Ten	Diez	dee-EHSS

Days of the Week		
Sunday	Domingo	doh-MEEN-goh
Monday	Lunes	LOO-nehss
Tuesday	Martes	MAHR-tehss
Wednesday	Miércoles	mee-EHR-koh-lehss
Thursday	Jueves	hoo-EH-vehs
Friday	Viernes	vee-EHR-nehs
Saturday	Sábado	SAH-vah-dough

words or syllables that can be pronounced in only one way. Syllables are divided by hyphens, and the accented syllable is always in capital letters. Practice reading some of the words aloud as you read through the list.

Knowledge of the primary language in which young children express themselves is necessary so you can tailor instruction to fit their needs effectively. Divergencies within the English language should also be understood by the teacher, for their original structure has special meaning to the group in which it is used. Such divergencies (dialects) result in different word forms, combinations of words, and pronunciations, and are often very difficult to understand. Consider these examples:

> Ey, brah, howzit? Woddascoops? Translation: Hey, man, how's it going? What's the news? (Hawaiian Pidgin)

> Grody to the max. (Valley Girl)

> Jones scooped up the scorching grasscutter and shoveled it to Smith, the keystone sacker, who whirled and fired it to Brown, the gateway guardian, who nipped the runner by a half-stride. The twin-killing in the final stanza nailed down the win for Johnson, the Bluebirds' fireballing southpaw. (Baseball announcer)

> My fellow citizens, it is an honor to be here with you today. When I embarked upon this campaign, I hoped it would be conducted on a high plane and that my opponent would be willing to stick to the issues. He has been inclined to be tractable instead—to eschew the use of outright lies in his description of me. I will not ignore these unvarnished fidelities no longer: his father is a Mormon who was secretly chagrined at least a dozen times by matters of a pecuniary nature. His son subscribes to a phonographic distributor and his great-aunt was an admitted sexagenarian. (Politician)

> Now, Greta, outen the dog and don't forget to make the door shut after! (Pennsylvania Dutch dialect)

> Tote the ball, James, 'fo' I give you one upside the haid. . . . That be mine! (Black dialect)

Since Black dialect is the one dialect most commonly heard in preschool settings, let's examine some of its major divergencies from standard English. Even though the dialect differs markedly from standard English, you will find that it is a rich, sophisticated language in itself.

1. *Phonological divergencies*–differences in speech sounds between standard English and the dialect. Some of the common phonological divergencies found in Black dialect include:
   a. the disappearing *r*: *poor* = "po," *for* = "fo," *morning* = "monin'," *Paris* = "Pass."
   b. the disappearing *l*: *rule* = "roo," *oil* = "aw," *help* = "hep," *roll* = "ro."
   c. the difficult *th*: *birthday* = "birfday," *with* = "wif."
   d. dropping sounds at end of words (especially *t* and *d*): *mild* = "mile," *soft* = "sof," *fast* = "fass," *meant* = "men."

2. *Grammatical divergencies*—differences in sentence structure between standard English and Black dialect. Some examples include:
   a. the use of the verb *to be*: absence or presence of the verb *is* indicates permanence or temporariness of action. Thus, "He home" means that he is home for the moment; "He *be* home" means that he has been home for some time and is expected to remain there for a while.
   b. lack of verbal agreement: "They *is* our friends." "She *don't* live here no more." "He *has ran* faster than me." "Tom *seen* him yesterday."

3. *Vocabulary divergencies*—differences in the words used in standard English and Black dialect. Examples include: "Cool it!" means "Be quiet!" "His jaws be set tight" means "He is very angry." "Those are cool vines, brother" means "That's a good looking set of clothes, friend."

Culturally different youngsters, then, may enter the preschool environment with a basic language characteristic: (1) they speak a language other than English (usually Spanish), or (2) they speak an altered version of standard English (usually Black dialect). Lack of facility in speaking standard English can, at times, create problems for these children and result in their having learning difficulties throughout their schooling if no special considerations are formulated. Several popular suggestions for approaching the problem of speakers of nonstandard English have been made over the years.

1. *Teach standard English to children prior to any other formal instruction.* Rapid drill and patterning provide young children with concentrated practice in standard English structure, vocabulary, and sound patterns. Proponents of this approach believe that bilingual education (the capacity to speak and think in two languages or dialects) should be "transitional," that is, children who do not speak standard English should be immersed in repetitive drill in the language as soon as possible, with classroom use of their native tongue kept at a minimum. As soon as these children have gained fluency in standard English, it is argued, they should be placed immediately into traditional English-only classes. This method is a refinement of the nineteenth century "melting pot" approach, where immigrant children were forced to learn standard English because no other language was allowed in the school.

2. *Teach standard English, but don't force the child to ignore his culture's primary language or dialect.* In this environment, the child is encouraged to speak in his native tongue, while standard English is taught informally in an atmosphere of play and activity-centered learning. The child learns standard English as he hears and tells stories, looks at picture books, sings songs and says rhymes, and talks about daily activities. The emphasis is on the functional use of life experiences. Advocates of this position argue that children unfamiliar with both standard English and American culture learn them gradually while holding onto their own valued cultural and ethnic identities. In this environment, the adults and children speak in both standard English and the second language in the context of spontaneous learning experiences. To use this approach in your teaching, refer to the nativistic position regarding language instruction as it was described earlier in this chapter.

3. *Teach standard English as a model.* This technique cuts across all preschool programs. Here, the teacher is the model for good language—she speaks carefully in standard English patterns. Common objects are labeled, actions are described, and language is used to describe actions and events during the day. Hearing standard English spoken by the teacher, it is argued, encourages children to imitate its use spontaneously.

The federal government has invested over $500 million to develop bilingual programs since the Bilingual Education Act was passed in 1968. Appropriations for programs set up under the act have increased yearly—$150 million was earmarked for 1979. Additional programs were developed under Title VII, Head Start, Follow Through, and under other public and private sources of funding. Bilingual education is a major area, and an issue of primary concern for early childhood educators today.

Being an issue in early childhood education implies that a basic controversy still exists on that topic. Basically, the controversy related to bilingual education involves these arguments:

1. Proponents of the English-only setting argue that current research studies show

that bilingual children learn standard English in English-only settings more effectively than they do in settings where both languages are used. Also, the children score better on standardized English reading comprehension tests at later grade levels.

2. Proponents of the dual-language setting argue that their program makes children feel more comfortable in school and helps them develop a more positive attitude toward school-related activities. They feel that test score gains from English-only settings will be short-lived while the standard English learned in their natural life situations will have more permanence.

Despite the controversy over which teaching strategy results in most effective learning, most educators do agree that knowledge of childhood bilingualism and of the alternative techniques for teaching English as a second language is essential for a sound bilingual program. This knowledge, combined with a sincere respect for cultural diversities, is of primary importance in any program designed to understand and eliminate the learning difficulties of the child exposed to a new culture and new language.

A Sample Program for Teaching Standard English

The Distar® program is an interesting example of special instructional designs originally created for culturally different children to learn standard English. The program structures its language lessons in small-step instructional units that are carefully broken down to offer the children a systematic introduction to standard English. Lessons proceed in complexity from simple word recognition to the development of complete sentences. Teachers work with small groups of five to six children for about 15 minutes per day; during this time a great deal of repetitive drill—through either choral or individual responses—is carried out. Immediate rewards in the form of praise ("You did it right!") or teacher approval (smiles, shaking hands, and so on) are essential when the children provide correct answers. Tokens or other forms of external reinforcement (food, toys) may be necessary if the teacher approval system seems to be initially unsuccessful.

Short drill sessions in which the teacher leads children in intensive, rhythmic instruction get them enthusiastically involved—like the student body being led by a cheerleader at a pep rally. The group is expected to respond to the teacher in a loud, rhythmic, whole-group response. It is a fast-paced experience with the oft-repeated direction "Say it fast" filling the air. Praise is a major reinforcer in this program; the teacher's instruction book offers these positive responses: "That was good remembering"; "You are smart; I can't fool you today"; "That was hard work, but you did a good job." See the following basic pattern of a sample lesson of the Distar® technique:

1. Identification
   Teacher: "This is a circle."
   Child (repeats phrase): "This is a circle."

2. Question
   Teacher: "Is this a circle?"
   Child: "Yes (*or no*) this is (*or is not*) a circle."

3. Selection
   Teacher: "Show me the circle."
   Child (child selects the proper geometric shape): "This is the circle."

4. Origination
   Teacher: "What is this?"
   Child: "This is a circle."

The goals of such dialogue are to expand the child's use of word labels, to increase his knowledge of word meanings, and to help him master the use of increasingly mature sentence patterns.

The following illustrative dialogue demonstrates how one teacher led the children through a complete lesson dealing with geometric shapes and the relative terms "in front of" and "in back of." The teacher draws a circle and a square on the chalkboard, the square partly hidden by the circle. The children, who are seated in a row facing the chalkboard, talk freely among themselves and to the teacher until she has completed the drawing and turns toward them. They then quiet down and attend to the figures on the chalkboard.

Teacher: Is the circle in front of the square?
Children: (in unison, rhythmically) Yes, the circle is in front of the square.
Teacher: How do you know?
Several children: (ad lib) Cause you can't see the whole square. . . . Cause it cover it up.
Teacher: Is the square in front of the circle?
Children: (ad lib) No. . . . In back. . . . No, circle in front.
Teacher: All right, give me the whole statement. Is the square in front of the circle? "No, the square is _____"
Children: (in unison) The square is *not* in front of the circle. The square is *in back of* the circle.
Teacher: (to James, who has stumbled through the last statement) James, where is the square?
James: Back.
Teacher: That's right. You're getting it. Now try to say the whole thing. "The square is *in back of* the circle." [Bereiter and Engelmann, 1966, pp.56–58]

After about four minutes devoted to elaborations of this task, the teacher switches to another activity.

Along with this heavy stress on speaking correctly, the children are required to listen carefully. To enhance listening skills, the teacher periodically attempts to "fool" the children. Consider the following example of a lesson containing a strong emphasis on both speech patterning and effective listening. Remember that the dialogue is carried on in a fast-paced

manner that generates the excitement of a football cheering section. Highly structured teacher's guides furnish word-by-word instructions that admonish the teacher to remind the children to "Say it fast" whenever the intensively paced drill seems to falter.

First comes a quick review of a previously learned—and popular—class concept.

Teacher: Tell me something that is a weapon.
Children (ad lib): A gun. . . . A rifle. . . . A sword. . . . Bow'n arrow . . .
Teacher: What's the rule? If you use it . . .
Children (in unison): If you use it to hurt someone, it's a weapon.
Teacher: Can you use a stick to hurt somebody?
Children (ad lib): No. . . . Yeah. . . . You can hit 'em. . . . You can throw it. . . . If it's a big stick . . .
Teacher: If you use a stick to hit somebody, then what do you know about it?
Children (more or less in unison): It's a weapon.
Teacher: Tell me something that is *not* a weapon.

After a review taking less than two minutes, the teacher then moves immediately into the presentation of a new concept—part:

Teacher (pointing): This is Tyrone. Now listen. *(Holding up Tyrone's hand and speaking slowly and methodically in a way that the children have learned to recognize as a signal that something new is being presented.)* This is *a part of* Tyrone. This part of Tyrone is a . . .
Children: Hand.
Teacher (pointing to Tyrone's nose): And this is a part of Tyrone. This part of Tyrone is a . . .
Children: Nose.

Several other parts of Tyrone are introduced in this way and then the teacher alters the presentation to require the children to provide more of the statement.

Teacher (pointing to Tyrone's ear): Is this a part of Tyrone?
Children: Yeah.
Teacher: Yes, this is a . . .
Children: Part of Tyrone.

Progressively the children are led to the point where they are supplying the entire pair of statements. Negative instances are introduced.

Teacher (pointing to Marie's nose): Is this a part of Tyrone?
Children: No, this is not a part of Tyrone.

Consideration is then shifted to parts of a chair and parts of an automobile (using a picture in a picture book). At the end of six minutes the children have achieved a tenuous mastery of the concept but have started to become restless and to make thoughtless errors. The teacher then shifts to a concept that had been introduced the day before—vehicle. She will return the next day to further work on the concept, part. During the closing minutes of the period, when some of the children are becoming inattentive, the teacher says, "Try real hard to get this, and then we'll have time to do some more jungle animals." This enticement serves to pull the group together for the final exercise on vehicles. [Bereiter and Engelmann, 1966, pp.57–58]

This example shows that direct instruction language programs are exclusively interested in using reinforcement techniques to establish imitative, patterned verbal responses to various stimuli within the child's environment. The Distar® program, of course, is only one application of this concept to preschool language instruction. Although Distar® is interpreted by some as too structured and formalized for preschool children, such intensive sessions are required only for about 10–15 minutes each day. Should you desire, the rest of the day could be used to present any of the other less formal, less structured language activities presented earlier in this chapter.

Factors Related to Self-Concept

A direct outgrowth of school performance and language ability is the child's self-concept. Should the child consistently experience failures in these two areas, his view of himself is likely to be diminished; repeated successes, of course, are likely to result in a good self-concept. Research has consistently shown that children from culturally different settings have low self-concepts in the school setting, primarily caused by lack of success. Even though these children come to school with the desire to succeed, continuous and cumulative failures cause a consistent lowering of their self-concept and a consequent drop in educational and personal aspirations. For these reasons, most current preschool programs evaluate the developmental levels of their children before entrance and establish learning tasks at which the children have high probabilities of success, rather than tasks at which they have low probabilities of success. Their methods of enhancing self-concepts generally fall into these categories:

1. *Helping children develop competence.* As mentioned previously, most children enter school with a drive to succeed. You can help them maintain this drive by establishing an environment in which they can experience success and do things for themselves—from putting a puzzle together to hanging their coats in the cubby.

2. *Giving sincere recognition and praise.* One of the most popular ways of enhancing a child's self-concept is to reward him with honest praise. Sincere appreciation of a job well done strengthens the child's character and motivates him to achieve new heights. A note of caution, however: A mechanical, free-flowing extension of praise is nearly as bad as extending no praise at all. Children may soon interpret constant gushy or flowery statements as insincere, and therefore meaningless. Nevertheless, children need encouragement, and praise must be given freely but honestly: "I'm proud of you, Carlos, you learned a new word today." "You really tried hard this time, Lawrence, I'm sure you'll learn

how to do it very soon." "I really like the way you cleaned the snack table today, Martha, you are a good worker."

3. *Respecting the child and his culture.* Often, prospective teachers of culturally different children suffer from prejudice based on lack of knowledge. Only a small percentage of such teachers has ever experienced a culturally different childhood, and they find it difficult to empathize with the children or their parents. Ignorance of the causes leading to lack of opportunity often brings out feelings of fear, mistrust, and negative attitudes toward the capabilities of culturally different children.

Before working with culturally different children, therefore, you must examine your inner thoughts honestly for feelings of prejudice and fear. For example, being brought up in a neighborhood that included many culturally different youngsters, I had friends whose homes were dilapidated and torn—some even had dirt floors. Later, as part of my professional training, I took a course titled "Disadvantaged Youth." The course instructor had obviously never lived in a culturally different setting as a youngster. Before the trip to a rural "disadvantaged" home, she warned, "Be careful not to drink coffee or eat food while you're there. Remember that these people are not very sanitary." Predictably, to welcome us to the house, the mother offered coffee and a cake that she had baked especially for our visit. After hearing polite refusals from the others in my group (including the instructor), I eagerly answered, "I'd enjoy some" (remembering my friends' parents and the pride they took in their ability to cook). The mother's response, as you might suspect, was precious. My biggest reward of the entire visit, though, came when the father delivered a sign that indicated total acceptance of a visitor in a low socioeconomic rural home—he shared his hunting rifle with me. This experience is included to illustrate how

preconceived ideas, even from respected professionals, can lead either to damaging or to improving self-concepts among the culturally different. And when you use a term such as *culturally different* to classify a child, think of who was actually culturally different in the vignette and what the resulting actions and words were. Can you apply such understandings to the children in your care?

Work toward understanding all children. Volunteer some time as a student assistant in preschool programs designed for the culturally different. Visit local community groups or neighborhood associations, talk to teachers of disadvantaged children, read about the particular culture in which you are interested, and observe culturally different children in their preschool setting or home environment. Be sure your feelings are not negative before you accept a position in a culturally different preschool setting. By experiencing the richness and pride reflected by people in all cultural groups, you will find that most of your feelings of apprehension quickly disappear. Children will soon sense your feelings and gain an impression of acceptance based on your words and actions.

As you keep in mind the positive ways to enhance self-concept, be aware, too, of the ways in which self-concept can be destroyed:

- *Through comparisons.* Comparing the efforts of one child with those of another frequently destroys a youngster's self-concept. This is done with comments such as: "Tina (a culturally different Appalachian child), why can't you learn to talk like Carol (an advantaged child)? I have a hard time understanding what you said."

- *Through giving too much or too little help.* Teachers often lower children's self-concept by doing too much for them. Speaking for the child instead of waiting for him to talk, putting the coat on the child instead of having the patience to let him try, or standing by with a mop as the child carries a glass of water are only a few of the many ways by which we overprotect children and cause them to develop poor self-concepts. Of course, by not providing appropriate help and guidance, we risk the same results.

- *Through stereotyping young children.* Often we develop ideas and expectancies of others from hearing what other people say about them. Sometimes this happens when teachers say or think, "I'm just wasting my time with these children. How can I teach them when they *don't want to learn?*" "I don't know what I'm going to do with these children—they're so *lazy.*" "Those children will never learn to speak well—they're just plainly *nonverbal.*" Stereotypes like these are unfounded and tend to stick only because of unthinking people whose value orientations have been prejudiced by others insensitive to the differences brought about by lack of opportunity. Avoid making such comments for they will only strengthen negative views of the children and result in a low self-concept. Instead, think of the value of each individual and show confidence and respect for what each can do.

To summarize, the prospective teacher of young children must be aware of the conditions caused by social, economic, and cultural differences and how these differences influence major areas of performance in school. The areas of difference usually emphasized by educators are those relating to language, concept development, and self-concept. Choosing teaching strategies in each area implies a knowledge of the effects of deprivation, an understanding of alternative instructional methods and materials, and a respect for the children being taught. Although this task responsibility is a challenging one, it can be one of the most rewarding of all.

SOME FINAL THOUGHTS

One of the most wondrous accomplishments of early childhood is the emergence of language. Within a short time youngsters accumulate words and eventually put those words together into sentences. They acquire language in such mystifying ways that some professionals have labeled children "linguistic geniuses." Children seem to recognize patterns of language and internalize them into their own system of communication, regardless of the fact that they tend to overregulate an imprecise English language ("I have five *toes* and two *foots.*"). Children's use of language tells you how they think. They attach word labels to actions or objects themselves, thereby using words to think. Children learn words through interactions with their environment. What does this mean for teachers?

Specifically, you serve to enhance language development by serving as a model and stimulator of good language throughout the entire day. You create a climate that promotes free, informal discussion; use stories, conversations and other planned activities; and provide special help for those children coming to school with specific language problems. Do not pressure the children into mature patterns of speaking until they are ready, for such pressures often cause children to develop patterns of stuttering or stammering. Children who are not allowed to progress at their own rate may even eventually lose the urge to talk in your classroom.

Language is a skill fundamental to the entire area of intellectual growth. As the child grows, her language and intelligence grow together—a process that should continually astonish and please you, especially since the acquisition of language is a uniquely human trait.

Supporting these ideas, ironically, is the Russian "father of behaviorism," Ivan Pavlov. Late in his life, Pavlov began to realize that human beings actually possess two "signal systems." *First signals* are all the stimuli to which animals *and* humans can respond (hunger, sleep, pain, and so on). Pavlov felt that his stimulus-response principles best applied to shaping behaviors of this type. *Second signals* are mainly *verbal* stimuli. Pavlov felt that this second signal system was the major feature separating humans from animal life. This dimension, according to Pavlov, has its own structures and functions, and, therefore, the established laws of classical conditioning are not applicable. Slobin (1966) quotes Pavlov thus, "The word created a second system of signals of reality which is peculiarly ours. . . . It is precisely speech which has made us human" (p.122).

Chapter 9

The Basic Academic Skills: Reading, Writing, and Math

"There's so much pressure," said Martha wistfully. "We must start Lisa early and push her so that she'll get into the best college when she's old enough. I want her to be aware of everything—the alphabet, numbers, words. I want her brain to soak up as much as possible." Martha, a publishing executive, sat with her husband Arthur, a lawyer, and discussed the serious business of their daughter's education. Lisa, three years old, had just managed to squeeze into one of the last openings of a prestigious sub-urban nursery school charging more than $2000 per year for tuition.

Many of today's children are being raised by success-oriented, professional parents like Martha and Arthur, who have been encouraged by recent findings about the influence of the early years on learning. Impressed with works such as Burton White's *The First Three Years of Life* (1975) and Glenn Doman's *Better Baby Institute,* many parents today are caught up in a quest to push their children to learn at an earlier age than ever before. They seize the messages offered others as they strive to raise the "smartest kid in America." Those who have not yet become engrossed in this movement often embrace it after observing other children's successes. All across the country people are caught up in what *Newsweek* (Langway, March 28, 1983) referred to as "Bringing Up Superbaby." The race is on as parents push their children to learn. Major universities and research hospitals assign teams of investigators to study learning patterns of children from the time of birth; some even are interested in how the baby's condition during pregnancy influences later learning.

This interest in pushing young children is, of course, well-intentioned, but some critics question whether such pressure places too much strain upon the children. More cases of stress in young children are reported by family therapists than ever before, and many of the cases are from families of young professionals who emphasize intellectual performance. Many couples wait to start families until they

Early experiences with books provide infants and toddlers with interests and attitudes prerequisite to the reading process itself.

dren's emotional and creative growth (1984). Burton White (1984) is concerned that his advice in *The First Three Years of Life* (1975) may have been unintentionally misinterpreted by some. "But we were interested in a *balanced* development," Dr. White noted (p. 61). "If large portions of time are spent in any narrowly focused direction, the child will probably have to pay a significant price in other developmental areas" (p. 70). The message White is giving us is that our responsibility is to provide experiences in all areas of development and, if we emphasize any single area at the expense of the others, we run the risk of hindering development in the others. Our major responsibility, then, is to understand as parents and as teachers, how to stimulate growth within *each* of the major areas of development: physical, intellectual, and social–emotional.

THE PRESCHOOL SETTING

Do we teach the academic areas in *preschool* classrooms? How we answer that question depends upon our definition of teaching the academic areas. If we think of beginning academic skills as memorizing the letters of the alphabet or reciting the numbers in sequence, the answer is a resounding no. Children who view the need to master academic skills in much the same way they do the need to drink warm milk will simply turn their noses up at us. But we can shout yes to the question if we understand that we are teaching the academic areas when we encourage children to ask questions and arouse interest in their world, even through the printed word. Given appropriate motivation and opportunity, young children will experience a natural desire to read, write, or recognize numerals; such desire is essential in building healthy learning appetites.

are successfully established in their careers and are financially secure. Now in their early- to mid-thirties, they plan to have only one child. They maintain a strong desire to do well in their careers while raising their children successfully, too. They see both responsibilities as important. They want to provide the best that money can buy for their children. The "best" is defined as intensive early learning.

How smart is it to place pressures on young children to learn basic academic skills such as reading, writing, and math? Although critics of high-pressure approaches to early learning worry about such things as stress and whether young children really care about things such as the difference between a Picasso and a Rembrandt, they all agree that young children *can learn* at an early age. But, they ask, is such an intensive technique the best form of instruction? T. Berry Brazelton fears that the current push on early academics shortchanges chil-

READING

The temptation to demonstrate just what a wonderful job we can do to teach even toddlers to read is very strong, indeed, especially with the popular acclaim positive results can bring. But, before such a decision can be made, we must examine the factors involved in the reading process in order to better understand what affects success in reading and all of academic learning.

Prerequisites to Reading

Perhaps the greatest factor in determining whether or not children are ready to read is whether or not they want to read. Such a desire appears to develop naturally as children listen to parents and teachers read to them and as they look through books for pleasure. Such initial experiences can actually begin at any age if the experience we provide is of interest to children and on their level of understanding. Does that mean that even infants can experience reading? According to Linda Lamme (1980), the answer is yes. Lamme's case for infant reading is based upon the premise that many important benefits are derived from reading and singing to infants. The lullabies we sing to infants while holding them as well as the books we share cause us to establish the physical contact so important in the parent–infant bonding process. Infants enjoy the physical contact, and, when they are able to associate books with such warm physical encounters, the basic positive attitude toward reading is developed before one year of age. Also, many basic reading skills can be developed by age one by competent caregivers. Lamme (1980) tells how:

> Through much interaction with books, infants become aware that pictures have meaning. They begin to use their eyes to discriminate between different objects in a picture, as someone points them out and names

them. They develop listening skills and the ability to differentiate among sounds. They also learn to turn the book's pages and become aware that books have a right side up. Each of these skills will help establish a sound foundation upon which future learning can build. [p. 286]

What kinds of books are appropriate for infants? Perhaps the most popular is the large picture book. Usually constructed of heavy, plastic-coated cardboard, these books are exemplified by clear, uncluttered pictures about things familiar to most infants: toys, animals, food, family members, vehicles, and so on. Some infant picture books are constructed of cloth or paper, both of which are somewhat less than desirable, at least as first books. Of course, we want the infant to handle the books, but infants have trouble with cloth books and often tear paper books. When sharing any picture books with children, you play a critical role. Point to the pictured object and name it, trying to associate it with the child's own world. For example, "See the bib? That looks just like Jamie's bib." After repeated experiences such as this, infants will point to pictures as you ask, "Where's the telephone? Can you find the telephone?" Infants can usually focus on pictures at two to four months; hence, after that time, many such directed experiences will eventually lead to the moment at about age one and a half when the infant will sit down with a book, turn its page, point, and proudly announce, "Ap-ple."

In addition to picture books, Mother Goose rhymes bring pleasure to infants. Mother Goose collections are excellent sources for rhythmical chanting and singing so greatly enjoyed by infants. Scratch and smell books have gained some measure of popularity in recent years. These books, as well as the touch-type books that invite infants to explore various textures, are excellent sources of sensory stimulation. Finally, early storybooks with their uncomplicated plots can be read to infants. Be sure that a clear picture appears on each page along with only a few words, hopefully with several repetitions.

Thus, the environment of the infant greatly influences the child's eventual acquisition of language and reading skills. Such knowledge should help to focus caregiver–infant interaction as an important component of the child's total academic development before the age of two.

What else, besides building a motivation to read within young children, contributes to the level of maturity necessary to becoming a reader? Perhaps the best way to answer that question is to examine the process that we commonly refer to as *reading.* The reading process has been defined by educators in many ways, but all the definitions include two things: (1) ability to recognize printed symbols (words) and (2) understanding the recognized words. The relationship between these two components of the reading process is effectively illustrated by Rudolph Flesch: "I once surprised a native of Prague by reading aloud from a Czech newspaper. 'Oh, you know Czech?' he asked. 'No, I don't understand a word of it,' I answered. 'I can only read it' " (1955, p. 23).

We may all have seen children learn to pronounce words without completely understanding them. If *word recognition* and *meaning* together constitute the reading process, those children were only name calling, not truly reading.

You may sense the common nature of learning to read and learning to speak. In Chapter 8, you learned that children acquire language by internalizing their life experiences, meaningfully assimilating their experiences into an established mental scheme, and attaching a spoken word label to that scheme. By providing verbal stimulation during life experiences, adults help children acquire greater numbers of word labels. Actually, youngsters are participating in a sophisticated communication process, involving both an input and output component. The input component is hearing someone attach word labels

to meaningful life experiences, while the output component is the generation of a spoken word itself.

Such interactions result in increasingly sophisticated input-output pairings as the child's language abilities continually grow. The words the child hears have no meaning by themselves; they become meaningful only by common agreement that certain sounds stand for certain things. Words, then, are arbitrary forms of communication and take on meaning only because groups agree on their meaning; for example, *glub* might be the chosen word label for *book* if it had been deemed appropriate when our arbitrary language system was developing. But it obviously wasn't, and the spoken word *book* has become a socially acceptable term to attach to the object you are presently reading. Likewise, the reading process involves a similar pattern of communication. It, too, is a communicative art involving understanding of arbitrary symbols (written words instead of spoken words) to which meaning can be attached.

Inherent in the process of acquiring skills in this communicative art is what is referred to as the development of *perceptual* skills. Perceptual skills involve a child's ability to receive sensory input, interpret it in some way, and then respond to it. The sensory input channels having the greatest impact on reading skills are the visual, the aural, and kinesthetic-tactile. Development of these three sensory input channels are, in turn, directly influenced by *neural development* and *experience background.* That is, when a child receives an impulse from any of these three channels, he interprets it and responds to it on the basis of his neural capabilities and his experiential background. If both areas have prepared him adequately, the child forms accurate perceptions of the new sensory impulses, and the reading process should develop normally. If, however, either area is inadequate in some way, sensory impulses may be incorrectly interpreted and the reading process most probably will be delayed. To see how a child's background of experiences can affect the ability to read, consider these questions: Did you ever read a popular book before you saw a movie based on that book? Which did you like better? If you said that you liked the book better, you responded in much the way most people would. The reason is that as you read the book, you associated *past experiences* with the plot and, as the events unfolded, those experiences caused you to picture the characters and settings in your own unique way. The same is true for each individual reading the same book, ultimately including the movie director. Of course, the director's experiences probably were much different from your own, thus causing disharmony—those movie scenes just weren't the way they happened in the book! Likewise, children call on past experiences when they learn to unlock the printed word— reading is a process that includes not only *word recognition* but also *word meaning*. The only way a child can get meaning from that printed word is to associate it with some past experience. Of course, the lack of or abundance of those past experiences can influence a child's progress either positively or negatively.

Because of this central role of perceptual development in the total reading process, many preschool programs are designed to enhance and nurture specific, related skills. Techniques for doing this range from highly formalized programs to unstructured, informal programs. Whatever technique is chosen, however, the major goal of perceptual instruction remains fairly constant: to develop visual, aural, and kinesthetic-tactile skills within the context of appropriate experience.

Visual Skills

1. *Visual discrimination:* the ability to differentiate among visual patterns—to see likenesses and differences, usually in size, shape, or color. Because children in a readiness program usually have difficulties distinguishing between an *o* and an *a*, a *d* and a *b*, an *n* and an *b*, they need to be provided with opportunities to observe likenesses and differences among the various stimuli in their environment that are more apparent.

2. *Visual memory:* the ability to observe visual stimuli and, when the stimuli have been removed for a period of time, to recall them from memory. Because learning to read involves the recall of letters, combinations of letters, and whole words, the readiness program is designed to help the child first remember simple items in the environment and then to move systematically to the more complex items such as letters of the alphabet or words.

Aural Skills

1. *Auditory discrimination:* the ability to differentiate among sounds—usually detecting likenesses and differences in tone, rhythm, volume, or source of sound. Since reading involves hearing the difference between *an* and *and,* or *gain* and *gang,* and telling which of the four words *ball, big, pin,* and *bone* begin with the same sound, auditory discrimination activities are vital in reading readiness programs.

2. *Auditory memory:* the ability to remember sounds and to recall them after a period of time. The child must not only perceive differences in sounds but he must also learn to remember them.

Kinesthetic-Tactile Skills   The ability to receive and interpret stimuli from outside sources through sensory channels other than the eyes or ears is referred to as kinesthetic-tactile skills. Body movement and the senses of touch, taste, and smell are especially attended to in this area of reading readiness. Some experts believe that the involvement of all the senses in the readiness phase strengthens the teaching of reading.

VISUAL SKILLS

Visual Discrimination Activities Visual discrimination activities generally fall into the following basic types.

- *Sorting objects:* Children identify objects that are alike and different. For example, sorting all the toy cars into one box and all the plastic horses into another.

- *Sorting by color:* Children identify different colors of objects and sort them by color.

- *Sorting by size:* Children identify big and little objects and sort them by size.

- *Sorting by shape:* Children identify basic shapes of objects (that is, round, square, triangle, and rectangle) and sort them according to likenesses.

- *Sorting by pattern:* Children observe a pattern on stimulus objects such as a bead arrangement or other pattern source. They then attempt to match or duplicate that pattern.

Some examples of these general categories of activities for visual discrimination follow.

1. Ask the children to use the separate compartments in the egg container to sort buttons by size, shape, color, or other criterion.

2. Cut 3-inch × 3-inch squares from fabric or wallpaper samples (two squares from each sample). Mount the squares on heavy tagboard, and mix them up well. Then ask the children to match pairs that are the same.

3. The children place the appropriate geometric shape cutouts into their corresponding holes on a frame.

4. The children duplicate a pattern by stringing together beads of appropriate color, size, and shape.

Visual Memory Activities

1. Show the child a geometric shape; then take it away and ask him to pick one just like it from a group of various shapes.

2. Show the child a simple, uncluttered picture. Then, take the first picture away and show him a second picture that has a simple addition or deletion. Ask him to tell you what is different about the second picture.

3. Show the child a series of three or four picture cards in random order. Then have him arrange the cards in order of their probable sequence and tell you the story as he goes along (see the picture cards). Similar card sets can be made for seeds sprouting, seasonal scenes, chicken hatching from an egg, and so on.

4. Place three objects in front of the child and ask him to name them. Then ask him to close his eyes while you take one object away. Then ask him to tell you what is gone (or what is new if you wish to add an object rather than take one away).

PICTURE CARDS

AUDITORY SKILLS

Auditory Discrimination Activities

1. Play a "mystery sound" game. Have the children close their eyes while you make a mystery sound such as knocking on the table, crumpling a sheet of paper, clapping your hands, snapping fingers, pouring water, and so on. The children then attempt to identify the sound.

2. Collect ten small plastic, metal, or glass containers such as juice cans, baby food bottles, or film containers. Cover each container with a colorful design and fill pairs of containers to about one-quarter full with five different noise-making materials—one pair with sand, another with water, a third with marbles, and so on, until five pairs are filled. Make sure each pair of sounds is distinct, then have the children shake the containers and match those with similar sounds.

3. Fill several jars or heavy glasses with different amounts of water. Have the children strike each container with a spoon and listen to each resulting sound. Have them try to put the containers in order from the lowest pitch to the highest pitch.

4. For children who are able to count: Have them turn their backs; then you tap on a table, strike a piano key, drop a marble in a pie tin, or hit a drum. Ask the children to tell you how many times they heard the sound from a single source. Then vary the game by making a series of sounds from two or more sources—for example, two taps on the table and one piano note.

5. *Listening exercises:* Children face the opposite direction and identify the actions that produce characteristic sounds: tearing paper, stamping feet, clapping hands, crunching paper, and so on. To extend this activity, clap your hands a different number of times and ask the children to repeat your pattern.

6. *Sounds of animals, vehicles, and so on:* Play recordings of characteristic sounds and ask the children to match the sound to a picture.

7. *Rhyming words:* Tell children that when words sound very much alike, we say that they *rhyme.* Which two words rhyme? For example,

Come watch me.
I'll climb the tree.

Later, ask the children to furnish the rhyming word:

Run, run, run,
We have such _____ .

Introduce riddles for rhyming:

A rabbit does this.
It rhymes with stop.
What is it? *(hop)*

Select a certain list of words, each beginning with the same consonant sound (or rhyme) except one, and ask the child which does not belong. For example,

- cat   car   boy   can

     (or)

- toy   boy   bird   joy

Auditory Memory Activities

1. Read or tell a short story to a child. Then have him put picture cards of the story events in order, and tell the story back to you as he does.

2. Ask the children to listen carefully as you say three or four colors, shapes, names, numbers, and so on. Then have them repeat the words back to you in the same sequence. For example, "Red, blue, green, yellow," or "Billy, Joan, Stan, and Jennifer."

3. Make a series of sounds by hitting a drum, by clapping, or by tapping on a table. Ask the children to repeat the pattern back to you.

4. Create a group story with a group of children. You start the story with a few interesting sentences. Have a child pick up from where you left off and continue the story by adding a few sentences of his own. Then have him turn it over to another child. Continue in this way until all children have had a chance. This activity works best if you choose stories that are familiar to the children.

KINESTHETIC-TACTILE SKILLS ▬▬▬▬▬▬▬▬▬▬▬▬▬▬▬▬▬▬▬▬▬▬▬▬▬▬▬

1. Use five pairs of empty soup cans and fill each pair with a different amount of a heavy material such as plaster of paris. For example, one pair would be empty; the second pair would be one-quarter full; the third, half full; the fourth, three-quarters full; and the last pair would be filled to the top. Cover the cans with a lid and decorate them with colorful construction paper. Begin the activity with one set of five cans of varying weight. Have the children first choose from among three cans the heaviest, the lightest, and the one in the middle. Then, add the two other cans in the set and ask the children to order the five cans from heaviest to lightest. Finally, introduce the second set of five cans and have the children make finer distinctions by matching pairs of containers that weigh the same.

2. Take ten small containers about the size of baby food jars and make five containers one color and five containers another color. Select five items with distinctive odors that can fit into the containers—cinnamon, pickle juice, liquid detergent, lemon extract, and mint, for example. Fill one container of each color with each item. You can place cotton balls into the containers to absorb the odoriferous materials, especially those in liquid form. When you finish, you should have five pairs of containers, each pair with one distinct odor. Begin by placing three different containers in front of a child and asking him to smell the different odors. "Can you smell the lemon . . . the pickle juice . . . the liquid detergent?" Then, introduce the three matching containers and see if the child is able to match each to its partner. Finally, for more sophisti-

cated distinctions, ask the children to match all five pairs.

3. Choose four common materials such as wood, styrofoam, carpet, and sandpaper. Make eight tablets—four identical pairs—all of the same size (2 inches × 3 inches) by gluing the materials to quarter-inch plywood. Have the children cover their eyes with a blindfold and run their fingers over each of the four different surfaces until they become aware of the distinctive feels. Then, ask them to match pairs of tablets according to texture.

4. Fill each of four baby food jars with one of the basic taste sensations (sweet, salty, sour, and bitter). Use sugar for the sweet taste, table salt for the salty taste, vinegar or pickle juice for the sour taste, and unsweetened chocolate for the bitter taste. You may wish to dilute each of the foods with water to avoid overloading your children's taste buds. That is, they can taste the different foods without being affected by the aftertaste of the previous one.

    Line the four bottles in front of a child and explain that each bottle contains a food representative of the four different taste groups. Dip a plastic spoon into the sugar solution and have the child taste it. Comment that: "This food is sweet." Continue with the other three solutions, emphasizing the taste sensation each time. Then, using a fresh plastic spoon, select a taste jar at random and ask the child to name the taste it contains. A word of caution: Use a different plastic spoon and a fresh set of jars for each child participating in this activity.

These three areas of perceptual skills can be developed in a reading program through dozens of different techniques, including those in the accompanying "Visual Skills," "Auditory Skills," and "Kinesthetic-Tactile Skills" boxes.

In addition to these valued perceptual skills, prerequisites to the actual reading process, or "readiness" for reading, must involve a planned period of experiences during which all of these basic skills and abilities are developed.

1. Physical abilities

   a. *Large muscle skills*—running, jumping, hopping, skipping, crawling, balancing, throwing, catching, and so on

   b. *Small muscle skills*—buckling, zipping, hooking, lacing, tying, tearing, folding, pasting, painting, drawing, cutting, holding a pencil, and so on

c. *State of health*—hearing and seeing well, being generally in a state of good health

2. Social-emotional maturity

   a. *Social growth*—sharing materials, participating in organized activities, playing well with peers, and adapting to routines

   b. *Emotional growth*—exhibiting self-control, displaying even temperament, respecting others, assuming responsibility, and showing self-confidence

3. Intellectual abilities

   Thinking skills—gaining meaning and understanding (after hearing a story, for example) by remembering main topics or information

4. Language skills

   a. *Language production*—exhibiting normal vocabulary growth and patterns of sentence formation

   b. *Listening*—analyzing and comprehending what is heard

5. Experience background

   a. *Direct experiences*—taking part in in-school and out-of-school trips, watching and participating in demonstrations, observing and interacting with guest speakers

   b. *Vicarious experiences*—listening to stories, viewing films or filmstrips, sharing pictures, watching television, and so on

6. Perceptual skills

   a. *Visual discrimination and visual memory*—differentiating among letters of the alphabet or words and recalling such differences after time has passed

   b. *Auditory discrimination and auditory memory*—detecting differences in sounds among letters or words and recalling such differences after time has passed

   c. *Kinesthetic-tactile skills*—discriminating among qualities of objects (rough, smooth; heavy, light; hard, soft) using senses other than seeing or listening

Many of these categories of essential prerequisite reading competencies are discussed in other sections of this book, because they are as important for other areas of the preschool program as they are for reading (physical abilities, Chapters 5 and 6; social-emotional maturity, Chapters 3 and 4; intellectual abilities, Chapter 7; language skills, Chapter 8; experience background, Chapters 7 and 10; perceptual skills, previous topic in this chapter). So, readiness for learning any academic concept or skill is seen as the sum total of the entire preschool program, not as any single criterion such as age or symbol recognition by itself.

Judging the Success of Your Program

You can judge the degree to which your readiness program has been successful either through formal or informal means. On the basis of those results, you will usually be able to determine if additional readiness experiences are required for continued growth or whether some introductory reading activities can be planned.

Many experienced preschool teachers can judge readiness by directed observation, as the children are playing or participating in various activities. However, most teachers who prefer this method use some type of informal checklist to help them. The observation checklist in Figure 9-1 illustrates one form in which these can be constructed, and many other observation techniques are discussed in Chapter 14.

Some teachers prefer to combine observation techniques and intelligence tests with standardized readiness tests. Many factors are involved in readiness to learn, and these readiness tests offer a broad selection of items and materials for testing purposes. Some contain manipulative devices; others, kits of activities; while still others involve only paper-and-pencil items. Some address only a single dimension of readiness, such as intellectual development or letter recognition; others cover several areas, including social awareness. Of course, some are much more effective in measuring readiness than others—and most, by themselves, are far from adequate in giving the total readiness picture of the child. You may wish to examine and compare some popular readiness tests. Readiness tests, in general, are administered as group tests and typically include items such as these:

1. *Associating the spoken word with pictured objects.* Four or five pictures are displayed in a line across the page. The child must put a cross on the one spoken by the teacher. For example, "Put a cross on the *clown.*"

2. *Visual discrimination.* Four or five similar objects or shapes are shown in a row. The first one has a cross on it. One other picture or shape in the row is exactly like the first one. The child marks the identical picture or shape. For example,

3. *Sentence comprehension.* Before the child is a row of pictures. For example, a calendar, lawnmower, clock, and automobile may be illustrated in one row. The teacher may say, "Mary's mother told her to be home at two o'clock. Mark the picture that tells Mary the time to come home."

4. *Copying a design.* A series of geometric figures or alphabet letters serve as models. The child is to copy the model.

5. *Auditory discrimination.* A row of four or five pictures is placed on the page. At the left is a stimulus picture; for example, a *dog.* The child marks each picture that begins with the same sound; for example, *doll* and *duck.*

6. *Drawing a human figure.* By examining the amount of detail, the teacher can estimate the stage of the child's physical and mental development. See page 332 for examples.

7. *Ability to count and write numbers.* The child is asked to put a cross on a numeral; to mark the first, second, or third object in a row; or to solve a simple mathematical problem such as, "Marlene had four cookies and gave one to each of her two friends. Put a cross on the number that shows how many cookies Marlene had left."

After you have assessed a child's readiness through informal observation procedures and a standardized test (if desired), you should try to reinforce areas in which the child is weak or to begin instruction if the child is ready. Most children are not ready for beginning instruction until the kindergarten year; their intellectual, physical, social-emotional, and perceptual development shows they are not normally ready for it until then. All four areas must mesh—the child may suffer harmful results if he is pushed into reading instruction before he is ready. An exchange of letters between a concerned mother who was not sure that her son was ready for reading instruction and Dr. Louise Bates Ames, a prominent authority at the Gesell Institute of Child Development, illustrates this point *(New Haven Register).*

Dear Doctor:

We recently moved to this state. And I learned immediately from well-meaning

```
                        Reading Readiness Checklist


        _____        _____
               (Child's Name)                        (Date)
```

		Yes	No
I.	**Physical** <u>Readiness</u> The child is . . .		
	A. healthy and free from persistent illnesses?		
	B. able to hop, skip, jump, run, etc.?		
	C. able to manipulate blocks, scissors, puzzles?		
	D. able to grasp pencils, crayons?		
	E. able to dress and care for self?		
II.	**Social-Emotional** <u>Readiness</u> The child is . . .		
	A. willing to share with others?		
	B. able to work with others?		
	C. eager to listen to stories and look at books?		
	D. apparently enjoying school?		
	E. able to see a task to completion?		
III.	**Intellectual** <u>Readiness</u> The child . . .		
	A. knows the basic colors and shapes?		
	B. can count to 20?		
	C. recognizes his name?		
	D. knows own address and phone number?		
	E. orients himself in space, i.e., understands relative terms <u>near</u>, <u>far</u>; <u>up</u>, <u>down</u>; <u>big</u>, <u>small</u>; etc.?		
IV.	**Language** <u>Readiness</u> The child . . .		
	A. understands simple directions and requests?		
	B. pronounces words accurately?		
	C. likes to talk about books?		
	D. speaks in complete thought units?		
	E. enjoys discussions of stories and pictures?		
V.	**Perceptual** <u>Readiness</u> The child . . .		
	A. recognizes likenesses and differences among letters of the alphabet?		
	B. can hear likenesses and differences among sounds?		
	C. can repeat series of objects, pictures, sounds, etc.?		
	D. notices signs, labels, etc.?		
	E. can remember rhymes, jingles, story sequences, etc?		

VI.   Recommendation

From my observation of _____ during

the daily routine, I presently feel that this child is

ready   not ready   for formal instruction in reading.
<u>(underline one)</u>

Figure 9-1   *Sample of an informal observation form for assessing reading readiness*

friends that my son, Tabor, who will be six in December, is eligible for first grade. I was completely taken aback as he would not have been eligible in our home state and I have never considered a five and one-half year-old ready for the work of first grade.

I couldn't bring myself to register him for the first grade, even though all our friends and neighbors urged it. Instead I started him in kindergarten. To begin with, Tabor is not ready for a full day of school. And in the second place, he is still very babyish. He still enjoys a two-hour nap each afternoon. Still likes to sit on my lap. Is just beginning to show an interest in coloring and cutting out, and his interest span is very short.

I don't mean to imply that my boy is not real bright because he is—bright but babyish. But what have I to lose by waiting? Next year will be quite soon enough for him to go to school all day and to cope with the pressures which first grade brings.

Before you read the response of Dr. Ames, think of how you would react to such a letter if it were sent to you. Make a list of your points and compare your ideas to those of Dr. Ames. Her response was the following:

Go to the head of the class, Mother. Your good letter needs no elaboration from us. Would that the day might come soon when all mothers see things as you do and no babyish nap-taking little five-year-old boy is forced to attempt the work of first grade, regardless of what antiquated state and local laws may permit.

Tabor was *babyish, immature,* not *physically ready,* he had a *short attention span*— all factors that could be easily observed by his mother (or a teacher). However, if he were assessed only by a standardized intelligence or reading readiness test, this youngster might have been proclaimed "ready to read." The point is that *you* are an important source of determining the child's readiness—that readiness should be viewed as the *total preparation* for moving from one level of learning to another.

At some point, then, usually between the ages of five and seven, many children become ready to move from readiness programs to beginning reading instruction. Such instruction varies from program to program—in fact, some skills identified as beginning reading skills by one program are considered readiness skills by others (identifying letters of the alphabet, for example). To draw a line in a sound, developmental program and say where readiness ends and reading begins is difficult, but for this discussion, readiness activities will be considered all those experiences that precede teaching children to recognize and understand the letters of the alphabet, words, and combinations of words.

Beginning Reading

Beginning reading programs can be broken down into two major categories, each reflecting an opposing view of how children should be introduced to words. On the one hand are those who structure instruction in ways that closely resemble natural language learning. Instead of focusing on sounds or letters, these theoreticians stress the teaching of whole words or complete thought patterns through labeling, experience stories, and play-type activities. On the other hand are theoreticians who view reading instruction as the process of helping children acquire separate, identifiable skills, beginning with the sounds of letters through structured, carefully sequenced activities. In this latter context, reading occurs after children learn patterned responses.

Informal Approaches to Beginning Reading Educators who use informal approaches follow instructional techniques that use whole words and sentences in contexts where children are able to use and understand them. These techniques are based upon the idea that children possess a natural potential for reading that is tapped when direct experiences create an intense desire to communicate thoughts and feelings to others through the printed word. Several types of techniques are used in preschool or kindergarten classrooms to provide informal experiences for the children, but perhaps the most popular are labeling activities, experience stories, and play-type activities.

Children are thrilled when they begin to recognize words, especially if the first word they recognize is their own name. You can help children recognize their names as well as other key words through a variety of *labeling activities*—such as those given in the box.

The *language experience approach* is often initiated with four- and five-year-olds. In this approach the teacher capitalizes on a direct experience and writes about it as it is dictated by a child or group of children. When children begin to recognize their spoken words in print, the experience chart becomes their first reading experience. The basic reading skills of word recognition and comprehension can be taught through follow-up activities to an experience story. The sequence shown in the "Experience Stories" box is recommended for use in the preschool or kindergarten classroom.

As the children gain experience with language charts, they will begin to recognize more and more words. Many preschool and kindergarten teachers use this approach because:

- It is firmly based on each child's background of direct experience.
- It uses familiar vocabulary and sentence patterns—the child's own.
- It introduces the printed word as "talk written down."
- It encourages the child to think.

Detractors argue that the language experience approach has several limitations; among these are:

- It lacks sequential skill development procedures.

- It is too unstructured for an inexperienced teacher to use as a main approach.
- It may introduce vocabulary that is too difficult or irregular.
- It relies heavily on a variety of direct experiences—which many schools are unable to provide.

Teachers using informal approaches to reading instruction often supplement their programs with varieties of *play-type* instructional materials. The teacher's basic role is similar to the role explained earlier in the reading readiness section but within a context of actual reading rather than of readiness. The idea behind this type of program is that through active involvement with manipulative activities the child will naturally draw out understandings from the materials. The teacher, of course, draws on every opportunity to ask the child questions and to help the child verbalize patterns and relationships he intuitively learned but was unable to clearly define. Some examples of the countless numbers of manipulative reading materials are given in the "Play-type Activities" box.

As a means of extending the children's reading interests to books, preschool teachers often arrange books and children's magazines in a special area of the room. Usually, the area is in a quiet section of the room where the children may go to comfortably look through the available reading materials. You may wish to arrange such an area where the lighting is especially good—near windows, if possible. If windows do not allow enough light into the area, consider bringing in old table or floor lamps to add a homey touch. Along that same line, some teachers arrange the reading corner similar to a cozy room, with carpeting, sofas, lounge chairs, rockers, tables, pillows, and so on. One enterprising teacher bought an old bathtub at an auction sale, painted it bright red, threw in a few cushions and stuffed animals, and placed it in the reading corner.

LABELING ACTIVITIES

1. On the first day of school, you may want to construct nametags for each child. Cut silhouetted shapes (of fish, birds, kittens, and so on) out of construction paper, print each child's name on one, and pin it to the child. Children take great pride in their nametags and enjoy looking for likenesses and differences among their own tags and those of their friends.

2. Label each child's storage box, locker, or coat hook with his name. On the first days of school, you may want to take each child's photograph with an instant camera, mount it on durable tagboard, print the child's name under it, and scatter all the labeled pictures on the floor. Ask the children, one at a time, to find their own tag, and take it to the locker where an aide can hang it. This procedure can be extended by informally including other reading skills—for example, "Jana did a wonderful job finding her name. Now, let's have someone whose name begins just like Jana . . . J . . . J . . . find his or hers. That's just great, Jimmy, you really did fine."

3. Write the child's name on a piece of finished artwork. Repeatedly exposing the child to his name is sure to help him in recalling it, and the child takes pride in seeing his name on something he created. When labeling, try to put the name in the upper left-hand corner so the child will become used to looking at that part of a page whenever he begins to read.

4. Label objects in the classroom, but only when these objects have the most meaning. For example, if new gerbils are brought into the classroom and the children's interest in the new additions is high, you may wish to print the word *gerbils* clearly on a bright piece of paper and attach it to the shelf on which the gerbil cage is placed. Discuss the word with the children. If the children decide to name the gerbils, you may want to print their names on a label and place it, too, near the cage. Labels like this can be made for a flower, the fish, the book area, and so on. Instead of simply placing the labels on the wall and seeing them receive no further attention, you may periodically take them away and see if your children are able to find out where each should be returned.

5. At times, children in a dramatic play area may ask you to provide certain labels for them as they try to make their play a bit more realistic. For example, one group of children set up an ice cream store and were about to open for business when they realized they needed a name for their store and a listing of the available flavors. So the teacher made a sign for the shop and listed the flavors: chocolate, vanilla, strawberry, and butterscotch. This variation of a labeling activity had real meaning for the children involved.

6. For snack time, use placemats made from wallpaper samples and label each mat with a child's name. Change the location of the placemats daily and encourage the children to find where their own is located. As the children begin to recognize each other's names, they may (one or two at a time) take turns arranging the placements for the entire group.

You can imagine the attention this lounging device received. Plants, aquariums, brightly decorated walls, or soft music add a comfortable touch to the area. All of this aside, though, the most important component of a reading area is a selection of good books. The following are some guidelines for choosing books.

1. Check the illustrations. They should be attractive, colorful, and simple in detail.

2. Examine the plot. It should be uncomplicated and directed toward things that interest young children, that is, repetition, catchy phrases, humor, action, rhyme, and a great deal of conversation.

3. Make sure the books are easy to handle. They should be easy for the children to hold, the construction should be of good quality paper and binding, and the pages should be easy to turn.

By making a reading area readily accessible to young children, the teacher following an informal approach extends the learnings acquired through other activities and helps the child to develop interest in books and reading.

Structured Approaches to Beginning Reading Structured approaches to reading instruction are not new, but they are receiving

EXPERIENCE STORIES

1. The teacher provides a direct experience that interests the children and stimulates them to talk informally.

2. The children dictate their ideas and feelings to the teacher, who writes them on chart paper (18 inches × 36 inches) exactly as they were spoken.

3. As each child's words are recorded, the teacher reads them back to the group, emphasizing left-to-right progression.

4. After each child has had an opportunity to contribute, the teacher reads the entire story back to the group.

5. The teacher may ask the children to read from the chart. Some may read only the title or a word. Others may be able to read the entire sentence they contributed as the teacher points to each word.

6. The teacher may use follow-up activities:
   a. "Find the sentence that Sharon told us."
   b. Hold up a card containing a key word in the story and see if anyone can recognize it on the chart.
   c. Ask questions to check on comprehension; for example, "What color are the hamster's eyes?"

7. Some children may like to illustrate the story when it is complete. The teacher should write the story title and the child's name at the top of the paper.

8. Some children may want to tell a related story as a result of the illustrating experience. Write down the words as the child says them on the space below the illustration or on a separate piece of paper.

9. Illustrated experience stories, from either the chart paper or individual illustrations, make attractive and interesting "library books" when they are given attractive covers and placed in an area where they are readily available to the children.

> **OUR HAMSTER**
>
> James said, "We have a pet hamster. His name is Fluffy."
>
> Joan said "He has brown fur and big brown eyes."
>
> Carmen said, "Fluffy is a funny hamster."
>
> Jackson said, "He always scratches and digs."
>
> Faith said, "We love Fluffy."

a great deal of attention, especially from teachers of children with learning problems. Through teaching machines or books, reading skills that are to be learned are subdivided into small units and organized sequentially, proceeding from simple skills to more complex ones (usually starting with letters, moving to combinations of letters, and eventually to words).

An example of one early reading system using a programmed approach is the Sullivan-Buchanan programmed material published by the Webster Division of McGraw-Hill Book Company. This program was designed especially for children who were able to respond to a programmed sequence in booklet form. The material consists of a series of sequenced workbooks through which the children move

PLAY-TYPE ACTIVITIES

Word Jars   Collect a number of objects small enough so that each fits easily into a baby food jar (coin, toy car, yarn, marble, eraser, paper, and so on). Place one object in each jar. Make a word label for each jar from heavy tagboard and encourage the children to place the appropriate word card in front of each jar.

Color Worms   Make a worm such as the one illustrated with each white construction paper segment having a color word printed on it. Make matching segments from colored construction paper so that they can be matched to the color names.

Word Match   Rule two pieces of tagboard into nine squares each. Draw or paste a picture in each square of the first sheet. For each picture, print a word on the second sheet. Cut the first sheet into separate squares, mix them, and encourage the children to place the pictures on the appropriate words.

Word Match   Make a 6-inch wheel from tagboard and place pictures of familiar objects around it. Laminate the wheel so that it is more durable. Print the word for each object on clothespins and mix them in a box. The children match the clothespins to the appropriate pictures.

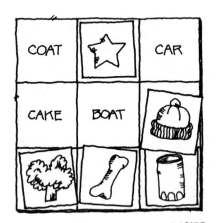

WORD MATCH SQUARE

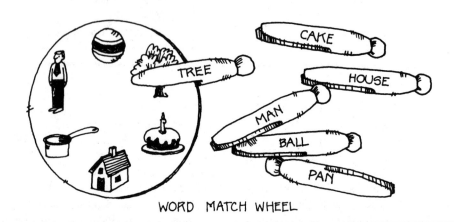

WORD MATCH WHEEL

Children are thrilled when they recognize their first word—usually their own names.

at their own individual rates of speed, beginning with the readiness material and progressing through beginning reading activities.

Beginning reading instruction starts when the children have demonstrated these identified readiness skills: (1) a knowledge of the alphabet and an ability to print upper and lowercase letters; (2) an ability to associate sounds with the letters *a, f, m, n, p, t, th,* and *i;* (3) the ability to recognize the words *yes, no, ant, man,* and *mat;* and (4) the ability to read the sentence *I am an ant.* These capabilities are required because the child progresses independently at his own rate with the first programmed booklet, and he must be able to make word choices about pictures of a *man, mat,* and an *ant* in order to begin. Figure 9-2 shows the first two pages of the programmed reader. The material increases in difficulty as the child adds new words to his vocabulary in much the same way as illustrated.

Another structured early reading program is the teacher-guided Distar® instructional system, published by Science Research Associates, Inc. The authors, Siegfried Engelmann and Elaine C. Bruner (1969), started with the idea that children will learn those concepts and skills that they should know, only if those concepts and skills are directly taught. In groups of four to ten children, the teacher is responsible for carrying out the direct instruction leading to the development of effective reading skills. Engelmann and Bruner advise the teacher that their direct approach can best be carried out if the following techniques are used:

1. Act as if you are having fun. Show off: "I can do it. Watch me. Don't you wish you could do it like that?"

2. React to the children. Act as if their accomplishments are big deals, because

Figure 9-2 *First pages of the Sullivan-Buchanan programmed reader*
(Reprinted from Programmed Reading, *Book 1A by C. D. Buchanan, copyright 1973, with permission of Webster/McGraw-Hill, New York, N.Y.)*

Figure 9-2 *(continued)*

for the children they are: "Did you see the way Irma did that? I didn't think she could do it, but she sure fooled me."

3. Give the children who are working hard some form of reinforcement. If praise does not seem sufficient, introduce privileges or tangible reinforcers: "John worked so hard today that he's going to get to erase the board. Good work, John. That's the rule: If you work hard, you get a handshake."

4. When children are working on difficult tasks, use tasks that are more fun as contingencies: "Tell you what: If you do a good job on this task, I'm going to let you do one of those stories where you get to see the pictures."

5. Treat the Take-Homes [homework assignments] as payoffs: "John worked so hard today that I'm going to give him a Take-Home. Tell me what it says, John, and you can take it home. I've never seen so many children get Take-Homes. You really work hard, don't you? And are you ever lucky, getting to take this home and show your mother."

6. Use a change of pace in your presentation: "Let's do it again, this time with great big voices.... Again.... Again.... Wow, what big voices! Now shhhhhhh. Listen." Pause. "Listen." Pause. "Let's rhyme with man.... What are we going to rhyme with?..." [p. 14]

Each reading lesson is highly teacher-directed and involves a great deal of verbal interaction between the teacher and the child. In the beginning phases of reading instruction, nine basic sounds are taught. The first is *a* (as in *and*), which is followed by *m, s, ē* (as in *eat*), *r, d, f, i* (as in *in*), and *th* (as in *this*). Here is an example of the technique the teacher uses to teach a combination of sounds to the children:

"Say it fast and I'll show you the picture. Listen." The children are inattentive. The teacher surreptitiously turns the page and looks at the picture. She laughs. "I like that picture. Who wants to see the picture?" Some of the children raise their hands.

"O.K., everybody listen." Most of the children attend. "Listen." All the children are attending. "Listen." The teacher pauses and slowly raises her index finger. All the children are attending. "Now you're listening. Listen: mmmaaa (pause) nnn. Say it fast! I can do it: man. Listen again: mmmaaa (pause) nnn. Say it fast: man. Your turn. Listen: mmmaaa (pause) nnn. Say it fast!" Some of the children say mmmaaannn. The teacher smiles at them. "Say it fast!" Some of the children again say mmmaaannn. Somewhat more demandingly, the teacher says, "Say it fast!" Again some of the children say mmmaaannn. The teacher says, "I can do it: mmmaaa (pause) nnn. Say it fast: man." She says the word *man* very fast. She acts pleased. That's saying it fast. "That's right. mmmaaannn. Say it fast: man." She turns to one of the children who had trouble with the response. "Did you see the way Irma said it fast? Watch, Irma, listen. This is for you: mmmaaa (pause) nnn. Say it fast!" The child produces the correct response. The teacher applauds and addresses the child who had trouble with the task. "Wasn't that good? Irma and I are the only ones here who can do that. We're really smart." Some of the other children object, saying that they too can say it fast. "Let's see. Everybody listen." Pause. "Listen: mmmaaa (pause) nnn. Say it fast!" Almost all the children respond correctly. "Yes, that's saying it fast. Let's do it one more time. Listen: mmmaaa (pause) nnn." One of the children interrupts saying "man." The teacher holds up her hand. "Wait! Don't tell me until I say 'Say it fast!' Listen: mmmaaa (pause) nnn." Pause and smile. "Say it fast!" Children respond loudly, "Oh, that was tough. I made you wait a long time. Let's see if you can wait a real long time. Remember—don't say the word until I say 'Say it fast!' Listen: mmmaaa (pause) nnn. Say it fast!" All the children respond appropriately. "Oh, that was so good." [p. 15]

The Distar® Reading program differs greatly from most preschool or kindergarten programs, in its step-by-step approach to acquiring basic reading skills. Results from research studies across the country have reported outstanding gains in reading effectiveness for children exposed to the Distar® instructional system. Teachers who have used the Distar® Reading program are highly enthusiastic about its results and are convinced of its value, especially when used with the mentally retarded, learning disabled, and children with other special needs.

Educators advocating a structured approach to beginning reading instruction support their methods as having these advantages:

- It works directly with the skills that need to be mastered and eliminates the time wasted on extraneous skills.

- It can stimulate the learner to elicit an automatic response.

- It leads to self-direction.

- It saves teacher time.

Those who oppose behavioral-based instruction present these arguments:

- It can be confusing if the program is not well developed.

- It puts an emphasis on the child's mechanistic performance.

- It assumes that if the child merely pronounces a word, he will automatically know its meaning.

- It presupposes that all children need to go through the same sequence of learning experiences.

HANDWRITING

Earlier in this chapter, you read about the intimacy of the listening–speaking relationship as the child gradually learns the language system of her particular culture. Likewise, an equal degree of correlation exists between two other communicative skills—reading (an input skill) and writing (an output skill)—as the children make their transition from spontaneous talk to graphic representations of talk. For example, consider the processes of labeling or constructing experience charts as discussed under the topic of reading. When the teacher writes down the children's exact words and the children read them back with the help of the teacher, the children begin to make the connection between listening, talking, reading, and writing. This is an important first step in learning to read *and* write, for children at this stage of development are just becoming aware of the idea that words are units of language. When children see these spoken words written down, their natural curiosity takes control and stimulates great interest in the printed word. Such interest is important in developing reading skills and is equally essential in generating spontaneous attempts to write. Should we teach children to *write* in the preschool or kindergarten setting? Is it reasonable to expect youngsters to recognize letters, to examine the parts of letters, or to accurately reproduce the straight lines and curves required by most handwriting programs?

Maria Montessori addressed those concerns when she wrote:

> Why . . . should we not write independently of such analysis. . .?
>
> It would be sad if we could *speak* only *after* we had studied grammar! It would be much the same as demanding before we *looked* at the stars in the firmament, we must study infinitesimal calculus; it is much the same thing to feel that before teaching an idiot to write, we must make him understand the abstract derivation of lines and the problems of geometry!
>
> No less are we to be pitied if, in order to write, we must follow analytically the parts constituting the alphabetical signs. [1964, p. 259]

What Montessori (1964) envisioned in place of analytical writing was handwriting instruction based on the *natural* growth characteristics of young children: "If I had thought of giving a name to this new method of writing, I should have called it . . . the *anthropological method*. Certainly, my studies in anthropology inspired the method, but experience has given me, as a surprise, another title which seems to me the natural one, "the method of *spontaneous* writing" (p. 260). Montessori's method of *spontaneous writing* involved planning a period of sensory experiences prior to the actual handwriting activity. During this prewriting phase, the children experienced repeated activities in which they exercised their hands in preparation for writing. Prewriting activities included sewing, weaving, and the manipulation of learning materials—all activities requiring children to use their fingers in ways similar to those used in writing. Once the children gained control over their large and small arm and hand muscles, Montessori (1964) introduced them to the writing process with only one special technique: "Seeing that I had already taught the children to touch the contours of . . . plane geometric insets, I had now only to teach them to touch with their fingers the *forms of the letters of the alphabet*" (p. 261). This procedure of tracing the forms of textured letters with the fingers, according to Montessori, led to *muscular memory* and superior penmanship because the correct letter forms were fixed within the child's neural framework. From this point on, says Montessori (1964), "Writing is very quickly learned, because we begin to teach it only to those children who show a desire for it by spontaneous attention to the lesson given by the directress to other children, or by watching the exercises in which the others are occupied" (p. 293). In general, Montessori found that by advancing through this procedure, *all* children by *four years* of age were intensely interested in writing and *some* children began to write by the age of *three and a half!* An example of writing done in pen and ink by a child of five years is shown in Figure 9-3.

Writing Readiness

Montessori described that period during which the child exhibits a spontaneous interest in writing as a *sensitive period*. This means that previous experiences have developed the prerequisite skills and motivation necessary for making a new learning task a successful, anticipated part of each child's life. In much the same way, we use the term *readiness* to describe the point at which previous experiences have resulted in the development of appropriate skills and attitudes necessary for beginning handwriting instruction. Some children may possess the prerequisite skills for handwriting when they enter the preschool classroom but others may not. For those who are ready for writing, we must know the types of learning activities considered appropriate for beginning writing; for those who are not ready, we must know the kinds of activities considered most appropriate to making them so. The following checklist contains key criteria that should be observed while judging whether or not any particular child is at the point where he can benefit from writing instruction:

HANDWRITING EVALUATION CHECKLIST

1. Uses crayons, scissors, brushes, and pencils easily?

2. Copies simple shapes?

3. Demonstrates established handedness?

4. Demonstrates interest in reading and writing?

5. Exhibits large and small muscle coordination?

6. Perceives likenesses and differences in sizes and shapes of objects?

7. Displays an attention span necessary for persisting at a new learning task?

Because some educators perceive handwriting as a *graphic art* (drawing letters) as well as a *tool of communication* (expressing

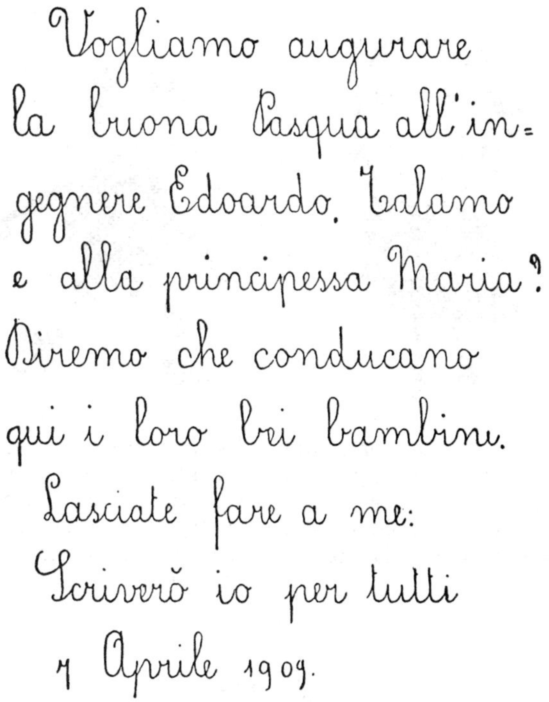

*Vogliamo augurare
la buona Pasqua all'in-
gegnere Edoardo Talamo
e alla principessa Maria?
Diremo che conducano
qui i loro bei bambini.
Lasciate fare a me:
Scriverò io per tutti
7 Aprile 1909.*

Figure 9-3 *Example of writing done with pen and ink by a child of five years. Translation: "We would like to wish a joyous Easter to the civil engineer Edoardo Talamo and the Princess Maria. We will ask them to bring their pretty children here. Leave it to me: I will write for all. April 7, 1909."*
(Reproduced by permission of Schocken Books, Inc., New York, N.Y., from The Montessori Method *by Maria Montessori, 1964).*

ideas), the skill a child attains in drawing is often used as a second source of predicting whether or not he will have success when he begins handwriting. Figure 9-4 shows crayon drawings done by kindergartners at various stages of mental and physical development considered appropriate for beginning handwriting instruction. It is advised that handwriting instruction be delayed until levels *d* and *e* are attained. Some children, of course, will be at those levels when they are four years old, and some won't be even in the first and second grades. Whatever the specific case, however, handwriting instruction should be delayed until the child has reflected the maturity characterized by levels *d* and *e*.

For the child who is judged *not* ready to write, and the great majority of your children will not be ready by the end of kindergarten, a planned program of activities can contribute to the development of skills prerequisite to handwriting. The prewriting activities usually parallel other areas of the curriculum that stress perceptual skills and muscular control. See the "Prewriting Activities" box.

Keep a watchful eye for relevant scribbles in the children's work and be sure to make appropriate comments that focus on special significant movements. For example, "You spent a lot of time on your drawing—I liked the way you made the lines go up and down."

a

Only a suggestion of form is evident; many details are missing; control of crayon is erratic.

b

Lack of perception of the relationship of the parts to the whole is apparent; details are missing; some details are overelaborated.

c

Keener observation of form is noticeable; significant details are included, such as ears, arms, hands; hair placement is more accurate.

d

An awareness of the relationship of the parts to the whole is shown; many details such as eyebrows, fingers, neck, and shoulders are included; broad strokes of the crayon are used consistently.

e

An understanding of body proportions is revealed; a variety of details makes a realistic picture; good crayon manipulation is evident.

Figure 9-4 *Forms drawn by children at various stages of maturity*
(From Handwriting in Kindergarten, *Seattle Public Schools, Seattle, WA, 1978. Used with permission.)*

PREWRITING ACTIVITIES

1. For development of perceptual skills and fine muscle control, collect a variety of sizes of nuts and bolts. Encourage the children to choose a bolt and find the matching nut. Then have them screw the nut onto the appropriate bolt.

2. Also for the development of perceptual skills and fine muscle control, select wooden inlay puzzles with small knobs on each piece for the children to grasp as they pick them up. These knobs encourage the children to coordinate the use of the two fingers and thumb in much the same way as they must be coordinated to hold a pencil properly.

3. Other manipulative experiences include:

    a. playing with building blocks

    b. working with clay or play dough

    c. painting, drawing, cutting, pasting, and coloring

    d. working with pegboards, Lincoln logs, tinker toys, and so on

    e. all of the physically oriented activities described in other sections of this book

4. Assist the children to develop sound overall language skills. Read them stories, show them pictures, label objects, create language experience charts. Ask them to describe objects, play games that require speaking and listening, retell stories, and, generally, play with their language. Specific suggestions for such activities are explained earlier in this chapter and in Chapter 8.

5. Encourage children to scribble at the art corner with crayons or paint. While scribbling, children often use strokes that are basic to letter formation even though they may not truly be making the letter itself. Children enjoy making large scribbles—either circular or up and down—that cover a whole paper when they paint or draw. You should see most of the nine basic strokes of writing (Figure 9-5) in the child's painting.

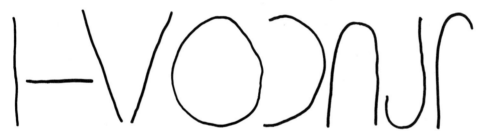

Figure 9-5 *Nine basic strokes of manuscript writing*

Or, "You drew some very nice circles—I'm so proud of you because that's very hard to do." The scribbler gains a great deal of pride by listening to such comments and begins to develop secure feelings about his growing muscular control and his various lines or shapes. As the children gain more and more experience and become increasingly interested in language, they will soon begin to attach names to their scribbles. For example, one little girl came up to her teacher with marks like these on her paper: "I can write!" exclaimed the girl. "Please tell me what you wrote," requested the teacher. "That's how my dad writes his name," said the girl. Although the girl certainly did not actually "write" her father's name, she was beginning to show a transitional progression from random scribbling toward purposeful handwriting instruction.

Notice the circles, half-circles, straight lines, and diagonal lines contained in this child's drawing. Such figures are basic to beginning letter formation.

Initial Handwriting Experiences

When children begin to show such interest in handwriting and are sufficiently mature in other significant areas of development, they are probably ready to write. The first word that most children want to write is their own name. The primary reason for this, of course, is that their names have such strong personal meaning. But we must remember too that the child sees his name more than any other word. You put it on his artwork, his storage locker, on his belongings, and on anything that goes home—so he also begins to copy it because it's familiar.

_Steven, a fairly advanced kindergartner, was especially busy at the painting easel this morn-_ing. _Using a paintbrush, he was studiously observing his name and reproducing each of the letters with green paint. Working slowly and methodically, Steven dipped his brush, studied a letter, and copied it onto his drawing. Letter by letter he was doing a reasonably good job of copying his name from another drawing of his that had been labeled by the teacher. Carefully, he plodded along:_ Stevon

As is often the case, Steven's beginning effort had some letters pointing backwards (reversals) and some of the other letters weren't exactly true to form.

These kinds of problems are very common and are simply indicative of most beginning efforts. The child has not yet learned the individual letters in his name—he is just copying from a model by reproducing its shape, and his visual skills may not be developed enough to allow greater accuracy. This manipulative and exploratory stage is an important part of beginning writing instruction. From such experimentation, handwriting is effectively born.

As children gain additional practice, these errors should gradually disappear. The type of initial practice provided, though, should be directed toward experimentation and manipulation rather than toward formal worksheets or handwriting guides. Since the child developed his interest in writing in a free and natural manner, it logically follows that initial handwriting experiences should follow a similar path. Initial experiences should involve a great deal of large muscle movement (in easel drawing or similar pursuits), which doesn't cause strain as does the sudden demand for small muscle control, which is necessary for writing with crayons or pencils. Such a transition should be gradual and carefully planned by the teacher. Some suggestions for beginning experiences are given in the box labeled "Initial Handwriting Experiences." In all cases, the visual image of the letter or word must be

These children are learning the basic letter forms by combining a set of curves and straight lines to construct letter shapes on a set of cards.

present so the child will have a model to reproduce, although the model need not be reproduced exactly.

As motivating experiences are provided for the beginner, he will develop a deeply satisfying feeling toward handwriting. This initially positive feeling is extremely important since the attitudes children develop at this early age strongly affect the degree to which they will meet related challenges later in their schooling.

As the children meet words other than their own names, especially in labels and experience stories, they will want to write them.

A group of five-year-olds had just completed an experience story about their trip to the zoo. The teacher, sensing the children's interest, asked each child who had contributed a thought to the chart to draw a picture of their idea. All children began working busily except Judy. The teacher was puzzled, and walked over to Judy to assess the situation. Judy informed her

teacher with determination, "I think I'll write what I said instead of draw it." The teacher, pleased with Judy's enthusiasm, took her to a table near the completed experience story and gave her an 18-inch × 24-inch sheet of newsprint paper and a large, soft lead pencil. Judy grasped the pencil, looked at the first word of her statement, and began to write her first sentence.

Judy took parts of a previous meaningful experience and personally joined them into a new learning experience. Children like Judy tend to spend large amounts of time sitting and copying when they are motivated at this stage.

Be careful to praise children for efforts such as Judy's. It is only too easy to approach a child at the beginning stages of handwriting development with statements like: "Your *m* looks like an *n*" or "Your capital letters should be bigger than your small letters." Remember that the child is only *beginning* and that such

INITIAL HANDWRITING EXPERIENCES

1. Let the children mold letters from modeling clay.

2. Provide smooth fingerpaint as a manipulative, sensorily stimulating writing medium.

3. Cut letters out of sandpaper and encourage the children to run their fingers over the shapes. Such feeling helps the children to remember the shapes of the letters when they draw them.

4. Spread colorful terrarium sand on the bottom of a shoe box lid. Encourage children to print words by running their index finger through the sand.

5. Ask the children to complete letter puzzles. Cut the letters comprising a child's name into two separate pieces. Ask the children to put the pieces together.

6. Provide many opportunities for the child to experiment and explore with a wide variety of writing materials: paint, chalkboard, large pencils, large crayons, fingerpaints, unlined 12 inches × 18 inches writing paper, and so on.

Secret Message

Lay waxed paper over plain drawing paper. Draw a geometric shape, a numeral, a letter, a word, a child's name, or a simple message on the waxed paper making sure you press hard as you do so. Give the drawing paper to a child, who then brushes watercolor over the paper. The watercolor will not stick to the clear wax, and the child will be able to guess the geometric shape, numeral, or whatever. (This activity is especially good at Halloween.)

Name Game

Cut a number of 1-inch squares from heavy cardboard. Print each child's name on the squares (one letter to a square). Draw squares on an envelope and print the child's name on the squares (again, one letter to a square). Put the cut-out squares inside the envelope. Have the child pour the letters from the envelope and match them to the name on the outside of the envelope.

Palm Trace

Provide a paintbrush and water soluble paint. Have children work in pairs. One child shuts her eyes as the other child traces a letter or numeral on her palm with the brush. The first child calls out the name of the letter or number and then looks to see if she was right.

Name Cookies

Cut out enough 3-inch letter shapes for each child in your group to have his first initial. Cover each letter with aluminum foil and give them to the children. Have the children mold cookie dough over the aluminum letters

CHILDREN WRITE IN EACH GUESSED LETTER ON THE CORRESPONDING PARTITION OF THE WORKSHEET

and put them into the oven. The children can paint their cookies with frosting when they come out of the oven.

Hint: Baking supply shops or variety shops often have letter or numeral cookie cutters.

Feel the Letter (or Numeral)

Get a carton that has partitions in it (such as a wine case). Stand it on its side, with the open partitions facing you.

Attach a piece of fabric to the top of each section of the carton, so that the fabric covers the open front of that section. On separate index cards, paste letters made from various materials, such as an *A* from sandpaper, a *B* from aluminum foil, and so on. Put one card on the bottom of each section of the carton.

Have a child reach into one of the sections and try to determine through his sense of touch which letter of the alphabet is on the card. You could place a worksheet with corresponding partitions at the learning area so that the children can write down the letter they chose for each section.

Letter Bags

Prepare eight drawstring bags and number them one through eight. Make or buy sturdy cardboard letters (or numerals). Place one letter in each bag.

Have a child place her hand into one of the bags and try to identify the letter by touch. She then takes a dittoed worksheet and circles the letter she believes to be in that bag. When all the bags are done, the teacher may check the worksheet.

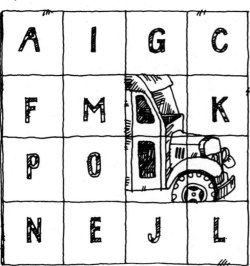

Letter Carrots

Cut carrot and leaf forms from orange and green tagboard, respectively. On the leaf form, print each of the lowercase letters; on the carrot form, print each of the uppercase letters. Put the carrots in one box and the leaves in another. Have the children take a carrot from one box and choose from the other a leaf form to match it.

Mitten Match

Using wallpaper samples or gift-wrapping paper mounted on heavy tagboard, cut out many pairs of mittens, each pair with one uppercase and one lowercase form of a letter. Put the mittens in a box and have the children match left and right mitten pairs.

Puzzle-Picture Letters

Cut a piece of tagboard 12 inches square. Divide it into sixteen 3-inch squares. Print a capital letter on each square. Cut another piece of 12- × 12-inch tagboard exactly like the first and divide it the same way. Put the two pieces face-to-face and identify which boxes on the second square match the boxes on the first square. Then, turning the second tagboard back toward you, print a corresponding small letter in each box. Draw or paste a large, colorful picture on the back of this second tagboard, and cut it into sixteen 3-inch squares. Mix up the squares. Have the children pick up a square, match it to the appropriate capital letter, and place it face down on the capital letter. They continue in this way until a puzzle picture appears.

problems will disappear with time. Be patient with your guidance. Focus on correctly formed letters rather than on mistakes. If these problems persist over a period of time and do not improve with your concerted efforts, then you may wish to initiate remedial instruction—but don't panic with four-, five-, or six-year-olds.

You must realize that some letters are more difficult to make than are others. This is why your children may be having more difficulty with certain letters. Edward R. and Hilda P. Lewis (1964) conducted a study to determine which letters cause children most difficulty. The following list, which combines capital and small letters, shows their results. The letters are listed from most difficult to easiest.

1. q	14. U	27. K	40. F
2. g	15. M	28. W	41. P
3. p	16. S	29. A	42. E
4. y	17. b	30. N	43. X
5. j	18. e	31. C	44. I
6. m	19. r	32. f	45. v
7. k	20. z	33. J	46. i
8. u	21. n	34. w	47. D
9. a	22. s	35. h	48. H
10. G	23. Q	36. T	49. O
11. R	24. B	37. x	50. L
12. d	25. t	38. c	51. o
13. Y	26. Z	39. V	52. l

[pp. 855–858]

As you can see, the letters that descend—*q, g, p, y,* and so on—are the most difficult. The easiest letters seem to be those that are either straight lines or circles. Primarily for this reason, you may see children use capital letters only in some words, mix capitals and smalls in others, or use all small letters in other words: LOVE, cAt, it.

In addition to providing a comfortable, accepting environment as they guide children's initial handwriting efforts, teachers are also models for good handwriting habits. Many teachers fear this responsibility because they are apprehensive about their own handwriting skills. This is an unfounded fear simply because all writing done by the teacher for

experience charts, labels, thank you notes, and so on is manuscript (printing) writing. Figure 9-6 illustrates model uppercase and lowercase manuscript letters. You will notice that they are all formed from the simple basic nine strokes described earlier in this section: The first five letters are a combination of circles (or circle parts) and straight lines. Make five circles like this ⬭⬭⬭⬭⬭ and then add the line segments or subtract the circle segments to form the first five letters: a b c d e.

The other letters can be easily made with similar rudimentary strokes. With only a few hours of practice on a tablet or on large chart paper, you should become skilled enough to be a good model for your children.

The Zaner-Bloser alphabet model illustrated in Figure 9-6 is, perhaps, the most popular alphabet model suggested for use with young children because it so closely approximates the letter forms they see in the books they read. Recently, however, a second writing program has emerged and is gaining widespread popularity. That program, *D'Nealian*™, is a system of handwriting instruction developed by the Scott, Foresman Company as a K-8 program. Basically, it is a system that moves away from the traditional circle and straight-line manuscript forms toward a flowing, rhythmic system of letter forms. If you carefully examine the D'Nealian™ manuscript in Figure 9-7, you should notice that each letter is made with a continuous stroke, except for the dotted letters *i* and *j* and the crossed letters *f, t,* and *x*. Aside from the flowing, rhythmic advantage, the developers of the D'Nealian™ handwriting system point out that even first-grade teachers find that their children are motivated to begin a transition to cursive writing—the way "big people" write.

In summary, handwriting experiences should be provided only for those children who demonstrate a readiness for it. Instruction should initially encourage large, free strokes in which the child attempts to copy a

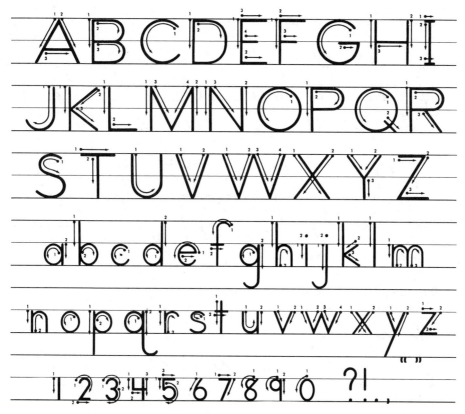

Figure 9-6 *Manuscript alphabet*
(Used with permission from Creative Growth With Handwriting. *Second Edition. Copyright ©*
1979. Zaner-Bloser, Inc., Columbus, Ohio.)

word of particular significance to him. Practice and reinforcement of this skill should be given through a variety of concrete, sensory experiences. Gradually, the child will begin to develop increased coordination and skill and will begin writing with crayons or large beginners' pencils on writing paper. Capital and small letters may be mixed, letter proportions may be off, and words and letters may be scattered over the paper—but remember that the children are still at a very early stage of developing a very difficult skill. Give careful guidance by praising the child for good efforts and not stifling motivation with undue criticism or nagging corrections.

Finally, you assume a key responsibility as a model for good manuscript writing. Much of what the children write (their name, labels, experience charts) will be copied from something you wrote. Therefore, you will want to develop a skill and ease in manuscript writing so your children will have a proper model to imitate.

Most children, at least by the end of kindergarten, will be able to write their names and a few other meaningful words. They will do so with great differences in individual ability and interest but, for those children who are willing and able, the preschool or kindergarten is a good place to start.

D'Nealian™ Manuscript Alphabet

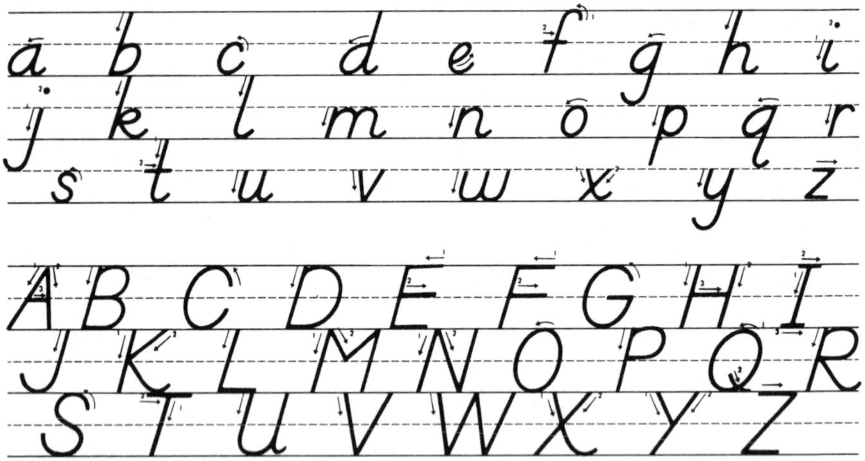

D'Nealian™ Cursive Alphabet

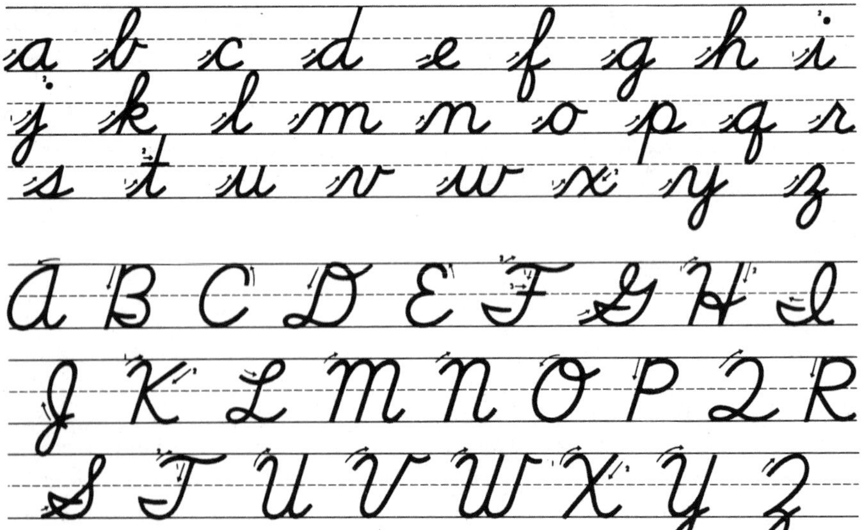

D'Nealian™ Numbers

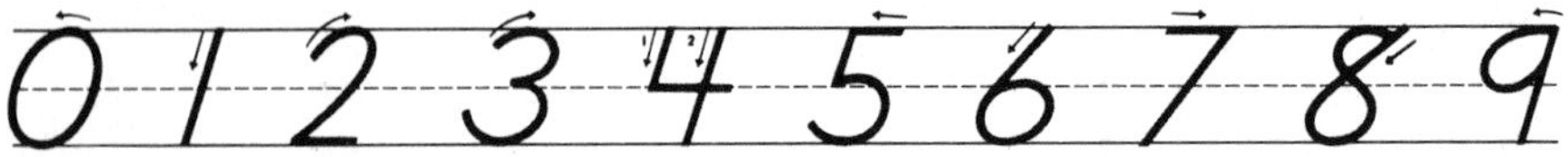

Figure 9-7 *D'Nealian™ manuscript*

(Used with permission from Scott, Foresman D'Nealian™ Handwriting. *Scott, Foresman and Company, Glenview, IL.)*

D'Nealian™ Handwriting, Book 2. © Scott, Foresman and Company.

MATHEMATICS

Each day in early childhood settings children learn mathematics whether or not it involves learning to add or even learning to count. Some of the first concepts these children master are those involved in daily routines such as saying to the child, "You may have *two* cookies if you like"; "Otis wants *half* of the banana," or "We need *one* more napkin." Think of the other possibilities associated with snack time—counting out plates, cups, chairs, tables, spoons—or any other routine time during the day. In their normal conversations with young children, teachers deliberately choose terms that enrich and strengthen basic mathematics concepts. Instead of saying, "Take some crackers if you want," these teachers seize opportunities to turn each statement into a valuable learning experience.

Informal Approach to Mathematics

Children will say and listen to mathematical terms at home and in the classroom long before they understand their true meanings. To illustrate this point, imagine that you are touring a preschool setting and are listening for all the comments related to the field of mathematics. You may hear comments like these:

- "My new ball cost *sixty cents.*"
- "We start school at *nine o'clock.*"
- "It snowed *yesterday.*"
- "We have *two* hammers, Arnie, *one* for you and *one* for Ginnie."
- "My little sister is *two-and-a-half* years old."
- "I want the *square* block."
- "*One, two* buckle my shoe. *Three, four* shut the door. . . ."
- "My car needs gas—give me a *hundred dollars'* worth."

- "My glass is only *half* full."
- "My teacher is *bigger* than me."
- "*Tomorrow* is Charlene's birthday. She'll be *five* years old."
- "Good boy, Charlie. You put *two* glasses on the snack table."
- "My mommy gave me a *dime.*"
- "I want *three* books."
- "Jimmy is using *two* paintbrushes."
- "Val painted *four* pictures."
- "He has *more* blocks *than* you."
- "I need *one more* piece to finish my puzzle."

Numbers are used throughout the day whenever opportunities present themselves or are created by innovative teachers. The child is viewed as the center of the curriculum and the teacher as the facilitator, or arranger of the environment. As an arranger, the teacher needs to create interesting phenomena that will stimulate the child's curiosity. Once stimulated, the child attacks a problem and seeks to solve it for himself. Martin Johnson and John Wilson (1976) explain further:

> While some modern proponents of this position . . . must be viewed as extreme, the common thread found . . . is that the curriculum for the child . . . should be developed from the interests of the child. In the case of mathematics, this approach has at different times in history given support to the "incidental learning" theory of arithmetic. That is, the introduction, development, maintenance, and extension of mathematical content and skills were a function of the incidental need for them in connection with what was usually an activity unit. [p. 169]

The method of incidental learning is to teach mathematics skills in the context of the child's own play activities, not to structure learning objectives or plan specific mathematics lessons. At the snack table, for example, the teacher may say, "There are four chairs, one for each of you." She may singly count the cups or cookies as they are passed out to each child. Children at the sandbox or water table may fill containers, empty them, and experiment with how much more sand or water is needed to fill a larger container than it takes to fill a smaller one. Cooking activities give the children practice in measuring ingredients with cups and measuring spoons. Size relationships are begun as the teacher asks the children to cut the pieces of celery "just as big as this one." During an informal tea party in the kitchen play area the children match the number of cups and saucers to the number of children participating. Boys or girls at the woodworking area plan to "measure" a piece of wood and saw it so that it is the same length as another piece. Block construction leads other children to choose the *biggest* block for the base of a building and the *smallest* block for the top. Separate shelves are provided for blocks of different shapes, so the children practice shape recognition as they remove and replace blocks used for construction projects. Weight relationships are discovered on the playground as children experiment to find which two children can make a seesaw balance. Number concepts are developed as children look for "one more piece to finish my puzzle."

Dozens of daily experiences can be capitalized upon for their informal mathematical value. The teacher (or other arranger) takes advantage of these opportunities because she believes every child is naturally curious and eager to find out things for himself. With the guidance and support of an alert teacher, the day's normal activities can be exploited for their contribution to mathematics learnings and can form the basis for the entire curriculum. Educators who use more formal approaches to mathematics teaching are warned that their artificial structure and limitations serve only to stifle open thinking abilities and lessen interest exploration and experimentation.

We have mentioned incidental, daily opportunities for emphasizing mathematics concepts, but there are many times during which planned activities can routinely introduce basic number concepts.

Calendars Because children experience great difficulty with concepts related to time, it is important to introduce such concepts in meaningful ways with a great deal of significant repetition. For this reason, the children should work with a calendar as part of their daily routine so they can learn what it represents and how it is used.

To begin, you should construct a large, attractive, sturdy calendar base with clearly marked numbers and the names of the month and days (not abbreviated) in bold letters. You may wish to add a colorful illustration appropriate for the particular month. This careful construction will attract the children and help them locate the significant information when it is needed.

Children should have many opportunities to handle parts of the calendar and derive greater meaning from the experience when allowed to do so. When introducing the name of the month, have it printed on a separate card so the children can focus on it while it is being held in your hands. Then a child can be asked to attach it to the appropriate location on the calendar base. Similarly, you may then introduce the location of the names of the days of the week and ask children to place the name cards in the appropriate slots. Emphasize the name of today ("Thursday," for example) and inform the children that it is the *first* day of the month. Ask the children to find the numeral 1 beneath Thursday. To prevent confusion from having too many numbers facing the child each day, some teachers place just one number on the calendar each day. Others prefer to cover the remainder of the days with seasonal numeral cards, removing one every day. For example, school bells cover the dates of Sep-

Many possible learnings can be accomplished through the daily use of calendars.

tember, apples for October, cornucopias for November, snowmen for December, and so on. Still other teachers decide to expose all the dates at the beginning of the month and ask the children to take turns covering each as the days pass by with illustrative cards. Initially, the entire month may be covered with identical cards, but then, in order to develop other concepts, you may choose to alternate colors for each row on the calendar, red apples for the first row, green for the second, red for the third, and green for the fourth. Then you may wish to alternate symbols for each column—for example, corn shucks for one column, cornucopias for the second, pilgrims for the third, and turkeys for the fourth. Think of the patterning skills being developed as you take advantage of the calendar in these ways. As you use the calendar with the children, think of promoting these number concepts:

- Calendars tell us the number of days in the year—365.

- Calendars divide the 365 days into groups of 12, called months.

- Many of the months have the same number of days, but some do not. Some children may like to learn this old rhyme:

Thirty days hath September,
April, June, and November;
All the rest have thirty-one,
Save February, which has twenty-eight in fine,
And leap year brings it twenty-nine.

- Calendars divide months into weeks—each week made up of seven days. How many weeks are in this month?

- Days of the week are given special names. What is the first day called? How many Mondays in this month? Tuesdays? What day does this month begin on?

- Calendars help us know when special days are coming. Thanksgiving is on the 25th day of this month. What day of the week is Thanksgiving?

- January 1st begins a new year. The last day of the year is the 31st of December. On what day of the week will the old year end? On what day will the new year begin?

- Calendars are divided into seasons: Winter begins on December 21, spring on March 21, summer on June 21, and fall on September 21. How can we mark the calendar to show when these seasons begin?

Counting Songs and Rhymes   We have spoken of the attraction of rhymes and songs in other sections of this book, emphasizing the joy children associate with such activity. Capitalize on such childhood pleasure by introducing these and other rhymes and jingles that help promote mathematics concepts:

> Baa, baa, black sheep
> Have you any wool?
> Yes, sir, yes, sir,
> Three bags full.
>
> One for my master,
> One for my dame,
> And one for the little boy
> Who lives down the lane.
>
> Five little squirrels sat in a tree.
> The first one said, "What do I see?"
> The second one said, "A man with a gun."
> The third one said, "We'd better run."
> The fourth one said, "Let's hide in the shade."
> The fifth one said, "I'm not afraid."
> Then BANG! went the gun,
> And away they did run!

> One, two, three, four, five—
> I caught a fish alive.
> Six, seven, eight, nine, ten—
> I let him go again.
> Why did you let him go?
> He bit my finger so.
> Which finger did he bite?
> The little one on the right.
>
> Rub-a-dub-dub,
> Three men in a tub,
> And who do you think they be?
> The butcher, the baker,
> The candlestick maker—
> Cast them out—knaves all three!

When you are satisfied that youngsters have achieved a level satisfactory to become introduced to counting itself, you may wish to initiate group activities designed to introduce *numbers, numerals,* and *sequence* in meaningful ways.

Counting   A sure understanding of mathematics concepts develops slowly because children need a lot of time to comprehend inherently abstract ideas in a meaningful way. Although some children may enrapture their parents by counting, "One, two, three, four . . . ten" or adding, "One and one is two," they may be simply parroting phrases heard over and over again and are not really counting or adding with understanding. They may be reciting with as much meaning as trick horses pounding their hooves at the signal of a trainer. To prevent situations like this from happening, you must provide many organized experiences to help the children develop the desired mathematical concepts. One teacher met this challenge by preparing a series of activities intended to build these counting skills:

1. Recognizing the amount of objects in a set *(number)*

2. Recognizing the number names *(numeral)*

3. Recognizing the proper ordering of the numerals *(sequence)*

Miss Kramer, a kindergarten teacher, realized that the best vehicle for developing the concept of number *was the* set *(a well-defined collection of objects), and she planned her first experiences with sets of concrete objects. She decided that the best way to begin would be to have the children make collections of things that were alike. Miss Kramer gave each of four children one paper clip and two rubber bands and asked them to separate the objects that belonged together.*

With the goal of comparing objects in a set, Miss Kramer asked the children questions designed to help them observe which group had "more than" and which group had "less than." At this point, the children were not yet ready for counting, so she asked them only to compare sets of different objects with one another. Gradually, Miss Kramer added sets of three erasers, four pencils, five crayons, and so on, and asked the children to group the objects accordingly. Through one-to-one matching and comparison activities, the children's concept of number grew as they grouped objects and determined which set had more (or fewer) elements than another.

After Miss Kramer had provided numerous activities of set comparison, she introduced her children to number names (numerals). *To prevent rote memorization of numerals—1, 2, 3 . . .—Miss Kramer decided to select numbers randomly to present to the group. For the sake of discussion, let us say that she selected the number* three. *She then proceeded through this sequence of activity:*

1. *Ask the child to place the same number of objects in front of him as you have in front of you.* (visual *recognition/ matching*)

2. *Present the child with a card containing three squares. Ask him to "place three counters on the card—one in each square."* (visual *and* verbal *stimuli*)

3. *Present the child with a card containing three squares and the numeral. Ask him to "place three counters on the card"* (numerical symbol *introduced*)

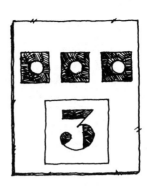

4. *Present the child with the symbol only and ask him to place as many counters on the table as indicated.* (numerical symbol *only*)

5. *After each numeral is introduced, give the child a card on which the numeral is cut in sandpaper. The teacher and child use the sandpaper numerals in three ways:*

   a. *The teacher shows the card to the child, asks him to move his fingers over the numeral, and says to the child, "This is three," or "This is four," and so forth.*

   b. *The teacher places the cards in front of the child and has him say, "Give me the three," "Give me the four," and so on.*

   c. *Still using the sandpaper numerals, the teacher asks, "What is this?" The child generates the number game.*

6. *For reinforcement, the teacher arranges the classroom with several center-based follow-up activities. For example, the children count the number of objects in each picture and match it to the appropriate numeral strip.*

As a final step in the counting procedure, Miss Kramer moved to the ordering of numbers. *While she was establishing the number names for the numbers, Miss Kramer had stimulated exploration of size relationships between numbers (more than, less than, and so on). Now she sought to encourage finer discrimi-*

nation among sets by developing the concept of "one more than." She began by asking the children to stack blocks and order number sticks such as cuisenaire rods. She started with one block and asked the children to make a stack that had one more block than she had. Then, she asked them to look at the stack of two blocks and make another stack with one block more than two. When the children had ordered the objects in sequence, she asked them to place a numeral card below each set. A number of creative, individual reinforcement activities were organized into learning stations for use following this initial introduction. Among these were the activities in the "Mathematics Activities" box.

As you have perceived, the major concern of Miss Kramer was to develop *meaningful* counting skills in an environment where the children are involved with concrete, manipulative materials and where they explore and experiment while making new discoveries. Her basic strategy followed this organizational plan:

1. Compare and contrast sets: "more than," "less than," and "same as."

2. Introduce number names (numerals).

3. Order numbers in sequence.

Techniques like this that involve the children are recommended by most early child-hood educators today. Dissenters align themselves with a behavioral philosophy, supporting expository, teacher-centered approaches to learning. Besides understanding numbers, other areas are covered in most preschool mathematics programs.

Understanding Terms of Comparison Understanding basic mathematical concepts evolves from the acquisition of relative terms that help young children describe their experiences meaningfully. Some of the more commonly used terms are given in the following list to help you as you begin to select materials and activities for your classroom:

- alike—different
- big—bigger—biggest
- more—less; most—least
- larger—smaller
- above—below
- before—after
- here—there
- near—far
- few—fewer—fewest
- fast—slow
- thick—thin
- in front of—in back of
- inside—outside

MATHEMATICS ACTIVITIES

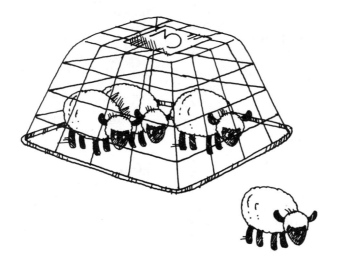

Zoo Animals

Collect a set of ten plastic strawberry containers and place a numeral from 1 to 10 on the bottom of each. These will serve as the zoo cages when turned upside down. Buy a set of plastic or rubber animals and ask the children to place the appropriate number of animals beneath the cages.

Number-Numeral Match

Cut out twenty 3-inch square tagboard cards. Put the numerals 1 to 10 on ten of the cards and the corresponding number of stick figures on the remaining cards. Put sets of two matching cards (numeral and same number of stick figures) together and punch a hole through both. Then, take two other matching cards and

(continued)

do the same, making sure that the hole is punched in a different location than the previous pair(s). Mix all the cards and ask the children to match numbers and numerals. They can tell if they are correct if the punched holes match.

Bean Drop

Number ten cups 1 to 10. Have the child count the number of dry beans that goes into each cup, drop them in, and arrange the cups in numerical order.

Number Train

Have the child hook each railroad car (made from half-pint milk cartons) in numerical order from 1 through 10 and place the appropriate number of counters into each car.

Number Balance

Ask the children to place a specified number of blocks into one pie tin on a balance scale and an equal number in the other. Then have them take a number of blocks away from one tin and ask them to count the number of blocks in each. Establish which tin has *more than* and which tin has *fewer than*. Basic operations of addition and subtraction can be reinforced when children are asked to determine the number of blocks needed to add or subtract in order to achieve a balance.

Chips

Sit on the floor with a group of children. Have the children take turns rolling a die and counting the number of dots on the top. Each child takes the same number of chips for her collection as shown by the dots on the

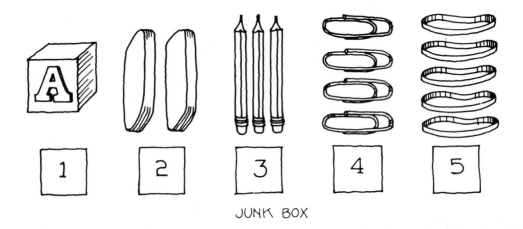

JUNK BOX

- up—down
- top—middle—bottom
- high—low
- tall—short
- close—closer—closest
- first—next—last
- all—none
- hot—cold
- big—little

As an illustration, to extend the concept of *more than* and *fewer than,* one teacher placed three crayons on the table in front of a small group of children. She had them look at the crayons carefully; then she asked the children to close their eyes and she secretly placed one more crayon with the set. She then had the children open their eyes and tell if there were now *more* or *fewer* crayons *than* there had been before. Think of creative ways to teach the terms of comparison as you read down the list.

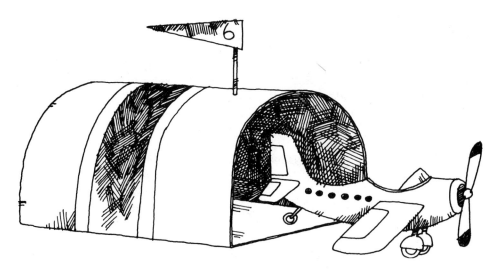

die. When all the chips are gone, the children stack them up and match columns. Because counting is the object of the game, not accumulating the most chips, compare and contrast the size of the columns ("Who has the tallest? the shortest?").

Junk Box Count

Collect a different number of various familiar objects, such as one building block, two pencils, three paper clips, and so on. Place all of the objects in a large box, labeled "Junk Box." Prepare 3- × 3-inch tagboard cards, each with a numeral from 1 to 10 on it.

Have the children take the objects out of the junk box and group identical objects in sets. Then ask them to take a tagboard numeral and place it under the set with which it corresponds.

Be near the child when the groupings are completed and ask questions such as, "How many rubber bands did you count?" "Do you have more paper clips or more pencils?" "Are there fewer pencils or fewer blocks?"

Number Airplanes

Make airplane hangars by cutting oatmeal boxes down the center and gluing each half onto heavy tagboard. Cover the hangars with colorful construction paper or paint them. Punch a hole in the top of each hangar and insert a wind sock (construction paper glued to a thin dowel) into each. Print a numeral on each wind sock. Have the children place plastic airplanes with from one to ten dots into the proper hangars.

Gaining Perspectives of Shape Young children as early as three years of age can learn to recognize basic geometric shapes. They can identify and compare *circles, squares, triangles,* and *rectangles*. As with the introduction of any new idea, though, children should experience shapes directly in various ways during their daily activities. Educators feel that the best way to do this is to informally call attention to shapes within the immediate environment and to use words describing shapes whenever referring to those specific objects. For example, instead of asking the child to put the crayons "into that box," say, "Please put the crayons into the *square* box." Normally, when beginning to start formal shape lessons, you should introduce only one new shape to the child at a time. You can do this by holding up a circle in front of a group of children and saying, "This is a circle," and then asking the children to say the word. You may also have several other geometric shapes cut from construction paper, among which the circle predominates. You can ask the children to search for a circle. When they have all found one, you may ask of each child, "Tell me what you have." The children may respond, "I have a red circle," or "I have a blue circle," and so on. Once one shape is understood well, others can be presented. However, you should remember to review a familiar shape before the new one is introduced. You can then encourage children to make discriminations among the familiar and the unfamiliar by asking, "How are the shapes alike?" and "How are these shapes different?"

Naturally, children need enjoyable follow-up activities to reinforce their ability to recognize and compare geometric shapes. Some classroom activities directed toward that goal are described in the "Geometric Shapes Activities" box.

Establishing Concepts of Time

Anyone experiencing a situation like the following can certainly verify that concepts of time are very difficult for young children to develop.

The Jones family, during an automobile trip to visit relatives, stopped at a diner for a quick lunch. Returning to the car, five-year-old Clarice inquired of her father, "Daddy, how much longer to grandma's?" "Only three more hours, Honey," replied Mr. Jones. Five minutes after resuming their driving, Clarice suddenly questioned, "Is it three hours yet?"

Since waiting three hours is incomprehensible for young children, we cannot reasonably expect them to grasp significantly time-related concepts of minutes, hours, days, weeks, months, and years when we teach them in a preschool classroom. These concepts are very difficult because they represent one major area of the preschool curriculum whose subject seems impossible to make concrete—the passage of time cannot be seen or felt. When they are learning to read, the children's original experiences involve them in associating words in print with real objects through labeling or experience stories. In learning numbers, children compare sets of concrete objects with numerals, as skills are developed and refined. But with time, we are faced with a monumental task of helping children conceptualize an abstract phenomenon with the use of abstract materials, such as clocks and calendars. Thus, asking preschool children to read clocks and calendars is an unrealistic expectation. Most are not ready for that type of instruction until they approach Piaget's stage of concrete operations (7–8 years).

This does not mean, however, that the topic of time should be avoided by preschool teachers. There is more to time than knowing how to read a watch or interpret a calendar. Children often hear references to time and must be led to sense its importance in their growing worlds—yet they are just beginning to understand. They are reminded: "It's time to get up to go to school.... It's time to go outdoors and play.... Snack time.... Time for a story.... Time to go home.... Time for lunch.... Just a minute and I'll be with you." How long is a minute to a four-year-old? It may be a fleeting moment if spent frolicking outdoors in an enjoyable game or it may be an eternity if spent in line awaiting a turn on a playground swing. How much is an hour? a day? a month? a year? As we grow and mature, even _our_ (adult) concepts of time constantly change. For example, when you were five years old, ten years old was old to you—to a ten-year-old, fifteen is old. But, to a fifteen-year-old, perish the thought of becoming an old timer of twenty! Time concepts are interesting and challenging. Someone once said that old is always five years older than your present age, and that person may be right. The point is that time is a difficult concept not only for preschoolers but for all of us. However, it dominates our daily lives, and there must be some value in teaching it. Some of the time-related vocabulary terms usually dealt with in preschool settings are:

GEOMETRIC SHAPES
ACTIVITIES

1. Have the children sort through cards containing pairs of geometric figures—some matched and some not matched—and decide whether the pairs are the *same* or *different*. If they are the same, have the children place them on the right side of the answer board (over the two geometric figures that are the same form). If they are different, have them place them on the left side (over the two geometric shapes that are different). At first, you may wish to vary the objects by shape only, but as the children gain experience, you may vary them in shape as well as other dimensions (color, size, texture).

2. Cut out a large assortment of each of the four basic shapes. Create four characters based on each of the shapes, that is, Ms. Circle, Ms. Square, Mr. Triangle, Mr. Rectangle. Mix all the shapes on the table and have the children sort the forms by placing them in front of the appropriate person. It may be valuable for the children to name the forms as they sort them.

3. Ask the children to look around the classroom for items or objects with the form of the four basic shapes—items like clocks, boxes, toys, utensils, blocks, and so on.

4. Provide a container through which the child can poke his hand, but which he can't see inside of. Have the child feel the shape within and identify the form felt.

Figure 9-8 A developmental strategy for teaching concepts of measurement

yesterday	minute	next week	never
today	hour	next time	always
tomorrow	clock	day	now
morning	calendar	week	early
afternoon	last night	month	late
tonight	long ago	year	birthday

Some ideas for teaching these concepts are given in the "Time Activities" box.

Developing Measurement Skills The preschool classroom should provide many opportunities to experience linear measurement (length, width, height), volume, and weight. Such beginning experiences should be informal and should deal with *arbitrary measurements* rather than with formal terminology such as *inch, foot, meter, gram, ounce, pound, pint, liter,* and so on. Some arbitrary measurements that often come up during water or sand play, for example, are "the *big* bottle," "the *small* spoon," "the *long* stick," "the *short* shovel," "the *tall* pile," and "the *heaviest* pail." The measurement program should begin with

such simple arbitrary comparisons and proceed to informal measurements with meaningful *nonstandard units.* An example of measurement with a nonstandard unit is to give a child a piece of string (the nonstandard unit) and ask him to sort from a group of objects those items that are *longer than, shorter than,* or the *same* length as his string.

When planning a program designed to foster skills in nonstandard measuring, it is important to begin with simple comparisons such as the one just illustrated and use concrete materials. With such a basic background, the child will form a sound foundation upon which more formal measurement with *standard units* can be introduced later in the primary grades (see Figure 9-8).

The development of measurement skills in the preschool years, then, is based on the idea of *comparison;* the child makes simple, direct comparisons among objects through linear measurements, estimates of volume, and weighing various objects in his environment.

TIME ACTIVITIES

1. Use time vocabulary during your daily dialogues with the children. Look at your watch or clock occasionally and show the children where the hands will be when it is time to go home, for example. Help the children plan events with you—for example, a special birthday party *later in the day* for Tammy's birthday, or a special field trip *tomorrow,* or Santa Claus's arrival *next week.* Ask the children to identify the television show they will want to watch *tonight.* These beginning time descriptions should first be given in terms of day and night and tied into routine activities, such as mealtimes, naps, or time to go home. They will soon begin to tell the difference between school days and weekends, school days and holidays, afternoon and morning, and so on.

2. Display a large, colorful calendar for each month and include days of special significance to the children—birthdays, holidays, special events, weekends, and so on.

3. Make a large clock with movable minute and hour hands. Set the hands to indicate what the real room clock will look like when it is time for a story, snack, nap, or any other special event.

4. Keep time records of special activities in your classroom. Count the days that pass between the time a seed was planted and when the sprout first appeared. Keep track of how many days must elapse before it is time to water the plants again. Observe the time it takes for a chicken egg to hatch. Count the number of days until Christmas or Halloween. Use a cooking timer to guide the children in estimating how long it will be until a batch of cookies is ready. In similar ways, teachers have put to good use various timekeeping paraphernalia such as hourglasses, stopwatches, or old alarm clocks.

Some suggested activities for each of these areas are given in the "Measurement Activities" box.

Outlined in this section were five basic areas of mathematics skills usually contained in programs for preschool children: (1) *counting skills,* (2) *understanding terms of comparison,* (3) *gaining perspectives of shape,* (4) *establishing concepts of time,* and (5) *developing measurement skills.* You should take advantage of informal environmental experiences, as well as plan organized classroom activities, to foster growth and development of these skills. These varieties of experiences help preschool children build a foundation of understandings that will later support and reinforce the more sophisticated expectancies of the primary grades. The concepts and skills should be taught in a developmental sequence appropriate to each group of children involved. Some teachers, especially those teaching children experiencing learning difficulties, may prefer a structured *behavioral* approach to such instruction; others may choose the more informal approach we have described up to this point. Again, a *strictly informal* approach would make little or no use of planned mathematics activities, but capitalize upon all life experiences to introduce and reinforce concepts. However, the work of Jean Piaget and his followers has caused some educators to reevaluate the informal approach and design the kinds of math experiences they view as most appropriate for young children because those children must be helped to develop the kinds of abilities corresponding to their particular stage of development. Those abilities that are common to children during the preschool years include *classification, seriation, spatial relationships, temporal relationships,* and *conservation.* Piaget tells us that unplanned mathematical learnings are, indeed, valuable, but that carefully planned and executed activities are also necessary if math learning is to be complete. He advocates not paper-and-pencil activities that confine the children to a right answer, but a system of manipulative

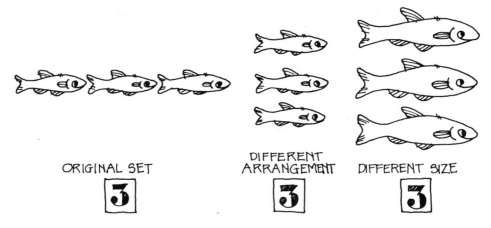

ORIGINAL SET

DIFFERENT ARRANGEMENT

DIFFERENT SIZE

Figure 9-9   *The ability to conserve number*

activities with problem-solving characteristics. That is why you were offered many kinds of suggestions for small-group or individual activity reflecting a play or game orientation in the preceding section.

Piaget believes that all reasoning powers are supported by the development of these abilities and that all mathematical learning, in particular, is based on an ability to conserve number. Figure 9-9 illustrates conservation of number. The number of items in a set remains three regardless of change in size or position. If the child realizes this characteristic, he demonstrates an ability to conserve number.

Piaget found that children learn to conserve number sometime between the ages of about five and seven, and developmentally progress to the conservation of length, weight, and area. He emphasized that an overall concept of number develops not only from conservation skills, but also primarily from classification and seriation tasks, as well as from other skills. Sample mathematics activities were described for each area in Chapter 7, but additional examples are given here for the sake of clarification. See the box "Piagetian Mathematical Concepts."

Many new programs were inspired by Piaget's theories. These programs are activity-based approaches that emphasize the manipulation of and experimentation with concrete materials as illustrated throughout this section. They emphasize a *set* approach similar to the one used by Miss Kramer earlier in this chapter, as well as the discovery of relational concepts such as "more than," "less than," and "the same as." All these programs believe that the selection of content and teaching methodology should be based on the logical structure of thinking proposed by Piaget.

The Behavioral Position

Behavioral instruction, of course, is based upon exposing children to teachers and materials that are designed to *teach* skills and concepts through a carefully planned sequence of tasks supported by a system of reinforcement and reward. Like reading, behaviorally oriented mathematics programs for young children are designed mainly for individuals experiencing learning problems. They can be divided into two major types: (1) those that are highly teacher-directed, and (2) those that utilize programmed materials. Perhaps the most popular teacher-directed program reflecting the behavioral philosophy is the Distar® Arithmetic program, written by Siegfried Engel-

MEASUREMENT ACTIVITIES

Linear Measurements

1. Compare the height of several children. Have them compare feet to see whose are longest or shortest.

2. Compare the length of different objects in the room. Have them guess which would be longer—for example, two straws laid end to end or five paper clips. Their guess can be verified by actual experimentation.

3. Have the children walk heel to toe from one area of the room or playground to another area and count the number of steps. Have them guess which of two objects is farthest from where they are standing, and then pace off the distances to see if they were correct.

4. Have the child use the width of his index finger to measure the length of a crayon, book, toy, or any other handy object.

Volume Measurements

1. Give the children a spoon with which they can scoop sand from a small sandbox. Have them spoon out the sand from the box into a cup, glass, and jar while counting the number of spoons necessary to fill each.

2. Have the children try to arrange four different containers in order by capacity. They can test their guess by pouring small cups of liquid or sand into the containers and counting which container held the most, which the next, and so on.

3. Have the children use a small cup as a measure and find out how many cups of rice, beans, and sand it would take to fill the same pot.

Weight Measurement   Make a simple balance scale from two lengths of wood, some string, and a pair of pie tins. Comparison activities can be carried out on this simple scale.

1. Children often will judge the larger object to be heavier when asked to distinguish between two items. They believe that the bigger the object is, the heavier it will be. Have the children use the scale to compare the weight of a large styrofoam ball with a smaller ball of clay. They will find that the clay is heavier than the styrofoam and that weight cannot always be determined by visual estimates.

2. Fill five cans with varying amounts of sand. Have the children use the scale to order the cans from lightest to heaviest.

3. Have the children experiment to see how many metal washers balance a cup, how many beans balance a crayon, how many nails balance a block, and so on.

4. Have the children measure one object in comparison to a number of other objects. For example, a block compared to nails, pencils, chalkboard erasers, washers, and so on.

mann and Doug Carnine (1969) and published by Science Research Associates (SRA). The program is based on *counting* objectives, beginning with rote counting tasks rather than set identification described earlier in this section. The philosophy behind the teaching approach is stated in the teacher's manual:

Distar® Arithmetic I teaches the basic rules about arithmetic that are needed if the children are to have a solid basis for remembering and classifying facts. The children take a step at a time. They do not move on in the program until they have mastered the steps that are needed for the operations that are to come. They are systematically taught the

PIAGETIAN MATHEMATICAL CONCEPTS

BY SIZE   **BY SHAPE**

Classification   The teacher uses shapes of squares and circles cut out of red construction paper to provide two ways of classifying (size and shape). To begin, the teacher and children identify the shapes, sizes, and color. Then, she tells the children, "Put together the ones that are the same." The children may decide to classify by size or by shape. The teacher asks the children to explain why they grouped the circles and squares the way they did.

Seriation   The teacher and children make a card set to be used for a variety of seriation purposes. The

teacher asks the children to "find the card that shows one dot." The children find the card and say, "This card shows one." The teacher then gives further instructions, for example, "Find another card that shows one," or "Let's look for the number that comes after one." Then, when three or four cards have been sequenced, the teacher may ask the children to identify groupings by number ("How many dots are on that card?") or to state which card contain *more, less,* or the *same* number of dots.

symbols, conventions, and operations that enable them to solve a broad range of problems. [p. 7]

The following is an example of an arithmetic exercise introduced fairly early in the Distar® program. The stress is placed on counting as the basic skill needed before more complex concepts and skills can be introduced. In this exercise, on "object counting," the children learn to count to five while the teacher follows the instructions in the teacher's manual exactly:

GROUP ACTIVITY

a. *(Point to the trees.)* These are trees. What are these? *(Wait.)*

b. Let's count all of the trees. What are we going to count? *(Wait.)*

c. I'll point, you count. *(Touch the objects from left to right. Do not count with the children unless it is necessary. Encourage all the children to count.)*

d. How many trees? *(Wait.)*

e. Let's count them again.

f. *(This time, touch the objects from right to left.)* Yes, how many trees? *(Wait.)*

g. *(Call on individual children to count the objects as you point to them. After a child has counted all the objects, ask him)* How many trees? *(Wait.)*

Programmed mathematics materials are normally organized into workbook formats and follow the same basic patterned presentation found in programmed reading materials.

If you choose behaviorally oriented ideas to support your mathematics program, you must be sure to:

1. specify the skill you want the child to develop

2. organize a sequential program aimed at developing that skill

3. establish a pattern of frequent verbal or written response

4. provide for positive reinforcement of successful responses

5. establish a program of periodic evaluation of goals

SOME FINAL THOUGHTS

Believing that children unable to perform skills such as reading and writing were surely destined to fall into the hands of the devil, the colonial legislature of the Massachusetts Bay Colony passed "the old deluder Satan" law in 1647. This piece of legislation required all settlements of 50 or more households to appoint a schoolmaster whose major responsibility would be to "teach all such children as shall resort to him to write & reade." Now, with almost 350 years experience, we still have not acquired answers to such important questions as "At what age should we begin teaching children to learn academic skills?" and "What is the best method of teaching these skills?"

Glenn Doman and other educators have argued that children can effectively learn academic skills prior to the age of two, but most early childhood educators have advised us that such practices are developmentally unwise. They see that period of life as being very important for establishing the base for subsequent academic skills. Children are occupied with sorting out sights, sounds, tastes, smells, and touches from all phenomena in their environment. They become aware of language; practice growing physical abilities; learn to play by themselves and cooperate with others; explore objects all around them; and, eventually, after an accumulation of all such experiences, indicate individual interest in learning to read, write, and recognize numbers. Usually, by kindergarten, the necessary accumulated experiences have been acquired, and some children have already begun to perform such skills, especially if they have been exposed to a stimulating environment at home or in prekindergarten programs.

What is the best method of instruction to use once children are judged ready to learn the basic academic skills? From all the accumulated research, it appears as though there is no single best method. However, certain basic elements of sound instruction appear to characterize all successful programs: systematic individual diagnosis, a broad base of life experiences, small-group teaching of specific skills, broad-based language experiences, a setting where each child experiences success, and an environment in which learning is seen as valuable and pleasurable.

Chapter **10**

Creativity: Encouraging the Spirit of Wonder and Magic

Joel enthusiastically turned to the easel to begin his favorite activity. He started to paint a warm, rich winter scene. His smiles and expressions of strong involvement indicated deep thought and careful planning—almost as if he were saying to himself, "This is a special picture because it is all mine." When it was completed, Joel stepped back to admire his work of art. With pleasure sweeping his face, Joel showed his picture to his best friend, Arthur. Both boys giggled and chatted as they surveyed the scene. All was going well until a strong voice intervened, "Whoever heard of a green sun? Do your picture over again and paint the sun yellow. I won't let you take home such a silly picture."

Later that day, Terri and Shana secluded themselves in a distant corner of the playground, participating in an activity that both seemed to greatly enjoy— expressing their thoughts to each other in spontaneous, colorful language. "Look at that blue bird," said Terri, "wouldn't it be funny to see a green checkered bird?" Shana laughed. "A green checkered bird? It would have to come from a green checkered egg!" The two girls continued to talk using joyful similar expressions. Their attention was focused on their surroundings, but their thoughts were running off into highly fanciful directions. Their kindergarten teacher, sensing the value of such imaginative thought as a means of developing creative self-expression, listened to the children and encouraged their verbal explorations. However, when it became time to move indoors, Mr. Carling announced, "The fun is over now, girls. It's time to go in and do our reading."

Many children enjoy fanciful experiences like these. They love to participate in activities where their minds are allowed to wander—seeking to find new relationships between the known and the unknown, experimenting with knowledge in new ways, or producing something in their own unique, original manner. Adults, however, often become confused about such common childhood en-

359

deavors and frown upon such originality with comments such as "Stop that *silliness,*" or "Do it the *right way.*" Such rigidity has a powerful influence on the child's confidence as well as on his willingness to try something new. Joel, for example, may now hesitate to join the others in a group finger-painting activity directed by the teacher because of the crushing experience he had. "What if I don't make a picture like my teacher wants?" may begin to characterize his thinking whenever new projects or activities are initiated.

Whenever children express their thoughts or actions in inventive, self-initiated, original ways, we say that they are *creative* children. Creative thinkers are those who produce truly unique reactions to their environment. The reactions may be similar to those discovered by millions of children before them, but the characteristic that makes any reaction creative is that it was *new to them.* This may show up in infants as they discover different ways to play with their toys or in adults as they seek to find an easier way to perform a household chore. Each person has some unique way of meeting a situation, but some people apparently feel freer to search for and express their unique ideas than do others. E. Paul Torrance feels that a great deal of what contributes to a person's ultimate ability to exhibit open-ended, original thinking as opposed to rigid, closed-end thinking occurs in the school:

> Creative imagination during early childhood seems to reach a peak between four- and four-and-a-half years, and is followed by a drop at about age five when the child enters school for the first time. This drop has generally been regarded as the inevitable phenomenon in nature. There are now indications, however, that this drop in five-year-olds is a man-made rather than a natural phenomenon. [1963, p. 79]

Some people argue that this phenomenon occurs because schools begin to clamp down and limit the freedom of children dur-ing the kindergarten year. "You're acting like a two-year-old," or "What do you think you are—a clown?" and similar sarcastic put-downs often accompany adventuresome, unique attempts at self-expression. Most children eventually conform to the growing rigidity of the school structure, but a few are reluctant to change—they clearly keep a "bit of that child" within them as they continue to meet life's challenges in independent, adventurous ways.

The noted Russian psychologist, Kornei Chukovsky (1963) believes that creative thought is extremely important since "without imaginative fantasy there would be complete stagnation in both physics and chemistry, because the formulation of new hypotheses, the invention of new implements, the discovery of new methods of experimental research, the conjecturing of new chemical fusions—all these are products of imagination and fantasy" (p. 116). Sidney Parnes (1971) added these thoughts: "We must cultivate talent in the way soil nurtures a seed. It provides for the growth of the seed but it does not tell the seed what to become" (p. 110). Arnold Toynbee (1971) warns Americans that a lack of emphasis on creativity in our schools could cause dire results:

> If America is to treasure and foster all the creative ability that she has in her, a new and bright spirit of change has to be injected into her educational philosophy. The rather rigid egalitarian models of educational selection and treatment, which seem to me to be tenaciously held by the . . . majority of American people, will, I should press, have to be refashioned to include the creative talents of the coming generation. . . . New educational philosophies and new institutions of learning need to be constructed to provide an opportunity for creative individuals to enhance their talents in schools. [p. 13]

Some highly creative people, including Einstein and Edison, were considered dunces by their teachers because they would not (or could not) conform to the inflexible patterns of thought expected by the teachers. V. Goertzel and Mildred Goertzel (1962) in their study of over 400 eminent people, most of whom would be regarded as highly creative, estimated that 60 percent had serious school problems. Those are only a few who had the persistence to "stick it out." But what has happened to the thousands of youngsters who surrendered their creative urges to conformity and, therefore, were never encouraged or allowed to make significant creative contributions to society? Teachers and parents should be highly concerned about such questions, as well as about providing encouragement and activity to help salvage neglected and wasted human resources. Let's explore more deeply the characteristics of creative behavior in preschool children.

CREATIVE BEHAVIOR OF PRESCHOOL CHILDREN

Perhaps the most significant studies of creativity in preschool children were those conducted by E. Paul Torrance of the University of Georgia (1969, pp. 4–12). His developmental and experimental studies were concerned with the characteristics of creative behavior in four- and five-year-olds. You should be aware of these characteristics so that you are able to arrange your environment in ways that encourage such patterns in all children. A sketch of his tentative conclusions and exemplary excerpts follows.

• *Creative preschool children learn in creative ways.* They enjoy experimenting, manipulating, and playing. They ask questions, make guesses, and offer their findings—sometimes quickly and emotionally, at other times tentatively and quietly.

Wilfredo always enjoyed participating in the various learning activities arranged about the room, and today was no exception. Moving to the science area, he quickly became engrossed in the manipulation of sound jars—glass containers filled to different levels with water. Each container, when struck with a small mallet, produced a different pitch. Wilfredo experimented with the various jars for some time until he discovered a pattern. Running to the teacher and asking her to come, he proudly announced, "Listen, here's the song we were singing before—I learned a song, I learned a song!" and plunked away at the first few notes of "Jingle Bells." "Oh, that's wonderful, Wilfredo," replied the teacher, "how did you learn?" "It was easy," he replied, "I just figured it out."

In similar ways, young children will always try to make sense of their environment by seeking out things that are wrong or missing or by finding answers to things they don't understand. They are uncomfortable until they do something about inconsistencies in their lives. You will find these children saying, "I'll have to figure this out" when faced with situations such as finishing a puzzle, moving a heavy object, building with blocks, or watching snow melt.

• *Creative preschool children have amazingly long attention spans when involved in creative endeavors.* Although many "experts" have established 15 minutes as the maximum attention span of a preschooler for one activity, Torrance found that creative youngsters were able to concentrate on creative tasks for as long as 30 minutes and, in some cases, for as long as 60 minutes at one time. For that reason, he recommends that children be allowed to continue with exciting activities even though the curriculum calls for something else. This point is illustrated in the following incident related by one of Torrance's students:

A three-year-old on a walk with the class was shown a snail. Completely fascinated, he spent the remaining school time (one-and-one-half hours) observing and touching the snail, rather to my annoyance, but I let him alone while the rest of us went on with crafts. The child consequently became so interested in nature's small creatures that at age five he is quite an authority on small creatures. He approaches them stealthily and while looking for lizards practically looked a rattlesnake in the eyes. He immediately recognized it and retreated just as quietly and was unharmed. [1969, pp. 6–7]

- *Creative children have a surprising capacity for organization.* Although these children can tolerate disorder for short periods of time, they demonstrate a need for orderliness and have strong capacities for organizing their environment. They want things to be organized and have a real interest and talent for making sure they are.

The block building corner was the center of activity this morning for Gina and Yi-Ming, two exceptionally talented four-year-olds. They cooperatively created a block building that was to represent an indoor swimming pool, planning and coordinating their efforts all along the way. The combination of blocks was decided upon after great periods of discussion and deliberation. Once completed, both children stood back and joyfully examined their majestic creation. "Isn't it nice?" asked Yi-Ming. "Yep—and we did it by ourselves," answered Gina, "It looks just like the pool at the YMCA." "Oh, . . ." thought Yi-Ming out loud, "but where will the people go in? We forgot the door!" Gina examined the structure for a minute and then offered a suggestion. "We can't put it there," complained Yi-Ming, "the water will leak out. Let's think this out." Both children studied the structure, offered alternative solutions, and finally came up with a plan that met their satisfaction. "It sure pays to think," offered Gina as they finally approved their structure.

Gina and Yi-Ming demonstrated a strong ability to organize their efforts in their

team construction of a large building, as well as in their formulation of a solution to their problem situation. They recognized that they needed to act in an organized manner if they were going to accomplish their task and took almost as much pride in their ability to organize their problem-solving efforts as in their final creation.

- *Creative children are able to return to familiar things and see them in different ways and in greater depth.* These children do not get bored when exposed to the same experience more than once. Surprisingly, they seem satisfied after the first experience, but are prepared to examine it more thoroughly the second time around.

Rose was most interested when her group visited the farm one day. They went into the barn and watched a number of hens sitting on their eggs. The teacher explained that the hen's warm body kept the eggs warm until they hatched, but that the chicks were not yet ready to be hatched. As the group moved on, the parent volunteer talked with Rose and answered many of the young girl's questions.

Upon returning home, Rose enthusiastically shared her new interests with her parents. Realizing her strong desire to observe the hatching of young chicks, Rose's parents arranged for a visit to the farm of a friend near the time when his eggs were to hatch. Rose, of course, was fascinated by the experience and stayed at the farm all day, watching the young chicks frolic.

Some adults hesitate to closely duplicate an experience for young children for fear they will be bored or inattentive. Creative youngsters, however, use a second experience to examine their recollections of the first more slowly and methodically. They can savor the first experience, extend it, and think more deeply about it.

- *Creative preprimary children learn a great deal through fantasy, and solve many of their problems of development through its use.* Fantasy is one of the young child's favorite ways of thinking, and it should be developed and guided in the preschool setting. Unfortunately, adults often eliminate expressions of fantasy in school (especially in the primary grades) because they view it as psychologically unhealthy. However, imaginative role-playing, storytelling, artwork, and language play are quite normal childhood activities and are a part of creative learning.

Mrs. Hernandez enjoys watching her children paint and appreciates all of their creative expressions. The children feel comfortable with their teacher because they know she will never say, "That's not right," or "Do it this way." Ronnie, for example, is a careful, methodical painter who likes to make neat paintings. He carefully dips his brush into green paint and draws a long line. He then adds a few dots on each side of the green line and draws a circle. He then dips his brush into the red paint and dabs a small amount inside the circle. "All done," Ronnie proclaims as he carefully puts his painting aside to dry.

Tara, on the other hand, expresses her creativity in a bolder, less controlled fashion. Tara starts her picture by putting her brush into the red paint and smearing it in the center of her paper, making large, bold strokes. She then adds blue and yellow, slopping on each color so that a considerable amount overflows and overlaps. She intently and actively paints her picture until the entire paper is covered with one color or another. She is content throughout the activity to explore all the possibilities of the medium, but in a different way from Ronnie.

Mrs. Hernandez obviously realized that both children were experiencing cognitive insights and emotional release during the process of their artwork and allowed each to work individually. She knew that the creative *process* in which

they were involved was much more important than the resulting *product,* so she allowed them to adopt a style that was most comfortable for them rather than imposing her own pattern. Likewise, we must encourage self-expression through art, music, creative dramatics, or language usage by allowing children to express their fanciful, personal thoughts in an atmosphere of freedom and acceptance.

- *Creative young children enjoy "playing" with words and seem to be natural storytellers.* Children's art seems to be appreciated by many people throughout the country; we see it displayed on advertisements, book or magazine illustrations, even postage stamps. Their verbal compositions, however, are seldom as widely appreciated or attractively treated in publications and displays. Many imaginative stories are created daily by young children and deserve much more recognition than they now receive.

Several four-year-old children in this classroom were becoming interested in experimenting with word sounds and story construction. As Cindy and Dee played at the outdoor water table, for example, they verbalized, "Drip, drip, drip. Splishy splashy, splishy splashy. . . ." "Look, I'm making it rain." "Rain, rain, you're a pain." "Rain splashing . . . the clouds are bumping together . . . wet trees, wet sidewalks, a flood!" "Get out the raincoats and 'brellas."

Their teacher, Mr. Jackson, enjoyed listening to such creative patter and often offered thought-provoking comments designed to encourage further verbal exploration. "That's a very nice story," he offered, "I like it very much. What if it rained all over the world right now?"

"I like rain," said Cindy. "It's fun to run through the puddles. My dog runs with me—splish, splash, splish, splash."

"I'm afraid of the thunder," said Dee. "Kaboom . . . kaboom. . . . ." Playfully, the two girls joined in shrieking laughter and ran to the porch roof for "cover."

There are many opportunities during the day to encourage such creative verbal self-expression. Perhaps the most important role of the teacher in these instances is to appreciate the children's expressions and listen to what they say. When they find that you value their creative endeavors, the children will enjoy expressing their thoughts and will eventually feel more comfortable using other avenues of creative expression, too.

One pitfall of encouraging creative verbalization should be emphasized at this point. Make a concerted effort to resist the temptation of requesting that the children tell you a story. Not all children can do so freely and asking them to express their thoughts at your request will be putting them in the position (sometimes frustrating) of trying to "please the teacher." Wait for them to want to express their thoughts—that personal interest in verbal expression can serve as a valuable pathway for finding creative delight, sharing thoughts with others, or for expressing emotions and fears.

ENCOURAGING CREATIVE THOUGHT

All individuals are born with some degree of creative potential and are subject to Piaget's (1964) suggestion that the basic goal of education should be to produce individuals who are capable of *creativity* (bringing new or original thinking to the solution of problems), *invention,* and *discovery.* Some people may look at such a statement and respond, "Don't look at me—I'm as *uncreative* as anyone can be!" Such people view creativity in an unrealistic light—they think of it as a magical ability that allows someone to design a new invention, compose a best-selling song, or paint a masterful picture. The teacher of young children must see youngsters in a wider, fuller sense. In this view, creativity means any way of reacting to a situation that goes beyond the mere imitation of what someone else did in that situation. Earl C. Kelley (1962) explained: "Every person needs the chance to be creative. This does not mean that everyone should paint a picture or write a symphony. Creativity occurs whenever a person contrives a new way out of a unique dilemma. It is simply meeting the problems of living and inventing new ways to solve them. Most of us do this every day in a greater or lesser degree." (p. 140).

Young children, because of their limited experiences, meet new problems daily. Whenever they develop original solutions to such problems, they are displaying some degree of creative thinking. Some children may display a higher degree of creativity than others, but no children are without some creativity. In infants, creativity may show up when the child invents a new way to play with a plastic ring; in toddlers it may be reflected in a new combination of words. Whatever the outward manifestation of the creative process, its essential feature is the ability to generate different ideas in the production of things or ideas. Of course, some children will possess more potential for creativity than others. We must not look unfavorably on those who do not—the less creative are valuable, too. Our main message here is to provide situations so that all children will be encouraged to bring out and nourish the creative potential with which they are endowed.

Understanding the Origin of Creativity

From where does children's creativity come? Recent research into brain functioning has focused upon exactly that question. Robert

Ornstein (1977) and David Galin (1976) are among researchers who have discovered that we actually have two interacting thinking systems housed in our heads—each located in a different place. These two systems are designated as *hemispheres* (left and right) of the brain. Each hemisphere is separated by a thick bundle of nerve fibers called the *corpus calossum,* which serves as a communications system between the two. In the past, researchers gave their attention primarily to only the left hemisphere because they believed that all the major thought processes originated there. They described the right hemisphere as basically a "partner" with very little or no functioning characteristics. The left hemisphere contains the thinking abilities traditionally rewarded in our schools—the desire for order and structure in our lives as well as the processes enabling us to perform well in reading, writing, and arithmetic. The left side looks at parts and processes and attempts to combine them into a meaningful product. Therefore, the left side is often called the "rational" or "logical" hemisphere.

Current research, however, has shown that some individuals are not able to think logically and rationally. They look at things differently, searching for new, creative avenues of expression. These individuals cannot conform to established standards and seek to do things "their own way." Instead of excelling in math, reading, spelling, and other school subjects requiring correct answers, these individuals prefer to express their thoughts in unbridled, free ways. They are guided by the right hemisphere, a side of the brain involving intuitive rather than logical thought. It seeks to shift from obvious ways of looking at things and strives to create new ways of looking at them.

In some ways, you might say we all are born with two minds in one head—the left for verbal and analytic thought and the right for intuition. Children dominated by right hemispheric thinking are very good at spatial forms—activities such as matching designs,

recognizing objects, copying geometric forms, or completing puzzles. Because of this skill, right-hemisphere functioning is often referred to as holistic thought; the person can perceive patterns even though parts of the whole are missing. On the other hand, the left hemisphere, or verbal-analytic hemisphere, specializes in logical thought. It learns best through sequential building of parts to make the whole. It stores its memories in words, thereby specializing in subject areas such as reading and writing. Each of these two modes of thought provides a dimension to our general pattern of thinking that the other lacks. However, cultural pressures for conformity and for performing in school such analytical tasks as reading or writing have caused our society to overemphasize analytic left hemispheric thinking at the expense of holistic right hemisphere skills. This phenomenon should be of special concern to education, because artists, musicians, writers, and other great thinkers have reported that their creative work is based on the ability to *integrate both modes of thinking.* Can this integration process be encouraged in young children and thereby foster the creative thinking process?

According to Galin (1976), the answer is yes because the corpus callosum, the great bridge of nerve fibers connecting the two hemispheres, is not mature at birth nor completely developed until sometime after the age of four. Therefore, dominance of one mode of hemispheric thinking is not yet established until that time. And, there is further evidence that the right hemisphere actually is the dominant mode of thinking and learning in the very young, particularly into the first two years of life. The organization of the brain is very plastic in young children. Thus, we have the opportunity to accomplish three goals: to cultivate creativity in young children by developing each mode equally, to integrate each mode into thinking patterns, and to encourage children to develop the ability to inhibit either one when it is inappropriate to a task.

Look for the creative children in your classroom.

Creative children

- Constantly demonstrate curiosity in many things.
- Enjoy asking questions.
- Bring many ideas to the solution of problems.
- Offer clever, unique, or unusual responses to questions or requests.
- Express personal opinions openly and vociferously.
- Demonstrate a keen sense of humor.
- Enjoy being different.
- Relish an opportunity to be adventurous or to take a risk.
- Fantasize, imagine, and like to pretend.
- Make up unique stories or ideas.
- Have large numbers of ideas to share.
- Delight in art, music, movement, or play rather than academic activities.

Test your own creative abilities by attempting to solve the following problem. Although this problem looks simple, it is actually quite difficult. As a matter of fact, only about one person in a hundred is able to solve it the *first time around.* Four volumes of Shakespeare's collected works are on the shelf: The pages of each volume are exactly 2 inches thick. The covers are each ⅙ inch thick. The bookworm started eating at page 1 of volume I and it ate through to the last page of volume IV. What is the distance the bookworm covered. Do not look at the answer until you have finished.

The answer is 5 inches. Remember that the bookworm started at page 1 of volume I. Put your finger on that point; do not count the back cover and all the pages in between. Are you catching on? Similarly, the bookworm ate only to the last page of the last volume; do not

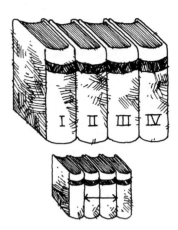

count the front cover and all the pages of the last volume. What causes so many of us to generate "correct" answers by looking only at obvious solutions to problems?

Children exhibiting creative thinking abilities are apparent in the preschool setting—we can see a steady progression in their ingenuity, imagination, and mastery of ways to use things available to them. They first understand the ways in which materials can be used normally and then begin to explore ways in which they can shape new products or find new uses for products. Children do this with many things in their environment: Plastic cups are not to be used merely for drinking liquids, they make wonderful scoops for the sand area, they can hold a pet hermit crab while its cage is being prepared, they can be used in pairs to simulate binoculars, and they can even be decorated with glue, sand, seashells, spangles, and pebbles, and sent home as colorful pencil holders. Paper clips, napkins, rubber bands, paper bags, straws, water, clay, paints, blocks, saws, hammers, leaves, twigs, and rhythm instruments are all fuel for the child's creative engine. The teacher is the key that turns on that engine and encourages it to continue running.

Tests designed to measure children's creativity tend to measure the creative thinking abilities. J. P. Guilford's *Unusual Uses Test* (1967) requires the children to propose unconventional uses for common objects. For example, the child is asked to tell all the ways he can think of to use a brick, a light bulb, or a piece of paper. M. A. Wallach and N. Kogan (1965) use a variety of techniques, among which is asking children to describe various kinds of pattern drawings. Figure 10-1 illustrates some of the patterns employed by Wallach and Kogan, as well as some of the more conventional and creative replies. These and similar tests may be useful to teachers who are interested in measuring the creative potential of their youngsters.

Teachers can and should encourage creativity in young children. Although all children will not become Mozarts, Michelangelos, Einsteins, or Curies as a result of their creative experiences, most educators believe that creative thinking is a valuable cognitive tool. Researchers have attempted to identify the conditions under which creativity seems to flourish in the schools and have come up with these general conditions:

- Time limits are removed from activities in which children are deeply involved.

- A free, open atmosphere is established where open expression is encouraged.

- The children are allowed to share ideas and to stimulate one another's thinking.

- Conditions where stress and anxiety are present are removed.

In order to establish such conditions, teachers apparently have to assume two important roles: (1) facilitator for the child's thinking and (2) arranger of classroom activities that encourage creative expression and free thinking.

Facilitating the Child's Thinking

You must develop the skills of listening to the children and encouraging their deeper explorations into creative thinking. You can do this by asking questions that encourage children to go beyond the obvious, that help them see relationships among ideas, and to improve or combine ideas. The following list offers some idea-spurring questions that indicate interest in the children's thinking and serve to encourage deeper thought:

- "What else can your boat do?"

- "What might happen if people knew how to fly?"

- "What if all the trees had red leaves?"

- "If you were a bird, how would you tell me you are hungry?"

- "Why do you suppose the ice melted?"

- "In how many different ways could you use the light bulb to get my attention?"

- "Have you ever thought of a new way that this ball could be used?"

- "Why is your painting like you?"

- "Does the stop sign take the place of anyone?"

- "What would you add to (or take away from) the story?"

- "What would happen if we slept during the day and were awake at night?"

- "What, instead of the shovel, could you use to dig in the garden?"

- "How would you feel if you saw a fly as big as a cow?"

- "If you had a chance to be any animal you wanted to be, which one would you choose?"

Notice that all questions deliberately went beyond the obvious and toward encouraging original ideas, many ideas (rather than only one), combinations of ideas, improvement of ideas, and free association among ideas. The ability to seize opportunities and ask questions like these is a sophisticated one that comes after a great deal of thought and practice. Be aware of the opportunities when they arise, for your children must be helped to experience the satisfactions associated with express-

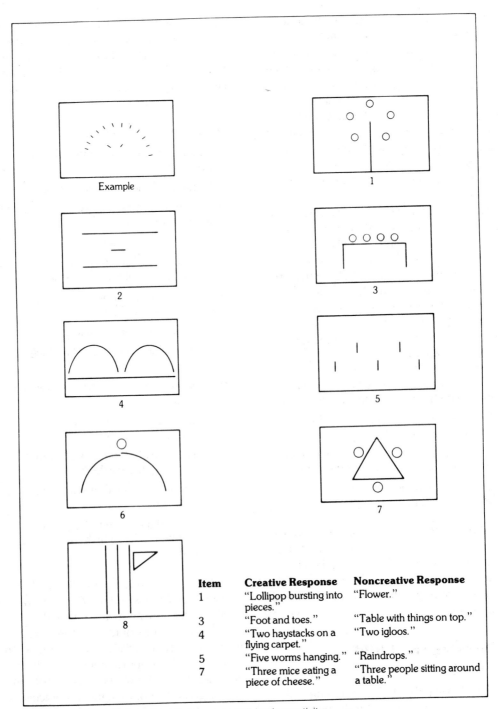

Item	Creative Response	Noncreative Response
1	"Lollipop bursting into pieces."	"Flower."
3	"Foot and toes."	"Table with things on top."
4	"Two haystacks on a flying carpet."	"Two igloos."
5	"Five worms hanging."	"Raindrops."
7	"Three mice eating a piece of cheese."	"Three people sitting around a table."

Figure 10-1 *Stimulus materials to assess children's creativity*

(From *Modes of Thinking in Young Children* by Michael A. Wallach and Nathan Kogan. Copyright © 1965 by Holt, Rinehart and Winston, Inc. Reprinted by permission of Holt, Rinehart and Winston, CBS College Publishing.)

ing oneself freely as a person, with confidence and approval.

In addition to *asking* good questions, you must learn to be a good listener. Creative children have a wealth of questions of their own to ask: "Why don't airplanes flap their wings?" "How do the clouds get so clean?" "Why do puppies have tails?" "Where does the water go when it goes down the tub?" Thomas Edison's last day in school, for example, came when he asked, "How can water run uphill?" after he noticed a river in Ohio did just that. Children come to us with a strong need to ask questions. Be respectful to them and guide them in exercising this childhood gift. Remember that this is a strange new world for youngsters and they are enthusiastic to understand what is incomprehensible to them. Whenever a child approaches you with a question, ask yourself, "Am I listening as carefully and sensitively as I am able?" When you do, you communicate to the child that he or she is a worthwhile individual whose thoughts are valued regardless how "silly" they might seem to be. This is something the children need to know.

Arranging Classroom Activities

Although each area of the preschool curriculum is ripe for creative endeavors, the areas of art and music are often more closely associated with creativity than some others. Preschool teachers understand the value of these areas and make sure that children have many opportunities for free expression through art and music.

ART

Art activities provide many opportunities for young children to release their creative abilities. They allow children to depict people or things in highly personal ways. Youngsters enjoy the possibilities presented by various art media and love to experiment with form and color or simply engage in sense-pleasure play without concern for the depiction of people or things. You may find that some children are content to swish their hands pleasurably through finger paints, while others are more concerned with representing clouds, grass, the sun, or trees. Whatever the individual inclination, children revel in the use of paints, crayons, and paper.

To some adults, whatever the children do with art materials is messy—their scribbles or sensory activities seem to be only unimportant blobs or meaningless jumbles of line and form. These adults often fail to understand or appreciate beginning artistic expression, and often resort to supplying follow-the-dot books, coloring books, or dittoed forms to their children. Such materials hinder the creative freedom that youngsters seek and start them on the road to learning that there is only one correct way to express oneself artistically— the way identified by the teacher or adult. Viktor Lowenfeld (1957) emphasized the importance of creative, free artistic expression as opposed to a guided, form-oriented approach:

> It has been proved beyond any doubt that such imitative procedures as found in coloring and workbooks make the child dependent in his thinking; they make the child inflexible, because he has to follow what he has been given. They do not provide *emotional relief* [italics mine] because they give the child no opportunity to press his own experience and thus acquire a release for his emotions; they do not even promote *skills* [italics mine] and discipline, because the child's urge for perfection grows out of his desire for expression; and finally they condition the child to adult concepts which he cannot produce alone, and which therefore frustrate his own creative ambitions. (p. 18)

By not allowing the young child to express himself freely with art media, we are stif ing creative potential, as well as hindering the youngster's developing *emotional* and *skills* growth. The *emotional* aspects of free artistic production are well exemplified by teachers, executives, businesspeople, or other employees involved in nonphysical labor who find great emotional release and satisfaction in sewing, painting, building, or producing unique materials with their hands during their free time. Such activities help drain accumulated nervous tension, frustration, and anger, and present opportunities to experience the joy and pleasure associated with creating something unique. The young child finds the same values when activities such as pounding and shaping in clay help release emotional strains, and painting a picture with brightly colored paint results in feelings of happiness and accomplishment. The *skills* aspects of free artistic involvement are illustrated in many ways:

- *small motor skills:* cutting; pasting; holding brushes, crayons, and pencils

- *eye-hand coordination:* painting the chimney so that it rests on the roof; cutting along a line with scissors; squeezing glue from a container so that it lands on the needed spot; placing a sunflower seed at just the right place on a collage

- *problem-solving skills:* deciding what color to paint a flower; determining how large to make a tree; settling on the proper materials to use for a collage

- *language skills:* talking to others as they participate; listening to adults as new words or directions are communicated ("Pull the string through the hole in the end of the box."); observing his name written by the teacher on a finished project

Although creativity may be the major purpose for advocating preschool art experiences, teachers should be aware of the important benefits of free uninhibited artistic pursuits.

The child's total personality emerges as she becomes involved in artistic endeavors.

But before you plan to offer art experiences to youngsters, you must be informed of *how* children develop their abilities and *what* they portray in their finished products. Such knowledge helps you interpret the child's work and set realistic expectation levels for their work, and helps guide you in selecting and planning your teaching strategies and materials.

The Developmental Dimension of Children's Art

The *developmental theory,* perhaps the most popular theory of art development, is primarily associated with Viktor Lowenfeld and W. Lambert Brittain (1970), who described children's growth in artistic abilities as progressing through a series of distinguishable, sequential stages. The three stages of art development normally associated with preschool youngsters are the scribble stage, the preschematic stage, and the schematic stage.

The Scribble Stage (2–4 years) The analogy that scribbling is to drawing as babbling is to speech illustrates the importance of this first stage. Before the age of two, the child is probably more interested in eating a crayon than drawing with it, but at about age two he begins to use it to scribble lines that are random and disorganized. As he matures, he moves to the *named scribble stage,* which can be described in the following anecdote.

Teodoro began his picture by putting two blobs of green paint on the easel paper. "Come see my tree," he proudly requested of the teacher. Although the painting was nowhere near the likeness of a tree, Teodoro nevertheless used this symbol to represent something he had thought about. In a short time, as he began a second painting, Teodoro again placed two green blobs on the easel paper, this time commenting, "This is my horse."

Adults are usually amused by this stage, as the child asserts that his scribbles are "mommy," "doggie," or "house." The child's interest in the process varies at this stage, and he often uses a great deal of paper for a few randomly scribbled lines.

After the named scribble stage come the *controlled scribble stage,* a transitional phase where the children are beginning to exercise some control over horizontal, circular, and vertical motions. The child is able to make his lines and circles go in the desired direction, but he is as yet unable to draw the object he wishes to represent. It is at the end of this period that the child moves away from using art media for the sensory pleasures he experiences, and begins to use them in a more conscious effort to represent something.

Preschematic Stage (4–7 years)   At this stage, the child first begins to represent the objects he sees in his everyday world, mostly people. In drawing people, the child usually begins to draw the head as a roughly circular line that encloses marks standing for eyes, nose, and mouth—although these facial features are often out of their usual location. The child also begins to represent other objects during this stage, usually with lines and crude circles or rectangles.

Schematic Stage (7–9 Years)   Although this stage has been identified as characteristic of the seven- to nine-year-old, Lowenfeld and Britain tell us that it may appear in some youngsters by the age of five. During this stage, the child seems to place his major efforts toward the representation of a human figure. He adds ears and hair (scribbles at the top of the head), sticklike arms sticking out the side of the head and ending in a club or sunburst of fingers, a set of legs that grow straight down from the head, again ending in a club or sunburst of toes. When the torso first appears, it will look like a crude oval or circle with the legs sticking straight out. By the age of five, the child will draw arms, legs, and torso of more realistic shape, usually represented by circles, ovals, and rectangles. Clothing and scenery may appear by this time.

Some educators believe that this interest in drawing the human figure is so significant that a child's ability to represent details in his picture can be used as a measure of intellectual maturity. Dale Harris (1963) revised and extended the Goodenough Draw-A-Man Test, and theorizes that increasingly sophisticated representations of the human figure indicate advanced levels of intellectual capabilities. Such thoughts have become controversial today (McWhinnie, 1971) but nevertheless they point out the value of art as more than a single-dimensional activity.

For an illustration of the artwork done by children during each of the developmental phases, refer to Figure 10-2.

Lowenfeld claimed that passage through each of the developmental stages is a natural phenomenon—that children must pass through one stage before they can attain the next. However, he felt that such movement could be stimulated not by outside teaching, but by providing an open environment in which the children freely bring forth and exercise what they already possess. When given opportunities to do so, they naturally progress through the developmental levels. In effect, the children are left alone to draw what they like while the teacher acts as a guide and inspiring force. Any application of external standards or patterns is considered a negative force producing only inhibitions and frustrations. R. Kellog (1969) stated:

> [The child is] a very experienced master of self-taught art. . . . In fact, Picasso said that adults should not teach children to draw but should learn from them. . . . Children left alone to draw what they like, without the interference of adult guidance, usually develop a store of gestalts, which enable them to reach the culminating stage of self-taught art. From there, if they are especially

gifted, they may develop into great artists, unspoiled by the stenciled minds of well-meaning adults. [pp. 12–21]

This developmental philosophy of preschool art education dominated the early childhood curriculum from the time of Froebel until the 1960s. It was during that time that all developmental theories came under assault, and the concept of teaching art by providing a challenging environment while waiting for children to grow and develop through predetermined stages became unpopular. Also during that time many art educators followed a philosophy that emphasized the formal teaching of art skills, developing cognitive goals through art experiences and advancing attitudes of art appreciation.

Sylvia F. Burns (1975) gives examples of some of the possible cognitive goals expected when activities are prepared with specific goals in mind:

> *Crayons:* Initial color perceptions, use of small muscles, perceptual-motor development, space and shape relationships, pictorial representation of the child's world. Counting, matching, grouping of colors, whole-part relationships, use of crayons for rubbings (paint over with thinned tempera—scientific learning that some things do not mix).
>
> *Paint:* More complex medium than crayons involving another approach to perceptual learning. A constantly changing medium good for scientific learnings: looks different wet than when dry, opaqueness can be covered over (What is underneath the visible color?). Variations in texture, fluidity, different textured effects depending upon brushes used. Can be mixed to change color, dripped into another color. Can be used on materials other than paper (Is the result the same?). Excellent vocabulary builder.
>
> *Paper collage:* Size relationships, shape discrimination, whole-part concepts, arrangement (design). A two-dimensional experience for reading. Problem solving (choosing from offered materials). Beginning math (classifying, counting shapes).
>
> *Three-dimensional collage:* Separating and putting together of items. Bringing together shapes and elements in the world (important for beginning reading). Sorting, comparing, seeing similarities in items, classifying items of same shape and/or material. Use of items in new ways (seeing alternatives). Problem solving (how to fasten).
>
> *Clay:* Sensory-tactile perceptions via shaping, rolling, pulling, pounding. Representation of personal ideas and perceptions of things in the world. Concepts of mass, change, relationship of parts to whole, fractions (whole, half, quarter). Math (many, few, larger, smaller, more), may also be used for addition and subtraction.
>
> *Finger paint:* Compare consistency. Motor development, change of form. Development of control (not confined to small area). Visual-motor coordination, figure-ground perception. Vocabulary builder. [p. 201]

Programs reflecting such goals emphasize cognitive growth at nearly the total exclusion of traditional goals. However, today, early childhood educators have retreated from such a drastic swing and have "rediscovered" to some extent the ideas of Viktor Lowenfeld. H. J. McWhinnie (1972) explains: "Lowenfeld's . . . ideas have new meaning for the 1970's. Someone with his orientation is now needed to redirect art education towards a greater concern for the individual and social ends and move it away from the excess of concern with the cognitive goals and discipline centeredness" (pp. 8–13).

The Feeling Dimension of Children's Art

A second contributing theory of artistic development holds that children draw what they *feel*—that art is one of the primary means of

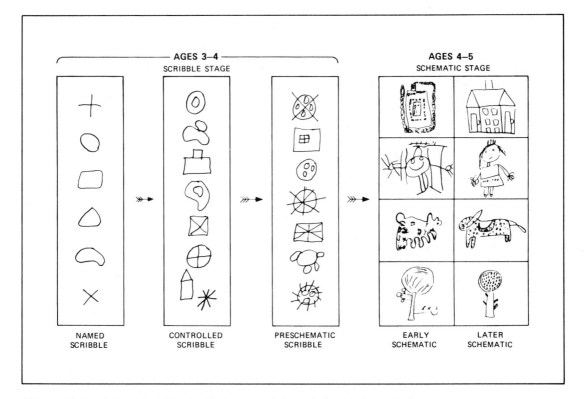

Figure 10-2   *A chart depicting shape, design, and stages in the development of children's drawings*
(Reproduced by permission of John Wiley and Sons, Inc., New York, N.Y., from *Development of the Child* by David Elkind and Irving B. Weiner, 1978.)

expressing what is deep down inside. Children's art, then, is seen to be a reflection of emotions as well as a reflection of general growth and development. The theory suggests that if a child draws himself as a large circle with sticks for arms and legs, it is not because he is unaware of his other body parts; rather, the large, prominent circle represents a preoccupation with the womb, breast, or other emotion-laden object. Likewise, if the child represents a mother in a family picture as being disproportionately larger than the father, it is because the mother assumes central importance for the child rather than because the child has a perceptual problem. Interpreta-tions can be readily made as the child draws a picture of his family room with an enormous television set, as he uses warm colors to paint a picture of his school setting, or as he aggres-sively splatters and heaps onto his easel paper blobs of angry reds after a discomforting sit-uation on the playground.

According to those who support this the-ory, the following characteristics, can reveal certain emotions in young children:

- *Color:* Bright colors are happy colors; dark colors indicate confusion or depression; pastel colors show calmness and ease.

- *Lines:* Smooth, steady lines indicate security and happiness. Scratchy, uneven lines represent insecurity or anxiousness.
- *Size:* Dimensions may indicate importance; out-of-proportion large people are more important and vice-versa.
- *Position:* The person in the center of the picture is most important; the one farthest away is least important.
- *Details:* If a person is drawn with more detail, the child sees that person as most important.

Don't act as an amateur psychologist as you review your children's artwork, however. One child, for example, had drawn a dark, foreboding picture resembling an explosion. His concerned teacher asked the child to tell her about it. His response: "This is Mt. Helen's explosion yesterday." Relieved, this teacher found that some interpretations have easy explanations. In other cases, however, the signals may have some potential value. Consider the five-year-old boy who had just become a new brother to a little baby girl. He had just completed a drawing of his family with a father, mother, and himself—the baby was omitted. The boy's teacher sensed his need and sensitively began a conversation by saying, "It looks as though you have some feelings about something that recently happened to your family." To be absolutely sure whether or not to intervene, however, you need to collect several pictures over a period of time.

This psychoanalytic theory of art development has influenced early childhood education over the years to a great degree, perhaps to an extent equal to the developmental theory of Lowenfeld. Many traditional preschool practices have been patterned after this thinking, with the idea that art materials allow for an effective release of the child's inner emotions, and provide valuable opportunities

for the release of aggressiveness or built-up tensions. Katherine Read, perhaps the leading educational advocate of this theory of art development, offers this view of art in the preschool setting:

> Experiences in the graphic and plastic arts offer [an] avenue through which individuals release their feelings and find satisfactions. It is [an] avenue of expression which may serve as an outlet throughout the life of the individual. . . . The anxious attention on the *product* [italics mine] rather than the *process* [italics mine], the coloring books, and other "patterns" that were imposed on us have all served pretty effectively to prevent most of us from expressing ourselves through art. Yet art is an important means of expression and of draining off feeling as well as a source of satisfaction. . . .
>
> As we ourselves work with children, we must try to safeguard their use of art media as a means of self-expression. For every child, art can serve as an outlet for feeling if the process is emphasized more than the product. It does not matter that there are differences in ability just as there are in music. Given an easel, paper, and paint, and no directions, every child will paint. For some children painting will remain an important avenue through which they can express feeling all through their lives. [1971, p. 235]

Read, therefore, advocates the use of free, unstructured painting as the major avenue of emotional release through art. Through such activity, she believes, we gain a great deal of insight into what children are feeling.

Your feelings regarding the merits of these theories bear an important relationship to the teaching strategies, activities, and materials that you will use with the children. They help you decide on the degree of guidance or freedom to give the children and on the kinds of activities the children seem ready to enjoy, and they make you aware of the kinds of products children are able to create. Whatever theory appeals to you most, however, you will certainly use many of the following popular suggestions for early childhood art activity.

Art Activities for Preschoolers

Teachers of preschool children are able to choose from a wide variety of suitable materials for their children. These materials can be used in a variety of creative ways. Remember that certain materials are more appropriate for some ages than for others.

SUGGESTED ART MATERIALS FOR THE TWO- TO FOUR-YEAR-OLD

- Pencils: kindergarten size
- Crayons of assorted colors and sizes
- Newsprint paper for drawing or painting (12 inch × 18 inch or 18 inch × 24 inch)
- Finger-paint paper: 12 inch × 18 inch or 18 inch × 24 inch
- Colored paper of assorted colors and sizes
- Brushes for easel painting (¼ inch to 1 inch width, round and flat bristle)
- Poster and tempera paint of assorted colors, liquid or powder form
- Paint containers: old cans or plastic containers
- Easels
- Smock or apron for each child
- Chalk of assorted colors and sizes
- Plastic modeling materials such as playdough, clay, salt and flour mixes
- Yarn of assorted sizes and colors
- Glue and scissors, paste
- Scrap materials for collages or texture experiences

SUGGESTED ART MATERIALS FOR THE FOUR- TO EIGHT-YEAR-OLD

- Poster paint of assorted colors
- Brushes of assorted sizes, round or flat bristle

Easel painting is enjoyed by nearly every preschool child, and is, therefore, one of the most frequently used avenues of creativity in early childhood facilities around the country.

- Crayons and chalk of various colors
- Modeling materials: clay, playdough, and so on
- Paper: construction, drawing, finger paint, easel, and so on
- Scrap materials for collages
- Easel painting supplies
- Glue, scissors, paste
- Magic markers or colored pencils
- Printmaking materials

Easel Painting and Other Painting Experiences   Easel painting is perhaps the most popular of all preschool art activities. It provides the child with initial opportunities to explore and discover growing artistic abilities.

Children enjoy painting at easels—some would probably prefer to spend most of the day drawing and scribbling. When first given opportunities to paint at the easel, the young child often engages in experiments with tempera or poster paints and a variety of brushes in sense-pleasure play, experiencing form and color with little concern for the depiction of objects. By about the age of four or five, experimental circular motions turn into heads and tree tops, while longer strokes become legs, arms, tree trunks, and horizontal lines. Such figures will not actually look as they appear to our eyes, but remember that young children are progressing through *first* experiences in depicting reality; this is a giant step in the development of their thinking abilities.

The easel painting area should be in a quiet, uncluttered part of the room near a sink or toilet facilities (important in the case of spills and other accidents). Newspaper or long sheets of butcher paper should be spread on the floor to catch drips and spills. Furnish small containers of creamy tempera paint (to be held within newspaper- or waxpaper-lined easel trays) and a variety of brushes for experimentation. Each child should know that he can paint when he wants to, so the easels should be available each day for painting opportunities.

In addition to preparing the easel area, your role includes helping the children get ready for their painting experiences. Help them into their protective smocks (usually old shirts or plastic aprons) and help them to use the brushes that feel comfortable in their hands. Encourage and assist the child during his efforts, making sure not to interfere unless a specific purpose can be achieved. For example:

Teacher: "You painted the whole paper green, Paul. It looks very pretty."

Paul: "I like green color."

Teacher: "I wonder how your painting would look if you added dots of another color."

Paul: "How do you make dots?"

Teacher: "Let me show you." (*On another piece of paper the teacher shows Paul how to use his brush to make dots.*)

Paul: "I want to make red dots." (*Paul experiments a bit with the red paint and makes some large, irregular dots. After some time, he proudly announces that he has finished his painting.*)

Such informal instruction opens the door to new possibilities for the child and helps him develop increasing creative skills. In the same way, children can be led to experiment with thick lines, thin lines, circles, swirls, and various color combinations.

After the children have begun to feel comfortable with easel painting and have learned to control brushes and paint, you may wish to introduce other painting experiences, such as those that can be done at tables. Note the examples in the painting activities box.

Drawing   In contrast to *painting* (a medium mainly emphasizing experimentation with form and color), *drawing* finds children attempting finer pictorial representations, most typically of people. Their ability to represent people was illustrated earlier; remember they pass through stages of scribbling and drawing until, by about the age of five or six, most children can represent people relatively accurately.

Your role in encouraging representation through drawing is essentially that of an arranger of the environment and stimulator of the child's thinking. Place *crayons, pencils, nontoxic marking pens,* or *colored chalk* on a large table along with an ample supply of drawing paper. As they are encouraged to experiment with these materials, children will add trees, houses, and flowers to their pictures of human figures. Because some children do not have opportunities to experience things beyond their immediate home environment, you may find those five- or six-year-olds getting stuck in a rut of drawing pictures only of people, houses showing all four walls, and tulips or "lollipop"

PAINTING ACTIVITIES

- *Ink blots:* Prefold paper; drop thick paint onto paper from tongue depressors; refold, open. Several colors may be used to produce interesting designs.

- *String painting:* Dip short lengths of string into bowls of paint and let them fall on paper. Paper may also be folded, then string pulled out while the paper is held shut with one hand.

- *"Block" printing:* Dip objects into bowls of paint and press or rub on paper. Objects may be spools, corks, sink stoppers, sponges, jar lids, small blocks, scrub brushes, potatoes cut in shapes, combs, Q-tips, and so on.

- *Dry powder painting:* Put dry powder tempera paint in dishes at the easel or on the table, and use wads of wet cotton. Dab the dry paint onto a paper that has been completely moistened with a sponge and water.

- *Textured paint:* Mix a textured substance with paint for different effects, adding a little glue to ensure sticking. Use salt (which sparkles when dry), sand, fine sawdust, coffee grounds, or soap flakes.

- *Spatter painting:* You will need small wire screens on wood frames, toothbrushes, pans of thin paint, and various designs to set under the screen on protective paper. Objects may be paper silhouettes, leaves, cookie cutters, or a variety such as keys, forks, spoons, scissors, tongue depressors, and so on. Dip the toothbrush into the paint and run it over the wire screen. The paint will produce an interesting effect on the object below.

- *Table painting:* Use bowls of paint and short-handled brushes for a variety of individual painting activities.

- *Fancy paper:* Cut easel paper into unusual shapes to stimulate more elaborate design painting on children's part: circles, triangles, free form, Easter eggs, Christmas trees, houses, and so on.

- *Different types of surfaces may be painted:* paper towels, colored construction paper, printed newsprint, finger-paint paper, cardboard boxes, egg cartons, wallpaper, magazine pages, dry-cleaning bags, wooden blocks, cloth, wood, clay, dried dough, seashells, stones, branches, paper bags, oil cloth, pine cones.

- Window painting: Bon Ami or Glass Wax may be colored with dry paint powder and used to paint windows.

- *Soap painting:* Whip soap powder and add dry paint powder. Paint on colored or white paper with brushes.

- *Crayon and paint:* Draw on paper with light-colored crayons, then cover with a wash of dark paint. Paint will not cover the crayon.

- *Detergent paint:* Paint mixed with detergent can be used to paint on glazed paper surfaces, plastic, aluminum foil, and glass.

- *Mixing colors:* The children can mix their own paints to be used at the table or easel. Put out colors in small amounts in paper cups or muffin tins and allow the children to mix. Mixing primary colors teaches pastel tints and grayed tones.

- *Water painting:* Large brushes and small pails of clear water can be used either outdoors or indoors to "paint" fences, walks, tricycles, sides of buildings, and so on.

---

trees. To move them away from such stereotyped production, provide them with a variety of experiences involving people, animals, flowers, buildings, and other kinds of places and events. Such experiences include trips to the zoo, farm, or areas of interest within the community; bringing animals to the classroom; or walking through the woods. During such experiences the child should be led to notice apparent features of objects and make creative interpretations of the objects they experience. The teacher can use questions or comments to stimulate thinking related to each of these areas. Questions like "Can you see the sunflower's seeds?" "Is the horse bigger than the dog?" "What color is the cake?" "Can you see the giraffe's long neck?" "Touch the flower. What does it feel like?" lead the child to observe more closely. To stimulate the child's creativity, the teacher can ask, "Did you ever imagine you were a spider?" "What would it feel like to be a tall tree?" "I wonder what the

DRAWING-RELATED ACTIVITIES

Crayon Activities

- *Crayon etching:* Cover paper with light-colored crayon, then cover light surface with dark crayon. Scratch through to light surface with edge of blunt scissors or tongue depressor.

- *Crayon leaf rubbing:* Place leaf under newsprint and scribble with crayon on top of paper to get impression of leaf. This can also be done with coins, string, pieces of paper, wire screening, burlap, and so on.

- *Crayon and paint:* Draw on paper with light-colored crayons; then cover with wash of dark paint. Paint with cover all but crayon markings.

- *Colored paper:* Using crayons on colored paper teaches children what happens when one color is applied to another.

- *Single colors:* Picking out one color to use for an entire picture offers a change from having a variety of colors to use.

- *Variety in diameter:* Wide crayons stimulate more extensive drawing; narrow crayons stimulate more detailed work. Using the entire flat side of crayon, after peeling paper, also adds variety.

- *Crayon stenciling:* Draw on cloth with a firm, even pattern of light, solidly applied color. Place material face down between two pieces of smooth paper and press with hot iron. Do not rub iron across paper.

Chalk Activities

- *Wet paper:* Paper dipped in water permits chalk to slide more easily, gives more fluid motion to drawing, and makes colors more brilliant. Construction paper or paper towels may be used.

- *Wet chalk:* Chalk is dipped in bowl of water before being used on dry paper. The effects are similar to those of dry chalk on wet paper.

- *Buttermilk or diluted plastic starch:* Apply these liquids to wet paper. The chalk will stick to the paper after it dries.

- *Fixative:* This may be sprayed on dried chalk drawings or added to water for wet paper drawings. Prevents chalk dust from rubbing off. Common fixatives include hair spray, liquid starch sprayed from a bottle, or special fixatives purchased from school supply stores.

- *Chalkboard:* This large surface encourages expansive, sweeping motions. Children love to draw with chalk on the chalkboard.

---

dog is trying to say." "How would you like to be able to fly like a bird?" "How would it feel to move as slowly as a caterpillar?"

This questioning-type approach offers the child an opportunity to rethink what he has experienced. This forces him to reconstruct the mental images needed to form the people, objects, or animals he wishes to draw.

But, to open up the child both to new experiences and to making a mental copy of those experiences is not all there is to the process of creative art. The child must *personalize* his association with the object, that is, he must transform it into an individually unique form that is free from any *standardized* expectancies. In effect, drawing activities should be motivated by varieties of direct experiences in which the children are led to think on levels that go beyond the mere recognition of objects. These creative thoughts should be directed toward the production of individually unique pictorial representations that demonstrate personalized awareness and increased insight.

Activities with crayon and chalk, other than drawing, are described in the "Drawing-related Activities" box.

Texture Experiences All children from their youngest years are fascinated by experimentation with different textures. Picture for a moment the infant who squeezes soft pudding between his fingers as he gurgles and laughs. This same attraction to sensory stimulation accompanies the child throughout his preschool years as he seeks to experiment with

TEXTURE-EXPERIENCE ACTIVITIES

Crayon Rubbings Place drawing paper over various textured surfaces such as sandpaper, a screen, the wall, floor, and so on. Rub a crayon over each surface and notice the different effects.

Finger Painting Place finger paint directly on paper or on the table. Make a design by smearing the paint with the whole hand, fingers, palm, fingernails, or knuckles. A suggested procedure for organizing the finger-painting experience is:

1. Cover a table top with paper or oil cloth, if preferred. At the early stages of finger painting, your children may feel less frustrated by sliding, tearing paper if the paint is directly applied to the table.

2. Allow plenty of "elbow room" so the children can experience free rhythmic body movement.

3. Put on smocks or aprons.

4. Apply finger paint to the shiny surface of finger-paint paper, or directly to the table.

5. Encourage the children to experiment freely.

6. Children should help clean their area when they finish with their design.

7. Have the children wash their hands immediately and remove smock or apron.

8. The children may wish to take their paper home. If the design was made on the table, simply press a sheet of paper onto the still-wet table, and a print will be made.

For a change of texture, add sand, salt, coffee grounds, or fine sawdust to the finger paint.

For a variation in color, put powder paint in salt shakers and let children add their own color to uncolored finger paint. This will help them learn color names, color concepts, and the concept of mixing colors to create new colors.

You should wet the smooth side of finger-paint paper for best results. However, such paper is not necessary. Children may finger-paint directly on formica-topped tables, or on large pieces of oil cloth. A print can be made by placing newsprint on top of the design, gently rubbing, then pulling off. Results can be cleaned off quickly with a sponge.

A large work area is best for finger painting—the child can, thus, use rhythmic movements with arms and perhaps the entire body.

Be sure that you have help from aides or volunteers during this time—supervision and cleanup will progress much more smoothly.

Plastic Materials The materials may be rolled, pounded, pinched, patted, and broken. Children first enjoy these materials (clay or play-dough) for their sensory appeal, but eventually they become interested in manipulating and shaping them into recognizable objects. Recipes for plastic materials follow:

COOKED DOUGH

2 cups boiling water

½ cup salt

½ cup flour

¼ cup cornstarch; blend with cold water

food coloring (optional)

Add salt to boiling water. Combine flour with cornstarch and water to make paste. Pour hot mixture into cold. Put over hot water in a double boiler and cook until glossy. Cool overnight. Knead in flour until right consistency, adding color with flour.

UNCOOKED DOUGH

3 parts flour to 1 part salt or

2 parts flour to 1 part salt

a small amount of vegetable oil (for a smoother texture)

food coloring (optional)

Mix flour and salt thoroughly. Add colored water, or add dry powder paint to flour and salt, mixing well before adding water. Add enough water to form dough into a ball. Knead on a floured surface until pliable but not sticky. One tablespoon alum may be added to each 2 cups of flour as a preservative.

PASTE RECIPES

HOBBY CRAFT PASTE

- ¾ cup water
- 2 tablespoons light Karo syrup
- 1 teaspoon white vinegar
- ½ cup Argo starch
- ¾ cup water
- ¼ teaspoon oil of wintergreen

  Combine ¾ cup water, corn syrup, and vinegar in a medium-sized saucepan; bring to a full boil. Stir cornstarch into ¾ cup water until smooth. Remove boiling mixture from heat. Slowly pour in cornstarch-water mixture, stirring constantly until smooth. If lumps form, smooth them out with the back of the spoon against the side of

the saucepan. Stir in oil of wintergreen. May be used immediately but will set to paste consistency in 24 hours. Store in covered jar. Keeps two months. Makes about 2½ cups.

BOOKMAKER PASTE

- 1 teaspoon flour
- 2 teaspoons salt
- ¼ teaspoon powdered alum
- 1 heaping teaspoon oil of cloves
- 1 pint cold water

  Mix dry ingredients with water slowly, stirring out lumps. Use a slow fire. Cook over a double boiler until it thickens.

various textures. Therefore, you should encourage children to explore textures as they become involved with a variety of art media. For examples, see the "Texture-experience Activities" box.

Cutting and Pasting Young children enjoy the prospect of using scissors, but may initially experience difficulty in manipulating them. For that reason, their first cutting experiences should be directed not to cutting out patterns or cutting along lines, but to random explorations with varieties of materials—construction paper, cloth, string, newspapers, magazines, tissue paper, and so on—using sharp scissors. The children take special pleasure in the cutting actions and will not be overly concerned about the form of the final product at this stage of development (at about the age of three or four). These cutting activities help the children get used to handling scissors and help them develop the hand and finger muscles necessary for opening and closing the scissors. When these skills become fairly refined (at about the age of four or five) the child is ready to cut out something he has thought

about. For example, Carlos had come to the cutting table from the creative dramatics area where he had been role-playing different scenes that fascinated him on a recent field trip. "I'm gonna make a punkin," he announced, and proceeded to cut out a figure crudely approximating an orange circle. The teacher held it up for the others to see and announced to the other children, "Maybe some of you would like to make pumpkins." Then she moved around the table and watched as several children gleefully cut out round, oblong, and other squiggly-shaped pumpkins. Whatever the final shape, though, the teacher was careful to praise and reassure each child for his cutting efforts.

As the children begin to cut out planned shapes, they soon will be interested in pasting things together. But, as with almost everything else in the preschool classroom, the young child needs to be guided and supported in his initial efforts. First attempts that result in failure will be frustrating for these children, so careful guidance is a necessity. Children's first attempts at using paste will find them experimenting freely, much as they did with easel paint or finger paint. They will often apply globs

Young children should not be expected to cut out planned shapes until they have accumulated experiences with random cutting. These children have had those experiences and reflect confidence in their current task.

of paste with their fingers to something they want to stick together with the idea that more paste ensures sticking. They quickly find out, though, that as their globs of paste dry and become hard, their objects fall apart. However, with your help, children quickly learn the proper amounts of paste to use and soon become interested in trying out a variety of different pasting media on different objects—trial-and-error learning that leads to careful observations of objects in their environment. There are commercially produced varieties of paste available, but you can also make your own. Two recipes for paste that you can use with preschool children appear in the "Paste Recipes" box.

Printing   The printing process involves using paint and a variety of objects to repeat a design over large pieces of drawing or butcher paper. The teacher prepares a printing area by first putting out several shallow pans and laying sponges or folded towels in the bottom of each. Then she pours heavy paint into each pan so that a type of printing pad is formed. The children press their printing tools onto the pad and stamp their repeated designs onto a piece of paper. Some of the possible printing tools available for preschool youngsters are given in the "Printing Activities" box.

Collages   The collage is a planned arrangement of one or several art media on one surface. Anything can be used to make collages: construction paper, drawn or painted objects, cloth scraps, or a variety of "junk" materials found in the environment. You may use a combination of such items or one item alone, but the goal is to create a collection of objects in a planned way. The following is a partial list of possible collage materials—use your imagination to think of ways they can be used.

TEXTURED MATERIALS

fur scraps	twigs
leather	pebbles
felt	dried flowers or
burlap or sacking	weeds
corrugated paper	feathers
egg carton dividers	cotton
carpet scraps	pipe cleaners
sandpaper	acorns
velvet	shells
corduroy	styrofoam
seeds	

PATTERNED MATERIALS

wallpaper samples	candy bar wrappers
magazines	catalogs
seasonal stickers	greeting cards
linoleum scraps	stamps
patterned gift-wrap	

TRANSPARENT AND
SEMITRANSPARENT MATERIALS

net fruit sacks	thin tissue paper
onion sacks	metal screening
crepe paper	colored cellophane
lace	paper lace doilies
plastic wrap	

SPARKLING OR
SHINY MATERIALS

sequins	paper from greet-
glitter	ing cards
aluminum foil	Christmas tinsel
ribbon	mica snow
seasonal wrapping paper	
metallic paper	

SHAPES

buttons	cupcake cups
drinking straws	macaroni, spaghetti
wooden applicators	heavy cotton rug
spools	yarn
scrap sponge	rubber bands
paper clips	toothpicks
metal washers	beads
cork	fluted candy cups
bottle caps	gummed stickers
keys	string
tongue depressors	old jewelry

SCATTERING MATERIALS

sand	beans
sawdust	seeds
yarn	twigs
rice	salt
tiny pebbles	popcorn
wood shavings	eggshells

Guiding Art Activities

The teacher's role in guiding art activities basically involves two tasks: (1) arranging the environment with equipment and materials, and (2) supervising the work in a warm and friendly manner. While *arranging* the room for creative art activities, you should always remember that children grow best when they are allowed to explore freely and imaginatively in a stimulating and challenging setting. Such a setting has an adequate amount of space so that children are able to work comfortably alone or in small groups. Materials and equipment should be easily obtainable at the area where the work is being done. Children must be unhurried and free to plan and carry out special projects in their own ways. Some suggestions are given in the "Activities for Designing Art Environments" box.

There are a number of guidelines you should follow as you *supervise* the children during their creative art endeavors:

1. Offer encouragement and praise while the children work. Let them know how much you value their unique efforts. As you observe their work and talk to them about it, do not pressure them to describe what they are doing—they may be merely exploring with the art media and may not be able to express anything in particular about their product. You may wish to comment about the color, shapes, sizes, or design of the product and show an interest and appreciation toward the work, but refrain from forcing conversation when none seems constructive.

2. Avoid tactless, silly comments such as "What is it?" or "What are you making?" when the children are engaging in media explorations. However, you can perfectly well lead off with the open-ended request, "Please tell me about your picture." Along the same line, refrain from being overly critical when children experience unavoidable acci-

PRINTING ACTIVITIES

- *Food printing:* Cut potatoes, green peppers, corn cobs, celery, apples, or a variety of other fruits or vegetables across the center to get a variety of natural printing stamps. Special designs may be cut into solid vegetables such as potatoes or carrots.
- *Potpourri:* Use thread spools, hair curlers, cookie cutters, the round ends of paper towel rolls, forks, cotton balls, carpet scraps, bottle caps, and other common scraps to make effective printing tools.
- *Rolling pin printing:* Rolling pins, cardboard tubing, or metal cans are equally effective for this activity. Glue yarn or string to the rolling pin so that it is strongly attached. Dip this printing tool into the paint and roll it over a surface.
- *Sponge printing:* Dip various sponge pieces into the paint and stamp them onto a surface.
- *Button printing:* Glue a variety of buttons to dowel sticks and use them for printing.

dents. Just as we would never admonish a house guest for spilling a drink by complaining, "Oh, you are so clumsy!" we must also never admonish children for their accidents.

3. Resist the use of patterns, outlines, or guides whenever possible. Of course, some special projects will necessitate the use of such structures, but excessive use of such materials limits the freedom of expression offered by unstructured art activity.

4. Help children and encourage their efforts, but refrain from fulfilling requests such as, "Will you draw a dog for me right here?" Do not allow children to become dependent on you— encourage them to think about ways in which they can accomplish their goal by themselves. Such requests for help from children usually come because of a desire to produce a "masterpiece" to please the teacher or parent. Let the children know that what they create should be pleasing to them and it is their own—not the teacher's.

5. Resist the temptation to recognize only the "best" works to be shown in a display area. Remember that your enthusiasm should be extended to all within your room, so an undue emphasis on the work of only a few children will soon discourage the rest.

6. Allow the children to take their productions home. Children often get frustrated when they are not allowed to share their artwork with their parents, so a question such as, "Do we get to take our pictures home tonight?" should not go unheeded. Encourage parents to value their children's artistic development and to display their children's work in a prominent place in the home.

7. Print the child's name in the upper left-hand corner of his drawing or painting. In this way you tend to personalize his efforts while giving him opportunity to begin developing reading skills.

When appropriate classroom arrangements are provided and free, creative exploration is encouraged, many values emerge from children's art activities. In such environments, we find a burst of individualism, self-expression, and confidence. Children naturally enjoy the sensory qualities of art and thoroughly delight in the satisfaction of produucing unique products. The enjoyment of creating, the fascination of working with art materials, and the creative processes involved in art activity all help to support the incorporation of a strong art program in the preschool curriculum.

ACTIVITIES FOR DESIGNING ART ENVIRONMENTS

- An easel painting corner should be basic to nearly all preschool settings. Place newspapers or butcher paper on the floor of a cleared area of the room (to catch drips or spills); provide some small containers of paint, some brushes, and an easel; and make sure that smocks are available for protection.

- Arrange a large table that features a special *art center*—this in addition to the classroom easel area. Art center activities may include finger painting, collage work, cutting and pasting, or any other special individual or small-group proj-

ect that can be done by the children as part of their daily planned program.

- Design a bulletin board or display area that can effectively exhibit the art creations of the children. Display the work at the children's eye level rather than at your own (see Figure 10–3).

- Play some soft music in the art area so the children can relax and think in comfort.

- Make handy various cleanup materials such as a sponge, water, or mops so that the children can easily clean up when they are finished or if there is an accident.

Special Art Projects

Although the major emphasis of an early childhood art program should be creativity and sensory stimulation, you may wish sometimes to lead the children in the production of special art projects. In connection with holidays or other particularly significant days, these projects bring a special reward when they are completed and taken home to proud family members. Because these activities are more highly structured and teacher-directed than the ones we have shared up to this point, they are not as fully recognized as suitable vehicles for the development of the child's rich imagination. For that reason, you must be sure that your directions for completing the project are clear and that the necessary physical skills for special manipulations are present so that the children experience joy rather than frustration. Also, be sure to offer these special projects only on special days so that the major emphasis of the children's basic art activities remains that of encountering sensory experiences designed to help children create and to foster cognitive, social, and motor skills.

Some suggestions are contained in the "Special Art Projects" box.

MUSIC

Listening to music, creating music, moving to music, and making music together should be joyous parts of the preschool curriculum. Children look forward to participating in music activities and should be given many opportunities to do so. As a matter of fact, even infants are attentive to and enjoy musical sounds in their environment. Very soon after birth they are able to distinguish musical sounds from other sounds that become part of their lives. Musical toys such as crib mobiles, trains, balls, bath toys, squeeze toys, rattles, and push-pull toys help focus the babies' attention to musical sounds. Caregivers enhance this interest by reciting rhythmical nursery rhymes such as those described earlier in this text, by singing lullabies or other enjoyable songs, and by engaging in a variety of vocal play. Clapping the baby's hands or manipulating the feet rhythmically as these songs are shared add to the enjoyment of the experience. Mimicking the trilling and cooing of the infant creates a fine degree of fascination for the baby. Infants enjoy these musical experiences and will tend to spend long periods of time at such vocal

ON BULLETIN
BOARDS OR
OTHER WALL
DISPLAYS

ON VARIOUS LEVELS
OF DISPLAY BOXES

ON ORDINARY
CLOTHESLINE
WITH CLOTHESPINS

ON VARIOUS
KINDS OF SHELVES

TACKED TO A BOARD
AND LEANING
AGAINST THE WALL

ON   FREE-
STANDING CORRU-
GATED CARDBOARD

Figure 10–3   *Some ways of displaying children's art*

SPECIAL ART PROJECTS

Spooky Pictures

Give the children orange and white crayons and ask them to draw a Halloween design or picture with them. Encourage the children to press hard because a thick layer of crayon is necessary. Then brush one coat of thin black tempera paint over the picture.

Rubbings

Furnish the children with a variety of objects with interesting textured surfaces, for example, keys, coins, doilies, combs, paper clips, and so on. Have the children put a piece of paper over the object and rub over it with a crayon.

Hairy Pumpkin

Scoop the seeds and meat from a medium-sized pumpkin. Place a styrofoam block or cylinder into the pumpkin so that it extends about 2 or 3 inches above the top. Encourage children to bring in colorful leaves from the playground or fall flowers (such as mums) from home. Stick the leaves and flowers into the styrofoam until a pleasant arrangement results.

Variation: You may wish to have each of your children make an individual pumpkin of this type to take home as a centerpiece gift. In this case, visit pumpkin farms and encourage children to search for small pumpkins for the project.

Snowman

Beat equal amounts of Ivory Snow and water until the mixture is very stiff. The children should take turns mixing. Have the children spoon the mixture onto a cardboard snowman shape and spread it evenly. Allow the snowman to set overnight.

The next day the children can decorate their snowman by painting on facial features and buttons with black tempera paint. They may wish to tie a fabric strip around the neck to serve as a scarf and add a construction paper top hat.

Easter Chicks

Cut apart several cups from styrofoam egg containers so that each child has one cup. Have the children cut two eyes from black construction paper and one orange triangle for the beak. Then have them dip a cotton ball into glue and set it into the cup. Brush the eyes and beak with glue and set them in place on the cotton ball.

Easter Eggs

Fill a large jar three-quarters full of liquid starch. Punch a hole in the lid. Place a ball of twine in the starch, thread one end through the lid, and place the lid back on the jar. Pull the string through the hole while a child wraps it around an inflated balloon. Encourage the child to wrap the balloon in several directions with phrases such as "around and around," "up and down," and so on. Once the balloon has been wrapped several times, have the child finish his wrapping at the top so the string can later be used as a hanger. Allow the balloon to dry overnight.

If the balloon has not popped by itself on the next day, prick it with a pin. The children can then push Easter basket grass through the openings in the yarn until the egg is full.

Tub Turtles

Gather a number of used plastic margarine tubs. Have the children paint pieces of styrofoam packing material for the legs, tail, and head of a turtle. Glue the styrofoam pieces to the tub as illustrated.

Turkey Ties

At Thanksgiving time, solicit some old neckties from the parents of your children. Make the basic turkey shape from construction paper and staple it to a bulletin board or mount it on heavy tagboard. Have the children staple or glue the old neckties onto the paper turkey to make the tail. The ties can then be used to discuss concepts related to size, shape, color, and so on.

Paperweight

Take the children on a nature walk and ask them to find a medium-sized stone. Bring the stones back to the classroom and wash them off. Have a variety of tissue paper available and have the children cut or tear the tissue paper into small pieces. First, the children brush a mixture of one-half water and one-half white glue on a small part of the stone. They cover this area with tissue paper and cover the paper with white glue. They repeat this procedure until the entire top of the stone is covered, overlapping the pieces to make it more attractive. Wait until the top is dry before covering the bottom in the same way.

Caterpillars

Cut apart enough cardboard egg cartons so that each child can have one three-cup section. Punch two holes in the first section. Make available pipe cleaners and three or four different colors of tempera paint. Have the children make caterpillars by painting the egg-carton sections and putting pipe cleaner antennae through the punched holes.

play. Recorded music also should be considered a vital part of the infant's musical environment. Be careful, though, to choose special times to play the recordings, since constant background music tends to be ignored after a period of time. Thus, the infant's early musical experiences with toys, jingles, rhymes, lullabies, action songs, and verbal interchange establish a sound foundation of interest in music that not only creates a pleasant and stimulating environment but also contributes to future desires to explore, manipulate, and experiment with music.

Child-Initiated Music

From these early musical encounters, children move to the child-initiated activities frequently found in preschool classrooms. Such activities capitalize on the young children's relative openness in expressing themselves. They often freely sing spontaneous songs, perform expressive bodily movements, or experiment with sounds all around them both indoors and out. You should communicate an acceptance and appreciation of such uninhibited behaviors since these music-oriented activities will tend to increase as the children sense your positive attitudes. You may go further by providing adequate space inside and out for free movement, by providing musical instruments for experimental use, and by your willingness to enter into singing, moving, or dancing activities with the children. In these ways, the child's enthusiasm is supported and his motivation to do more will be reinforced.

The primary aim of music in the preschool setting is not to develop musical talent per se, but to think of music as an enjoyable art form and a creative means of self-expression. The key word in the previous statement is *enjoyable:* Every child should find music to be a rewarding experience and should never be forced to participate in a music activity in which he has no interest. Such unfair demands eventually create negative attitudes toward this

inherently pleasant childhood activity. As an example of what can be done to create negative attitudes toward music, consider the misguided kindergarten teacher who required each of her children to stand in front of the entire class and sing a memorized solo. This performance was evaluated by the teacher and used as the criterion for each child's report card grade in music! Contrast that musical program to the following classroom that stresses incidental teaching.

In Ms. Carpenter's kindergarten classroom, music was looked upon as something natural and spontaneous—it could be expected to come at any time from anyone. Bea walked into school this morning and began to sing her favorite seasonal song to the aide: "Jingle bells, jingle bells, jingle all the way. . . ." Other children soon caught the pattern and chimed in, "Oh what fun it is to ride . . ."

The aide sang along with the children and all ended the song with a great deal of laughter and excitement.

Later on in the morning, the children returned from a trip to a toy store—a part of the teacher's seasonal activity. During free play, Ms. Carpenter observed a boy marching in a circle pounding an imaginary drum as he went along. He was chanting, "See the drummer boy, boom . . . boom . . . boom!" in rhythmic movement. He was an especially outgoing youngster, so Ms. Carpenter offered him a drum from her set of percussion instruments as he continued to portray a working drummer boy toy he saw at the toy store. Ms. Carpenter then went to the piano and added a soft, marching rhythm accompaniment to the boy's activity. Other children began to join the marching activity with other kinds of rhythm instruments. The marching continued for several minutes while the children's attention remained high.

Of course, Ms. Carpenter did not always become directly involved in the children's musical experiences; such a practice is neither appropriate nor advisable. This illustration was only an example; on most occasions, you must only provide the space, materials, and encouragement—the children will enthusiastically take it from there.

Teacher-Initiated Music

Good music programs on the preschool or kindergarten level are closely integrated with regular classroom routines. Songs and creative movement may be related to a field trip, a special weather condition such as rainfall, a certain seasonal or holiday observance, or a special topic being explored in the classroom such as learning basic colors and shapes. Whatever the situation, combining musical experiences with other parts of the daily program demonstrates to the child that music is something to be enjoyed as an integral part of their lives rather than as a separate entity. Teacher-initiated musical activity can be more completely understood if we reexamine Ms. Carpenter's classroom.

Ms. Carpenter welcomed natural musical expression, but also provided regularly planned musical activities during the daily sessions. Such periods were always relaxed and comfortable, and the music was suitable for preschool children. On this particular day, Ms. Carpenter capitalized on the children's interest in "Jingle Bells" and planned group rhythm activities to accompany the song. First, Ms. Carpenter asked the children to think of themselves as Santa's reindeer. They were all to sit in a group and rest because it was Christmas Eve and Santa was about to begin his long, tiring journey to deliver presents to children all over the world. The twinkling sound of "Jingle Bells" on the piano signalled the children to stand in pairs, with one child (Rudolph) as the leader. As the twinkling music played, the reindeer pranced about as they pulled Santa and his sleigh on his merry rounds. They made small stops as Santa delivered his presents to each house, but quickly started again as Santa signalled the reindeer to prance and pull again. After about five such stops, Ms. Carpenter saw that some of

the children were becoming tired, so slowly and at a lower pitch on the piano, she asked the reindeer to plod back to the North Pole where they all flopped down to sleep.

In addition to such planned and unplanned musical experiences, Ms. Carpenter provided many informal interludes during the session. Four keys on the piano signalled the start of rest time for those who were ready for it, a short lullaby accompanied back rubs for children ready for a rest period, short tunes signalled cleanup time or snack, and a record player was kept in a corner where children could slip on earphones to listen to favorite records.

Children enjoyed these pleasant musical experiences and looked forward to participating in them. Ms. Carpenter understood the importance of such activities and applied her knowledge to design pleasurable experiences that invited voluntary participation from each child.

Music can contribute in many ways to the growth and development of young children. Because you must be able to provide many types of opportunities for participation, guidelines and resources are presented in the following sections.

When you plan to initiate a music activity, the first step is to determine which teaching vehicle is to be focused upon: *movement, singing, rhythm,* or a combination. This decision, in turn, will influence your choice of materials and activity.

Movement

A discussion of locomotor activities (movement) was presented in Chapter 6. However, certain elements of that discussion need to be reemphasized and applied to music experiences because these two areas are interrelated in many ways. Movement is a fundamental component of music; music is rhythmical with various patterns and beats. For that reason, songs, chants, and rhythm activities should be utilized while teaching youngsters about the

Where Is Thumbkin?

(Are You Sleeping?)

human body and its capabilities. Learning about the body includes concepts such as the names, locations, and functions of the body parts. Musical activities provide many opportunities for exploring and experimenting with all parts of the body. Consider the following examples.

Singing

Children in the preschool setting are often uninhibited in the adult sense, and frequently enjoy opportunities to express themselves in spontaneous song. Because young children have such natural inclinations for song, they should all be provided with chances to develop their interest. How can we do this? Certain developmental cues can guide you in answering this question.

Children enjoy listening to others sing and sing spontaneously as they play. To encourage them, make singing an integral part of your daily routine. Sing melodious tunes whenever it is time for toileting,

Clap, Clap, Clap, Your Hands

Key: F
Starting tone: F

American Traditional

Clap, clap, clap your hands, Clap your hands to - geth - er.

Clap, clap, clap your hands, Clap your hands to - geth - er.

Tap your head, wave your hand, point your toe. and many
other actions will be suggested.

Head, Shoulders, Knees, and Toes
(Tavern in the Town)

My head, my shoul – ders, knees and toes (knees and toes) my head, my

shoul – ders, knees and toes (knees and toes) and eyes and ears and

(Repeat movement)

mou – th an – d nose, my head, my shoul – ders, knees and toes – (knees and

(Repeat movement) *(Very fast)*

toes)

rest, play, or snack. Show the children that you enjoy singing and are not inhibited or embarrassed to sing in front of them. This *enjoyment* characteristic is the first necessary ingredient in your musical program—if you feel self-conscious in front of the children, you will likely make them feel the same way and they will suppress their desire to sing with you. It may sound surprising, but children will actually enjoy listening to you in much the same way you enjoyed listening to a parent, grandparent, caregiver, or teacher. So, instead of calling to a child who needs assistance, you may wish to sing something—for example, this adaptation was sung by one teacher to the tune of "Twinkle Twinkle Little Star."

> Let me help you, if I may,
> We'll get that shoe tied today.

You can compose simple lyrics to accompany other enjoyable activities. For example, this song (to the tune of "Clementine") was composed by a teacher during a cooking activity:

> Cut the carrots,
> Cut the carrots,
> Cut the carrots, one by one,
> Our soup needs lots of carrots,
> Isn't this a lot of fun?

One teacher adapted "Here We Go Round the Mulberry Bush" for cleanup time:

> This is the way we wash our hands,
> Wash our hands, wash our hands,
> This is the way we wash our hands.
> So early in the morning.

The most important advice for you in this phase of developing a singing program for young children is to have confidence in your musical ability and to lose your musical inhibitions. Children are not music critics—they are generally oblivious of your shortcomings

and appreciate your efforts to make routines enjoyable. Their response to your efforts will be gratifying and professionally rewarding. Perhaps a personal note might convince those of you who remain skeptical.

For reasons not appropriate to detail here, I always felt ill at ease in a singing situation—whether it was singing "Happy Birthday" or bellowing a tune in the shower. It was more painful for me to sing a song, for example, than it was to have a tooth pulled. So, whenever my family got together during a holiday, everyone joyously sang along while I quietly watched in envy. The same attitude accompanied my undergraduate education, as silent lip movements helped me to mask self-consciousness and survive in music methods class. However, when I walked into my first kindergarten class as a student teacher and saw the children react positively to my sex and size, I began to understand that personal inhibitions regarding singing would soon need to be overcome. At this point, I decided that the best way to do so would be to "sink or swim."

The opportunity presented itself on that first morning with the children—Jenny was having a birthday and her mother had sent cupcakes for all the children to share. Naturally, a group singing of "Happy Birthday" was in order and the cooperating teacher turned to me (perhaps sensing my feeling) and asked, "Would Mr. Maxim care to lead us today?" Swallowing hard, I managed to force out the response, "I would love to," all the while picturing a fog horn-voiced giant leading children in song. Needless to say, the children were more interested in Jenny's birthday than in my voice. You know, I never really noticed that they knew I was singing—and they loved it!

From that rewarding point on, I have found that, like it or not, I get involved in any excuse for singing: family gatherings, ballgames, birthday parties, and especially activities with children.

Like me, you may suffer from a bit of initial stage fright. However, if you face your respon-

Children are absorbed by the enthusiasm generated by teachers who truly enjoy music in the early childhood setting. They often are encouraged to experiment with instruments after watching adults play them.

sibility maturely, the blending of voices in your classroom will convince you that your self-imposed constraints on your musical talents were both unnecessary and exaggerated.

As you sing to the children and praise them for their own spontaneous efforts, some simple songs may be slowly introduced.

Children enjoy singing songs that have simple, repetitive lyrics, unsophisticated melodies, and narrow, low melodic range. Group singing for preschoolers should be started when you sense that the children are ready for it. Such sessions should not be made part of a rigid schedule, but should arise whenever a positive reaction seems apparent. These following guidelines may help you as you plan activities to bridge the gap between spontaneous singing and group-oriented song:

1. First songs should be action songs—relatively fast-paced songs that involve some types of body movements. The standard action songs of "Eency Weency Spider" and "Where is Thumbkin?" are two such favorites. Another popular song is the following:

2. Sing the song all the way through and invite the children to join in the actions. If the children wish to hear the song a second time, sing it again. However, do not *ask* if the children want to hear it another time—someone will say no. Some children will learn the words quickly and will soon join in. Do not insist that the others join in with comments such as "Everyone sing now" (a sure way to quiet the children), or "Buddy knows the words already—everyone listen to him sing" (a sure way to discourage anyone from learning the words). *Stay away from* the practice of

The Bus

1. The peo-ple on the bus go   up and down,   up and down,   up and down.
   (Stand up, then sit or squat down.)

The   peo - ple on the bus go   up and down,   all   through the   town.

2. The wheels on the bus go round and round. *(Move arms in circles.)*
3. The horn on the bus goes toot, toot, toot. *(Make beeping motion with hands.)*
4. The money in the box goes ding, ding, ding.
5. The wipers on the glass go swish, swish, swish. *(Move arms back and forth, together.)*
6. The driver on the bus says, "Move on back." *(Turn head to side, put hand to side of mouth, imitate bus driver's voice.)*
7. The baby on the bus cries "Wah, wah, wah." *(Rub eyes with fists.)*

singing a line over and over again until the children learn it and then moving from line to line until the entire song is learned—this type of dissection leads to certain boredom and eventual loss of interest.

3. Pick up the song again the next day and repeat the previous procedure. By this time the children should be fairly familiar with the lyrics, and many of them will join you as you sing. If the children have not begun to join you willingly by about the third day, there is no point in continuing to push it. Find another song that may attract the children.

4. Kindergarten and early primary grade children enjoy associating a game orientation with their music. Such selections usually involve the entire group in a circle with one or two children singled out for some specific purpose. Consider these examples:

Old King Glory of the Mountain

Old king glo - ry of the   moun   - tain.   The moun-tain was so high, it

near - ly reached the sky.   The   first   one, the sec-ond one, the third   fol - low me.

The Noble Duke of York

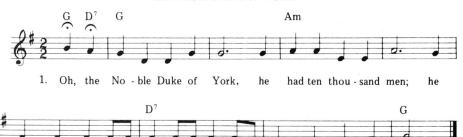

1. Oh, the No-ble Duke of York, he had ten thou-sand men; he
marched them up to the top of the hill, and he marched them down a - gain.

2. And when they were up, they were up,
And when they were down, they were down,
And when they were only half way up,
They were neither up nor down.

Arrange the children in a circle and designate one child to be "king." The king parades around the outside of the circle as the others stand and sing. As the words *first, second,* and *third* are sung, the king taps the shoulder of the child he is passing at the time. Only the *third* person, however, leaves the circle to follow the king on his parade. The song then begins again with the king choosing additional children for the parade. The song is repeated until all children are in the parade except one, who then becomes the king for a new game.

Form a circle and designate one child to be the "duke." The duke leads the other children during the first verse as they march in a circle. During the second verse, the children stand in the circle and stand straight during the words "when they were up, they were up"; sit down during the words "when they were down, they were down"; and squat or kneel during the words "when they were only halfway up, they were neither up nor down."

Some beginning teachers feel that their inability to play an instrument is a handicap for teaching young children to sing. However, children do not need musical accompaniment to enjoy singing—as a matter of fact, pianos or other instruments often distract young children. Unless you are skilled enough to play an instrument by ear, children may be helped more by having no accompanying music than by having it.

Despite these cautions, there are two *chording* instruments that are fairly easy to learn and furnish delightful accompanying music for children's songs: the guitar and autoharp. The soft, simple chords produced by these instruments provide enjoyable backgrounds for songs. With the guitar, you will need to learn the finger positions required for basic chords, but you will need to learn only a *few* chords because children's songs are relatively unsophisticated. The autoharp is even more easily learned since it uses preset chords—as a matter of fact, three-year-olds often enjoy playing it. You only have to press down on a chord bar and strum the strings to produce the desired sound—the chord bar leaves the correct strings free while stopping all the rest. Each chord bar is marked on the autoharp and you need only press the right

London Bridge

bar to play the accompaniment. Many books have chords marked for the teacher. They look like this:

As you can see, the song contains only two different chords, each repeated several times before the other is reintroduced. Only a few minutes' practice with a guitar or autoharp should make you ready to share this favorite song with your children.

Your responsibility in creating an environment for music in the preschool setting, then, is to establish an atmosphere of comfort and acceptance, and use music throughout the day. Children will enjoy your enthusiasm and appreciation for singing, and will themselves compose and sing simple tunes in their work and play. When you sense their strong interest in group singing, capitalize on it and share with them some appropriate, lively, action-oriented tunes.

Rhythmic Activities

Young children are conscious of musical rhythm and enjoy moving to the beat of musical selections. Evidence of this interest can be shown by observing children as they play in unstructured settings: they chant in rhythm as they swing or jump rope; experiment with words or sounds such as "quack-quack" or "bow-wow"; twirl in a circle while "dancing"

to a favorite song; or sway and tap as a catchy tune is heard. These and many other forms of rhythmic movement can be easily seen in an environment of freedom and acceptance where children can express their feelings openly.

Like singing, rhythmic expression should at first be encouraged through spontaneous activity. Allow the children opportunities to move rhythmically in their own ways for short periods of time during the day. Often, children will do so if different kinds of music are played on the record player. You will find them clapping or tapping as they attempt to "keep time" to a regular beat. Other children will be content to twirl and move to the music. Still others will enjoy holding colorful scarves in their hands and allowing them to trail as they glide smoothly to the beat of the music. Such random bodily movements eventually become more controlled as children are exposed to planned rhythm experiences. These initial experiences should involve steady rhythmic patterns that are not necessarily from songs. For example, you may steadily beat on a drum or tambourine as the children walk in a circle. You may ask the chidren to alter their gait as the beating is either speeded up or slowed down. Other initial activities are described in the "Rhythmic Activities" box.

As the children gain opportunities to experience such creative rhythmic activities,

Youngsters enjoy the sounds of rhythm instruments and take pride in learning how to establish basic rhythmic patterns.

they will begin to anticipate the prospect of using rhythm instruments. If the instruments are all brought out at one time, you will probably find that the children become too excited about them. It is best to simply introduce one or two instruments at a time so the children will have opportunities to experiment with them freely. Of course, there will be some "noise" at first, but if you alternate their use between the outdoors and indoors, most problems can be overcome. At this point, you should talk informally with the children about their instruments, focusing on the sounds emitted by them. You may identify the instruments for the children by using the appropriate terms—say "triangle," for example, instead of "clang-clang." As the children explore the instruments, you may help them discover the proper way to hold them. Have the child tap a triangle while holding it by one side as he had been doing and then tap it while holding it by the string. Don't say, "See, you were hold-

ing it wrong," but keep your comment open-ended, "Which way sounds better?" As the children become used to playing an instrument properly, they may be asked to furnish the rhythmic pattern in rhythm activities.

As such informal, creative experiences are provided for young children, they will slowly become able to manipulate the instruments properly and will gain sufficient control for group experiences. If you choose to group your children as a "rhythm band," you will at first need to develop sections of instruments. Those instruments most popularly used in preschool settings include *triangles, drums, rhythm sticks, cymbals,* and *bells.* Give each section enough time to work together so that they are able to coordinate their efforts. Rarely should you expect all sections to play together in unison—the responsibility of each section playing together is demanding for preschool youngsters. Only at the end, for one or two beats, should you expect all the children to

RHYTHMIC ACTIVITIES

- Play the high-pitched piano keys in a spirited way as the children prance like elves or fairies around a circle. Then play some low keys in a deliberate way, and ask the children to march like giants around the circle. Other contrasting combinations include: hopping like grasshoppers and plodding like bears; flitting like bees and lumbering like elephants; and cavorting like ponies and trudging like rhinos.

- Use even rhythms on the drum or tambourine during patterns of walking, marching, galloping, and skipping. (Skipping is a very difficult skill for four- and five-year-olds to acquire. Don't force a child to skip if he has difficulty doing so—give him help, but allow him the satisfaction of choosing his own rhythmic movement.)

- Use some of the many excellent records that contain rhythmic tunes and encourage creative movement to music. Hap Palmer records are especially good for such activities, but there are several more that are as good.

- Encourage the use of chants for children's actions, including jump rope chants. One popular jump rope chant follows:

  Teddy Bear, Teddy Bear, go upstairs.
  Teddy Bear, Teddy Bear, say your prayers.
  Teddy Bear, Teddy Bear, turn out the light.
  Teddy Bear, Teddy Bear, say good-night.

HOMEMADE INSTRUMENTS

Wood Chimes   Hang different materials from a straight bar or a triangular wooden frame or a circular band of metal stripping so that they will strike each other when they are moved by the wind. For a variety of sounds, use different sizes and kinds of materials, such as nails, metal scraps, pieces of glass, strips of wood, dowels, pieces of bamboo, and pieces of pipe.

the wood block. Make sure the hole is wide enough so the cap will slide freely along the nail. (Maybe make the hole in the cap first—with a larger-sized nail—then attach it to the wood.) Use as many nails and as many caps on each nail as desired.

Nail Scraper   You will need blocks of wood about 2 inches × 2 inches × 8 inches and nails of different sizes. Hammer a few nails into a block of wood so that they are all the same height. Leave a space and repeat the process with different sized nails—or use the same size, but hammer them in deeper. To play, run a large nail along the separate rows of nails.

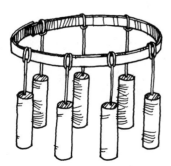

Wood Block Tambourine   You will need blocks of wood about ¾ inch × ½ inch × 6 inches, bottle caps, and nails with wide heads. Remove the cork from the bottle caps. Place a bottle cap on the wood block and hammer a nail through the cap and partway into

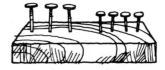

play together. The following is a suggested procedure for organizing a rhythm band experience:

1. Choose a record with an appropriate beat, or select a suitable song to be played on a musical instrument.

2. Decide on the sequence in which each instrument will be played. For example, one teacher developed this plan for "Jingle Bells":

Jingle bells, jingle bells (*bells only*)
Jingle all the way (*triangles only*)
Oh, what fun (*cymbals only*)
It is to ride (*drums only*)
In a one horse open sleigh.. (*rhythm sticks only*)
(*Repeat verse exactly as before.*)
"Jingle bells!" (*everyone together*)

3. Develop cues with which to signal each group to enter the song. You may choose to hold up the instrument to be played, show the children a picture of the instrument, use a cue word such as "cymbals," or simply point to the next group to play.

The suggested rhythm instruments can be purchased from any of several school supply outfits. However, many teachers have found that teacher- or child-made instruments are often just as effective. Some of the many instruments you might make yourself include those found in the "Homemade Instruments" box.

As the children gain increased coordination and skill in using these rhythm instruments, you will be able to supplement your total program in many ways. Poetry, music, creative movement, and musical accompani-

---

String Guitar   This is the most complicated instrument to make. You will need a strip of wood about 2 inches × 24 inches × ¾ inch, two screw eyes, 36-inch nylon fishline (squidding is best), two popsicle sticks, and a large nail for each one.

1. Insert a screw eye near each end of the wood strip.
2. About 1½ inches from each end of the wood strip, saw a ¼-inch deep groove across the strip for the popsicle stick.
3. Insert the popsicle stick sideways into the grooves, and tie the fishline between the two screw eyes.

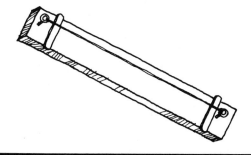

4. Tighten the fishline by turning one of the screw eyes with the large nail.
5. Use as a rhythm instrument, or make several string guitars (each tuned to a different note).

Drums   Use old coffee cans or large vegetable cans that can be obtained from the school cafeteria. Cover the open end with inner tube rubber as tightly as possible and secure it with heavy cord or wire. A drumstick is easily made with a dowel rod and piece of foam rubber at the end.

Kitchen Cymbals   Collect discarded kettle lids (with knobs on top) and use them as cymbals.

Rattles   Some containers you might use are paper cups, plastic bottles, small plastic boxes and cans, wooden match boxes, and metal bandage cans. These can be partly filled with one or more of the following: dried beans, peas, grain, or seeds; table salt; rock salt; marbles; pebbles; feathers; sand.

(Many of these homemade musical instruments are based on the ideas of two creative teachers, Pearl Bailes and Mary Alice Felleisen.)

RECORDS

Appropriate records of good quality should be available for use in the preschool setting. Such records can benefit your program in several ways: (1) they can be listened to for pure enjoyment, (2) they can guide marching, dancing, or singing activities, and (3) they can be used to teach basic concepts. Several companies have produced records of high quality for preschool youngsters. Among the most widely used are:

1. HAP PALMER RECORDS available from: Educational Activities, Inc., Freeport, New York 11520.

AR 514	Learning Basic Skills Through Music, Volume 1
AR 522	Learning Basic Skills Through Music, Volume 2
AR 521	Learning Basic Skills Through Music: Building Vocabulary
AR 526	Learning Basic Skills Through Music: Health and Safety
AR 519	Patriotic and Morning Time Songs
AR 523	Modern Tunes for Rhythms and Instruments
AR 524	Folk Song Carnival
AR 527	Mod Marches
AR 518	Simplified Folk Songs
AR 531	Aprendizage De Conocimientos Basicos A Traves De La Musica
AR 533	Creative Movement and Rhythmic Exploration
AR 538	Holiday Songs and Rhythms
AR 540	Math Readiness: Vocabulary and Concepts
AR 541	Math Readiness: Addition and Subtraction
AR 543	Getting to Know Myself
AR 545	Homemade Band
AR 546	Movin'
AR 556	The Feel of Music
AR 563	Pretend
AR 581	Easy Does It: Activity Songs for Basic Motor Skill Development
AR 597	Tickly Toddle

2. ELLA JENKINS RECORDS (*Adventures in Rhythm*) available from: Adventures in Rhythm, 1844 North Mohawk Street, Chicago, Illinois 60614.

7631	Little Johnny Brown
7638	Call and Response Rhythmic Group Singing
7664	You'll Sing a Song and I'll Sing a Song
7665	Play Your Instruments and Make a Pretty Sound

3. SESAME STREET RECORDS available from: Children's Records of America, Inc., 159 West 53rd Street, New York, New York 10019.

22051	Bert's Blockbusters
22052	The Electric Company
22053	Bob and Susan Sing Songs from Sesame Street
22054	Tu Me Gustas (I Like You)
22055	Letters and Numbers
22056	Ernie's Hits
22057	Sing the Hit Songs from Sesame Street
22058	"C" Is for Cookie
22059	Big Bird Sings!
22060	Somebody Come and Play
22061	Let a Frown Be Your Umbrella

ment are only a few of the areas that can be more exciting when the children can supply their own music.

Recordings

Appropriate records of good quality should be available for use in the preschool setting. Such records can benefit your program in several ways: (1) they can be listened to for pure enjoyment; (2) they can be used as a guide for marching, dancing, or singing activities; and (3) they can be used to teach basic concepts. Several companies that produce high-quality records for preschool youngsters are identified in the "Records" box.

Music activities can be used in many contexts during the preschool day. Singing, dancing, listening, moving, and playing instruments are all enjoyable activities for young children. Plan musical activities for your children, keeping in mind their level of development and their interests. Choose songs that are simple and activities that are active and involving. Don't be concerned about your personal musical talent; all confident teachers can provide a wealth of delightful musical experiences for young children.

22062   Pete Seeger and Brother Kirk Visit Sesame Street
22063   Sesame Street Story Time
22064   Sesame Street 1—Original Cast
22065   Sesame Street Zoo
22066   Grover Sings the Blues
CC25503   The Muppet Alphabet Album
CTW 79005   Sesame Street Fever

4. TOM GLAZER RECORDS available from: CMS Records, Inc., 14 Warren Street, New York, New York 10007.
CMS649   Music for Ones and Twos
CMS657   Activity and Game Songs for Children, Volume I
CMS658   Activity and Game Songs for Children, Volume II
CMS688   Let's Sing Fingerplays

5. SONG AND PLAY TIME WITH PETE SEEGER available from: Folkway Records, 701 Seventh Avenue, New York, New York 10036.

6. MISS JACKIE RECORDS available from: Miss Jackie, 10001 El Monte, Overland Park, Kansas 66207.
Lollipops and Spaghetti
Peanut Butter, Tarzan and Roosters

7. STEVE MILLANG AND GREG SCELSA RECORDS available from: Youngheart Music Education Service, Los Angeles, California 90027.
We All Live Together, Volume 1
We All Live Together, Volume 2
We All Live Together, Volume 3

8. MAKING MUSIC YOUR OWN (Kindergarten set) available from: Silver Burdett Company, 250 James Street, Morristown, New Jersey 07960.

9. SONGS TO GROW ON (FC 7005), Volume 1—Nursery Days by Woody Guthrie available from: Folkways Records, 701 Seventh Avenue, New York, New York 10036.

Use other records for various activities, including popular music, holiday music, classical music (surprise!—children like it), ethnic music, and so on.

10. OTHER MUSIC, RHYTHM, AND MOVEMENT RECORDS available from:

Bowmar Records
622 Rodler Drive
Glendale, California
91201

RCA Records
Educational Sales
P.O. Box RCA 1000
Indianapolis, Indiana
46291

Columbia Children's Record Library
CBS Inc.
15 West 52nd Street
New York, New York 10019

Folkways Records
701 Seventh Avenue
New York, New York 10036

SOME FINAL THOUGHTS

Research beginning in the late 1960s has given us extensive knowledge about brain functioning. Perhaps the most dramatic advance has been the discovery that individuals have two interacting thinking systems, housed in the left and right hemispheres of the brain, each complete with its own thinking mode. There is reason to believe that infants and young children have the capacity for interchange between hemispheres; that is, they use both sides equally up to at least the age of four. This allows youngsters to eagerly pursue self-initiated exploration of objects or conditions through all sensory channels. But, for some reason (perhaps the rigidity and conformity of many elementary schools), this capacity for creativity slowly diminishes as the children progress through the primary grades. As a teacher of young children, however, you can encourage this impulse in many ways including the artistic and musical pursuits described within this chapter.

Young children enjoy drawing, painting, and expressing themselves through a variety of art media. Because most preschool children are not yet inhibited by adults imposing a right or wrong way to scribble and draw, their artistic expressions are often freely and openly generated. Starting with simple scribbles, which is often done for sheer sensory pleasure, and progressing through stages until they begin to represent things such as people, trees, houses, animals, or other objects very close to their own lives, children experience an avenue of expression that has no parallel in their lives. Besides this obvious pleasurable aspect of artistic expression, researchers have studied young children and found that artwork can give us clear information about three other areas of the child's development: (1) the amount of detail and accuracy shown in drawings gives us an indication of the child's mental maturity, (2) the degree of detail and accuracy gives us an indication of the child's small muscle control, and (3) the content of a child's artwork may illustrate a variety of moods and emotions.

Motivate your children to enjoy art by providing a sufficient supply of materials and encouraging them to express themselves in well-organized areas of the room where they can work without worrying about being messy. Show interest in the children's work, but try to refrain from pressing them to explain their work. Your major concern is to encourage creative artistic expression, or a foundation upon which growing skill and aesthetic sensitivity can be built.

Music, like art, should be an enriching part of each day for preschool youngsters. Whether included as a pleasurable accompaniment to daily routines (washing up or dressing, for example) or simply channeling energy by moving freely to rhythm, informal music can bring a special sense of well-being and joy to you as well as to the child. Don't be afraid to make up your own times or words to songs as you fit them to almost any activity the child is involved in. You will be astonished at how skilled you become at this activity and gratified to see how the young children are drawn to your spontaneous efforts.

Although children differ markedly in their ability to make music, nearly all respond to melody and want to sing as well as to dance. Still others simply prefer to listen. Whatever the case, music experiences should be provided for the very young. You need not read music, play an instrument, or sing like Barbra Streisand in order to bring music into your classroom. Did you think you had to be Picasso in order to set up an easel painting area in your room? There is one central requirement for a good preschool music program—a sense of enjoyment in singing and dancing. Your spirit, not a perceived bad voice or clumsy dance movement, is what will register with the children. If you augment your program with simple songs, basic musical instruments, and well-chosen records, your children will be eager to explore music and movement while allowing their creativity to flourish.

Chapter 11

The Child's Physical and Social World: Science and Social Studies

What a wonderful bird the frog are—
When he stand he sit almost;
When he hop, he fly almost.
He ain't got no sense hardly;
He ain't got no tail hardly either.
When he sit, he sit on what he ain't got
   almost.

—Anonymous

Children often approach their physical and social worlds with a spirit of magic and wonder. In the rhythm and rhyme of fantasy, they regularly transform the ordinary into the extraordinary. It is within the physical and social realms that children's direct experiences begin to inform them about all of the wonderful things in their environment—trees, mountains, clouds, rain, sunshine, flowers, bugs, firefighters, police officers, doctors, libraries, post offices, and stores. Their relatively unsophisticated experiential backgrounds, however, affect the way they interpret or make sense of these new wonders. Because some new discoveries cannot be associated with anything previously experienced or understood, imaginative, fanciful thought is summoned to provide an explanation: "Look, Meghan, it's dark because the sun went to sleep." Children are fascinated by their dynamic new world and naturally want to find out all about it as quickly as possible by manipulating, observing, touching, trying out, and handling everything. Young children are curious; they want to know: "Why?" "What is it?" "How does it work?" "Where does it come from?" And that's only the beginning; they have hundreds more of these questions. They are, in effect, natural inquirers, who spontaneously and ingeniously use all their senses to act on their environment while searching for answers to questions that perplex and mystify them. Whoever first suggested the process of inquiry as a learning technique must have developed those ideas after observing young children as they freely and enthusiastically explored their environment.

Basically, all we know about the things that surround us can be broken down into two major categories: (1) the physical world and (2) the social world. Both offer unique ways of looking at natural phenomena, and those who become "scientists" in either category study related occurrences in special ways. For example, if the "young scientist" in your classroom wanted to know why chestnuts fall from certain trees during the fall season, he would be using a questioning approach of a physical scientist. If another wished to find out why people celebrate Halloween by dressing in costumes and carving a pumpkin, she would be acting much as a social scientist. The physical sciences, then, deal with the earth and nature, while the social sciences (or social studies) deal with people and the characteristics of societies. Because these two areas provide the bulk of direct experiences for the children in your early childhood setting, separate descriptions and suggestions will be provided within this chapter.

SCIENCE

Strategies for Teaching Science

The preschool science curriculum has a major role in building a foundation to support "natural scientists" and to encourage their active investigations into scientific pursuits. In such a program, preschool teachers use *process* approaches—strategies intended to capitalize on the children's natural tendencies to question and investigate. Such strategies emphasize and value the involvement of children in direct experiences and active exploration. A process approach can be contrasted with a *product* approach in which the attainment of knowledge or specific skills is emphasized and valued more highly than scientific, investigative thinking. In a process approach to teaching science in the preschool classroom, the teacher uses several basic strategies.

One thing a teacher can do is to *capitalize on informal happenings during the school day.* Be aware of the numerous opportunities that allow children to use the questioning methods of a scientist. For example, this event occurred one day on the playground of a private nursery school:

On a bright, warm morning the children were allowed to spend a great deal of time pursuing outdoor activities. They moved from one play activity to another and seemed to enjoy the inviting comforts of the weather. After a while, three children moved to the shade of a large tree for a short period of rest. When the teacher noticed that the children had remained in the shade for a longer amount of time than usual, she moved to the area to see if a problem had arisen. One hadn't. The teacher found the three children concentrating intently on the busy efforts of a swarm of ants. "Look at that hole—that's where they live," said Jana. "They live under the ground?" questioned Will. "Yep, and that's where those ants are dragging the food," offered Carrie. "Mrs. Long, do the ants really live underground?" asked Will. Mrs. Long, in an effort to maintain the scientific curiosity already so effectively raised, simply answered, "Let's watch them carefully and see if Jana and Carrie are right."

To capitalize on this incidental experience, Mrs. Long later went to another area populated by ants and dug up a shovelful of dirt and ants. She placed the mixture into a gallon jar, secured the lid carefully, and wrapped the jar with construction paper so that no light would be allowed inside. The darkness was necessary so that the ants would sense that they were underground and safe to begin digging a new pathway of tunnels. When the dark paper was removed, Will, Carrie, and Jana all became enthused about the passageways constructed by the ants. From this excitement, others began to ask: "What do they eat?" "Can we feed them?" "Do they drink water?" and other questions that extended their understandings.

The project continued throughout the year. Children fed the ants in small quantities: dead insects, food scraps, and almost any other organic substance. They also occasionally provided small amounts of water.

Your task is to help children place their informal experiences into meaningful contexts so that this background of accurate information can help form higher-order concepts and generalizations. This is an important professional task, because random exposure to unrelated events with little or no guidance from the teacher is not sufficient—children must be led to discover that phenomena just don't happen. Skillful leadership is essential to encourage children to observe, question, and make discoveries leading to these higher-level concepts and generalizations.

You can *guide scientific thinking through the use of skillful questions and comments.* Children have a limited background of experiences—thus, their foundation for examining and making sense of new physical phenomena is also limited. For this reason, they may often misinterpret their new experiences. One child, for example, after observing a chick break through its shell, commented, "My cat is going to hatch some kittens real soon." Carol Seefeldt (1974) offered additional thoughts on this subject:

> Observing young children, talking to them, asking them questions about how they think engines work or why they think clouds move reveals to the adult the level of their scientific thinking. Often the children have misconceptions that need clarification and revision. They may believe, for example, that the wind moves because it is happy or the shadows move to get out of their way. . . . Engines, air, the clouds, according to the young child, move because they want to. Often the young child's egocentricity influences his concepts: He may believe that the sun sets because he goes to bed or that the rain is falling because it does not want him to go outside. [pp. 176–177]

Skillful guidance during science experiences can be an effective weapon against the formation of such misconceptions. Examples of some pertinent questions and comments that can be used during scientific experiences include:

- "I wonder if the ants will eat this cracker crumb. Let's try it and see what happens.""Let's try it again and see if the same thing happens."
- "Maybe we can find out if we watch it carefully."
- "How can we find out?"
- "Martin's snail ate a piece of lettuce. Do you think we should feed lettuce to these snails, too?"
- "How can we find out for sure?"
- "Which worm is longer?"
- "What food does the rabbit eat?"
- "What's wrong with the plant?" "It's drooping."
- "How many little hamsters were born?"

Several of the questions, of course, were designed to help the children observe an object or event; others were designed to encourage higher thought processes such as predicting and finding relationships. Through such questions and comments, the teacher helps the children to evaluate and extend their experiences.

You should be familiar with the scientific process so that children can be led to make new discoveries and, hopefully, have fun. Basic investigative, or process, skills include observing, inferring, classifying, and communicating. A description of each of these four processes follows (Neuman, 1972).

1. *Observing.* Children should be encouraged to examine objects using all or as many of their five senses as possible: seeing, hearing, smelling, tasting, and touching. Some activities that might be used to help children develop skills in the process of observation are included in Table 11-1.

Table 11-1 *Using the Process of Observing*

Process	Materials Suggested	Activities
Observing: Visual	Colors (paints, crayons, food coloring), living plants, seeds, leaves, rocks, minerals, pieces of wood (sawdust from the wood), small animals, fish	Multiple opportunities to examine objects visually. Look for general and specific properties, changes in appearance.
Observing: Smell	Perfumes, fresh-cut flowers, plants, common household products with distinctive odors, fresh fruits, fresh vegetables	Describe smells. Use the sense of smell to identify and describe objects.
Observing: Touch	Cloth material of varying textures, wood of varying grains, various grades of sandpaper, objects of various temperatures	Use the sense of touch to increase the quality of one's observations.
Observing: Taste	Variety of foodstuffs, harmless drinkable liquids	Taste a variety of edible products to increase the accuracy of one's observations. Identify characteristics of objects on the basis of taste.
Observing: Hearing	Musical instruments, variety of noisemakers, phonograph records (music and sound effects), tape recorder	Identify voices and commonly heard sounds. Identify degree of loudness, pitch, quality. Increase child's awareness of sounds around him and how they enable him to make better observations.

2. *Inferring.* When observations of an event or object are limited, children should learn to associate previous experiences to the limited observation to discover new information about the event or object. This process involves "risk taking" on the part of the children. In order to make an inference, they must feel secure enough to take a chance in being "wrong." Your approach to encouraging scientific investigation should be one that encourages risk taking. Some activities that help children develop inferencing skills are included in Table 11-2.

3. *Classifying.* Usually referred to as "sorting" by preschool children, the process of classifying involves sorting a group of objects on the basis of a single property or dimension such as color, hardness, or size. When children classify scientifically, they should be allowed to decide upon

their own classification schemes, not have a scheme imposed upon them by their teacher. Table 11-3 offers some suggested activities that help children develop classification skills.

4. *Communicating.* Children should be encouraged to tell what they have observed, inferred, or classified. Such experiences should be shared with teachers and other adults as well as with their peers. Table 11-4 suggests some communicating experiences.

You can *convey a positive attitude toward the children's interests.* The children's world is filled with items and experiences that fascinate them. However, they do not always receive reinforcement and encouragement from the adults around them as they explore these new wonders, simply because those adults may either frown on certain types of active exploration or lack interest in a particular area in

Table 11-2 *Using the Process of Inferring*

Process	Materials Suggested	Activities
Inferring	"Gift box," sealed bags of materials	Infer what is in the gift box or sealed bag without looking inside.
	Variety of clear liquids	Infer which liquid is water without smelling or tasting the various liquids.
	Closed container with small living insect inside	Infer whether the object inside the container is alive.
	Sound effects (records or tapes)	Infer whether noise is being made in the city or in the country. Describe object making noise from its sound.
	Hot and cold objects	Infer how objects became hot or cold. Is entire object hot or only part of it?

Table 11-3 *Using the Process of Classifying*

Process	Materials Suggested	Activities
Classifying	Bags of buttons, bags containing a variety of materials; sandpaper squares consisting of a variety of grades and painted a variety of colors; tagboard pieces in a variety of shapes, sizes, and colors; bags of rocks; shells	Have children sort materials according to properties of their own choosing. Encourage children to think about and tell why they sorted objects in the way that they did. Also encourage them to try to find another way to sort their objects.

Table 11-4 *Using the Process of Communicating*

Process	Materials Suggested	Activities
Communicating	Any and all of the materials used in developing the skills of observing, inferring, and classifying can be used in developing this process skill. In addition, small sets of objects composed of specific properties can be used to help children develop a useful vocabulary for communicating. The sets may include objects that are shiny and dull, hard and soft, rough and smooth, heavy and light, hot and cold, fat and thin, or noisy and quiet.	Describe materials and/or recognizable objects. Name materials and objects. Tell about perceived relationships among materials and objects. Learn descriptive terms.

which the child is interested. For those reasons, you may often hear comments or see reactions like the one described in this hypothetical situation:

Digging in the garden, Marcianne and Dennis uncovered two small, white, wiggling, wormlike creatures. Calling to their teacher, the youngsters each picked up one of the Japanese beetle grubs, held them in their hands, and asked what they were. Her face turning ashen, the teacher drew back and commanded, "Put those things right back where you found them and get inside to wash your hands right now."

Although you cannot treat every area of the children's interest with equal time and enthusiasm, you should be prepared to make new experiences pleasant for them. If you cringe at the sight of worms and other crawling creatures, either don't introduce them at all to the children or ask someone else to do it for you. Your queasiness in these situations will, of course, be sensed by the children and have an effect on their enthusiasm for future explorations. When these situations arise by chance, you should exhibit enough insight and self-control to show interest in the child's discovery.

On the other hand, your own interests can be capitalized on and enthusiastically shared with the children. Such strong positive feelings are sure to be contagious and result in new and exciting interests for the youngsters. You may have a "green thumb" and work well with plants. Your interest in machines may result in many valuable simple experiments. Whenever your own personal interests are brought to the classroom, however, remember to be aware of where the children are experientially—you don't want to overwhelm them with too much, too soon.

You should *be knowledgeable about basic scientific concepts and able to communicate those concepts to the children in appropriate terms.* It is not necessary for you to have complete command over every scientific concept handled in the preschool setting, but you should have enough knowledge to be able to help the children whenever they need your support. G. Craig (1947) emphasized that "the teacher need not be appalled by the extensiveness and complexity of science as a whole, for she is responsible for imparting only a small portion of the total scientific knowledge, namely that portion pertinent to a group of children at a given age level" (p. 60).

That portion that is pertinent for your age group can be gathered from many sources. It is both enjoyable and informative to leaf through children's reference books in the library, for example. These books are well illustrated and contain the basic information you need. Films, filmstrips, pictures, magazines, and other sources serve the same purpose. Often, the major problem with such self-education is finding the time to do it. However, once you have convinced yourself that such a project is needed, the experience will be, without doubt, a delightful one. Many teachers who have experienced nature themselves, for example, find it easy to pass on their new enthusiasm to their young children.

Having the basic scientific knowledge required to talk with children is only one part of the teacher's responsibility; the other part is to develop skill in communicating that information to the children when necessary. Often, children's observations, questions, and experiments will need to be enlarged and verbalized by the teacher. But note that sometimes the teacher's commments can be too involved, as in this case:

Karen: "Why did the puddle go away?"

Teacher: "The heat from the sun's rays made the water disappear into the air. That's called evaporation."

Instead of this difficult answer, the teacher should have offered a simple explanation:

Young children enjoy investigating living creatures of all different shapes and sizes, including these earthworms and "Hermie" the hermit crab. Be careful not to stifle this curiosity by communicating negative feelings about spiders, bugs, or other creeping, crawling animals.

Karen: "Why did the puddle go away?"

Teacher: "The heat from the sun dried it up."

Teachers sometimes cause problems, too, when they fabricate stories in an attempt to explain scientific concepts. Examine this situation, for example:

Richard: "What happens to our dead gerbil?"

Teacher: "He goes to gerbil heaven—where all the good little gerbils go."

Richard: "Is it nice there?"

Teacher: "Oh yes. He will have a clean, comfortable home and plenty of food to eat. And, even better, our gerbil will see his mother and father along with many of his friends who died, too."

Obviously, there is a better approach:

Richard: "What happens to our dead gerbil?"

Teacher: "The gerbil died because it was very old. If we keep it here it will start to smell. Let's get the shovel and bury it outdoors."

Interpretations of scientific events by the teacher to the children should be free of intricate explanation and mystical description. Your role is a challenging one—to find the balance and sensitivity needed to make a preschool science program uncomplicated and fascinating. Anything that goes beyond these characteristics causes misunderstandings and frustrations that may be difficult or impossible to eradicate later on. Remember simply to stick to the scientific facts and keep fantasy in its proper place; otherwise children may think of physical science as "magic" rather than as a description of the physical environment.

When you plan to enrich scientific discoveries by creating an environment ripe for scientific investigation, a great deal of careful planning is involved. Choices must be made

regarding appropriate materials and equipment suitable for the children's interest and developmental levels. Lists of supplies are available from many sources; none are included here because they can be overwhelming to education students who have not yet taught young children. Instead, we will discuss various equipment and materials under topics of investigation popularly experienced in the preschool setting.

Science Centers

Equipment or supplies are normally set up in a special corner or section of the room established as the "science center." In these areas, you must choose materials for children who wish to experiment with them. There should be no predetermined teaching objectives or specific directions for the children to follow. Your role is fairly minimal. You serve mainly to set up and maintain materials in the center and to make sure that the children are free to work on their own. Of course, you should always be aware of what is going on in the science center. You must determine whether to intervene should one child seem to approach frustration with an activity or another child appear to be doing something that might endanger herself or others.

Animals   Young children are fascinated by all kinds of animals—from imaginary storybook animals with human characteristics to real animals with cold, wet noses so exciting to touch. They can be observed watching in surprise and wonder, mouths agape, as a mother robin feeds and cares for her young. They are captivated by the industriousness and strength of ants as they gather food or materials for their growing colony, and can watch for long periods of time.

The preschool environment should reflect these childhood interests and provide for many experiences with all kinds of animals. In addition to becoming aware of the physical characteristics of living organisms other than human beings, young children acquire strong feelings of importance as they feed the classroom animals and provide for their care. Rarely do young children have opportunities to practice themselves the care and treatment they receive at home from their parents. With animals, however, young children become directly involved in caring for other living beings and soon develop an awareness of the value of good diet, cleanliness, and protection.

The animals described in the "Indoor Animals for Young Children" box are appropriate for the preschool classroom. With the best of care, they should become interesting and valuable science materials in your classroom. The environment outside the classroom walls is an exciting place for youngsters, too. Some suggestions for utilizing the animals outdoors are located in the "Outdoor Animals" box.

To obtain the greatest value from having animals in the preschool classroom, either indoor or out, you must constantly watch out for their health and safety. Lack of concern in this area only serves to develop a feeling of disrespect in the children; this often leads to abuse of the animal, followed by its injury, sickness, or death. If the children are to respect animal life, they must learn to understand and appreciate suitable environments and patterns of care; they must understand that all living things depend upon each other for survival.

Plants Plants are often used in the preschool program for three main purposes: (1) to beautify the classroom, (2) to involve the children in caring for and nurturing them, and (3) to help children learn about plant life through experimentation and observation. Plants can brighten the preschool environment and make it an attractive and pleasant place for the children. However, because plants are often placed in hanging baskets or on tall shelves, the children rarely have opportunities to look at them closely. They become,

unintentionally, the *teacher's plants* as they blend into the environment and become ignored by the children. To be *children's plants* and, therefore, to become a more meaningful part of the children's environment, they must be brought down to the level of the children—where they can be watched, touched, and cared for by the children themselves. Children's initial experiences with plants will undoubtedly involve accidents: overwatering, breaking off of leaves or branches, pulling up the plant with the roots, or even destroying a plant. However, if the children are going to learn to treat plants properly and to respect them, they must be taught to do so. In any event, most of the accidents will occur, not from mischievousness, but from lack of knowledge about how to treat and care for plants properly. A child's actual experiences while caring for and observing plants go a long way toward helping him understand why it is important to protect the environment around him. Some good plants to have in the preschool classroom include:

- *Spider plant:* large clusters of flowing grasslike leaves, usually with dark- and light-green tones. Plant reproduces by sending out small plantlets. Ideal for hanging basket.

- *Philodendron:* a durable tropical vine with small, waxy leaves. Can be a climber or can be put in a hanging basket. Small, versatile, and hardy.

- *Wandering Jew:* attractive vinelike specimen for a hanging basket. Delightful purple leaves with silvery bands. Very fast growing. Branches easily. Roots quickly in water or damp soil.

- *Geranium:* a flowering plant with red, white, or pink petals. Cuttings root very easily.

- *Snake plant:* long, spearlike leaves grow up to four feet tall. Attractive bands of dark and light green on the succulent leaves.

INDOOR ANIMALS FOR YOUNG CHILDREN

Ants   Ants provide long periods of entertainment for young children as they tunnel through the soft dirt in a jar or purchased ant farm. Ants require no special care except for periodic feeding (they will eat almost anything) and watering. Cover the side of the jar with dark paper to encourage tunneling out to the sides where they can be seen.

Caterpillars and Butterflies   Caterpillars or their cocoons can be found in the autumn clinging to the leaves of bushes, trees, or weeds. If a caterpillar is found, be sure to pick a large amount of leaves of the type on which it was feeding and give them to the caterpillar until it spins into a cocoon. If the cocoon is found, keep it attached to the branch or twig and carefully bring it into the classroom to be stored in a cool, relatively moist area until the butterfly or moth emerges. The Monarch butterfly caterpillar or cocoon (chrysalis), found on milkweed, is an exceptionally good insect for the children to observe.

Cocoons occasionally have surprising contents, however. One child brought a cocoon she had found to school. When the cocoon opened sometime later, the room (luckily empty since it was recess time) filled with grasshopper-like insects—lots of them. So you may want to keep caterpillars and cocoons in a covered aquarium.

Earthworms   Earthworms can be purchased at a fishing supply store or can be readily found in soft soil, especially after a rain. They can be easily kept in an aerated container filled with a mixture of loose earth and coffee grounds. Children can watch them tunnel into the dirt and create passageways similar to those of ants. Let the children handle the earthworms if they want to—the rough texture and squiggly feelings in their hands delight many youngsters.

Tadpoles and Frogs   Tadpole eggs look like small marbles of clear jelly with a tiny dark dot in the center. They are found along the edge of a pond and are easily scooped up and placed into a container of water. When the tadpoles hatch, they eat either the algae and microscopic organisms formed in the pond water or goldfish food. Young tadpoles spend all of their time completely submerged in the water, but as they grow and develop legs, they need to get out of the water. A large rock or floating piece of wood serves this purpose. Be careful to cover the top of the container with a mesh screen or you will have trouble keeping the tadpoles inside. When the tadpole completely loses its tail, it becomes a frog and requires different food: tiny bits of fish, meat, or leafy vegetables; and especially live flies, gnats, or worms. A frog is nearly

impossible to keep in the classroom so it might be best to return developed frogs to the pond in which they were found.

Goldfish   The goldfish is perhaps the easiest fish to care for in the preschool classroom as it requires much less special care than tropical fish. Goldfish, or any other kind of fish, rarely survive for any length of time in a small goldfish bowl, so it is recommended that you use a balanced, aerated aquarium for any fish you plan to keep.

When setting up the aquarium, be sure to wash it clean with plain water (no soap!). Add successive layers of sand and coarse gravel to the bottom and secure some live plants into this base. Put a small jar or plate on the gravel so that excessive dust does not stir up as you slowly add water. Hook up an aeration and filtration system for proper balance. Allow the aquarium to set for a few days while the chlorine and other harmful chemicals dissipate. Snails, catfish, and other scavengers help to control algae and waste materials. If all precautions are heeded, very little additional care is needed.

Turtles   Until recently, turtles were found in nearly every preschool classroom. However, it has been discovered that some carry salmonella, a serious intestinal disease. Some turtles, though, can be successfully kept in your classroom. The best way to determine whether or not the turtle you choose is a safe one is to check with a reputable pet shop.

Turtles are very easy to care for. They eat worms, ground meat, some vegetable greens, and small insects. Turtles must eat in the water, so it is important that all foods be placed in an area where the turtle is able to submerge its head while eating.

Hermit Crabs   The hermit crab is an increasingly popular classroom animal mainly because it requires so little care and is so fascinating for young children to observe. These tiny creatures can be bought in a pet store or large department store. They use abandoned shells for their homes and to watch them carry their homes on their backs as they move from place to place is a joy for the children.

Keep your hermit crabs in a well-ventilated enclosure. Spread coarse gravel at the bototm of the container and scatter a few empty shells on the surface. Except for a diet of almost any type of food scraps, these amusing creatures need little or no care.

Gerbils   All children enjoy these small, furry, friendly animals. They are clean, playful animals requiring little care, so they make almost the ideal classroom pet.

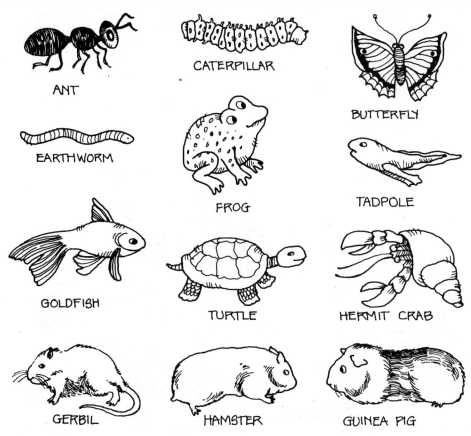

ANT

CATERPILLAR

BUTTERFLY

EARTHWORM

FROG

TADPOLE

GOLDFISH

TURTLE

HERMIT CRAB

GERBIL

HAMSTER

GUINEA PIG

Gerbils are usually kept in a wire cage lined with newspaper and cedar shavings. These materials form a hygienic bed for the gerbil's wastes, which are nearly nonexistent. Gerbils gnaw on the shavings and shred the newspaper; then they completely cover themselves with the shredded newspaper and shavings mixture as they sleep. The gerbil cage should include a special hanging water bottle, an exercise wheel, and an aluminum can for moments of privacy. Be sure to avoid a gerbil cage and any accessories made of plastic. Gerbils gnaw and chew almost any materials that are not metal or glass.

Gerbils reproduce readily and often have a litter every month or two. Children delight in watching the mother and father care for the tiny pink babies, but the frequency of reproduction often results in extreme crowding.

Feed the gerbils a mixture of grains, cereals, breads, or vegetables such as carrots or lettuce. Special treats such as potato chips are especially appreciated.

Hamsters Like gerbils, hamsters can be purchased very reasonably at pet stores. An old aquarium fitted with a wire mesh screen at the top makes an ideal home for hamsters and gerbils alike. Hamsters are similar to gerbils and require the same basic care. The main reason some teachers select gerbils rather than hamsters is that hamsters are nocturnal animals, and usually sleep during the hours when the children are in school. The gerbils, however, are often awake and active during the hours of the normal school day.

Guinea Pigs In contrast to the active gerbils and hamsters, guinea pigs are quiet, docile animals who are content to cuddle and snuggle in a person's arms. Their cage should be similar to the gerbil cage, but should contain a bit more shavings or straw to absorb greater amounts of moisture. Because guinea pigs eliminate greater amounts and do so with greater frequency, their cages must be cleaned more often. Guinea pigs are vegetarians and especially enjoy eating lettuce, apples, grass, or commercial food from the pet store.

OUTDOOR ANIMALS

Insect Zoo Small, simple cages containing insects give children an opportunity to watch the habits of small animals and to view their developmental changes. Cages are easily made and can be adapted to a variety of insects. Keep the insects for a day and then release them to nature.

Water Microscope Cut three circles from the sides of a small plastic pail with a good cutting knife. The circles should be large enough to accommodate a child's hand, but not so large as to make the pail weak. Get a piece of plastic wrap slightly larger than the top of the pail and fit it over the top. Keep it in place

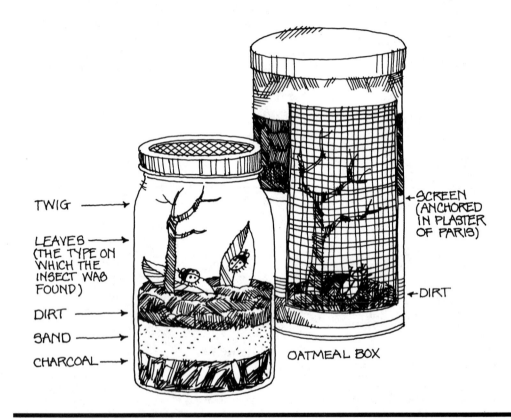

TWIG

LEAVES
(THE TYPE ON
WHICH THE
INSECT WAS
FOUND)

DIRT

SAND

CHARCOAL

SCREEN
(ANCHORED
IN PLASTER
OF PARIS)

DIRT

OATMEAL BOX

- *Asparagus fern:* ideal for a hanging basket. Foliage is delightfully airy with billows of soft green lacy stems.

- *Umbrella tree* (Schefflera): a good-looking, fast-growing tree that reaches a height of six feet or more.

- *Jade plant:* looks like a miniature tree. Leaves are full and succulent, and look like little mittens extending from

branching stems. Grows from 18 to 30 inches.

- *Rubber plant:* popular treelike plant. Broad, shiny leaves extend from a center stalk that grows to five feet or more.

- *English ivy:* a good hanging or climbing plant. Typical bushy, ivy-leaf foliage on many branches. Hardy plant that can survive in nearly any environment.

with a snug-fitting rubber band or string. Pour water (not cold) slowly onto the plastic until the plastic sags into the shape of a lens. View tiny insects (or other objects) through this magnifying glass by inserting them under the plastic-wrap lens through the holes in the side of the pail and allow them to feed on food scraps.

Look for Underwater Animals   Get a large juice can for each child and cut out both ends. Cut a piece of cleaner's plastic wrap and cover one end of the can. Secure the wrap with a strong rubber band. Leave the other end of the can open.

Have the children put their can, wrap-end first, into a stream to view the rocks, vegetation, or animal life there through the opening. The wrap acts as a mag-

nifying lens as the water pushes it up, allowing the children to see things at the stream's bottom in bigger-than-life proportions.

Bird Feeder I   Make a hole through the center of two jar lids by hammering a 3-inch nail through both. Put the nail through one lid, through a large chunk of bread, cake, or doughnut, and then through the other lid. Bend the pointed end of the nail to keep it from pulling through the bottom lid. Tie a piece of string below the nail head and hang up the feeder.

Bird Feeder II   Tie a long string onto a pine cone. Smear the cone with gobs of peanut butter and roll in bird seed. This quick "feeder" is ready for hanging and for attracting numbers of birds to your playground.

JUICE CAN →

CLEAR
PLASTIC →
WRAP

All of these plants are very easy to grow and care for. Their light and temperature requirements cover a wide range of conditions but are not unnecessarily exacting. Once these plants have adjusted to your room—to the light, temperature, and humidity—they can be fed and watered routinely by the children with your guidance. Most of these plants are extremely hardy; the wandering Jew and phil-

odendron, for example, can grow in water as easily as they can grow in soil. Several of these plants, especially the vinelike ones, can be rooted simply by cutting off a shoot and placing it in water. Roots, the part of the plant nearly always hidden from the children, will soon appear. Children enjoy taking these cuttings to start new plants of their own. When deciding upon the collection of plants for your classroom, you may wish to follow this guideline and include at least one *flowering plant,* at least one *vine,* one or two *hanging varieties,* at least one *fern,* and at least one *treelike plant.* When you choose plants for the classroom, be especially watchful that you select nonpoisonous varieties. Toddlers frequently put things into their mouths, and a poisonous leaf or stem is not beyond their interests.

You can add to the child's experiences with plants in the late winter or early spring through various planting activities, either indoors or outdoors. Bean seeds, melon seeds, pumpkin seeds, grass seeds, radish seeds, and the like germinate very easily. You can handle experiences with growing plants from these seeds in one or two ways: (1) you can plant the seeds in wet soil and wait for the sprout, or (2) you can place folded wet paper towels in the bottom of glass containers and lay seeds on each pad. In the second method, the children see not only the sprout, but the formation of the roots as well.

When the plants begin to mature, the children can move some of them to a garden plot outdoors if the space is available and the climate appropriate. Flowers and vegetables offer variety and excitement as they are grown for their aesthetic appeal or simply to be eaten. The digging, weeding, and watering responsibilities add to the children's awareness of life within their environment and to the concept of what plants need to grow.

Many creative activities can follow up direct planting experiences, such as those described in the "Activities with Plants" box. For example, fingerplays can help children understand the essentials of good gardening:

MY GARDEN

This is my garden. (*Spread arms outward.*)
I'll rake it with care. (*Make raking motions.*)
Here are the seeds
I'll plant in there. (*Plant each seed.*)
The sun will shine. (*Make circle above head with arms.*)

The rain will fall. (*Make fluttering motions with fingers.*)
The seeds will sprout
And grow up tall. (*Stretch arms above head.*)

Also, planting activities can turn into creative art-related construction projects. For example, try the potato activity described in the box.

Several of the activities suggested in the box are scientific experiments involving plants that are appropriate for young children. They are used most effectively after the children have already had some opportunities to grow their own plants from seeds or cuttings and to transplant the seedlings.

The Climate   Science experiences dealing with the climate are normally very welcome in the preschool classroom because young children are curious about the climatic features of *weather* and *seasons.* Children are greatly affected by these features as they adjust their play and dress to seasonal demands. Experienced parents and teachers also attest to the fact that the children's emotional states are strongly affected by changes in weather and climate; they agree that children sometimes seem like "human barometers"—some adults can even predict rain or snow as the children's restless behavior increases. When it is too warm, children may become lethargic; when it is too cool, they may become irritable. Two or three snow or rain days in a row may cause increased behavior problems because the children will be unable to release physical energies through vigorous outdoor play. The teacher can capitalize on atmospheric changes during the planned and unplanned preschool science program. Consider these climate concepts as you develop your science program, but keep in mind the climate of your own region.

WEATHER

• The weather changes daily and is influenced by the sun, clouds, and winds—

"The dark clouds are coming near. Let's go inside because it will rain very soon."

• The weather influences the clothing we wear—"It's raining today so you will need to put on your raincoats before you go home."

• The weather may influence how we feel—"Come here and lie on the cot for a while, Jerry. Sometimes the rainy weather makes us sleepy."

• The weather influences our choice of play activity—"Today is so sunny and warm. We'll be able to use the water table for the first time."

Each *season* has its own set of characteristics.

FALL

• Leaves change colors and drop from the trees.

• Animals gather food for the winter.

• People harvest food from gardens and farms.

• The first frost follows increasingly colder nights.

• Apples, pumpkins, and squash are characteristic fall foods.

• The days become shorter and cooler.

• Rakes and harvesting tools are characteristic of the season.

WINTER

• Trees are bare, except for the evergreens.

• Snow, ice, and sleet accompany the cold weather.

• Heavy coats, mittens, hats, sweaters, and boots help us feel warmer.

• Some animals sleep through the winter.

• Building snowmen and sliding on the ice are but two of the many special winter play activities enjoyed by children.

• Hot soup and hot chocolate are enjoyed during a particularly cold day.

Stimulate your children to observe and experience the wonders associated with seasonal changes throughout the school year.

• Days become short—the sun sets much earlier.

• Heat from furnaces keeps us warm inside buildings.

• Snow shovels, snowplows, and winter tires are characteristic of the season.

SPRING

• Days become warmer, windier, and rainier.

• Snow and ice begin to thaw.

• People are busily cleaning up after winter.

• Flowers, leaves, and plants begin to emerge.

• Many animals break out of their long winter sleeps or return from their southern migration.

• Longer, warmer days mean more hours in the sun playing in the sandpile, on the tricycle, and so on.

• Berries begin to ripen and are enjoyed as one of the fresh foods of that season.

ACTIVITIES WITH PLANTS

Indoor Garden Soil

Get a large plastic or wooden box and help the children fill it half full with dirt. They can add dead leaves, grass clippings, cow manure, and other organic matter. Loosen the soil with a trowel and mix it thoroughly. Moisten the soil.

After the soil is prepared, the children can use it for activities involving the planting of flowers or vegetables.

Seed Germination

Place a damp paper towel, cotton wad, or sponge in the bottom of a clear jar or dish. Sprinkle some lawn seed on the pad. Keep the pad moist and watch the seeds germinate.

How Plants Get Water

Put a sponge into a clear glass jar and place some radish seeds between the sponge and the glass. Moisten the sponge and be sure to keep it moist. Place the jar in a warm place until the seeds sprout. The children can observe that the plants send out roots to absorb the moisture that is so essential to their lives.

Sock Plot

Ask your children to bring in old socks from their parents that are ready to be thrown away. Take the children to a grassy field with weeds and grass high enough to reach their knees (fall is the best time for this trip). Have the children put the old socks over their shoes and run or walk through the field. Then have them take off the socks and examine them. Discuss the things that are stuck. Back in the classroom, put three to five socks in the bottoms of flat plastic boxes (or line cardboard boxes with plastic film). Cover the socks with potting soil and keep the mixture watered. In seven to ten days, a good number of young plants should begin to emerge.

Green or Pale?

Plant bean seeds in two separate containers and allow the plants to sprout. Keep one pot in direct sunlight on the window and cover the other pot with a paper bag. Continue this procedure for about two weeks, removing the bag for observation purposes only. After that time, the uncovered plant should be green, robust, and healthy, while the covered plant is stunted and pale.

May I Have a Drink, Please?

Have the children stir some food coloring into a glass of water. Take a piece of celery and slice it across the bottom. Allow the children some time to examine the stalk. Let the celery stand in the tinted water for about one hour. The celery stalk will change color as the water travels upward.

Take the celery out of the water, slice it, and examine the stalk again. Try the same experiment with a carrot or white carnation.

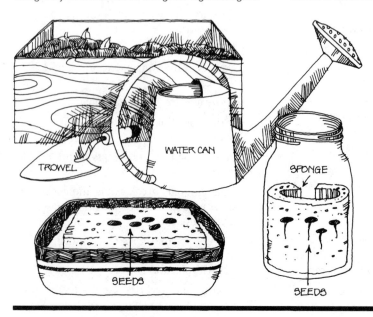

TROWEL

WATER CAN

SPONGE

SEEDS

SEEDS

Potato Head

Start with a large potato (A). Scoop off the top and line the shallow hole with a wet paper towel, sponge, or blotting paper. Stand the potato in a large dish of water. Sprinkle the wet paper towel with grass seed (B). Keep the towel moist at all times. Shortly, the seeds will begin to sprout and the "potato head" will begin to grow "green hair." Furnish cloves to the children so they can add eyes, nose, and mouth to their potato creature's face.

Which Way to Go?

Plant bean seeds in soil and water them daily. After the seeds have sprouted, place one plant in a box with a window cut out of one end. That window should be the only light source for the bean plant. Have the children observe how the plant bends toward the window and continues to grow in that direction.

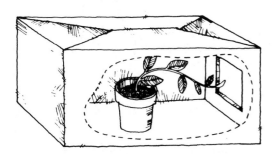

My Sweet Potato

Carefully wash a fresh sweet potato and suspend it in a jar of water so it is about one-half to two-thirds above the water. The potato can be supported with toothpicks. Have the children observe the emergence of an attractive new plant.

Terrarium

Place a handful of charcoal at the bottom of a glass container—this will keep the soil from getting "stale." Put in some pebbles or sand; make it as colorful and attractive as you can. Fill the container with good, rich potting soil and plant a variety of dwarf or slow-growing plants. Arrange pieces of rock, toy animals, driftwood, or a variety of other items to enhance the terrarium's attractiveness. Sprinkle the garden lightly and cover with a glass lid.

Other Plant Ideas

- Bring in many different kinds of flowers. Have the children compare color, shape, smell, size, and so on.
- Encourage the children to classify plants or flowers according to color, shape, and so on.
- Visit a nursery. Arrange for the children to purchase a small plant or seeds to grow once they return to the classroom.
- Observe the formation of seeds on plants, especially in the fall. Go outdoors and collect as many different kinds of seeds as possible.
- Plant a variety of seeds—grass, flower, bean, or whatever your choice. Keep the ground moistened. Continue observing the differences in growth among the different seeds.
- Grow a fruit-bearing plant such as a tomato or pepper plant. Examine the seeds within the fruit. Dry the seeds and plant them so the children can see the plant develop its life cycle from seed to plant to flower to fruit to seed again.
- Make your own potting soil from dirt, leaves, grass, and other biodegradable materials.
- Visit a farm or orchard.
- Make seed collages.

WEATHER CHARTS

Some teachers choose to discuss the weather each day with the children and ask them to compile a weather chart to summarize those conditions. Weather charts help to promote and guide the children's thoughts. As the conditions are described, you may want to guide comments toward the types of clothing appropriate for people to wear. Some suggestions for weather charts follow.

- Make a chart or bulletin board displaying various climatic conditions. Print the word representing each condition beneath each condition. Cut out a pair of clock hands from construction

paper and attach them to the chart with a brass fastener. The children can then move the hands to signify combinations of conditions such as "sunny and hot."

- Place a dress-up doll near the weather chart. Invite the children to dress the doll with appropriate clothing for the day's weather.

- Make a dress-up chart similar to the weather chart with specific clothing pictured for each weather condition. Ask the children to turn the clock hands to the clothing suitable for the prevailing weather condition that day.

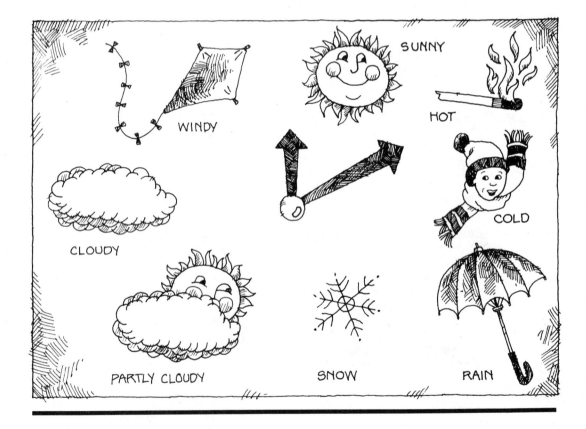

- Garden tools, construction equipment, and construction workers are characteristic of the season.

SUMMER

- Hot, humid, active days call for light clothing, water, and plenty of rest.
- Many animals are active.
- Plants are actively growing and in full bloom.
- Many schools do not continue through the summer.
- People relax and have fun during summer vacations.
- Swimming and baseball are enjoyable summer pastimes.
- Lawnmowers, outdoors grills, garden tools, and refreshment stands characterize the season.

These suggestions are offered only as directions by which you can guide the children's thinking as the days go by through the school year. You must remember that three- or four-year-olds in your classroom are relative newcomers to this world and may be experiencing the first seasons that have any significant meaning for them. As a result, they seek answers to the seemingly magical wonders around them. And you can stimulate their thinking by providing opportunities to observe and discuss the characteristics of all these interesting climatic conditions. One way of stimulating discussion on a daily basis is a weather chart, as shown in the following box.

Other Areas of Interest in the Environment Plants, animals, and climate are the scientific areas that are most interesting to young children, but other areas stimulate their powers of inquiry, too. "What is it?" "Why did that happen?" and "How does it work?" are questions that reflect the children's curiosity about the many other remarkable

things found in their ever-growing world. The children are not seeking technical answers— in fact, they are satisfied with a direct demonstration of a phenomenon. For example, during one particular warm day in the winter, one group of children showed a great deal of interest in a large sheet of ice that was beginning to melt. They were puzzled at this phenomenon and wanted to know why it was happening. They seemed satisfied with an explanation that the sun was out and the resulting warmth melted the ice. However, their continued interest in the melting snow and dripping icicles led the teacher to think of a classroom activity that would help demonstrate the effect of heat on frozen water. Back inside, the teacher brought out a tray of ice cubes and placed it on the table. She asked the children to observe the tray carefully and to guess what would happen if it were allowed to stay outside the refrigerator. Then, the teacher left the tray on the table and asked the children to check on it periodically to see what happened. At no time during the experience was an explanation given other than that ice melts when it gets warm and freezes when it gets cold.

There is no one recommended guide for preschool teachers to follow in determining exactly *what* and *how many* other scientific concepts or topics should be handled in the preschool classroom. You must use the children's interests and your professional judgment in deciding what else should be experienced. The topics described in the box entitled "Other Areas of Science Activities" have been taught as separate units or as individual activities in preschool classrooms throughout the country. You can also help your children to understand the world around them by thinking up activities for these topics:

- *Electricity:* dry cell batteries, bell wire with alligator clips at each end, simple switches, bells, or motors.

This child is being assisted by the teacher after he wondered what would keep his roller skates from sticking. The teacher explained that they might turn better if they were oiled. She capitalized on his interest and helped the youngster proceed from there.

- *Water:* floating and sinking materials, graduated cylinders, sieves, strainers, basters, and so on.

- *Weather:* rain gauge, wind vane, thermometer.

- *Senses:* a world of things for creative seeing, touching, hearing, smelling, and tasting; "freely boxes."

In Table 11-5 Donald Neuman (1972) summarized how all of these planned and informal science activities help children make sense of their environment and develop the important conceptual underpinnings so essential to later academic success. Can you, either individually or as a class of early childhood students, add to this important contribution of Neuman's?

It must be reemphasized that the science areas on which the preschool curriculum draws are so all-encompassing that it is impossible to identify the specific informational, observational, and experimental projects that comprise regular parts of instruction. Therefore, to recommend what every "four-year-old should know or do" cannot be done. However, you should capitalize on those facets that interest your children and turn them into activities that meet the general, overall goal of science in the preschool classroom: *to interest the children in their world and help them develop meaningful concepts by involving them in active experimentation.*

OTHER AREAS OF SCIENCE ACTIVITIES

Air

- Have the children blow into a container of water with a straw. Call their attention to the resulting air bubbles in the water.

- Place a deflated balloon beneath a book on the table. Blow up the balloon and have the children observe how the air makes the book rise.

- Discuss how the wind makes a pinwheel turn, the leaves flutter, or a kite fly.

- Have the children observe each other's breath on a cold day. Explain that they can see the air that comes from their body.

Magnetism

- Allow the children to manipulate a bar magnet and/or horseshoe magnet freely as they experiment to see which objects can or cannot be picked up.

- Ask the children to separate the objects that are attracted by a magnet from those that are not by sorting a variety of objects into two separate boxes.

- Have the children decide which of a group of magnets is strongest by comparing the number of tacks or pins they can each pick up.

- Put some iron filings on a paper plate. Ask the children to move a magnet around beneath the plate and observe what happens.

Machines and Tools

- Take your children to a farm, construction site, factory, or any other place where a large number of tools or machines are used so that they can observe their operation firsthand.

- Make a carpentry or plumbing area within your classroom. Encourage the children to manipulate and construct with the tools there.

- Discuss with the children how the wheels of their wagon make it easier to transport heavy objects than pushing or pulling the objects.

- Call attention to the adjustments made on a tee-ter-totter as it accommodates children of different weights.

THE SOCIAL WORLD

Our children's understanding of their social world involves all of the learnings they accomplish related to understanding themselves, others, and the environmental phenomena that influence relationships between themselves and others. In Chapters 3 and 4 and parts of other chapters, we have defined and described the child's social world in terms of the interpersonal skills and behaviors that children acquire as they interact with their peers, parents, teachers, and significant others. By itself such an interpretation would supply a very limited explanation of all the dynamics accounting for how children develop a sense of who they are and how they fit into this world where they were born. Thus far we have examined the factors accounting for the development of self-concept, including areas such as the following:

- becoming comfortable and safe in the classroom environment

- knowing their names and the names of others

- expecting sound leadership qualities from the teacher

- interacting with others in the classroom environment

- playing with others both indoors and out

Table 11-5 *Sample Science Topics for the Early Childhood Setting*

Topic	Materials Suggested
1. *Objects are alike, objects are different. How are they different?*	*Rocks, twigs, leaves, coins, glasses of water (add various food colors), common toys, small insects, fruits, animal pictures, flowers, assorted yard goods, buttons, seeds, two-dimensional shapes, assortment of tiles, building blocks, small musical instruments or noisemakers.*

2. *Objects have definite properties. What are some common properties of objects?*
   a. color
   b. shape
   c. size
   d. bounciness
   e. shine
   f. texture
   g. smell
   h. sound (pitch, tone, loudness)
   i. hardness
	Felt pieces (variety of shapes and colors), wooden dowels, two- and three-dimensional shapes, pieces of cloth (variety of colors, shapes, and textures), common fruit, cords, metallic pieces, plastic or ceramic tiles, paint color cards, rug samples, phonograph and records, bells, super ball, rubber ball, clay, sandpaper, food coloring, perfume, other materials with a distinctive odor.

3. *Some objects are living, some are not. How can you tell if an object is living? How can you tell if it is not living?*	*Common insects, mealworms, small rodents, algae, rocks, aquatic plants, seeds, seedlings, sand, soil, aquarium, goldfish, fossils, crystals (such as sugar), mechanical toys, living plants, plastic flowers, sponges, common fruits and vegetables.*
4. *Some objects are solid, some are liquid, some are gas. How are solids alike? How are liquids alike? How are gases alike? How are solids, liquids, and gases different from one another?*	*Talcum powder, sand, salt, sugar, wood, metal, plastic, ice, oil, glycerin, water, rubbing alcohol, balloons filled with oxygen, air, carbon dioxide, freon, or steam.*

Source: Neuman, D., "Sciencing for Young Children," Young Children, April, 1972, 27, p. 221.
© 1972 by the National Association for the Education of Young Children, 1834 Connecticut Avenue, N.W., Washington, DC 20009. Reprinted by permission.

- feeling competent in all areas of development

- having confidence to express creative ideas

- expressing emotions freely

The total environment of the school is designed in one way or the other to help children grow and develop in a social atmosphere of psychological safety. Our present discussion will move from a discussion of the interpersonal social skills presented so far to a consideration of special areas that lead to a growing sense of personal and social awareness.

Developing a Sense-of-Self (Body Image)

Full-length, unbreakable mirrors can be found in nearly all early childhood facilities. "That's me!" often accompanies comments about the physical self as youngsters examine the special features making each of them unique individuals. Youngsters enjoy looking at their hair, eyes, cheeks, legs, eyebrows, and other body parts; they also soon become interested in comparisons with the other children. From these early impressions, we find that youngsters become affected by how attractive they feel they are and how others, in turn, respond to them because of their appearance. I recall one teacher, for example, who often failed to choose an obese child in her classroom whenever an activity called for voluntary, vigorous physical activity. The child's physique appeared to elicit this seemingly unconscious response. Discrimination of this type—even from loving parents, teachers, or peers—plays a significant part in the development of a child's low self-image. Focusing again on the obese child, studies showed that fat children are viewed negatively even by their families. In an attempt to examine attitudes of parents toward their preschooler's body type, one study (Waitzkin, 1983) sent researchers to a zoo, an amusement park, and a shopping center to take pictures of both fat and lean children. In three days, no parent of an overweight child gave permission for a photograph to be taken, while each parent of lean children gave consent. Even more surprising, parents having both fat and lean children allowed only the lean child to be photographed. Other studies, too numerous to elaborate upon here, have found that preschoolers perceive obese peers as "ugly," "stupid," "sloppy," "mean," "lazy," or "sad."

Appearance, therefore, appears to influence attitudes toward preschool youngsters. What stereotypic attitudes might be attached toward a child in a wheelchair? a child with a facial disfigurement? a sturdy, stocky boy? a short, frail-looking boy? a little girl with frilly dress and bright ribbon in her curly hair? a lean, well-coordinated girl in patched blue jeans? Any of these special individual descriptions can consciously or unconsciously influence the behavior and attitudes of teachers, too. But, what can be done about it?

Such a question is very difficult to answer and even the most experienced child psychologists are uncertain about exactly what to do. However, the most popular suggestion is that teachers must be aware of their feelings toward certain physical features of children and look beyond physical appearance to what the child has inside. This simple awareness often helps prevent the accumulation of subtle messages that communicate, often without words, that you may value some children over others because of the way they look. A second valuable suggestion is to avoid making comparisons among children that cause one child to feel inferior to another. Try not to assign responsibilities on the basis of strength, height, age, weight, speed, sex, or other physical characteristics simply because you feel that single feature makes one child more valuable or desirable than another. The danger, then, in body image activities is to prevent the emergence of stereotyped attitudes or the unnecessary comparisons that lead to low self-esteem. Here are some suggestions for body image activities:

- *Use photographs whenever possible.* Children's photos could be used on cubbies, on helpers' charts, on attendance charts, or in books containing individual photos of all the children. In these "Books About Me," have children tell about such things as their home, favorite food, favorite story, or what they can do best. Print their comments below their photographs.

- *Play guessing games such as "Police Officer and Lost Child."* Select one child to be the police officer and another to be the parent. The parent implores, "Police officer, can you help me find my lost child?" The parent then describes one child in the group while the police officer and others in the group try to make the identification.

- Ask children to bring in photographs of themselves as babies. Discuss the physical changes they have gone through. Arrange "then and now" photographs on a bulletin board display.

- Ask individuals to complete this rhyme as they look into a full-length mirror: "The magic mirror sees all with me. Tell me, mirror, what do you see? The mirror tells me that I am _____ ."

• Use many action rhymes and fingerplays, such as:

Hands on hips,
Now on toes.
Touch your shoulders,
Head and nose.

Touch your knees,
Now your feet.
Touch your elbows,
And take a seat.

Developing Attitudes toward Members of One's Own Sex and of the Opposite Sex

Developing sex-role identity and positive attitudes toward members of the opposite sex are important aspects of personal and social awareness. Most young children develop feelings toward sexuality during their early years. Judy Corder-Bolz (Pickhardt, 1983), a sociologist specializing in sex-role development, believes that society and its traditional sex-role attitudes lead children from sexual awareness toward some degree of sexism, but, she says, sexism often springs from other causes, too. For example, at the age of about five, children go through a fascinating stage labeled by Corder-Bolz as "developmental sexism." What this means is that they are enormously sexist in their sex-role perception and choice of play activities. Despite the most rigid attempts of adults to shape a nonsexist environment, at this age boys still remain pilots and girls do the dishes. Developmental sexism is viewed as a natural phenomenon influenced by something called "gender constancy." That is, children understand that they belong to a certain sex and that a person's sex cannot change. Prior to about age five, children are unsure about whether or not boys can change into girls or vice-versa.

Once they grasp the concept that one's sex cannot change, they begin to organize the world into "girl" or "boy" categories. Such a connection to sexual identity helps children grow in the area of sense-of-self that they began during infancy. When observing children stereotyping through play, many parents and teachers will attempt to reason with them in order to create more objective attitudes about sex roles. For example, if the child says, "Only boys can grow up to be carpenters," teachers may say something like, "That's not true. Women are carpenters, too." This approach often fails. The child's way of classifying the world into male and female is new and not open to exceptions. A child may even become upset that the teacher fails to see the world in the same light and defend his case even more strongly. We can even compound the problem, therefore, by trying to reason with a child. This presents us with an interesting dilemma: We don't want a girl to feel bad, for example, because she does many "girl things" such as cooking a meal or setting the table during a dramatic play, and, yet, we don't want her to continue to accept the limited view she seems to be accepting for future aspirations. What can we do? Here are some suggestions to keep in mind as you handle the area of sex roles with young children:

• Let children know you understand their new system of organizing their world. Oftentimes, they come to you with or display in other ways an excitement about new discoveries in life. Accept their explanations as a developmental characteristic, but lead them toward understanding exceptions. For example, one five-year-old girl yelled at a young man walking by her group during a field trip: "Men aren't s'posed to wear earrings!" Remembering the advice about reasoning with youngsters, the teacher told the child, "I know you have never seen a man wear earrings before, so it's hard to see a man do something different." Don't try to offer a seemingly logical statement such as, "It's okay for men

Table 11-6 *Checklist for Sex-stereotyped Behavior*

1. *Number of illustrations of males_____ females_____*

2. *Number of times adults are shown:*

	Male	Female
in active play	_____	_____
using initiative	_____	_____
playing independently	_____	_____
solving problems	_____	_____
earning money	_____	_____
receiving recognition	_____	_____
displaying inventiveness	_____	_____
involved in sports	_____	_____
being passive	_____	_____
appearing fearful	_____	_____
showing helplessness	_____	_____
receiving help	_____	_____
playing quietly	_____	_____

3. *Number of times adults are shown:*

	Male	Female
in different occupations	_____	_____
playing with children	_____	_____
taking children on outings	_____	_____
teaching skills	_____	_____
giving tenderness	_____	_____
scolding children	_____	_____

4. *Ask these questions:*

   Are boys allowed to show emotions?

   Are girls rewarded for intelligence rather than for beauty?

   Are there any derogatory comments directed at girls in general?

   Is mother shown working outside the home? What kind of job?

   Are there any stories about one-parent families? Families without children? Are baby-sitters shown?

to wear earrings, too." Such a statement might provoke a response such as "Men *shouldn't* wear earrings!" and create even more distress.

• Set up a nonsexist classroom. Because children do not like to be "told," the activities and equipment in your classroom should be used equally by boys and girls alike. Examine books and other teaching materials carefully to see

whether sex-stereotyped behavior is evident. Check for the points listed in Table 11-6.

• Talk with children about changing sex roles. Give them information about how our culture is changing. Read them stories or discuss ideas about everyone's potential to choose careers and about all the different ways men and women are choosing to live.

- Despite your best intentions, overt sexism can catch you by surprise and frustrate you in your efforts to stress a single, humanistic role for all human beings. Be forewarned and understand how you can extend the children's views about what men and women do.

Learning about the World Around Them

As the children grow in self-esteem and understand that significant people around them want to help them grow to their full potential, they become very anxious to learn about the world around them. Being accused by my own students (in jest) of using overly trite analogies, I find it very difficult not to include this analogy to emphasize the point. Let us imagine for a moment that you have suddenly found yourself in the company of space beings, say from Mars, and that you and a friend are standing at the doorway of a huge space vehicle looking out at a strange land much different than you had even imagined before. The orange and green Martians are uttering some sounds that are totally incomprehensible to you and your apprehension is quickly turning to anxiety. "Oh, dear, what's happening to me!" Rather than succumb to panic behavior, you eventually work out a system of communication with the Martians that informs you they are well-intentioned and friendly. Learning that the outside environment will not be a threat to your well-being, you eagerly venture out to experience all the fascinating wonders in waiting. Likewise, children are eager, anxious inquirers into their world but have the willingness to do so only if they know they are capable individuals, that their learning experiences will not threaten their health or safety, and that their teacher is an encouraging, helpful individual who makes learning as much fun as possible. Classroom visitors, field trips, and other concrete experiences, therefore, serve to absorb youngsters in their quest to

investigate the world; however, by using excessive telling and talking strategies, we accomplish little more than our Martians did in informing you about Mars.

You had to learn by exploration—the same is true of children. What are some areas of social exploration appropriate for preschool and kindergarten children? We have talked about numerous possibilities for field trips and resource people in Chapter 7; in this chapter we will look more specifically at those areas normally labeled as "social sciences" or "social studies" by elementary school teachers. Of course, preschool and kindergarten teachers do not organize their day by subjects such as these, but they do teach many concepts associated with them during the daily routine. Therefore, in order to demonstrate how certain ideas fit into the overall picture of a child's education, further suggestions will be organized into those categories established by educators to facilitate investigation into our world.

The basic content of the *social studies* is drawn from six separate *social sciences:*

- *History*—inquiry into what has happened in the lives of people in the past
- *Geography*—the study of natural resources and how they affect human life
- *Civics*—investigation of the rights and responsibilities of citizenship
- *Economics*—study of the production, distribution, and consumption of goods and services, including occupations and career education
- *Sociology*—inquiry into the development and organization of people living together in groups such as families, neighborhoods, and communities
- *Anthropology*—study of the customs, myths, and institutions of various cultures and ethnic groups.

You may, at this point, feel certain anxieties about these subject areas: "These social sciences are so broad!" "What do I teach about them?" "What can the children understand?" Don't look at such concerns as problems, but as strengths. You have the whole world from which to choose and, assuming that Bruner was correct when he said that if any appropriately chosen concept is communicated *at the child's level,* we can use it as a source of instruction. Additional examples and illustrations will be shared throughout the rest of this chapter, but, for the sake of clarification at this point, consider the following information about the social sciences just listed.

History

Young children have extremely poor concepts of time, so the introduction and development of ideas related to history are very difficult. Their problems with time were explained in Chapter 9. Such problems create learning limitations that prevent concentrated exposure to concepts in history. This does not mean, however, that all concepts related to the study of history should be ignored. History deals not only with specific names, dates, and events of isolated times of the past, but it also deals with the concept of *change* and the forces that cause it. To develop a good sense of chronology, children must first understand the consequence of the passage of time: change. Change permeates the child's environment—seasons change, friends change, clothes change, weather changes, and skills change. As children learn how change affects us all, focus their attention on such events and characteristics.

1. *Encourage children to observe the changes they are personally experiencing.* "I couldn't do that when I was lit-tler," is a prideful comment heard from youngsters when they learn a new skill or task. "The fairy gave me a quarter for my baby tooth," or "I got new glasses. The doctor said my eyes were weaker than last year," are comments that afford

you opportunities to talk about the physical changes that accompany the passage of time. In addition to seizing on informal opportunities such as these, you may wish to introduce simple comparison activities to help the children focus on other changes in their physical appearance. Ask the parents to send to school with each child a picture of the child as a baby. Have the children compare their appearance then and now. Or, bring in items of clothing that are normally worn by babies. Have the children examine them and discuss why they do not now wear clothing like this. Finally, keep a growth record on one classroom wall; mark the children's height at the beginning of the year, the middle of the year, and the end of the year. After marking each child's height at the beginning of the year, ask each child to predict what his height will be at the end of the year and mark that height. At the end of the year, discuss the change: "Did you grow? As much as you thought? Why? Why not?"

2. *Help children observe the changes that occur in things in their environment.* "Look, the leaves are red," is a child's comment that gives the teacher an opportunity to help children observe changes that occur throughout the year. "Yes, aren't they beautiful?" asks the teacher. "Do you remember what color they were in the summer?" "What will happen to the leaves in the winter?" By helping children focus on seasonal changes in clothing, plants, and animals (discussed in the science section of this chapter), the teacher helps them understand environmental change.

3. *Emphasize that change can be regular* (as experienced in the previous examples) *or sudden and unplanned.* Excellent opportunities to help them learn this occur, for example, when "Big Bird came to talk about conservation so our story time must be cancelled today," or "We won't be able to play outdoors

today because of the rain—what would you like to do now?" or "The police officer is sick and will not come today. She will be here tomorrow." Through such experiences, children learn that things are constantly changing whether or not we anticipate those changes.

In addition to *change,* the historical concept of *long ago* is often introduced by some preschool teachers. Although children find it impossible to conceptualize "long ago," they are nevertheless interested in the characteristics of past times. They love to hear stories of the past and to handle or observe objects from other eras. K. Wann, M. Dorn, and E. Liddle (1962) tell us that we must allow children to experience such activity even though they may not yet be ready to put such experiences into a realistic time framework. The authors state: "This dipping into the past without concern for a logical development of chronology from the past to the present does not violate basic principles of learning. To wait until they can handle true chronology is to deprive children of one of the most important learnings of early childhood" (p. 53). The "History Activities" box describes resources that can be used to provide experiences for young children related to the past.

Geography

Like history, geography has a reputation for encouraging only memorization of meaningless facts. Most of us remember classroom exercises that were aimed solely at recalling place locations, land formations, capital cities, major exports, population figures, and so on. Little attention was paid to going beyond these facts and examining the influence of humans on their physical environment and vice-versa. Because schools used to accept this factual recall view of geography completely, the subject has been traditionally viewed as inappropriate for the curriculum of young children. However, with the contemporary view that geography is concerned not only with the characteristics of the *earth's environment* but also with the relationship of that environment of the *people* who live in it, preschool educators have begun to have renewed interest in making it an integral part of the early childhood curriculum. There is great danger in introducing geographical concepts to young children before they are ready for them; consequently, the preschool teacher faces a challenge in designing meaningful activities. Some popular activities designed to promote geographic understandings are included in the "Geography Activities" box.

HISTORY ACTIVITIES

- Invite resource persons, especially senior citizens, to come to your school to tell stories, share objects, or demonstrate skills that were used in the past.

- Bring in objects from the past (butter churns, toys, clothes, and so on) and place them in an interest center or in any area where you can demonstrate their use. Encourage the children to manipulate the objects and to talk about their experiences.

- Take the children to a local museum or old building where they can observe things as they

were long ago. Of course, the youngsters cannot comprehend the time period in which the objects from the past were most popularly used, but they will be able to compare the use of such objects with their newer versions.

- Read or tell children stories about things that occurred long ago. Through such listening experiences, young children learn about games of the past, occupations, jobs, challenges, or accomplishments.

GEOGRAPHY ACTIVITIES

Representation   Maps are abstract representations of real places on the earth's surface. Because they are so abstract, their use may be beyond the capabilities of preschool youngsters. Nevertheless, readiness experiences that help children understand that certain objects or symbols can be used to represent others should be an important part of every preschool program. Several activities designed to promote this representation aspect of initial map readiness instruction follow:

- Encourage free play in the sand or water play areas with trucks, cars, boats, and the like. As children "build" road, bridges, canals, and other geographic features, they begin to understand how their miniature environment simulates the larger world.

- Take a class trip around the neighborhood and photograph the buildings as you go along. Mount the pictures on blocks of wood and encourage the children to use them in much the same way as they would use regular blocks in their play.

- Use photographs of the children to illustrate that familiar things can be represented by scale models: "The picture shows you, but the picture is very small and you are really much bigger." Take photographs or draw pictures of a variety of classroom features and ask the children to point to or pick up the real object. In this way, the children can be led to understand that symbols represent real things or real places, but in much smaller ways.

Physical Features   Present knowledge of child growth and development seems to indicate that focusing on the children's immediate environment is a logical place to start examining physical features. Encourage the children to look not only for the physical appearance of the geographical features around them, but also to discuss the ways in which each feature influences their activities and the activities of others:

- If your playground comprises several different surfaces, that is, sand, dirt, grass, asphalt, concrete, and so on, you may want to have the children observe each carefully and decide which is best, for example, for riding a tricycle. Discuss why the hardest surface is easiest and why the softest is least desirable. Ask the children to find the area that would be best for digging, for tumbling, for resting, or for any other activity.

- Sand and water play can be used to help children build model rivers, lakes, roads, mountains, farms, cities, and the like. Toy vehicles add additional fantasy to free play and help

develop an awareness of the different types of geographical features on the earth's surface and of how people use those features in their daily lives.

- Take a walk outside the school and locate various physical features. The children can identify churches, houses, apartment buildings, trailers, row homes, stores, parking lots, and parks. You should lead discussions designed to help the children compare and contrast the ways in which these neighborhood features are used.

- Take a trip to an area more remote than the one in which your school is located—to a rural area, for example. Encourage the children to look for different land formations and buildings such as rivers, ponds, mountains, valleys, fields, farm houses, or barns. Lead a discussion of the ways in which this environment differs from their own, especially in terms of the people's clothing, work, play, and living arrangements.

The Earth   A complete understanding of the earth and its features is certainly impossible for young children. Consider, for example, the youngster who busily burrows with his shovel because he wants to "dig all the way down to the bottom of the world." Despite such maturational limitations, it is important for children to participate in experiences that focus their attention on some apparent features of the earth's surface:

- When standing in the sun, ask the children to look carefully and find their shadows. Explain that the sun's strong light makes the shadow. Move into the shade and talk about the differences.

- Digging in the dirt and playing with water introduce the children to the two basic features of the earth. Take the children to a lake or pond to help them more fully understand large bodies of water covering the land surface. Have the children classify objects or pictures that belong primarily on *land* or on the *water*.

- Have the children look at the sky (away from the sun) to explore the many varieties of cloud formations. They will learn that large, puffy, white clouds mean fair weather; white large, dark, thick clouds warn of rain or snow.

- Point out the nature of wind. On a particularly windy day, for example, ask the children to run into the wind and then turn away from the wind and run. Discuss the differences in effort expended.

- Observe seasonal changes—for activities, refer to the preceding section dealing with science in the preschool classroom.

CIVICS ACTIVITIES

The Classroom Governing Process "Mrs. Jackson is the boss," said Valerie, "and she said to put the puzzle away." Valerie obviously identified her teacher as the classroom authority figure and interpreted the role of authority figure as one that allows the person to "boss" others around. That kind of "boss" is seen by some children as the only or primary control over their actions and behaviors. They view teachers as power figures who rule over all children, and they view the child's role as one of being bossed by others. A basic knowledge of the democratic process cannot be developed if the child lives in an environment that perpetuates such beliefs, for authoritative environments prepare children not for life in a democracy, but for life in a dictatorial form of government. Therefore, to expect the child to respond positively toward you simply because you are the "boss" is a type of expectation that fails to help children become self-disciplined, responsible members of a group. To achieve the goal of classroom democracy, the following suggestions may be of use:

- Establish rules that are necessary for the care and protection of your children, and help children realize that those rules are made to protect them and others. In all types of governments, including a democracy, citizens have a certain amount of responsibility to follow rules. For example, three-year-olds must realize that city streets present certain hazards, and that certain restrictions are necessary when the group is on the steet. Katherine H. Read (1971) presents a good argument for such considerations:

Because we feel confidence that cars on the cross streets will stop when the light is green for us, we are free to drive through an intersection. The child who feels confidence that his parent will stop him is likely to act with less hesitation, to explore more freely. He feels safe when he can feel sure that he will be stopped should his impulsiveness lead him in dangerous directions. If the stopping or the limiting is done with love and without humiliation, he is helped to trust himself, to develop as a spontaneous, creative person. . . . He is free because he has parents who take responsibility. . . . They are setting a pattern which he can follow as he takes over the task of setting and maintaining limits for himself. They give him a model to follow when they act as responsible people. [p. 315]

So, a first step in establishing the democratic classroom is to create an atmosphere in which the children understand (1) that some rules are necessary for their protection and the protection of others and (2) that each child has the eventual responsibility to guide and adjust his own behaviors on the basis of those rules.

Civics

Civics deals with the rights and responsibilities of good citizenship, and especially with understanding the governing process—that is, the relationship between authority figures and those subjected to authoritative power. According to John Jarolimek (1971), three concepts are basic to an understanding of this process:

- the methods of establishing and maintaining order
- the power exerted by an authority figure over the people subjected to it
- the behaviors expected by individuals who are living within the particular governing framework

Naturally, the preschool curriculum would not initiate a formal study of the local, state, or national government to further these understandings. Children are exposed to concepts of government, however, at various times in their daily lives. Teachers, parents, other adults, brothers, sisters, peers, and a host of other significant human beings make and enforce rules that govern each child's actions in the home, at school, and throughout the neighborhood and community. This exposure

- Invite the children to participate in democratic decision-making activities. "Our new pet hermit crab needs a name. Does anyone have a suggestion?" After the names Herman and Harry were suggested, the teacher asked the children to vote for the name they liked best. Another class was asked to vote for making either popcorn or Jello for a snack. Such voting experiences give the children opportunities for group decision making and for following the will of the majority. Learning to live in a democracy also involves the ability to choose individual pursuits, so children may be asked, for example, to decide between two activities. "Those of you who want to swing may follow Mr. Adams and those of you who want to play Red Rover come with me to the grass area." Similarly, choices can be made concerning classroom learning activity, amounts of food during snack time, nap requirements, and so on.

The Governing Process Outside the Classroom   Many of the concepts related to this phase of understanding are taught in an informal manner:

- During dramatic play, the children may be encouraged to use miniature street signs similar to those normally found around their home or

school. Make favorable comments when the signs are properly used: "Very nice, Robert. You stopped your car at the stop sign and allowed Becky to cross the street."

- While on a field trip, make it a point to call the children's attention to safety rules. "We must go to the next corner in order to cross the street. There is a sign to tell us when it is safe to go."

- Invite police officers to visit the classroom. They can explain their duties and help the children understand the importance of following rules. Also, be sure to strengthen the knowledge that certain rules exist for the benefit of members of a group by guiding children's behavior when needed. State what the rule is and explain the limits. Accept the children's questioning of the rule—this helps them understand why the rule is necessary.

- Help the children recognize some of the symbols and ceremonies that represent our country without expecting them to memorize passages or understand their underlying meanings completely: Display the flag and explain what it means; play the national anthem before a special event; sing patriotic songs or read patriotic stories; have police badges or caps available for dramatic play; attend patriotic parades or special civic observances.

offers many excellent opportunities to demonstrate the importance of rules for governing personal and group behaviors. See the "Civics Activities" box.

Economics

The ear-shattering cry of a youngster appealing to his parents for a new toy during a shopping trip or the round-eyed gaze that accompanies "Mommy, I wanna new ball for my birfday" reminds us of the many ways in which economics concepts permeate the daily lives of young children. Many of today's critical problems are related to economics, so this

subject should be made a part of the preschool curriculum. Seefeldt (1977) pointed out that "if all people had everything they wanted, then knowledge of economic concepts would not be so critical. But today there are critical differences between people's needs and the things they can have. The concept of scarcity—the difference between the unlimited wants of people and the limited goods, services, and materials available—is a major concern of economic education" (p. 125).

The field of economics examines and describes the ways in which people produce, distribute, exchange, and consume goods or services. Although children have many oppor-

ECONOMICS ACTIVITIES

After taking a trip to the bakery, you can develop these concepts:

- *Production.* Bakers use goods furnished by other people: milk, flour, sugar, shortening, and so on. The bakery is a source for many goods: bread, rolls, cakes, cookies, and so on. The work in the bakery is divided into specialized tasks for more efficient production.

- *Distribution.* The bakery sells some of the goods it prepares in its own store and distributes other goods to other stores. Many different workers help to get the baked goods from the bakery to the stores. Packaging, handling, and transportation are important elements of the distribution process.

- *Exchange.* The dealer uses attractive displays and advertisements to encourage people to buy his goods. Some dealers sell baked goods at lower prices than others. The price people pay is directly related to how expensive it is to produce the goods and how badly the people want them. Dealers make profits when they sell the goods to buyers.

- *Consumption.* We buy what we want after deciding what is wanted and needed most. We buy some things because they satisfy basic needs and others because they bring us enjoyment. We examine the goods carefully so that we can select those that give us the most for our money.

These concepts can be expanded on during most trips or other experiences that involve monetary exchange or the use of a person's services. For example, trips to grocery stores, toy stores, drugstores, construction sites, gasoline stations, train stations, farms, and dairies can all be used to develop economic concepts, along with related concepts in many other curricular areas.

Arrange the classroom environment into different areas that help children participate in activities involving the responsibilities of people who produce, distribute, exchange, or consume goods. For example, experimental play with plumbing equipment helps children understand the services rendered by plumbers. Woodworking activities involve the children in real work—similar to the type grown-ups do. A classroom ice cream store, clothing store, shoe store, grocery store, and so on, place the children in the creative roles of customer and seller. Vivian Todd and Helen Heffernan (1970) illustrated one creative teacher's approach to this suggestion:

One day [the teacher] has individual cans of fruit juice and drinking straws for the children to purchase at the store at juice time. Another day, she provides the store with fresh carrots that are sold to feed the guinea pig and also to provide carrot sticks at refreshment time. The day she reads from *I Want to Be a Storekeeper* [Carla Greene (Chicago: Children's Press, 1958)], the store has boxes of cereals for sale, and the children have refreshments of cereal flakes in a sandwich bag. When she uses the flannelboard to talk about good things to eat, she makes the children aware that their store does not sell candy. In short, she makes the store an integral part of the school program and the roles of the store personnel a reality to the children. [p. 280]

Illustrate the advantages of division of labor as you assign two children the responsibility of preparing tables for snack time. The children can be led to understand that their work will probably go more smoothly if one child places all the cups and pitchers on the tables while the second child arranges the placemats and plates.

The understanding that our immediate wants and needs cannot always be immediately satisfied can be effectively communicated through creative classroom experiences: "I know you would like to use the shovel now, Chelsea. But Rhonda is using the only one we have. You will have to wait until she is finished." Similar comments can be shared with the children as economics-related experiences evolve in the classroom.

Also, you can make attractive gift package outlines from colorful construction paper. Encourage the children to search through catalogs or magazines and pick out the one or two gifts they would most like to have. They could then cut out their choices and paste them on the package outline. Stimulate discussion of the gift packages as the children complete their work.

Help the children appreciate the contributions of various workers within the community by capitalizing on the workers' eagerness to come to your classroom. Most telephone companies are willing to send a telephone installer to explain how the telephone works and to give the children an opportunity to talk to each other on real telephones that are connected and workable. Some companies even allow classrooms to keep these phones for short periods of time. The wee-ooo of a fire siren when the firetruck comes to the school brings excitement and motivation to learn about the responsibilities of a firefighter. If a delivery person brings your milk, ask him to arrange his schedule so that he and his truck can be seen by the children as the delivery is made. The ice cream vendor is another source of economic learnings. If possible, obtain some cash from the petty cash fund and give each child a quarter. Arrange one day for the vendor to stop at your school during snack time and sell the children some ice cream for which they will pay with their own money.

By sharing responsibilities during creative play, young children learn positive attitudes about an individual's contribution to the success of a group.

tunities to experience these concepts, a lack of explanation, continuity, or guidance may have left them with false understandings or fragmented information. For example, many children resent being told no by a parent when they want a particular toy; they cannot understand why these unending fountains of cash refuse their important requests. To help them gain such basic understandings, a planned, organized presentation is essential. See the "Economics Activities" box.

Sociology

Sociology involves the study of people's apparent natural tendencies to live together in groups. Such group orientation is one of the foremost characteristics of human beings. Dorothy Skeel (1974) stated that the sociologist investigates the characteristic aspects of human groups such as "the family, school, church, and government.... He attempts to determine the influence of these groups upon their members—to recognize the behavioral

changes ... exhibited by the members.... He attempts to explain why members of a group behave as they do" (p. 21).

Although forming groups appears to be a natural tendency in human behavior, young children start out in this world as anti-group-oriented beings. They are extremely self-centered—the only existence they are aware of is their own. Gradually, they seek contact with others in their environment, and, once they begin to develop language, they gain enough understanding to realize that they are not, indeed, alone in this world. Initial dependencies are directed toward the parents, but, by about three years of age, most children are spending less and less time with their parents and more and more time with other people, especially other children. From that point on, group orientations begin to have increasingly important control over their behavior. (Review Chapter 3 for a more complete discussion of this topic.)

Children need to be helped toward gaining an awareness of group membership and

SOCIOLOGY ACTIVITIES

- Give children opportunities to share, either in pairs or in larger groups, common classroom chores: setting the table for a snack, feeding the animals, watering the plants, or filling the paint jars. In this way, they develop strong feelings of their own self-worth, and positive feelings about helpful contributions to the group.

- Create a climate that encourages peer cooperation—praise or reward behaviors that contribute to the welfare of the group. A pat on the back and warm words of praise, for example, for Matt and Marty when Matt helped Marty turn a screw into a block of wood encourage similar group-oriented behaviors in the future.

- Help the children accept each other into various play activities within the classroom. Comments such as, "Let's go to the doll corner and see if they need a doctor to look after the sick baby," can help some children approach others.

- Arrange periods during the day in which children work together toward the completion of a group activity. Examples of activities requiring group cooperation include: (1) playing group games such as Duck, Duck, Goose; (2) completing murals or other large art projects; (3) cooking projects; (4) planting and keeping up a garden; (5) singing songs, telling stories, or doing fingerplays; and (6) building with blocks.

of the behaviors necessary for attaining effective group relationships. They must be led to do so through a great number of direct interpersonal experiences in all areas of the preschool curriculum. The best types of experiences are those that include a rich variety of play. Children's play, we learned, can be characterized as a hierarchical, developmental process in which children gradually expand the quality and quantity of social interaction with other children.

Some popular activities that can lead to effective membership in social groups are described in the "Sociology Activities" box.

Anthropology

Children begin to learn about anthropology when they experience the practices and traditions of various cultural groups: their art, music, institutions, beliefs, celebrations, and so on. Although the preschool child's world centers around himself, his home, and his school, and he demonstrates a strong interest in learning more about those who are close to him, he is also beginning to indicate a budding fascination about the lives of other people, people from backgrounds similar to his own as well as those whose backgrounds are quite

different. Such motivation may come from exposure to a diversity of backgrounds within the preschool center or from within the child's own neighborhood. Regardless of its cause, however, the important consideration is that the interest is beginning to grow from within the child. Therefore, it becomes your responsibility to develop a system of instruction in which the various contributions of cultural groups, including those represented in the preschool setting, can be recognized. The cultural heritage of all children should be handled in a natural way as an integral part of each day's activities. Suggestions for initiating such instruction are given in the "Anthropology Activities" box.

Halloween The popular tradition of dressing in costumes and masks should be approached extremely carefully with preschool children because they often have a great deal of difficulty separating reality from fantasy. Therefore, the well-meaning teacher who "surprises" the children dressed as a scary "skeleton" with a mask and costume may be greeted with sobs and tears rather than with joyful laughter. These young children are at an age where they are not quite sure whether or not a "real skeleton" walked in, and that uncertainty could cause traumatic reactions. However, if dressing up is shared in an atmosphere of play and fun, the children will have a great deal of enjoyment because they know they are safe.

You may wish to consider the suggestions for Halloween-related activities given in the box.

Thanksgiving Because of their difficulty with time concepts, the historical aspects of Thanksgiving should be avoided with young children. But since the traditionally special meal is so widely accepted, having the group pre-pare and share it can be a very meaningful activity. However, try to stay away from cele-brating the meal after dressing the children in feathers, Pilgrim's hats, buckskin vests, and other time-worn paraphernalia. This practice often leads to unwarranted stereotypes and confusion about the holiday itself. (Ramsey, 1979). Let them participate in the preparation of their meal by helping to make the stuffing and to place it into the turkey. They can also make cranberry sauce, prepare applesauce, dice the vegetables, and bake the bread. After the food has been prepared, the entire class can sit together and eat the meal. During the meal,

ANTHROPOLOGY ACTIVITIES

- Read or tell stories that describe the lives of people in other cultures. The following books are only a few of the many excellent stories for young children: *Homes* by Virginia Parsons, *Little Leo* by Leo Politi, *Meet Miki Tabino* by Helen Copeland, *The Little House* by Virginia Lee Burton, *Nine Days to Christmas* by Marie Hall Ets and Aurora Labastida, *The Story About Ping* by Marjorie Flack, *Wee Gillis* by Munro Leaf, and *Crow Boy* by Taro Yashima.

- Invite guest speakers into your room. Special information and great enthusiasm can be generated by an effective speaker who has a great deal of information and/or concrete materials to share. Often, cultural or ethnic community centers provide speakers for such purposes.

- Visit museums, cultural or ethnic centers, or historical societies that offer concrete experiences with other cultures. Large cities, especially, have museums where children can learn about the lives of people from many backgrounds.

- Introduce games and toys that represent the types of recreation enjoyed by children in this country and throughout the world. This popular game from the Congo is a good rhythm and movement activity. Gather the children into a circle and designate one child who is "It." Begin clapping rhythmically and encourage the children to join you. While everyone is clapping, "It" stands in front of someone and does some steps in rhythm to the clapping. The person he faces must then imitate the exact foot movements of "It." If he fails, he becomes "It" and

proceeds in the same manner with someone else. If the child imitates "It" exactly, "It" must move on to someone else and repeat the procedure until he defeats someone.

- Encourage children to sample a variety of foods associated with various cultures. Preparing such foods will often interest children to try them, especially if the foods from different cultures are experienced each day in a natural setting. Stay away from the temptation of treating the children as if they are going to eat something that is strange or different. Try tortillas, bagels, fry bread, and so on.

- Celebrate popular local or national holidays. Some days during the school year are *especially* noteworthy (although *each* day in the pre-school should be noteworthy) because of their significance to the child. By being given opportunities to observe such important days, young children are provided with the most popular means of sharing cultural customs and traditions within their preschool setting. Special songs, stories, food treats, poems, or art projects add to the observance of special days; parents or volunteers can serve as resource persons or additional supervisory help for special projects. Some special days and their customary traditions are given in the following sections. In order not to offend any single cultural group, only those special days having general national exposure are used for illustration. Of course, the suggestions can easily be applied to other observances.

HALLOWEEN-RELATED ACTIVITIES

- Visit a farm having apple or nut trees or grapes ready for harvest. Have each child pick enough to fill a small bag. Share their collections at snack time.

- Visit a cider mill and bring back a fresh gallon of cider for snack or mealtime.

- Bring to the classroom a large pumpkin suitable for decoration, or visit a pumpkin farm where the children can select their own. Have the children cut open the top of the pumpkin, reach inside, and scoop out the slimy seeds. Making pumpkin pie from the meat or drying out the seeds for spring planting (or for eating) can be valuable follow-up suggestions, depending on the level of your children. Tempera paint can be used to decorate the pumpkin shell as a group activity.

- Read or tell stories of Halloween or pumpkins.

- Bake cookies in the shape of pumpkins. Children may cover them with orange frosting and decorate them with chocolate chips or raisins.

- Make orange gelatin and serve for a snack.

- Arrange the dramatic play center with a variety of Halloween costumes or accessories.

- As a visual discrimination activity when children are dressed in Halloween costumes, ask each child to say a simple phrase such as "trick or treat." The other children must guess the identity of the speaker.

- Use orange and black paint at the easel or finger-painting table.

- Make paper plate masks for those children who may feel uncomfortable with a traditional mask. Attach a popsicle stick to a decorated plate so the children can cover and uncover their faces whenever they feel like it.

- Make trick or treat bags as large group art projects. Use orange and black paper (either with plain or fringed edges) and crayon-rawn cats, owls, or pumpkins to decorate a shopping bag.

- Create joyful songs or fingerplays to share with the children, such as this verse sung to the tune of "Frère Jacques":

Ghosts and goblins,
Ghosts and goblins,
Halloween, Halloween.
Today's the day for ghosts,
And for little goblins,
Halloween, Halloween.

---

the teacher can lead conversations emphasizing thankfulness and friendship. Other appropriate Thanksgiving-time activities are described in the box.

Hanukkah Hanukkah is an 8-day Jewish holiday that comes in either November or December, on the 25th day of the Hebrew month *Kislev.* It is a solemn festival celebrating religious freedom for the Jews. Traditional components of the celebration include:

1. The *menorah,* a special candleholder with eight branches and a place for a smaller candle called the *shamash.* The shamash is lit first and is then used to light the other candles. Starting on the right and moving to the left, one candle is lit the first night, two the second, and so on, until there are nine (including the shamash) in the menorah on the last night.

2. The *dreidel,* a four-sided top that is enjoyed by the children. There is one Hebrew letter printed on each side, collectively reading, "A Great Miracle Happened There," referring to the first Hanukkah when only one little jar of oil lit the holy lamp in the temple for eight days.

3. *Gelt,* coins often given as gifts to the children, one each night. Although Hanukkah often occurs during the Christmas season and gifts are exchanged for both celebrations, Hanukkah should not be referred to as the Jewish Christmas.

THANKSGIVING-TIME ACTIVITIES

- Arrange a trip to a turkey farm. Examine turkey feathers. Note how they differ from feathers of other birds.
- Read stories or sing songs with special Thanksgiving flavor. Creative movement can add to the fun; ask the children to strut like a turkey while they sing the "Gobble, gobble, gobble" of a song's lyrics.
- Involve children in creative art projects, such as making mosaics from seeds, grasses, or corn.

- Encourage children to portray Thanksgiving customs at the dramatic play corner.
- Discuss things that the children are thankful for.
- Direct the children to stuff a small, lunch-type paper bag with newspaper and to wrap a red pipe cleaner around the top. They should allow a portion of the cleaner to hang down. Then, using red tempera paint, they paint the turkey's head. Colored construction paper strips are glued to the back of the bag to form a colorful tail.

Some activities appropriate for Hanukkah are found in the "Hanukkah Activities" box.

Christmas Although this holiday has become overcommercialized and ostentatious over the past few years, children nevertheless look forward to this day more than any other day except, in some instances, to their birthday. Naturally, the gifts and special holi-

day magic have a great deal to do with this extremely popular holiday. However, because the children in your preschool facility may be from various ethnic backgrounds or non-Christian homes, it may be wise to emphasize winter customs and the spirit of giving that accompanies Christmas-time, rather than its religious significance. Only if your school is affiliated with a Christian church-related orga-

HANUKKAH ACTIVITIES

- Display a menorah, dreidel, or gelt along with pictures in a special area of the room.
- Invite a Jewish parent or a rabbi to share the traditions of Hanukkah with the children.
- Make dreidels from styrofoam blocks through which dowels have been inserted and held in

THERE

WAS

GREAT

MIRACLE

place by glue. The four sides of the dreidel should have these symbols:

- Play a dreidel game by giving each child a number of nuts. Each child places one nut in the center of the group. Taking turns, the children each spin the dreidel. If the first symbol faces up, that child puts a nut in the center; the second symbol, the child gets half the nuts; the third symbol, the child gets nothing; and the fourth symbol, the child wins all.
- Visit a nearby Jewish temple or synagogue.
- Make potato *latkes* (pancakes) for a snack during Hanukkah. Latkes are traditionally eaten during Hanukkah.
- Use the dreidel in any classroom games normally requiring a spinner or dice.
- Use sponge prints to make Hanukkah decorations.

CHRISTMAS-TIME ACTIVITIES

- Decorate the Christmas tree with creative ornaments made by the children. Stringing popcorn, using glue and glitter on pine cones (or styrofoam balls), or fashioning paper chains are tree decorating suggestions that have been used by preschool teachers over the years.

- Read fanciful stories (such as Moore's *The Night Before Christmas*) or sing lively songs (such as *Jingle Bells*) that reflect the spirit of the holiday season. Asking the children to prance like reindeer, flitter like snowflakes, or laugh like Santa adds to the joyfulness of such activities.

- Make special handmade gifts for parents or for janitors, cooks, and other support personnel in your preschool facility. For example, napkin rings can be easily constructed by most four- and five-year-olds. Cut paper towel rolls into 1-inch sections. Cut several 1-inch strips from

construction paper, long enough to wrap completely around the sections. Have the children cut a bell, tree, or any seasonal design out of construction paper and glue it to the strip of construction paper. Then have them staple the paper strip to the roll and insert a seasonal paper napkin.

- Have a special Christmas party with class-made cookies, milk, and, perhaps, a scoop of ice cream. If desired, a parent may be asked to dress as Santa and entertain the children as they listen to stories or sing carols. Special inexpensive gifts may be shared.

- Visit a senior citizens' home or hospital. Sing one or two carols or perform a simple seasonal skit that will entertain those who are away from their normal home life during the holidays.

---

nization should you stress the religious aspect of Christmas—but don't start too early. Having a tree for three weeks, for example, makes it hard for the children to wait and may overstimulate them to the point of frustrating the teacher. Some activities that can be used to enhance the holiday season are described in the "Christmas-time Activities" box.

Some Spanish Americans or Mexican Americans celebrate *Las Posadas* beginning on December 16 as a reenactment of Joseph and Mary's trip to Bethlehem. The celebration often includes the whole community in feasts, parades, and other festivities. Much of the celebration is like Christmas, but special customs characterize Las Posadas; chief among these is a nightly search of homes to see where statues of Joseph and Mary could be housed. Prearranged, such a home is found on the ninth night (Christmas Eve) where coffee, punch, wine, tortillas, tamales, and other special foods are served. Special experiences designed to communicate the characteristics of Las Posadas include the following:

- Make *piñatas*. Fill them with wrapped candy or nuts and small unbreakable toys. Children are blindfolded, spun around one by one a time or two, and given chances to swing a stick to break the piñata.

- Invite a Spanish American or Mexican American parent to your classroom to explain Las Posadas.

- Prepare tortillas, tamales, or other traditional foods.

- Read stories of Las Posadas to the children (see Marie Hall Ets and Aurora Labastida, *Nine Days to Christmas* [New York: Viking, 1959]).

- Provide materials and costumes for the dramatic play area so the children can play out the events of Las Posadas.

Valentine's Day   This holiday is especially appropriate for young children because it deals with one of the most pervasive attributes of the young child's life: love. The time-honored tradition of sending and receiving Valentine's

Day cards makes this day especially valuable for studying the mail system. Valentines can be made by the children out of precut hearts for their parents and put into envelopes; the envelopes can be stamped and addressed to their parents by the teacher. Then, a trip to the post office, where the children can see the envelopes cancelled and routed into the proper channels can be a valuable field trip activity. Other appropriate Valentine's Day activities include:

- A Valentine's Day party where the children prepare heart-shaped Jello molds, cakes, or cookies for treats is always a happy experience. Valentines can be exchanged, but be sure that each child brings one for every member in the room. Since most of the children will be unable to read or write, it is not necessary to address the cards.

- Craft activities can be used to design a gift to take home for a parent or other member of the family. Provide heavy cardboard tracers for one large heart and one small heart. The children trace around the large shape onto white construction paper and around the small shape onto red construction paper to form the basic ingredients for a placemat. The red heart can be glued on top of the white heart, and the entire product decorated with glitter, stickers, or frilly paper.

Easter   Usually signalling the coming of spring, Easter is a delightful time of the year for the preschool child. Buds can be seen popping out on trees, bulbs poke their way through the cold ground, and birds twitter as they build their nests. An awareness of these wonders of nature helps the child later understand the religious significance of Easter and Passover when and if those holidays are observed by his family. However, at this early period of their lives, children seem more concerned

about the Easter Bunny, little chicks, and candy. Therefore, they should be given opportunities to enjoy the season through a variety of enjoyable activities in the classroom. See some suggestions in the "Easter-time Activities" box.

Other Special Days   Patriotic days such as Columbus Day, Lincoln's and Washington's birthdays, Martin Luther King, Jr. Day, or other special cultural or ethnic observances stimulate an appreciation for our community or country. Teachers may focus on patriotic stories, songs, or special trips to parades or displays in order to stress the way in which the accomplishments of great people are observed.

Other special days such as Earth Day reflect different concerns. Cleaning the playground or planting a sapling may help the children become aware of the growing concern for the total environment.

Contemporary concerns demand that equal treatment of all ethnic groups and cultures represented in American society be stressed. Learning about the traditions of the many groups in the country helps foster greater interpersonal understanding as well as increased self-pride. It is imperative, then, that preschool teachers seize upon opportunities to share days that are important for different groups within the framework of the activities suggested earlier. The Chinese New Year, St. Lucia's Day, Tanabata, Mardi Gras, Kwanzaa, and other special days should be recognized and integrated into the school day. Often, children will experience difficulty understanding the significance of holidays they have never observed before, but it is still important to include a variety of holidays so children are made aware of and are exposed to other important celebrations. Creative teaching suggestions and further information concerning holidays can be easily found in teacher resource guides.

The basic content, then, for social studies comes from the six social sciences: history,

EASTER-TIME ACTIVITIES

- Easter-time signals the beginning of spring and the reawakening of plant and animal life. Have the children plan their own flower or vegetable gardens, select the seeds, and look after the plants as they grow.

- This is an excellent time to introduce pets to your classroom, if you do not yet have any. The care and feeding of pets is an important part of any child's preschool experience.

- Color hard-boiled eggs with a food dye solution. Refrigerate the eggs. At an Easter party, the children can peel the eggs and eat them. Use the discarded shells for a group art activity—make a mosaic design with colored egg shells and glue.

- Read or tell stories (*The Runaway Bunny* by Margaret Wise Brown [New York: Harper & Row, 1977]) or sing special Easter songs (*Peter Cottontail*).

- Hatching chicken or duck eggs in a classroom incubator is both challenging and enjoyable.

- Craft activities offer creative ways for children to make special Easter gifts for loved ones. For

instance, you can poke a small hole with a compass into half of an egg shell. Have the child paint the shell with tempera paint and push a pipe cleaner through the hole, bending the inside end slightly to keep it in place. Then have the child place his flower(s) into an empty film container vase filled halfway with plaster of paris. When the plaster of paris hardens, the flower will stand rigidly in place.

geography, civics, economics, sociology, and anthropology. As a preschool teacher, you will have many opportunities to "teach" anthropology, but, as you can see from our previous discussion, you will not be doing so at 9:30 in the morning under the heading of "anthropology period." Anthropology, like each of the other social sciences, is an area that can cohesively integrate other areas of the curriculum. In other words, it furnishes the content, or raw material, necessary for the child to be able to play purposefully with blocks, create an art project, or sing and listen to stories. Betty L. Broman (1978) explained: "The social studies are one of the two content areas of instruction (the other is science); therefore, whenever you are teaching a skill subject (language arts or math, for example) generally you are teaching social studies at the same time. Social studies is the 'glue' that bonds together

the elements of the curriculum for young children" (p. 192).

The present approach to teaching the content of social studies has been patterned after the time-honored "here and now" philosophy advocated by Lucy Sprague Mitchell (1934) and the "object-oriented" practical philosophy of Caroline Pratt (1924). Repulsed by the historically popular technique of making the children memorize social studies facts about things they had absolutely no experience of, these educators sought to make the subject serve a real function in the school. Influenced by John Dewey, they argued that the first step in the education of all young children was to help them experience things for themselves. Mitchell's "here and now" philosophy, for example, stressed that anything that was given to the child outside the realm of direct experience and observation was dangerous. Therefore, she recommended "here and now," firsthand experiences for young children—trips, objects, and resource persons. Caroline Pratt stressed that the real function of the school was to provide the child with practical experiences (projects) that would serve to integrate all the subjects taught (this is similar to Broman's description of the role of social studies). Pratt felt that through useful activities and emotional support, the child would build a foundation of practical skills that would serve him all throughout his life.

Because of this stress on direct experience and involvement in the preschool social studies program, three direct contact sources are identified as essential for all teachers: *taking field trips, utilizing resource persons,* and *examining real things.* Refresh your knowledge of these important firsthand sources of knowledge by reviewing the pertinent sections in Chapter 7.

SOME FINAL THOUGHTS

At the beginning of this chapter you may have wondered: "Science and social studies in the same chapter? How can two such comprehensive areas be treated satisfactorily that way? Isn't it 'elementary schoolish' to take such a subject-oriented approach?" These questions are valid ones and can best be addressed by remembering that both subjects call for active exploration of all the exciting phenomena of the young child's world. Science and social studies involve more than isolated facts to be expounded on by a teacher and passively absorbed by children. In fact, this approach can lead to a troublesome dilemma: "How can I explain science and social studies to young children? I don't know enough about those

subjects!" It's important for you to realize that science and social studies are more than academic subjects—they are areas in which children and adults learn together about the world. They study worms, ants, trees, construction workers, police officers, firefighters, and other aspects of our environment that encourage speculation and questions. These direct experiences help children associate the known with the unknown; they help to organize random discoveries into a meaningful foundation upon which to build deeper understandings; they answer some of the many questions that youngsters naturally express; and they stimulate further queries as the children gain keener interests in and awareness of their world.

Your role in science and social studies, then, is to encourage children to meaningfully experience their environment. Even though we call these two areas of the curriculum "science" and "social studies," they shouldn't be treated in the context of "science class" or "social studies class." Instead, they should be viewed as a system of challenging discoveries that give meaning to the children's world. Consider the following scene: On a cold, gray, wintery day, some soft white flakes of snow begin to fall, covering the stark landscape with a powdery shell. As the teacher gazes out the window, she thinks of all the ways this event might contribute to her students' learning. Recollections of songs, poems, art activities, stories, and fingerplays enter her head. "Surely these reliable activities will bring enjoyment to the children," she thinks, "but I should be able to seize this opportunity to help my youngsters understand what is happening out there, too." This teacher's concerns involve science and social studies even though she did not think of them specifically in that way; many things the children might learn about the snow would fall into one of those categories. The lists below offer a few questions that will encourage children's learning. Add your own ideas to the list.

SCIENCE LEARNING

1. What makes snow?

2. How cold must it be before we can expect snow to fall?

3. Could we bring snow into the classroom and save it on the table until we go home?

4. How can birds and other animals find food when the ground is covered with snow? Can we help them?

SOCIAL STUDIES LEARNING

1. Who will clean the roads and sidewalks of snow?

2. If the snow gets so deep that animals can't eat, who can help them?

3. Will school be cancelled tomorrow? Who makes that decision?

4. Who are some people that rely on snowy weather to make money?

We can see that both science and social studies deal with questions about the environment and that when we encourage children to explore the world it is nearly impossible for them not to learn something about either science or social studies. Both areas help children develop techniques of questioning, observing, testing, and forming new concepts. This is the basis for scientific thinking and the best way to encourage learning in the very young.

Chapter 12

Providing for Children with Special Needs

Bob H., 14 years old, entered his sixth grade class-room on the first day of school in September antic-ipating another year of ridicule and failure. Able to read only at the primer level, Bob had been the favorite target of teachers' frustrations. In fact, Bob's new teacher (Mr. Bowles—his first year on the job) was warned by several colleagues and even by the ele-mentary supervisor "not to worry because there's nothing that can be done for Bob anyway—he's pretty much of a lost cause." Perhaps because of a high degree of optimism or a strong sense of human-ism, Mr. Bowles refused to accept their admonitions. Before planning a program for Bob, though, Mr. Bowles wanted to check the student's personal file. The file gave some useful information, but seemed heavily weighted with comments about Bob's aca-demic failures. Mr. Bowles was not convinced, how-ever, that he should think of Bob as a lost cause without first trying to help him.

Mr. Bowles greeted his children on that first day of school and, as they walked in, was particularly caught by Bob's physical maturity. Much larger than the other children, Bob seemed out of place in the room. For several weeks Mr. Bowles observed Bob's activ-ities both with other children and with his school work. Bob seemed to get along with the others on the playground and at lunch but exhibited his strongest feelings during academic pursuits. Often these feelings came out as misbehaviors. Mr. Bowles immediately planned an individualized program for Bob in which he could work at his own level but without being subjected to materials below his maturity level; that is, Bob worked with manipula-tive materials and individualized practice sheets rather than pages from a first grade arithmetic book. Mr. Bowles's observation also uncovered some interesting information—Bob was actually very skilled in some areas of his development, especially in the physical realm. Bob was an expert planner and builder, for example, and always assumed natural leadership whenever building situations arose in or out of the classroom. Also, Bob focused his library book selections on one area in particular: construction machinery. Mr. Bowles seized this dis-

covery and used construction and construction machinery to motivate Bob in several curricular areas. As Bob experienced repeated successes and became motivated while being exposed to topics of personal interest by a teacher who was sincerely interested in him, despite previous circumstances, Bob steadily blossomed and grew throughout the year. By the end of the year, Bob's physical maturity was still far beyond that of the other children, but now his social, emotional, academic, and creative talents were growing, too.

Mr. Bowles kept in contact with Bob for the next few years until he took another teaching position in a distant state. His rewarding experiences with Bob were nearly forgotten until one day he picked up a newspaper from the town of his original position and focused on an advertisement with Bob's photograph prominently placed: "Bob H.'s Earth Moving and Excavation Company." If we measure success even in the most materialistic sense, Bob must certainly be near the top of all the students who were in Mr. Bowles's first sixth grade class.

What does all this mean to you, teachers who will be working with youngsters up through third grade rather than sixth? First, Mr. Bowles reflected a characteristic that should describe teachers at all levels, that is, he was primarily a teacher of children rather than a teacher of subjects. That means Mr. Bowles was aware of more than Bob's academic performance. He knew that intellectual development is only one area of the *whole child* and that children have strengths in other areas of development that should be addressed, too. He realized that we should accept the child at his present stage of development and capitalize on strengths to foster growth in areas that may need special attention. Second, Mr. Bowles realized that the preconceived stereotype of Bob that other teachers tried to communicate to him at the beginning of the year should not dictate how Bob would be treated that year. Mr. Bowles knew that negative statements are often made as an unconscious effort to cover up our own

failures, not the child's. In addition, Mr. Bowles realized that all children must be treated fairly and given equal opportunities to excel; that just because some children may appear brighter or come from better homes, they should not be given greater opportunities than the "dull" child or the child from "the wrong side of the tracks."

Like Mr. Bowles, teachers throughout the United States at all levels of instruction are being made more sensitive to the special needs of children, especially those children who, because of certain limitations, require some adjustment to their educational programs to help them approach their maximum developmental potentials more fully.

THE HANDICAPPED CHILD

> There are more than eight million handicapped children in the United States today, and the special educational needs of these children are not being met. More than one half do not receive appropriate services . . . and one million are excluded entirely from the public school system.
> —Introduction to PL 94–142 (1975)

Public Law 94–142

It was because of concerns like these that the Education for All Handicapped Children Act of 1975 (Public Law 94–142) was passed. Signed by President Ford in November 1975, PL 94–142 was primarily a funding bill; it offered fiscal support to states in return for their compliance with its provisions. Basically, the law mandated that by September 1, 1980, each state must provide access to a free educational program within the public educational system to all handicapped children between the ages of three and eighteen. The government required those programs to be as self-sufficient and productive as possible within a "least restrictive environment"—an environment suited to a handicapped child's special needs, but one that is as close as possible to a normal child's environment.

Local school districts responded to PL 94–142 in a three-part approach to making adjustments to their regular school programs. The approach included these components: (1) *identification* of those children in need of special services, including mentally retarded, hard of hearing, deaf, orthopedically impaired, other health impaired, speech impaired, visually impaired, seriously emotionally disturbed, and children with specific learning disabilities; (2) *assessment,* or evaluation, of the degree of impairment including formal and/or informal techniques involving the cooperative efforts of parents and professionals; and (3) *intervention,* or planning and monitoring a well-defined, individualized educational program for each child. All three parts are carefully prepared and presented in writing for each handicapped child in the form of an Individual Educational Program (IEP). The IEP is a written statement jointly developed by a qualified school official, the child's teacher, the child's parents or guardian, and, if possible, the child. The written IEP must include these sections:

1. an analysis of the child's present level of achievement

2. a listing of long- and short-range goals

3. a statement of specific services that will be provided to help the child reach those goals

4. an indication of the extent to which the child will become involved in the regular school program.

The particular characteristic of the law that interests early childhood educators is that it encourages the development of programs for preschool children by creating a *special incentive grant* for states that provide services to handicapped children aged three to five. These special incentive grants can be up to $300 for each child served.

Obviously, this law makes new demands on all teachers, including both regular and special education teachers in public and private schools. Although the law calls for education of handicapped children in "the least restricted educational environment" it does not mention *mainstreaming,* that is, placing handicapped children in a regular classroom. However, in 1975 the Council for Exceptional Children (CEC), a leading recommending body for teachers affected by PL 94–142, officially described mainstreaming as necessary for handicapped children—children whose special needs are such that they can be satisfied in an environment that includes nonexceptional children. Their position identified the regular classroom teacher, alone or with help, as the optimal instructor for all students. Underlying this philosophy of mainstreaming is the recognition that when handicapped and nonhandicapped children have a chance to learn, grow, and play together, they grow in self-esteem, social skill, and understanding.

How do you fit into all of this? You should know as much as possible about PL 94–142 because every school district in the country is affected by it. As more and more handicapped children become integrated into the classrooms of public and private schools, regular teachers are more likely to provide appropriate educational experiences for them. To get ready for such an experience, you should:

1. Learn all about the handicaps with which you will be dealing.

2. Visit classrooms where handicapped children have been successfully mainstreamed.

3. Talk to teachers who have worked with handicapped children and gather useful suggestions from them.

4. Seek help from special education teachers who may have worked with children

handicaped in ways similar to your children.

5. Attend special conferences, workshops, or other in-service training sessions designed to assist you in IEP writing and/or designing special learning materials and teaching techniques.

6. Talk to the child's parents and previous teachers. They can offer suggestions and advice as the school year progresses.

7. Seek special assistance through publications and nonprint media (speakers, films, and so on) from local, state, or national agencies.

Special Handicaps

It has been long agreed among early childhood educators that every child is unique and special. For that reason, all of education should be _special education_ and all educational practices should be directed toward meeting each individual's unique needs. Some children, however, may possess certain extreme mental or physical difficulties that restrict them from reaching the same stages of development as other children. Such handicaps cause some children to differ markedly from the typical child at a particular age level and result in behaviors or characteristics that deviate in an extreme manner. The rest of this chapter will help you identify children with these special handicaps and will share ideas designed to help you develop skills in working with them. The charge of identifying children with special handicaps is a particularly difficult one, though. Philip Safford (1978) elaborates:

> One of the most difficult tasks facing the teachers of young children is that of determining which among the varying patterns of individual differences among children constitute "problems." A 4-year-old boy seems to be acting out themes of anger and destruction in his play with dolls. A 6-year-old frequently reverses the direction of certain numerals and letters of the alphabet as he learns to copy them from the board. A 3-

year-old makes essentially no use of expressive language. Do such patterns of behavior indicate the presence of problems or handicaps, or are they within the bounds of normalcy, given the individuality of children's development? [p. 11]

Such determinations can be effectively made by a sensitive, informed teacher who is aware of both the characteristics of typical children at various levels of development and the behaviors or characteristics of children having developmental difficulties. Early identification of developmental handicaps is extremely important, for the earlier they are identified, the easier it often is to improve or eliminate them. Nothing, however, can be done until the child is identified as needing assistance, and it is the adult working with early childhood youngsters who often sees the children enough to become aware of such difficulties. You have been presented with many descriptions of developmental standards throughout this book, and it is hoped that your ability to recognize the typical behaviors of children at various ages has been strengthened. Now you will be exposed to the characteristics of children who are developing so far from the normal patterns that they require certain adjustments to their environment.

Mentally Retarded Children Mental retardation is an extremely sensitive problem and one that has been defined differently by different educators throughout the years. Earlier systems classified mental retardation into levels such as _moron, imbecile,_ and _idiot_ in order to describe degrees of _feeblemindedness._ Certainly, you are aware of the derogatory nature of these labels and realize that their professional use is today condemned. Such labels usually were accompanied by feelings of hopelessness toward the child and a consensus that he was unable to benefit from any kind of education.

Fortunately, our view of mental retardation has now changed, although universal agreement has not yet been achieved. Many educators describe the degrees of mental retardation caused by brain injury or environmental factors according to performance on standardized tests of intelligence (IQ). The IQ, as discussed in Chapter 14, is the most traditional yet the most criticized method of assessing children's intelligence. The IQ test was developed by Alfred Binet, a French psychologist attempting to identify slow learners in France in 1905. The test quickly reached the United States, where Lewis Terman of Stanford University revised it for use in this country and gave it the name Stanford-Binet Test of Intelligence, the name it is known by even today.

Binet saw intelligence not as a single ability, but as a number of related factors that work together. For example, he felt that as children grow older, their intellectual ability increases, but not necessarily at the same rate as their chronological age. To account for this difference, Binet converted scores on his test into a *mental age,* that is, the age at which a certain level of performance on his test would be considered chronologically normal. For example, a child of four would be considered normal if his mental age was also 4; however, a mental age of 2 for that same child would indicate a lag of two years below the norm.

The IQ, or *intelligence quotient,* is a formula designed to express this relationship between chronological age (CA) and mental age (MA). It expresses intelligence as the ratio of MA to CA multiplied by 100 to avoid the problem of using decimals.

$$IQ = MA/CA \times 100$$

Therefore, if a child's mental age is 24 months and his chronological age is 48 months, his IQ is:

$$IQ = 24/48 \times 100$$
$$IQ = 1/2 \times 100$$
$$IQ = 50$$

This tells you that the four-year-old child has the intellectual level of a two-year-old. An IQ of 100 is considered normal (average).

$$IQ = 48(MA)/48(CA) \times 100$$
$$IQ = 1 \times 100$$
$$IQ = 100$$

The *standard deviation* of IQ tests is 16; this means that we can categorize *normal* or *average* intelligence as the range of scores from 84 to 116. However, average intelligence is usually associated with IQ scores that fall within the 80–120 range. The American Association of Mental Deficiency (AAMD) examined the use of IQ scores to indicate mental retardation, and designed a classificational system to describe the levels of retardation for children falling below the normal levels of intelligence. Their work is shown in Table 12–1.

According to this system, degrees of mental retardation are identified solely through scores attained on two popular childhood tests of general intelligence. Samuel A. Kirk has also used intelligence test scores to classify levels of mental retardation, but has added a new dimension—explanations of potential growth within each level of retardation (see Table 12–2).

Many professionals today question the classification of young children into levels of

Table 12-1 *AAMD Classification of Mental Retardation*

Level	Intelligence Quotient Scores	
	Stanford-Binet	*Wechsler Intelligence Scale for Children*
Mild	67–52	69–55
Moderate	51–36	54–40
Severe	35–20	39–25
Profound	<19	<25

Source: Gearheart and Lifton, 1979.

Table 12—2   *Classification of Mental Retardation and the Potential for Growth within Each Level*

Level	IQ Score	Definition
Educable mentally retarded (EMR)	50–75/80	Unable to profit sufficiently from a regular program but has potentialities in (1) academic subjects, (2) social adjustment, and (3) minimal occupational adequacies.
Trainable mentally retarded (TMR)	25/30–49	Not educable in the traditional sense but has potentialities for training in (1) self-help skills, (2) social adjustment in the family, and (3) economic usefulness.
Totally dependent	25/30	Unable to be trained in total self-care, socialization, or economic usefulness, and requires almost complete care and supervision throughout life.

Source: Kirk, 1972.

retardation based solely on IQ scores. As a matter of fact, federal regulations now *prohibit* educational placement decisions (that is, placement in special education classes) solely on the basis of a single test of intelligence. Despite such obvious rejection of the intelligence test as a single source of information regarding the evaluation of a child's intellectual abilities, controversy surrounds the issue even until today. The controversy centers on two viewpoints: (1) the belief that intelligence is primarily inherited and that efforts to improve it are largely fruitless; and (2) the belief that intelligence is largely a product of experience and that one can structure the environment to increase intelligence.

Arthur R. Jensen is the leading spokesperson for the first belief, a belief that educators today find unacceptable because of its strong racist overtones. Although I in no way support Jensen's ideas, I believe that all ideas (however unpopular they may be) should be shared in order to give learners an understanding of the dangers involved in looking at only one source of information.

Jensen contends that Black youngsters perform at a lower level on intelligence tests than their white counterparts because of genetic differences. He uses this argument to explain the lack of adequate standard-English speaking patterns among Blacks—that is, limited language comes from limited intelligence. Jensen believes that this limited intelligence results in Blacks' inability to learn conceptual material. He asserts that Blacks are able to learn through memorization but that material taught through problem solving and discovery is beyond their native ability. Consequently, Jensen believes that although programs can be designed to improve the *achievement* of Black youngsters, it is futile to expect growth in intelligence. Programs based on Jensen's premises would most probably find children being drilled in repetitive patterns until they can respond quickly and uniformly.

Jensen has been roundly criticized throughout the country for racism. Oscar Jarvis and Marian Rice (1972) summarize these feelings:

> Racist explanations [of intelligence] were developed in part to justify the institution of chattel slavery in the New World. As a slave, the Negro never participated in the total culture.... A hundred years after obtaining his freedom in the United States, he is still discriminated against in terms of education, housing, jobs, and social participation in the general culture. A genetic explanation of I.Q. differences, as reviewed by A. R. Jensen, simply does not take into account cultural history of the Negro in the United States.

Mentally retarded youngsters find joy and happiness when provided with experiences designed to meet their special developmental needs. (© Nikolay Zurek/Jeroboam)

Negroes are disproportionately represented in the lower income groups. It is inevitable that differences in intelligence and achievement may appear as racial differences when the differences are primarily class differences. [p. 491]

Jerome Kagan (1973) attacked the genetic view of intelligence with these comments:

Since middle-class children are more consistently encouraged than are lower-class children to learn to read, spell, add, and write, rather than to keep away from police or defend oneself from peers, the child's I.Q., social class, and school grades are all positively related. The I.Q. is an efficient way to summarize the degree to which a child has learned the vocabulary, beliefs, and rules of middle-class American society. . . . The child is asked to define the word "shilling" rather than the word "rap"; he is asked to state the similarity between a "fly" and a "tree," rather than the similarity between "fuzz" and "Uncle Tom"; he is asked what he should do if he lost one of his friend's toys, rather than what he should do if he were attacked by three bullies. [p. 199]

These first two major arguments attacking the genetic view of intelligence are directed, then, toward the social and economic limitations placed on Blacks and toward the cultural bias of intelligence tests. A third refutation of genetically fixed intelligence is based on studies by Benjamin Bloom (1964) that demonstrate that not only is IQ *not* fixed, but also that it can be altered with training, experience, and changes in teaching patterns. (See Chapter 2.) Bloom's conclusions were that the long-term overall effect of living in a "deprived" as opposed to an "abundant" environment is 20 IQ points, and that providing early experiences is the key to raising intellectual levels. This hypothesis found many supporters in the 1960s, and research evidence accumulated since then has convinced the vast majority of educators today that preschools can do a lot to prepare environments that provide experiences leading to changes in intelligence. Refer to Chapter 2 for a more complete discussion of this issue.

Based on today's accepted view, that the intelligence of all people can be altered by the environment, a number of innovative *compensatory* preschool programs have been developed. These programs were designed to provide the kinds of experiences and stimulating environments that could compensate for the social and economic conditions causing developmental lags, especially in the area of intelligence. Many of these programs, stimulated by Head Start and other federal, state, local, or private funding, showed positive results in achieving their goals. Some of the most popular model programs are:

BEHAVIORAL APPROACHES

• Behavioral Analysis Model
Donald Bushnell, Project Director
University of Kansas

Academic Preschool (Distar®)
Wesley Becker and Siegfried Englemann, Project Directors
University of Oregon

COGNITIVE APPROACHES

• The Cognitive Curriculum
David Weikart, Project Director
High/Scope Educational Research Foundation
Ypsilanti, Michigan

INFORMAL MODELS

• Bank Street Approach
Elisabeth Gilkeson, Project Director
Bank Street College
New York, New York

Tucson Early Education Model (TEEM)
Ronald Henderson, Project Director
University of Arizona
Tucson, Arizona

Because of the possibility of prejudice or unfair labeling of young children, you should be aware of alternative methods of determining to what extent mental retardation may exist in young children:

1. Observe the child for any characteristics or behaviors that are obviously immature for his chronological age.

2. Examine the child's cumulative records for information regarding the development of such skills as crawling, creeping, walking, and talking.

3. Evaluate the child's ability to remember things over a period of time.

4. Check the child's attention span and frustration level.

5. Examine the child's ability to get along with others and determine whether he is accepted or rejected by his peers.

6. Observe the child's interest in books or other learning-related materials.

The severity of mental retardation obviously varies widely—from the mildly retarded youngster who fits well into the normal daily routine to the severely retarded child who needs special care and understanding. Most preschool teachers are flexible individuals: normally they have little difficulty absorbing the mentally retarded child into the classroom or providing special educational services. Those who have done so usually followed general recommendations such as the following:

RECOMMENDATIONS FOR WORKING WITH MENTALLY RETARDED CHILDREN

1. Initiate a systematic procedure for diagnosing the child's level of development, and plan a step-by-step program in which the child can experience repeated success.

2. Use as many direct experiences as possible.

3. Use manipulative, real learning materials so the child can experience as many sensory modalities as possible (hearing, seeing, touching, tasting, and smelling) in his learning. Don't rely on talking to the child!

4. Plan for patient repetition because the mentally retarded child needs more time than his normal counterpart to grasp ideas—be tolerant and understanding.

5. Provide constant reinforcement through reward and praise for each accomplishment.

6. Provide many opportunities for the child to speak. Piaget, Chomsky, and other prominent writers describe the interrelated development of language and intelligence and emphasize the importance of language as an evolving process of intelligence.

7. Encourage the child to persist and let him know that you like him and want to help him.

8. Be consistent in your behaviors. Mentally retarded children become anxious and frustrated when their authority figure fluctuates in her behavior patterns.

9. Respond to the child's questions and comments. The mentally retarded youngster will feel better about himself if he knows that his questions and comments are sincerely accepted by his teacher.

10. Be sure to avoid comparisons with the normal children in your classroom and eliminate a competitive climate. Help the child adjust to regular routines and get along with the other children.

The key to an effective program for mentally retarded youngsters is your ability to individualize the program and to stimulate the child to learn with challenging tasks presented at his present ability level. With patience and understanding, these children are capable of doing many of the same things normal children can do, except on a slower and more delayed scale. The hypotheses of Bloom (1964) and Hunt (1961) (discussed in Chapter 2) during the 1960s enlightened educators to the fact that properly designed programs for pre-school children can raise IQ scores by 20 or 25 points. If we go back to Tables 12-1 and 12-2, it is apparent that enriching environments during the early years can move children from the category of moderately retarded (Table 12-1) or educable mentally retarded (Table 12-2) to a low normal category (above IQ score of 80). Because of this and other evidence, early childhood educators have become convinced that planning educational experiences in terms of the child's developmental level rather than his chronological age is imperative. If this is done, there is no reason why mentally retarded young children cannot successfully adjust to and learn in regular preschool classrooms.

Hearing Impaired Children   The incidence of hearing problems in the nation's schools has been the subject of conflicting evidence over the years, especially among reports describing the hearing problems of preschool youngsters. S. R. Silverman and H. S. Lane (1970), however, conducted an exhaustive study of hard of hearing and deaf youngsters and discovered that "of 18,926 children enrolled in public residential schools for the deaf in the United States, 1028 were under the age of 6; of 15,370 children in public day schools and classes, 2,453 were of preschool age; and of the 3686 children in denominational and private schools, 1646 were under the age of 6" (p. 385).

Although total deafness is relatively rare in preschool classrooms (only 4 percent of all hearing problems result in deafness), mild or moderate hearing problems are found about as often as any other form of physical or mental handicap. The degrees of handicap are based on the extent of hearing loss as measured in *decibels* (db), standard units for measuring the volume of sound. Table 12–3 differentiates six classes of handicapped hearing in terms of extent of hearing loss, and describes the ability to understand speech within each category.

Table 12-3 *Levels and Characteristics of Handicapped Hearing*

Handicap Level	Amount of Loss	Ability to Understand Speech
No significant handicap	< 25 db	No significant difficulty with faint speech
Slight handicap	25–40 db	Difficulty only with faint speech
Mild handicap	40–55 db	Frequent difficulty with normal speech
Marked handicap	55–70 db	Frequent difficulty with loud speech
Severe handicap	70–90 db	Can understand only shouted or amplified speech
Extreme handicap	> 90 db	Usually cannot understand even amplified speech

Source: Davis and Silverman, 1970.

Although physical examinations and parental observations uncover some cases of hearing difficulty before the child comes to school, many mild or moderate hearing problems remain undiscovered until the child enters the preschool classroom. Thus, the teacher must be watchful of the children under her care so that possible hearing problems can be uncovered before complications accumulate. Symptoms of hearing difficulties include the following (Safford, 1978):

1. Shows speech problems:
   a. reluctance to speak
   b. speech very loud, very soft, or very slow
   c. articulation (forms words or speech sounds) poor
2. Is unresponsive when spoken to; may often ask "Huh?" or "What?"
3. Watches the speaker's face while the speaker is talking
4. Cocks or turns head toward a speaker
5. Has difficulty maintaining attention when spoken to
6. Complains about earaches or demonstrates actions that indicate pain in the ear.

In keeping with the spirit of PL 94–142, you are responsible for helping *identify* youngsters with hearing impairments and for *planning* programs that provide least restrictive environments for them. This is not as threatening a situation for you as it may seem, for R. A. Stassen (1973) points out, "Of all handicapped pupils, those with amplifiable hearing losses are among the most potentially teachable" (p. 3). The preschool setting should be the same for children with impaired hearing as it is for everyone else, except for the following recommendations.

RECOMMENDATIONS FOR WORKING WITH HEARING IMPAIRED CHILDREN

1. Develop an attitude of readiness to listen. Use special signals to remind the child that you are about to speak. Encourage him to let you know when he's ready to listen to you.
2. Use the voice for getting the child's attention. Say the child's name when you wish to talk to him. Tapping him on the shoulder and similar measures only serve to bring unnecessary attention to the child's handicap.
3. Keep within close range when speaking. Turn toward the child so he can see

your face. He is helped when he is able to interpret your lip movements as well as your facial expressions.

4. Use a normal conversational tone of voice. Speak in short sentences with a clear voice. Clarity is much more important than loudness, for increasing your volume will only single out the handicapped child and begin to label him as "different." Besides, clear speech is much easier to lip-read than is exaggerated speech.

5. Serve as a good speech model. Avoid overuse of gestures or overexaggerated lip movements or facial expressions. Children benefit more when they observe normal speech behaviors than otherwise.

6. Use frequent repetition. Talk to the hearing impaired child and repeat your words when it seems necessary. If you develop an accepting environment, the child will feel free to let you know when your words need to be repeated.

7. Encourage parents to expand your work in the home. Parental cooperation is essential to the success of any preschool program, but especially when special measures have been instituted to compensate for hearing handicaps.

8. Develop a favorable attitude toward the child. The single most important variable in working with the hearing impaired is an understanding teacher. You should treat the child as an able individual and be empathetic (not sympathetic) with his condition. Overprotection of such children is unnecessary; except for these few special recommendations they need to be treated like others in your room.

Deaf children, of course, present a different situation from those who possess some degree of hearing. The ultimate goal, again, is to integrate the children into the regular classroom, but it is unlikely that they will make a

These hearing impaired youngsters have been mainstreamed into a regular classroom after being trained in the use of special hearing devices. (© Elizabeth Crews/Icon)

good adjustment unless at least *some communicative* speech patterns have been developed in the home or in special school settings before the child comes to the regular classroom. W. M. Northcott (1970) believes that integration of the deaf into the regular classroom is not appropriate if these conditions are present:

1. The hearing loss was recently diagnosed and there has been no parent guidance to ensure transfer and maintenance of educational gains through home stimulation, and

2. The child is not yet aware that his hearing aid brings in meaningful environmental sounds, including speech, or that he must look at faces to gain understanding from moving lips and facial expression. [p. 368]

Once it has been determined that the deaf child can be mainstreamed, he must be placed in a situation where he can gain optimum benefit from his experience, much as any other child. This means that the major goal of his early preschool experiences should be *socialization*. Thus the child will have an opportunity to adjust to the room and to the other children. This is as much a benefit to the normal hearing child as it is to the deaf child, for he begins to understand and befriend the handicapped at an early age. Once the socialization process has begun, and the deaf child indicates an interest in formal learning, you may wish to contact hearing specialists or other resource persons for suggestions of supplementary teaching materials. However, special materials or methods should be used within the context of the regular classroom whenever possible so that the deaf child is generally treated like any other in your care.

Northcott (1973) observed hearing impaired children who were mainstreamed into regular classrooms and found that, even though these characteristics were not evident beforehand, the children had several features in common:

1. Active utilization of residual hearing and full-time hearing-aid usage, if prescribed

2. Demonstrated social, academic cognitive, and communicative (auditory and oral) skills within the normal range of behaviors of hearing classmates at a particular grade level

3. Intelligible speech and the ability to comprehend and exchange ideas with others through spoken, written, and read language

4. Increased confidence and independence in giving self-direction to the tasks at hand [p. 3]

Children with hearing problems, then, are able to feel good about themselves, and can gain from the educational setting if they are integrated with normal hearing children. The sensitive teacher must look at these children with an understanding eye and match their unique needs with her program's resources. Except for following the special recommendations, the hearing impaired child should be treated as any other in your care.

Visually Impaired Children   A physical handicap that is often found in the preschool setting is the inability to see clearly. Like the hearing impaired, the visually impaired child is most often normal in all other areas of development, so he needs much the same kind of educational environment as the normal seeing child, except, of course, for certain special considerations.

Visually impaired children are normally classified into two categories:

1. *The partially seeing:* children whose field of vision is 20/200 (that is, they can see at 20 feet what a normally sighted person can see at 200 feet) or better in the corrected better eye, but not greater than 20/70.

2. *The blind:* children whose field of vision is 20/200 or less vision in the corrected better eye.

Children with visual impairments exhibit distinct symptoms—you should be constantly alert to these. Some common symptoms include (Rogers, 1977; Kirk, 1972):

1. crossed eyes (strabismus)

2. involuntary, rapid movements of the eyeballs (nystagmus)

3. squinting

4. rubbing the eyes

5. crusts, sties, or swollen lids

6. reddened or watery eyes

7. tilting the head to one side

8. pupils of uneven size

9. sensitivity to light

10. awkwardness in eye–hand coordination (in puzzles, dressing, and so on)

11. facial distortions while doing close work

12. avoiding tasks requiring good vision

13. complaints of pain in the eyes, head-aches, dizziness, or nausea following close eye work

14. lack of interest in normally appealing visual experiences

15. tendency to regularly confuse letters, words, or numerals: 6 and 9, *d* and *b*, or *bad* and *dad*.

Like teachers of other handicapped children, the teacher of young children with visual problems must follow a number of special practices if mainstreaming is to be successful. The following suggestions have been recommended by Rose C. Engel (1973):

RECOMMENDATIONS FOR WORKING WITH VISUALLY IMPAIRED CHILDREN

1. The sense of touch helps to round out what the child hears.

2. "Puppy" is only a word until experiences of its wiggling, tail-wagging, cold nose, and wet tongue add meaning.

3. Listen and refuse a request if you need to but do not ignore it by not responding.

4. Many of the child's concepts are built and clarified by what he hears. Tell him where and why he is going before moving him. Talk about the type of flooring the child is crossing, such as "Now you are on the grass (cement, asphalt, tile, wooden floors)."

5. Thoughtfully arrange the environment for free movement with safety. Encourage independence.

6. Tell him what is going on. When you touch him, tell him who you are. Teach other children to identify themselves when touching him.

7. Let him make as many movements as possible by himself. Tell him to "come to your voice." Let him open doors with his own effort, when possible.

8. Hearing is the child's main channel for learning. Don't be afraid of a sensory overload on this channel for the visually impaired.

9. Give him opportunities to help others. He is so often on the receiving end.

10. Expect the standards of courtesy and waiting expected of others. A handicap is not to be used to take advantage of the rights of others.

11. Care for him rather than always taking care of him.

12. Adapt the environment or situation so that each child can be part of the activities enjoyed by others in the group.

13. Work for communication and praise the child for each success, remembering that receptive language always precedes expressive language.

14. Use a multisensory approach in teaching.

15. Be a good language model.

16. Use many kinesthetic experiences and sensory art activities to encourage manual dexterity and manipulation.

17. Physically take the child through what is expected before asking him to do it alone.

18. Encourage the child to verbalize his needs rather than anticipating them. In a situation where there is some problem in relation to another child, help him use a verbal rather than a physical approach.

19. Work with the child's parents and therapists. Parents are the prime educators of their children.

20. Listen! Give him time to talk by waiting for his response and try not to answer for him.

Blind children can be provided with regular academic or play activities when main-streamed into preschool classrooms. The young girl is being helped to write while the young boy is being helped in the block corner by a child with normal vision. (Left: ©️ Mitchell Payne/Jeroboam. Right: ©️ Charles Harbutt/Magnum Photos)

21. Respect the contribution and opinion of each child, including the visually handicapped child.

22. Use concrete experiences.

23. Repeat, but VARY, the situation to keep the child interested.

24. Encourage free physical movement.

With certain limitations, visually handicapped preschoolers—like children with normal eyesight—should be provided with an environment in which they can explore, discover, and manipulate. The teacher must respond to the children's interests and lead them to master special skills and abilities. If a young blind child can trust a teacher in such a setting, he will be able to move toward autonomy and increased skill with greater confidence.

In addition to the recommended teaching practices, you might contact a teacher or supervisor who has had special training in the field for other suggestions. Close cooperation among resource people, the classroom teacher,

and parents can lead to special practices and procedures that will make the visually handicapped youngster's adjustment to the regular classroom a successful one.

Physically Handicapped Children

Some children are born with a physical handicap; others acquire it after birth. The type and degree of each child's physical problem require the teacher to make appropriate adjustments within the context of the regular classroom. Since the special skills required to work with the wide range of physical disorders is a topic too broad for this text, the physical handicaps that appear to be most commonly found in preschool children have simply been listed and general suggestions have been made for meeting the affected children's unique needs. See Table 12-4.

Obviously, your chief role is to be aware of these conditions and try as hard as possible to design programs to fit the physically handicapped within the regular preschool setting. Be especially mindful that physically handicapped children suffer from many disadvantages brought about by their condition. Dorothy Rogers (1977) explains:

> Physically handicapped children experience many disadvantages. For one thing their developmental progress suffers, leaving them out of step with children of the same age. Blind children, for instance, are slower in learning to walk, eat, dress, and bathe. In addition, the physically handicapped individual is often an underachiever. The child with poor vision may not see the blackboard well; the crippled child feels isolated and hence can't relax and enjoy school activities. Teachers, although generally sympathetic with younger children, may be less tolerant of older ones. This intolerance is most common in the case of milder defects—notably of speech, hearing, or sight—that reduce academic achievement and reflect on the teacher's effectiveness.
>
> Handicaps also impede social adjustment. A child lacking motor skills rarely plays an important role among peers. Activities are restricted, so one child grows envious, resentful, and withdrawn—sustained only by the successes of fantasy. Another may become anxious and angry, engaging in offensive aggression. Afterward he feels guilty, but his efforts to "make up" are rebuffed. Still another child may, either consciously or unconsciously, use her handicap to gain selfish ends. In any case, her mood and attitude may make her such poor company that she becomes more rejected still—a vicious cycle. She may employ the handicap as an excuse to escape growing up or to take advantage of others and may even feel a masochistic enjoyment, feeding on the sympathy of others.
>
> The handicapped child also suffers simply by being a child. Children are frequently insensitive to the feelings of less favored persons. They can be brutally frank, causing deep wounds. In one case, a lame child was called "Crip." In another instance, children mimicked a boy with a cleft palate, taking no pains to remove themselves from his hearing....
>
> The handicapped also suffer from societal attitudes toward them. While ostensibly heeding their welfare, people often feel pity or repulsion—or even an unconscious resentment that such people must be pro-

Table 12-4   *Common Physical Handicaps in Preschool Children*

Condition	Characteristics
Cerebral palsy	A nonprogressive condition in which the child is unable to control muscle reflexes voluntarily. The condition results from damage to the brain due to causes such as infection to the mother during pregnancy, insufficient oxygen during birth, Rh incompatibility between father and mother, birth trauma, or heredity. It can also result from brain injury or brain infection during the early developmental years.
Epilepsy	A convulsive disorder that often accompanies neurological disabilities such as cerebral palsy. Seizures, or "fits," characterize epilepsy. These seizures range from those in which the pupils constrict and dilate, the mouth froths due to an inability to swallow, respiration becomes irregular, and the body goes through a short period of quivering (the most dramatic type lasting up to two minutes) to the small seizure in which the child merely seems to be engaged in a daydreaming or staring spell (about 10 seconds).
Spina bifida	A condition caused by malformation of the spinal cord. The condition results in impaired mobility, usually paralysis of the legs. Other handicapping characteristics include mental retardation or lack of bladder and bowel control.
Amputation	Loss of any of the limbs through surgery. Artificial limbs are often supplied.
Paralysis	Brought about by a variety of neurological disorders, paralysis renders the child unable to control parts of his body, especially the limbs.

vided for. The handicapped, in turn, come to expect society's negative attitudes toward them, and they often acquire deep-seated inferiority complexes. Despite intermittent struggles, the majority are unhappy and often doomed to social isolation. [pp. 94–95]

Since the regular preschool classroom may be one of the first intensive exposures to normal children, the physically handicapped child should be made to feel comfortable by an understanding, helpful teacher. Again, be careful not to be overly helpful or to communicate pity. These children have come from hospitals or institutions where they have been exposed to therapy procedures encouraging self-help and positive self-concept. Your role is to build on this foundation by providing an accepting environment of warmth and tolerance. Kirk (1972) explains how the previous therapy received by the child can be supported and extended within the regular preschool setting:

1. Develop motor abilities in the child through special materials, special aids and supports for mobility, and through special methods provided by the physiotherapist, the occupational therapist, and the special teacher. In the school situation the teacher is the coordinator of the program even though specific prescriptions are given by the attending pediatrician or orthopedic specialist.

2. Develop language and speech, especially in the cerebral-palsied child, since this is one area where the majority are retarded or defective. This includes the ability to perceive oral language and to express it, to perceive visual stimuli and interpret them, and to express oneself in motor terms. The latter includes both speech and gestures. This phase of the child's development is assisted by a speech correctionist, the parents, and the special teacher.

3. Develop in the child the psychological factors of visual and auditory perception, discrimination, memory, and other factors considered intellectual. These functions are best developed through the school program which includes language usage, listening, planning, problem solving, dramatization, imagination and creative expression (through art and music media), creative rhythms, visual and auditory memory and discrimination, and perception. At this age level an environment with toys, sand tables, doll corners, and so forth, is provided so that the children will learn to respond to the attraction of the environment both physically and mentally. Through the addition of materials and the verbal and manual suggestions of the special teacher the children are helped to progress from one developmental stage to the next.

4. Develop social and emotional adequacy in the child at home and in the school by providing him with opportunities for acquiring emotional security, belongingness, and independence. The school situation is probably superior to the home in not overprotecting the child and in giving him opportunities to do things himself. The environment of the school which includes other children of the same age gives the child an opportunity to learn to interact with others, to share, and to cooperate. It offers him examples of activities which he can imitate, and at the same time the protection and help which he needs when he really needs it. [pp. 258–259]

If the child can learn to overcome problems related to physical handicaps at an early age in a regular preschool setting, chances are increased that he will accept the handicap and be willing to work toward the development of other assets. Such results are possible in schools for young children because the schools' flexibility allows them to meet unique individual needs and their desire to help enables each individual to grow toward his maximum potential.

Learning Disabled Children *Learning disabled* (LD) is a term that has emerged during the late 1970s to describe any condition or set of conditions that prevents a child from functioning at the level of development normally expected for children at a particular age. These conditions may include perceptual disorders, motor disorders, mild brain damage, or "learning blocks" that affect learning in only one area such as reading or math. Although these children are not mentally retarded (often they are of average or above-average intelligence) and are essentially like all other children, they do have special educational needs.

The early diagnosis of learning disabilities is a primary responsibility of the early childhood educator, for the condition can best be remediated when discovered during the early years. A number of factors may lead you to suspect a learning disabled child (there are about 8 million learning disabled children in our schools):

1. the inability to follow simple instructions
2. the inability to repeat patterns and processes
3. low levels of cognitive functioning
4. confusion in spatial orientation—looking left when told to look right, and so on
5. poor gross or fine motor control
6. lack of established handedness
7. poor appetite or craving for certain foods

Although teacher observation is important for discovering learning disabilities in young children, resource personnel such as school psychologists should be contacted before a formal diagnosis is made. Once such a diagnosis has been made, however, an individualized enrichment program should be developed immediately with the aid of parents and other professionals such as reading specialists, pediatricians, or neurologists. The two learning disabilities most often uncovered in the preschool setting are *dyslexia* and *minimal brain dysfunction (MBD)*.

This physically handicapped child is grasping onto special hanging strings in order to encourage muscle growth through exercise. (© Jean-Claude Lejeune/ Stock, Boston)

Dyslexia is broadly defined as any retardation in the development of reading, that is, reading at a level that appears to be below the learner's level of intelligence. It is often thought of as a neurological disorder causing the learner to see reversed letters or mirror images. For example, *saw* for *was* (reversal) or боу for *boy* (mirror image). To understand the extent of the problem, hold this page in front of a mirror, and try reading the next few sentences, or hold a mirror above Figure 12-1 and look only at the mirror as you attempt to complete the maze, going from start to finish by keeping a smooth pencil line. Although there are many other forms of dyslexia, these two (reversal and mirror image) are among the most common.

Many approaches have been suggested for treating the dyslexic. Since many educators feel that dyslexia is an outgrowth of failure to

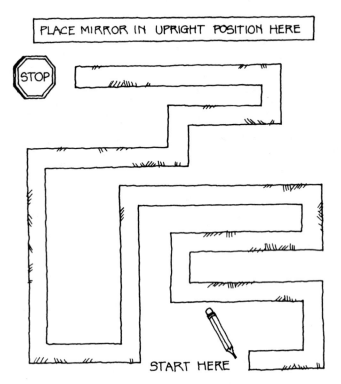

PLACE MIRROR IN UPRIGHT POSITION HERE

STOP

START HERE

Figure 12-1 *Illustration of dyslexic functioning*

establish clear hand, eye, or foot preferences—a condition affecting the ability to read or write—most approaches focus on forms of patterning to encourage the establishing of *dominance* (handedness, eyedness, or footedness). These programs can be categorized into three major approaches: the Frostig program, characterized by materials involving various activities to promote visual perception; the Doman-Delacato approach, characterized by physical activity to overcome neurological problems; and the Fernald Tracing Method, emphasizing repeated tracing activities. Marianne Frostig and D. Horne (1964) felt that special educational intervention for learning problems should be directed toward the development of *visual perception*. Figure 12-2 illustrates the types of patterning activities she developed. In this activity, the children are

to focus their eyes on the separate paths of each feature pictured and to trace each with a pencil or crayon. Many other activities like this are provided in the Frostig materials.

The Doman-Delacato program is directed toward treating not the visible results of brain injury (learning disabilities) but the injured brain itself. Robert J. Doman, Glenn Doman, and Carl H. Delacato (1963) knew that normal children develop by successfully accomplishing certain tasks at different ages; for example, successful attempts at crawling and creeping during infancy involve sending sensory nerve messages to the area of the brain governing those movements. Repeated successes gradually build up neurological patterns in that part of the brain enabling the child to make those and other related coordinated movements without much conscious planning. Hypothe-

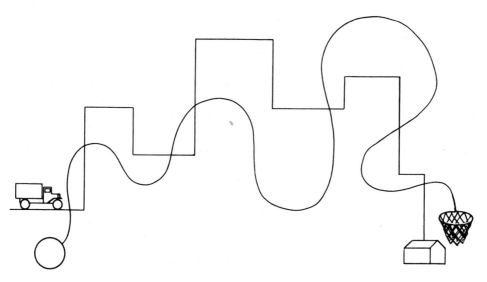

Figure 12-2   *Sample work page from the Frostig Visual Perception program*
(From Frostig Visual Program, copyright 1964. Published with permission from Follett Publishing Company, a division of Follett Corporation.)

sizing that brain-injured children could be helped to activate brain cells in other parts of their brain to take over the functions of their dead ones (especially the ones governing patterned movements), the developers planned a group of patterning movements normally the responsibility of the damaged level of the child's brain. They felt that if these early developmental movements were repeated over and over (even with adults), the undamaged cells in the other parts of a brain would eventually receive the sensory messages that the exercises were feeding into it. Gradually, the child would be able to perform the movement patterns he once had been unable to perform. When the child exhibits the ability to crawl and creep in the Doman-Delacato program, for example, he is moved toward normal standing and walking, and eventually is patterned to improve other physical skills such as hearing, vision, manual dexterity, and, eventually, reading skills. A sample Doman-Delacato room is illustrated in Figure 12-3.

The Fernald (1943) Tracing Method is based on the idea of the efficacy of repeated practice. It emphasizes the use of a patterned kinesthetic approach (touch and sight) to improve reading skills. The basic procedure is outlined as follows:

STAGE 1

1. Child chooses words he wishes to know.
2. Word is written for the child with crayon.
3. Child traces the word while touching it, pronouncing each part as he proceeds.
4. Process is repeated until child can write it on his own.
5. He uses it in the story he is writing.
6. Story is typed when child is finished.

STAGE 2

1. Same as stage 1 except tracing is no longer necessary.

2. Child learns word by looking at it, says it to himself, and writes it.

3. Each word _must_ be pronounced as it is written.

STAGE 3

1. Child looks at printed word and says it to himself before writing it.

2. Child starts reading from books.

3. Permitted to read anything and as much as he likes.

STAGE 4

1. Child begins to make relationships between words he knows and new words.

The early childhood teacher is important in the treatment of a dyslexic child. She must look for the symptoms of dyslexia and examine possible remediation procedures so that the young child can be provided with the program best suited to his needs. This program, whatever it may be, requires specialization—consultations with experts in the field are usually the most effective procedure.

Minimal brain dysfunction (MBD) is a general term characterizing a variety of learning and behavioral disorders commonly found in the preschool setting. Many of the characteristics associated with dyslexia can also be associated with MBD, except that MBD involves severe learning problems in _all_ developmental areas, including reading and language. Characteristics of MBD include:

1. developmental lags—slowness in maturation

2. immature speech

3. poor visual-motor coordination

4. early cognitive failures

5. poor motor control—awkwardness or clumsiness

MBD can be _congenital_ (inherited) or _acquired_ (disease or accident causing injury to the brain). Your chief role is to make classroom observations and _refer_ the suspected cases of MBD for further testing to appropriate specialists. As you can see, the signs of MBD do not differ greatly from those of dyslexia, and methods of diagnosis are similar. Some educators criticize educational literature for separating MBD from dyslexia in discussions of learning disabilities. Rather than enter into this argument, however, I will only note that it is important to identify the learning disabled child and to search through various resources to try to find how this child can best be helped within the regular preschool setting.

Here are some special tips for working with learning disabled children in your classroom:

1. Try to work on a one-to-one basis with the LD child.

2. Offer two or three short sessions throughout the day; a maximum time allotment of 20–30 minutes for each session is usually satisfactory.

3. Go slowly as you work with the child. LD children need a relaxed pace and frequent repetition.

4. Make sure the child listens to you as you speak. You can do this by requesting her to feed back your message at intervals.

5. Insist that the child has mastered one level before you move to the next.

6. Offer much praise at frequent intervals. Make the session a successful and fun-filled experience.

7. Use many concrete elements as you teach. Make sure to focus on the child's accurate visual perception of each object.

8. Try to stick to a rigid routine. LD children need structure and order in their lives.

Principles and practices for aiding the _seriously emotionally disturbed_ and the _speech impaired_ have been introduced throughout this

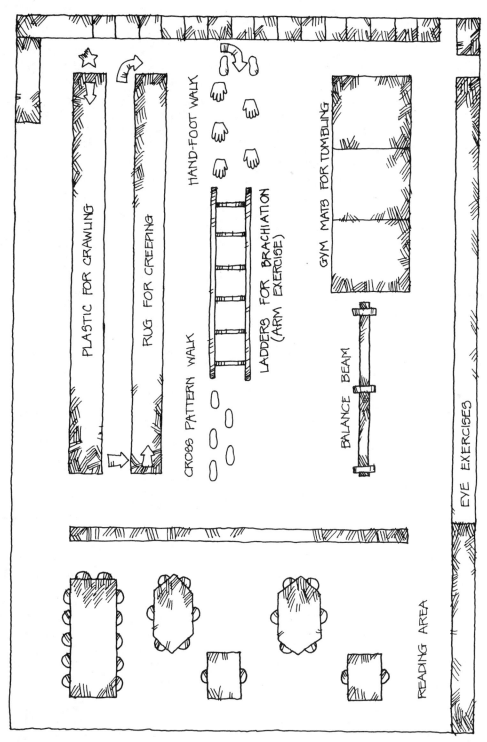

Figure 12-3 *A sample Doman–Delacato Room*

book. Note that in some truly exceptional cases you may seriously question whether you are able to offer sufficient help. Constant extreme behaviors such as rapid changes in moods or "blowing his stack" may indicate special needs requiring help beyond what you are able to provide. When this happens, feel free to admit your frustrations and seek the advice of a qualified professional. Behaviors in this category include those that: (1) are extreme and seemingly uncontrollable; (2) occur regularly; and (3) persist over an extended period of time.

MAINSTREAMING

Since our mission in early childhood education is equal education for all, the concept of mainstreaming physically and mentally handicapped children should be met enthusiastically by classroom teachers. In mainstreaming children aged six and younger, we build on all we know about the importance of the early years to all aspects of the child's development. There have been many suggestions for aiding the teacher in the process of mainstreaming preschool youngsters into the regular classroom setting. Some of the most popular recommendations are listed here:

1. View the child as a *whole child* with strengths as well as weaknesses. Avoid looking at the handicapped youngster as an "epileptic" or a "dyslexic," but rather as a child like any other child.

2. Learn all you can about the mainstreamed child's specific disability. Gain awareness of therapy techniques and become familiar with technical terminology.

3. Involve parents in dealing with their child both in the school and at home. They should learn what you are doing in school so that your practices can be reinforced and extended in the home.

4. Maximize interactions between the handicapped and nonhandicapped children.

   a. Give simple explanations about a child's handicap, when needed. Youngsters are curious and will often want to know about a new child and will be satisfied by an open, honest explanation. ("Jeannie's legs don't work well so she needs a wheelchair.") Such a gesture on your part will set the stage for acceptance.

   b. Read books or tell stories about children with differences.

   c. Encourage the handicapped child to share strong capabilities. For example, the wheelchair-bound youngster may well help another child in a project demanding manual dexterity and soon gain that child's appreciation for outstanding manual skill.

   d. Look for special programs designed to introduce your regular students to the special needs of the handicapped. Barbara Aiello has developed a special program called "Kids on the Block," which includes puppets with different types of impairments. Each puppet displays a vibrant personality. "The Great Renaldo," for example, jauntily announces that he "sees nothing and knows all," carrying his white cane and happily describing how he can tell time with his Braille wristwatch. Mark explains how his wheelchair ("cruiser" as he calls it) helps him enjoy life—he once went to a Halloween party as a tractor (only a "handicapped kid" can do that!). Children can ask the puppets questions. Mark, for example, is often asked how he can go to the bathroom. He explains that bathrooms are equipped with special rails to help him get up and down. Life-size and dressed in real clothes, these puppets become ideal educators in every way. For more information on this complete curriculum on disabilities, contact

Mrs. Barbara Aiello
3509 M Street, N.W.
Washington, DC 20007
(202) 342-9177

5. Individualize your program. Start where the child is and plan a sequential program to encourge him to build one skill upon another. Build on continuous success rather than tearing down with repeated failures.

6. Make appropriate spatial and environmental changes in and around the school. Ramps may need to be built for physically handicapped youngsters, or grab bars may need to be placed in the bathrooms, for example.

7. Take special in-service training through workshops or seminars. Keep up on the current principles and practices of mainstreaming.

SOME FINAL THOUGHTS

"What is it, a boy or a girl?" That's usually the first question parents ask when they await the birth of a child. Without hesitation, their second question nearly always is, "Is it okay? I mean is everything normal?" In most cases, parents' anxieties are relieved when they find out that they are gifted with a normal, healthy infant. According to 1980 figures released by the National Foundation/March of Dimes, 93 percent of the babies born in the United States are normal. But, for the remaining 7 percent, a problem is present at birth and may remain throughout life. Some of these problems are minor and can eventually be overcome, but others will directly affect one or more of the key developmental areas. Even babies who are born healthy are not immune to illness or injury and, may later experience problems or deficiencies that cause them to be viewed as "spe-cial" children, "exceptional" children, or as "handicapped."

Research on child development supports the contention that intervention during the early years is the most important factor in preventing handicapping conditions from interferring with children's future development. This view is so strong that, since 1972, federal guidelines have stipulated that 10 percent of children in Head Start programs must be children with handicaps. Most importantly, Public Law 94–142 (The Education for All Handicapped Children Act of 1975) states that a "free and appropriate public education will be available for all handicapped children between the ages of three and eighteen...." This law has been interpreted to mean that even handicapped preschoolers will benefit from participating in school activities with their normal peers, where social, affective, and cognitive learning can be experienced. The implications of this legislation for early childhood teachers is tremendous, for once an accurate assessment of a handicapped child's needs is made, the intervention process can begin. Most early childhood teachers, however, know little about dealing with children requiring special needs. They are unfamiliar with the community agencies serving the children's families. This is why the subject of mainstreaming provokes so much controversy today.

Various educational models have been used with the very young, and various teaching suggestions for all developmental areas have been offered. However, the key responsibilities you have as an early childhood teacher are: (1) to learn as much about specific developmental disorders demonstrated by the children in your classroom as possible and (2) to teach in a skilled, flexible, tolerant manner. Although you may not receive all the help you hope for in learning about this critical area during your pre-professional education, make every effort to educate yourself by attending meetings, informal discussions, or staff development sessions and by reading pertinent professional newsletters and journals.

Chapter 13

Establishing a Safe, Healthful Environment

Lois and Evan are four-year-olds who attend a suburban nursery school. They both enjoy playing outdoors—and the messier the activity, the more they enjoy it. After a short swing and a climb on the jungle gym one day, the two youngsters moved to the garden plot where they began to dig excitedly for worms. After uncovering four or five of the wiggly creatures, they decided to place some dirt in a small pail so their new discoveries could be shared with the teacher when it was time to return indoors.

In a little while, the teacher signalled the children to return to the classroom, where they were to remove their wraps and prepare for a short snack. Lois and Evan rushed up to the teacher and shared the worms they had found. The teacher congratulated the youngsters on their fine work and invited them to tell the others about their worms during group time after the snack. But first, she reminded the two, they had to wash their hands. Into the bathroom went Lois and Evan, where they giggled their way through the hand-washing experience, mixing the soap and water to make bubbles. Finding it necessary to use the toilet again, Lois and Evan both stopped to urinate before returning to the classroom. Lois was particularly interested in the fact that Evan was able to stand while urinating, so she watched until he was finished. Turning to her teacher in the doorway, Lois asked why Evan was able to stand and she couldn't. The teacher, realizing that this was not a good time to gloss over the situation, commented, "There is a difference between a girl and a boy. Boys stand up to urinate. You are a girl. Girls sit down— mommies sit down, too." Satisfied with this explanation, Lois sat on the toilet and completed her tasks in the bathroom.

Lois and Evan returned to the classroom and joined the other children at the tables for a short, healthful snack. Today the teacher had prepared their favorite, milk and oatmeal cookies. When the snack was finished, the teacher invited the children to join her in a group for a short, quiet period of sharing. This group period not only gave the children a chance to express themselves to the others, but it also provided them with an opportunity to relax and regain some of the energy they had expended on the play-

ground. Of course, Lois and Evan beamed as they shared their story of digging up the worms from the school's garden plot.

This brief vignette describing a morning in a preschool illustrates a teacher's ability to arrange a safe, healthful environment. In this case, the teacher met health and safety concerns in the following ways:

1. Outdoor activity encouraged healthful exercise.

2. Proper clothing was worn to meet the demands of the weather.

3. Cleanup experiences were an integral part of the plan.

4. Toileting was encouraged in a warm, accepting environment.

5. Nutritious snacks helped fulfill basic physical needs.

6. A short period of rest helped balance active times with quiet times.

Health and safety education in the preschool is generally informal. It evolves from activities that are basic to daily living rather than from short scheduled lessons or discussions. Safety and good health practices are two important goals that all preschool centers should strive to attain.

PROMOTING GOOD HEALTH

Until the early 1960s many people in the United States were appalled at the idea of placing children up to age five together in the same facility, in close contact with each other. This age range is particularly susceptible to illnesses and infectious diseases, particularly common childhood diseases such as measles, chicken pox, and mumps, and many parents at the time felt it would be safer to keep their youngsters

at home. Also, medical science was not as advanced as it is today, and if the children did develop such illnesses, medicine was often unable to prevent serious complications. The results were sometimes devastating: Hospitalization or death led to grief and great financial burdens, and possible lengthy quarantines led to loss of jobs—and remember that unemployment and other benefits were not available during much of this period. The problem of infectious diseases, then, caused many families to question the value of close situations, such as those found in preschool settings. Because of these strong parental concerns, strict health and safety measures were instituted by the first nursery schools. For example, children were not admitted until they had passed a health examination administered by a physician or nurse. When this was done, and other basic health precautions were followed, it was found that children in preschool groups remained as healthy as those not in contact with other children.

Common Communicable Diseases

Today, immunization programs have drastically reduced the threat of childhood illnesses, but there are still some with which you should be familiar. Table 13-1 summarizes these.

Although highly effective vaccines have reduced the incidence of these communicable diseases, the organisms that cause them are still very much with us. For example, a serious polio outbreak occurred in Texas in 1970, and in Connecticut a school suffered a rash of polio cases that left seven children partially or severely paralyzed. Diphtheria claimed the life of a five-year-old New York City girl in 1977 and hospitalized her six-year-old sister and four-year-old brother. During an outbreak of 2500 reported cases of measles in Los Angeles in May 1977, two persons died and five cases of encephalitis (brain inflam-

Table 13-1   *Common Communicable Diseases among Preschool Children*

Contagious Disease	Symptoms	Incubation Period	Isolation Period
Chicken pox	Slight fever; itchy rash; eruptions on face and trunk	14–21 days; usually 14–16	10 days or until disappearance of scabs
German measles	Swollen glands; fever; stiff neck; rash	14–21 days; usually 16–18	4–7 days
Measles	Red, watery eyes; fever; cough; runny nose; rash after third or fourth day	About 10 days	From beginning of symptoms until 4 or 5 days following appearance or rash
Mumps	Swollen glands in front of and below ear; fever	12–26 days; usually 18	7–10 days, or until swelling has diminished
Polio	Fever; headache; stiff neck; sore throat; nausea; vomiting	7–14 days	Duration of the fever or one week following the appearance of symptoms
Scarlet fever	Fever; headache; sore throat; vomiting; rash with flaky skin	1–9 days; usually 2–4	7–10 days
Tuberculosis	Fever; persistent cough; weight loss	6–8 weeks	Until disappearance of infection
Whooping cough	Cold accompanied by hacking cough; followed in 2 or 3 weeks by periodic, sharp, sudden, heavy coughing spells; perhaps vomiting	7–16 days; usually 5–7	3 weeks after appearance of cough

mation) set in. The incidence of diphtheria, mumps, whooping cough, and the other communicable diseases has clearly dropped over the decades, but occasional scattered cases arise, and unimmunized children are even more susceptible to such diseases than were the children of the prevaccine generation—and this susceptibility is particularly worrisome. In the 1930s and 1940s communicable disease was so common that some youngsters were able to develop natural immunities. Today, however, children no longer have an opportunity to develop natural immunity, and unvaccinated children are totally open to attack by viruses.

Many educational and health authorities have expressed concern over the growing laxity regarding immunization. They want the laws requiring proof of immunization enforced before children can enter into any child–group

situation, including nursery school and day care, rather than only before elementary school. Enforcement of these laws could stimulate interest in getting infants and preschoolers immunized. During the previously mentioned measles outbreak in Los Angeles, for example, the city declared that any child not having proof of vaccination would be barred from school. Lines formed quickly, and eventually 99.9 percent of the school children had been immunized, an incredible figure compared to national immunization figures of 59.6 percent in nonpoverty areas and 38 percent in poverty areas. This percentage is an ideal goal for the entire country, but even a coordinated community effort involving parents and concerned groups could push up current immunization rates.

Your role, then, should be to become aware of such diseases because their occur-

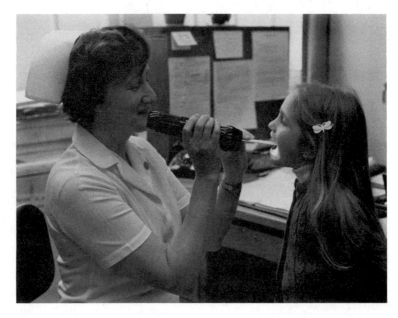

Sound medical information is crucial to the establishment of a healthy preschool environment.

rence among children is certainly possible. Be aware of the various symptoms and notify appropriate authorities when a contagious disease is suspected. Help parents become aware of the value of immunizations—if necessary, launch a drive to reach the parents of prospective preschoolers so proper vaccine protection can be provided before the children enter your nursery school or day-care facility.

Common Skin Infections

Another common health problem for young children is contagious skin infections. Many skin infections are difficult to cure, and you may need a doctor's advice to determine if a child should be kept in school. However, knowing what to look for can help you catch the disease before it spreads on the individual or among other children. Table 13-2 summarizes common skin infections.

Lice infestation is also sometimes found, especially where habits of good hygiene are not regularly practiced. Unwashed hair and unclean bodies make good breeding places for lice—especially the hair and seams of clothing. Symptoms usually include itching and irritation, but proof can best be obtained by examining the child's hair or clothing carefully for signs of the lice. If lice are found, the best remedy is to disinfect—a task that should be referred to and done by proper medical authorities such as the school nurse or your child-care supervisor.

CLEANLINESS AND SELF-CARE

Basic to the prevention of disease and infections is a pattern of cleanliness and self-care. Skills and attitudes related to these areas must

Table 13-2 *Common Skin Infections among Preschool Children*

Disease	Symptoms	Cause
Impetigo	Yellow, crusted sores filled with pus; usually found near nostrils	Staphylococcus bacteria
Scabies	Itchy, red blotches on the skin	Mites burrowing under the skin and depositing eggs
Ringworm	Ring-shaped, discolored patches of skin, especially found about the scalp; itching	Variety of fungus burrowing beneath the skin
Athlete's foot	Small blisters between the toes; itching	Fungus

be stressed so children develop a positive attitude toward them and begin to look forward to increasing competence in each area. Young children must be taught how to care for their physical selves. They must learn particularly about using the toilet facilities and about washing themselves before and after eating or sleeping and after strenuous activity.

Using Toilet Facilities

Learning to use the toilet facilities is a major accomplishment for children during the preschool years. Most children tend to be nearly fully toilet trained by the age of three, but younger boys and girls cannot, in most cases, control their elimination, so you must assume a supportive role in caring for them. Such care can become very complicated if all the mechanics are picked up on a trial-and-error basis. The following suggestions are presented so that the tricks of diapering will more quickly become a part of your repertoire and result in more pleasurable child-care experiences.

- To prevent a sore back, change the baby on a waist-high table.
- Wash the baby's bottom with a soapy cloth each time you change him. Rinse it with clear water and pat it dry. This helps control rashes and chafed skin caused by bacteria and the saltiness of

urine. This procedure is especially crucial if you are using waterproof pants or disposable diapers.

- Spread baby powder or petroleum jelly on the baby's bottom to prevent rashes or chafed skin.
- Fix a mobile above the baby's head. This will capture his attention and will usually prevent excessive squirming while you are changing him.
- At about nine months, the baby may be changed while standing. Give him a special toy to hold in each hand for balance.
- Sing or talk to the youngster as you clean and change him. Make the situation one in which the baby feels comfortable and encouraged to form better habits of control.

Even when youngsters gain control of their bladders and sphincters, they will continue to experience some accidents. Learn to accept them—they are typical of this age group—and avoid communicating any initial feelings of repulsion at the sight of a child's accidental excretions. If you communicate queasiness or disgust to the child, you may make him ashamed and confused instead of comfortable and secure in the situation. If a child is told, for example, "Change into these dry pants and you'll feel better," instead of, "Oh, you're such a bad boy—aren't you ashamed of yourself?" he will gain self-assurance and learn to control his own needs, knowing that you understand. Under no condition should a child be make to feel ashamed for a toileting accident in school. Such an attitude can only breed conflict and resistance. Meet incidents with a matter-of-fact attitude and direct your attention to the child's successes rather than to his failures.

If you understand the reasons for accidents like this, you may be able to handle such situations with greater insight. The following are some common reasons for accidents.

1. Children are often strained and nervous during the first few weeks of the new preschool year or during other highly exciting times. Reassure the child that it is not bad to have accidents.

2. Some children get so involved in their activity that they fail to heed signs of their physical distress. Remind the child to go to the bathroom at the times you have observed were routine for him. Reinforce him with praise when bathroom experiences are successful.

3. Sometimes a simple relapse occurs. Such regressions will stop with time so try not to draw attention to them. Simply offer the child a change of clothing and reassure him that there is nothing wrong with what happened.

4. An emotional problem may cause a child to have accidents fairly regularly. Confer with the child's parents to see if something at home could be contributing to the problem. Children often have severe toileting problems at home, caused by uncertain adults who set unreasonable toileting standards before the children can comprehend them. In such instances, emotional distress can contribute to several toileting problems, such as wetting the bed for periods of time longer than normal or excessive numbers of "accidents."

5. Kidney or bladder infections may cause toileting problems. If such problems persist and the child appears to be free of emotional influences, a talk with the parents or appropriate medical personnel could be in line.

Regular toileting routines should be carried out in a casual, free atmosphere. You will quickly discover through observation how often each child needs to use the bathroom, and you will be able to make any necessary adjustments. A pleasant "It's time to go to the bathroom," will help the child feel confidence in the teacher's concern for him. After a while, as the child shows increasing ability to regulate his condition, the teacher may simply ask the child, "Do you need to go to the bathroom now?" Slowly the responsibility is shifted to the child, where it must eventually remain. Of course, there will still be accidents, and you must always be on the lookout for them.

The following list of suggestions may be helpful in getting young children adjusted to a sound toileting schedule.

1. Make sure that the bathroom facilities are clean, attractive, and inviting. Maintain a comfortable atmosphere that will help children relax and give them calm confidence.

2. If legally possible, remove the door from the bathroom so toilet provisions can be viewed by the children as part of the normal classroom routine.

3. Allow the children plenty of time to complete their toileting. Being rushed through the process makes it difficult for them to maintain a positive attitude.

4. Be aware of some children who will need help at toilet time, particularly after a bowel movement. Help the child to help himself or to watch others as they gain more skill and confidence.

5. Help those children having difficulty with clothing. Pay particular attention to complicated buttons, fasteners, and buckles, and too tight clothing—this will

help prevent accidents. Children often wait until the last moment to use the toilet, so every second wasted by fumbling with a complicated buckle or snap can contribute to the possibility of accidents.

6. Request that parents send a change of clothes for each child so that a proper cleanup operation can be done after inevitable accidents. Some teachers have found, however, that keeping a few sets of unisex clothing on hand is preferable to keeping track of separate clothing for each child.

7. Be constantly aware of the children and look for signs of a toileting accident. Often, the last child to let you know of such incidents is the one who has the problem. If you don't discover it quickly, the other children in the room are bound to do so. And their reactions will often be unintentionally shattering: "Ugh, Kelly just peed in her pants!" If this happens often enough, the child will soon develop feelings of disapproval or shame over her toileting failures.

8. Some teachers of young children believe that toileting should become a specified part of the daily schedule for all children in the room. For instance, all children may be encouraged to use the toilet when they come to school, then after outdoor play in the middle of the morning, and again just before lunch. Those on the full-day schedule will have similar intervals in the afternoon. These teachers believe that such practices encourage the acquisition of greater routine and control. Those who favor a more individualized approach, however, argue that a set schedule ignores the personal needs of each child and that all children must go to toilet when their personal needs dictate. Others offer a compromise—they establish a schedule to encourage children to develop a routine in their toileting, but it is a flexible one; that is, within the schedule children are allowed to go when they need to. They see this system as being easier to control than the individualized approach but more individualized than the rigid schedule approach.

Since young children of both sexes often share the same bathroom facilities, it is common for boys and girls during the toileting period to begin to show a strong interest in each other's bodies. At about the age of four, they begin to realize that boys and girls are not alike, and this is a confusing discovery. Their faces, arms, legs, and belly buttons look alike—and even their behinds look the same. Now comes the reality that one place indeed looks different—the boy has a penis and scrotum and the girl has a vagina. "Why does Ginny's look like that and mine look like this?" "Why are boys and girls different?" Such questions are not meant to startle adults, but are children's honest efforts to find out about something that is most important to them at this age—their bodies.

Adults, however, often react in strange ways to such natural curiosity. We recall one incident reported recently in "Dear Abby," a newspaper advice column, where a six-year-old was caught examining the genital area of his five-year-old female cousin. The mother became so upset that she painted the boy's genitals red with Mercurochrome and forced him to sit naked in front of all the relatives while they laughed and made fun of him. This humiliating experience was a cruel punishment, especially since the boy was simply acting out of natural curiosity. Of course, if the boy persisted at such activity regularly and demonstrated an unnatural tendency in this regard, you would need to involve the parents and seek outside advice as to what should be done to correct the situation. However, *at no time* should making such a horrifying example of children's deeds be done in your classroom. The situation brought such a response from the public that "Dear Abby" reported the number of letters received exceeded any total for any situation on her record.

What do you tell children when they ask such questions about their new interests? Through your responses, show acceptance and understanding, and explain that all little boys are made with a penis and all little girls are made with a vagina. Avoid substitute names such as wee-wee, tinkler, pee-pee, or ding-dong. If the children pursue your explanation with the question "Why," give them accurate information about sexual matters but without going into a full account of sexual intercourse. Simply explain that when a father and mother want to have a baby, a special fluid comes from the father's body through the penis and joins with an egg in the mother's body where the baby starts to grow. When the baby is born, it comes out through the vagina. Stay away from explanations such as "Daddy plants a seed in mommy." Explanations such as this only confuse young children, as they undoubtedly picture daddy forcing mommy to swallow a peach pit or doing some similar act. Explain that because of these special body functions, it is perfectly natural for boys to stand up to urinate while girls sit down. Remember that young children are not shocked by such explanations. Only when parents or teachers communicate uncomfortable feelings about such information do children feel shock or anxiety. One child, for example, was so surprised when his teacher asked, "Do you need to *urinate* now?" that he immediately blurted, "You used a dirty word!" Keep in mind that young children will react to your unspoken feelings. This is why your attitudes in this area must first be clarified and your feelings of worry and embarrassment modified.

Washing and Keeping Clean

Cleanliness is an important consideration for teachers and caretakers of young children. Of course, the ways in which such care is extended vary with the age groups under their care—infants require specialized techniques that differ from those used with toddlers or young children. The following suggestions are designed to assist you in washing infants.

- Once the baby loses his umbilical cord (usually at about 10 days), he is ready for his first sponge bath. Wash the baby in a sink or basin. You may want to cushion the bottom of the sink or basin with a towel or sponge and add several inches of warm water (not much warmer than your body temperature).

- Use a mild soap and soap the baby all over, even his head. Be careful because the baby will become very slippery.

- Talk and sing to the baby during the bath—make it an enjoyable time. Say each body part as you wash—this encourages language growth.

- Once rinsed and dried, the baby should be rubbed with lotion because skin oils were removed by the water. Some babies will enjoy being rubbed with cooling bath powder, also.

- After a few months, the baby will become more and more excitable in the water. At this time you may want to move him to a tub for his bath (oh, your sore back!).

- To prevent many fears of children in bathtubs, always make sure you remove the child from the tub before you pull the drain plug. Otherwise, youngsters may fear going down the drain with the bath water. Some children are afraid to have their hair washed, probably because they cannot see what's happening to them. Hold a mirror in front of the child as you joyfully sculpt sudsy forms on his head. He may want to join you after a while!

- Baths are important, but they should not be given each time the infant or toddler becomes soiled. Take comfort, he won't catch a disease simply because he is slightly dirty. As a matter of fact, some pediatricians argue that one of the reasons for the high rate of childhood disease among young children in this country is that they have been kept *too clean* and haven't had a great opportunity to build up natural immunities.

Washing the hands and keeping clean could be encouraged with older children following a toileting routine, but it should not constantly be considered a virtual necessity. It is a habit that young children develop in time, especially if motivated by adults or older children whom they admire. However, in order to maintain an attitude favorable to sound health and hygiene, hand washing should be compulsory before, and in some instances after, eating. In addition, vigorous activity during play, such as digging in dirt or hammering nails, will frequently require a freshening up period, including washing the face and hands. When children awaken from afternoon naps, they have another opportunity to wash. A pleasant, friendly reminder encourages them to refresh themselves after this comfortable period of sleep.

PROPER REST

Strenuous activity is a major cause of fatigue, but there are other causes, including stress, improper nutrition, excessively warm temperatures, or a body constitution that simply requires more rest. Of course, the effects of these conditions vary from child to child, but they are sometimes expressed as crankiness, unreasonableness, shortness of attention span, crying, excitability, and, perhaps, listlessness and inactivity. The following story illustrates the effect fatigue may have on children in your classroom:

Usually Marlene gets plenty of rest and arrives at her school full of vigor and ready to participate in each day's new adventures. However, on this particular morning, she seemed somewhat tired and listless. While on the playground, Marlene is usually one of the most active children—running, climbing, jumping, sliding or swinging. However, on this morning, she was content to sit somberly under a shade tree watching the others. Inside, Marlene spent some time aimlessly leafing through books in the reading corner and eventually she wandered over to the water table. She seemed content to pour water from containers and stayed at this activity until it was time for the children to go to the sinks to clean up for snack break. Miss Jackson, the teacher, walked over to Marlene and said to her, "Marlene, it's time for you to put away your toys and get ready for snack time." Marlene answered with a quick, "No, I don't want a snack today." The teacher answered, "I know you'd like to stay and play, but we have to go now." Marlene, eyes welling, haltingly announced, "I don't like ... (pause). ... I don't like ... " and suddenly burst into tears. Miss Jackson placed her arm reassuringly around Marlene and led her to the area where the sleeping cots were kept. She had Marlene lie down, and then she slowly stroked the girl's back, offering comforting words to soothe her feelings. Slowly Marlene stopped crying and fell off into a quiet, comfortable nap.

Later on, when Marlene's mother arrived to pick her up, Miss Jackson found out that unexpected company the night before had kept Marlene up for two hours past her bedtime. The resulting overstimulation and lack of sleep had caused behaviors that were not normally part of Marlene's emotional constitution. However, by allowing her to rest during a big part of the morning, Miss Jackson had recognized the situation and, by allowing her to sleep, had made a proper adjustment for it.

To avoid fatigue, children need an individualized program of sleep, relaxation, and activity. Naturally, not all children need the same kind or amount of rest, so the program

A program of rest, relaxation, or sleep should be organized on an individual basis so that varying needs can be met.

should be flexible enough to allow individuals to relax in whatever manner they choose, as long as it is not disturbing to others. Some children may require a long nap in a dark quiet room; others may rest on their cots, read a book, or play quietly with a toy. Whatever the choice, young children should be given an opportunity for rest or relaxation periods, especially if the program is a day-long one. Many teachers arrange a schedule that allows frequent changes of pace. These changes alternate quiet periods with more active periods, and follow concentrated, rigorous activities with more relaxed ones. Some teachers even eliminate rest periods, especially if their children are particularly energetic and need only a minimum of rest.

Day-long programs normally include a period of rest or relaxation in the afternoon,

a quiet, relaxed period of about one hour for those children not needing sleep and a longer period of time for those who do. The half-day program normally includes only a short period of relaxation, usually about 15 minutes, during which the children rest from a vigorous outdoor or indoor activity. During this time, the tables may be prepared for a snack while the children listen to pleasant, soft music. The success or failure of any rest period, however, rests squarely on the shoulders of the teacher. It is her responsibility to create the proper atmosphere for relaxation and to help the children settle down whenever a comfortable, quiet interval is needed. That responsibility, as uncomplicated as it may sound, is one of the most challenging teachers face in their daily programs, for although rest is needed by all children it is resisted by many. Often the situation becomes a battle of wills with one side firing, "Do what I say is best for you," and the other responding with, "I dare you to try and make me!"

If you have determined that an extended period of reclining rest or sleep is needed by your children (this case may differ from one preschool setting to another), the following guidelines may be of use.

1. Rapidly growing children need a great deal of sleep. For example, an 18-month-old child needs approximately 16 hours of sleep per day while a two-year-old may need only 12 hours of sleep; a three- or four-year-old may need 11½; a five-year-old, 11. Daytime naps, of course, help children meet these average sleep requirements. Children up to age three, then, will undoubtedly require additional sleep in the preschool setting while three-, four-, and five-year-olds may have received all the sleep they needed the night before. It must be emphasized that the *amount* of sleep is much less important than the *quality* of sleep. A good rest period, for those in need of one, is a quiet, relaxing period before bedtime, with a comfortable cot, a darkened room, and an emotional climate of comfort and happiness.

2. Make the restless child feel comfortable and reassured. Some children need more time to quiet down than others, so help them along. Walk quietly over to the child and whisper a reminder to him or comment about a particularly enjoyable experience that both the teacher and child can remember with pleasure. Perhaps some gentle stroking on the back will soothe and relax the child. Often a favorite stuffed animal or blanket will help these children to rest.

3. Help the children who are afraid to sleep because of unreasonable fears. Encourage them to talk about what bothers them, and let them know you care. However, be careful not to make comments that will help perpetuate the fears. For example, a child who fears falling asleep because "the monsters will get me" will find his beliefs reinforced by an adult's comment, "Don't worry, I'll stay here and chase them away when they come." Instead, reassure the child that there is nothing to be afraid of, that there are no monsters (or whatever), and that you will be near if he needs you.

4. Allow the children to sleep for as long as they like, but remember that each child has a natural sleep tendency. For this reason, some parents will not want their children to have a long afternoon nap because a longer nap than necessary tends to delay their falling asleep at night. With experience, you will be able to judge each child's needs and adjust their rest times as necessary.

5. Before the nap and immediately afterward, provide for a period of toileting, face washing, and clothing change. After the nap, children often look forward to a refreshing snack.

6. Remember your valuable role as a model for the children. As you supervise the rest time, assume a position of rest yourself. Stretch out on a cot or relax in a chair, but be careful to avoid record-keeping, busy room preparation duties, and any other activity that communicates "Do as I say, not as I do."

If you set the appropriate conditions, children will regulate their sleep to the amount they need. But to do this, they must be free from strain, pressure, nagging, and the like. The teacher must find a way to combine freedom, reasonable restrictions, and guidance so that the nap period will be a valued experience for each child. You can do this primarily by getting to know your children and becoming familiar with their needs.

ACCIDENTS AND INJURIES

In addition to childhood diseases, teachers of young children face other common health hazards in the form of accidents, mishaps, and injuries. As the teacher, you will probably be the first adult on the scene in the case of such emergencies. The guidelines in Table 13-3 on how to respond to common accidents explain what steps to take. Diagnosis and treatment of severe injuries should be left to the school nurse or other trained medical personnel, but many common emergencies can be effectively handled with common medical knowledge and basic first aid supplies. Whatever the situation, try to remain calm and in control—the child will not be reassured by a frightened, tense adult.

Knowing how to handle medical crises is extremely important to the adult working with young children because, as a teacher in a nursery school or child-care facility, you automatically acquire certain legal responsibilities related to what takes place during school hours. Robert Hess and Doreen Croft explain:

> In essence, the administration and staff become liable for the health and safety of the students and, if legally challenged, must provide suitable explanation for the way they met this responsibility.
>
> Nursery school liability is essentially different from that of other schools, because when a young child is injured, there is deemed to be no contributory negligence on his part. If older children are injured, lost, kidnapped, or in some other way harmed while at school, the courts hold that they may conceivably have contributed to their condition. In cases involving nursery schools, however, the law is clear that young children are not expected to take care of themselves. Because caretaking, not education, is interpreted to be the primary purpose of a nursery school, a special burden is placed on the school and its teachers. [1972, p. 353]

Your legal responsibility is referred to as *tort liability*. Specifically, within the area of tort liability is a category referred to as "unintentional acts," or those acts defined as an unintentional breach of legal duty leading to injury or damage. According to Polly K. Adams and Michael K. Taylor (1981), as a trained professional, you become negligent in your duties and therefore liable for damages if you do not provide positive action in establishing responsible rules and regulations, providing adequate supervision, employing responsible staff, maintaining safe playgrounds, and ensuring safe conditions throughout the center.

Because of this special burden, several remedial steps should be taken to lessen the possibility of costly legal problems:

1. Check the safety of the overall physical plant:
   a. fireproof construction (alarms, extinguishers, fire escapes)
   b. open and free hallways, stairs, or doors
   c. heating plant shut off by fire doors
   d. freedom from chipping paint (especially paint containing lead)
   e. playground free from broken glass, nails, sharp metal edges, and the like
   f. safe and sturdy environment

2. Provide constant supervision both within and outside the classroom. Children should be constantly supervised by a teacher who is alert to the entire situation.

3. Set realistic limits for the children. Let them know that there are constraints essential for the protection of their health and safety. Make such limits known in simple, concrete terms so they understand exactly what is expected of them: "Walk around the swings to get to the jungle gym." Avoid overly frightening the child with irresponsible com-

Table 13-3   *Treatment of Minor Injuries*

Minor Injury	Condition	Guideline
Abrasion	Oozing blood, as from a scraped knee	Clean out with soap and water; bandage if necessary.
Laceration	Deep cut that bleeds more freely than an abrasion	Apply pressure to wound; clean with soap and water; bandage; notify medical personnel.
Burn	Redness of skin or blistering	Keep under cold running water or wrapped in clean cloth; if blistering, get medical help.
Sprain	Swollen and discolored joint	Keep pressure off the injured joint; apply cold packs; contact medical personnel.
Fracture	Difficulty moving arm or leg; swelling; hard to distinguish from sprain unless bone punctures skin	Do not move the child; summon medical help at once.
Head injury	Sometimes, no apparent signs of injury; bump or bruise often accompanies, however	Calm the child; summon medical help; apply cold pack to minor bumps.
Foreign object in eye	Burning eyes; watery; turning red	Keep child from rubbing eye; wash eye with cool water; summon medical help.
Bee sting	Part of body red, swollen, and warm to touch; if allergic, child may have difficulty breathing, become cold, feel clammy, or even pass out	Apply a cold pack; if allergic, get medical help at once.
Fainting	Loss of consciousness due to insufficient supply of blood to the brain	Keep child lying down and summon medical assistance.
Nose bleed	Trickle of blood from the nose	Keep child quiet; hold head back and apply cold pack; squeeze nostrils together for a few minutes.
Choking	Foreign matter becomes lodged in air passage	Use the Heimlich maneuver.
Convulsions	Child falls unconsious; muscles stiffen, relax, and so on, in a series of rhythmical contractions	Make sure breathing passages are open; keep child from bruising self; roll up cloth and place between teeth; place child face down on soft surface.

ments such as, "If you keep walking so close to the swings, someday you'll get your head knocked off."

4. Report all accidents and injuries to appropriate medical personnel and to parents, regardless of how minor they may seem. Record such accidents on the child's health record.

5. Obtain insurance to cover you if you get involved in a legal suit and to cover the children in case of physical injury.

6. Keep an up-to-date accident report form as a means of pinpointing accidents and avoiding repetitions. Such a report should include the child's name, time, date, cause of injury, first aid administered, and any recommendations to prevent similar accidents from happening.

Accidents and injuries, then, are sometimes part of a day's unscheduled activites. Since the responsibility for meeting these situations normally falls on the teacher, it is up to you to select and maintain safe equipment and to enforce safety measures in and around the school.

CHILD ABUSE

Nearly every preschool has children with histories of neglect and abuse. This is a very sensitive area and one in which many teachers hesitate to become involved. However, the problem of child abuse is a serious one and reflects some interesting statistics:

> Child battery is a major killer of children today.

> If no family therapeutic program is initiated, the child once released from a physician's care stands a 25 percent to 50 percent risk of further permanent injury or death.

> Eighty-five percent of the children abused are under six years of age, 75 percent under four years of age, 25 percent under one year, and 16 percent under six months. [Sanders, 1975, p. 334]

Since only a small percentage of child abuse cases are ever reported, these estimates should be considered to be very conservative.

People looking at such statistics often tend to feel that the abusive parent is undereducated, poor, mentally imbalanced, or a basic child hater. However, according to E. F. Lenoski (1975) "Ninety percent of a group of parents reported are married and employed. They come from all walks of life, professions, ethnic groups. They are voters. Eighty percent confess to a religious belief. Only 10 percent are mentally ill. Only 8 percent are drinkers and only 2 percent are drug addicts." Child abusers come from all walks of life. They cannot be classified according to any stereotypes— but one characteristic does seem to be present in most: They were abused themselves as children.

You need to be alert to the signs and symptoms that point to the possibility of neglect or abuse and know the steps you can take to bring help to those children whose needs are not being met at home. Consider the following example.

Jerry was a quiet, withdrawn child who was usually lethargic and listless at school. He very rarely engaged in vigorous activity and seemed to prefer sleeping or daydreaming most of the day. Jerry had a history of missing school regularly—nearly always for flimsy reasons and lame excuses. Despite his withdrawn, passive personality, Jerry often came to school with cuts and welts or in obvious pain. When questioned by his teacher, Jerry always attributed his injuries to accidents incurred while running, to falling off his bicycle, and to similar forms of strong physical activity.

Jerry's teacher was concerned with such inconsistencies. One day he arrived at school with a cast on one arm and a series of swellings and bruises on his face. When questioned, he of course attributed his injuries to falling off his bicycle. But when she examined the injuries closely, the teacher found that the cuts and marks were not the type you would expect in a fall from a bicycle. The teacher was by now confused. She strongly suspected parental abuse and wanted to help the child, but she didn't know what to do.

This situation is not unique—it probably occurs every day in the nation's schools. So that you won't find yourself in the same predicament as Jerry's teacher, carefully examine the following information.

First, Jerry's teacher should be commended on her willingness to do something about the situation. All too often teachers fear personal retribution from angry, raging parents. In addition, many teachers see themselves as having a "righteous" image and fear to come close to situations that are so far removed from their own thinking. In other words, because the situation is so foreign to their backgrounds or views of parenthood, they tend to shy away from it and, in effect, "pretend it isn't there." However, if our concern for the total welfare of children is genuine, we must be willing to confront cases of child abuse and try to do something about them.

Child abuse can be classified into three distinct categories: *physical abuse, mental abuse,* and *sexual abuse.* If children experiencing any of these forms of abuse are identified when they show the first symptoms, they may be helped when their problems can be most readily solved. However, too often problems are not recognized until the conditions of neglect become acute and intolerable. And by then it may be too late to salvage the child or the home. The following is a list of symptoms of possible neglect and abuse that you can look for.

CHILD'S APPEARANCE

1. Does child appear dirty and unkempt?
2. Does child appear hungry, malnourished, or waiflike?
3. Does child have regular swellings, cuts, bruises, burns, and so on?
4. Does child exhibit difficulty or pain when moving?
5. Does child have injuries related to sexual molestation?
6. Does child wear "cover-up" clothing in warm weather?

CHILD'S BEHAVIOR

1. Does child have difficulty explaining regular injuries?
2. Does child refuse to admit cause of injuries?
3. Does child appear "afraid" when questioned about injuries?
4. Is child chronically late or absent?
5. Does child explain lateness or absence with flimsy reasons?
6. Is child passive or withdrawn?

7. Does child daydream or seem out of touch with reality?
8. Is child aggressive, disruptive, or destructive?
9. Does child appear to be acting out of need for attention?

Once you have reason to suspect child abuse, it is important to report the case directly to your immediate supervisor or to a child protective agency, depending on the regulations of your child-care facility. Such a procedure is not now simply a humanitarian gesture as it once was, since in several states (including California and Pennsylvania) professionals may be guilty of a misdemeanor if they fail to report incidents of suspected child abuse to the proper authorities.

Teachers who do report such cases rarely, if ever, get involved beyond this point. The protective agencies normally contact the parents, develop the facts in each case, and diagnose the type and quality of service needed to rehabilitate the home without ever bringing the teacher into the picture. This rehabilitation philosophy is based on

> a "reaching out" with social services to stabilize family life. It seeks to preserve the family unit by strengthening parental capacity and ability to provide good child care. Its special attention is focused on families where unresolved problems have produced visible signs of neglect or abuse and the home situation presents actual and potentially greater hazard to the physical or emotional well-being of children. [de Francis. 1968, pp. 130-131]

Many parents, after having their initial anger or resentment calmed by a case worker who convinces them that she is there to help and not to punish, are willing to undergo therapeutic intervention. Strange as it may sound, they are willing to do so because their neglect and abuse were probably not willful or deliberate. The treatment of their children usually results from frustrations associated with their inadequacy or inability to live up to or practice parental roles. And if they are, for example, unable to control their child's behavior, their frustration builds and they may feel that severe physical or mental abuse of the child is the only solution. The role of the protective agency in such a case is to educate these parents and help them become more acceptable and confident in their functioning.

By working together with the proper agencies, you help the child in need of protection. If help is given in time, the emotional impact of serious neglect and abuse can be forestalled and the blocks that inhibit the development of a whole child can be removed.

A SOUND, NUTRITIOUS DIET

Involved in the responsibility of maintaining a healthful environment is providing a program of sound nutrition. Perhaps the most obvious product of an unbalanced program of nutrition is an overweight or underweight child. The reasons why a child becomes overweight may be either constitutional or environmental (too much exercise with the fork), but many authorities today feel that our affluent society and its wealth of "junk foods" has contributed more to the problem than any other source. Soda pop, candy bars, chewing gum, cakes, cookies, and fast food restaurants (often referred to as "franchised malnutrition") all appeal to children and parents to the extent that America's calorie intake is at an all-time high, but related nutritional benefits have not increased proportionately. Concern about this situation has become so intense today that complaints from special interest groups have pressured food manufacturers and advertisers to soften their hard-sell approach to marketing "junk food" that contains largely starches and sugars. We still have a long way to go, but

such public reaction helps to allay somewhat a situation that some authorities view as a major health problem of young children.

Less well recognized are the problems of underweight children. These children, too, need to be understood, for they may suffer as much as overweight children. "Beanpole" or "Stick" and similar taunts can cause children to become shy and sensitive about their condition. Also, they may lack the stamina to engage in some of the more active games.

Both underweight and overweight children have a basic problem with sound nutritional practices. However, in some cases, the underlying problem may be physical. If you are in doubt, check with a physician to see what weight is best for the child and to what extent the condition is physical or psychological.

The need for more effective nutritional practices is noted not only for the physical and behavioral advantages to be gained, but also because there is a relationship between a good early diet and the fulfillment of a child's mental capabilities. R. Lewin (1975) has argued that "an infant deprived of nutrition or stimulation will never develop to full mental capacity" (p. 30). Dorothy Rogers (1977) substantiates this claim:

> The infant's brain has reached 25% of its final weight at birth; and by 6 months it is halfway there. By contrast, total body weight at birth is only 5% of its final weight and reaches the halfway mark only by age 10. As a group, severely malnourished children lag behind in language at the age of 6 months. If both *adequate food and supplementary schooling* are provided children by the age of 3½, deficiencies attributed to early malnutrition may be overcome. However, if these children do not get the additional foods until after that age they do not show such gains, because the critical brain-growth period has passed. [Italics are mine.] [p. 89]

Similar observations have been made over the years, but only recently have early childhood professionals so strongly stressed the relationship between inadequate diet and reduced learning power. We have become concerned because of our commitment to provide opportunities for optimal development and functioning. Herbert Birch and Joan Gussow (1970) report that the *most important* factor in determining the child's growth and functioning is probably nutrition. They go on to explain that "there is no question that the child's ability to repond appropriately to significant stimuli in his environment is retarded during the period of chronic malnutrition; and that continued malnutrition is accompanied by progressive behavioral regression" (p. 39). These are powerful statements—perhaps as important as Bloom's (1964) and Hunt's (1961) research findings (discussed in Chapter 2) that awakened us to the importance of stimulation during the early years for later intellectual functioning.

Mealtime

Child-care centers should recognize the importance of sound nutrition both in their mealtimes and in their educational programs. Although sound nutrition is not fully valued by some, it is as important to the success of a complete early childhood program as any other component. The following guidelines should be carefully considered by child-care facilities catering to infants.

GUIDELINES FOR INFANT NUTRITION

1. Feed infants when they become hungry. They develop many of their feelings of trust by being fed when they are hungry.

2. Hold the infant comfortably during feeding. He will understand that the world is a safe place and that you can be trusted.

3. Smile, chat, and respond to the infant as he is fed. Make the feeding experience a pleasant one.

4. Have a well-trained nursery attendant in charge of one or two infants, and allow each child to determine his own feeding schedule.

5. Ask the mother to bring in the child's formula or to prepare it at the center. However, label each bottle so that formulas cannot be confused.

6. Some infants start on solid food during the first month of life; others start much later. Keep in constant touch with the home so that your practices are consistent.

7. At about six or seven months, the infant can be placed in a high chair for short periods of time.

8. At six to seven months, babies begin to show preferences for food, so it should be selected to agree with individual tastes. Introduce the baby to new foods by encouraging him to explore a variety of foods placed before him—mashed bananas, pears, or apples are especially appealing.

9. Encourage the baby to do things for himself. Reinforce any attempts at self-feeding and provide items such as carrot sticks, bread crusts, and hard cookies to encourage such tendencies. From about age one until age two, the child assumes increasing responsibility for his own feeding.

10. When the child moves toward eating solid foods, a new challenge awaits you—getting him to use eating utensils. Follow these suggestions:

   • Allow the child to use his fingers during feeding time, but remember that he will be messy. This is an important initial step to get the infant to feed himself.

   • Give the infant a spoon to play with as you feed him. Soon you will be able to help him fill the spoon, and put it into his mouth. Naturally, he will miss the target a few times at first, but have patience, he will slowly improve with practice.

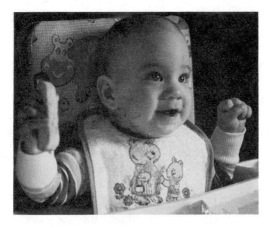

Infants need regular, nutritionally balanced meals, but they also need much practice while learning to eat and drink.

• Let the infant play with an unbreakable empty cup while you are feeding him. When he seems to gain control, fill the cup with a few drops of a favorite liquid and let him try to drink from it. Again, there is bound to be some spilling so give a small portion at a time and allow plenty of practice. Perhaps you may want to put a rubber band around the cup to help prevent it from slipping.

Toddlers and young children attending child-care facilities may need one or several mealtimes during the day: breakfast, mid-morning or mid-afternoon snack, lunch, and, in some cases, dinner. These meals should be carefully planned, preferably by a qualified nutritionist, and prepared by capable cooks in clean, sanitary kitchens. The number and kinds of meals, of course, depend on how long a particular child spends at the preschool center. For example, a child attending a center for a half day may be given only breakfast and a snack; a child attending a full day may require each meal. Whatever the case, each menu should be planned around a sound nutritional base, such as the following, which are based on Head Start guidelines. Menus for major meals—breakfast, lunch, and dinner—should

include items from each of the four basic food groups plus water:

1. Milk, cheese, eggs, and related dairy products (3 servings per full day)
2. Meat, fish, and poultry (2 servings per full day)
3. Fruits and vegetables (3 servings per full day)
4. Breads and cereals (4 servings per full day)
5. Water (6–8 glasses per day)

Basically, young children require the same foods as adults, but in smaller proportions. Sample food guides for full meals and snacks are given in the accompanying box.

Remember that children this age manage best with small helpings of food and that their appetites vary from day to day. Thus, don't pressure children to eat food they may not feel like eating on a particular day—when they are ready, they will most certainly eat. Conversely, have additional servings ready for children who want them. The following is a list of basic rules of thumb to follow in deciding on a serving size for young children:

• ½–1 cup of milk
• ⅓–⅔ cup of juice
• 1–3 ounces of meat, poultry, or fish
• 1–2 tablespoons of vegetable or fruit
• ½–1 slice of bread
• 1–2 cookies or crackers

It is important that children have their meals in a clean, cheerful environment. Mealtimes should be periods of calmness and happiness for children.

During these periods adults help them establish food habits that are the foundation of good health throughout their lives. Several guidelines should be followed in creating such an atmosphere. They will help teachers and other child-care workers realize the most effective means of facilitating the goals of sound nutrition.

GUIDELINES FOR A GOOD NUTRITION PROGRAM

1. Children differ in their reactions to food.

   a. Allow them to become acquainted with *new* foods *slowly.* Introducing several new foods at one meal will certainly cause problems.

   b. Allow them to make some choices as to what they eat. For example, let a child who dislikes vegetables choose between two of them—you may get him to eat one.

   c. Keep home and cultural patterns in mind. The foods children will openly accept or reject are those that are likely to be accepted or rejected by their family and culture.

2. A good physical and emotional environment is important.

   a. Provide a bright, clean eating area.

   b. Furnish plates, cups, and eating utensils that can be comfortably managed by small hands.

   c. Have suitably sized tables and chairs so children will be physically comfortable.

   d. Seat four or five children together with one adult at a table, and encourage calm, interesting conversation. Many concepts can be extended during this time by discussing: *yellow* corn, *orange* carrots, or *green* beans; *crisp* vegetables, *soft* pudding; *more* milk, *less* juice; *one* cookie, *two* cookies.

   e. Never withhold foods, such as a special anticipated treat, for punishment.

   f. Try playing soft music at times.

   g. Accept table accidents as a normal part of life. Don't create a fuss by admonishing the child to be more careful—simply assist him in a cleanup operation.

   h. Plan an orderly schedule for mealtimes. However, don't overemphasize regularity to the point of causing emotional concerns. Some children have trouble regulating themselves to a routine and need understanding and guidance from an adult.

MEAL GUIDES: SHADYSIDE DAY-CARE CENTER

BREAKFAST

½–1 cup cereal

½–1 cup milk

1–2 pieces cheese cube

1–2 wedges apple

MORNING SNACK

⅓–⅔ cup orange juice

½–1 slice whole wheat bread and butter

LUNCH

½–1 ounce fish pattie

2–4 raw carrot strips

1–2 tablespoons cooked corn

½–1 slice whole wheat bread and butter

¼–1½ cup pudding

½–1 cup milk

AFTERNOON SNACK

½–1 cup milk

1–2 oatmeal cookies

Children learn good eating habits and develop a positive feeling for good nutrition if mealtime is conducted in an organized, cheerful manner.

3. The way in which food is served to the children may determine whether or not they eat it.

   a. Serve small portions—to a small child a heaping plate may be an impossible challenge. Children respond more positively to a small serving and assurances of seconds than to a huge original portion.

   b. Serve bite-sized pieces of food that may be eaten with the fingers. Even those who can use a fork do so more easily when faced with small pieces of food.

   c. Serve the meal as soon as the children are seated around the table.

   d. Serve some raw vegetables and some cooked—children may prefer one over the other. Cauliflower, carrots, celery, turnips, and rutabagas provide interesting assortments of this type.

   e. Serve foods with a variety of colors and textures. Cut the food into a vari-

ety of sizes and shapes to interest the children—cheese may be cut into diamonds and squares or carrots into strips and circles.

   f. Avoid mixing foods together on the children's plates. Many children avoid eating foods if they even touch one another on the same plate. For this reason, never mix vegetables on the same plate or serve a gravy or sauce that will spill over to another food on the same plate. Many teachers prefer plastic plates that are sectioned off into separate areas.

4. Children should develop a sense of responsibility for establishing good nutritional habits.

   a. Encourage them to wash their hands and faces before each meal. While waiting for others to get ready, children finished early may read books, sit with a friend, or engage in other quiet activities.

   b. Urge children to help set the tables. Napkins, eating utensils, and cups can be arranged by the children and tied into cognitive learning that occurs during other parts of the day. For example, telling the child to "put five napkins at this table," or to "pour a little more juice for Amy," helps to reinforce skills worked on earlier.

   c. Older children (3½ years and up) can pass serving bowls or pitchers to one another as they wish to help themselves to extra portions.

5. A smooth, orderly transition should be made between a preceding activity and mealtime. One teacher, for example, after reading a story filled with animals, had the children move to the eating area one group at a time—the mice "creeping," the elephants "clumping," the lions "stalking," and so on.

Mealtime in a child-care facility, then, must be organized, clean, and cheerful. Wholesome food, attractively prepared and served, will encourage most children to develop a positive attitude toward eating nutritious meals. However, should eating problems persist over a period of time, it would be wise to consult with the parents, school nurse, or a physician.

COOKING WITH YOUNG CHILDREN

Because of the increased emphasis on nutrition education, cooking programs are finding their way into more and more early childhood programs. Such projects are valuable for two reasons: (1) They involve children with the food and (2) they are meaningful learning activities. Both of these features are illustrated in the following discussion.

When creating a cooking program, keep in mind a principle that weaves its way through nearly every theory of learning: Start with the simple and move to the more complex. Beginning cooking experiences should contain activities in which all young children can participate with a reasonable degree of success. These activities are usually referred to as "precooking" activities, but they can be character-ized as tasks that help children become familiar with the various skills necessary for an effective cooking program. The accompanying box describes some "precooking" activities you can have the children do.

Beginning activities such as these help familiarize children with the cooking process. If they are properly guided, most youngsters become excited about their growing accomplishments and are highly motivated to enter into more complex cooking projects. However, successful cooking projects don't happen just by chance—they must be carefully planned in advance so the maximum learning potential can be derived. Keep the following ideas uppermost in mind as you plan any cooking project with your young children.

1. Allow all children who want to do so to participate actively.

2. Require that children wash their hands and faces before the cooking project starts.

3. Scrub the cooking counter with soap and water before the cooking activity begins.

4. Encourage children to experiment as they work with the food (smell, taste, chop, and so on).

5. Emphasize the many areas of learning as the cooking project evolves:

PRECOOKING ACTIVITES

1. Scrub vegetables (carrots, celery) with brushes.
2. Spread peanut butter on a half slice of bread.
3. Measure and pour dry ingredients (rice, popcorn) from a cup into a bowl.
4. Measure and pour liquids (water, milk) from a cup into a bowl.
5. Blend together two ingredients (water and Jello powder).
6. Shake something (cream to make butter).
7. Roll something with the hands (cookies).
8. Use cooking utensils: table knives (soft to hard foods), hand grinder (peanut butter), hand grater (cheese, carrots), rolling pin (cookie dough), egg beater (pudding ingredients), scraper (peeling carrots or potatoes), hand juicer (oranges), food chopper (nuts).

- following directions (pour the milk into the bowl)
- listening (pour syrup over the oats)
- learning new words (*avocado*)
- working as a group member (help to peel the apples)
- learning about foods (where they came from, how they grow; their nutritional value)
- understanding changes in states of matter (liquid to gelatin)
- measuring ingredients (½ cup, 1 teaspoon)
- developing muscle control (mixing, pouring, grasping)

6. Maintain a safe environment:

- Discuss safety measures for appropriate projects.
- Use care while working at a hot stove or with hot liquids.
- Encourage children to respect (not fear) sharp knives and other potentially dangerous kitchen utensils.
- Provide constant, alert supervision.

7. Allow children the opportunity to have fun and enjoy the cooking experience. The time should be one of pleasant socializing rather than of stony silence or petty arguments.

8. Cooking can be more fun if the children prepare foods they have grown themselves. Beans, spinach, peas, and lettuce are all easily raised in a small garden plot and provide sound, nutritious meals.

9. It is becoming common to hear about doing away with "junk foods" containing sugars, saturated fats, and large amounts of starches. A back-to-nature approach is gaining strength—a program that emphasizes natural fruits, vegetables, nuts, and dairy foods rather than pre-packaged foods, cake mixes, pudding, candy, and other sweets. Try to eliminate such "junk food" snacks or meals and move toward more nutritious foods.

Initial cooking projects should be fairly simple—many teachers begin with gelatin, pudding, popcorn, vegetables, and the like. Increased interest and skill will gradually lead to more sophisticated experiences. Be careful, though, to suit the project to the level of the children because if it is too difficult, too long, or has too many steps to follow, children will become distracted and frustrated with the idea, "Here's another thing I can't do!" The following anecdote illustrates how one teacher combined all of these suggestions in creating a cooking experience.

Mrs. Hollister had already done some basic food preparation activities and seen the children respond favorably to them. Now she was encouraged to try making a tossed salad with them. In developing the project, Mrs. Hollister found it useful to complete a planning form (similar to the one illustrated in Figure 13-1). This task helped her to organize her thinking and kept the project moving along in a confident, constructive manner.

Mrs. Hollister served as the "cooking coordinator," the person responsible for guiding the efforts of four small groups of children, each group working with volunteer "cooking mothers." The groups were located at four separate tables. Each group used its time to do a specific task leading to the completion of the salad. At one table children were busily washing and tearing lettuce and spinach. Similarities and differences between the two vegetables were brought out as the cooking mother encouraged the children to observe the dark green spinach leaves and compare them to the lighter green lettuce leaves. The children were also asked to compare differences in texture, size, taste, and other features. As the cooking mother asked questions about the leave's growth and their other uses, the children were motivated to hypothesize, and predict answers.

Cleaning and scrubbing are important steps in preparing an area before and after the children's cooking experiences.

In much the same manner, cooking mothers at other tables sparked conversation about their tasks—at the slicing table, about how cucumbers, tomatoes, and radishes change in appearance from outside to the inside; at the grating table, about the smell and texture or appearance of the carrots and cheese as they are being grated. Meanwhile, a fourth group of children was making a simple salad dressing that would eventually turn the salad creation into a masterpiece! The children at each table were guided by the cooking mothers and a simplified recipe guide in determining just how much of their ingredients were needed for the salad. (Sample children's recipe guides are illustrated in Figure 13-2.)

As the children worked along toward the completion of their separate projects, Mrs. Hollister and the cooking mothers observed them to determine levels of motor skill development (eye-hand coordination, manipulation of utensils, and so on), perception, listening skills, ability to follow directions, and concept development (quantity, texture, time, and so on). When each separate table completed its task, the children were brought together by Mrs. Hollister at a fifth, central table where all the

ingredients were combined. As each table's ingredients were added to a large bowl, the children were asked to talk about what their group did so the whole group could learn to appreciate the efforts of small groups in a large community activity.

When the salad was eventually completed, Mrs. Hollister asked everyone to sit at their tables and then passed out a small bowl of the finished product to everyone. "Yumm, it smells so good" or "This is the best salad I ever ate" were the general comments heard. However, one or two hesitant children couldn't be convinced to try the salad. They were simply asked to, "Please stay and keep the rest of us company." Mrs. Hollister chose to capitalize on the children's pride of accomplishment for this project by developing an experience chart later in the day. In this way, all the experiences were summarized in a meaningful beginning reading activity. Those who wished to do so added illustrations for the story during the quiet time that followed.

Enthusiasm for Mrs. Hollister's project soon reached the children's homes. Parents contacted her and made comments such as, "What

COOKING PROJECT

Date _____   Project _____

Whole group activity   Small group activity

1. Purpose for the project:

    ☐ New food experience   ☐ Observing texture changes in
                                              cooking
    ☐ Fun experience   ☐ Noting similarities and differences

    ☐ Language development   ☐ Small muscle skills

    ☐ Following directions   ☐ Learning about different foods

    ☐ Cooking skills   ☐ Encourage experimentation

    ☐ Sensory experience   ☐ Listening experience

    ☐ Observing changes in matter   ☐ Social experience

2. Cooking supplies needed:

    _____   _____   _____
    _____   _____   _____
    _____   _____   _____
    _____   _____   _____

3. Ingredients needed:

    _____   _____   _____
    _____   _____   _____
    _____   _____   _____
    _____   _____   _____

4. Step-by-step procedure:

    a. _____   f. _____

    b. _____   g. _____

    c. _____   h. _____

    d. _____   i. _____

    e. _____   j. _____

Figure 13-1   *Planning form for a cooking project*

Figure 13-2 *Children's recipe guides*

kind of salad did you make in school? Billy never wanted to eat salad before and now I can't feed him enough of it." This example illustrates the extent to which teachers can influence good nutrition in the home. Mrs. Hollister decided to take advantage of the parental interest by sending home a recipe letter each time a new recipe was created in her class. The following is a copy of one of her letters.

March 16, 1985

Dear Parents,

We made a tasty tossed salad in school today! We would like to share our recipe with you.

8 cups	iceberg lettuce
3 cups	raw spinach
¼ cup	thinly sliced carrots
½ cup	sliced cucumbers
¼ cup	diced onions
¼ cup	sliced radishes
¼ cup	diced green peppers
2	sliced tomatoes

Wash or scrub all of the vegetables. Tear the lettuce and spinach leaves and place them into a large bowl. Add each of the other ingredients. When all have been added, toss them until the salad is evenly mixed. Store the salad in the refrigerator until it is to be served. Then prepare this dressing and pour it over the top.

Mix

2 cups mayonnaise
1 cup sour cream
4 tablespoons finely chopped green onion.

The salad was delicious!

With love,
Mrs. Hollister's Five-Year-Old Group
Sunnydale Day-Care Center

Cooking as a Sensory Experience

Seeing, tasting, touching, smelling, and listening provide sensory experiences as the children work with their food in cooking expe-

Numerous values result from well-planned cooking experiences. First cooking experiences should be simple enough to help familiarize children with basic tools used in the cooking process.

riences. Children learn as you stimulate them to think and observe through questions such as these possibilities for a classroom "Popcorn Party":

1. What does the popcorn *look like* before popping? After popping?

2. How does the popcorn *feel* before popping? After popping?

3. *Listen* to it pop. How does it *sound*?

4. Can you think of some words to describe how it *smells* as it is popping?

5. What does it *taste* like before we add salt? After? How do you like it better?

Popcorn was used, of course, only as an illustrative example. Think of how the questioning strategy would be altered or kept the same for these foods as they are compared prior to, during, and after cooking: carrots, jello, eggs, peanut butter, grilled cheese sandwiches, soft pretzels, bread, vegetable soup, powdered milk, or pudding.

Cooking as a Conceptual Experience

Children can reinforce basic conceptual skills through cooking when they discover that apples can be red, green, or yellow. They experience red as they work with meat and tomatoes; shades of green can be differentiated as they enjoy broccoli, lettuce, spinach, and other leafy vegetables; orange is encountered with carrots and sweet potatoes; yellow is met as the children peel a banana or slice a squash.

In addition to color, children can learn to use conceptual terms while describing a food's size and shape. Bananas are *long*, peas are *little*, tomatoes are *soft and round*. A slice of bread is usually *square*, a cross-section of grapefruit *triangular*, and a sliced carrot *round*. Other food, such as cheese, is found in just about any shape. Play games with children as they are preparing food or eating to help them reinforce old ideas or learn new ones: "I'm thinking of something on your plate that is brown and square. Can you tell me what it is?"

Table 13-4 *Activities for Learning the Food Groups*

Milk	Meat and Meat Alternatives	Fruits and Vegetables	Bread and Cereals
Milk	**Meat**	**Vegetables**	**Breads**
Reconstitute and taste evaporated and powdered milk. Taste and compare whole and skim milk. Make creamed soups such as cream of potato. Make pudding and custard. Make ice cream and/or cottage cheese.	Grind meat for hamburger, meat loaf, or meat balls. Prepare hot dogs at a cookout. Dip liver slices in flour and fry.	Wash and tear lettuce, cabbage, and other greens for a salad. Scrub potatoes and bake. Husk corn; shell peas; peel carrots, potatoes, and onions. Pick broccoli, cauliflower, green peppers, cucumbers, carrots, and so on. Wash and cut for tasting raw. Grow tomatoes. Make tomato juice. Prepare different tomato products. Prepare an assortment of vegetables to make vegetable soup.	Mix, shape, and bake biscuits, muffins, popovers, pancakes, waffles, and cornbread. Mix and knead yeast bread. Toast bread in a toaster or in the oven. Taste different kinds of breads. Feel the difference between cake and all-purpose flour. Thicken sauces such as gravy with flour. Make a pizza crust, top with tomato sauce and cheese. Add seasoning, vegetables or meats.
Whipping cream	**Fish and poultry**		
Make butter. Whip cream.	Prepare by frying or baking.		
Cheese	**Dried beans**	**Fruits**	**Cereals**
Grate cheese and roll cheese balls. Prepare grilled cheese sandwiches. Dice cheese for macaroni and cheese. Taste and compare different kinds of cheese for flavor, texture, and color. Make cheese dips and fill celery or dip other raw vegetables.	Make bean soup, baked beans, or bean dip. Grow dried beans in a cup or can.	Dry fruits such as grapes or apples. Peel and taste citrus fruit. Juice oranges, grapefruit, lemons, or limes. Pick apples and make applesauce. Grind cranberries and oranges. Compare taste, color and shape of different melons. Compare fruit seeds. Plant seeds in cups or cans	Cook oatmeal, rice, or noodles. Make crunchy "grainola." Grind grains such as wheat.
	Eggs		
	Hard-cook eggs and peel shell. Prepare deviled eggs and egg salad sandwiches. Beat egg whites. Crack an egg. Mix for scrambled eggs.		
	Nuts		
	Make peanut butter in a blender (see instruction booklet) or grind for chunky style. Spread on bread or crackers, apple slices or banana. Gather nuts and crack them.		

Source: Marilyn Blossom and Ann A. Hertzler, *The Food Curriculum,* United States Department of Agriculture, Cooperative Extension Service, University of Missouri (Columbia), no date.

Learning the Food Groups

As the children work with foods, you may wish to help them understand that a balanced diet includes eating a number of different kinds of foods, commonly classified into four major food groups. Table 13-4 offers some suggestions for working with foods in each category.

Cooking then, provides for a variety of learning experiences. Children learn to follow directions, to work together, to measure, to watch a clock or oven timer, to recognize new

NONCOOKING RECIPES

WALDORF SALAD

4 cups diced apples

2 cups diced celery

⅔ cup chopped walnuts

1 cup raisins

1 cup mayonnaise

Mix apple, celery, walnuts, raisins, and mayonnaise; toss. If desired, serve on a bed of fresh lettuce and top with a bing cherry.

COLESLAW

8 cups finely shredded cabbage

½ cup finely chopped onion

1 cup sour cream

½ cup mayonnaise

1 teaspoon salt

1 teaspoon dry mustard

Combine cabbage and onion in large bowl. Blend the remaining ingredients together in a separate container and pour over the cabbage and onion. Mix.

BUTTER

1 pint heavy whipping cream

½ cup salt

Small baby food jar for each child

Pour about 3 tablespoons of whipping cream and a dash of salt into a small baby food jar. Shake the jars vigorously until butter forms (5–10 minutes). The liquid remaining is butter-milk and the children should taste it.

THREE-BEAN SALAD

1 can green string beans (drained)

1 can yellow wax beans (drained)

1 can red kidney beans (drained)

½ cup chopped green onions

¼ cup chopped fresh parsley

8 oz. Italian salad dressing

1 tablespoon sugar

2 cloves garlic (crushed)

Crisp fresh lettuce

Mix beans, onions, and parsley together in a large salad bowl. Combine salad dressing, sugar, and garlic. Pour over bean mixture and toss. Cover and refrigerate for at least 3 hours, stirring periodically.
Serve on fresh lettuce leaves.

SUMMER FRUIT SALAD

3 bananas (sliced)

3 cups oranges (sectioned)

1 cup seedless green grapes

1 cup fresh pineapple (squares)

1 cup fresh pitted cherries

2 cups fresh grapefruit (sectioned)

2 cups pears (squares)

2 cups peaches (squares)

Cut and prepare all fruits. Place into a large salad bowl and leave in the refrigerator to chill. Cover with the following dressing:
Blend 1 cup sour cream, 2 tablespoons honey, and 2 tablespoons orange juice.

words, or to see how things change as they are sliced, frozen, mixed, or cooked. They exercise their small muscles as they spread peanut butter, knead bread dough, or crack a nut. They discover how things grow, where food comes from (milk does not grow in a bottle), and how to prepare nutritious meals. Youngsters learn about food through experiences provided in your classroom—at meals, snacks, or play.

You can help parents, especially low-income parents, realize the power of experience as a teaching tool to help their children learn about nutrition. Remember, however, that families with larger incomes often need guidance, but problems of poor nutrition are more commonly confined to lower income levels. Because of greater resources, though, families with larger incomes can afford to make mistakes and still receive an adequate diet for

COOKING RECIPES

APPLESAUCE

8 apples (pared and quartered)

1 cup water

½ cup brown sugar

¼ teaspoon cinnamon

⅛ teaspoon nutmeg

Heat apples in water until boiling. Reduce heat and simmer 5–10 minutes until tender; stir periodically and add water if necessary. Mash apples with a potato masher and add the remaining ingredients and stir. Heat to boiling and remove from stove.

OATMEAL CRUNCH

½ cup butter

½ cup sugar

¼ cup dark corn syrup

1 tablespoon molasses

2½ cups oats

Heat oven to 350°. Grease square pan, 8 × 8 × 2 inches with unsalted shortening; line bottom of pan with foil and grease foil. Melt butter over moderate heat. Remove pan from heat, stir in sugar, dark corn syrup, and molasses. Add the oats and stir thoroughly. Press the mixture into the pan and bake 35 minutes. Set pan aside for 10 minutes to cool. Loosen the edges and cut. Let pieces cool completely before serving.

SOFT PRETZELS

4 cups flour

1 tablespoon salt

1 tablespoon sugar

1 package dry yeast

1½ cups warm water

2 eggs (beaten)

1 cup kosher salt

Combine flour, salt, and sugar. Stir in yeast mixed with warm water. Knead the dough until elastic. Give each child a small ball of dough to form a pretzel in any shape desired. Brush dough with the beaten egg and sprinkle with kosher salt. Bake for 20 minutes at 425°.

APPLE CRISP

4 cups sliced apples

¾ cup brown sugar

½ cup unbleached flour

½ cup oats

¾ teaspoon cinnamon

¾ teaspoon nutmeg

⅓ cup softened butter or margarine

Heat oven to 375°. Grease square pan, 8 × 8 × 2 inches. Place apple slices in pan. Mix remaining ingredients thoroughly in large bowl. Sprinkle over apples.

Bake 30 minutes until topping is golden brown. Serve warm.

---

maintaining good health. The following resources can help guide families in need of information on good nutrition:

1. Home visits by nutrition professionals (or teachers if they are specifically knowledgeable in nutrition)

2. Food demonstration classes in which parents are shown methods of preparing food that will preserve the greatest nutritive value

3. Printed materials periodically sent to the home in all forms (pamphlets, leaflets, letters, and so on) and in all languages

4. The U.S.D.A. Home Economist in your area who can help in efforts toward good nutrition.

Thus, two practical approaches to meeting the concern for good nutrition are available to early childhood educators today: (1) providing sound, nutritious meals and snacks in the child-care facility and (2) educating parents about basic principles of good nutrition. It is the responsibility of all of us to be aware of these two major options and to develop innovative, imaginative, practical approaches to nutrition education for young children.

Recipes

The recipes on pp. 496–97 have been successfully used in various types of preschools around the country. They require only simple mixing and measuring, and varied amounts of cooking time. Other recipes are readily available in special cookbooks for children or in general cookbooks.

SOME FINAL THOUGHTS

There is much you can do to provide for the health and safety of the youngsters in your care. Try to convince parents that physical examinations and vaccinations are needed before their children enter a group setting. Be prepared to recognize the symptoms of contagious diseases and to care for the children should illness or injuries occur while they are under your supervision. Along the same line, help the children understand their role in maintaining a healthful environment by encouraging them to develop desirable health and safety habits.

Chapter **14**

Putting It All Together: Creating a Challenging Preschool Environment

The true excitement of beginning teaching usually comes with the process of planning and selecting the equipment and materials for a given group of children, and in designing the actual physical facility. This process is an extremely sensitive one because the experience of spending time with teachers in the preschool setting is important for young children. Your children are probably leaving their homes for the very first time, and when they arrive in this strange, new environment, they are surrounded by new children (probably more of the same age than they have ever seen), new play areas, different toys, strange adults, unfamiliar toilet facilities, and a variety of other untried experiences. The children must be led into these new experiences by a trusting and knowledgeable adult, for such a person can give children a feeling of confidence and a spirit of adventure that is basic to an enthusiastic, emotionally safe introduction. One question that beginning teachers often ask is, "But what kind of experiences *should* I provide in order to make the environment as safe and as rewarding as possible?" This is extremely difficult to answer because there is no agreement today as to which approach to creating classroom environments is most effective. All the individuals or groups offering recommendations, however, agree on one basic guideline: The young child should be foremost in the minds of educators responsible for developing preschool programs. So, before any thoughts about the actual physical characteristics, teaching materials or strategies, and other features of the setting can be made, we must first consider the client.

FOUNDATIONS OF PROGRAM PLANNING

How do we view the development of the child? What theories of instruction best explain the learning process? These questions must be answered

499

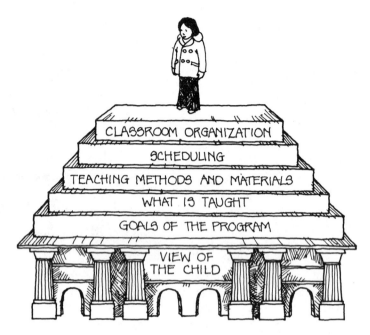

CLASSROOM ORGANIZATION

SCHEDULING

TEACHING METHODS AND MATERIALS

WHAT IS TAUGHT

GOALS OF THE PROGRAM

VIEW OF THE CHILD

Figure 14-1   _The foundation of program planning_

openly and honestly, for the decisions you make provide the foundation of your program (see Figure 14-1). Without a carefully formed view of the child as your foundation, your program stands a strong chance of falling and crumbling for lack of focus and well-defined design. However, if your foundation is strengthened and nourished in a sound, well-informed manner, it will dictate the goals of the program: what is taught, the materials and methods used by the teacher, the scheduling of daily activities, and the ways in which the classroom is physically organized.

Preschool programs today are supported by a wide range of current opinions in the field of child development. Such programs take this information and turn it into basic program models that serve as guides for teachers developing their own programs. Currently, there appear to be three broad categories into which model programs fall:

- _Informal models_—These programs have evolved through the years from the early, traditional, child-centered preschools designed for middle-class children to today's informal settings for all children. The primary emphases of these programs today are the needs of the "whole child": (1) habits of health and personal care, (2) motor skills, (3) self-concept, (4) social and emotional development, (5) satisfactory behavior, and (6) language and intellectual development.

- _Skills-oriented models_—These programs emerged during the late 1960s and are primarily geared toward the formal, direct teaching of specific skills or information, especially in the areas of reading, math, and language. These programs are mainly teacher- or subject-oriented rather than child-centered; this means that the teacher directs the learning activities while the child participates in prescribed ways. Other developmental processes are considered important, but the major purpose of these programs is to develop academic skills within a highly structured learning environment.

• *Cognitive developmental models—* These programs, which also emerged during the late 1960s, are concerned mainly with two areas: (1) the development of effective learning processes such as problem solving, concept formation, observation, experimentation, and manipulation with particular emphases placed on Piagetian tasks and language development, and (2) the acquisition of positive attitudes toward learning. The teaching strategies designed to meet these aims consist of teacher direction (sometimes formal and at other times informal) in activities, some of which may be highly structured and others more flexible. Because of this program flexibility, cognitive developmental programs range from high-structured approaches similar to the skills model to low-structured approaches similar to the child-centered informal model.

The philosophies of each approach have been discussed in detail throughout this text. A summary of each position is found in Table 14-1.

You will notice that there are many basic differences among philosophies in early childhood education—these differences affect the ways teachers prepare and use methods and materials of instruction. Within these separate models, the teacher must be fully aware of her unique role and of the expectations for the children. Once this awareness has been achieved, the teacher must be willing to carry through her responsibilities and prescribed functions enthusiastically. Successful program implementation, then, strongly depends on (1) an awareness of the teacher's

Your foundation for program planning should be solidly formed by a deep understanding of young children and the experiences to which they should be exposed.

role as prescribed by the model and (2) a willingness by the teacher to carry out that role at all times. Although there are differences among models, as listed in Table 14-1, certain characteristics are held in common. Eleanor Maccoby and Miriam Zellner (1970) summarized those common considerations.

1. Individual differences among the children are recognized and dealt with as they enter the program.

2. Preevaluation is necessary in order to determine those individual differences.

3. Children's needs can best be met if they are properly identified and matched with the appropriate resources.

4. Children must be interested in school and motivated to learn before any behavioral changes can be expected.

Table 14-1   *Comparison of Three Basic Models of Preschool Programming*

	Informal Models	Skills-Oriented Models	Cognitive Developmental Models
Objectives	Focus on social and emotional development, language skills, health and personal care, and intellectual abilities	Focus on academic knowledge and skills; also concerned about other areas of development, primarily personal and social behavior	Focus on development of Piagetian skills: sensorimotor, language, and cognitive; value play and social interaction as a tool to move child from egocentricity toward socialized behaviors
Source of child's motivation	Satisfaction of personal needs essential before learning can take place; personal needs include love and security; motivation mainly intrinsic	Motivation seen as capable of being manipulated from the outside through a reward system; such rewards can be material or social, but motivation seen as an aftermath (reward) rather than a precondition of learning	Child intrinsically driven toward seeking equilibrium; solving problems and gaining increasingly mature levels of logical thought seen as a motivation in itself
Learning environment	A balanced curriculum encouraging freedom and direct experience within well-defined limits; learning activities based on developmental principles and adjusted to each child's interests and needs; teacher responsive to the child's intellectual, social, and physical needs; emphasis on an integrated project approach (such as cooking) where many learnings are encouraged	Very specific methods of classroom management and teaching; detailed methods and sequential skills development advocated; emphasis on programmed materials and teaching machines	Definite teaching strategies, but classroom free enough for exploration and discovery; materials designed to develop basic Piagetian skills such as classification, seriation, conservation, and problem solving

5. Teachers must provide activities and experiences that lead to successful challenges for the children in their environments.

6. All children can experience success in any program provided that the activities are presented in such a way that they make sense to the children.

Perhaps, by now, you have begun to formulate some ideas that tend to influence you toward one particular program model or another. Such a decision requires deep thought and planning—you do not just appear in the room on the first day of school and "do what comes naturally." You must read, talk to other teachers, observe other classrooms, and study how others have organized their programs. A *good* program does not happen simply by chance. As you participate in professional field experiences or student teaching, make the most of your opportunities and begin to make choices about the type of early childhood program that appeals to you.

Observe and evaluate with a good program checklist as your guide, while you compare and contrast programs for young children. Ask for help from teachers at preschool centers or from your college instructors. They are all members of a team entrusted with your education and are as concerned about your professional education as you are about the education of the children you will teach. All early childhood professionals have a joint interest—the development of young children. Your commitment to this interest will be maintained and strengthened as you cooperate and share ideas with those in the field of early childhood education.

PLANNING PRESCHOOL PROGRAMS

The process of implementing philosophical decisions into actual program designs can be illustrated by comparing it to the process of planning a vacation. Assume that it is term break and an opportunity exists for you and a group of friends to visit any one of four possible vacation spots: Bermuda, Paris, the Florida beaches, or Vail, Colorado. Such a situation would probably involve a great deal of discussion as to the merits of each place, since individual interests and values would affect the final decision. Perhaps after a great deal of give-and-take some compromises could be reached among all members of the group and an eventual decision made. The teacher planning her preschool program is faced with similar considerations. She does not simply choose one

approach out of thin air and use it in her teaching. She is a member of a team—a team comprising *herself, parents, children,* and *administrators.*

- *The teacher.* You are an individual and have professional characteristics all your own. Your personality, your training, and your experience all influence the type of classroom practices you feel are most appropriate for your children. You must be true to these feelings and teach in a way that is most agreeable and most comfortable for you, for an uncomfortable or unappealing technique will most certainly result in artificiality and an unnatural style of teaching. Your children will sense the resulting feelings of unhappiness and will most likely respond to you and the classroom in a similar way. So, your knowledge of teaching methods and materials should be brought into the open and shared with others as the goals and techniques for your preschool program unfold.

- *The parents.* Parents looking for a preschool setting for their children often provide positive input into the strengths and weaknesses of the program. Encourage parents to share their ideas and to voice their concerns about what is being provided for their children. Parents are, in actuality, "consumers" who have a right to examine a program and make suggestions on the things that they would like to have provided for their children.

- *The children.* Remember that the children are the major reason why your preschool exists—the program is for them. Examine the backgrounds of your children, recall your knowledge of child growth and development, and think of all you know about the interests and abilities of youngsters as you plan your program. Keep these thoughts in mind, because the final program you choose should be affected by many variables directly affecting the children, including their families; whether they come from urban, suburban, or rural settings; whether they come from low-income, middle-income, or high-income homes; whether they speak English or another language; or whether or not they have had varieties of educational experiences before entering school. A good program respects these variables and is designed to promote areas that need to be strengthened and extended.

• *The administrators.* Although some preschools allow individual teachers sufficient freedom to plan and execute whatever program they desire, many require new teachers to accept the principles and policies established by the school itself. They desire this conformity because they want a coordinated program in which all involved are constantly aware of each other's responsibilities. Such programs range from those requiring strict teacher conformity to those allowing the teacher some degree of freedom within a basic curricular structure. Be sure to find out the type of teacher-freedom that is extended by the administration of the school you are considering for employment—if you are the kind of person who needs to follow a set curriculum and have the major plan of organization outlined for you, then you may feel awkward in a school that asks all teachers to assume full responsibility for planning and executing their own curriculum. Of course, the opposite is true for those of you who need freedom and openness in their planning.

Being a member of a team, then, implies that all members should have appropriate input into any decisions and, ideally, that such give-and-take will result in a decision that all can accept. Therefore, as you and your friends must choose one from among four vacation spots, the teacher and her teammates must choose from among the major philosophies of pre-

school education: informal models, skills-oriented models, and cognitive developmental models.

Goals

Once you have decided on the basic philosophy for your program, the next issue that arises is where you wish to go with it. To relate this decision to our vacation analogy, let us suppose that the group decided that Florida would be the most attractive and interesting place for you to go. You therefore established a major direction, but the decision-making process is still not finished. Your travel plans must now address the question of what you want to do once you get there. You must establish *goals*—what do you want to accomplish? Suppose the individuals involved in making the decision eventually choose these four major goals:

1. To visit Disney World
2. To swim, surf, and bask in the sun at the beach
3. To visit Cape Canaveral and other points of interest
4. To sample the entertainment at the various night spots

Of course, other possibilities for travel goals existed and were discussed in your group's deliberations—possibilities such as shopping, boating, fishing, jai alai, dog racing, and the like. But, after considering the variety of factors, your group eliminated those and settled on these particular four goals. If the group had not effectively planned the vacation in this way, you might have found yourselves fluttering from one activity to another when you got to Florida, and not really spending enough time at one to make it worthwhile, or you might have devoted so much time to one activity that you didn't have enough time for the others. In much the same way, the teacher

Good early childhood programs differ in their philosophical orientations, but they all share one common characteristic: they attempt to provide the types of experiences best suited to the needs of their children.

must identify goals for her preschool program—statements that identify *what* she wishes to accomplish from the program she is developing so that it will operate as efficiently as possible. Before we examine goals of specific preschool programs, let's analyze the two major mistakes often made by teachers in stating such goals:

1. *Stating too many goals.* Some teachers list as many as 40 or 50 goals for their program. Such a figure is unrealistic and virtually impossible to accomplish. This is analogous to fluttering from one activity to another on your vacation trip and not spending enough time on any one activity to make it worthwhile.

2. *Stating goals too vaguely.* At times, the goals of a preschool program are stated in such a general way that they lack real meaning. This problem is analogous to the situation of saying, "I'm going on vacation to have fun." Such a statement lacks focus and would probably apply just as well to a trip to Antarctica as it would to a trip to Florida.

For most purposes, three to six well-stated goals, bearing directly on the chosen program approach, would be sufficient. Examples of goals for sample programs representing each of the three major directions of preschool programming follow.

INFORMAL PROGRAMS

1. To help the children care for their bodies and establish healthful routines

2. To develop control of the large and small muscles

3. To help the children acquire effective patterns of speaking

4. To encourage feelings of friendliness, cooperation, and sharing

5. To develop an intellectual base necessary for successful learning

SKILLS-ORIENTED PROGRAMS

(The skills-oriented descriptions are loosely based on: The Behavior Analysis Model, Department of Human Development, University of Kansas, Lawrence, Kansas 66044)

1. To teach young children *academic skills* that will enable them to compete effectively in the public schools

2. To teach young children *social skills* that are necessary for successful adjustment to school

3. To train teachers, aides, and parents to use positive reinforcement to develop these skills

COGNITIVE DEVELOPMENTAL PROGRAMS

(The cognitive descriptions are loosely based on: The Cognitive Curriculum, High/Scope Educational Research Foundation, 125 North Huron, Ypsilanti, Michigan 48107)

1. To help the child develop logical modes of thought through concept formation:
a. to gain knowledge about himself and objects
b. to see relationships between himself and things in his environment
c. to group and order objects and events

2. To help the child develop the capacity to manipulate symbols and thus to act on and represent the environment

As you compared and contrasted the goals for each area, it is hoped that you understood that the illustrative programs described the goals for only *one* program under each heading and that even the various separate programs under each heading vary in their goal statements. Take, for example, two separate groups of students opting for a vacation trip to Florida. Obviously, their major direction is the same (program model), but their expected accomplishments (goals) may vary slightly (for example, swimming for one group and fishing for another). Likewise, teachers closely associated with each philosophy may disagree to some extent on exactly what they hope to accomplish.

Curriculum Organization

Teaching Techniques The types of learning experiences provided for the children should be closely aligned with the stated goals. For example, if we are to satisfy the four goals stated for our vacation trip to Florida, we must ask ourselves the question, "Now that we've determined where we're going and what we'd like to accomplish when we get there, what is the *best mode of transportation* to get us there?" In answering this question, we can examine the possibilities: airplane, boat, car, bus, bicycle, motorcycle, van, truck, pogo stick, walk, run, swim, balloon, hitchhike, crawl, or skip. Choices are numerous and varied—some are ridiculous and would never help us achieve our goals; others are more realistic and appear to be more reasonably suited to helping us accomplish the goals. In the same way, you must choose the most appropriate teaching strategies and materials as you move the children toward stated program goals. This analogy between the method of transportation for the Florida vacation and choosing appropriate techniques and materials for the classroom may appear trite; however, each day in thousands of preschool settings across the country, children suffer because their teachers fail to understand the obvious logic inherent in *choosing the most appropriate methods and materials for accomplishing any chosen goal.* Too often, approaches to teaching are chosen because they are "cute" or "gimmicky" and not because they were identified as valued strategies for accomplishing particular goals. Remember that your responsibility is to develop a professionally sound curriculum, and that such a project should result from effective, mature decision-making processes.

Theories of learning and development, as well as their practical applications to working with young children, were discussed and illustrated throughout this book. As you read through each section, you were asked to become a decision maker—you were asked to compare and contrast approaches to the education of young children and decide on the one, or combination of several, that appealed most to you. Now you are at the point where a commitment must be made. What should young children experience in the preschool setting and what is your role in that setting? Answers to this question may be arrived at using the kinds of if-then statements we used in making decisions regarding our Florida vacation. For example, we may have decided:

- *If* we want to get to Florida as soon as possible to accomplish our goals, *then* an airplane might be the best mode of transportation to get us there.
- *If* we've never before been to Florida and want to see the sights along the way, *then* an automobile might be the best mode of transportation to get us there.
- *If* we'd like to join the numbers of others who are seeking to break unusual world records, *then* we'll try to see if we can hop all the way to Florida on a pogo stick.

In the same way, we must examine those techniques ("modes of transportation") that appear to be the best vehicle for accomplishing the goals we have identified as important for the children to be served. So, if-then statements may serve the same purpose in this decision as they did in the Florida vacation decision. For example:

- *If* we seek to meet the needs of the "whole child" (social-emotional, physical, intellectual), *then* we must attempt to combine a trusting environment and informal experiences for learning. (Informal)
- *If* the children need to develop sound reading, math, and language skills in order to be successful in their later schooling, *then* a highly teacher-directed, formalized approach should be the method of instruction. (Skills-oriented)
- *If* the processes of problem solving and concept formation are valued, *then* the best classroom environment would be one in which there is student-centered activity such as observation, manipulation, and experimentation. (Cognitive developmental)

To illustrate how these approaches differ in actual preschool settings, consider these examples from the programs whose goals we identified on page 506.

INFORMAL PROGRAMS

Willie, four years old and an only child, is brought to school by his mother. After exchanging a few words with the teacher, Willie's mother leaves for home. Willie takes off his coat and hangs it in his locker. He looks around the room for a moment and then walks toward the art corner where he becomes engrossed in water color painting at the easel. He grabs a brush and covers the entire paper with bright, vivid colors. After three paintings, Willie leaves the easel and joins a group of children in the block corner. He finds that the children are

You must decide whether it is more appropriate to guide young children through their learning experiences or to allow their free exploration into various learning activities. You also need to choose the most desirable learning materials to achieve your goals.

playing with toy cars, the blocks serving as buildings on a street. The group soon has an argument over an accident, which the teacher sensitively handles. After this period of free play activity, the teacher calls the group together and guides individuals to interest centers dealing with topics in reading, writing, math, science, social studies, music, construction, and games. Jennifer is to begin with the science center where she will become involved in experiments with magnets. After she moves from the science center, Jennifer enters the math center where she and four other heterogeneously grouped children enjoy playing games centering on numbers. Following this learning center, Jennifer freely chooses to participate in a cooking acitivity led by the teacher and her aide. All through the cooking activity the teacher emphasizes concepts from different subject areas. For example, children use math skills to count and measure the ingredients, reading skills to learn new vocabulary and read the recipe, science while observing changes in matter, social skills while cooperating in special tasks, and language skills as they discuss each phase of the project. After making their no-bake cookies, the teacher asks the children to join together for snack time when they will eat the cookies and drink a glass of milk.

*Following the snack time, children are given the choice of listening to a story (*The Snowy Day*) read by the teacher or going out to play. Jennifer joins her friends on the playground and plays jump rope games for 15 minutes. Coming back into the classroom, Jennifer finds that she is just in time for a music activity, or, if she prefers, she can choose a free period at a learning center. She chooses to sing along in a seasonal song led by the teacher while other children become involved with drawing, puzzles, games, blocks, and the like.*

Jennifer and her friends find their classroom full of interesting activites. They are given free time to pursue activities in which they are particularly interested, and at other times, they are led by the teacher to activities identified as necessary for improvement in some area of development. The teachers constantly encourage children to succeed in what they under-

take, and they accept each child as an individual. Continuous praise and reinforcement accompany the children's efforts: "You painted a very nice picture. I like it very much." Teachers encourage cooperative play and working as a member of a group. This informal program *is designed to help children develop in all areas, including beginning to learn academic-type skills.*

SKILLS-ORIENTED PROGRAMS

Vera, a five-year-old child from an urban ghetto area, comes through the door this morning to be warmly greeted by her teacher. "Good morning, Vera," say her teacher. "Good morning," replies Vera. "That was very nice, Vera," says the teacher, "I like the way you said good morning." Vera's program was designed to overcome the educational disadvantage that she reflected through scores attained on diagnostic tests. To ensure that such problems could be eliminated, her teacher designed a program that was structured so that Vera mastered one skill before she moved on to the next.

Vera is directed to a table where a trained aide is working with a group of four other children. The aide instructs the children to pick up their crayons and "circle the largest *ball" on a worksheet. Vera does her task correctly and is immediately given a bright red token, directly followed by the teacher's praise, "That was a very good job, Vera." After two similar tasks on the same worksheet, Arnold slams down his crayon and yells at the top of his voice. Ignoring Arnold, the teacher instead praises Vera because she is working so well. Picking up his crayon once more, Arnold reaches back and throws it across the table. Sensing that this potentially dangerous situation cannot be further ignored, the teacher calmly removes Arnold from the table to a chair that is isolated from the other children. "You threw a crayon at someone, Arnold, and we do not allow that in this room." After explaining the broken rule to Arnold, the teacher sets a kitchen timer for three minutes and allows Arnold to return after the three-minute period is over. Arnold's punishment is that he is not able to gain tokens for the period spent during "time out."*

Vera and the others in her group work with the aide for 15 minutes, after which they are free to exchange their accumulated tokens for special activities such as easel painting or puzzles. Vera chooses the easel painting and enjoys her activity for the next 20 minutes. For the rest of the morning, Vera works at learning tasks related to mathematics and reading, and is rewarded for her accomplishments all along the way with tokens and praise. After each 10- to 15-minute work period, Vera is given a chance to exchange tokens for special activities.

After completing her morning's work, Vera is helped with her coat and boots and waits for her older sister to pick her up. As she is ready to leave, her teacher says, "Good-bye, Vera. You were a very good worker today," and brings to an end another day in a behavioral skills-oriented preschool classroom.

COGNITIVE DEVELOPMENT PROGRAMS

Sarah, a four-year-old, begins her day in the cognitive developmental program with a short planning period. In order to give children an opportunity to set goals and plan ahead, Sarah's teacher provides 20 minutes at the start of each day for the children to select the areas in which they would like to work. Each day, the children are free to choose among four work time areas: the art area, large motor area, doll corner, *or* quiet area.

Today, Sarah chooses to start in the doll corner, then move to the art area, to the large motor area, and, if there is time, to the quiet area. Approximately 40 minutes of the morning is allotted to work time, so the teacher is on constant watch to encourage children to finish one task before they move to another. Sarah moves quickly to the doll corner where she is free to play in the company of an aide. The aide, serving as a guide for the child, uses language techniques during each learning experience: "The doll is near the table." "Is the chair far from the table?" "Find something that is near the shelf."

Sarah moves from the doll corner to the art area. She selects an easel and begins to make a series of lines. The aide stationed at this cor-

ner also uses language techniques while Sarah works. "The long green line is next to the bright red circle." Satisfied with her painting, Sarah hangs it up to dry and moves enthusiastically to the large motor area. This is one of her favorite areas; she enjoys equipment such as riding toys, hollow blocks, and boards. Again, an aide is near to stimulate language development by teaching spatial concepts such as up *and* down *or* above *and* below *or by encouraging the children to verbalize their actions.*

Although Sarah will not have time to join the teacher in the quiet area, she notices what the others are doing. The teacher has read a short story and is following it up with a discussion of the story's sequential events. She asks questions such as, "What was the first thing Harold did?" Then the teacher and the children cut out magazine pictures and place them in a sequence to tell a story. The sequences involve no more than four pictures. The teacher first discusses with the children what was happening in each picture, then asks the children to put the pictures together so they tell a story, and finally encourages those who were able to tell a story from the sequence of pictures.

After work time, Sarah and her classmates put away their materials and go to the bathroom. Even during this 15-minute cleanup period, the children are exposed to language as the teacher leads their work with comments such as, "All the big *blocks go on the* bottom *shelf," and so on.*

Following the cleanup period, the children are divided into groups for a juice time of approximately 30 minutes. This period again gives the teacher and her aides opportunities to extend language skills. When Sarah is being served juice, for example, she is asked, "Do you want more *juice than Megan?" and, when the cookies are being passed, the teacher says, "Kelly is* first, *Jeanie is* next, . . . "

A 20-minute activity time provides the children with a choice of staying indoors or going outdoors. Today, the teacher combines both an outdoor and indoor activity for this period. The children are taken outside on the play-

ground where they find a variety of leaves—some big, some little; some leaves with the same shape and some with different shapes. When they come back into the room, the children are asked to select a big leaf and a little leaf of the same shape from their assortment. After the children select their leaves, they place the big leaf on the gummed side of a piece of clear contact paper first, and then they place the little leaf in another spot. During this time, the teacher guides conceptual development by interjecting terms such as on, off, above, below, big, little, and so on. After the leaves are placed on the contact paper by the children, they are instructed to fold one side over the design. In this way, the leaves are encased in a folded piece of contact paper, and the entire project has resulted in a personal placemat for juice time or an attractive gift for a parent.

Sarah's teacher, then, used informal activities during the day as one technique in furthering certain aspects of cognitive development. In addition, she provided specific times during the day when the children worked in small groups, investigating situations within a Piagetian framework. Today, the group activities focused on the Piagetian skill of classification. Sarah joins a group of three other children in a corner where the teacher has prepared a large container of water and a variety of objects (sponges, wood blocks, fork, stone, rubber band, crayon, styrofoam, cups, and so on). The object of this activity is to encourage the children to experiment and classify the objects in the large group into two separate groups: things that float and things that sink.

The final part of the cognitive developmental preschool day involves dismissal. Sarah is given her last bit of conceptual stimulation during this time—she is advised to "put the mitten on your hand."

These examples illustrate the fact that a rich variety of preschool programming exists today. Sometimes it is difficult to choose from among the alternative programs because there appear to be so many positive features associated with each approach. However, you must make a choice in a way that reflects the needs of your children and your conception of the teaching style that best suits you. Although this is difficult, it can be most rewarding—your creativity and professional skills are reflected in the smiles and sounds of delight of the children under your care.

To illustrate how important this phase of planning is, let me invite you to close your eyes for a moment and travel back to that wonderful time in your life filled with fantasy and imagination. Reach back and recall some of the exciting experiences of your own childhood—that vital period that should still be part of every teacher of young children. Riffle through the memories of bubble gum, playground swings, scraped knees, favorite pets . . . and the time an adventure led you to a secret corner of a dark closet which concealed a brightly wrapped gift meant especially for you! "I think I know what's in the box—but could it really be . . . ? I just can't wait to open it and see what it holds—just for me!"

Anticipating what the classroom environment will contain should be just as exciting for the young child as guessing the contents of a gift package. The experiences and adventures in store should be so interesting that they produce intensive anticipation and the desire for extensive personal involvement in the challenging projects available. It doesn't take long, though, for the child's feeling of exquisite anticipation to be squelched by uninspired or poorly planned classroom experiences. Just as a poorly planned trip that results in detours, delays, stopovers, breakdowns, reroutings, or cancellations would affect our trip to Florida, so would an unimaginative, poorly planned classroom environment affect the extent to which educational goals are achieved. Besides *teaching technique,* then, two factors that affect curriculum organization are *classroom organization* and planning a *time schedule.*

Classroom Organization Planning and arranging the children's physical environment is an important extension of your philosophy of teaching—the way you arrange the room and the materials you choose all reflect your feelings about the ways in which children grow and develop. Therefore, in order for the facilities to be of maximum benefit to the young child, they must be consistent with the philosophy and goals you have established for your teaching. Basic to any philosophy, though, is the recognition that *children are alike in many ways and different in many others.* For that reason, all planning should keep in mind the varying degrees of ability, creativity, curiosity, and interest that any group of children bring to their preschool experience. The preschool room is arranged and furnished with one general goal in mind: *to meet the individual developmental needs of all the children.* Much as car sickness, air sickness, or a variety of other individual problems may affect the mode of transportation chosen for our group vacation in Florida, so do individual differences in a preschool group affect the total success of a program.

Many suggestions for establishing a sound classroom environment were provided in Chapter 4, emphasizing the need for a warm, friendly environment to help children make the important adjustment from home to school. Remember that, in many instances, you are providing the children with their first real educational experience and that the feelings they develop during this experience will most likely accompany them throughout the remainder of their schooling. For that reason, the rooms they enter should be friendly and alluring. This does not mean that an interior decorator has to design the room, but only that even the most unattractive room can be transformed into a more attractive one by painting, using colorful draperies, decorating with discarded store displays (such as animals, cartoon characters, story characters), exhibiting children's artwork, providing a small carpeted area, and a variety of other techniques.

To the beginning teacher, these suggestions may seem unattainable, since she may certainly ask, "But where can I get all of that? I can't afford it and the school won't buy it for me." That is a vital concern and one that must be addressed realistically. Understand, though, that you are not alone in your attempt to make the children's preschool experience a good one. Parents are often eager to contribute supplies; community agencies may be able to furnish used toys or furniture; maintenance workers can turn a drab room into a majestically colorful one with their skills; local stores and businesses often supply carpet remnants or old displays; and other groups are all eager to lend some support by offering free materials, equipment, or labor to help you achieve your goal. Encourage their honest interest and accept their willingness to help you transform your less than adequate facility into an attractive one. Following is a comprehensive list of free and inexpensive materials.

Millwork or Lumber Company: Wood "scraps" suitable for the carpentry table or art cabinet are given away by the box load. Sawdust is available as well as fascinating curls of wood created by planing. Leave a marked box and come back for it. Lathed scraps are available for purchase in some places and add special pieces for young builders. Button molds (used as wheels in the display) are available for purchase in 1", 1½", and 2" sizes.

Grocery Store: Boxes, boxes, boxes and a purpose for every size. Try a box corner for a table easel, a larger size for a puppet theater, a post office, or store, and of course, several for dramatic play of any sort desired by the children. Many cardboard displays disposed of by stores are suitable for various purposes in the classroom. Cardboard soft drink cartons are excellent for holding paint containers (prevent spilling at the table), and one painted white will be welcomed by your school "milkman."

Telephone Company: Empty telephone cable spools are wonderful additions to the outside play area. Small (3 ft. in diameter) ones make lovely doll corner tables. Stop a telephone man and put your name on the waiting list. On occasion, they may part with old instruments, but colorful, scrap telephone wire is always available.

Soft-Drink Companies: Wooden soft-drink crates are available at a minimal charge. Painted bright colors (children may do this in small numbers using leftover latex paint) they serve as excellent substitutes for the commercial hollow blocks. A set of casters on one will create a durable wagon for hauling blocks or friends. Set the casters in far enough to allow stacking. Wet strength fiberboard beer cases are excellent storage units. The children can easily handle them.

Ice Cream Stores: Ask at your favorite restaurant for their empty 3 gallon cardboard ice cream containers. Uses range from space helmets through spatter paint screen forms.

Gas Stations and Garages: Here you may obtain tires for playground swings, inner tubes to supplement materials at the carpentry table, and bottle caps from the drink machines. You may find a garage willing to cut the steering wheel from a wrecked automobile for the children to use in their play. Old tractor tires make fabulous bouncy sand boxes.

Wallpaper Stores: Wallpaper books of discontinued patterns are usually available on the first come, first serve basis. Use textured sheets for easel painting. Those with fabric samples are especially nice. Precut samples make excellent puppet skirts.

Carpet Shop: Many carpet shops have samples of discontinued rug patterns available for 10¢ a piece. Larger samples cost more but can be used as rest mats. Here, too, you will find the soft foam underpadding pieces.

Tile Stores: Tile stores frequently have broken patterns of mosaic tile available for a minimal charge. Children enjoy matching, counting, and creating with these colorful squares. You can supplement by making parquetry boards on cardboard.

Boat Rentals and Marinas: At the beginning or end of the season, many rowboats or sailboats no longer "seaworthy" are destroyed.

If you can find a truck and some help, they are yours.

Moving Companies: Overseas moving companies may occasionally part with a large, amazingly well-built packing crate for the cost of transportation. They make excellent play houses. It's worth a try. . . .

Print Shops: Print shops have assorted sizes of "scrap" paper. . . . Leave a box under the counter of [your] favorite print shop, and go to empty it every 2 weeks or so. Colored cardboard tickets, letter sheets, and all sorts of paper for collage can be obtained this way.

Builders and Road Construction: New construction offers at least the possibility of obtaining an unused sewer pipe for the playground.

Paint Shops: Paint color cards are fun color experiences and excellent collage. Old paint brushes are great for painting buildings with water. Cardboard paint buckets made the ball and bean bag game.

Fabric Shops or Departments: Stores that carry material dispose of the inner cardboard form which makes an excellent plaque for children's artwork. You may also find ribbon scraps to add to your art materials and fabric remnants if you don't get enough from sewing mothers.

Home: Dress-up clothes (maternity tops are ideal, need no hemming), ties, shoes (men's and women's), hats, costume jewelry. Old petticoats make lovely skirts, frilly nylon blouses, a bridal veil can be made by attaching old curtains to a clip hat. (Supplement by thrift shop sales.)

Empty food containers for store or building, paper towel rolls, empty detergent bottles, bleach bottles, cookie sheets for easy to clean finger painting, buttons, spools for bubble blowing, flashlight, yarn, scraps of material, empty egg cartons, aluminum pie plates, small juice cans and baby food jars for easel, newspapers for paper-mâché, magazines for cutting and pasting, scarves for dancing (dyed cheesecloth will work equally well) as butterflies, wind, kites; empty shoe polish bottles to refill with paint, cracker crumb container for sprinkling sand over glue patterns. [Quill, no date, pp. 2–3]

You must also remain constantly aware of the new supplies that are being developed commercially for preschool youngsters. However, creative teachers have for many years transformed "junk" materials into some very creative and valuable classroom tools. One teacher designed and created these "junk" toys:

1. Stacked cans—Easy to do. Use assorted sizes and colors of cans and ask the children to stack them in sequential order.

2. Color lotto—Squares of construction paper mounted on cardboard and covered with clear contact. Children match the colored squares.

3. Parquetry—Floor covering samples used as pattern tiles for sorting and counting activities. Tiles are available in several sizes and can be used to create individual or patterned designs.

4. Sound shakers—Small plastic 30mm film containers filled with various materials—rice, beans, toothpicks, screws. Seal the lids. Which is loud, which is soft?

Choose only equipment that leads to the fulfillment of the basic goals of your program. Although some preschool programs require special equipment (for example, typewriters, programmed materials, videotape equipment) to achieve their goals, some basic supplies and materials are commonly found in most preschool settings. A listing of that basic equipment is presented here. As you read through the list, you should observe that it is a *general list*, which is not representative of all schools.

INFANT MATERIALS

mobiles	bounce chairs
rocking chairs	small bathtubs
cribs	green plants
rattles	record player
soft terry or sponge	plastic bracelets
toys	household items
cradle gyms	pacifiers

nesting toys	texture books
wall mirror	wind chimes
yarn balls	music boxes
hand mirrors (safe)	

ART AREA

easels	crayons
paint	pencils
brushes	tablets
clay	construction paper
paste	marking pens
scissors	aprons or smocks
yarn	junk box (variety of
drawing paper	materials)

LARGE MUSCLE ACTIVITY AREA

balance boards	jungle gym
wagons	tunnels
tricycles	sandbox
traffic signs	ladders
wheelbarrow	blocks
trucks	platforms
tractors	

DRAMATIC PLAY AREA

furniture	variety of dress-up
puppets	clothes
puppet stage	dolls
	props

LIBRARY AREA

books	experience stories
chairs	tape recorder
carpet	record player
catalogs	flannelboards
homemade books	pictures

MANIPULATIVE AREA

dominoes	Tinkertoys
beads	nesting toys
puzzles	blocks
dressing frames	table games (such
lotto games	as "Candy Land")
pegboards and pegs	

WOODWORKING AREA

hammers	paintbrushes
nails	paint (tempera or
soft wood	poster)
screwdriver	pliers
screws	saws

files
vise
wrench
planes
nuts and bolts

hand drills
workbench
sandpaper
rulers

WATER AND SAND PLAY AREA

plastic wading pool
funnels
food coloring
various containers
water table with
  dishpan
coffee pots

doll clothes
construction
  equipment
squirt bottles
sponges
detergent
straws

MUSIC SUPPLIES

piano
autoharp
guitar
record player
records
rhythm sticks
bells
triangles

xylophones
drums
tape recorder
shakers
tambourines
handmade
  instruments

SCIENCE CORNER

balancing scales
magnets
seeds
gardening tools
plants
simple machines
aquarium
terrarium
animals

rocks
seashells
compasses
magnifying glasses
various materials to
  dismantle (such
  as clocks, pencil
  sharpeners, old
  toys)

Choosing the classroom materials and deciding how to use them are only two of the three major decisions necessary for organizing the curriculum. The third, *planning the schedule of activity,* answers questions such as: "What should I have the children do first?" "How often should the children rest?" "When do I ask the children to change from one activity to another?" "Should I follow the same basic routine each day?"

Planning a Daily Schedule Planning the daily schedule as a framework for your curriculum is important for these reasons:

1. It provides a basic time structure into which you can plan activities.

2. It gives the children a sequential guide by which they can plan a series of classroom activities with minimal guidance from the teacher. John, for example, moved from the block corner to the bathroom to urinate. He washed his hands and sat down at the snack table with the other children. Following the snack, he headed directly to the carpeted area to hear a story from the teacher. At no time did John need to be told what to do—this basic sequence of events occured each day and John had adjusted to the routine. Children need such established routine to feel safe and comfortable; they gain confidence in doing for themselves what is expected of them. A frequent cause of misbehavior or anxiety in young children is a quickly changing environment that is unplanned and unorganized.

3. It accommodates the parents who need to know when to arrive with their children, when to pick them up, when to arrive for a special event, or when to visit for a special purpose.

Sample time plans describing the difference between a full-day and half-day program were presented in Chapter 1. Tables 14-2 to 14-4 illustrate time plans reflecting the philosophical emphases of different programs for half-day programs.

As you compared and contrasted these daily schedules, it should have been apparent how the philosophy of the program dictates the amount of time spent on the various activities and, in particular, exactly what activities are provided for the children. Whatever the chosen direction, however, always keep the children in mind, for their interest (or lack of it) may require adjustments to the framework. The inflexible teacher who stops a child just before she "puts her baby to sleep" in the doll corner may have destroyed in one minute all

Table 14—2   *Time Plan for Informal Program*

9:00–10:30	Free-choice activities—children are able to explore whatever games, toys, or equipment have been chosen for display. They may listen to records or play with blocks, puzzles, cuisenaire rods, and so on. These activities are selected to foster certain skills, concepts, or attitudes for that day, week, or month. The teacher or aide works with individuals or small groups on selected materials.
10:30–10:45	Snack time
10:45–11:00	Group time—this period is devoted to large-group activities such as singing, listening to a story, sharing, or participating in a group project such as cooking. These activities are designed to develop skills in all areas of the child's development.
11:00–11:30	Outdoor play
11:30	Dismissal

Table 14—3   *Time Plan for Skills-Oriented Program*

8:00–8:30	Staff planning
8:30–8:45	Greeting
8:45–9:05	Instruction period 1—children are assigned to the reading, mathematics, or handwriting group.
9:05–9:30	Special activity 1—children exchange tokens acquired during the instructional period for art projects, puzzles, outdoor play, or games in which they might be interested.
9:30–9:50	Instruction period 2—children move to a group dealing with another skills area.
9:50–10:15	Special activity 2 (choices like those in special activity 1)
10:15–10:30	Snack time
10:30–10:50	Instruction period 3
10:50–11:15	Special activity 3
11:15–11:30	Dismissal

Table 14—4   *Time Plan for Cognitive Developmental Program*

8:30–8:45	Greeting as children arrive
8:45–9:05	Planning time—children select activities in which they would like to work.
9:05–9:45	The children work in self-selected areas: the art area, large motor area, doll corner, or quiet area.
9:45–10:00	Cleanup—put away materials and equipment and use toilet facilities.
10:00–10:15	Juice time
10:15–10:45	Group time—teacher and aides work on special concepts with small groups of children.
10:45–11:10	Activity time: (indoors) music or circle games; (outdoors) playground equipment
11:10–11:30	Circle time—review what was done during the day.
11:30	Dismissal

the good things that had transpired in the previous 20 minutes. Certainly, an extra minute or two for that particular child would have made the activity a valuable learning experience. And extending an unpopular activity beyond its usefulness would be just as detrimental to your program as cutting off activities that are popular. By keeping a sensitive eye on the children and interpreting their reactions to daily activities, you can adjust the time blocks in your daily schedule and provide for the individual needs and interests of your children.

Up to this point in our program decision-making process, you have (1) identified a basic framework upon which to build, (2) formulated a set of goals to be achieved, and (3) chosen the teaching strategies and materials to help you reach those goals. Now comes the task of deciding which methods to use to judge how well your program has influenced the children's growth and development. That is, you are asking, "How effectively are my methods and materials helping the children progress toward the program goals?" The answers to this question constitute the last part of the decision-making process: *evaluation.*

Evaluating the Program

On our vacation to Florida, we may often hear two kinds of comments: "Wow, that was a lot of fun—I really enjoyed it," and "Let's go somewhere else—this is a bore." The experiences we have are constantly being judged as good, bad, or indifferent on the basis of how well they fullfilled our original expectations. Naturally, if the experiences are judged good, we are happy about our choices and satisfied with the trip. If the experiences do not meet our vacation expectations, we may feel negative or hostile, and our vacation goals may not be accomplished.

In the same way, you should constantly look at the goals of your program to judge whether they are being accomplished in a suc-

cessful and enjoyable manner. To do so, you must thoroughly understand the process of evaluation, for without such knowledge your teaching effectiveness and relations with the parents may be jeopardized. Before we examine the various evaluation processes, however, let's establish what evaluation is. *Evaluation* can be considered to be any formal or informal process by which teachers gather and analyze pupil data to determine whether changes should be made in the program to meet unique individual needs and interests more adequately. Many formal and informal techniques can be used to evaluate the progress of young children. These are discussed in the following sections.

Teacher Observation   Simply watching the children during the school day is perhaps the most popular technique for evaluating young children's skills, interests, understandings, feelings, emotions, or social abilities in the preschool. Data gathered during this type of evaluation procedure are normally recorded on one or both of these types of recording forms: (1) *anecdotal record forms* or (2) *checklists.*

Teachers often prefer to record short, but detailed comments about a child based on observations of his activity in the preschool setting. These comments, often jotted on 3-inch × 5-inch index cards, should describe only the child's behavior, not your interpretation of that behavior. For example, one misguided teacher made this comment about Arnie and included it in his permanent file: "Arnie caused a disruption in the block corner today by pinching Jerome. His social skills are much below the other children and may cause him problems in first grade." By recording your opinion, especially after experiencing some negative aspect of the child's behavior, you run the danger of stereotyping that child for the remainder of his school experience. How many times have we seen youngsters live up to the expectancies we establish for them (self-

---

NAME ___Johnny Smith_____   AGE ___4 yrs. 6 mos._____

Monday (10-18-80)

    Worked for 20 minutes alone in the mathematics corner. Johnny now recognizes the numerals 1-10 and can place the number of corresponding objects with each numeral. He still becomes upset, though, when he leaves his mother in the morning.

Wednesday (10-20-80)

    Johnny worked at solitary activities again today and experienced a tantrum when asked to share a toy with another child. He appears to be reluctant to work with others or to share his possessions with them.

Figure 14-2   *Sample anecdotal card*

fullfilling prophecy)? If you must enter negative comments about children, balance them with positive comments so that future teachers will be aware of the child's strengths as well as his weaknesses. A sample anecdotal card for one child is illustrated in Figure 14-2.

These general suggestions should help you as you prepare anecdotal comments about individual children:

1. Record only the child's behavior and avoid making hasty judgments about that behavior.

2. Avoid stereotyping a child by predicting future behavior in terms of past experiences.

3. Refrain from viewing overconforming children too favorably and underconforming children unfavorably. One of the primary characteristics of highly creative youngsters is their inability to conform to normal routines or expectancies. We often shut off their creative potential by forcing them into patterns that destroy their originality and desire for uniqueness.

4. Record only the material that is useful. All too often, we teachers bury ourselves under mounds of observational data that lack focus. To make our observations useful, remember to select only those behaviors that describe a particular dimension of an individual's behavior.

Normally, anecdotal records are kept only for those few children who need to be observed for some special reason—temper tantrums or destructive behavior, for example. Whenever observations of all the children need to be made, *checklists* can be particularly useful. Checklists contain items that can focus on many areas of children's development and can be filled out in a much shorter period of time than can anecdotal records. A sample checklist is illustrated in Figure 14-3. It is a very short, somewhat imprecise form, but space limitations prohibit the use of more complicated, highly detailed forms used by some teachers.

Work Samples   Many preschool teachers maintain folders containing work samples for each child. Naturally, not every piece of each

PRESCHOOL CHECKLIST

	Inappropriate for age	Appropriate for age
1. Visual acuity		
2. Visual discrimination		
3. Left-to-right sequence		
4. Auditory acuity		
5. Auditory discrimination		
6. Listens to stories		
7. Follows simple directions		
8. Articulates common sounds		
9. Uses appropriate words and sentences		
10. Conversations with others		
11. Large motor coordination		
12. Small motor skills		
13. Cooperates with other children		
14. Attends to personal needs		
15. Self-confidence (feelings of adequacy)		
16. Attention span		
17. Accepts limits		
18. Respects adults		
19. Recognizes numerals 1-10		
20. Distinguishes among the basic shapes		
21. Knows the eight basic colors		
22. Recognizes own name in print		
23. Interest in learning		
24. Respects classroom materials		
25. Curious about the environment		
26. Works independently		

Figure 14-3   *Sample evaluation checklist*

child's work is kept for the folder, only periodic samples throughout the school year. Some teachers prefer to take weekly, bi-weekly, or monthly samples, which they date and place into the child's folder. In this way, the teacher can look at a child's former work and compare it to what he is now doing. This accumulation of work gives the teacher an idea of how well an individual is progressing and of what steps might be necessary to reinforce certain areas of development.

Tests Many early childhood professionals agree that _subjective_ means of evaluation (that is, anecdotal records, checklists, and work samples) are important, but they argue that more specific measures are necessary in order to give an unbiased view of the child's progress. Such specific measures, referred to as _objective_ tests, are useful, but only if they are properly carried out. Helen Robinson (1977) explained some difficulties in testing young children:

> It is not easy to test young children. They react to the tester, the test situation, and to their inner needs with much less inhibition than older children or adults. Test results with young children are notoriously _unreliable_. You can get wildly different results on the same test within a brief period. The _validity_ of many tests for young children is difficult to establish. The test may or may not measure what it purports to measure, and what it purports to measure may not be a valid indication of the child's development or learning. Children's sef-concepts, for example, are a very relevant aspect of child development. So far, however, it has not been satisfactorily established that any of the instruments or procedures used for testing reliably reflect this construct. [p. 531]

Keeping these problems in mind, educators nonetheless find tests to be a valuable measure in determining to what degree their program goals have been met. Their proce-

dure in doing so usually consists of administering a _pretest_ as well as a _posttest_. The pretest measures the child's abilities as he enters the program, and the posttest gives an indication of how much he has grown as a result of it. Some means of continual evaluation is recommended for children who appear to have the greatest needs.

As with the tests themselves, the pre- and posttest procedure may have its shortcomings. For example, I can recall with horror observing the testing program designed for infants of low socioeconomic parents. During the pretest phase, the infants were kept waiting in groups of three or four with their parents while another child was being tested in a separate room. Naturally, feeding and rest schedules were disrupted as the infants were kept waiting for their turns, some for as long as one hour. The children became cranky and often cried as a result of the wait, but when they were separated from their mothers for testing, they became even more anxious and disruptive. I expressed my concern to the tester as to the reliability of the pretest since the infants were in such an unsettled environment. "Oh, don't worry," was the reply, "we want low scores on the pretest. We'll control the situation more effectively on the posttest and get greater positive results for the program than people would expect!" Testing, then, is open to many misuses, so whenever you need to use tests of any kind, be sure to do so in a professional manner.

There are many standardized, formal tests for preschool youngsters, mostly _achievement_ or _intelligence_ tests. _Achievement tests_ are the type you probably remember most. They measure certain skills and abilities that result from instruction (reading, math, language, and so on). The type of achievement test that seems to be most popular among preschool teachers is the _readiness test,_ a measure designed to indicate whether or not a child possesses the prerequisite abilities necessary to begin formal instruction. The most widely used readiness test is the Metropolitan Reading Readiness Test.

Intelligence tests are designed to measure a child's inherent ability for cognitive or creative functioning. (See samples of test-items in the "Intelligence Test-items" box.) The widely controversial IQ test is perhaps the most popular intelligence test. IQ tests have been roundly criticized in recent years for several reasons.

1. IQ scores reflect cultural bias because they were developed for the white middle-class youngster. This bias, then, accounts for one's score on the test.

2. IQ tests are used in ways to stereotype a child. Many educators have falsely used IQ scores to predict children's progress through school.

3. IQ scores were originally thought to be fixed throughout life and not affected by the child's environment. Surely, the experimentation of the 1960s put an end to this myth.

In recent years, educators have begun to seek a more comprehensive view of intelligence than merely a score on an IQ test. They have begun placing heavy emphasis on the processes of problem solving and creative thought. Tests of these processes assess the child's ability to think in logical, fluent, and original ways while solving unique problems.

Despite their problems, if they are used properly, achievement and intelligence tests can be effective measures of how well each child in your room compares to other children of the same age level. For example, you may find that the child's score of 105 on a reading readiness test places him at the 75th percentile. This means that when compared to all children taking the test, he scored in the top 25 percent. Such information is important, but should not be used as the sole source of information about a child.

Formal tests, then, provide early childhood educators with important measures of

intellectual and achievement levels if they are treated in a professional manner. The most appropriate professional use seems to be when such measures are utilized in conjunction with other evaluation techniques for the purpose of improving instruction.

Children's Self-Evaluation A final and less frequently used form of evaluation in the preschool setting is the process of children's self-evaluation. Often we are surprised at the reactions of children when they are given an opportunity to evaluate themselves and their day at school. Remember that children are not informed educational critics and cannot evaluate your pedagogical methods, but they are quite willing to let you know whether your routines and activities are pleasing or not. You can often gain important feedback when you informally ask questions such as: "What did you think about school today?" "What did you enjoy most this morning? Least?" "Show me that you can skip."

Some simple types of record forms can be used for student self-evaluation, especially if you are using learning centers in your classroom. They can gather information about how meaningful, interesting, enjoyable, or appropriate the children found the centers to be. Two special self-evaluation checklists are shown in Figure 14-4.

Obviously, most preschool youngsters will be unable to read the directions on the self-evaluation record forms. They were placed on the form simply to describe the kind of statement you may wish to read or say to the children as they respond. Because children's standards of appreciation may be much different from your own, these bits of feedback may offer valuable information to the wise teacher who welcomes and respects the opinions of the children she teaches.

The lists on p. 524 describe ways in which the three philosophically different programs we have been discussing might evaluate their own effectiveness.

INTELLIGENCE TEST-ITEMS

Auditory Perception

Number and Syllable Recall: Ask the child to repeat three series of two digits (example: 4–6, 3–8, and 9–2); then move to three series of three digits (example: 2–8–9, 7–1–3, and 4–5–9); and finally to three series of four digits (example: 3–5–1–7, 4–2–9–6, and 7–3–8–2).

The same procedure can be used as you ask the child to repeat 2 syllables:

a. green car

b. big boy

c. cold ice

6–7 syllables:

a. The dog barked at the man.

b. The girl kicked the red ball.

c. I jumped over the fence.

12–13 syllables:

a. The little kitten was frightened by the big brown dog.

b. We all played outdoors on the warm, sunny day.

c. Jimmy kicked the big blue ball over the tall fence.

Visual Memory

Sit across a table from a child. On the table are six commonly used objects, such as a block, ball, crayon, scissors, clay, and toy horse. Tell the child you are going to play a game and that he must close his eyes. While his eyes are closed, you remove one of the objects. The child must identify the missing object when he reopens his eyes.

Perception

Have a set of beads that vary in size, shape, and color. Make a model for the child and ask him to repeat it.

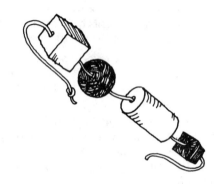

Visual Discrimination

Prepare a set of about ten cards on which a picture at the top serves as the model the child uses to choose a matching picture from among three pictures at the bottom. Ask the child to find which of the pictures at the bottom is most like the one at the top. Pictures may vary in color, design, or position.

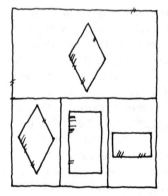
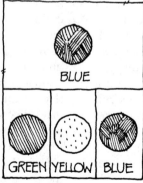
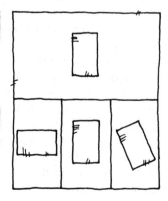

Conceptualization

Three common tasks, each having to do with body concept, may be used to judge conceptual development.

a. Glue a picture of a person on a large sheet of tagboard and cut it horizontally into five sections. Ask the child to put the person together.

b. Draw a picture of an incomplete man with the following parts missing: one ear, one eye, part of the hair, neck, one arm and hand, one leg and foot. Ask the child what is wrong with it.

c. Some tests prefer to ask the child to draw a complete person by himself. Judgments of conceptual maturity are made on the basis of how sophisticated the body is drawn.

Sequencing

Have a set of cards picturing objects familiar to the child. Ask him to place the cards in line so that the one with the fewest red balls comes first and the one with the most red balls comes last.

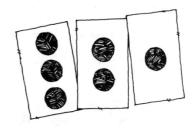

Vocabulary

Prepare ten cards, each containing three or four pictures showing different relationships among the elements. Ask the child to look at each picture and decide which one shows what you said. For example, you may say, "The box is *under* the table."

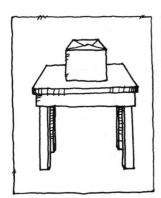

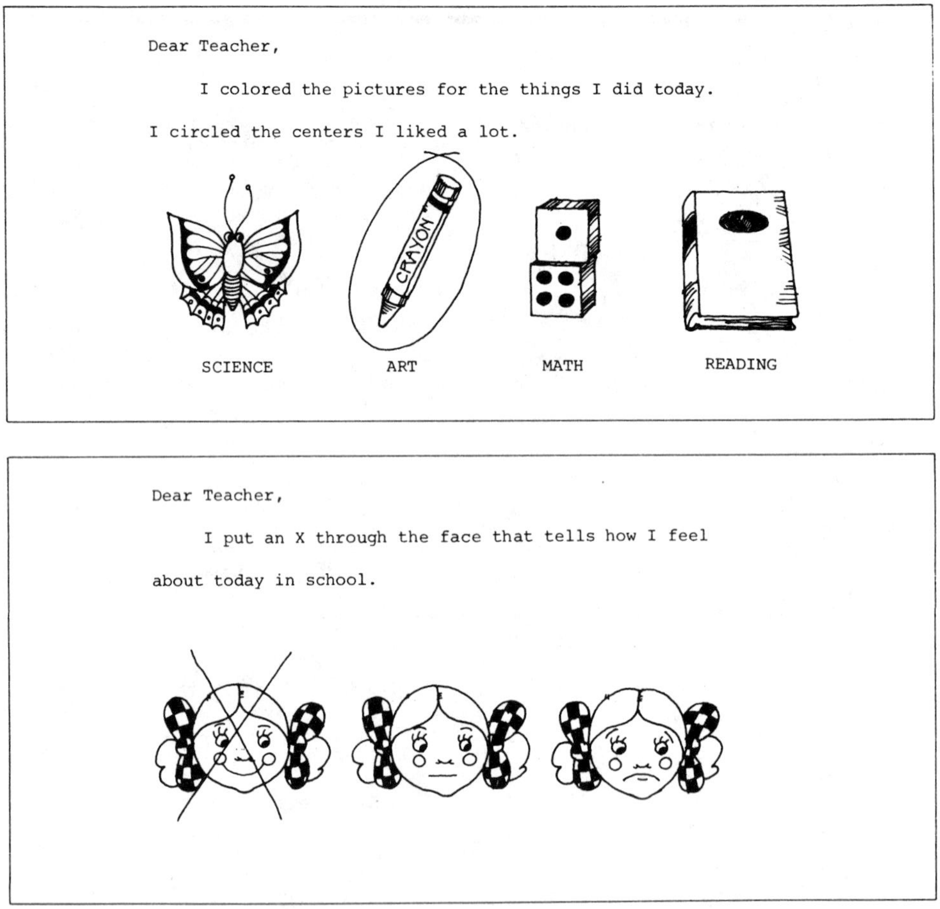

Dear Teacher,

    I colored the pictures for the things I did today.

I circled the centers I liked a lot.

SCIENCE   ART   MATH   READING

Dear Teacher,

    I put an X through the face that tells how I feel

about today in school.

Figure 14-4   *Two examples of self-evaluation checklists*

INFORMAL MODEL

1. Observation
2. Anecdotal records
3. Teacher checklists
4. Metropolitan Achievement Test
5. Self-evaluation

SKILLS-ORIENTED MODEL

1. Progress Achievement Test
   The Behavior Analysis Model
   Department of Human Development
   University of Kansas
   Lawrence, Kansas 66044

2. Teacher checklists
3. Observation
4. Achievement tests related to the curricular areas

COGNITIVE DEVELOPMENTAL MODEL

1. Stanford-Binet IQ test
2. Teacher checklists
3. Personality tests
4. Achievement tests
5. Tests of cognitive functioning (Piagetian tasks)

Sound, professional evaluation is a key to the success of preschool programs. It tells us how the programs need to be extended and enriched in order to make each youngster's schooling experience personally rewarding and profitable. Every preschool educator should strive to formulate an evaluation plan that is consistent with the basic philosophy of the established program and to interpret the results of such feedback in ways that will ensure that each child's unique educational needs can be met.

KNOWING WHETHER YOU ARE A GOOD TEACHER

Related to continuous growth in teaching is the ability to evaluate whether or not you are doing an effective job at any given time. There are many sources of such evidence, including these:

1. *Feedback from the children.* Young children are openly honest about their feelings. Often their reactions toward you and your activities effectively communicate acceptance and affection or rejection and apathy.

2. *Feedback from your associates.* Other professionals often are a valuable source of information about your teaching effectiveness. Accept such advice from your colleagues in an open way and realize that they are being helpful by offering it to you. Positive feedback is often welcomed and openly accepted, but negative feedback is helpful, too. However, the tendency of many teachers is to accept positive feedback eagerly because it is a valuable ego booster while initially rejecting or angrily reacting to negative feedback because it is a blow to one's pride. However, in order to improve, it is necessary to pay equal

attention to both forms of evaluative feedback and to examine your practices on its basis.

3. *Feedback from parents.* Parents often provide an important source of information related to your effectiveness as a teacher. You will find that they frequently shy away from beginning teachers until they prove themselves. These parents will often justify such behaviors with reasons such as: "Mrs. Lawrence has been in this school for fifteen years. She knows more about my child than that new teacher." Or, "Mrs. Jemison has her own young children and that new teacher doesn't have any. I'll trust Mrs. Jemison before that new teacher." One way of telling how successful you are is the speed at which this attitude changes. Are parents opening up to you and seeking your advice? Other sources of feedback include candid statements from parents about their feelings toward you, willingness of parents to help in your program, enthusiasm of parents to carry out your suggestions in the home, and friendly gestures such as gifts or dinner invitations.

If your feedback indicates a need for improvement, your willingness to change is an essential part of a healthy approach to teaching. By being reluctant to change, you often bring about recurring professional and personal frustrations that can be reflected in your teaching. Getting up in the morning and dragging yourself to work becomes routine. You become dissatisfied with your work, depressed, and exhausted. You soon find yourself inwardly screaming, "Let me out of here!" To some, you've become a victim of what is commonly becoming known as "teacher burnout." Burnout can appear at any time during a career and occur at three levels:

• *First-degree burnout (mild):* Short-lived bouts of irritability, fatigue, worry, and frustration.

- *Second-degree burnout (moderate):* Same as mild but lasts for two weeks or more.

- *Third-degree burnout (severe):* Physical ailments occur such as ulcers, chronic back pain, migraine headaches, and so on.

Many sources of irritation, ranging from inadequate professional training to concerns about salary and increasing clerical duties, can contribute to such conditions. Mild and moderate burnout are the easiest to remedy. They require a simple "recharging" of your career. Consider these suggestions:

1. Break away from established routines and consider new challenges, including switching to a new group of children.

2. Try to communicate to others the necessity of providing positive feedback. Nothing helps more than a friendly compliment. Practice this technique and encourage others to do likewise.

3. Keep alert to changing methods and activities. Attend conferences, workshops, and in-service programs designed to introduce you to new ideas.

4. Join organizations in the community or socialize with people outside the profession. Often we tend to overwork ourselves by talking only about school after hours.

5. Do something different in the summer. Find a job completely divorced from early childhood education or take a relaxed vacation. Renew your spirits and your energies by forgetting about your profession for a short period of time.

6. Avoid making picky little demands. Often, insignificant demands are blown out of proportion and cause strained relations between you and your supervisor.

Severe burnouts are the most difficult to remedy and require the most extreme remedial procedures. Mortimer Feinberg recommends the following: "First, we have to determine if the depression is internalized. If you have trouble sleeping, no appetite or sexual drive, emotional outbursts of anger, you probably have internalized kinds of problems and need professional counseling. Maybe the solution is retirement or changing jobs. (1979, p. 57)."

This last recommendation may appear harsh, but it was offered by an outstanding consultant who has worked with many depressed, burned-out people. The general feeling is that the health of our educational system depends upon the mental attitudes of its teachers. By being aware of the different stages, you may be able to take steps to head off further progress of the condition and eliminate professional weariness. This "revival" aspect of professional development may seem to be insignificant or one that can be cynically attacked, but it nevertheless provides interesting fuel for thought should boredom and fatigue begin to enter your professional frame of mind.

SOME FINAL THOUGHTS

Effective teachers are effective, logical decision makers. They must examine the current recommendations of early childhood professionals, weigh the consequences of each alternative form, and settle on a program that is satisfactory for the parents, the children, and themselves. This is a challenging task, and one that should be enthusiastically met by those who are ready to enter the field. Nothing can be as exciting and rewarding as molding and creating a personal program that dynamically grows and develops under your careful guidance. The true reward of developing such a program comes not from weekly paychecks or outstanding observation reports but from your tingling spine when, on the last day of school at the end of the year, a tearful group of youngsters announce, "I don't want to go home. School was so much fun this year."

The following list summarizes the major decisions necessary for effective program development. Examine it as you begin to design your personal plan for the parents and children you are to serve.

- *Philosophy:* How do I view the development of the child? What theory best explains the process of learning?

- *Goals:* What are the needs of the parents? The children? What do I hope to achieve?

- *Curriculum:* What is my role? The child's role? What materials and activities will be used? How will I arrange the classroom? How will I schedule the daily activities?

- *Evaluation:* To what extent did my program achieve its goal? How favorably do my children compare to others of the same age and background?

What you may end up with after studying these questions is an *eclectic approach.* When describing the eclectic approach, I think of the well-meaning student a few years back who reacted in a very concerned voice when a professor announced that he was *eclectic.* "Oh my," said the student, "how serious a problem is it?" Stunned, the professor went on to explain that being eclectic was not a health problem, but an approach to teaching that selects several aspects of different learning theories and combines them into a personalized strategy. Some educators agree that each theory has something valuable to offer and that combining aspects of each approach can be a valuable part of a true child-oriented classroom. They find it difficult to accept the view that any one single learning theory can effectively explain a process so personal and complex as the learning process.

These educators also believe that all teachers are, in a sense, eclectic, and that it is nearly impossible to plan an early childhood program that avoids eclecticism. For example, you may accept the behaviorists' contention that reinforcement of correct responses encourages learning while rejecting their ideas regarding structure and strict teacher direction. You may wish to pattern your basic instructional program, instead, after Piaget's philosophy, and do so within an informal classroom environment. Whether you choose one basic theory to follow or seek to combine the strengths of several into your personalized philosophy, the main thing is to examine the needs of your children and to choose the technique that seems to have the greatest potential for encouraging their success.

A Final Word from Your Author

You are on your way to becoming a professional in the field of early childhood education. That is certainly an exciting prospect and one with a great amount of responsibility, for you are now at the point of your professional development where you are expected to make personal, informed decisions regarding the principles and practices you will use with any group of preschool children. The decisions you make and the ways in which you carry them through make you one of the most important factors in the future growth and development of each child with whom you have contact. This is a tremendous responsibility and one that must not be taken lightly. You will need to think and act on your own, without the immediate aid of Jean Piaget, B. F. Skinner, your instructor, your classmates, your textbooks, and other aids. Don't feel alone, though—every teacher must go through the process: "How do I do that?" "If only I had a chance to talk with my college instructor!" "Where can I get help?" And don't stop looking for answers to your questions or concerns. Make your future the brightest one possible by constantly growing in your field. Strive toward self-improvement and for increased professionalism. Although your career will be filled with hard work, your efforts will be rewarded with smiling faces and hugs aplenty. Best wishes for a long and fruitful career with young children.

As you progress through the approaching stages of your professional career, make every effort to keep up with what's new in the field. Look for magazines and professional organizations recognized as having a productive record in helping our young children. Some of the popular ones are listed on the next page.

528

PROFESSIONAL ORGANIZATIONS

National Association for the
Education of Young Children
(NAEYC)
1834 Connecticut Avenue, N.W.
Washington, D.C. 20009

Association for Childhood
Education International (ACEI)
3615 Wisconsin Avenue, N.W.
Washington, D.C. 20016

National Education Association
(NEA)
1201 16th Street, N.W.
Washington, D.C. 20036

Child Welfare League of America
(Day Care)
44 East 23rd Street
New York, New York 10010

Day Care and Child Development
Council of America
1401 K Street, N.W.
Washington, D.C. 20005

American Association of
Elementary-Kindergarten-Nursery
Educators
1201 16th Street, N.W.
Washington, D.C. 20036

Educational Resources Information
Center/Early Childhood Education
(ERIC/ECE)
805 West Pennsylvania Avenue
Urbana, Illinois 61801

American Montessori Society
(AMS)
175 Fifth Avenue
New York, New York 10010

MAGAZINES AND JOURNALS

Young Children (Journal of NAEYC)
National Association for the
Education of Young Children
1834 Connecticut Avenue, N.W.
Washington, D.C. 20009

Childhood Education (Journal of ACEI)
Association for Childhood
Education International
3615 Wisconsin Avenue, N.W.
Washington, D.C. 20016

Today's Education (Journal of NEA)
National Education Association
1201 16th Street, N.W.
Washington, D.C. 20036

Day Care and Early Education
Human Science Press
72 Fifth Avenue
New York, New York 10011

Early Years
Allen Raymond, Inc.
P.O. Box 1223
11 Hale Lane
Darien, Connecticut 06820

Teacher
Macmillan Professional Magazines,
Inc.
262 Mason Street
Greenwich, Conneticut 06830

Instructor
The Instructor Publications, Inc.
P.O. Box 6099
Duluth, Minnesota 55806

Learning
Education Today Company, Inc.
530 University Avenue
Palo Alto, California 94301

References

Abt Associates, Inc. *Education as experimentation: A planned variation approach.* Cambridge, Mass.: Abt Associates, 1977.

Adams, P. K., and Taylor, M. K. Liability: How much do you really know? *Day Care and Early Education,* Spring 1981, *8,* 15–18.

Allen, K. E., and Hart, B. *The early years.* Englewood Cliffs, N.J.: Prentice-Hall, 1984.

Aries, P. *Centuries of childhood.* New York: Vantage Books, 1962.

Armstrong, R. D., and Gage, W. J. In L. M. Logan, V. G. Logan, and L. Paterson (Eds.), *Creative communication: Teaching the language arts.* Montreal: McGraw-Hill Ryerson Limited, 1972.

Aukerman, R. C. *Approaches to beginning reading.* New York: Wiley, 1971.

Baker, K. R., and Fane, X. F. *Understanding and guiding young children.* Englewood Cliffs, N.J.: Prentice-Hall, 1971.

Bandura, A., and Walters, R. *Social learning and personality development.* New York: Holt, Rinehart and Winston, 1963.

Barman, A. S. Four-year-old development. In J. Wylie (Ed.), *A creative guide for preschool teachers.* (no city given): Western Publishing, 1969.

Barnes, K. Preschool play norms: A replication. *Developmental Psychology,* 1971, *51,* 99–103.

Baumrind, D., New directions in socialization research. *American Psychologist,* 1980, *35,* 639–652.

Bell, R. Q., and Harper, L. V. *The effect of children on parents.* Hillsdale, N.J.: Erlbaum Associates, 1977.

Belsky, J., and Steinberg, L. D. What does research teach us about day care: A follow-up report. *Children Today,* July–August 1979, 21–26.

Bereiter, C., and Englemann, C. Observations on the use of direct instruction with young disadvantaged children. *Journal of School Psychology,* Spring 1966, *4,* 56–58.

Bierstedt, R. *The social order* (4th ed.). New York: McGraw-Hill, 1974.

Birch, H. G., and Gussow, J. D. *Disadvantaged children: Health, nutrition and school failure.* New York: Harcourt, Brace and World, 1970.

Birch, L. The turtle's corner. *Classroom Computer News,* April 1983, *3,* 29–32.

Black, I. S. (Ed.). *More about readiness experiences* (to accompany *Bank Street readers*). New York: Macmillan, 1972.

Bloom, B. S. *Stability and change in human characteristics.* New York: Wiley, 1964.

Bower, T. G. R. *A primer of infant development.* San Francisco: W. H. Freeman, 1977.

Brazelton, T. B., in Berkman, S. See the baby. See the better baby. *American Baby,* May 1984, *46,* 58–61; 70–80.

Broman, B. C. *The early years in childhood education.* Chicago: Rand McNally, 1978.

Bronfenbrenner, U. Contexts of child rearing: Problems and prospects. *American Psychologist,* 1979, *34,* 844–850.

Bruner, J. S. *The process of education.* Cambridge, Mass.: Harvard University Press, 1960.

Bruner, J. S. Play is serious business. *Psychology Today,* 1975, *8,* 80–83.

Buchanan, C. D., and Dodson, B. *Programmed reading: Teacher's guide to the primer.* St. Louis: Webster Division, McGraw-Hill, 1973.

Burns, S. F. Children's art: A vehicle for learning. *Young children,* March 1975, *30,* 201.

Burrows, A. T. Children's language. In Paul S. Anderson (Ed.), *Linguistics in the elementary school classroom.* New York: Macmillan, 1971.

Butler, A., Gotts, E. E., and Quisenberry, N. L. *Play as development.* Columbus, Ohio: Charles E. Merrill, 1978.

Caldwell, B. M. Aggression and hostility in young children. *Young Children,* 1977, *32,* 4–13.

Caldwell, B. M. Mother-infant interaction in monomatric and polymatric families. *American Journal of Orthopsychiatry,* July 1963, *33,* 653–664.

Cazden, C. B. Suggestions from studies of early language acquisition. In DeStefano, J. S., and S. E. Fox (Eds.), *Language and the language arts.* Boston: Little, Brown, 1974.

Chandler, E. O. Verses taken from her handwritten notebook. Cited in S. J. Braun and E. P. Edwards. *History and theory of early childhood education.* Belmont, Calif.: Wadsworth, 1972.

Charlesworth, R. *Understanding child development*. Albany, New York: Delmar Publishers, 1983.

Chukovsky, K. From two to five (M. Morton, trans.). Berkeley, Calif.: University of California Press, 1963 and 1968.

Clifford, M., and Walster, E. The effect of physical attractiveness on teacher expectations. *Sociology of Education,* Spring 1973, *46,* 248–258.

Cohen, D.J., in collaboration with Brandegee, A.S. Serving Preschool Children. Washington, D.C.: Office of Child Development, 1975.

Cook, R. Report to Sargent Shriver, Director, Office of Economic Opportunity. Washington, D.C.: U.S. Government Printing Office, no date.

Craig, G. *Science for the elementary school teacher*. Boston: Ginn and Company, 1947.

Croft, D. J. *Parents and teachers*. Belmont, Calif.: Wadsworth, 1979.

Davis, H., and Silverman, S. R. (Eds.). *Hearing and deafness* (3rd ed.). New York: Holt, Rinehart and Winston, 1970.

D'Evelyn, K. E. *Individual parent-teacher conferences*. New York: Teacher's College Press, Columbia University, 1963.

deFrancis, V. The status of child protective services. In R. E. Helfer, and C. H. Kempe (Eds.), *Helping the battered child and his family*. Chicago: University of Chicago Press, 1968.

DeGuimps, R. *Pestalozzi: His life and work*. New York: D. Appleton, 1890.

Delacato, C. H. *The treatment and prevention of reading problems*. Springfield, Ill: Charles C Thomas, 1963.

DeMause, L. *The history of childhood*. New York: Psychohistory Press, 1974.

DeMause, L. Our forebears made childhood a nightmare. *Psychology Today,* April 1975, *8,* 85–88.

Deutsch, M. Facilitating development in the pre-school child: Social and psychological perspectives. *Merrill-Palmer Quarterly,* July 1964, *10,* 249–263.

Dion, K. Young children's stereotyping on facial attractiveness. *Developmental Psychology,* 1973, *9,* 183–188.

Dion, K. Physical attractiveness and evaluations of children's transgressions. *Journal of Personality and Social Psychology,* 1977, *24,* 207–213.

Duckworth, E. Piaget rediscovered. *ESS Newsletter,* June 1964, Elementary Science Study, Educational Services, Inc. Watertown, Mass., p. 3.

Duncan, G. 1., et al. (Eds.). Policies, procedures, and standards for certification of professional school personnel. Harrisburg: Pennsylvania Department of Education, 1977.

Durkin, D. *Teaching young children to read*. Boston: Allyn and Bacon, 1976.

Dworkin, M. S. *Dewey on education: Selections, with an introduction and notes*. New York: Teachers College Bureau of Publications, 1959.

Earle, J. *Microcosmography, or a piece of the world discovered in essays and characters*. London, 1934. In R. Aldington (Trans.), *A book of characters*. New York: Dutton, 1928.

Elkind, D. The case for the academic preschool: Fact or fiction? *Young Children,* January 1970, *25,* 133.

Engel, R. C. *Language motivating experiences for young children*. Van Nuys, Calif.: DFA Publishers, 1973.

Engelmann, S., and Becker, W. *Distar reading I*. Chicago: Science Research Associates, 1970.

Engelmann, S., and Bruner, E. C. *Distar reading I and II: Teacher's guide*. Chicago: Science Research Associates, 1969.

Engelmann, S., and Carnine, D. *Distar arithmetic I: An instructional system, Teacher's Guide*. Chicago: Science Research Associates, 1969.

Erikson, E. H. *Childhood and society*. New York: Norton, 1963.

Evertts, E. L., Weiss, B. J., and Cruikshank, S. B. *About me, Level 1: Teacher's Guide*. New York: Holt, Rinehart and Winston, 1977.

Fagg, L. F. Play today? *Young Children,* January 1975, *30,* 93.

Feinberg, M. Cited in (no author listed) Teacher burnout. *Instructor,* January 1979, *88,* 57.

Fernald, G. *Remedial techniques in basic school subjects*. New York: McGraw-Hill, 1943.

Fisk, L., and Lindgren, H. C. *Learning Centers:* Glen Ridge, N.J.: Exceptional Press, 1974.

Flesch, R. *Why Johnny can't read*. New York: Harper and Row, 1955.

Ford, P. L. The New England primer: A history of its origin and development. New York: Dodd, Mead, 1879.

Fordyce, W. K. A worm in the teacher's apple. *Childhood Education,* May/June 1982, *58,* 287–291.

Fowler, W. Cognitive learning in infancy and early childhood. *Psychology Bulletin,* February 1962, *25,* 116–152.

Frank, L. Play is valid. *Childhood Education,* March 1968, *44,* 433–440.

Frostig, M., and Horne, D. *The Frostig program for the development of visual perception.* Chicago: Follett, 1964.

Galbraith, R. E., and Jones, T. M. *Moral reasoning: A teaching handbook for adapting Kohlberg to the classroom.* Minneapolis, Minn.: Greenhaven Press, 1967.

Galin, D. Educating both halves of the brain. *Childhood Education,* 1976, *53,* 17–20.

Galler, B. Providing CDA training with an interactive model. *Young Children,* March 1981, *36,* 25–31.

Gander, M. J., and Gardiner, H. W. *Child and Adolescent Development.* Boston: Little, Brown, 1981.

Gearheart, B. R., and Litton, F. W. *The trainable retarded: A foundations approach* (2nd ed.). St. Louis: C. V. Mosby, Adapted from H. Grossman (Ed.). *Manual on terminology and classification in mental retardation.* Baltimore: Garamond/Pridemark Press, 1977.

Gesell, A. *The pre-school child: From the standpoint of public hygiene and education.* Boston: Houghton Mifflin, 1923.

Goertzel, V., and Goertzel, M. G. *Cradles of eminence.* Boston: Little, Brown, 1962.

Graham, L. B., and Persky, B. A. Who should work with young children? In L. B. Graham, and B. A. Persky, *Early childhood.* Wayne, N.J.: Avery Publishing Group, 1977.

Grant, E. The tale of Peter and the rabbit. *Phi Delta Kappa,* November 1967, *44,* back cover.

Greenberg, H. M. *Teaching with feeling.* New York: Macmillan, 1969.

Griffiths, R. *A study of imagination in early childhoodanditsfunctioninmentaldevelopment.* London: Trench, Trucher, and Company, 1935.

Guilford, J. P. *The nature of human intelligence.* New York: McGraw-Hill, 1967.

Hammerman, A., and Morse, S. Open teaching: Classroom. *Young Children,* October 1972, *28,* 43–52.

Harmin, M., and Gregory, T. *Teaching is . . .* Chicago: Science Research Associates, 1974.

Harris, D. B. *Children's drawings as a measure of intellectual maturity.* New York: Harcourt, Brace and World, 1963.

Harris, E. D. (Ed.). *Report on educational research* (Vol. 9). Washington, D.C.: Capitol Publications, 1977.

Headley, N. E. *Education in the kindergarten.* New York: Van Nostrand, 1966.

Hess, R. D., and Croft, D. J. *Teachers of young children* (2nd ed.). Boston: Houghton Mifflin, 1972.

Hildebrand, V. *Introduction to early childhood education* (2nd ed.). New York: Macmillan, 1976.

Hill, P. S. Kindergarten in *American educators' encyclopedia.* Lake Bluff, Ill.: United Educators, 1941.

Holt, J. *How children learn.* New York: Pittman, 1967.

Hunt, J. M. *Intelligence and experience.* New York: Ronald Press, 1961.

Hunter, B. *My students use computers.* Reston, Va.: Reston Publishing Company, 1984.

Hymes, J. L., Jr. *Teaching the child under six.* Columbus, Ohio: Charles E. Merrill, 1968.

Hymes, J. L. *Teaching the child under six.* (3rd ed.). Columbus, Ohio: Charles E. Merrill, 1981.

Illick, J. E. Child-rearing in seventeenth century England and America. In L. DeMause (Ed.), *The history of childhood.* New York: Psychohistory Press, 1974.

Jarolimek, J. *Social studies in elementary education.* New York: Macmillan, 1971.

Jarvis, O. T., and Rice, M. J. *An introduction to teaching in the elementary school.* Dubuque, Iowa: Wm. C. Brown, 1972.

Jenkins, G. G., and Shacter, H. S. *These are your children.* Glenview, Ill.: Scott, Foresman, 1975.

Johnson, M. L., and Wilson, J. W. Mathematics. In C. Seefeldt (Ed.), *Curriculum for the preschool-primary child.* Columbus, Ohio: Charles E. Merrill, 1976.

Juluis, A. K. "Focus on movement: Practice and theory." *Young Children,* November 1978, *34,* 19–26.

Kagan, J. Preschool enrichment and learning. In J. L. Frost (Ed.), *Revisiting early childhood education.* New York: Holt, Rinehart and Winston, 1973.

Kamii, C. An application of Piaget's theory to the conceptualization of a preschool curriculum. A paper written for presentation at the Conceptualization of Preschool Curricula Conference sponsored by the Department of Educational Psychology, The City University of New York, May 22–24, 1970, 9.

Kamii, C. A sketch of the Piaget-derived preschool curriculum developed by the Ypsilanti Early Education Program. In S. J. Braun, and E. P. Edwards. *History and theory of early childhood education.* Belmont, Calif.: Wadsworth, 1972.

Katz, L. G. Developmental stages of preschool teachers. *Elementary School Journal,* October 1972, *58,* 50–54.

Katz, L. G., and Ward, E. H. *Ethical behavior in early childhood education.* Washington, D.C.: National Association for the Education of Young Children, 1978.

Kelley, E. C. *In defense of youth.* Englewood Cliffs, N.J.: Prentice-Hall, 1962.

Kellog, R. *Analyzing children's art.* Palo Alto, Calif.: National Principle Books, 1969.

Kessen, W. *The child.* New York: Wiley, 1965.

Keyserling, M. D. *Windows in day care.* New York: National Council of Jewish Women, 1972.

Kilpatrick, W. H. *Source book in philosophy of education.* New York: Macmillan, 1937.

Kirk, S. A. *Educating exceptional children* (2nd ed.). Boston: Houghton Mifflin, 1972.

Kohlberg, L. The child as a moral philosopher. *Psychology Today,* September 1968, *2,* 25–30.

Kohlberg, L. The claim to moral adequacy of a highest state of moral judgment. *Journal of Philosophy,* October 1973, *70,* 631–632.

Lamb, P. (Ed.). *Guiding children's language learning* (2nd ed.). Dubuque, Iowa: William C. Brown, 1971.

Lamme, L. L. Reading with an infant. *Childhood Education.* April/May 1980, *56,* 285–290.

Langway, L., et al. Bringing up superbaby. *Newsweek,* March 28, 1983, *101,* 62–68.

Lazerson, M. *The historical antecedents of early childhood education.* Seventy-first yearbook of the National Society for the Study of Education.

Chicago: National Society for the Study of Education, 1972.

Leeb-Lundberg, K. Friedrich Froebel: A friend. *Childhood Education,* April/May 1977, *53,* 302–306.

Leeper, S. H., Dales, R. J., Skipper, D. S., and Witherspoon, R. L. *Good schools for young children* (3rd ed.). New York: Macmillan, 1974.

Lefrancois, G. R. *Of children* (1st and 4th eds.). Belmont, Calif.: Wadsworth, 1973, 1983.

Lenneberg, E. H. The capacity for language acquisition. In J. A. Foder and J. J. Katz. *The structure of language.* Englewood Cliffs, N.J.: Prentice-Hall, 1964.

Lenoski, E. F. What's happening in child abuse? Workshop comments in L. Sanders, R. W. Kibby, S. Creaghan, and E. Tyrrel. Child abuse: detection and prevention. *Young Children,* July 1975, *30,* 334.

Lewin, R. Starved brains. *Psychology Today,* 1975, *9,* 30.

Lewis, E. R., and Lewis, H. P. Which manuscript letters are hard for first graders? *Elementary English,* December 1964, *41,* 855–858.

Lewis, M. M. *Language and the child.* The Mere, Bucks, England: National Foundation for Educational Research, 1969.

Lowenfeld, V. *Creative and mental growth.* New York: Macmillan, 1957.

Lowenfeld, V., and Brittain, W. L. *Creative and mental growth.* New York: Macmillan, 1970.

Maccoby, E. E., and Zellner, M. *Experiments in primary education: Aspects of Project Follow Through.* New York: Harcourt Brace Jovanovich, 1970.

Marion, M. C. Create a parent-space: A place to stop, look and read. *Young Children,* April 1973, *27,* 221–222.

McCarthy, M. A., and Houston, J. P. *Fundamentals of early childhood education.* Cambridge, Mass.: Winthrop Publishers, 1980.

McMillan, M. *The nursery school.* New York: E. P. Dutton, 1919.

McNeill, D. Developmental psycholinguistics. In F. Smith and G.A. Miller (Eds.), *The genesis of language.* Cambridge, Mass.: MIT Press, 1966.

McWhinnie, H. J. Reviews of recent literature on figure drawing tests as related to research problems in art education. *Review of Educational Research,* 1971, *41,* 115–131.

McWhinnie, H. J. Viktor Lowenfeld: Art education for the 1970s. *Studies in Art Education,* 1972, *4,* 8–13.

Meltzoff, A. N., and Moore, M.K. Imitation of facial and manual gestures by human neonates. *Science,* October 1977, *198,* 75–78.

Merton, R.K. *Social theory and social structure.* New York: Free Press, 1968.

Mitchell, L. S. *Young geographers.* New York: John Day, 1934.

Montessori, M. *The Montessori method.* New York: Schocken Books, 1964.

Morrison, G. S. *Parent involvement in the home, school, and community.* Columbus, Ohio: Charles E. Merrill, 1978.

Morrison, G.S. *Early childhood education today* (2nd ed.), Columbus, Ohio: Charles E. Merrill, 1980.

Neuman, D. Sciencing for young children. *Young Children,* April 1972, *27,* 219–221.

New Haven Register, September 11, 1968. In C. L. Bush and M. H. Huebner, *Strategies for reading in the elementary school.* New York: Macmillan, 1970.

Newman, B. M., and Newman, P. R. *Infancy and childhood.* New York: Wiley, 1978.

Nixon, R. M. *Weekly compilation of presidential documents,* August 8, 1969.

Northcott, W. H. Candidate for integration: A hearing impaired child in a regular nursery school. *Young Children,* September 1970, *25,* 368.

Northcott, W. H. (Ed.). *The hearing impaired child in a regular classroom: preschool, elementary, and secondary years.* Washington, D.C.: Alexander Graham Bell Association for the Deaf, 1973.

O'Leary, K. D., and O'Leary, S. G. *Classroom management: The successful use of behavior modification.* New York: Pergamon Press, 1977.

Olsen, M. It makes me feel bad when you call me "Stinky." *Young Children,* December 1970, *26,* 120–121.

Ornstein, A. C. Who are the disadvantaged? *Young Children,* May 1971, *26,* 267–268.

Ornstein, R. E. *The psychology of consciousness* (2nd ed.). New York: Harcourt Brace Jovanovich, 1977

Owen, G. *Nursery school education.* London: Methuen, 1920.

Parker, B. Some observations on psychiatric consultation with nursery school teachers. *Mental Hygiene,* 1962, *46,* 559–566.

Parnes, S. Quoted in *Igniting creative potential.* Salt Lake City, Utah: Bella Vista Elementary School, 1971.

Parten, M. Social participation among preschool children. *Journal of Abnormal and Social Psychology,* 1932, *27,* 243–369.

Pearce, J. C. *Magical child: Rediscovering nature's plan for our children.* New York: Bantam Books, 1977.

Pennsylvania Department of Education. Program Approval Standards: Undergraduate and Graduate Programs. Part II. Policies, procedures, and standards for certification of professional school personnel. 1977.

Pennsylvania Department of Public Welfare. *Regulations for child day care centers.* Harrisburg, Pa.: Department of Public Welfare, 1981.

Pestalozzi, J. Letter to Heinrich Gessner about his orphanage at Stanz, Switzerland. In S. J. Braun and E. P. Edwards, *History and theory of early childhood education.* Belmont, Calif.: Wadsworth, 1972.

Piaget, J. *The psychology of intelligence* (M. Percy and D. E. Berlyne, trans.). London: Routledge and Kegan Paul, 1956.

Piaget, J. *Play, dreams, and imitation in childhood.* New York: W. W. Norton, 1962.

Piaget, J. Development and learning. In R. E. Ripple and V. N. Rockcastle (Eds.), *Piaget rediscovered.* Ithaca, N.Y.: Cornell University Press, 1964.

Pickhardt, I. Sexist piglets. *Parents,* December 1983, *58,* 32–37.

Pines, M. *Revolution in learning: The years from birth to six.* New York: Harper and Row, 1966.

Plumb, J. H. The great change in children. *Intellectual Digest,* 1972, *2,* 82–84.

Pratt, C. *Experimental practice in city and country schools.* New York: Dutton, 1924.

Quill, J. *Beautiful junk.* Washington, D.C.: Office of Child Development, Project Head Start, no date.

Ramsey, P. G. Beyond ten little indians and turkeys. *Young Children,* September 1979, *34,* 28–51.

Read, K. H. *The nursery school: A human relations laboratory*. Philadelphia: W. B. Saunders, 1971.

Rice, J. M. A general consideration of the American school system. In *The Public School System of the United States*. New York: Century Company, 1893.

Riley, S. S. Some reflections on the value of children's play. *Young Children,* February 1973, *28,* 146–153.

Robinson, H. F. *Exploring teaching in early childhood education*. Boston: Allyn and Bacon, 1977.

Rogers, C. Forget you are a teacher. In M. D. Gall, and B. A. Ward (Eds.), *Critical issues in educational psychology*. Boston: Little, Brown, 1974.

Rogers, C. R. Toward a modern approach to values: The valuing process in the mature person. In H. Kirschenbaum, and S. B. Simon, (Eds.), *Readings in values clarification*. Minneapolis, Minn.: Winston Press, 1973, pp. 75–91.

Rogers, D. *Child psychology* (2nd ed.). Belmont, Calif.: Wadsworth, 1977.

Rousseau, J. J. *Emile, or a treatise on education* (B. Foxley, trans.). London: Dent, 1911. The first French edition was published in 1762.

Safford, P. L. *Teaching young children with special needs*. St. Louis: C. V. Mosby, 1978.

Sanders, L. Child abuse: Detection and prevention. *Young Children,* July 1975, *30,* 334.

Schaffer, H. R., and Emerson, P. The development of social attachments in infancy. *Monographs of the society for research in child development, 29,* 1964, 48.

Seefeldt, C. *A curriculum for child care centers*. Columbus, Ohio: Charles E. Merrill, 1974.

Seefeldt, C. *Social studies for the preschool-primary child*. Columbus, Ohio: Charles E. Merrill, 1977.

Shavelson, F. J., Hubner, J. J., and Stanton, G. C. Self-concept: Validation of construct interpretation. *Review of Educational Research,* 1976, *46,* 413.

Shirley, M. M. *The first two years*. Minneapolis: University of Minnesota Press, 1933.

Silverman, S. R., and Lane, H. S. Deaf children. In H. Davis, and S. R. Silverman (Eds.), *Hearing and deafness* (3rd ed.). New York: Holt, Rinehart and Winston, 1970.

Skeel, D. J. *The challenge of teaching social studies in the elementary school*. Pacific Palisades, Calif.: Goodyear, 1974.

Slobin, D. I. Soviet psycholinguistics. In N. O'Connor, *Present-day soviet psychology*. Oxford: Pergamon Press, 1966.

Smilansky, S. *The effects of socio-dramatic play on disadvantaged preschool children*. New York: Wiley, 1968.

Smith, E. B., Goodman, K. S., and Meredith, R. *Language and thinking in school* (2nd ed.). New York: Holt, Rinehart and Winston, 1976.

Smith, J. A. *Adventures in communication*. Boston: Allyn and Bacon, 1972.

Spodek, B. *Early childhood education*. Englewood Cliffs, N.J.: Prentice-Hall, 1973.

Stanton, J. On behavior modification. *Young Children,* November 1975, *31,* 22.

Stassen, R. A. I have one in my class who's wearing hearing aids! In W. H. Northcott (Ed.), *The hearing impaired child in the regular classroom: preschool, elementary, and secondary years*. Washington, D.C.: Alexander Graham Bell Association for the Deaf, 1973.

Stendler, C. B. Aspects of Piaget's theory that have implications for teacher education. *Journal of Teacher Education,* September 1965, *16,* 330.

Stone, L. J., and Church, J. *Childhood and adolescence*. New York: Random House, 1973.

Strother, D. B. The importance of play. *Practical Applications of Research,* December 1982, *5,* 1. Newsletter of Phi Delta Kappa's Center on Evaluation, Development, and Research.

Todd, V. E., and Heffernan, H. *The years before school* (2nd ed.). New York: Macmillan, 1970.

Torrance, E. P. Adventuring in creativity. *Childhood Education,* 1963, *40,* 79.

Torrance, E. P. *Creativity*. Belmont, Calif: Fearon, 1969.

Toynbee, A. Quoted in C. W. Taylor, Introduction to *Igniting creative potential*. Salt Lake City, Utah: Bella Vista Elementary School, 1971.

Vygotsky, L. S. *Thought and Language,* 1934. (E. Haufmann and G. Vakar, trans.) Cambridge, Mass.: M I T Press, 1962.

Waitzkin, B. The fat child. *Parents,* November 1983, *85,* 110–114.

Wallace, I., Wallechinsky, D., and Wallace, A. Significa. *Parade,* 29 November 1981.

Wallach, M. A., and Kogan, N. *Modes of thinking in young children*. New York: Holt, Rinehart and Winston, 1965.

Walzer, J. F. A period of ambivalence: Eighteenth-century American childhood. In L. DeMause, *The history of childhood*. New York: Psychohistory Press, 1974.

Wann, K., Dorn, M., and Liddle, D. *Fostering intellectual development in young children*. New York: Teacher's College Press, Bureau of Publications, Columbia University, 1962.

Watson, J. B. Psychology as the behaviorist views it. *Psychological Review*, 1913, *20*, 158–177.

Watson, J. B. *Behaviorism*. New York: W. W. Norton, 1930, 1970.

Weir, M. K., and Eggelston, P. J. Teacher's first words. In *Readings in early childhood education 78/79*. Guilford, Conn.: Dushkin Publishing Group, 1978.

Westinghouse Learning Corporation–Ohio University. The impact of Head Start, June 1970. In J. L. Frost (Ed.), *Revisiting early childhood education*. New York: Holt, Rinehart and Winston, 1973, pp. 400–404.

White, B. L., in Berkman, S. See the baby. See the better baby. *American Baby*, May 1984, *46*, 58–61; 70–80.

White, B. L. *The first three years of life*. Englewood Cliffs, N.J.: Prentice-Hall, 1975.

Zaremba, S. W. Spanish in the preschool: A bilingual aid for the English-speaking staff. *Young Children*, March 1975, *30*, 174–177.

Credits

ASCPA: Photos courtesy of ASPCA Archives. (P. 30.) Brooks/ Cole Publishing Company: Excerpt from *Child Psychology*, Second Edition, by Dorothy Rogers. ©1977 by Wadsworth Publishing Company, Inc. Reprinted by permission of the publisher, Brooks/Cole Publishing Company, Monterey, California. (pp. 459–460.) W. H. Freeman and Company: Excerpts from *A Primer of Infant Development* by T. G. R. Bower, 1977. Reprinted by permission of the publisher. (P. 78.) Holt, Rinehart and Winston: (1) Excerpt from *Language and Thinking in School*, Second Edition, by E. Brooks Smith, Kenneth S. Goodman, and Robert Meredith. Copyright ©1970 by Holt, Rinehart and Winston, Inc.; ©1976 by Holt, Rinehart and Winston. Reprinted by permission of the publisher. (p. 297.) (2) Table from *Hearing and Deafness*, Third Edition, edited by Hallowell Davis and S. Richard Silverman. Copyright 1947, ©1960, 1970 by Holt, Rinehart and Winston, Inc. Reprinted and adapted by permission of Holt, Rinehart and Winston, CBS College Publishing. (Table 12-3, p. 454.) Human Sciences Press: Excerpts from "Observations on the Use of Direct Instruction With Young Disadvantaged Children," by Carl Bereiter and Siegfried Engelmann. *Journal of School Psychology*, Vol. 4, No. 3, 1964, pp. 56–58. Reprinted by permission of Human Sciences Press, New York, N.Y. (pp. 303, 304.) National Association for the Education of Young Children: (1) Excerpt from "The Case for the Academic Preschool: Fact or Fiction?" by David Elkind. Reprinted by permission from *Young Children*, Vol. 25, No. 4, January 1970, p. 139. Copyright ©1970, National Association for the Education of Young Children, 1834 Connecticut Avenue, N.W., Washington, D.C. 20009. (pp. 61–62.) (2) "Play Today" by Leila P. Fagg. Reprinted by permission from *Young Children*, Vol. 30, No. 2, January 1975, p. 93. Copyright ©1975, National Association for the Education of Young Children, 1834 Connecticut Avenue, N.W., Washington, D.C. 20009. (P. 213.) (3) Excerpt from "Open Teaching: Piaget in the Classroom" by Ann Hammerman and Susan Morse. Reprinted by permission from *Young Children*, Vol. 28, No. 1, October 1972, pp. 43–44. Copyright © 1972, National Association for the Education of Young Children, 1834 Connecticut Avenue, N.W., Washington, D.C. 20009. (pp. 238–239.) (4) "On Behavior Modification" by Jessie Stanton. Reprinted by permission from *Young Children*, Vol. 31, No. 1, November 1975, p. 22. Copyright ©1975, National Association for the Education of Young Children, 1834 Connecticut Avenue, N.W., Washington, D.C. 20009. (P. 254.) (5) Excerpt from Children's Art: "A Vehicle for Learning" by Sylvia F. Burns. Reprinted by permission from *Young Children*, Vol. 30, No. 3, March 1975, p. 201. Copyright ©1975, National Association for the Education of Young Children, 1834 Connecticut Avenue, N.W., Washington, D.C. 20009. (P. 372) (6) Excerpt from "Initial Code of Ethics for Early Childhood Educators" in *Ethical Behavior in Early Childhood Education* by Lillian E. Katz and Evangeline H. Ward (Washington, D.C.: NAEYC), 1978: 20–21. ©1978 by the National Association for the Education of Young Children. Reprinted by permission from NAEYC. (pp. 18–19.) National Council of Teachers of English: Excerpt from "Which Manuscript Letters Are Hard for First Graders?" by Edward R. Lewis and Hilda P. Lewis, *Elementary English*, Vol. 41, December 1964, pp. 855–858. Copyright © 1964 by National Council of Teachers of English. Reprinted by permission of the publisher. (P. 338.) Phi Delta Kappa: Excerpt from D. B. Strother, "The Importance of Play," *Practical Applications of Research 5*, No. 2, December 1982. Reprinted by permission of the publisher. (p. 143.) Random House, Inc.: Excerpts from *Childhood and Adolescence: A Psychology of the Growing Person*, Third Edition, by Joseph L. Stone and Joseph Church, 1973. Reprinted by permission of the publisher. (p. 80.) Schocken Books, Inc.: Excerpt from *The Montessori Method* by Maria Montessori, 1964. Reprinted by permission of Schocken Books, Inc. (P. 45.) Science Research Associates, Inc.: (1) Excerpts from *Distar® Reading I*, Teacher's Guide, by Siegfried Engelmann and Elaine C. Bruner. ©1969, Science Research Associates, Inc. Reprinted by permission of the publisher. (pp. 325, 328–329.) (2) Excerpt from *Distar® Arithmetic I*, Teacher's Guide, by Siegfried Engelmann and Doug Carnine. ©1969, Science Research Associates, Inc. Reprinted by permission of the publisher. (pp. 355–356.) Significa: "Little Mary Ellen," *Parade*, November 29, 1981. Reprinted by permission of Irving Wallace, David Wallechinsky, and Amy Wallace. *Significa*, E. P. Dutton, Inc. New York, N.Y., 1983. (p. 30.) W. B. Saunders Company: Excerpt from *The Nursery School*, Fifth Edition, by Katherine H. Read, 1971. Reprinted by permission of the publisher. (p. 374.) Wadsworth Publishing Company: Excerpt from Constance Kamii, "A Sketch of the Piaget-Derived Preschool Curriculum Developed by the Ypsilanti Early Education Program," Ypsilanti Public Schools, Ypsilanti, Michigan, August 1971. Selection appears in *History and Theory of Early Childhood Education* by Samuel J. Braun and Esther P. Edwards. ©1972 by Wadsworth Publishing Company, Inc. Reprinted by permission of Wadsworth Publishing Company, Belmont, California 94002. (P. 238.)